The World Guide to CSR

The World Guide to
CSR

A Country-by-Country Analysis of Corporate Sustainability and Responsibility

Edited by **Wayne Visser** and **Nick Tolhurst**

Greenleaf
PUBLISHING

© 2010 Greenleaf Publishing Limited

Published by Greenleaf Publishing Limited
Aizlewood's Mill
Nursery Street
Sheffield S3 8GG
UK
http://www.greenleaf-publishing.com

Printed in Great Britain on acid-free paper by
CPI Antony Rowe, Chippenham and Eastbourne

FSC
www.fsc.org
MIX
Paper from
responsible sources
FSC® C013604

Cover by LaliAbril.com

British Library Cataloguing in Publication Data:
  A catalogue record for this book is available from the British Library.

Paperback: ISBN-13: 9781906093389
Hardback: ISBN-13: 9781906093372
ePub: ISBN-13: 9780955450563
PDF: ISBN-13: 9781907643095

Contents

Acknowledgements

First and foremost, we wish to thank all the contributors to this volume, who have given generously of their time in writing the regional and country profiles. We trust that your thought leadership will be recognised and appreciated.

We are grateful to the organisational supporters of *The World Guide to CSR*, including CSR International and Deutsche Gesellschaft für Technische Zusammenarbeit (GTZ).

And thank you also to Greenleaf Publishing, for believing in the potential of this publication, for their patience in waiting for the final manuscript and their diligence in producing the book. Greenleaf has undoubtedly become the world's leading publisher in CSR.

About the supporting organisations

CSR International

CSR International is a global think-tank, launched in 2009 by social entrepreneur, writer and academic, Dr Wayne Visser. The motto of the organisation is 'CSR is dead — long live CSR!' This is based on the belief that the old understanding of CSR (corporate social responsibility, which we call CSR 1.0) is no longer fit for purpose and the new CSR (corporate sustainability and responsibility, which we call CSR 2.0) has only just been born.

Hence, CSR International strives to be an incubator for a new, evolved concept of CSR. CSR 2.0 moves beyond CSR as public relations, philanthropy or incremental improvement to CSR as a transformative concept based on the five principles of creativity, scalability, responsiveness, glocality and circularity. CSR 2.0 is embedded as a new DNA code for business, with four components: value creation, good governance, societal contribution and environmental integrity.

CSR International acts as a networking hub for those who are deeply concerned about the world's social and environmental problems and profoundly inspired by the potential of business to contribute to the solutions. Therefore, our members are CSR professionals, students and enthusiasts from business, government, academia and civil society, who are focused on transforming business into a positive agent for change in the economy, society and the environment.

CSR International promotes CSR as an integrated solution through thought leadership, research, best practice benchmarking and shared learning. We offer a number of knowledge-based resources, including CSR research, news and book review digests, a blog and a searchable Wikipedia. The CSR research archives include summaries of over 500 research studies published over the past five years. The website also has information about CSR jobs, events and an archive of videos with leading thinkers and practitioners in CSR.

For more information, email **info@csrinternational.org** or visit **http://www.csrinternational.org**.

GTZ's Centre for Cooperation with the Private Sector (CCPS)

As an international cooperation enterprise for sustainable development with worldwide operations, the federally owned Deutsche Gesellschaft für Technische Zusammenarbeit (GTZ) GmbH supports the German government in achieving its development-policy objectives. It provides viable, forward looking solutions for political, economic, ecological and social development in a globalised world. Working under difficult conditions, GTZ promotes complex reforms and change processes. Its corporate objective is to improve people's living conditions on a sustainable basis.

The private sector plays a crucial role in the sustainable development of societies as they influence their social and ecological environment. To support private companies, GTZ has run a worldwide programme to enhance responsible business practices since 2002. As part of this, GTZ's Centre for Cooperation with the Private Sector (CCPS) promotes the socially and environmentally considerate business behaviour of companies in Sub-Saharan Africa. The CCPS:

- Helps companies to identify crucial areas for corporate responsible engagement and the corresponding needs for support

- Assists companies to analyse and overcome hindering factors for corporate responsibility

- Supports the development of companies' networking capacity

- Links businesses with other networking initiatives for mutual learning

- Systematically identifies and shares relevant information and knowledge

In addition to the direct engagement with the target group, CCPS liaises with partner organisations as intermediaries. These are local academic institutions and multi-stakeholder networks as well as non-governmental organisations that promote the same principles as CCPS.

Major current topics are: anti-corruption, water sustainability, the financial wellness of employees, responsible business investment in post-conflict zones, food security, responsible leadership and energy efficiency. Its websites are: **http://www.gtz.de** and **http://www.gtzccps.org**.

About the editors

Dr **Wayne Visser** is Founder and Director of the think-tank CSR International and author/editor of nine previous books, including seven on the role of business in society, the most recent of which are *The Top 50 Sustainability Books, Landmarks for Sustainability* and *The A to Z of Corporate Social Responsibility*. Wayne is also Senior Associate at the University of Cambridge Programme for Sustainability Leadership, where he is contributing to various research and teaching programmes and where he previously held the position of Research Director. Before getting his PhD in Corporate Social Responsibility (Nottingham University, UK), Wayne was Director of Sustainability Services for KPMG and Strategy Analyst for Cap Gemini in South Africa. His other qualifications include an MSc in Human Ecology (Edinburgh University, UK) and a Bachelor of Business Science with Honours in Marketing (Cape Town University, South Africa). Wayne is a Fellow of the RSA (Royal Society for the Encouragement of Arts, Manufactures and Commerce), lives in London, UK, and enjoys art, writing poetry, spending time outdoors and travelling. In 2010, Wayne embarked on a 'CSR Quest' world tour, to share best practices in corporate sustainability and responsibility. More information about the CSR Quest tour is available on **http://www.csrinternational.org** and a full biography and much of his writing and art is on **http://www.waynevisser.com**.

Nick Tolhurst was Director of the Institute for Corporate Culture Affairs (ICCA) from 2004 to 2010. He is a Fellow of the Institute for Cultural Diplomacy and a lecturer on CSR at the Steinbeis University in Berlin. Before joining ICCA, Nick worked for the British Foreign Ministry in Germany, advising British companies in Germany and German companies investing in the UK. Previously, Nick worked for the European Commission at DG II (Economics and Financial Affairs) preparing for the introduction of the euro in differing cultures and economic systems. Nick studied at London Metropolitan University (UK) and completed a master's degree at Osnabrück University (Germany), both in European Studies, specialising in Economics and Cultural Studies. Nick has written and edited many publications on CSR, corporate culture and economics including, most recently, *Responsible Business, The A to Z of Corporate Social Responsibility* and the *ICCA Handbook on CSR*.

List of contributors

Inge Aarhus (contributor for **Norway**) was Project Manager in the Ministry of the Environment for the Lillehammer Olympics. She is also Director responsible for operations of the Green Business Network Norway, which has organised four national conferences on CSR. Inge has an MSc from the Norwegian University of Life Sciences.

Cristian Loza Adaui (contributor for **Perú**) has researched and taught Business Ethics and CSR at the San Pablo Catholic University, Perú. He is founder of DesarrollaRSE, Perú and is co-founder and associate consultant of ProyectaRSE Consulting Group, Perú. He holds a master's in Management and CSR from LUMSA University, Italy, and is finishing his PhD in economics at the Catholic University Eichstätt-Ingolstadt, Germany.

Niaz Alam (contributor for **Bangladesh**) is a Board Member of the London Pensions Fund Authority. A solicitor by background, Niaz has worked on corporate responsibility and ethical investment issues since 1992. He was formerly Deputy Director of the Ethical Trading Initiative and Head of Social Issues at the Ethical Investment Research Service.

Felipe B. Alfonso (contributor for **Asia**) is Executive Director of the Ramon V. del Rosario Sr. Center for Corporate Social Responsibility. He has extensive experience in conducting management development programmes and is currently Vice Chairman of the AIM Board of Trustees. Previously, Professor Alfonso was President of AIM, Associate Dean for Research and Associate Dean of the Center for Development Management in the Philippines.

José Manuel Almela (contributor for **Spain**) is a CSR specialist with a bachelor's in Economics, and master's degrees in Audit and Business Management, and in CSR and Accountability. He has carried out most of his professional work through the CSR Commission of the Economists' Association of Alicante. Owner of the consulting company Erresece, he specialises in the management of SMEs.

Kenneth Amaeshi PhD (contributor for **Nigeria**) is a faculty member of the Doughty Centre for Corporate Responsibility, Cranfield School of Management, UK, and a Visiting Professor of Comparative Corporate Governance at the Lagos Business School Nigeria. He holds a PhD in Political Economy and International Business from the University of Warwick, UK.

Liliana Anam (contributor for **Poland**) is a Founder and Manager of CSRinfo, as well as being a CSR advisor and expert in the international Working Group on ISO 26000. She works with companies, NGOs and governmental institutions, conducts research, writes articles and takes an active part in the CSR debate in Poland. She manages the everyday business of CSRinfo.

Bimal Arora PhD (contributor for **India**) is an independent CSR scholar based in India, with a PhD in CSR from Nottingham University, UK. His research interests include management of CSR in large organisations, the political economy of CSR in India and inclusive business models. Bimal is associated with several organisations in India and beyond.

Khadeeja Ashaah Balkhi (contributor for **Pakistan**) is a sustainability consultant and Editorial Director of the magazine *tbl — triple bottom-line*, which she co-founded. As Senior Vice-Chair, CSR Standing Committee, FPCCI (Federation of Pakistan Chambers of Commerce and Industry), she focuses on leveraging CSR towards inclusive economic prosperity. She volunteers at the grass roots and co-founded the RSD Foundation.

Leeora Black PhD (contributor for **Australia**) is a CSR consultant and thought-leader. She focuses on solving complex CSR problems and building organisational CSR capacity. She advises business on integration of CSR into operations and strategies, stakeholder engagement and sustainability reporting. A speaker and trainer on corporate social responsibility, she founded ACCSR in 2003 and is an Honorary Visitor at the La Trobe University Graduate School of Management.

René Carapinha (contributor for **South Africa**) is associated with the Centre for Responsible Leadership at the University of Pretoria and the Sloan Center on Aging and Work at Boston College. Her research focuses on the work–life interface, global corporate citizenship, and social development. René is interested in business models and strategies that enhance employee, family and community well-being and development. Previously René worked at the Boston College Center for Corporate Citizenship and as a researcher at the Centre for Social Development in Africa at the University of Johannesburg. René is currently working towards her doctorate degree at Boston College.

Leonardo J. Cárdenas (contributor for **Mexico**) is a CSR teacher, graduate programme coordinator, consultant, speaker and member of national councils. He has been advisor to the UN, chair of the government stakeholder group for ISO 26000, chair of the Mexican national standardisation committees on social responsibility and America's representative at the ISO SAG for Social Responsibility.

Liviu Chelcea, PhD (contributor for **Romania**) is a Senior Lecturer at the University of Bucharest, specialising in economic anthropology and urban sociology. Over the last four years he has been participating in a large-scale project on the economic culture of Eastern Europe which aims to analyse the interaction between the work culture of Western Countries and that of Eastern countries.

Derick de Jongh DCom (contributor for **South Africa**) is Director of the Centre for Responsible Leadership in the Faculty of Economic and Management Sciences at the University of Pretoria. Prior to this, Professor de Jongh founded the Centre for Corporate Citizenship at the University of South Africa in 2002. His core area of expertise lies in the field of leadership and sustainability.

Jonas Eder-Hansen (contributor for **Denmark**) holds an MSc in intercultural management from Copenhagen Business School (CBS). He has more than seven years experience within CSR research and project management. Jonas is responsible for embedding the UN PRME at CBS through integrating sustainability into all core activities of the business school (education, research and administration).

Tania Ellis (contributor for **Denmark**) holds an Executive MBA and is a Danish-British speaker, writer, consultant and CEO of Inspiratorium®, which gives advice and inspiration on social business trends to private, public and civic organisations. She is the author of articles and books on CSR, social innovation and social entrepreneurship, including *The New Pioneers*.

Aron Embaye (contributor for **Germany**) has been CSR project advisor at ICCA since 2005. He received his MBA from the University of Natal in South Africa after obtaining his first degree at Asmara University in Eritrea where he also worked for two years as part of the academic staff. He is currently completing his PhD at Frankfurt University, Faculty of Economics and Business Administration, focusing on CSR and business strategy. He has contributed towards a number of publications including *The A to Z of Corporate Social Responsibility*.

Tareq Emtairah PhD (contributor for **Saudi Arabia**) is Research Fellow for the International Institute for Industrial Environmental Economics, Lund University. His areas of interest include sustainability and innovations in the banking sector, buildings, utilities and tourism. Tareq consults on public policy, innovations and sustainability issues, and is a special advisor with the Sustainability Advisory Group in Dubai.

Ravi Fernando (contributor for **Sri Lanka**) is CEO of the Sri Lanka Institute of Nanotechnology (Pvt) Ltd. He holds an MBA from the University of Colombo, Fellowship of the Chartered Institute of Marketing (UK), a Diploma from the International Management and Advanced Management Programme INSEAD (France) and a postgraduate Certificate in Sustainable Business from Cambridge University. He won a Global Strategy Leadership Award at the World Strategy Summit (2007) and is the UN Global Compact Focal point in Sri Lanka.

Dena Freeman PhD (contributor for **Israel**) is an independent CSR consultant with many years' experience in Israel, Africa and the UK. She is also a lecturer in Social Anthropology at the Hebrew University of Jerusalem and a Fellow of the Harry S. Truman Institute for the Advancement of Peace.

Germán Granda (contributor for **Spain**) is Managing Director of Forética and has degrees in Business Sciences from CUNEF, Political Sciences from UNED and Economics from Université Catholique de Louvain (Belgium). He is also member of CERSE and member of the Board of CSR Europe.

David Grayson CBE (contributor for the **United Kingdom**) joined Cranfield as Director of the new Doughty Centre for Corporate Responsibility in 2007, after a 30-year career as a social entrepreneur and campaigner for responsible business, diversity and small business development. This included the chairmanship of the UK's National Disability Council and serving as a joint managing director of Business in the Community.

Lalith Gunaratne (contributor for **Sri Lanka**) established a solar energy business for rural electrification in Sri Lanka in the 1980s, which he sold to Shell Renewables International in 1999. He then developed an international consulting business in renewable and rural energy in Africa and Asia. In 2002 he established Sage Training to focus on human resource development. Lalith has a Diploma in Mechanical Engineering (Nuclear) from Ontario, Canada; Diploma in Marketing (CIM-UK) and MSc in Responsibility and Business Practice from University of Bath, UK.

Maria Elena Baltazar Herrera PhD (contributor for **Asia** and **Philippines**) is a member of the faculty of the Asian Institute of Management. Her areas of research interest include corporate social responsibility, health policy and finance, and performance measurement and management. She is co-author of the book *Doing Good in Business Matters* (2007).

Dermot Hikisch (contributor for **Canada**) has a master's in Sustainability from Sweden and works as a Research Manager for ENDS Carbon. His recent projects have included co-chairing the UK Green Business Awards, launching the Brand Emissions Leaders Project, and presenting on strategic sustainable development across the British Isles. Dermot loves mountains and especially fresh snow.

Roger Haw Boon Hong PhD (contributor for **Malaysia**) is the Founder and Chairman of the Ansted Social Responsibility International Awards (ASRIA). He is an international academic (professor), institution and organisation developer and sustainability expert. Roger has demonstrated his commitment to a variety of CSR practices, education and environmental sciences development activities.

Jennifer Iansen-Rogers (contributor for **The Netherlands**) is a Senior Manager of KPMG Global Sustainability Services. She is a leading professional in CSR reporting and assurance, working with clients such as AkzoNobel, Carlsberg, Vodafone, Rabobank and KPN. She is closely involved in professional practice development and was a director of AccountAbility until April 2009. Jennifer regularly lectures and contributes to publications in this field.

María Irigoyen (contributor for **Argentina**), is Project Director at ReporteSocial.com. With an MSc in International Development from the University of Bath and a graduate of the University of Cambridge Sustainability Leadership Programme, Maria currently leads corporate advisory projects in sustainability and related fields. Her professional experience also includes work in civil society organisations and academic institutions.

Audra Jones (contributor for **United States of America**) has worked in private sector business development, corporate social responsibility and international development. Currently Audra is the Americas Director for the International Business Leaders Forum. Audra's background includes roles at the United Nations Foundation, Inter-American Foundation, Citibank, General Electric Trading Company, Lever Brothers, Louis Berger International and USAID.

Angela Joo-Hyun Kang (contributor for **South Korea**) is Founder and CEO of G-CEF (Global Competitiveness Empowerment Forum). Holding a mid-career master's degree in Public Administration from Harvard Kennedy School and with business and nonprofit sector experiences, she serves as an advisor to the Korea Human Rights Foundation, Community Relations Center and Presidential Council of Nation Branding.

David Katamba (contributor for **Uganda**) is a professional business manager and marketer. He is Chairman of the Uganda Chapter for Corporate Social Responsibility Initiatives (UCCSRI) and Assistant Lecturer in Marketing at Makerere University Business School (MUBS). He has developed a number of manuals and also facilitated a series of training initiatives in CSR, marketing, entrepreneurship and business planning.

Ahad Kazimov (contributor for **Azerbaijan**) is Corporate Social Investment Program Manager for Eurasia Partnership Foundation. He was born in Baku, Azerbaijan and received an MA in Social Psychology from Baku State University (Azerbaijan) and an MA in Public Affairs at Indiana University (USA). The sphere of his professional and research interests are corporate social responsibility and philanthropy in Azerbaijan.

Mervyn E. King (contributor for **South Africa**) is a Senior Counsel, Professor Extraordinaire at the University of South Africa on Corporate Citizenship and has an honorary Doctor of Laws from the University of the Witwatersrand. He is Chairman of the King Committee on Corporate Governance in South Africa and of the Global Reporting Initiative (GRI) in Amsterdam. He chaired the United Nations Committee on Governance and Oversight within the UN.

Ullrich Klins PhD (contributor for **Africa**) started his career as an academic, working for the Technische Universität München. He has been with the German Development Service (DED) since 2006 and until March 2010 was seconded to the GTZ Centre of Cooperation with the Private Sector (CCPS), which focuses on Corporate Responsibility in Sub-Saharan Africa.

Kiara Konti (contributor for **Greece**) has completed an MSc in Business & Community (University of Bath, UK, 2006), has worked for leading Greek CSR boutique consultancies, and has published a number of articles on CSR in the Greek press. Since 2008, she has been working for Ernst & Young in Greece, supporting the provision of both CSR advisory and assurance services.

Alexey Kostin PhD (contributor for **Russian Federation**) graduated in Economics from Moscow State University (1976), where he was later Deputy Dean. He is currently working as Executive Director at the CSR–Russian Centre in Moscow, *inter alia* consulting to UNDP and UNECE as a noted Russian expert in CSR and sustainable development. He worked on the EU-TASIS project on environmental monitoring for ex-Soviet countries at the European Environment Agency in 2002–2003.

Arno Kourula DSc (contributor for **Finland**) is Project Manager at Aalto University School of Economics. His focus areas are CSR, NGOs and Base of the Pyramid. Arno's background is in academia (as a researcher at Helsinki School of Economics and a visiting scholar at Stanford University), public and private sector consulting, NGO fundraising and development cooperation at the United Nations.

Attila Kun PhD (contributor for **Hungary**) is a labour lawyer, Senior Assistant Professor at Károli Gáspár University, Budapest, and lecturer on the first official Hungarian CSR course (at BKF: Budapesti Kommunikációs és Üzleti Főiskola [Budapest College of Communication and Business]). His fields of research in CSR include corporate accountability, regulation versus self-regulation, and labour law. In 2009, he was the member of the jury in the first Hungarian CSR MarketPlace Initiative.

Sarah Lauwo (contributor for **Tanzania**) is a PhD student in Accounting at the Essex Business School, UK. Her thesis is on CSR and Accountability Practices in Developing Countries, focusing on the mining sector of Tanzania. She has been teaching at the University of Dar es Salaam and her research interest is on social and environmental accounting, corporate governance, corporate regulation and accountability, and globalisation.

Sam Yoon-Suk Lee (contributor for **China** and **South Korea**) is the founder and CEO of InnoCSR, a consultancy dedicated to sustainable CSR programmes. Prior to InnoCSR, Sam worked as a consultant for Trilogy and for UNICEF. Sam holds an MBA from China Europe International Business School and a BA from Korea University.

Maria Lemos (contributor for **Portugal**) is the owner and founder of Sustainable Side of the Street, a Portuguese company for Responsible Tourism created in 2007. Prior to that she worked as a chemical engineer for a Portuguese oil company in the assessment of the quality of liquid effluents. She has a Postgraduate Certificate in Conference Management, awarded by the University of Westminster (2006), and has been working in the Meetings Industry since 2004. She is a Special Advisor to Travelmole VISION on Sustainable Tourism and was specifically identified as a meeting and event industry leader by Meeting Professionals International (MPI).

Abbe Le Pelley (contributor for **Middle East**) is a Senior Associate with the Sustainability Advisory Group. She has over a decade of experience in CSR, socially responsible investment and corporate communications. Previously, Abbe helped found the Centre for Responsible Business at the Dubai Chamber of Commerce and Industry and worked for Barclays plc and Jupiter Asset Management in London, and Hill and Knowlton in Dubai.

Nadejda Loumbeva (contributor for **Bulgaria**) works in knowledge sharing and organisational learning and has consulted for various international organisations on knowledge-sharing issues. Nadejda also has private sector experience and is interested in how sharing and learning can be applied to integrate CSR, ethics and sustainability.

Dima Abdeljalil Maaytah (contributor for **Jordan**) is a senior strategic advisor and trainer on risk associated with organisational responsibility, typically in the areas of CSR and sustainable development. She has developed CSR strategies for a number of organisations such as the Greater Amman Municipality, and conducted studies on the status of CSR in the MENA region.

Laura Maanavilja (contributor for **Europe**) joined CSR Europe in 2007 to coordinate the network's internal and external communications. She also manages a portfolio of corporate and national partner accounts and coordinates working groups and information services for members. Prior to joining CSR Europe, Laura worked in international media relations for Finnish industry associations. She holds a master's degree in business communication from the Helsinki School of Economics.

Aparna Mahajan (contributor for **India** and **United Arab Emirates**) is a Management, CSR and Development Consultant. She has been an International Technical Expert for UNDP Somalia in Kenya, Consultant to UNDP India, Country Specialist to UNDP/UNV India, Programs Specialist for the Dubai Chamber of Commerce and Industry, UAE, and Advisor, Corporate Communications for The Energy and Resources Institute.

Deyana Marcheva (contributor for **Bulgaria**) is currently a PhD student at the Law Faculty of Sofia University Saint Kliment Ohridski, Bulgaria. In 2002 she was awarded a research scholarship at the University of Oxford for her studies in feminist jurisprudence. Her research interests include public sector governance, public–private sector partnerships and concessions, CSR and gender studies.

Alex P. Mavro Jr (contributor for **Thailand**) is an American who grew up in Thailand and experienced the western development model up close. During 20 years in the service industry, he began seeing corporate social responsibility as the link between development and sustainability. Today he helps Asia-based organisations develop their internal capacities to implement multi-stakeholder-based business strategies.

Judy N. Muthuri PhD (contributor for **Kenya**) is a Lecturer in CSR at the Nottingham University Business School, UK. Her research interests are in corporations and development; SME integration in business value chains; and CSR in developing countries. Her published work appears in various leading journals and she has co-authored a series of practitioner reports on corporate community involvement for the Charities Aid Foundation (UK).

Kiarie Mwaura PhD (contributor for **Kenya**) is a Senior Lecturer at the University of Nairobi and his main research interests lie in the area of corporate law, especially CSR, corporate governance, business and human rights, and constitutional regulation of corporations. He has published and consulted widely in these areas and has recently served as an expert researcher for the International Commission of Jurists' Expert Legal Panel on Corporate Complicity in International Crimes and has held a Visiting Fellowship at Harvard Law School.

Cedric Marvin Nkiko (contributor for **Uganda**) is a professional CSR practitioner and researcher holding a BSc and MSc in Business Strategy and Governance from University of Derby and currently completing his DBA/PhD at Portsmouth Business School, UK. In addition to his present Stakeholder Engagement role at Derbyshire County Council, Cedric has contributed towards numerous SME/CSR research projects for WBCSD and SVN Netherlands. He recently served on the multi-stakeholder ISO Ad-Hoc Group on Social Responsibility towards the development of ISO 26000.

Yanuar Nugroho (contributor for **Indonesia**) is an Indonesian activist–scholar. He is currently a Research Associate with Manchester Business School, UK, having finished his PhD in technological innovation and social change in Manchester in 2007. His research interests revolve around the topics of innovation and the third sector, sustainable development, new communications media, and social change and business in society.

Dixie O'Donnell (contributor for **Turkey**) is a security and development consultant for international organisations and businesses with expertise in terrorism, energy security, development, CSR and soft security in Eurasia. She holds an MSc in Anthropology and Development from the London School of Economics and a BA in International Studies from the University of Washington.

Daniel F. Ofori PhD (contributor for **Ghana**) is Senior Lecturer at the University of Ghana Business School. Dan is an academic with considerable teaching, research and consulting experience in applied management. He has presented papers on CSR at international conferences and workshops and published widely. He has also authored three books.

Chris Ogbechie (contributor for **Nigeria**) holds a First Class Honours bachelor's degree in Mechanical Engineering from Manchester University and an MBA from Manchester Business School. He is a Senior Fellow at the Lagos Business School, Nigeria and currently a doctoral student in the Brunel

Business School. His main research interests are on upper echelons theory, board effectiveness and corporate governance.

Alireza Omidvar (contributor for **Iran**) advises on industrial and commercial opportunities for investors. He is the author of *Government Policy Making in Promoting CSR* and teaches courses on CSR in EFQM and CSR as a business strategy. He holds a Professional Certificate in CSR from Nottingham University, a BA in Political Science and an MA in Public Policy from Tehran University.

Estrella Peinado-Vara (contributor for **Latin America**) is a Private Sector Specialist at the Multilateral Investment Fund (FOMIN) of the Inter-American Development Bank (IDB). She has been working at the IDB since 2002 on private sector development and corporate social responsibility with a special focus on small and medium enterprises. She has an MBA from Georgetown University.

Adhitya Hadi Permana (contributor for **Indonesia**) joined Business Watch Indonesia in 2005 as a field researcher, where he later became the editor of their bi-monthly magazine *CSR-Review* and has carried out research that focuses on sustainable tea initiatives.

Renginee G. Pillay LLB, LLM, PhD (contributor for **Mauritius**) is a Lecturer in Law at the University of Surrey, UK. She received her doctorate from the University of Kent. Her most recent publication is a book chapter titled 'Corporate Social Responsibility in a Neoliberal Age' co-authored with Professor Paddy Ireland in *Corporate Social Responsibility and Regulatory Governance* (Palgrave Macmillan, 2009).

Luke Poliszcuk (contributor for **Japan**) is CEO of eQualC Sustainability Communications, a Tokyo-based firm focused on sustainable management strategies and effective bilingual communication. Among many other activities, he is a member of the American Chamber of Commerce in Japan's CSR and Environment committees, and a founding member of the International Society of Sustainability Professionals Japan chapter.

Nicole Porto (contributor for **Sierra Leone**) is an independent consultant who has been working in Sierra Leone for several years on CSR issues primarily within the extractive sector. She has worked with NGOs and businesses to improve partnerships and devise strategies to increase the capacity of the private sector to meaningfully contribute to poverty reduction. She holds a bachelor's degree in International Relations and Political Science from the University of Southern California and a master's degree in Human Rights from the London School of Economics.

Ulf Richter PhD (contributor for **Côte d'Ivoire**) received his doctorate in Economic Sciences from the University of Lausanne. He currently serves at Centrum Católica, Pontificia Universidad Católica del Perú. Previously, he taught at the International University of Grand Bassam, and CERAP in Côte d'Ivoire. In 2007, he was a visiting fellow at Harvard University.

Francisco L. Roman DBA (contributor for **Asia** and **Philippines**) is the Deputy Executive Director of the Ramon V. del Rosario Sr. Center for Corporate Social Responsibility. He is also the Don Andres Soriano Professor of Business Management of the Washington SyCip Graduate School of Business at AIM. Professor Roman completed his DBA at Harvard Business School.

Motoko Sakashita (contributor for **Japan**) is an Insight Supervisor at McCann Erickson, a New York-based advertising agency. She belongs to Planet McCann, a global community which provides information and communication advice on environmental and social themes. She is also a member of the McCann PULSE™ programme, which seeks to understand people's insights across various countries.

Alice Schmidt (contributor for **Austria**) is an independent consultant advising businesses and other organisations on CSR and international development. She has lived in Africa, Asia, Australia and Europe, working for UN agencies, NGOs, businesses, universities and the media. Alice is particularly interested in questions around ethical supply chain management and CSR strategy.

Nazareth Seferian (contributor for **Armenia**) is Programmes Manager, British Council Armenia. He is a graduate of the University of Cambridge Sustainability Leadership Programme and has been working to promote Corporate Sustainability and Responsibility in Armenia since March 2008. As part of his work at the British Council, he helped found the CSR Working Group, an informal partnership of four nonprofit organisations in Armenia.

Tomás Sercovich (contributor for **Ireland**) is Membership Services Manager, Business in the Community Ireland and has been working in corporate responsibility (CR) advisory services since 2002. His areas of expertise are strategy and governance, and measurement and communication of CR performance. He is a member of the Board of CSR Europe, the Chambers Ireland Policy Council on CR and the IBEC Sustainable Enterprise Group.

Arnold Smit PhD (contributor for **Africa**) has, over a career of 15 years, established himself as a consultant in three areas: change management, leadership development and corporate responsibility. He is currently the Executive: Business in Society at the University of Stellenbosch Business School — Executive Development Ltd. The centre supports companies with their corporate responsibility and sustainable development agendas and builds the capacity of NPOs to become more effective and sustainable.

Heiko Spitzeck PhD (contributor for **Switzerland**) is a lecturer at Cranfield University's Doughty Centre for Corporate Responsibility in the UK. He obtained his PhD in Business Ethics at the University of St Gallen in Switzerland and held visiting scholar positions at the University of California at Berkeley and Fordham University in New York.

Alin Stancu, PhD (contributor for **Romania**) is Assistant Professor at the Academy of Economic Studies in Bucharest. His current research interests include: business ethics, corporate social responsibility and marketing-management. He is involved in eight national funded research projects. He teaches marketing, public relations and services marketing. He has written several articles and conference papers on corporate social responsibility.

Oumhany Sy (contributor for **Senegal**) is Corporate Responsibility Officer of ArcelorMittal Mining in Senegal, where she has developed various CSR/HSE projects. Passionate about sustainable development issues in Africa, Oumhany is a graduate in Sociology of Organisations from Lyon II University. As a consultant, she supported many organisations in defining and implementing their projects on social dialogue, rural development and gender.

Perla Puterman Szomstein (contributor for **Venezuela**) is the Founder and Moderator of the Ibero-American Virtual Forum on Social Responsibility. She is also an ISO instructor for promoting standardisation on Social Responsibility and former President of the Commission of Social Responsibility of the national Chamber of Commerce and Industry. She teaches at several universities on international CSR standards. She is also former General Director of the NSB FONDONORMA.

Jimmy Tanaya (contributor for **Indonesia**) is studying for his PhD at Manchester Business School, focusing on CSR and palm oil in Indonesia. His work with Business Watch Indonesia has included general implementation guidelines and standards of good business practices for companies in Indonesia. His research interests are business strategy, CSR, and environmental–economic–social trade-offs.

Thomas Thomas (contributor for **Singapore**) is Executive Director of the Singapore Compact for CSR, the national country network focal point of the UN Global Compact. He was the Co-chairperson of the National Tripartite Initiative on CSR and has been involved in the development of ISO 26000 as an expert, a member of the Chairman's Advisory Group and Convenor of Singapore Working Group.

Hanna Thorsteinsdottir (contributor for **Iceland**) is a CSR professional working at Société Générale in Paris. Her CSR experience includes posts at ING Bank and the GRI in Amsterdam. Hanna holds a BSc in Business Administration from Reykjavik University and an MA in European Studies from the University of Amsterdam.

Nick Tolhurst (contributor for **Germany**) is Managing Director of the Institute for Corporate Culture Affairs (ICCA), a fellow of the Institute for Cultural Diplomacy and a lecturer on CSR at the Steinbeis University in Berlin. Nick has written and edited many publications on CSR, corporate culture and economics including *The A to Z of Corporate Social Responsibility* and the *ICCA Handbook on CSR*.

Ricardo Trujillo (contributor for **Spain**) is a CSR Analyst in Forética. He has a bachelor's in Business and Law from UPNA and a master's in International Business from Centro de Estudios Comerciales y Económicos (CECO). He has participated (and coordinated) several projects within different organisations and he has contributed to several publications, including *Informe Forética*.

Tarcila Reis Ursini (contributor for **Brazil**) is Ekobé's Director. She holds an MSc in Development from the University of London and bachelors' degrees in Economics and Law. She was Ethos Institute's Manager from 2003–2007, an expert contributor to the ISO 26000 development and member of GRI's International Stakeholder Council (2007–2009). She is co-author of *Innovation, Legislation and Social Inclusion*.

Angela Pinilla Urzola (contributor for **Colombia**) has a multidisciplinary background with an MSc in Environmental Engineering, an MA in Human Ecology and a PhD focused on social and environmental accountability issues in the UK. Previously, Angela has been involved in higher education and research in Bogotá, Colombia, and undertook environment-related consultancy services in Colombia, Kenya, Belgium and the UK.

Jurie van Niekerk (contributor for **Africa**) is a professional sustainable development practitioner and researcher. He has more than 20 years' experience in Sub-Saharan Africa in project design and management as well as monitoring and evaluation with EC, USAID, NZAID, DFID, World Bank, foundations, public sector and private sector companies. He holds a master's in Development Studies, currently completing Doctorate Strategic Leadership and Entrepreneurship with Regent University, USA.

Ivri Verbin PhD (contributor for **Israel**) is the CEO and founder of Goodvision, the Israeli pioneer CSR consulting firm. Prior to this he served as advisor to H.E. Shimon Peres. Mr Verbin is a Lt Col. (res) and a board member of the Society for the Protection of Nature.

Antonio Vives PhD (contributor for **Latin America**) is Principal Associate, Cumpetere, an infrastructure investment and sustainability consultancy, as well as Consulting Professor at Stanford University. He was a former Manager of Sustainable Development at the Inter-American Development Bank, and a member of the Sustainability Advisory Council of CEMEX, the Board of Trustees of IBLF Americas and the Public Infrastructure Commission of California.

Joshua Wickerham (contributor for **China**) is the China Representative for AccountAbility. He splits his time between Asia, North America and Europe researching and sharing insights into China's sustainable international development. He opened the China office for the international non-profit research organisation AccountAbility. Besides playing the *guqin* and writing, he also enjoys vermiculture and organic gardening.

Theresia Widiyanti (contributor for **Indonesia**) is from Solo, Central Java, Indonesia. She was trained in occupational health and safety at Diponegoro University before joining Business Watch Indonesia as a researcher in 2005, where her work has been focusing on, among others, the role of business in agriculture, retail and sustainable tourism.

Marcus S. Wleh (contributor for **Liberia**) is Corporate Responsibility Manager for ArcelorMittal Liberia. He is a development practitioner with over ten years' experience in humanitarian relief and aid coordination in Africa and Asia. He is interested in grassroots development issues. He recently co-authored the chapter 'Transparent Business Practices: ArcelorMittal's participation in Liberia's EITI' in *Advancing the Mining Sector* (EITI, 2009).

Camila Yamahaki (contributor for **Brazil**) is a PhD student in CSR at Middlesex University. She holds a BA in Public Administration from EAESP-FGV (Brazil) and an MA in CSR from the University of Nottingham. She has held earlier positions as a consultant and researcher in Brazil and in the UK. She is co-author of *Innovation, Legislation and Social Inclusion*.

Rodica Milena Zaharia PhD (contributor for **Romania**) is professor at the Department of International Business and Economics, Academy of Economic Studies, Bucharest, and is interested in areas such as globalisation, economic development, research methodology and CSR. She is the editor for the *European Journal of Interdisciplinary Studies* and coordinates grants focused on CSR and interdisciplinarity.

Foreword

Wayne Visser

The idea for this book came in 2007 and 2008 during the international book launch tour of *The A to Z of Corporate Social Responsibility*. As my co-editor, Professor Dirk Matten, and I introduced the book in countries as diverse as Canada, China, Guatemala, South Africa, Switzerland, Thailand and the UK, it became clear that there is no universal model of CSR. Nor should there be. Although we may agree on some underlying principles and best practices — most recently encapsulated by ISO 26000 — the concept and practice of CSR must be defined by its national and cultural context, if it is to be relevant and effective.

At the time, there were a few good country comparative reports, including for example *The CSR Navigator* (GTZ 2008, covering 13 countries), *Corporate Citizenship around the World* (Global Education Research Network with Boston College Center for Corporate Citizenship 2009, nine countries) and *A Guide to CSR in Europe* (CSR Europe 2009, 20 countries). While incredibly useful and insightful, these reports still left large gaps on the map. *The World Guide to CSR* is an attempt to fill some of those gaps. With five regions and 58 countries profiled,[1] it is still not truly global or comprehensive, but I think it is a good start.

The sentiments behind the book also led me to embark on a 'CSR Quest' tour in 2010, visiting over 20 countries on five continents, with the aim of capturing and sharing CSR best practices from around the world. My experience to date, especially in travelling to developing countries, is that many companies (and governments) still have a very narrow view of CSR — at best equating it with philanthropy or community investment, and at worst using it as a superficial public relations or marketing tactic. The tour is an attempt to correct that perception.

At the same time, I have noticed that many of the greatest innovations in CSR are coming from those same countries (think of M-PESA in Kenya, or A Little World in India, for example). So the tour, much like the book, is a way to discover, capture and share these case studies. The way I see it, the *World Guide* represents the past and the present. It tells

---

1 The chapters are a result of an open 'Call for Contributors' that was issued in October 2008.

us how far we have come and is testimony to some great progress across many nations. However, I hope it also reminds us of how far we still have to go. Despite decades of CSR, in virtually every country, across just about every social, environmental and ethical indicator, we are still headed in the wrong direction.

This is why I am calling for a renaissance in CSR — for a new model, which I call Radical CSR or CSR 2.0, where CSR stands for 'Corporate Sustainability and Responsibility' and is based on five fundamental principles: Creativity, Scalability, Responsiveness, Glocality[2] (thinking globally and acting locally) and Circularity (closed-loop thinking and business processes). CSR 2.0 is the subject of another book,[3] but I believe the *World Guide* represents a crucial step on our journey to transforming CSR, especially to achieving Glocality.

I hope that, in the years to come (and in future editions of this book), we will continue to fill the gaps in our knowledge of CSR around the world. We are at a crucial juncture in the evolution of CSR. If countries and companies fail to adopt a holistic, embedded, scalable model of CSR, it will continue to suffer from 'the three curses' of the status quo, in which CSR tends to be incremental, peripheral and uneconomic. Even worse, it will allow companies to feel good about themselves, while communities crumble, ecosystems collapse and economies descend into chaos.

If, on the other hand, we learn from the lessons of history — including the limitations of old-style CSR (remember, Enron ticked virtually all of the explicit CSR boxes before its collapse in 2001) — then CSR can become a powerful strategy for political, social and environmental change. One thing is for sure: CSR will not disappear. But will it be part of the problem or part of the solution? Will the popular perception of business continue to be like the extractives company portrayed in the movie blockbuster *Avatar* (or, for that matter, BP, in the wake of its latest oil spill catastrophe), or will CSR make it part of a new, more caring mythology?

The jury is still out on that question, but I trust the *World Guide* will inspire CSR enthusiasts, scholars, managers, regulators, activists, students and others to make sure that business lives up to its potential as a force for good in the world.

London, UK
June 2010

2   The term 'glocalisation' comes from the Japanese word *dochakuka*, which simply means global localisation.
3   *The Age of Responsibility: CSR 2.0 and the New DNA of Business* (Wiley, 2010).

Introduction

Nick Tolhurst

The debate on Corporate Social Responsibility (CSR) has grown rapidly over the last two decades. There are many reasons for this but one of the main drivers has been the growing realisation that globalisation has spread and accelerated both the benefits, as well as the disadvantages, of economic development throughout the world.

As more and more countries came to participate in the global capitalist system, the role of business took on an ever more decisive role across all levels of society. However the very fact of an ever more interconnected global economy makes the way different societies deal with, and react to, economic change so crucially important. As trade barriers break down, industrial investment globalises and national governments experience a corresponding decline in power, issues such as sustainable production, labour standards or indeed the cultural and social implications of development cannot be assumed to be converging to a 'global norm', nor can they be left to be decided solely in the marketplace.

There are a number of reasons for this. Differences in the way societies approach business are as much a reflection of a rich and diverse history and development as other cultural attributes. More fundamentally though, with the rise of non-Western economies and growing scepticism about the 'Western economic paradigm' — with regard to ecological sustainability, lifestyles or more recently financial stability — a diversity of ideas and new thinking may well be of vital importance in dealing with the myriad of challenges our world faces.

With this in mind, the *World Guide* is both a timely and intriguing glimpse across the richness of global business cultures. It will be of interest not only to academics in the field of CSR, but also to all those who deal with, or have an interest in, business or public organisations across different cultures and countries. In terms of content, this volume not only provides a rich seam of different perspectives on CSR and best practices, but also offers highly practical information on trends, legal codes and important organisations, as well as backgrounds to academic CSR centres in the respective countries.

The book is structured around five **Regions** (Africa, Asia, Europe, Latin America[1] and the Middle East) and 58 **Countries**, including profiles for each. In order to make the publication as accessible and as useful as possible, each regional and country profile is structured in a similar fashion.

First, each chapter sets the CSR ideas and practices in **Context**, describing the cultural, historical and religious traditions that have supported CSR, philanthropy and related beliefs, values or practices. Then (where applicable) country-specific **CSR models** which illustrate how CSR has developed are included. For each country profile, we also include **Priority issues**, which describe the most important issues faced by the country/ region, whether environmental, social, political, economic or governance related. Further, a section on **Trends** describes key studies on CSR-related topics, typically based on academic research and other surveys. For example, findings may include the level of awareness of CSR-type issues, CSR reporting and implementation of CSR standards. Each country profile also includes information on **Legislation and codes**, summarising the key social, environmental and ethical legislation or national and global codes applicable in each country. Country profiles are completed with backgrounds on the key **Organisations** that are promoting CSR, **Case studies** describing those companies widely regarded as being the best-performing in CSR and the state of CSR **Education**, including university centres for CSR, and courses.

This unique publication is truly the first to attempt such a broad sweep of comparative CSR across so many different countries, regions and business cultures. We are hopeful that it will provide a highly useful, practical and accessible guide for all those interested in how global society tackles the most pressing challenges ahead. We welcome all feedback at **info@csrinternational.org**.

Frankfurt, Germany
June 2010

---

1   Since North America only has two countries — Canada and the USA, both of which have profiles included — a regional profile was not deemed necessary.

Regional profiles

A

I Africa

Ullrich Klins
Project Manager, Centre for Cooperation
with the Private Sector (CCPS)

Jurie H. Van Niekerk
Managing Director, JvN & Associates

Arnold Smit
Executive Director: Business in Society,
University of Stellenbosch Business School —
Executive Development Ltd

▌ Context

In the vast majority of Africa's 53 countries, CSR is still in its infancy. At worst, it is regarded with suspicion as an agenda of the North imposed on countries of the South. At best, it is embedded within the African context and used to address the continent's economic, social and sustainable developmental challenges.

Africa consists of two very distinct regions. The predominantly Muslim/Arabic region north of the Sahara is commonly referred to as Middle East and North Africa (MENA), while Sub-Saharan Africa (SSA) covers the bulk of African states.

The World Bank (2009a) gives a glimpse of Africa's development challenges: poverty is the highest among all the world's regions, with the largest increase in people living on less than USD1.25/day; only 60% of children complete primary education (20% less than other regions); 5% of the adult population is infected with HIV (2007 figures); population growth in urban and rural areas is the highest in the world; and entrepreneurs face greater regulatory and administrative burdens than any other region.

These socioeconomic realities, combined with generally weak public administration and service delivery, have a significant impact on the drivers, role and function of CSR for companies operating in Africa. Typically, legislation and enforcement are poor, civil society scrutiny is largely absent and consumer activism for responsibly produced products is relatively weak. Even when international funding agencies such as the World Bank require major development projects in Africa to comply with standards and codes (for example the Equator Principles), this has a very limited trickle-down effect on suppliers and multinational companies operating in the region.

As a result, much of the CSR discourse and research in Africa is focused on ethics, anti-corruption measures and counteracting weak public service delivery in key sectors such as healthcare and education (Visser *et al.* 2006; Zimmer and Rieth 2007; Hamann *et al.* 2008; Imani Development 2009).

Africa's cultural context is another important factor in defining CSR on the continent. The very communal culture is manifested in the following African indigenous concepts:

- **Harambee** embodies and reflects the strong ancient value of mutual assistance, joint effort, social responsibility and community self-reliance. It is guided by the principle of collective good rather than individual gain (Winston and Ryan 2008).

- **Tsekada** is about behaving as a 'righteous person', fulfilling obligations to society (Ararat 2006).

- **Ubuntu** in Southern Africa reflects an interdependent, communal, harmonious, relationship-aware and respectful community culture — meaning each person can only be fully functioning through other people (Nussbaum 2003).

- **Zekat** (or *Zakat*) can be translated as charity or alms to the poor.

Hence, CSR activities aspire to resolve challenges faced by communities, which governments cannot fully address. By contrast, the environment, workplace issues, product quality and health and safety get much lower priority.

CSR in Africa is most often associated with medium to large companies, and particularly with multinationals or large foreign investors. Given the relative wealth of these companies in comparison to the poverty of the countries and societies in which they are operating, CSR can be a way to counteract negative perceptions of business, as well as a way to make a genuine difference to social and environmental challenges. As a result, CSR is seldom related to the companies' core business, but rather tends to be 'positive payback' philanthropy, with public relations benefits.

As a result, CSR activities and projects in Africa are mainly focused on creating a positive corporate image, as well as addressing weak public sector service delivery in the areas of healthcare (particularly HIV/AIDS), education or labour skills development and the prevention of child labour. CSR is a particularly prominent theme among mining, oil and gas companies in Southern Africa, due to their significant social and environmental impacts, although telecommunications companies have gained a high profile more recently (Hamann and Kapelus 2004).

▌ Models

Defining a comprehensive model for CSR in Africa is problematic, not only because CSR is in its infancy, but also because it tends to be characterised by ad hoc projects focused at the community level and driven by the dominant cultural context of the individual countries within the region. These ad hoc projects are a result of limited attention paid by companies to CSR and the general absence of supportive national strategies, policies and structures.

Visser (2006) proposes a CSR Pyramid for Africa — adapted from Archie Carroll's classic CSR Pyramid of economic, legal, ethical and philanthropic responsibilities — whereby CSR priorities have a different order of importance on the continent, namely economic, philanthropic, ethical and legal responsibilities. There are also distinctive approaches and cultural contexts in the MENA and SSA sub-regions.

MENA region

Although some countries and companies in the Arab world are further ahead than others, CSR is still primarily considered as something peripheral to business, rather than an internal process that is mainstreamed into core operations, strategy and long-term planning. Studies reveal that philanthropy is the most common manifestation of the social agenda of corporations in the MENA (Middle East and North Africa) countries (Ararat 2006). Furthermore, CSR in the region is generally driven by rational choices of business or political choice rather than by the expectations of societies or pressure from the grassroots level (World Bank Institute *et al.* 2007).

Sub-Saharan region

CSR in Sub-Saharan Africa also resembles corporate philanthropy more than an embedded practice. However, this also varies. For example, Ofori and Hinson (2007) compared the adoption of social responsibilities by internationally connected firms with those of indigenous Ghanaian firms and found that the former are more strategic, moral and ethical in their approach to CSR. By contrast, the legacy of colonialism and apartheid in South Africa has resulted in Broad-Based Black Economic Empowerment becoming a strong CSR-related factor, driven by government (Hanks *et al.* 2008). A similar approach can be found in Namibia, where a preference in procurement is given to companies that empower previously disadvantaged people.

▌ Priority issues

Poverty reduction

While poverty reduction in other parts of the world has been generally positive, the situation has been deteriorating in Africa as a whole. In Sub-Saharan Africa, the USD1.25 a day poverty rate showed no sustained decline between 1981 and 2005, remaining at around 50%. In absolute terms, the number of poor people has nearly doubled, from 200 million in 1981 to 380 million in 2005 (World Bank 2009b).

Health and HIV/AIDS

HIV/AIDS increasingly plays a crucial role at all levels. In particular, in Southern African countries the prevalence rates on a national level are estimated to be between 12% and 26% of the population (World Bank 2009a), with higher rates in some provinces. Though most companies have reacted rather slowly, HIV/AIDS workplace programmes, health programmes, provision of antiretroviral drugs and support of hospitals have now become a crucial part of CSR-related activities in the region.

Skills development and education

In no region is the challenge of skills development and the provision of universal basic education more acute than in Africa. Both areas are important to economic growth and poverty reduction, but the fiscal and administrative capacity of African states to meet these goals is limited. The presence of HIV/AIDS and its decimation of the labour force only serve to compound the problem (Johanson and Adams 2004).

Youth development

The World Bank Institute *et al.* (2007) indicate that one area that resonates strongly among companies and governments in the MENA region, and where a manifestation of CSR could have a positive multiplier effect on the region's growth, is in the private sector's engagement with youth. Creating meaningful employment and opportunities for young people throughout the Arab world is one of the most critical sustainable development challenges facing the region.

Socioeconomic development

In the SSA region, the priority for CSR is typically on socioeconomic development, i.e. providing the means for sustainable access to the mainstream economy for poor and marginalised communities. In particular, the focal areas and projects of the private sector in the region generally focus on education, training, health, environment, sport, cultural events and poverty alleviation or social welfare.

National priorities

The following are a few examples of national socioeconomic priorities in Africa.

Democratic Republic of Congo (DRC)

Under the Responsible Business Investment in the DRC programme, the following strategic focus areas are targeted: creating awareness about corporate citizenship, developing SMEs through supply chain management, and linking public with private interests.

Ghana

In Ghana, a coalition of companies has agreed on the Ghana Business Code, which is aligned to the UN Global Compact and its ten principles. The Ghana Club 100 also produces a ranking of Ghana's best performing companies.

Kenya

In recent times, the Kenya Bureau of Standards has been involved in drafting some guidelines on CSR. These standards, as well as those that companies have voluntarily adopted and the ISO standards being developed, form a backdrop against which to measure CSR in Kenya (Gathii 2008).

Malawi

In Malawi, CSR projects cover the construction of marketplaces, school blocks and hospitals, as well as donations in kind, such as blankets, computers and bore holes. Another priority in Malawi is combating corruption. Business Action Against Corruption (BAAC) is an initiative of 35 companies that is implementing a code of conduct. It was recently awarded with the World Bank Anti-Corruption Collective Action Award.

South Africa

In South Africa, priorities are focused on Broad-Based Black Economic Empowerment (BBBEE), skills development and HIV/AIDS. Many so-called CSR activities and projects are more related to Corporate Social Investment (CSI). In the BBBEE-related Code of Good Practice, CSI 'refers to an enterprise's contributions to society and a community that are extraneous to its regular business activities and hence include initiatives in the areas of development, health, education, training, environment, arts and culture and sport' (Njenga and Smit 2007). CSR has also been embedded through a Socially Responsible Index on the stock exchange.

Uganda

In Uganda, an initiative called the CSR Consultative Group has been started recently. This aims at enabling each member to deliver high-quality CSR services and advocates for better CSR practices and policies, according to the Institute of Corporate Governance of Uganda (ICGU). In addition, it is striving for development of a CSR curriculum at a major Ugandan university.

▌ Trends

A major new development in African trade is that trading groups — such as the Common Market of the East and Southern Africa (COMESA), Southern African Development Community (SADC), East African Community (EAC) and the Economic Community of West African States (ECOWAS) — are beginning to look at CSR, although this remains secondary to increasing trade to the US and Europe.

In several African countries, local networks of the UN Global Compact have emerged. In a few cases, these network activities have led to collective actions on CSR, corporate citizenship or the Millennium Development Goals — for example, in Malawi on combating corruption and in Zambia on HIV/AIDS at the workplace.

The exception is South Africa, where the CSR landscape is well developed, incorporating initiatives like the OECD Guidelines for Multinational Enterprises, the King Report on Corporate Governance, UN Global Compact, ISO 14001, GRI and the Social Responsibility Index of the Johannesburg Securities Exchange. There are also sector agreements, like the Kimberly Process diamond certification scheme, the Extractive Industries Transparency Initiative (EITI) and the Equator Principles for the finance sector. While CSR is generally well incorporated by larger companies, SMEs still struggle with the blurred boundaries between CSR and CSI (corporate social investment).

Elsewhere in Africa, the research suggests that CSR is often seen as an 'add-on', peripheral to the core business (Imani Development 2009). Most CSR practitioners only allocate about 20–40% of their work time to CSR matters. CSR departments are rare and many operate from within marketing, communications, corporate affairs, training or human resources departments. Even where CSR policies are established, they often refer to philanthropic approaches.

CSR policy adherence is typically not evaluated. Corporate leadership involvement in CSR matters tends to be focused on launching community projects, supporting CSR policies and ensuring resources for CSR projects, rather than embedding CSR in business processes. Reporting is established in many of the larger companies, but the scope and depth is limited. Several firms have been delisted from the UN Global Compact for failing to comply with reporting requirements.

According to companies surveyed by Imani Development (2009), critical success factors for implementing successful CSR projects in Africa are (in ranked order of importance):

1. Project management skills

2. Staff commitment and involvement

3. Stakeholder/partnership involvement

4. Alignment to company objectives

5. Executive/management commitment

Notably, the involvement of government (e.g. through regulations, incentives or support for CSR dialogues) was deemed critical in successful CSR projects. In both Deutsche Gesellschaft für Technische Zusammenarbeit (GTZ) GmbH research studies (Zimmer and Rieth 2007; Imani Development 2009) the private sector called for more CSR regulation and stronger government support for CSR. For instance, communication experts in Ghana requested that the government set up a National Corporate Social Responsibility Framework to define parameters for CSR in the country.

Government was also identified as a hindrance to CSR in some cases, with particular reference to restrictive policies, bureaucratic practices and lack of exemplary leadership in the CSR space.

Studies for the MENA and SSA regions make the following recommendations for moving CSR forward in Africa (World Bank Institute *et al.* 2007; Imani Development 2009):

- Moving from purely philanthropic activities to sustainable programmes to address development challenges

- Raising awareness and clearly defining CSR and its role, as companies' activities often are scattered and haphazard

- Making a stronger business case for CSR

- Expanding beyond social responsibility to corporate citizenship, which captures not only the obligations of business but also its rights

- Exploring ways in which CSR programmes on the local level can be made to complement efforts of multinationals and their supply chains

- Promoting the role of business associations in promoting business engagement in development

- Encouraging partnerships with universities and academia to inculcate a culture of awareness and ethical behaviour in young and future leaders

- Concentrating on practical CSR 'how-to' guides and advisory services

■ Legislation and codes

MENA region

In many ways, the MENA region is ahead of others due to the fact that it is taking an approach to CSR that is regional, organised and driven at the policy level. There are signs of a growing governmental buy-in to the concepts of CSR, sustainable development and environmental responsibility. Indeed, governments are beginning to realise that CSR can significantly and positively contribute to enhancing competitiveness, attracting investment and maximising the value of wealth creation.

At the regional level, steps have been taken to institutionalise the idea of CSR. For example, in the first phase of the MENA–OECD development plan (2005–2007), a regional Institute for Corporate Governance (HAWKAMA) was established in Dubai in 2006. At a national level, many MENA governments are engaging business to achieve environmental and social objectives through public–private partnerships (PPP).

Sub-Saharan region

There is no comprehensive or concrete CSR policy or law in most countries in the SSA region, apart from some rather ad hoc legislative and non-regulatory activities. An exception is the previously mentioned Broad-Based Black Economic Empowerment (BBBEE) Act in South Africa.

CSR aspects can be discovered most often in the mosaic of state policies and laws on economic development, environment, labour, health and safety, transparency and other related issues. Beyond this, regulations, which have an impact on CSR, are often based on the ratification and subsequent domestication of international conventions. For instance, in Kenya these conventions are mainly focused on workplace issues and the physical environment. Other policy and developmental instruments like CSR codes of conduct, labels, certification, partnerships, guidelines, management systems and awards are rare in many countries.

The African Union's involvement in CSR approaches is still relatively low. However, the newly established EU–Africa Business Forum now considers, in addition to market and trade issues, CSR matters like anti-corruption and good governance.

National legislation

Examples of specific national CSR-related legislation include:

- **Kenya**. Vision 2030, Kenya National Environment Action Plan and draft guidelines for CSR, recently developed by the Kenya Bureau of Standards

- **Malawi**. Employment Act, Corrupt Practices Act

- **Mozambique**. Conventions to promote the Declaration on Fundamental Principles and Rights at Work

- **Namibia**. Vision 2030, Transformation Economic and Social Empowerment Framework (TESEF), Affirmative Action (Employment) Act

- **South Africa**. The Broad-Based Black Economic Empowerment Act (BBBEE) and its various derivatives, such as the Codes of Good Practice, the Generic Scorecard, and industry charters in financial services and mining

■ Organisations

MENA region

■ The **Center for International Private Enterprise (CIPE)** introduced the Arabic term for corporate governance, *hawkamat ash-sharika*, thus initiating business dialogue on the subject in the Middle East. CIPE produces periodical newsletters and articles in both Arabic and English on corporate governance trends. **http://www.hawkama.net** and **http://www.cipe.org**

■ In Tunisia, CIPE partner **Institut Arabe des Chefs d'Entreprise (IACE)** launched a *Code of Best Practice of Corporate Governance* in 2008. They convened a high-profile conference on corporate governance in 2009 where IACE announced recipients of the Best Corporate Governance Article Award, and launched the Center for Corporate Governance — the first of its kind in North Africa — as well as a competitive corporate awards programme. **http://www.cipe-arabia.org**

■ In Egypt, CIPE works closely with the **Egyptian Junior Business Association (EJB)**, which established a taskforce on corporate governance and published a manual, *Corporate Governance in Family Businesses* — the first of its kind in the MENA region. **http://www.ejb.org.eg**

■ In Jordan, **Al Urdun Al Jadid Research Center (UJRC)** successfully implemented a distinctive regional project entitled 'Strengthening Responsible Corporate Citizenship in the Businesses of the MENA Region'. This project was executed within the framework of the Fifth MENA Development Forum (MDF5), a partnership conference of the World Bank Group, UNDP and MENA think-tanks, seeking to build a regional coalition to strengthen CSR culture and practices. The project included two North African case studies for Egypt and Morocco. **http://www.ujrc-jordan.org**

Sub-Saharan Africa

Malawi

■ The **African Institute of Corporate Citizenship (AICC)**, an NGO that promotes sustainable business practice in Africa, is the focal point of the Global Compact local network. The AICC is recognised internationally as a centre of excellence in corporate citizenship. **http://www.aiccafrica.org**

Democratic Republic of Congo

■ The **Fédération des Entreprises du Congo (FEC)** is the DRC Chamber of Commerce, Industry, Agriculture and Trade, and also functions as an Employer Federation. FEC is involved in the 'Responsible Business Investment in the DRC' initiative and engages in anti-corruption measures and codes for the mining and forestry sector. **http://www.fec.cd**

Ghana

■ The **Chamber of Mines** represents member companies, which produce over 90% of Ghana's mineral output. It has signed the UN Global Compact and encourages its member companies to regard CSR as a core component of their business. **http://www.ghanachamberofmines.org**

∎ The **Private Enterprise Foundation (PEF)**, a member of the UN Global Compact Local Network, is an umbrella organisation for business associations, active in the field of corporate governance. **http://www.pefghana.org**

Kenya

∎ The **Federation of Kenya Employers (FKE)** has been committed to the fight against HIV/AIDS. It is a signatory of the UN Global Compact and also involved in Kenya's Vision 2030. **http://www.fke-kenya.org**

∎ The **Kenya Association of Manufacturers (KAM)** has about 600 members from 13 industrial sectors. KAM established the Centre for Energy Efficiency and Conservation (CEEC) and has been the Focal Point of the Global Compact Local Network in Kenya since September 2009. **http://www.kam.co.ke**

∎ The **Kenya Private Sector Alliance (KEPSA)** is the umbrella body of the private sector having 180 corporate members, as well as 30 business associations and 30 sectors or multi-sector institutions. KEPSA is promoting the UN Global Compact and active in the field of anti-corruption. **http://www.kepsa.or.ke**

Mozambique

∎ **Fórum Empresarial para o Meio Ambiente (FEMA)** is a member-based NGO dedicated to representing and securing the involvement of the private sector in environmental and social matters in Mozambique, also acting as the Focal Point of the UN Global Compact Local Network. **http://www.fema.org.mz**

Namibia

∎ The **Namibian Employer Federation (NEF)** has 120 direct corporate members and nine associate members and is the Focal Point of the Global Compact Local Network in Namibia. **http://www.ioe-emp.org/en**

South Africa

∎ **Business Unity South Africa (BUSA)** is an employer federation with 43 business associations connected as members. It is strongly involved in black economic empowerment and anti-corruption activities in South Africa. **http://www.busa.org.za**

∎ The **National Business Initiative South Africa (NBI)** is a voluntary group of leading companies with about 140 members. NBI is signatory of the UN Global Compact and Focal Point of its Local Network in South Africa. The NBI provides a platform for business leadership and a vision of how companies can contribute to a sustainable society. **http://www.nbi.org.za**

Uganda

∎ The **Uganda Chapter for Corporate Social Responsibility Initiatives (UCCSRI)** is a founder member of the emerging CSR Consultative Group, a body that brings together major CSR stakeholders in Uganda. **http://www.uccsri.com**

■ Case studies

Coca-Cola (Egypt)

Coca-Cola has entered into a partnership with the Egyptian Ministry of Irrigation and Water Resources and USAID to launch the Global Development Alliance — an initiative to provide clean water and solid and liquid waste treatment for communities in Upper Egypt and the Delta. **http://www.thecoca-colacompany.com/citizenship/community_initiatives/Egypt_031808.pdf**

De Beers Group

The De Beers Group, which has operations throughout Africa, developed the Diamond Trading Company Best Practice Principles (BPP) to define the way it does business, to inform its understanding of what is right and wrong and to describe what is important to the company. These are supported by an extended set of guiding principles that cover economic, ethical, employee, community and environment aspects, being developed by over 300 stakeholders, thereby providing a collective view of what constitutes best practice (Van der Walt 2007). **http://www.debeersgroup.com/en/Sustainability/policies**

Satemwa (Malawi)

Satemwa is a tea producing company with good CSR practices applied to the market-place, workplace, community and environment. It is involved in fair trade, engages in labour rights, and HIV/AIDS and health issues. It is also a member of the UN Global Compact Local Network and strives to apply each of the UN Global Compact's ten principles to the company (Kambalame 2007). **http://www.satemwa.com**

Shell (Nigeria)

In Nigeria, because of (and despite) ongoing criticism and controversy since 1995, Shell has made considerable efforts to bring its corporate strategy in line with the principles of sustainable development and has committed to extensive stakeholder engagement and transparent reporting on its environmental and social performance (Boele *et al.* 2001). **http://www.shell.com/nigeria**

Unilever (South Africa)

An extensive economic impact assessment study on Unilever in South Africa was made by Kapstein (2008). The findings show that Unilever's direct impacts include its 3,000 suppliers and their 20,000 employees, while indirect impacts include supporting approximately 100,000 jobs. This means that for every job directly created by Unilever, another 22 workers depend on the company for some part of their livelihood. **http://www.unilever.co.za**

Other cases

There are many other positive case studies, company codes and excellent examples of business performed in a responsible manner, which can be found in the publications *Africa Leads* (UNISA Centre for Corporate Citizenship *et al.* 2006), *The Business of Sus-*

tainable Development in Africa (Hamann *et al.* 2008), *Corporate Social Responsibility and the United Nations Global Compact in South Africa 2007* (Hanks *et al.* 2008) and *Corporate Social Responsibility in Sub-Saharan Africa* (Imani Development 2009).

▌ Education

South Africa

Most of the leading universities with CSR-related degrees and courses are located in South Africa. However, only the University of Cape Town (UCT) offers a comprehensive core module on corporate citizenship. Some schools provide either core modules on business ethics or on 'business in society' or on 'HIV/AIDS policy and strategy'. Most offer elective courses on CSR topics, e.g. corporate governance or environmental management. In addition, the following short courses are offered:

- **Gordon Institute of Business Science (GIBS).** Corporate citizenship, including a seminar with Harvard Business School (*Making Markets Work* by Martyn Davies). **http://www.gibs.co.za**

- **Institute of Directors.** Corporate governance. **http://www.iodsa.co.za**

- **Leadership Centre at the University of KwaZulu-Natal.** Corporate citizenship. **http://www.leadershipcentre.co.za**

- **Sustainability Institute at the University of Stellenbosch.** Corporate citizenship. **http://www.sustainabilityinstitute.net**

- **UNISA Centre for Corporate Citizenship (CCC).** Two six-month courses, emphasising corporate citizenship and corporate governance, plus various short courses. **http://www.unisa.ac.za**

- **University of Cape Town Graduate School of Business.** Business ethics and black economic empowerment, integrating the Centre for Leadership and Public Values; also offering a postgraduate Diploma in Corporate Social Responsibility. **http://www.gsb.uct.ac.za**

Beyond South Africa

- **Uganda.** Makerere University Business School (MUBS) is planning a separate course on the Principles of CSR, which integrates CSR topics into basic courses in marketing, strategy and entrepreneurship, as part of a bachelor's degree in CSR. **http://www.mubs.ac.ug**

- **Ghana.** The University of Ghana Business School (UGBS) has already integrated CSR into some courses, e.g. Business Policy and Strategic Management, and will establish a CSR Centre of Excellence to develop courses/modules for undergraduate and postgraduate programmes in mid 2010. Courses and training materials are intended to enhance private and public stakeholder proactive engagement in CSR. **http://www.ugbs.edu.gh**

References

Ararat, M. (2006) *Corporate Social Responsibility Across Middle East And North Africa* (Sabanci University, Turkey: Corporate Governance Forum [CGFT], **http://ssrn.com/abstract=1015925**, accessed 17 March 2010).

Bertelsmann Stiftung and Deutsche Gesellschaft für Technische Zusammenarbeit (GTZ) GmbH (2007) *The CSR Navigator: Public Policies in Africa, the Americas, Asia and Europe* (Gütersloh: Bertelsmann Stiftung).

Boele, R., H. Fabig and D. Wheeler (2001) 'Shell, Nigeria and Ogoni: A Study in Unsustainable Development: II. Corporate Social Responsibility and "Stakeholder Management" versus a Rights Based Approach to Sustainable Development', *Sustainable Development* 9.2: 121-135.

Centre for International Private Enterprise (CIPE) and Global Corporate Governance Forum (2003) *Corporate Governance in Morocco, Egypt, Lebanon and Jordan* (Washington, DC: CIPE).

Crane, A., D. Matten and L. Spence (2008) *Corporate Social Responsibility: Readings and Cases in a Global Context* (London: Routledge).

Gathii, J.T. (2008) 'Kenya: What does CSR really mean?', *Business Daily Nairobi*, 6 May 2008; **http://allafrica.com/stories/200805061150.html**, accessed 30 October 2009.

Hamann, R. and P. Kapelus (2004) 'CSR Practices in the Mining Sector in South Africa and Zambia', *Development* 47.3: 85-92.

——, S. Woolman and C. Sprague (2008) *The Business of Sustainable Development in Africa* (Pretoria: UNISA Press/Deutsche Gesellschaft für Technische Zusammenarbeit (GTZ) GmbH/BMZ).

Hanks, J., R. Hamann and V. Sayers (2008) *Corporate Social Responsibility and the United Nations Global Compact in South Africa 2007* (Johannesburg: Global Compact Network South Africa, National Business Initiative [NBI] and Deutsche Gesellschaft für Technische Zusammenarbeit [GTZ] GmbH).

Imani Development (2009) *Corporate Social Responsibility in Sub-Saharan Africa — Built In or Bolted On? A Survey on Promoting and Hindering Factors* (Eschborn, Germany: Deutsche Gesellschaft für Technische Zusammenarbeit [GTZ] GmbH/BMZ/British High Commission South Africa).

Johanson, R.K., and A. Adams (2004) *Skills Development in Sub-Saharan Africa* (Washington, DC: World Bank).

Kambalame, D. (2007) *Satemwa Tea Estate Limited: Case Study* (Pretoria: UN Global Compact Regional Learning Forum/Deutsche Gesellschaft für Technische Zusammenarbeit [GTZ] GmbH, unpublished).

Kapstein, E.B. (2008) *Measuring Unilever's Economic Footprint: The Case of South Africa* (Kloof, South Africa: Famous Publishing).

Njenga, S., and A. Smit (2007) *Leading the Way through CSI: A Guidebook for Corporate Social Investment Practitioners* (Rosebank, Johannesburg: Knowledge Resources).

Nussbaum, B. (2003) 'Ubuntu: Reflections of a South African on our Common Humanity', *Reflections* 4.4; **http://www.barbaranussbaum.com/downloads/reflections.pdf**, accessed 2 November 2009.

Ofori, D., and R. Hinson (2007) 'Corporate Social Responsibility (CSR) Perspectives of Leading Firms in Ghana', *Corporate Governance: The International Journal of Business in Society* 7.2: 178-193.

UNISA Centre for Corporate Citizenship, Deutsche Gesellschaft für Technische Zusammenarbeit (GTZ) GmbH, UN Global Compact and Barloworld (2006) *Africa Leads* (Pretoria: University of South Africa [UNISA] Press).

Van der Walt, H. (2007) *Global Compact Case Study: De Beers. Raising the Bar: From Legal and Risk-Based Compliance to Values and Principles-Based Responsibility and Assurance* (Pretoria: UN Global Compact Regional Learning Forum/Deutsche Gesellschaft für Technische Zusammenarbeit [GTZ] GmbH, unpublished).

Visser, W. (2006) 'Revisiting Carroll's CSR Pyramid: An African Perspective', in E.R. Pedersen and M. Huniche (eds.), *Corporate Citizenship in Developing Countries* (Copenhagen: Copenhagen Business School Press): 29-56.

—— (2008) 'Corporate Social Responsibility in Developing Countries', in A. Crane, A. McWilliams, D. Matten, J. Moon and D. Siegel (eds.), *The Oxford Handbook of Corporate Social Responsibility* (Oxford: Oxford University Press): 473-479.

——, M. McIntosh and C. Middleton (eds.) (2006) *Corporate Citizenship in Africa: Lessons from the Past; Paths to the Future* (Sheffield, UK: Greenleaf Publishing).

Winston, B., and B. Ryan (2008) 'Servant Leadership as a Humane Orientation: Using the GLOBE Study Construct of Humane Orientation to Show that Servant Leadership is More Global than Western', *International Journal of Leadership Studies* 3.2: 212-222.

World Bank (2009a) *Key Development Data and Statistics* (Washington, DC: World Bank).

—— (2009b) *Heavily Indebted Poor Countries* (World Bank; **http://web.worldbank.org**, accessed 30 October 2009).

World Bank Institute, Centre for International Private Enterprise (CIPE), Egyptian Institute of Directors and Arab Labour Organisation (2007). 'Corporate Social Responsibility and Corporate Citizenship in the Arab World', report on a meeting in Cairo, Egypt 21-22 November 2007, Washington, DC: World Bank.

Zimmer, M. and L. Rieth (2007). *Impact of Voluntary CSR Initiatives — The Global Compact and its Regional Learning Forum* (Eschborn, Germany: Deutsche Gesellschaft für Technische Zusammenarbeit (GTZ) GmbH/BMZ/British High Commission South Africa).

II Asia

Felipe B. Alfonso
Executive Director and Professor, Ramon V. del Rosario, Sr.
Center for Corporate Social Responsibility, Asian Institute of Management

Maria Elena B. Herrera
Faculty Fellow, Ramon V. del Rosario, Sr.
Center for Corporate Social Responsibility, Asian Institute of Management

Francisco L. Roman
Deputy Executive Director and Professor, Ramon V. del Rosario, Sr.
Center for Corporate Social Responsibility, Asian Institute of Management

■ Context

In the 2005 Asian Forum on Corporate Social Responsibility Survey, 63% said that CSR goes beyond compliance with rules and regulations. Despite differences in history and culture, Asian CSR is linked to underlying value systems, such as placing the good of the family and larger society over that of the individual.

Two-thirds of all listed companies, and a substantial number of private companies, are family controlled and managed. For example, the 15 top family groupings in Indonesia, holding 62% of all listed assets, comprise 21.5% of the country's GDP (Adams 2003). In Hong Kong, the top 15 family groupings hold 34% of all listed assets and comprise 84% of the country's GDP. Thus, CSR in Asia is a natural extension of the family corporation. A failure of the corporation is often seen as a failure of the family.

CSR in Asia is also rooted in specific cultural traditions. For example, in Indonesia, there is the concept of *gotong royong*, which literally means 'joint bearing of burdens'. This is a tradition of helping out other people in the community by providing assistance to victims of natural disasters, volunteering for community projects, or even just coming together to help make an occasion such as a wedding successful.

A similar tradition in the Philippines is called *bayanihan* — *bayan* meaning country and *bayani* meaning hero. *Bayanihan* means individuals and small groups coming together in order to help those in need or to accomplish a goal for the larger community.

In Hong Kong, the practice of CSR is attributed to Confucianism — emphasising the social roles of individuals towards the collective, with an ethical mandate that the greatest good is for the community. The common Confucian heritage is often used to explain the value that many Asians place on relationships among family and friends and is reflected in the respect and courtesy shown for age, wisdom, leadership, neighbours and customs (Whelan 2007).

Asian CSR also has a long tradition of philanthropy, through implicit obligations that were embedded in business practices and institutional frameworks. Furthermore, these responsibilities lay with the owner of the corporation, and did not imply the creation of a distinct and separate organisational mechanism (Debroux 2008).

In Japan, *shonindo* — the way of the merchant — means that work needs to be disciplined, honest and efficient in providing service to society and leading to a business culture of benevolent responsibility towards direct stakeholders.

The core values in Japan, China and, to some extent, Korea are faith and trust drawn from Buddhism and Confucianism. In South-East Asia, CSR retains a paternalistic overtone, where CSR emanates from the personal responsibility of organisational leaders (often also owners) rather than organisational responsibility.

However, there is no single Asian approach to CSR because Asia itself is so diverse.

▋ Priority issues

In Asia, CSR activities are tied to three factors: localised issues, cultural traditions at a country level and historical events. The predominant social issues in Asia are education, poverty, environment and human rights.

Poverty

Extreme poverty — especially in the less developed Asian economies — leads to poor nutrition and impacts access to such basic needs as shelter, education and healthcare, thus creating the potential for extending the poverty problem across generations of families. Many of the philanthropy-based CSR programmes in Asia focus on poverty reduction (e.g. livelihood, free clinics, housing and scholarship).

Education

Education is related to the problem of poverty, as evidenced by low human development statistics in countries such as Sri Lanka, India, Pakistan and the Philippines. In contrast, in Singapore and Malaysia, the objective of education is to maintain economic growth in the context of an ageing population and to equip graduates to deal with international competition.

Labour and supply chain

The most prominent workplace issue is labour standards. Others include such matters as sexual harassment, HIV/AIDS, diversity and employee privacy.

As suppliers to global manufacturers, for many South-East Asian countries (Vietnam, Cambodia and Indonesia), the main focus is on economic development. According to Welford and Frost (2006), they face numerous challenges such as:

- **Divergence of codes**. Numerous different codes of conduct may in certain cases have contradictory elements depending on the type of customers and industry;

- **Complication of the structure**. Many companies are unable to undertake 'green supervision' beyond one or at two levels in the supply chain; and

- **Cooperation**. The main challenge is to move away from inspection and auditing and towards capacity building, working with governments and business in developing sound laws and frameworks, building long-term trust relationships down the supply chain and working with NGOs.

Environment

Environmental degradation in Asia results in increased health problems and scarcity of resources. Environmental protection is recognised as a priority issue in countries as diverse as South Korea, the Philippines, Sri Lanka, India and Malaysia. Nevertheless, the ecosystem continues to be degraded or used unsustainably. For example, mono-crop plantations (e.g. palm oil in Indonesia) are prevalent across Asia, but often fail to take into account the interests of local people (Clay 2004).

The use of chemical fertilisers and insecticides, resulting in an unhealthy concentration of harmful chemicals, are causing degradation of the environment, destroying biodiversity and putting food resources at risk. The loss of forests is also contributing to global warming, increasing the risk of flooding and causing the destruction of many plant species.

There are, however, examples of new initiatives. In the Philippines, an economic resource model for valuing coastal resources is in use, and in China and Thailand there are large-scale projects to address water management concerns.

Products

Marketplace issues spring from a company's relationship with its customers and other stakeholders. Marketplace categories (Zhang 2008) include such issues as:

- Integrity of product manufacturing and quality
- Disclosure, labelling and packaging
- Responsible marketing and advertising
- Responsible selling practices
- Pricing, distribution and access

Community

The relationship with local communities and indigenous peoples is slowly becoming a priority for industries such as power generation and mining. Emerging issues include obesity and nutrition, integrity of the food chain, privacy and technology, drug pricing for the poor and elderly, marketing to children, heightened expectations for product safety and extended product responsibility. There are, however, varying perspectives on these different concerns.

Governance

Many would argue that at the heart of Asia's problems are poor public and corporate governance due to weak institutional frameworks. Agencies such as Transparency International note the debilitating corruption that impedes social and economic progress in Asia.

▮ Trends

Due to these pressing social and environmental problems faced by Asian countries, companies are expected to do more for the communities they operate in. CSR is practised because internal and external stakeholders place pressure on companies to address these concerns. CSR is increasingly being recognised as a kind of 'social licence to operate', since business cannot thrive in a society where many remain poor (Asia Business Council 2008).

Driving forces

Asian CSR tends to emanate from culture, values and tradition. Formal and written approaches such as Codes of Conduct are more Western in origin, but are nevertheless adopted as appropriate.

Tradition

Drivers of CSR range from religious traditions, notions of trusteeship, family philanthropy and role models within the country, to company responses to regulation, NGO and civil society pressure, and requirements of national and international business partners in a more global world. The values of employees and organisations also play an essential role in motivating CSR practice.

Market forces

Asian practitioners of CSR believe that community trust and reputation are the most important motives for CSR, followed by internal customer satisfaction, sustainability and customer loyalty (APEC Secretariat 2005). This finding is similar to the results of the 2005 opinion survey conducted by the Ramon V. del Rosario Sr. Center for Corporate Social Responsibility where 40% of the respondents reported that one objective of CSR programmes is to enhance company reputation.

Regulation

Laws and regulations, corporate governance and other compliance programmes are becoming part of corporate policy in Asia. Asian executives and officers have begun to bring their management expertise to bear on CSR plans and programmes in so far as they may positively influence the regulatory environment (RVR CSR Center 2005).

Forms of CSR

In Asia, responsible corporations are perceived as those concerned and active in community welfare and offering top-quality products and services. External CSR programmes tend to focus on the environment and social community issues such as education and health, whereas internal CSR programmes are directed towards employee welfare or workplace conditions.

CSR is still practised through gift giving, donations and volunteering throughout the region. In some cases, even though the CSR concept is evident at the individual level due to the Asian 'charitable' culture, practices may not actually translate at the corporate level. When corporations do give, they tend to give cash to charities rather than crafting strategic responses to clearly defined corporate social issues (APEC Secretariat 2005).

Another approach taken by corporations is to create their own foundation to implement their CSR programmes. As noted by Dr Filemon Uriarte of the ASEAN Foundation, corporate foundations play an important role in human development. Asian CSR, still in its early stages, typically takes two approaches: the philanthropic mode or community relations, as appropriate to their situation. For example, many companies (e.g. in India and Indonesia) are still in philanthropic mode and practise CSR through community partnerships, employee codes and corporate foundations.

Most CSR-practising Indonesian companies are in the compliance stage (according to Zadek's corporate citizenship model [APEC Secretariat 2005]), where they adopt policy-based compliance as a cost of doing business.

Implementing CSR

Partnerships

In most developing Asian countries, the development of NGOs as grassroots organisations acts as a corporate conscience or watchdog and offers an alternative response to the needs of the community. For example, in Indonesia and the Philippines, NGOs play an important role in supporting the labour movement.

Collaboration with government and private corporations also provides a method of harnessing different complementary resources in order to achieve shared goals more successfully. A study by the Ramon V. del Rosario Sr. Center for Corporate Social Responsibility (2005) noted that 74% of the respondents believed that partnerships with NGOs or other external organisations make CSR programmes more credible.

One of the growing trends in Asia is the growth of social enterprise, which merges business and NGO models (Welford 2009).

CSR reporting

In Asia, the notion of the extended family results in a strong preference by firms for direct dialogue with stakeholders, rather than issuing standardised reports to the public. A study on CSR website reporting — analysing the corporate websites of the top 50 companies in seven Asian countries — noted that the percentage of companies reporting extensively, with the exclusion of Japan, is very low (Chambers *et al.* 2005). These findings are similar to the APEC study (2005), which shows evidence of CSR activity in Asia, yet low awareness and reporting.

Nevertheless, in recent years there is a growing trend for Asian companies to publish CSR reports, especially in South Korea and Japan. According to Japan's Ministry of the Environment there has been an increase in the number of CSR-reporting companies from 169 (6.5%) in 1997 to 1,049 (37.8%) in 2006 (Adachi 2008).

Integrating CSR

Businesses are adapting CSR policies not so much to 'save the planet' as to survive and prosper. The Grant Thornton International Business Report concluded that firms are adopting CSR as a strategy (Enterprise Innovation 2008). Countries like mainland China (rank 1, 74%), Thailand (rank 4, 64%), the Philippines (rank 6, 59%) and Malaysia (rank 8, 58%) are leading in integrating CSR as a business strategy in Asia.

In an IBM (2008) study involving 1,130 CEOs in 40 countries, it was reported that business leaders in Asia Pacific are faster in spending more on CSR efforts than any of their international peers. This study also noted that Asia Pacific companies are increasing their CSR investment at an average of 42%, as compared to a global average of 25%. CSR was seen as a key and differentiating component of their business strategy, as evident in the study where 81% of Asia Pacific CEOs and 84% in Greater China[1] confirm they have high expectations of CSR compared to 69% of CEOs globally. Moreover, case studies in various conferences acknowledge that there have already been substantial changes in accountability.

Emerging business models

There are three emerging business models in Asia, each described briefly below (Beshouri 2006). They are all examples of serving the bottom of the pyramid through community-based strategies reflecting the distinct characteristics of low income markets, while creating growth opportunities for companies. These initiatives bridge cultural gaps between the company and the community, and benefit both the community (through promotion of micro-market activity) and the company (by creating a positive association with the company's brand).

Collective accountability

The core issue addressed is problems with fee collection and pilferage. The solution is that small groups monitor usage, promote compliance and provide social insurance. Relevant industries include utilities and finance.

An example is Manila Water (MW) in the Philippines. A large number of households in MW's target market live in shanties (informal dwellings) that lack proper sanitation facilities. The cost of installing basic plumbing is substantial, so consumers felt they had to make illegal connections to obtain water. MW allowed community collective installation, metering and billing. Collective metering may refer to either one meter for three or four households or a bulk meter for 40–50 households. Everyone who is on a group or bulk meter shares the responsibility for the whole bill. This has ensured timely payment of bills for MW (up from 30% prior to the initiative, to 100%). This cheaper, higher-quality water service helps to free up income for other purchases and raises the quality of life and health for the households being served.

Livelihood partnership

The core issue addressed is a lack of brand equity and cultural divisions that can separate the interests of consumers and producers. The solution is that business offers additional services around core products or services that promote primary demand, while

---

1   Greater China includes Hong Kong, Macau and Taiwan.

providing training or cooperative business programmes to the community. Relevant industries include telephone services, utilities and agriculture.

Scalable, embedded distribution

The core issue addressed is that traditional service delivery is too costly relative to purchase size and density of consumers. The solution is low-cost, community-based distribution points that employ key workers in low income areas. Relevant industries include fast-moving and/or low-value consumer goods, and telecoms.

An example is Hindustan Lever (HL) in India. The company developed Shakti, a programme that trained rural women to operate as distributors of consumer products in villages of fewer than 1,000 people. HL created a four-week training programme and employed some of the company's leading entrepreneurs as trainers. The Shakti programme now covers 80,000 villages with 25,000 women entrepreneurs. It generates annual sales of around USD250 million in villages that would otherwise be uneconomic to serve.

▌ Legislation and codes

While CSR-related laws exist in the areas of environment, workplace and labour, corporate governance, and social development, enforcement of legal responsibilities tends to be weak. This is mainly due to poorly developed legal infrastructure in many developing countries or the government's lack of necessary resources and political will to implement these laws (Visser 2008).

Environment

Most Asian countries have also adopted Agenda 21, along with the Rio Declaration on Environment and Development and the Statement of Principles for Sustainable Management of Forests. Countries like the Philippines and Indonesia have adopted laws on marine life protection and coastal conservation, such as the UN Convention on the Law of the Sea.

Other national laws include forest conservation Acts in China, India and Bangladesh, and clean air and clean water Acts in the Philippines and Japan.

An increasing number of Asian countries are also enacting laws that require environmental impact assessment (EIA) for large-scale projects, especially for the extractive industry. In the Philippines, mining companies are required to submit an EIA as early as the exploration stage.

Multinational corporations are also adopting international standards such as ISO 14001 on environmental management.

Labour

Many countries in Asia are signatories to the various International Labour Organization (ILO) conventions, especially the core ILO conventions against child labour and discrimination in the workplace. The labour laws protect employees by stipulating minimum wage, overtime pay, and workplace health and safety requirements.

Corporate governance

Several countries have implemented codes of conduct and anti-corruption laws, such as the Securities Regulation Code in the Philippines, the Code of Corporate Governance in Singapore and anti-corruption legislation in South Korea. These are designed to encourage good governance among companies by promoting accountability and transparency in their operations.

Social development

In 2007, Indonesia passed Law 40/2007 on Limited Liability Companies, which makes CSR mandatory for almost all companies (excluding the financial and information technology sectors). Article 74 stipulates that all companies engaged in the use of natural resources must conduct environmental and social responsibility programmes. The revised law also mandates disclosure of activities related to environmental and social responsibility programmes in the company's annual reports (Darwin and Guntensperger 2007).

In the Philippines, mining companies are required under the Philippine Mining Act to allocate at least 1% of milling and mining costs to social development projects to affected communities. Companies or individuals giving donations to registered non-profit organisations are also given tax deductions.

▌ Organisations

▌ The **Asia Pacific Philanthropy Consortium (APPC)**. An independent association of grant-making and philanthropic institutions. **http://www.asiapacificphilanthropy.org**

▌ The **Association for Sustainable and Responsible Investment in Asia**. A nonprofit membership association dedicated to promoting CSR and sustainable investment practices in the Asia Pacific region, with 52 voting members and 73 associate members. **http://www.asria.org**

▌ **Community Business Hong Kong**. A membership-based nonprofit organisation, with a mission to 'lead, support and inspire businesses to continually improve their positive impact on people and communities'. It provides training, facilitation and advice to some of the world's leading companies on diversity in the workplace, corporate community investment and CSR strategy and policy. **http://www.communitybusiness.org.hk**

▌ **Confederation of Indian Industries (CII)**. This industry led and managed nonprofit organisation has a membership base of over 7,800 organisations from the private sector. The CII established the Social Development Council to ensure the participation of companies in social development and to provide an institutional base for the social activities of the corporate sector. **http://cii.in**

▌ **CSR Asia**. This social enterprise is one of the leading providers of 'information, training, research and consultancy services on sustainable business practices in Asia'. CSR Asia works with its partners in different countries of operations to promote and develop CSR strategies. **http://www.csr-asia.com**

▌**Indonesia Business Links**. This not-for-profit foundation was established in the wake of the Indonesian economic crisis. A major aim of the organisation is to contribute to the creation of sound and ethical business practices in the country. **http://www.ibl.or.id**

▌**The Nippon Keidanren (Japanese Business Federation)**. This federation was created by the Japan Federation of Economic Organisations and the Japan Federation of Employers' Associations, with over 1,600 members from industrial associations and regional economic organisations. It adopted the Charter for Good Corporate Behaviour in 1991. In 2003, the organisation also established a subcommittee on socially responsible management. **http://www.keidanren.or.jp**

▌**Philippine Business for Social Progress (PBSP)**. A private, nonprofit foundation dedicated to promoting business sector commitment to social development. Organised in the 1970s by prominent business leaders in the Philippines, it has since grown to become the nation's largest business-led social development foundation with around 238 members. In 1991, it established a Center for Corporate Citizenship. **http://www.pbsp. org.ph**

▌The **Population and Community Development Association**. This association has around 100 members and supports rural sector development in Thailand through its Thai Business for Rural Development Initiative in partnership with different corporations. **http://www.pda.or.th/eng**

▌The **Singapore Compact for CSR**. This group functions as a national society in furthering the CSR movement through ongoing dialogues, training, collaboration and practical project implementation. It is also a participant of the UN Global Compact. **http://www. csrsingapore.org**

▌**Vietnam Chamber of Commerce and Industry**. This chamber promotes CSR through various conferences and dialogues and by recognising, through awards, companies that operate in a socially responsible manner. **http://vibforum.vcci.com.vn**

▌Case studies

City Development Limited (Singapore)

City Development Limited (CDL) focuses on giving back to the community, through its commitment to long-term sustainable CSR programmes aimed at caring for the underprivileged, raising awareness about the environment, nurturing the youth and promoting the arts. CDL was conferred the prestigious President's Social Service Award and President's Award for the Environment in 2007 and was recently honoured as the nation's first BCA Green Mark Champion for developing the highest number of exemplary green buildings in Singapore. **http://www.cdl.com.sg**

Siam Cement Group (Thailand)

Siam Cement Group has an extensive CSR programme focusing on social and community development and environment protection. Due to the increasing cost of raw materials and waste elimination, SCG has set its target on achieving zero waste through the concept of the 3Rs (reduce, reuse and recycle). The company also established the SCG Foundation that implements programmes on education and youth development as well as providing disaster relief assistance. **http://www.siamcement.com/en**

Smart Communications (Philippines)

Smart Communications is the leading wireless telecommunications services provider in the Philippines. It provides quality services at prices that the lower income consumer can afford. Smart also implements programmes for the environment and social development. An example is its Smart Wireless Engineering Education Program, which aims to raise the level of engineering education in the country by providing wireless laboratories to more than half of the schools that offer electronic and communications engineering in the country (de Jesus 2007). **http://www.smartsweep.ph** and **http://www.smart.com.ph**

Tata Group (India)

Tata Group spearheaded the corporate citizenship movement in India. Almost 30% of the company's profits are invested in community development programmes across India. The Group has a centrally administered Tata Council for Community Initiatives that helps its companies through specific processes in social development, environmental management and employee volunteering. The company, in partnership with UNDP India, crafted the Tata Index for Sustainable Human Development, a 'pioneering effort aimed at directing, measuring and enhancing the community work that the group enterprises undertake' (Branzei and Nadkarni 2008). **http://www.tata.com**

Toyota (Japan)

Toyota follows strict environmental standards in its operations worldwide. It also participates in programmes such as reforestation in China. With its Toyota Foundation, the company supports and funds different projects all over Asia. For example, through its Asian Neighbors Program it supports problem-solving projects that address the relationship between nature, culture and social systems. **http://www.toyotafound.or.jp/english** and **http://www.toyota.co.jp/en**

▌ Education

In Asia only two schools were ranked in *Beyond Grey Pinstripes* (2009), which ranks MBAs on social and environmental criteria: the **Asian Institute of Management, Philippines** (Rank: 97) and the **Seoul School of Integrated Sciences and Technologies (aSSIST), Korea** (Rank 100).

However, there are other schools that have previously been ranked by *Beyond Grey Pinstripes*:

- **China Europe International Business School** (2003)

- **Korea Advanced Institute of Science and Technology** (2001)

- **Indian Institute of Management, Bangalore, India** (2003)

- **Indian Institute of Management, Calcutta, India** (2003)

- **Indonesian Institute for Management** (2003)

- **National University of Singapore, Singapore** (2007)

- **SP Jain Institute of Management and Research, India** (2003)

References

Adachi, N. (2008) 'How to Choose the Right Media to Communicate with Stakeholders — to be Printed or Wired?', presentation to the Asian Forum on Corporate Social Responsibility (unpublished).

Adams, I. (2003) 'The Morality of Corporate Governance: Issues of Quality and Quantity', delivered at the 2003 conference of the Economic Society of South Africa, Somerset West, South Africa, 17–19 September 2003; http://www.essa.org.za/download/2003Conference/AdamsI_The%20Morality%20of%20Corporate%20Governance.pdf.

APEC (Asia Pacific Economic Cooperation Secretariat) (2005) 'Corporate Social Responsibility in the APEC Region' (prepared by the Institute for International Studies and Training, Tokyo, Japan).

Asia Business Council (2008) 'Corporate Social Responsibility: Business Solutions to Global Challenges'; http://www.asiabusinesscouncil.org/docs/BSR.pdf, accessed 2 June 2010.

Aspen Institute Center for Business Education (2010) 'Beyond Grey Pinstripes 2009–2010'; http://www.beyondgreypinstripes.org/pdf/2009-2010BGP_Brochure.pdf, accessed 2 June 2010.

Beshouri, C. (2006) 'A Grassroots Approach to Emerging Market Consumers', *The McKinsey Quarterly*, 4: 60-71.

Branzei, O., and Nadkarni, A. (2008) 'The Tata Way: Evolving and Executing Sustainable Business Strategies', *Ivey Business Journal*, March/April 2008; http://www.iveybusinessjournal.com/article.asp?intArticle_ID=750, accessed 18 March 2010.

Business for Social Responsibility (2007) *Beyond Monitoring: A New Vision for Sustainable Supply Chains* (Business for Social Responsibility; http://www.bsr.org/reports/BSR_Beyond-Monitoring-Report.pdf, accessed 18 March 2010).

Catalyst Consortium (2002) *Corporate Social Responsibility Resources*, Catalyst Consortium; http://www.rhcatalyst.org/site/DocServer/CSRResources.pdf?docID=104.

Chambers, E., W. Chapple, J. Moon and M. Sullivan (2005) *CSR in Asia: A Seven Country Study of CSR Website Reporting* (Nottingham, UK: Nottingham University Business School; http://www.nottingham.ac.uk/nubs/ICCSR/research.php, accessed 18 March 2010).

Chapple, W., and J. Moon (2007) 'Introduction: CSR Agendas for Asia', *Corporate Social Responsibility and Environmental Management* 14.3: 183-188.

Clay, J. (2004) *World Agriculture and the Environment: A Commodity-by-Commodity Guide to Impacts and Practices* (Washington, DC: Island Press).

CSR Asia (2008) *CSR Asia Business Barometer: The State of CSR Disclosure in Asia*, October 2008; http://www.csr-asia.com/upload/Report_Business_Barometer_2008.pdf, accessed 18 March 2010.

Darwin, A., and P. Guntensperger (2007) 'Mandatory CSR: Waiting for Details', *Jakarta Post*, 21 November 2007 (Supplement on Corporate Social Responsibility).

Debroux, P. (2006) 'Corporate Social Responsibility in Asia: the Beginning of the Road' (Japan: Soka University; http://keiei.soka.ac.jp/assets/images/ctg07/review/data/soka200603/soka200603_02.pdf, accessed 18 March 2010).

—— (2008) 'CSR and Sustainable Development in Asia: A Growing Awareness' (Japan: Soka University; http://keiei.soka.ac.jp/assets/pdf/keieironsyu/vol32_no1-3/philippe_debroux.pdf, accessed 18 March 2010).

De Jesus, M. (2007) 'Smart and Gawad Kalinga: Restoring the Hope of the Poor', in *Doing Good in Business Matters. CSR in the Philippines: The Practice* (Makati City, Philippines: Asian Institute of Management and De La Salle Professional Schools, Ramon V. del Rosario, Sr. Graduate School of Business): 281-315.

Enterprise Innovation (2008) 'China Tops CSR Survey with HK and Taiwan Scoring Poorly', Enterprise Innovation, 18 December 2008; **http://www.enterpriseinnovation.net/content/china-tops-csr-survey-hk-and-taiwan-scoring-poorly**, accessed 18 March 2010.

IBM (2008a) 'The Enterprise of the Future', IBM; **http://www-931.ibm.com/tela/servlet/Asset/214647/GBE03035-USEN-02.pdf**, accessed 18 March 2010).

—— (2008b) 'Asia Pacific Findings of IBM 2008 Global CEO Study', IBM 20 May 2008; **http://www.ibm.com/news/hk/en/2008/05/29/u020625i16462m07.html**,, accessed 18 March 2010).

RVR CSR Center (Ramon V. del Rosario Sr. Center for Corporate Social Responsibility) (2005) 'AFCSR Executive Survey' (unpublished).

—— (2008) 'Corporate Social Responsibility in Asia: Getting it Done the Intel Way' (Manila: Asian Institute of Management).

Silos, L. (1998) *Management and the Tao: Organisation as Community* (Manila: Asian Institute of Management).

UNDP (United Nations Environment Programme) (undated) 'The Global Programme of Action for the Protection of the Marine Environment from Land-Based Activities'; **http://www.gpa.unep.org**, accessed 18 March 2010.

Uriarte, F. (2009) 'ASEAN Foundation and Emerging CSR Issues and Challenges'; **http://www.aseanfoundation.org/documents/brochure/AF_CSR_Booklet.pdf**, accessed 18 March 2010.

Visser, W. (2008) 'Corporate Social Responsibility in Developing Countries'; **http://www.waynevisser.com/chapter_wvisser_csr_dev_countries.pdf**, accessed 18 March 2010.

Welford, R. (2007) 'Corporate Governance and Corporate Social Responsibility', *Corporate Social Responsibility and Environmental Management* 14.1: 42-51.

—— (2009) 'CSR in 10: Emerging Trends and Issues for Corporate Social Responsibility over the Next Decade', CSR Asia; **http://www.csr-asia.com/upload/news/118283040347.pdf**, accessed 18 March 2010.

—— and S. Frost (2006) 'CSR in Asian Supply Chains', *Corporate Social Responsibility and Environmental Management* 13: 166-176.

Whelan, G. (2007) 'Corporate Social Responsibility in Asia: A Confucian Context', in S. May, G. Cheney and J. Roper (eds.), *The Debate over Corporate Social Responsibility* (New York: Oxford University Press): 105-118.

Zhang, F. (2008) *Corporate Social Responsibility in Emerging Markets: The Role of Multinational Corporations* (London: The Foreign Policy Centre; **http://fpc.org.uk/fsblob/919.pdf**, accessed 18 March 2010).

III Europe

Laura Maanavilja

Communications Manager, CSR Europe

▮ Context

The interaction between business and society in Europe is shaped by the diversity of economic, political and cultural landscapes across the continent. The idea that companies can contribute to societal well-being beyond their legal obligations has a long tradition in many parts of the region. In general, the development of CSR has been driven by proactive strategies adopted by pioneering businesses, European institutions and national governments, as well as by external pressures from other stakeholders such as civil society and the investor community, among others.

In Western Europe, the development of the welfare state system during the second half of the 20th century emphasised the role of the state as the primary provider of welfare, while companies were expected to fulfil their societal obligations mainly by complying with laws, paying taxes and providing employment (Kinnicutt and Mirvis 2009).

Over more recent decades, however, economic and socio-political factors in many Western European countries have led to a partial redefinition of the boundaries between the public and private sector as well as their respective roles in society. In this context, growing attention is being paid to the voluntary actions that companies take as part of their CSR strategies to manage their economic, social and environmental impacts and to contribute to wider societal development.

In post-communist Central and Eastern Europe, environmental and social concerns have tended to receive less attention than the significant economic challenges associated with the transition to a market economy. However, CSR awareness and implementation in the region are advancing rapidly. In contrast to Western Europe, it is mainly companies themselves — often foreign multinational corporations — that are the main agents of change, whereas external pressure from civil society, media and public authorities has so far been fairly low (Line and Braun 2007).

In Europe, as well as in other parts of the world, the CSR movement has traditionally been led by large companies, yet 99% of European companies are small and medium-sized enterprises (SMEs), and about two-thirds of jobs in the private sector are in SMEs (Audtrecsh *et al.* 2009). Many small companies are by nature attuned to the values of their founder or owner as well as to the needs of their local communities, but today increasing attention is being paid to the implementation of a more structured CSR approach in European SMEs.

As a relatively wealthy, stable region with a developed economic and societal structure, the current CSR issues and challenges in Europe naturally differ to some extent from those faced by the world's less developed regions. Many social and environmental responsibilities, which may fall under companies' voluntary CSR engagement elsewhere are legally defined in Europe.

However, the increasing interest in business opportunities associated with innovative CSR approaches, together with the growing stakeholder expectations for corporate accountability and responsible business practices both within and outside Europe, continue to push the CSR agenda forward.

Furthermore, as a result of the financial and economic crisis, the level of public trust in business has recently fallen significantly in many European countries.[1] In this context, it can be said that the credit crisis and the ensuing recession have highlighted the need for companies to contribute to rebuilding trust in business and shaping a more responsible and sustainable economy in Europe and globally.

∎ Priority issues

The CSR priorities of companies in Europe reflect the economic, social and environmental challenges faced by European societies today, as well as the business challenges faced by companies operating in an increasingly globalised and interconnected marketplace.

In 2005, CSR Europe, a network which brings together more than 2,000 companies throughout the continent, outlined a business roadmap based on some of the key CSR issues for companies in Europe (CSR Europe 2005). These included environmental protection, health and safety, equal opportunities and diversity, skills and competence building, and innovation and entrepreneurship. The roadmap also identified strategies for addressing these issues: through mainstreaming CSR in the company, stakeholder engagement, leadership and governance, communications and reporting, and business partnerships.

Environment

European countries have some of the highest environmental standards in the world. In the 2008 Environmental Performance Index, which compares the environmental performance of nearly 150 countries worldwide, 16 out of the top 20 countries were in Europe, with Switzerland, Norway, Sweden and Finland leading the ranking (Yale University and Columbia University 2008).

Despite its relatively well-developed regulatory frameworks, environmental management systems and public awareness on environmental issues, Europe faces serious environmental challenges. Key priorities include combating climate change, preserving biodiversity, reducing health problems from pollution and using natural resources more responsibly.

1 http://www.edelman.com/trust/2009

In terms of climate change mitigation, the European Union (EU) aims to reduce its overall emissions to at least 20% below 1990 levels by 2020 and to increase the share of renewables in energy use to 20% by 2020 (European Commission 2008). Central to the European climate strategy is the EU Emissions Trading System (EU ETS), which rewards companies that reduce their CO_2 emissions and penalises those that exceed limits. Introduced in 2005, the scheme covers about 12,000 factories and plants responsible for about half the EU's emissions of CO_2 (European Commission 2004). Furthermore, many European companies in different sectors are defining their own emissions reduction targets.

Looking at the broader sustainable development agenda, the challenge for European economies today is to integrate environmental sustainability with economic growth and welfare. From the CSR perspective, companies have to develop strategies to achieve energy and resource efficiencies in their production processes, reduce the environmental impact of their products throughout the entire product life-cycle and contribute to a shift towards more sustainable consumption patterns.

Demographic change

Europe has a population of around 732 million, or about 11% of the world population. By 2050, Europe's share of the global population is projected to fall to 6–8% (United Nations DESA 2009).

Over the next decades, many European regions will face major economic and social challenges associated with an ageing and stagnating — or in some cases declining — population, mainly as a consequence of declining fertility rates and increasing life expectancy in most European countries.

There are, however, significant disparities in the demographic prospects of different regions in Europe. A 2008 study based on 24 social and economic indicators found that Scandinavia, the UK, Benelux countries, southern Germany, Switzerland, Austria and France seem to face the best future in terms of their demographic sustainability, while many regions in eastern and southern Europe struggle to deal with an array of negative demographic phenomena (Hoßman *et al.* 2008).

Compared to other continents, Europe already has the oldest population, with a median age of nearly 40 years today, which is projected to rise to 47 years in 2050 (United Nations DESA 2009). In terms of CSR, companies thus have to take into account the needs and characteristics of an ageing workforce, for example in the areas of lifelong learning and the promotion of health and well-being in the workplace. On the other hand, demographic change can also be seen as a driver of CSR innovation in products and services that respond to the needs of the ageing population.

Europe's demographic development is also shaped by intra- and intercontinental migration. Some European countries, mainly the UK, Spain, Italy, Germany and France, are among the major net receivers of international migrants, after the US and Canada (United Nations DESA 2009). The integration of immigrants in the labour market and society is a challenge faced by many European countries. According to MIPEX (2008), labour market access in the EU-25 is, on average, only halfway to best practice. Companies have a crucial role in this field through their employment practices, including recruitment and training, and their contribution to building social cohesion, for example through community engagement.

Education and skills development

The EU's Lisbon Strategy, launched in 2000, aimed at making Europe 'the world's most dynamic knowledge-based economy by 2010'. Developing an economy based on knowledge and innovation is also one of the priorities of the EU's Europe 2020 Strategy launched in spring 2010.

Education levels in Europe are relatively high in global comparison. However, one third of the EU working age population still has low educational qualifications (below upper secondary level), and the share of 25–64 year-olds with high educational attainment in the EU is, at 23%, far behind the 40% of both the US and Japan. According to recent projections, in 2015 almost a third of jobs in the EU are expected to require higher education and almost half will require at least medium level qualifications (Hingel *et al.* 2008: Chapter 7).

Advancing adult participation in lifelong learning remains a challenge in many European countries. It is estimated that currently less than 10% of adults in the EU participate in lifelong learning (Hingel *et al.* 2008: Chapter 1). For businesses, ensuring a skilled workforce today and in the future is a key CSR issue. As part of their CSR approach, many European companies invest in building the skills and competences of their own employees as well as supporting long-term education and employability initiatives in their communities. These types of initiatives often focus in particular on disadvantaged groups such as women, minorities or young people from disadvantaged backgrounds.

Health and safety

Ensuring a high level of consumer product safety is a key priority of both regulatory authorities and companies in Europe. In response to media exposure of product safety scandals or as part of a proactive approach to risk and reputation management, companies are increasingly incorporating product health and safety considerations in their CSR strategies and engaging in voluntary industry initiatives in this area. For example, the food and advertising industries have over past years intensified their self-regulation efforts in response to growing concerns over unhealthy lifestyles and rising obesity rates, particularly among children in Europe.

Regarding occupational health and safety, companies' CSR initiatives focus on a number of issues related to various health support services and prevention of ill health (CSR Europe 2008). As a whole, EU countries have made considerable progress in reducing the incidence of work-related accidents and illnesses, to a large extent as a result of a variety of legislative measures. Between 2000 and 2004, the rate of fatal accidents at work in the EU-15 fell by 17%, while the rate of workplace accidents leading to absences of more than three days fell by 20%.

However, many workers in Europe continue to perceive that their jobs pose a threat to their health or safety. According to a 2007 survey, almost 28% of workers in Europe say that they suffer from work-related health problems (European Commission 2007). A growing CSR challenge in this area is the management of psychosocial risks and the promotion of mental well-being in the workplace, including the issue of stress, which is the second most common work-related health problem across the EU-15, second only to back pain (Eurofound 2007).

Moreover, health and safety considerations related to products and production processes are a core focus area of the responsible supply chain management standards and practices being implemented by European companies with operations or suppliers abroad.

Poverty and social exclusion

In spite of the overall wealth of the European Union, nearly one in seven people in the EU are considered to be at risk of poverty, and the figures are even higher for some groups such as children and older people (Frazer 2009). Poverty in most EU countries is generally understood as relative poverty, in other words people are said to be living in poverty if their income and resources are so inadequate as to preclude them from having a standard of living considered acceptable in the society in which they live (European Commission DG EMPL 2004).

The debate on poverty in Europe is often closely associated with social exclusion or vulnerability. Some key issues in this area are reflected in the EU policy challenges in the field of social inclusion, which include: eradicating child poverty; making labour markets truly inclusive; ensuring decent housing for everyone; overcoming discrimination and increasing the integration of people with disabilities, ethnic minorities and immigrants; and tackling financial exclusion and over-indebtedness (European Commission 2010).

Preventing and combating exclusion demands involvement on all sides. For companies, this can mean for instance developing inclusive recruitment and HR management practices, fostering employability and job creation in the communities they operate in, and engaging in community initiatives targeting particularly deprived areas or marginalised groups.

Diversity and equal opportunities

Despite widespread legal protection, discrimination continues to exist within European societies and businesses. According to a 2008 survey, a third of Europeans report witnessing discrimination or harassment in the past year. Discrimination based on ethnic origin (62%) is seen to be the most widespread form of discrimination in the EU, followed by discrimination on the grounds of sexual orientation (51%) and disability (45%) (Eurobarometer 2008a). However, there are significant differences between the specific issues and how they are perceived in different European countries.

At the EU level, anti-discrimination legislation is based on numerous laws adopted in past decades to fight gender discrimination as well as the Racial Equality Directive and the Employment Framework Directive (European Council 2000a, 2000b), which aim at preventing discrimination on the grounds of race and ethnic origin, religion or belief, disability, age or sexual orientation.

To give an example of one of these areas, gender equality continues to be an important issue in Europe. Across the EU, women earn on average around 17% less than men, and in some countries the gender pay gap is widening. Gender inequality is linked to a number of legal, social and economic factors related to discrimination and segregation in the labour market. For example, women often work in sectors where their work is given a lower value than in sectors dominated by men. Furthermore, women are underrepresented in managerial and senior positions, representing only 32% of managers in companies within the EU and 10% of board members of the largest companies (European Commission DG EMPL 2009).

In recent years, more and more European companies have started to develop diversity management strategies in the workplace. In a recent pan-European survey, 56% of the companies surveyed had some kind of diversity policies and practices in place (European Commission DG EMPL 2008). In another study, 82% of the respondents recognised there were business benefits associated with diversity, for example with regard to enhanced employee recruitment and retention, an improved corporate image and reputation, greater levels of innovation and better marketing opportunities (European Commission 2005).

▌ Trends

Awareness and attitudes towards CSR

Even though approaches vary in different European countries, in many cases stakeholder groups such as NGOs and the media have played a key role in drawing attention to CSR-related issues. Recently, growing emphasis has been put on the role of consumers and investors as drivers of CSR.

In the first European survey on consumer attitudes towards CSR (CSR Europe 2000), 70% of consumers said that a company's commitment to social responsibility is important when buying a product or service and 44% said they would be willing to pay more for products that are socially and environmentally responsible.

Levels of consumer awareness and action vary to some extent between different European countries. Moreover, CSR opinion polls tend to be subject to a certain degree of survey bias. For example, a recent survey found that while 75% of European consumers said they are ready to buy environmentally friendly products even if they are more expensive, only 17% had actually done so in the month before the survey (Eurobarometer 2008b).

However, the market growth for organic products — an estimated 10–15% annually (FIBL and IFOAM 2007) — and Fair Trade products (according to FLO International (2009) more than 50% in many European countries in 2008) indicate that a increasing number of Europeans are voting with their wallets for more sustainable products.

Regarding the role of investors, the growth of the European market for socially responsible investment (SRI) is driven by an increasing demand from institutional investors for whom responsible investment is becoming a matter of risk management (particularly around climate change). There has also been a further mainstreaming of environmental, social and governance (ESG) considerations into traditional financial services, and a growing interest from NGOs, media and individuals (Eurosif 2008).

As an example, a 2008 survey of institutional investors in Europe's top three SRI markets — France, the UK and the Netherlands — found that 70% of institutional investors believe they are responsible for the ESG strategies of the companies in which they invest. Their main environmental focus tends to be on climate change, while on the social side a key issue is child labour. In the area of corporate governance, the clearest concern to emerge is corporate reporting on ESG issues (Novethic 2008).

Promoting increased transparency and disclosure of ESG information is also a key issue on the EU agenda, for example in the framework of initiatives such as the European Multi-Stakeholder Forum on CSR.

CSR Reporting

A growing number of companies in Europe are reporting on their sustainability performance as part of their annual reports or in separate CSR reports. Globally, Europe is often considered the leading region for CSR reporting.

For large companies, CSR reporting is becoming the norm. The UK is leading the pack, with more than 90 of the 100 largest companies reporting on CSR. In most Western European countries, this figure tends to fall between 40 and 60. There has been a rapid rise in reporting over past years — for example, among the 100 largest companies in Spain, the number of reporters jumped from 25 in 2005 to 59 in 2008. In Eastern Europe, the reporting rates are generally lower, but first movers in the region are keen to show leadership in this area (Bartels 2008).

In recent years, some European governments have made CSR reporting mandatory for large companies or decided to lead by example by pushing state-owned companies to report on their sustainability performance. These requirements often rely on existing reporting frameworks such as the Global Reporting Initiative (GRI) guidelines or the UN Global Compact. The aim is to push companies to improve their sustainability performance and to promote greater transparency towards stakeholders.

As a relatively early example of national reporting requirements, all listed companies in France have had to disclose information on social and environmental conditions in their annual reports since 2001. In the Nordic region, Sweden has made sustainability reporting based on the GRI guidelines obligatory for all state-owned companies as of 2009, and the largest Danish companies are required to report on their sustainability efforts as of 2010.

▌ Legislation and codes

CSR has become an increasingly important topic on the European agenda since the 1990s. At the EU level, no legislation on CSR as such has been introduced, but existing EU and national regulatory frameworks cover a wide range of issues related to CSR, for instance in the areas of environmental protection, health and safety, and employment practices. Furthermore, public policies on CSR in different European countries evolve rapidly, as CSR is increasingly seen as an innovative and flexible means to address some of the challenges facing European societies.

EU strategies and policies

A milestone in the EU approach to CSR was passed at the European Council in March 2000, when the EU set a new strategic goal for 2010 through the Lisbon Strategy and the European Council made a special appeal to companies' sense of social responsibility.

In July 2001 the European Commission presented a Green Paper entitled 'Promoting a European Framework for Corporate Social Responsibility'. It introduced a definition of CSR as 'a concept whereby companies integrate social and environmental concerns in their business operations and in their interaction with their stakeholders on a voluntary basis', which has become widely used in Europe (European Commission 2001).

The Green Paper was followed by a Communication by the European Commission in July 2002. It stated that CSR can contribute to achieving the goals of European strategies on competitiveness and sustainable development, and proposed an EU strategy to promote CSR. The principles underlying this strategy included among others the recognition of the voluntary nature of CSR, an all-encompassing approach to CSR (including economic, social and environmental issues as well as consumer interests), and support and compatibility with existing international agreements and instruments (European Commission 2001). The Commission also launched the European Multi-Stakeholder Forum on CSR, which brings together European representative organisations of employers, business networks, trade unions and NGOs to promote innovation, convergence and transparency in existing CSR practices and tools. The Forum published its final report in 2004 and has subsequently held two review meetings in 2006 and 2009 (EMSF 2004).

In its second Communication on CSR in March 2006, the Commission reiterated the importance of CSR in the context of the renewed Lisbon Strategy and the European Sustainable Development Strategy (2005). It called on the European business community to step up its commitment to CSR and announced its support to the European Alliance for CSR, an open partnership for European enterprises and their stakeholders to promote and further develop CSR (European Commission 2006). In 2008, a major contribution to this increased cooperation between business and stakeholders was reached with 18 collaborative 'CSR Laboratory' projects, which launched their outputs as a joint European Toolbox for CSR.[2] Recent EU initiatives have continued to highlight the links between CSR and economic performance, the role of CSR in the shift towards sustainable production and consumption, and the integration of CSR considerations into EU policies in various areas. For example, the annual European Competitiveness Report (European Commission DG ENTR 2008) included for the first time an in-depth discussion on the links between CSR and competitiveness in the EU.

National strategies and policies

In recent years, several European governments have introduced national CSR strategies or integrated CSR in their sustainable development plans. In some countries, CSR is progressively being integrated into a wide range of policies, whereas in others awareness-raising initiatives are mostly being developed at present.

In 2007, the European Commission compiled a compendium of public policies on CSR across the 27 member states of the EU. It showed that national CSR policies reflect the diversity of economic, cultural and political contexts in Europe, but their main objectives are similar: promoting stakeholder dialogue and public private partnerships; enhancing transparency and credibility of CSR practices and instruments; raising awareness, increasing knowledge, disseminating and awarding best practices; and ensuring a more solid and consistent link between sustainable development objectives and public policies (European Commission DG EMPL 2007).

A 2007 study comparing CSR policy approaches in 13 countries worldwide divided the studied countries into groups based on their CSR policy approach and instruments (Welzel *et al.* 2007). Some European countries, such as the UK and Sweden, were identified as 'outspoken CSR countries' which have a wide range of incentives and instruments in place to help CSR to effectively complement other policy goals. Other countries, such as France and Germany, can be described as 'solid CSR countries'. With a longstand-

2   **http://www.csreurope.org/toolbox**, accessed 19 March 2010.

ing CSR-related policy background (for instance on environmental issues), they tend to regard international standards as important and rely heavily on 'soft law'. In the new EU member states and candidate countries in Eastern Europe, the direct involvement of governments in CSR is diverse. In most countries of the region, systematic incentives and initiatives on CSR are generally missing (Line and Braun 2007).

▮ Organisations

▮ **CSR Europe**. The leading European business network for CSR, consisting of around 75 corporate members and a national partner network of 27 European CSR organisations reaching out to more than 2,000 companies in Europe. **http://www.csreurope.org**

▮ **Academy of Business in Society (EABIS)**. An alliance of companies, business schools and academic institutions, with the support of the European Commission, committed to integrating 'business in society' issues into the heart of business theory and practice in Europe. **http://www.eabis.org**

▮ **European Commission**. Includes European policy perspectives on CSR and EU initiatives such as the European Multi-Stakeholder Forum on CSR. **http://ec.europa.eu/enterprise/csr/index_en.htm**

▮ **UN Global Compact Local Networks**. UN Global Compact local networks are clusters of participants who come together to advance the Global Compact and its principles within a particular geographic context. There are around 30 local networks in Europe and the Commonwealth of Independent States (CIS). **http://www.unglobalcompact.org/NetworksAroundTheWorld**

▮ Case studies

CSR Europe has compiled a database of more than 600 examples of company initiatives related to various CSR issues.[3]

Education

CSR is moving up the management education agenda in European universities and business schools, and the business community is increasingly stressing the need for educational institutions to develop new knowledge and skills for current and future leaders on this topic.

In the 2009–2010 *Beyond Grey Pinstripes* ranking by the Aspen Institute (2010), the top ten European MBA programmes integrating social and environmental stewardship into curricula and research were **Rotterdam School of Management** (The Netherlands), **IE Business School** (Spain), **Nottingham University Business School** (UK), INSEAD (France), **ESADE Business School** (Spain), **University of Navarra** (Spain), **HEC Genève** (Switzerland), **University of Jyväskylä** (Finland), **Copenhagen Business School** (Denmark) and **Vlerick Leuven Gent Management School** (Belgium).

3   http://www.csreurope.org/solutions

Further information on the activities of universities and business schools in the domains of CSR research, education and training in Europe is included in the Business in Society Gateway website developed by the European Academy of Business in Society (EABIS) and the European Foundation for Management Development (EFMD). The website provides information on relevant educational programmes, specialised research centres and academic experts. **http://www.businessinsociety.eu**

References

Aspen Institute Center for Business Education (2010) 'Aspen's Global 100: Beyond Grey Pinstripes 2009–2010' (New York: Aspen Institute Center for Business Education; **http://www.beyondgreypinstripes.org/pdf/2009-2010BGP_Brochure.pdf**, accessed 24 May 2010).

Audretsch, D., R. van der Horst, K. Ton and R. Thurik (2009) 'First Section of the Annual Report on EU Small and Medium-sized Enterprises' (Zoetermeer, Netherlands: EIM Business and Policy Research).

Bartels, W. (2008) 'KPMG International Survey of Corporate Responsibility Reporting' (Amstelveen, Netherlands: KPMG International).

CSR Europe (2000) 'The First Ever European Survey of Consumers' Attitudes towards Corporate Social Responsibility' (Brussels: CSR Europe).

—— (2005) 'A European Roadmap for Businesses: Towards a Sustainable and Competitive Enterprise' (Brussels: CSR Europe).

—— (2008) 'Wellbeing in the Workplace: A Guide with Best Practices and Tips for Implementing a Successful Wellbeing Strategy at Work' (Brussels: CSR Europe).

EMSF (European Multi-Stakeholder Forum) (2004) 'The European Multi-Stakeholder Forum on CSR Final Results and Recommendations, The European Multi-Stakeholder Forum on CSR; **http://www.responsabilitasociale.org/emsf_final_report.pdf**, accessed 19 March 2010).

Eurobarometer (2008a) 'Discrimination in the European Union: Perceptions, Experiences and Attitudes' (Special Eurobarometer Report 296; Brussels: European Commission).

—— (2008b) 'Attitudes of European Citizens towards the Environment' (Special Eurobarometer Report 295; Brussels: European Commission).

Eurofound (2007) 'Work-Related Stress' (Dublin: Eurofound; **http://www.eurofound.europa.eu/ewco/reports/TN0502TR01/TN0502TR01.pdf**, accessed 19 March 2010).

European Commission (2001) 'Green Paper: Promoting a European Framework for Corporate Social Responsibility' (COM[2001]366 final; Brussels: European Commission).

—— (2002) 'Corporate Social Responsibility: A Business Contribution to Sustainable Development '(COM[2002]347 final; Brussels: European Commission).

—— (2004) 'Questions and Answers on Emissions Trading and National Allocation Plans' (MEMO/04/44; Brussels: European Commission).

—— (2005) 'The Business Case for Diversity: Good Practices in the Workplace' (Brussels: European Commission).

—— (2006) 'Implementing the Partnership for Growth and Jobs: Making Europe a Pole of Excellence on CSR' (COM[2006]136 final; Brussels: European Commission).

—— (2007) 'Improving Quality and Productivity at Work: Community Strategy 2007–2012 on Health and Safety at Work' (COM[2007]0062 final; Brussels: European Commission).

—— (2008) '20 20 by 2020: Europe's Climate Change Opportunity' (COM[2008]30 final; Brussels: European Commission).

—— (2010) 'Poverty and Social Exclusion' (Brussels: European Commission; **http://ec.europa.eu/social/main.jsp?catId=751&langId=en**, accessed 24 May 2010).

European Commission DG EMPL (Employment, Social Affairs and Equal Opportunities) (2004) 'Joint Report on Social Inclusion 2004' (Brussels: European Commission).

—— (2007) 'Corporate Social Responsibility: National Public Policies in the European Union' (Brussels: European Commission).

—— (2008) 'Continuing the Diversity Journey' (Brussels: European Commission).

—— (2009) 'Gender Pay Gap: Which are the Causes?' (Brussels: European Commission; http://ec.europa.eu/social/main.jsp?catId=682&langId=en, accessed 7 November 2009).

European Commission DG ENTR (Enterprise and Industry) (2008) 'European Competitiveness Report 2008' (Brussels: European Commission).

European Council (2000a) 'Council Directive 2000/43/EC of 29 June 2000 Implementing the Principle of Equal Treatment Between Persons Irrespective of Racial or Ethnic Origin' (Brussels: European Council).

—— (2000b) 'Council Directive 2000/78/EC of 27 November 2000 Establishing a General Framework for Equal Treatment in Employment and Occupation' (Brussels: European Council).

Eurosif (European Social Investment Forum) (2008) 'European SRI Study', Eurosif; http://www.eurosif.org/publications/sri_studies, accessed 19 March 2010.

FIBL and IFOAM (2007) 'The World of Organic Agriculture: Statistics and Emerging Trends 2007' (Bonn, Germany: IFOAM; Frick, Germany: FIBL).

FLO International (2009) 'Global Fairtrade Sales Increase by 22%' (Bonn: FLO International; http://www.fairtrade.net, accessed 6 November 2009).

Frazer, H. (2009) 'Poverty and Inequality in the EU' (Social Inclusion Working Group, EAPN; http://www.eapn.org/images/docs/poverty%20explainer_web_en.pdf, accessed 19 March 2010).

Hingel, A., O. Bjerkestrand, R. Deiss, M. Hrabinska, L.B. Jakobsen, M. Kuzma, C. Marcone, F. Dewar, M. Le Bourhis, A. Saltelli, M. Nardo, M. Badescu, M. Deluca, B. d'Hombres, B. Hoskins, M. Saisana, D. Vidoni, E. Villalba, J.-L. Mercy, L. Mejer, M. Beck-Domzalska, E. Gere, G. Istrate and F. Reis (2008) 'Progress towards the Lisbon Objectives in Education and Training: Indicators and Benchmarks 2008' (Brussels: European Commission).

Hoßman, I., M. Karsch, R. Klingholz, Y. Köhncke, S. Kröhnert, C. Pietschmann and S. Sütterlin (2008) *Europe's Demographic Future: Growing Imbalances* (Berlin: The Berlin Institute for Population and Development).

Kinnicutt, S., and P. Mirvis (2009) 'Trends in Corporate Citizenship: Global versus Local Forces', in *Corporate Citizenship Around the World: How Local Flavor Seasons the Global Practice* (GERN; http://www.cccdeutschland.org/pics/medien/1_1224173416/GERN_for_web.pdf, accessed 19 March 2010): 4-10.

Line, M., and R. Braun (2007) 'Baseline Study on CSR Practices in the New EU Member States and Candidate Countries' (United Nations Development Programme; http://www.acceleratingcsr.eu/uploads/docs/BASELINE_STUDY_ON.pdf, accessed 24 May 2010).

MIPEX (Migrant Integration Policy Index) (2008) 'Key Findings'; http://www.integrationindex.eu/topics/2636.html, accessed 7 November 2009.

Novethic (2008) 'Institutional Investors' Perspective on their Responsibility for ESG Policies of the Companies in which they Invest', Novethic; http://www.novethic.com/novethic/v3_uk/upload/ESG_Study.pdf, accessed 7 November 2009.

United Nations DESA (Department of Economic and Social Affairs) (2009) 'World Population Prospects: The 2008 Revision' (New York: DESA/UN; http://esa.un.org/unpd/wpp2008/index.htm, accessed 19 March 2010).

Welzel, C., A. Peters, U. Höcker, and V. Scholz (eds.) (2007) *The CSR Navigator: Public Policies in Africa, the Americas, Asia and Europe* (Gütersloh, Germany: Bertelsmann Stiftung).

Yale University and Columbia University (2008) 'Environmental Performance Index'; http://epi.yale.edu, accessed 7 November 2009.

IV Latin America

Estrella Peinado-Vara
Operations Officer, Inter-American Development Bank

Antonio Vives
Principal Associate, Cumpetere

▌ Context

Traditionally, philanthropy in the region has been motivated by the need to alleviate extreme poverty in the midst of large inequalities and extreme wealth. This charitable activity has been led by the church and its organisations, stemming from concern for the poor and its role, begun in colonial times, as provider of health and education services. Economic elites have joined more recently, in great part as a response to growing inequality and the perceived need to increase social cohesion.

Philanthropy in Latin America typically revolves around *asistencialismo*, charitable giving for poverty alleviation (not poverty reduction), to help those in need to go from one day to the next, with the beneficiaries being the poor, children and disadvantaged youth. There was, and still is, a parallel track for promotion of the arts and culture, and private education.

In the last few decades, there has been some progress. Philanthropic practices in the region have evolved from traditional giving for poverty alleviation to a more organised form that expands its concerns to include civil society development, community and institutional development, and public policies and governance. Some of these practices are implemented through foundations, subject to regulations and under the scrutiny and participation of civil society.

This evolution has also led to the involvement of high net worth individuals through the companies they own, control or manage and has also stimulated corporate philanthropy. In the same way, corporate philanthropy has moved towards strategic philanthropy and, in the more 'enlightened' firms, to some forms of CSR.

Nevertheless, these CSR efforts are still limited to relatively few firms, either because they are multinationals or subsidiaries of multinationals, or are large family-owned companies with a philanthropic bent, or because they are led by a new generation of leaders, already educated on the broader responsibilities of business in society.

Obviously most companies, large and small, engage in an array of responsible practices that are a natural part of any sensible management strategy, or are required by law, such as complying with labour conditions and environmental concerns. What is not yet mainstreamed, however, is to think beyond these basic activities to those that require additional effort.

There is a dearth of statistical evidence at the regional level and it is not yet possible to ascertain the relative development of CSR in the countries or its general evolution. Most of the evidence is circumstantial and hard to compare between countries. One region-wide study (Vives and Peinado-Vara 2006) compared the CSR practices in SMEs for eight countries in the region and found that practices are relatively extensive, mostly without acknowledging or naming them CSR. In this survey, the most advanced countries in the region were Chile, Argentina and Mexico. This result may not hold for larger firms, where circumstantial evidence (cases, institutional development and exposure to globalisation) would lead us to think that the most advanced countries in the region by far are Brazil, followed by Chile and Mexico and to a lesser extent Colombia.

■ Priority issues

As the countries in the region are developing countries or emerging economies, the priorities for business and the expectations of stakeholders are different from those traditionally expected in developed countries. There are also global issues, such as environment, human rights, child and slave labour and basic labour conditions that all companies should consider regardless of local or regional context.

Labour issues

Apart from these universal issues, concerns relating to labour practices and benefits tend to be a priority as many countries do not have strong legal frameworks or enforcement mechanisms. There is generally high inequality in income distribution in Latin America: the Gini coefficient for the region is around 0.5 (the higher, the worst income distribution), which is higher than Sub-Saharan Africa. Bolivia, Brazil, Honduras and Colombia have Gini coefficients higher than 0.58 and the best distribution exists in Uruguay with 0.45 (ECLAC 2008). Typically, poverty affects the indigenous populations worst; hence, practices related to social inclusion — incorporating the poor, less educated, marginalised and women — are especially welcomed by the population.

Environment

Broad environmental issues like water and air pollution are a priority, but climate change is generally given less emphasis, even though there is interest among governments and large business. Biodiversity loss in the rainforest is an issue in countries such as Brazil and Colombia, and countries heavily dependent on extractive industries like Chile and Perú, but it is not a generalised priority for most businesses. Eco-efficiency practices are of more interest for companies than their stakeholders.

Social services

The private sector in Latin America contributes to these priorities by showing some social responsibility, but not as a systemic effort. Business in the region faces government and market failures, with many basic needs partially unmet. For example, social services such as education and healthcare are generally lacking, while infrastructure services (e.g. water and sanitation, transportation and energy) are relatively deficient. While the private sector is not automatically expected to provide these services, in some cases, particularly in remote regions or where local governments are weak, companies may be forced to step into the breach in order to enhance their own position. Expectations also increase if the company has a relatively large influence in the local context. In this regard, community development activities are also a high priority.

Corporate governance

As local capital markets are relatively underdeveloped, there is less interest in issues such as corporate governance and corporate reporting. This is not to say that they are irrelevant, only that they are less important than other issues more closely related to development problems. In some countries, for instance Brazil, reporting is taking off but only among the relatively large firms. Similarly, corporate governance initiatives such as Novo Mercado in BOVESPA (the São Paulo Stock Exchange) are mostly exceptional.

Corruption

Corruption is a major problem, but mostly it is perceived by the population to be a government issue more than a company failing, although both parties are involved. Most countries of Latin America are ranked below position 67 in the Corruption Perception Index of Transparency International (only three are ranked higher — Chile, Uruguay and Costa Rica [a high ranking indicates good practice]). In a recent survey of 22 leading exporting countries, two Latin American countries ranked in the last five in the Bribe Payers Index, together with India, China and Russia.

∎ Trends

CSR as an integral concept is relatively new to Latin America and in its broadest expression is confined to relatively large firms with global exposure. Most companies that have responsible practices do not frame them in the context of CSR, but rather in terms of compliance with legislation and good management practices. There is a dearth of published studies of trends in the region; nevertheless, some trends are visible in certain countries.

For instance, in Brazil, the CSR agenda is moving towards sustainable production and consumption with a strong focus on environmental issues, transparency, tackling corruption and working conditions (GERN 2008). The public sector is also more involved in promoting a national CSR agenda. However, because of the impact of the 2008–2009 financial crisis, these issues are likely to diminish in importance relative to issues of corporate governance, at least for the larger corporations. In fact, this global economic turmoil is a great opportunity to think about what brought us to this situation and to use CSR to avoid it happening again in the future.

In reporting by large enterprises there is also some progress. By December 2008, 114 organisations in Latin America had published a sustainability report following the Global Reporting Initiative (GRI), out of a total of 942 globally. Among the 114 companies,

61 are based in Brazil followed by Chile with 17 and Colombia with six. Although timid, there is a trend towards sustainability reporting assurance in Latin America, with an increase of 22% annually in the number of sustainability reports that have gone through external verification over the period 1997–2007. Other regions are leading this trend, such as Asia, where assurance has been growing at 31% annually.

■ Legislation and codes

Legislation and codes in Latin America cover CSR practices in a relatively indirect way. In general, CSR has not been included as part of the government agenda or in public policies. All countries have the traditional labour and environmental legislation that cover these practices in some form. Nevertheless, for some aspects, the national laws do not reach the minimum considered acceptable in more developed countries. In these cases, larger companies are expected to go beyond mere compliance.

There have been some attempts at a more comprehensive approach. Argentina has been discussing a CSR law, Mexico and Colombia have developed non-certifiable CSR norms ('Norma' in Mexico, 'Guía Técnica' in Colombia) and the city of Buenos Aires has a law requiring the publication of a social and environmental report for larger enterprises.

■ Organisations

At the beginning of the decade, there was only a handful of organisations devoted to the promotion of CSR. Now all countries in Latin America have one or several major institutions promoting CSR practices.

■ **Forum Empresa and BSR.** This pan-American CSR organisation, with 19 countries represented in its membership, was originally promoted by the US organisation Business for Social Responsibility (BSR), which is still a member, to coordinate activities and carry out some research on best practices at the regional level. Many of the Latin American institutions have links with BSR, the leading CSR organisation in the US. **http://www. empresa.org** and **http://www.bsr.org**

■ **World Business Council for Sustainable Development (WBCSD).** Many companies are members of WBCSD. Its precursor, BCSD, was founded by businessman Stephen Schmidheiny, who is regarded as an influential individual leader in CSR in the region. Similarly, Manuel Arango in Mexico and Robert Murray in El Salvador have led by example in their businesses and through the creation and support of institutions promoting CSR, and business associations. **http://www.wbcsd.org**

■ **Ethos.** Probably the leading national CSR organisation, both in terms of size and activities, is Ethos in Brazil, founded in 1998 and now with over 1,300 members, mostly from the private sector (representing 35% of Brazilian GDP). It has led the development of printed and online materials in the region, producing CSR indicators, promoting private participation in the Millennium Development Goals and holding many conferences and training events. **http://www.ethos.org.br**

■ **CEMEFI**. Another of the early leaders was CEMEFI (Centro Mexicano para la Filantropia) in Mexico, created in 1988. It now has over 700 members. Although originally created to promote philanthropic activities, it has been moving, together with the trends in Latin America, towards a broader concept of CSR practices. The association created an award to recognise the most responsible practices in Mexican corporations, besides hosting in conferences, training courses and producing some publications. **http://www.cemefi.org**

■ **Convertirse**. At a sub-regional level, Convertirse is a network of six organisations in Central America, some of them already mentioned: Centrarse (Guatemala, **http://www.centrarse.org**); Fundemás (El Salvador, **http://www.fundemas.org**); Fundahrse (Honduras, **http://www.fundahrse.org**); Unirse (Nicaragua, **http://www.unirse.org**); AED (Costa Rica, **http://www.aed.com**) and Integrarse (Panama, **http://www.integrarse.org.pa**).

■ **Inter-American Development Bank**. Another key institution has been the Inter-American Development Bank, currently acting through its Multilateral Investment Fund which has been promoting responsible practices through research, publications, training materials and conferences. The best known of these is the Inter-American Conference on Corporate Social Responsibility, held every year since 2002, following a mandate from the Summit of the Americas on 2000.[1] It also finances, through grants, the application of responsible practices in partnerships with private corporations, particularly through the supply chain and through its own lending operations. **http://www.iadb.org/mif**

■ **Other organisations**. There are many other national institutions, the best known of which are IARSE in Argentina (**http://www.iarse.org**), AccionRSE (**http://www.accionrse.cl**) and Prohumana (**http://www.prohumana.cl**) in Chile, Perú 2021 in Perú (**http://www.peru2021.org**), CentraRSE in Guatemala (**http://www.centrarse.org**) and FUNDEMAS in El Salvador (**http://www.fundemas.org**).

■ Case studies

It is risky to highlight companies that are widely recognised as leaders in responsible practices, as it is almost impossible for them to be uniformly and consistently responsible over the whole spectrum of operations. The following cases highlight particular practices that are considered worthy.

CEMEX

CEMEX produces, distributes and sells cement, ready-mix concrete, aggregates and related construction materials. It operates in more than 50 countries in the Americas, Europe, Asia, Africa and the Middle East and is one of the largest providers of building materials worldwide, employing more than 50,000 people. Its operations have significant environmental impacts, ranging from CO_2 emissions and the effects on biodiversity from quarrying to local impacts from transportation and dust. CEMEX has developed a

---

1 A summit of the presidents of the countries of the Western Hemisphere which meets periodically to set hemispheric priorities and areas of collaboration in the Americas.

Sustainability Management System (SMS), which includes both environmental (health and safety) and socioeconomic (engagement with local communities) aspects. Cemex is a core member of the Cement Sustainability Initiative (CSI) developed as part of the WBCSD. It also cultivates relationships with the Global Leadership Network, UN Global Compact, World Environment Center and Boston College's Center for Corporate Citizenship, among others. Cemex has developed several CSR projects in Latin America. Construmex, a project that was developed for Mexico, was concerned with the remittances that immigrants in the US were sending to their families in Mexico, mostly intended to assist with housing improvements. Another project, Let's Fix Our Block, aims to improve the conditions of the streets and pavements of a given community. The community members help raise money for the project and provide labour, while the government funds part of the project and Cemex provides the necessary materials. **http://www.cemex.com**

Empresas Públicas de Medellín (EPM)

EPM operates as a convergent utilities service provider and telecommunications company, and is the largest company of its kind in Colombia.Its operations include hydroelectric facilities, power generation, transmission and distribution, gas distribution, wastewater treatment and telecommunications services. It was founded in 1955 and is the property of the city of Medellín. With the project Integral Policy of Corporate Social Responsibility, apart from an exemplary management of a municipality-owned company in terms of transparency, EPM considers CSR as a cross-cutting concept. Among its projects are educational programmes within a development plan for Medellín, scholarships for youth at risk and support for housing improvement through access to finance for energy, water and sanitation at preferential terms. It has developed a new business model for customers at the bottom of the economic pyramid, as well as providing support to local forms of government to improve infrastructure, education, cultural development, productive chains in agribusiness, micro-entrepreneur development, conservation activities and solid waste management. **http://www.epm.com.co**

Grupo Bimbo

Grupo Bimbo produces, distributes and markets over 5,000 bakery products. It owns more than 100 brands in Mexico, the US, Argentina, Brazil, Colombia, Costa Rica, Panama, Chile, El Salvador, Guatemala, Honduras, Nicaragua, Perú, Venezuela, Uruguay, Paraguay, the Czech Republic and China. The group has 83 plants, five associates and three trading agencies. Grupo Bimbo's net sales amounted to USD6,700 million in 2007, the company employing over 97,500 people and trading on the Mexican Stock Exchange since 1980. The company has obtained national and international certificates including ISO 9000:2000, HACCP and Clean Industry, awarded by the Mexican Environmental Authority. The firm takes responsibility for the development of employees in balancing and reconciling work and family life and the role of each professional in society so that all can assume their full social responsibilities. With respect to the climate of labour relations, a joint exercise is mounted with the unions to provide continual evaluation of working conditions. Grupo Bimbo and the microfinance institution FinComun formed an alliance with funds from the Multilateral Investment Fund (MIF) that helps FinComun improve its operations to serve more shopkeepers in Grupo Bimbo's distribution network (more than 450,000 small store operators in Mexico) offering them new products and services, including microloans to modernise their stores or improve their homes and life, health and education insurance coverage. Grupo Bimbo also participates in environmental projects, such as the reforestation of protected natural areas in Mexico, as well as in a series of social investments. **http://www.grupobimbo.com**

GrupoNueva

GrupoNueva produces piping systems for drinking water and sewage, irrigation systems, housing construction materials and wood products. The company has commercial operations in 25 countries, mostly in Latin America, and employs 13,000 people. CSR and sustainable development are key elements within GrupoNueva's strategy. It focuses on the generation of eco-efficiency, economic value and social development in the communities where GrupoNueva has any kind of influence. The Sustainability Scorecard is one of the main management tools used by GrupoNueva to promote performance improvement and to generate value for shareholders, other stakeholders and the environment. GrupoNueva is very active in socially inclusive business to provide economic opportunities to fight poverty. For example, it produces low-cost furniture for low-cost housing, and training for small and medium-sized furniture-making entrepreneurs in Chile. It also provides access to drip irrigation systems for small farmers in Guatemala. **http://www.gruponueva.com**

Natura

The Natura company is a Brazilian leader in cosmetics, fragrance and personal hygiene, with direct sales to customers through home representatives. It has been publicly owned since 2004 and its brand is one of the most valuable in Brazil. Natura has a presence in Argentina, Chile, Perú, Mexico, Venezuela, Colombia and France. In 2007, its gross revenues were BRL4,301.6 million (USD1,860 million). Natura seeks to contribute to sustainable development by using natural inputs and helping the producing communities to generate income to improve their standard of living. The relationship with the supplying communities is based on fair trade, paying on average a 15% fair trade premium. Natura is NBR ISO 14001 and NBR ISO 9001 certified and approximately 60% of its raw materials are FSC (Forest Stewardship Council) certified. Its Annual Report integrates the GRI G3 indicators that allow a common view of the financial, social and environmental performance of the company. **http://www.natura.com.br**

▌ Education

Education on CSR at the university level is just becoming available, but is changing fast. There are already four schools in the top 100 ranking of *Beyond Grey Pinstripes*: *Instituto Tecnologico de Monterrey*[2] (Mexico, ranked 17), *IESA* (the graduate business schools in Venezuela, 75), *Fundação Getúlio Vargas* (Brazil, 79) and *Universidad de los Andes* (Colombia, 95). It is significant that out of the eight schools from developing countries in the top 100, four are from Latin America.

---

2 *Beyond Grey Pinstripes*: a periodic online publication of the Aspen Institute: **http://www.beyondgreypinstripes.org**.

The survey only evaluates 112 schools and as such it has a bias towards developed countries and the US and Europe in particular. Nevertheless, there are other well-known universities that incorporate responsible practices in the curricula, particularly at the MBA level, for instance *INCAE* in Central America (based in Costa Rica), universities such as **Universidad de Chile, Católica de Chile** and **Andres Bello** in **Chile, Universidad del Pacífico** in **Perú**, and **Universidad de San Andrés** and **Universidad Argentina de la Empresa** in **Argentina**. This is only a small sample and the chapters on each country contain more information.

For many years the Social Enterprise Knowledge Network (SEKN), led by Harvard Business School and comprising ten universities in the region, have been promoting social entrepreneurship and alliances between NGOs, corporations and public institutions to advance social enterprise. Lately, they have also been moving towards incorporating a broader concept of CSR.

Executive education is relatively underdeveloped and a significant portion of education for the private sector takes place through conferences. Besides the Inter-American conferences mentioned above, almost all countries in the region hold national conferences. Some of the best attended are the annual ones organised by Ethos in Brazil, CEMEFI in Argentina and ANDI (Asociación Nacional de Industriales) in Colombia.

There are no research journals devoted specifically to CSR in Latin America but relevant research often appears in CSR-related journals (e.g. *Journal of Corporate Citizenship* or the *Journal of Business Ethics*) and in more general management journals such as *Harvard Business Review América Latina* or magazines. There are some magazines devoted to CSR (most notably *Stakeholders* in Perú and *Sinergia* in Argentina). Books with local content have started to appear such as Paladino 2007 and Flores *et al.* 2007. Most of the CSR organisations listed above have newsletters that include articles, interviews, best-practice examples and in some cases include self-evaluation tools. There is, for example, a blog (**http://www.cumpetere.blogspot.com**) and a virtual group devoted to the issues (**forode_responsabilidadsocial@yahoogroups.com**). There are no institutions evaluating CSR education in Latin America or compiling information on CSR programmes, so it is hard to get good information on these.

References

Cici, C., and F. Ranghieri (2008) 'Recommended Actions to Foster the Adoption of Corporate Social Responsibility (CSR) Practices in Small and Medium Enterprises (SMEs)' (Washington, DC: Inter-American Development Bank; **http://idbdocs.iadb.org/wsdocs/getdocument. aspx?docnum=1353696**, accessed 2 June 2010).

Corral, A., I. Isuzi, E. Peinado-Vara and T. Perez (2007) 'La responsabilidad social y medioambiental de la microempresa en Latinoamérica' (Washington, DC: Inter-American Development Bank; **http://idbdocs.iadb.org/wsdocs/getdocument.aspx?docnum=1580927**, accessed 2 June 2010).

ECLAC (2008) *Social Panorama 2008* (Santiago de Chile: ECLAC).

Flores, J., E. Ogliastri, E. Peinado-Vara and I. Petry, (2007) 'El argumento empresarial de la RSE: 9 casos de América Latina y el Caribe' (Washington, DC: Inter-American Development Bank; **http://idbdocs.iadb.org/wsdocs/getDocument.aspx?DOCNUM=1337282**, accessed 2 June 2010).

GERN (Global Education Research Network) (2008) 'Corporate Citizenship around the World. How Local Flavor Seasons the Global Practice' (Boston, MA: GERN/Boston College Center for Corporate Citizenship; **http://www.cccdeutschland.org/pics/medien/1_1224173416/GERN_for_web.pdf**, accessed 19 March 2010).

Instituto Argentino de Responsabilidad Social Empresarial (2005) 'Indicadores de responsabilidad social para PyMEs' (Translation and adaptation of the Ethos Indicators [Indicadores Ethos de Responsabilidade Social Empresarial]; Buenos Aires: IARSE).

Paladino, M. (ed.) (2007) *La responsabiliad de la empresa en la sociedad: Construyendo la sociedad desde la tarea directiva* (Buenos Aires: Colección Emecé IAEpress, 2nd edn).

Peinado-Vara, E. (2005) 'Corporate Social Responsibility in Latin America: Responsible Solutions to Business and Social Problems' (Washington, DC: Inter-American Development Bank; **http://www.iadb.org/sds/publication/publication_4551_e.htm**, accessed 19 March 2010).

Puppim de Oliveira, J.A. (ed.) (2006) *Journal of Corporate Citizenship* 21 (a special theme issue on 'Corporate Citizenship in Latin America: New Challenges for Business').

Vives, A., A. Corral and I. Isusi (2006) 'La Responsabilidad social de la empresa en las PyMEs de Latinoamérica' (Washington, DC: Inter-American Development Bank; **http://idbdocs.iadb.org/wsdocs/getdocument.aspx?docnum=1580927**, accessed 2 June 2010).

—— and E. Peinado-Vara (eds.) (2003–200) 'Proceedings of the Inter-American Conferences on CSR', Inter-American Development Bank; **http://idbdocs.iadb.org/wsdocs/getDocument.aspx?DOCNUM=1771441**; **http://idbdocs.iadb.org/wsdocs/getDocument.aspx?DOCNUM=1163475**; **http://idbdocs.iadb.org/wsdocs/getDocument.aspx?DOCNUM=1596836;http://idbdocs.iadb.org/wsdocs/getDocument.aspx?DOCNUM=1597232**, all accessed 2 June 2010).

V Middle East

Abbe Le Pelley

Senior Associate, Sustainability Advisory Group

■ Context

Regional description

When we talk of the Middle East today, two thoughts spring to mind: 'sand' and 'oil'. Both of these have played major roles in shaping the region's traditions and cultures. All six of the Gulf Cooperation Council's (GCC) member states (Saudi Arabia, Kuwait, Bahrain, Qatar, Oman and the UAE) are desert nations and oil exporters. The international oil cartel OPEC is dominated by Middle Eastern countries, with around half of the world's oil (and natural gas) estimated to be in this arid region. This resource has nurtured both the creation of the welfare state system within the oil producing countries, and the strategic importance of the region internationally. For instance, matters such as the precarious balance of peace and security across the region are increasingly seen as issues for public concern on the global stage, one in which many have a vested interest.

As a region, the Middle East is not clearly defined but generally constitutes the land joining Asia and Africa. This chapter covers the Arabian Peninsula, the Levant and Iran. Traditionally the region's strategic advantage was founded upon its geographic position, which offers direct avenues for international trade. Although still of advantage today, the focus is no longer predominately on trade, but on maximising business development in general. Consequently, some Arab nations are becoming international hubs of commerce and industry.

This unique positioning has for decades resulted in the Middle East being exposed to, and impacted by, global influences. As a result, these countries are rapidly transforming their economies, promoting themselves as the next holiday destination, international financial centre or regional hub for sport and culture. With the globalisation of Arab brands (Emirates, Aramex, etc.) and the influx of multinational companies and Foreign Direct Investment (FDI) across the region, it is clear that the Middle East is becoming a major player in today's global business market. As such, many countries are adapting their traditional business approaches to reflect new paradigms, management philosophies and international expectations.

Summarising the state of CSR across a region, particularly one incorporating some of the world's richest and poorest countries, is challenging. The phenomenon, in its Western sense, remains in its infancy in the Middle East — even in the more mature, dynamic and rapidly developing markets. However, as much of the Arab world is guided by Islamic principles, there are overlapping similarities between traditional business cultures and the foundations of CSR. As such, some deeply rooted traditions embedded in Arab cultures correspond with elements of our modern understanding of corporate responsibility, particularly a sense of personal duty, an obligation to society and a bond of trust in business. This profile intends to provide a snapshot of the status of CSR in the region, identifying some cross-border issues and trends in a regional context.

Development of CSR

If you were to mention CSR to a businessperson in the Middle East ten years ago, you would have been met with a blank expression. Today, this still holds true for much of the region. Yet inroads have been made. Development began five years ago when the concept of corporate governance started to take root. Elements of this agenda became topical across the Arab world in order to support the Western injection of FDI into Middle Eastern economies. Other supportive trends were family and state owned entities going public, the globalisation of large regional companies, the proliferation of sovereign wealth funds into international markets and the surge of Western-orientated migrant workers throughout the region. Thus the term CSR is increasingly recognised by professionals in the region — though still in a somewhat fluid, undefined and regionalised manner.

In general, CSR in the Arab world is synonymous with charity. It is about a company's contribution to society and is misunderstood to be predominantly about philanthropy. It is becoming apparent that CSR in the region is entangled with a sense of religious duties and, at times, it is proving difficult to differentiate between them. Recent studies conducted by Chambers of Commerce and Industry in the region show that there is great confusion between what company owners spend personally in almsgiving and what the organisations themselves offer in support of the community (Al Harthy 2009). There is little evidence of businesses demonstrating a connection between CSR and corporate strategy or long-term sustainability. Consequently, the area of philanthropy remains the most traditional and prominent of all CSR initiatives.

From this perspective, CSR is not new. The culture of giving back to society is well established in the region, guided by the tradition that it is one's duty to direct a company in line with personal values and religious beliefs. In fact, the Arab culture and Islam both consider charity as a duty that leads to social prosperity and it is still a notable influence on individuals today. This tradition is reflected through *Zakat*, one of the five pillars of Islam. It stipulates that Muslims should contribute a portion of their wealth to society's poor. As such, corporate social contributions have been evident in Arab states throughout history, traditionally focused on community structures such as schools and mosques.

However, in line with these religious origins, it is believed that societal contributions should remain confidential. To promote or discuss charitable donations is regarded as vulgar, as individuals are seen to capitalise on this societal obligation for self gain. Consequently, multinational companies operating in the region often communicate their CSR (or charitable initiatives) more than local firms.

The business case

Despite this focus on charitable donations, the concept of strategic philanthropy does not exist. Corporate giving remains predominantly driven by media attention given to international disasters. Few companies use philanthropy to advance their own interests, possibly a result of the traditional view that contributions should remain private and provided at respectful times of giving, such as during Ramadan. Humility and conformity, in light of tradition, culture and religious beliefs have meant that, although giving is entwined with business, communicating this support has been slow to follow. There are signs of change however, as can be witnessed by the rising number of companies disclosing their corporate giving to the public.

This ad hoc approach to charity, and absence of any sense of strategic philanthropy, combined with the local view that contributions should not be promoted for personal or commercial gain, mean that community initiatives are not harnessed to provide the 'win–win' potential they offer companies and society in the West. In fact, there are many differences that make it hard to highlight the Western business case for CSR in the Middle East, most notably the lack of Western-focused drivers. This results from the unique social structures, religious backgrounds and traditional norms that constitute the fabric of Middle East nations.

The consumer voice is generally absent. Collective bargaining is not allowed in many states, nor are pressure groups. There is a varying, but limited, freedom of speech in the media. Economies of the Gulf are often producer-driven rather than consumer or demand-focused. Consequently, there is a lack of any comprehensive sense of stakeholder engagement, or pressure, in the region. Add to this the growing and transient expatriate population, many of whom do not intend to stay in their host countries for an extended period of time, and it is clear that the sense of activism found in the West is lacking in the Arab world.

Hence, CSR in the region has not arisen from consumer pressure or demands. Rather, governments and businesses in the Middle East are defining the term for themselves. This contrast with Europe, where collaboration with the public leads the way. Consequently, government initiatives and quasi-governmental not-for-profit organisations are driving the agenda forward, as evident in Iran, Saudi Arabia, Qatar, Jordan and the UAE.

Mainstreaming CSR

CSR in the region remains in its infancy. It will take time before the concept is accepted in the mainstream or companies look past ad hoc social and environmental initiatives to help secure long term business benefits. Although the promise of change is in the air, the current economic climate seems to have affected the momentum that began to generate around the case for CSR. As the more mature markets in the region embark on this journey only time will tell what shape its definition of sustainability will take.

For certain, it is not for the West to impose its definition. A cut- and-paste approach will not work in this environment. At the moment, a CSR model is evolving and it is heavily focused on religion, social giving, legal compliance and eco-efficiency. There is still a need to link this with the mitigation of risk and the optimisation of strategic business opportunities. It is likely to happen, but, as with the rest of the world, it will take time to develop. Some countries and companies (predominately large state and family-owned entities) are already cooperating to drive the CSR concept forward across the region.

■ Priority issues

National employment

With a very young population profile in the Middle East, there is considerable pressure to provide jobs in the region's already overstretched labour markets. According to Dunlop (2006), 60% of the region's population is under the age of 24 and faces bleak employment prospects. Some 100 million jobs have to be created in the next 20 years just to absorb new entrants to the job market and another 20 million to reduce the present level of unemployment. Projected growth rates may not be enough to accommodate this influx of people into the marketplace, particularly given existing rates of unemployment.

This problem is exacerbated by the employment of expatriate workers (and significant number of regional refugees), who tend to come from relatively poor countries and are paid a fraction of the salary it would cost to employ or train a national worker. In addition, national citizens have traditionally sought employment in the public sector, an area of work that has limited scope for growth and future job creation. Consequently, the private sector is of growing importance to nationals. Solving this problem, and relieving the current dependency on expatriate workers, has become a primary concern confronting the region today.

In order to tackle this challenge Arab governments have imposed national employee quota systems on businesses. Operating in Oman, Saudi Arabia, Bahrain, Qatar, Yemen and the UAE, this approach intends to drive nationals onto the job market and reduce the dependency on foreign workers. It usually operates by setting targets for different industries and a reward or penalty system to encourage companies to comply. In the case of Oman, the quota system has been in operation since 1988 with targets (set between 15% and 60%) for six industry sectors. In addition, companies are encouraged to register their nationalisation plans and, in 1998, the government introduced a 'green card' award system, offering firms that meet their targets preferential treatment in their dealings with the government.

The corporate sector has responded to this challenge by working towards these quotas, while recognising the opportunity of introducing business solutions that enhance their own competitiveness. In the UAE for instance, banks such as NBAD and Emirates NBD offer programmes that provide training, funding and support to young national entrepreneurs who are likely to become future loyal customers. Other popular responses include the provision of national and graduate employee training programmes, or partnership programmes, such as that provided by Dubai Holding, Clifford Chance and Trowers & Hamlins to train young nationals as future in-house lawyers through their Legal Graduate Training Program.

Diet and lifestyle

The Middle East is facing huge health-related issues ranging from malnutrition (Iraq and Jordan), to obesity and related diseases (GCC states). In the region's more developed nations, key health issues appear to be a result of globalisation and the adoption of a Western-influenced lifestyle. This has resulted in a reduction in general activity and changes to the traditional diet, resulting in increased consumption of high-energy foods. This is exacerbated by a lack of nutritional education, accepted social opportunities for Arab women to exercise and experienced healthcare professionals in the region.

Kuwait has been ranked 8th in the World's Fattest Countries table, ahead of the US. Figures suggest that around 60% of Emirati nationals, 60% of those living in Bahrain and 36% of those in the Kingdom of Saudi Arabia (KSA), are either overweight or obese. For women, the percentages appear to be higher with 66% of women in Saudi believed to be overweight (AMEinfo 2009). The International Obesity Task Force, a London-based think-tank, finds 83% of women obese or overweight in Bahrain, 74% in the UAE and 75% in Lebanon (Pipes 2009).

Obesity creates a major risk for diet-related chronic diseases, including diabetes, heart disease, gastric illnesses, hypertension, strokes and cancer. Official figures in the UAE state that 41% of deaths in the country are caused by cardiovascular diseases. Predictions for the next two decades suggest a tripling of deaths from strokes and coronary heart disease in the Middle East and Africa (AMEinfo 2007). Obesity-related illnesses now account for one-third of total health costs in the Middle East, the most prominent of which is diabetes.

Diabetes is considered to be an epidemic today. Globally, a person dies from diabetes-related illnesses and two more develop the disease every ten seconds. The UAE has the second highest global diabetes prevalence, at an estimated one in five people (Johnson and Johnson 2008). This is causing a huge strain on the productivity of Arab nations, as it is a major cause of school drop-outs and inefficiency of employees. The high cost of treatment is also putting pressure on government resources. Approximately AED6 billion (USD1.6 billion) was spent on the management of the disease in the UAE in 2008. The country's National Health Insurance Company (Daman) predicts that diabetes will cost the country an estimated AED10 billion by 2020.

In order to tackle this, international organisations and regional public bodies are setting up partnerships. With the support of the Ministry of Health, UNICEF Gulf Area has introduced the Childhood Obesity Prevention Initiative, an awareness campaign on childhood obesity in the UAE. In conjunction with the Emirates Diabetes Society and the Ministries of Health and Education, Johnson & Johnson has established a Juvenile Diabetes Education Center to train diabetes educator nurses, while serving the needs of children with diabetes, their parents and school teaching staff.

The Middle East Healthcare Leadership Program is a more regionally-focused initiative driven through the Johnson & Johnson Corporate Citizenship Trust Middle East branch. Partnering with INSEAD and the UAE Ministry of Health this programme addresses the skill gaps of healthcare leaders in the region. It equips participants with the techniques necessary to undertake leadership roles in challenging and rapidly changing healthcare environments. It is unique in its pan-Arab scope and has already engaged representatives from Lebanon, the UAE, Bahrain, Saudi Arabia, Kuwait, Oman, Iraq and Qatar.

Workers' rights

Much of the Arab world, particularly the GCC, has developed at an astounding pace over the last decade. The corresponding construction boom relied on the import of cheap, migrant workers from poor countries in Asia. The influx of these workers, and the drive for rapid development, pushed issues such as human rights and employee health and safety to the forefront of the CSR agenda.

Worker health and safety is becoming more stringent in the Middle East, in response to mounting international pressure, high level debates at pan-Arab conferences and an increase in regional media coverage on the subject. Countries such as the UAE, Kuwait and Saudi Arabia have been widely criticised for their poor standards of worker health and safety, but there is evidence that they are trying to tackle this problem. The UAE introduced federal-level legislation to resolve issues such as poor housing conditions, heat exhaustion and access to healthcare for migrant workers. Despite the efforts of regional governments, though, challenges persist.

Generally, health and safety standards adopted by companies in the region tend to be motivated by legal compliance. As such, worker-related accidents are often a direct result of poor management, which is compounded by the fact that many workers themselves often lack basic experience, skills and training. However, through increasing corporate dialogue on issues of transparency and handling of health and safety, this situation may well change. The Institution of Occupational Safety and Health has launched a virtual branch to address legal complications surrounding health and safety in the Arab world, which is resulting in an increased understanding of the financial implications of establishing robust health and safety policies.

Despite this progress, Middle Eastern corporations need to do more in this area, particularly those working on large construction projects where there is a tendency to offload direct responsibility for such matters to contractors and sub-contractors.

Environmental sustainability

Parts of the Middle East are hot and arid. Environmental challenges, such as water scarcity and efficiency and pressure on energy consumption, are critical to its population and business community. However, having never experienced an environmental movement, nor vocal environmental interest groups, levels of awareness and concern are low. There is also a highly consumer-orientated culture in the region, with much of today's lifestyle coming at the expense of the environment. The UAE is said to have one of the highest per capita levels of resource consumption and ecological footprints in the world (WWF 2010).

To date, business-led solutions have gravitated around a range of basic initiatives: recycling, clean-up days, environmental management systems and internal green offices/teams. These have been seen as quick and easy wins for corporations that are feeling pressure to demonstrate practice in CSR. However, the regional environmental imperative is emerging and phenomena such as the trend for green buildings are really beginning to take off.

The construction boom experienced by the GCC has presented a unique opportunity. With a blank canvas on which to build iconic structures (e.g. Bahrain's World Trade Centre — the world's first example of integrated large-scale wind turbines in a commercial development), local governments have come to recognise the potential to position the region as a leader in green buildings and technology. Outlined as a priority issue in both the Dubai Strategic Plan 2015 and Abu Dhabi's Plan for 2030, the UAE is working on initiatives to tackle regional challenges such as low levels of environmental awareness, increased pollution, extreme consumerism, inefficient energy and water consumption and climate change.

Dubai has launched green buildings legislation and the Emirates Green Building Council, whilst Abu Dhabi is developing a new building rating system, Estidama, and the Masdar initiative. Through the inception of Masdar, Abu Dhabi hopes to nurture a global hub for Cleantech education, research, development and production. It also hopes to partner with international leaders and innovative companies in the Cleantech industry, to diversify away from its oil-based economy and focus on renewable energies and to develop the world's most sustainable city with the lowest environmental footprint.

Although these initiatives are symbols of the Middle East's intentions to support alternative energy, issues that are assumed to be hugely pressing to the region (e.g. water scarcity, climate change and ecological health) are not really prioritised as major concerns. This is highlighted in the Saudi Arabia profile and through instances such as the lack of exploration within the region for clean development mechanisms, for which the Middle East is eligible under the Kyoto Protocol.

Overall the level of environmental awareness is growing, but its focus varies from country to country. Education is paramount in furthering this issue. As Ralph Thrum said at the launch of Aramex's first sustainability report, 'there is no such thing as a sustainable company in an unsustainable world',[1] a concept that is still to hit home to regional firms today.

■ Trends

The concept of CSR itself is an evolving regional trend. Access to data and practical examples to support the business case are still limited. The first CSR conferences to take place in the Middle East were hosted by the UAE and Kuwait in 2004. Since then they have appeared in countries such as Qatar, Bahrain and Lebanon. In 2005, Al Urdun Al Jadid Research Centre (UJRC) and the Mediterranean Development Forum, with the help of regional organisations, assimilated country case studies on CSR from the Middle East. This was the first regional CSR benchmarking exercise. Since then research in this field has been supported by the programmes directed by national bodies such as the Dubai Chamber and Hawkamah.

In addition to conferences and reports, the Middle East is keen on recognition through awards. In 2008 the 'CSR Arabia Award' and the 'CSR Award Scheme' were launched by the Emirates Environmental Group and IIR (Institute of International Research) respectively. Additionally, many pre-existing awards have grown to include sustainability criteria in their processes. For instance, in Saudi Arabia, the Responsible Competitiveness

---

1 Ralph Thrum, Associate Director Business Engagement and Development, Global Reporting Initiative, speaking at the launch of Aramex's sustainability report, Dubai, UAE, September 2007.

Initiative, linked with the King Khalid Award for Responsible Competitiveness, now measures national companies on several indicators of social responsibility.

Corporate governance

Regionally, economies are opening up and issues of transparency and accountability are being encouraged. Awareness of the concept of corporate governance is growing, though its development and origins are different from the West and there remains a lack of understanding of its connection with CSR. Companies that are aware of corporate governance matters tend to be those reacting to, and complying with, new listing requirements (e.g. by Abu Dhabi Securities Market, Nasdaq Dubai, Dubai Financial Market, Tehran Stock Exchange, etc.). Few firms are actually taking the initiative and looking to understand the benefits themselves.

In comparison with mature international markets, the Middle East has only just begun to develop its financial systems regulations, reporting and bankruptcy laws. Consequently, reports and conferences on this subject are prevalent and tend to address prominent regional challenges, such as the role of corporate governance for family and state-owned enterprises. Particularly noteworthy here is the work of the Hawkamah Institute for Corporate Governance which has published reports, facilitated conferences and established awards to drive the agenda across the region.

Sustainability reporting

Overall, the Arab world is fairly new to the concept of corporate reporting, whether financial or non-financial. The first stand-alone sustainability reports were published in the GCC in 2007. Previously examples were restricted to Health, Safety and Environment (HSE) reports for companies operating in high risk sectors (e.g. ADNOC, from the oil extraction industry), or some inclusion of sustainability issues in annual reports or on corporate websites. Multinational enterprises with subsidiaries in the Gulf tended to document their local sustainability activity in their global reports.

In general, regional reports are at the commitment stage of the journey, with examples originating from Aramex in Jordan, Jumeirah in the UAE and Burgan Bank in Kuwait. Little comparable data on issues of materiality or evidence of strategic alignment and stakeholder engagement exists. However, prior to the economic downturn, this was set to change, with numerous companies expected to publish reports.

In 2008 two groups were founded to push the sustainability management and reporting agenda in the region. The Arab Leaders Sustainability Group, which spans five countries across the Middle East, was established by Her Highness Queen Rania of Jordan and the Abu Dhabi Sustainability Group, and was launched by the Environment Agency Abu Dhabi. To support this trend, a number of sustainability reporting events have been held, such as that hosted by the Dubai Chamber in collaboration with the Global Reporting Initiative (GRI).

▎ Organisations

▎ **Al Urdun Al Jadid Research Centre (UJRC).** Jordanian NGO, promoting sustainability in the region. http://www.ujrc-jordan.org

▎ **Arab Business Women's Council**. Regional NGO based in Egypt; convened under the Arab League. http://www.abwoc.org

▎ **Arab Forum for Environment and Development**. A Lebanese NGO endorsed by the League of Arab States and UNEP. http://www.afedonline.org/en

▎ **Centre for Responsible Business, Dubai Chamber**. A not-for-profit organisation promoting CSR in the UAE. http://www.dubaichamber.ae

▎ **Environment Agency Abu Dhabi**. A government organisation established to protect the environment and promote sustainability. http://www.ead.ae/en

▎ **Hawkamah**. A Dubai-based institute promoting corporate governance in the region. http://www.hawkamah.org

▎ **Lebanese Transparency Association**. Promoting transparency, anti-corruption and disclosure in Lebanon. http://www.transparency-lebanon.org

▎ **Sustainability Advisory Group**. An international federation of sustainability professionals, with a regional focus, that works with companies to embed principles of sustainability. http://www.sustainabilityadvisory.net

▎ **Young Arab Leaders**. A pan-Arab, not-for-profit organisation promoting leadership and entrepreneurship among Arab youth. http://www.yaleaders.org

▎ Case studies

Aramex, Jordan

Aramex is a global provider of logistics and transportation services. It aims to be a world leader in sustainability and is already recognised as a trailblazer in the Middle East. In 2007 Aramex published its first sustainability report, *Changing Today, Protecting Tomorrow*. It was the first GRI Third Generation (G3)-rated report in the Middle East, and remains one of the best examples of sustainability reporting in the region. Although it does not contain many facts and figures, it makes some strong commitments; tells a story of how, why and what the company thinks is important; and how it is improving areas of strategy and governance. Aramex has begun the process of aligning its systems with international reporting standards. It received a B+ rating from GRI for its report and has committed to using comparable international standards in future, for instance AA1000.[2] Aramex is demonstrating a link between its focus on sustainability and its core business strategy. In 2008 it became the first logistics company in the region to use

---

2   http://www.accountability.org/aa1000series

hybrid cars, and has outlined plans to become the first carbon-neutral global logistics and transportation company in the world. **http://www.aramex.com**

Qatar Airways, Qatar

Qatar Airways operates in over 80 destinations worldwide. It has undergone phenomenal expansion, with around 35% growth every year for the past ten years. It is demonstrating a commitment to CSR through a focus on developing quality new-generation fuel research, and social giving. Qatar Airways has created a Five Pillar CSR Program, known as 'The Oryx Flies Green', which embraces change management, environment, integrated fuel management, communication and sustainable development. Qatar Airways is becoming one of the region's leading players with respect to its environmental footprint, and is working to link such initiatives with its core business. The company has a dedicated environment department and is preparing to comply with the EU Emissions Trading Scheme for the aviation industry. The company has a fuel optimisation department whose primary focus is to identify ways in which to reduce its dependence on fossil fuels as part of its integrated fuel management programme. **http://www. qatarairways.com**

See the individual country chapters for other case studies.

References

Al Harthy (2009) Speech by Mohammad Bakar Al Harthy, Chief Executive Officer of Society Benefits, Community Development Authority (CDA), at the Centre for Responsible Business 2009 Responsible Business Dialogue, Dubai, UAE, 'The CSR . . . The Reality and Aspiration'; **http://web2.dubaichamber.ae/pdf/crb/Al_Harthy_Centre_for_Responsible_Business_Conference.pdf**, accessed 10 June 2010.

AMEinfo (2007) 'Heart disease causes 41% of UAE deaths', AMEinfo, 6 December 2007; **http://www. ameinfo.com/140866.html**, accessed 10 June 2010.

—— (2009) '60% of Emiratis classified as overweight; obesity levels in expatriates equally high', AMEinfo.com, 23 April 2009; **http://www.ameinfo.com/193820.html**, accessed 10 June 2010.

Brady, C., M. Jarvis and D. Petkoski (2009) 'From Corporate Philanthropy to Strategic Partnerships: The Potential of Inclusive and Sustainable Business Models in MENA', in *The World Bank. The Role of the Private Sector in Development: Assessments and Prospects* (Lebanon: Arab Planning Institute).

Dunlop, I. (2006) 'Business and Youth in the Arab World: Partnerships for Youth Employment and Enterprise Development' (International Business Leaders Forum; **http://www.iblf.org/docs/ BizYouthArab.pdf**, accessed 20 March 2010).

Emtairah, T., S. Påhlman and D. Pamlin (2007) 'Arab Companies in the 21st Century, Oil Revenues, Urbanisation and Emerging Economies: Converging Opportunities for Global Leadership' (UK: WWF; **http://assets.panda.org/downloads/arab_report_070115.pdf**, accessed 20 March 2010).

GERN (Global Education Research Network) (2008) 'Corporate Citizenship around the World: How Local Flavour Seasons the Global Practice' (Boston, MA: GERN/Boston College Center for Corporate Citizenship' **http://www.cccdeutschland.org/pics/medien/1_1224173416/GERN_for_web.pdf**, accessed 19 March 2010).

Human Rights Watch (2006) 'Building Towers; Cheating Workers, Exploitation of Migrant Construction Workers in the United Arab Emirates' (18.8[E]: 75; New York: Human Rights Watch).

—— (2009) ' "The Island of Happiness"; Exploitation of Migrant Workers on Saadiyat Island, Abu Dhabi' (New York: Human Rights Watch).

Jagannathan, N.V., A.S. Mohamed and A. Kremer (eds.) (2009) 'Water in the Arab World: Management Perspectives and Innovations' (Washington, DC: The World Bank, Middle East and North Africa Region).

Johnson & Johnson (2008) 'Citizenship and Community Investment Middle East Report' (Dubai, UAE: Johnson & Johnson Corporate Citizenship Trust Middle East).

Pipes, D. (2009) 'The Middle East Explodes with Obesity', Daniel Pipes Blog, 29 December 2004, updated 11 July 2009; **http://www.danielpipes.org/blog/2004/12/the-middle-east-explodes-with-obesity**, accessed 10 June 2010.

WWF (2010) 'UAE Government institutions urged to lead by example and reduce "carbon footprint" ' (WWF; **http://wwf.panda.org/about_our_earth/search_wwf_news/?uNewsID=188381**, accessed 10 June 2010).

Zalami, A. (2006) 'CSR in the UAE, A Preliminary Assessment', in *Dubai Ethics Resource Centre Mediterranean Development Forum* 5 (Dubai, UAE: Dubai Ethics Resource Centre).

B
Country profiles

1 Argentina

María Irigoyen
Project Director, ReporteSocial.com.

■ Context

CSR in Argentina has gradually evolved through the years, influenced by the country's cultural, historical and religious traditions. Its origins date back to the period of the Spanish viceroyalty, when the Catholic Church helped the poor through the Christian concept of charity. When Argentina became an independent state in 1816, the governing class took over this role, mostly through philanthropic activities.

During the mid 20th century, Peron's welfare state was marked by the concept of social justice, and in the 1980s civil society organisations played a stronger role in addressing society's needs through solidarity. In the 1990s, the concept of CSR was introduced in the media and some corporate circles (Milberg *et al.* 2003).

In 2001, Argentina suffered a severe economic, political and social crisis that had a profound impact on poverty, social exclusion and insecurity, generating mistrust in practically all institutions. In this context, companies developed philanthropic activities to meet basic community needs, compensating for a weak state and orientating their CSR activities to short-term poverty alleviation (Paladino *et al.* 2006).

However, once out of this situation, a new interest in responsible business practices emerged, and the beginning of the 21st century saw the rise of many CSR organisations, university courses, a new interest in the media, public–private partnerships, and seminars in related fields. Community contributions became increasingly seen as just one of the many dimensions of CSR, understood as a broader concept covering all stakeholder relationships (Berger *et al.* 2005).

Best practices began to include stakeholder engagement to inform decision-making processes, ethical supply chains, CSR reports and CSR governance structures. Many of these initiatives were promoted and disseminated by multinational companies.

Despite this evolution, CSR practices are still to a great extent the business of a few large companies and have yet to be further integrated into small and medium enterprises. Many organisations continue to focus on community activities, but there is greater CSR awareness, and these practices co-exist and are gradually evolving into a model where responsibility is integrated into all business areas.

∎ Priority issues

Sustainable economic growth

After a period of strong growth, in 2008 the Argentine economy started to decelerate due to domestic and international factors. In this context, and given Argentina's history of economic instability, achieving sustainable growth is challenging and requires ensuring a predictable institutional environment favourable to long-term planning. Priority issues for sustaining economic growth with social equity include: macroeconomic stability through prudent fiscal policies; investment to address bottlenecks to expanded economic activity; private sector development to improve productivity performance; trade policies that create new opportunities; and education policies that build a skilled labour force for future economic demands (World Bank 2006).

Building transparency

According to the Transparency International 2009 Corruption Perception Index, Argentina rates 106 out of 180 countries (where 1st means least corruption). Transparency policy needs to be deepened in the executive power of government, and extended to the judicial and legislative branches. Promoting judicial independence remains crucial: out of 750 corruption cases analysed, only 7% resulted in convictions, judicial investigations last an average of 15 years, and little has been done to guarantee the physical safety of witnesses (Gruenberg 2008). The manipulation of statistical data also remains a major concern.

Informal employment

In Argentina, 39.1% of workers are in the informal market, and this situation is worse for women and youth: 57.4% of informal workers are under 24 years and women are also disproportionately represented in this sector (Encuesta Permanente de Hogares 2007). Informality is linked to vulnerable living conditions, as workers have no access to social safety nets or credit. They also lack legal protection and have lower wages and unstable employment.

Quality education

Even though Argentina has done well in achieving universal education, improving educational quality remains a priority; the country was bottom of the Latin American countries participating in the 2006 Programme for International Student Assessment (PISA) evaluations of reading comprehension skills. An average of 50% of students who enter secondary school do not graduate, and only one in four students from families in the poorest population quintile graduates (World Bank 2006).

Desertification

Eighty per cent of Argentine territory is used for farming, livestock and forestry activities, with 60 million acres affected by different degrees and processes of desertification. This situation is critical in arid and semiarid zones, which constitute 75% of the national territory and are home to 30% of the population, and where productivity loss also results in the deterioration of living conditions (Secretaría de Ambiente y Desarrollo Sustentable de la Nación 2009).

∎ Trends

Aligned with the CSR focus in the 1990s, many studies analysed community investment and philanthropic business trends (for an example see Berger 1998). As a broader notion of CSR developed, research on trends expanded.

The CSR survey conducted by Berger *et al.* (2005) with over 150 of the largest Argentine companies found that 86% had a code of ethics and 56% an ethics committee. Those with an annual community donations budget increased this from 51% in 1997 to 61% in 2005. Regarding responsible value chain practices, 71% have explicit rules to prevent discrimination, 48% require their suppliers to meet social and environmental criteria beyond legal obligations and 48% have education programmes to inform consumers on product and services risks. Approximately one-third of these companies publish an annual CSR report, and of these, 61% do it according to recognised standards.

The survey results suggest that CSR is definitely on the agendas of the largest Argentinian companies, but the degree of institutionalisation and implementation of specific practices is still a challenge. A recent survey by PwC (PricewaterhouseCoopers) found that some of the main difficulties encountered by local companies in implementing sustainability practices include the economic investment needed (48%), little consumer appreciation for these initiatives (21%) and lack of top management awareness (17%) (Redolfi *et al.* 2009).

Another survey, conducted by *datosclaros* for the business magazine *Mercado*, shows that CSR continues to be a largely unknown public issue: six out of ten people interviewed had never heard of CSR (Rodríguez Petersen 2008a).

Nonetheless, society agrees with a more responsible role for business: 94% of people interviewed thought it was essential for companies to communicate their CSR actions, compared to 87% in 2007 and 74% in 2006; and 87% of companies had implemented a CSR-related action during 2008, with a large focus on education and environment (Rodríguez Petersen 2008b).

Despite this progress, 41% of company directors interpret CSR as making contributions to society, and 33% of the public agree. The public almost unanimously agree that beneficiaries should be included in decision-making processes, while 36% of the companies said that during 2008 this did not occur. Only 28% of businesses agree with the state evaluating the impact of CSR on society, compared with 50% of the public who think this is a good idea.

∎ Legislation and codes

In recent years several legislative projects on CSR-related issues have emerged. In 2005 a project was proposed to establish mandatory reporting on economic, social and environmental performance for companies with more than 300 employees. Similar initiatives have also been proposed in the province and city of Buenos Aires. It is also relevant to mention the Social Volunteering Law (Ley 25.855) which promotes citizen participation in community nonprofit activities, but has yet to be implemented.

Other national laws which touch on key ethical, social and environmental issues include:

- **Public Ethics Law (Ley 25.188)** which introduces ethical criteria in the exercise of public functions

- **National Employment Law (Ley 20.744)** includes ethical work-related aspects such as discrimination, and has been modified and complemented by norms that expand on these issues: occupational health and safety (Ley 24.557), social employee benefits (Ley 26.341), child labour (Ley 26.390) and maternity rights (Ley 21.824)

- **Environmental Protection Norms** are addressed in the 1994 reform of the Argentine National Constitution, which incorporated new rights and guarantees. Among these, Article 41 established the right to a healthy environment and, in this context, the National Congress sanctioned environmental protection norms including laws on Industrial and Service Activities Waste Integral Management (Ley 25.612); PCBs Management and Elimination (Ley 25.670); General Environmental Law (Ley 25.675); Environmental Water Management (Ley 25.688); Access to Public Environmental Information (Ley 25.831); Domiciliary Waste Management (Ley 25.916); and Deforestation (Ley 26.331). Of these, the General Environmental Law is key as it establishes the principles, objectives and instruments of the Argentine National Environmental Policy.

International standards are also part of the Argentine CSR landscape. The number of Global Reporting Initiative (GRI) reporters is increasing, and by July 2008 305 organisations had adhered to the local network of the UN Global Compact. There is also growing interest in the new ISO 26000 guideline on CSR.

▮ Organisations

In recent years many organisations have emerged across the country to promote CSR. Key business associations and other member-based organisations include:

▮ **Consejo Empresario para el Desarrollo Sostenible**. As the Argentinian chapter of the World Business Council for Sustainable Development, this business association promotes sustainable development and currently has more than 50 corporate members. **http://www.ceads.org.ar**

▮ **Foro del Sector Social**. In 1999, 43 business leaders signed a collaboration agreement with this organisation that groups 3,000 of the most important NGOs in the country, and 70 others joined the CSR Programme that was created. **http://www.forodelsectorsocial. org.ar**

▮ **Fundación del Tucumán**. A member of Forum Empresa, this business association with more than 100 members promotes sustainable business practices with a focus in Northwest Argentina. **http://www.fundaciondeltucuman.org.ar**

▮ **Grupo de Fundaciones y Empresas**. This group promotes social private investment in Argentina and currently includes 27 companies and company foundations. **http://www. gdfe.org.ar**

▌ **Instituto Argentino de Responsabilidad Social Empresaria**. Founded in Córdoba, this NGO is a key CSR promoter and currently has more than 100 members. **http://www. iarse.org**

▌ **MoveRSE**. With a focus in the City of Rosario, this organisation promotes sustainable inclusive business practices and has 20 members. **http://www.moverse.org**

▌ **VALOS**. Created to promote sustainable business practices in Mendoza, this business association currently has more than 70 members. **http://www.valos.org.ar**

International business chambers and national sector chambers also play a significant role in CSR promotion in Argentina. Other CSR promoters include the **Instituto para el Desarrollo Empresarial de la Argentina** which has a CSR working group and various published documents, and the **Asociación Cristiana de Dirigentes de Empresa** which promotes Christian values and ethics in business.

▌ Case studies

The following cases represent emblematic CSR practices of leading companies in Argentina:

Grupo Arcor

Founded in 1951, this leading Argentine industrial group, specialising in the manufacture of confectionery, cookies, ice cream and foodstuff, has followed a development model based on generating economic, social and environmental value. Through a participative CSR process, the company integrates ethical criteria throughout its supply chain, contributes to creating equal childhood opportunities, promotes healthy living habits and protects the environment through eco-efficient production models. **http:// www.arcor.com.ar**

Banco Galicia

Created in 1905, this bank seeks to enhance its role as a social actor, integrating sustainability into business operations to help improve the welfare of Argentinian people. It was the first bank in Argentina to adhere to the Equator Principles; it supports microfinance organisations and provides financial products for the development of the agricultural sector. **http://www.e-galicia.com**

Gas Natural BAN

Part of the Spanish multinational Grupo Gas Natural, this company has distributed natural gas in the Buenos Aires Province since 1992. Through inclusive business practices, it has begun supplying gas to vulnerable neighbourhoods, developing a social management model based on community participation to install natural gas networks. With a B+ GRI Third Generation (G3) rating, its 2008 CSR Report describes how the company has introduced CSR aspects in its top management and business strategy. **http://www. gasnaturalban.com.ar**

Manpower

This US employment services company, present in Argentina since 1965, integrates CSR into its core business, with a focus on workplace development, disaster recovery, refugees and human trafficking. Key programmes include the creation of work opportunities for disabled people, initiatives for preventing child labour, and the promotion of opportunities for women to engage and thrive in the workforce. **http://www.manpower. com.ar**

▌ Education

- **Escuela de Dirección y Negocios de la Universidad Austral**. The MBA and the executive business programmes include a mandatory CSR course. **http://www. iae.edu.ar**

- **Pontificia Universidad Católica Argentina**. CSR is part of a Business Ethics course in graduate and postgraduate programmes in the Faculty of Economic and Social Sciences. **http://www.uca.edu.ar**

- **Universidad Argentina de la Empresa**. The Faculty of Economic Sciences, the MBA and other postgraduate programmes include mandatory Business Ethics and Social Responsibility courses, and the Faculty of Communication offers an elective CSR course. **http://www.uade.edu.ar**

- **Universidad Católica de Córdoba**. Through its Ethics and Social Responsibility Business Center the university offers a CSR executive business course. **http:// www.ucc.edu.ar**

- **Universidad de Buenos Aires**. The Faculty of Economic Sciences has created the National Center for CSR and Social Capital, and the Faculty of Agronomy has an Institute for Ethics in Agronomy. **http://www.uba.ar**

- **Universidad de San Andrés**. The Center for Social Innovation has an Executive CSR Training Program, and mandatory and elective CSR Seminars are included in the MBA. **http://www.udesa.edu.ar**

- Other centres dedicated to research on CSR-related issues are the **Centro de Estudios de Estado y Sociedad** and the **Instituto de Estudios para la Sustentabilidad Corporativa**. **http://www.cedes.org** and **http://www.sustentabilidad.org.ar**

References

Balián de Tagtachian, B. (2004) 'Responsabilidad Social Empresaria, un Estudio Empírico de 147 Empresas', 'Colección Documentos de Trabajo', July 2004, Serie F–N1, Pontificia Universidad Católica Argentina.

Berger, G. (1998) 'Estudio de Filantropía Empresaria' (Buenos Aires, Argentina: Universidad de San Andrés and Gallup Argentina).

——, E. Reficco and R. Hermelo (2005) 'Encuesta de Responsabilidad Social Empresaria en la Argentina — Año 2005' (Buenos Aires, Argentina: Universidad de San Andrés/TNS-Gallup; **http://www.udesa.edu.ar**, accessed 20 March 2010).

Encuesta Permanente de Hogares (2007) (INDEC) 'Tasa de Empleo no Registrado Según Características Socio-Económicas, Excluyendo Beneficiarios de Planes de Empleo (Primer Trimestre)' (INDEC; http://www.indec.gov.ar, accessed 20 March 2009).

Gruenberg, C. (2008) 'Transparencia', in *Agenda Pública a 25 Años de Democracia* (Buenos Aires, Argentina: CIPPEC): 40-49.

Milberg, A., M. Paladino and R. Vassolo (2003) 'Revisión de la Responsabilidad Social Empresarial en Argentina' ('A Review of Corporate Social Responsibility in Argentina'), in *III Iberoamerican Academy of Management Annual Meeting*, São Paulo, Brazil, November 2003.

Paladino, M. (ed.) (2007) *La Responsabilidad de la Empresa en la Sociedad: Construyendo la Sociedad desde la Tarea Directiva* (Buenos Aires, Argentina: Colección Emecé IAEpress, 2nd edn).

——, P. Debeljuh and P. Scarinci de Delbosco (2007) *Integridad: Un liderazgo Diferente* (Buenos Aires, Argentina: Colección Emecé IAEpress).

——, A. Milberg and F. Sánchez Iriondo (2006) *Emprendedores Sociales y Empresarios Responsables* (Editorial; Buenos Aires, Argentina: Temas Grupo).

Redolfi, N., M. Spitale and B. Bradford (2009) 'Desarrollo Sostenible: ¿un Nuevo Paradigm de Gestión?', in *CEO Argentina Hot Topics* (Responsabilidad Social Corporativa, Año 5.11, PricewaterhouseCoopers; http://www.pwc.com/ar/es/publicaciones/assets/ceo-desost.pdf, accessed 21 March 2010): 14-23.

Rodríguez Petersen, J. (2008a) 'Las Grandes Objeciones', in *Mercado. RSE: El Debate de Hoy. Y el Debate de Mañana* (Buenos Aires: Editorial Coyuntura S.A., November 2008): 24-34.

—— (2008b) 'Ranking de la RSE', in: *Mercado. RSE: el debate de hoy. Y el debate de mañana* (Buenos Aires: Editorial Coyuntura S.A., November 2008): 36-66.

Roitter, M. (1996) *La Razón Social de las Empresas. Una Investigación Sobre los Vínculos Entre Empresa y Sociedad en Argentina* (Buenos Aires, Argentina: CEDES).

—— and M. Camerlo M (2005) 'Corporate Social Action in a Context of Crisis: Reflections on the Argentine Case', in C. Sanborn and F. Portocarrero (eds.), *Philanthropy and Social Changes in Latin America* (The David Rockefeller Center Series on Latin American Studies; Cambridge, MA: Harvard University).

Secretaría de Ambiente y Desarrollo Sustentable de la Nación (2009) 'Programa de Acción Nacional de Lucha contra la Desertificación: PAN, Documento de Base'; http://www.ambiente.gov.ar/?idseccion=143, accessed 21 March 2010.

World Bank (2006) 'Country Assistance Strategy for the Argentine Republic: 2006–2008' (Report No. 34015-AR; World Bank; http://siteresources.worldbank.org/INTARGENTINA/Resources/1CASAr.pdf, accessed 21 March 2010).

Acknowledgements

I would like to thank the many professionals in CSR-related fields who provided me with their insights and valuable opinions on the issues covered in this chapter.[1] A special thanks to my husband Pedro and the rest of my family and friends for their endless support on every project I embark on.

---

1 In particular Mercedes Occhi, María Eugenia Bellazzi and Victoria Benvenuto from ReporteSocial.com, Gabriel Berger and Ana Reyes (Udesa), Patricia Debeljuh (UADE), Alberto Willy (IAE), Mario Roitter (CEDES), Sebastián Bigorito, María José Alzary and Virginia Vilariño (CEADS), Luis Ulla and Alejandro Rocca (IARSE), Nicolás Ducoté (CIPPEC), Agustina Paglayan and Verónica Raffo (World Bank), María Amelia Videla and Lucas Utrera (Manpower), and Amalia Milberg and Nicola Helfert for revising the final version of the chapter.

2 Armenia

Nazareth Seferian
Programmes Manager, British Council Armenia

∎ Context

The smallest of the 15 republics formed after the collapse of the Soviet Union, Armenia is a landlocked country with a population of around 3 million people. Poor in resources compared to its neighbours and with two out of four land borders closed due to political issues, Armenia is not considered a priority country for investment by many international companies, and relatively few of them have local offices. The major share of businesses in the country is either owned by locals or by Russian companies and individuals.

The concept of CSR, corporate sustainability or community investment is poorly understood in Armenia. While local representatives of international companies are relatively clear on the concept, there is not much visible activity in this area. Most of the large local companies are owned by the so-called oligarchs, Armenians who grew rich in the transition period from communism to capitalism, when state assets were privatised. The tax practices in the country also blur the perception of corporate responsibility — the oligarchs, many of whom also have influential positions in government, avoid paying their full due in taxes. This leads to a highly skewed understanding of corporate responsibility locally, namely that 'if my company pays its taxes, then it is a responsible business'.

This belief is further reinforced by the state position on CSR. For the first time in the country's history, the new government, led by President Serzh Sargsyan and Prime Minister Tigran Sargsyan, included the 'Promotion of Corporate Social Responsibility' as a separate point in the government's 2008–2012 programme. While this was not elaborated further in the text, the Prime Minister and Ministry of Economy representatives have said on a number of occasions that their priority at this stage is to level the tax playing field. The indication is that the first step to corporate responsibility is for a company to pay its taxes — everything else can come later. But in a country where the tax authorities are viewed with suspicion and where the discovery of 'tax irregularities' is sometimes used as a tool against the enterprises of political opponents, this approach to CSR may well slow down the country's progress to a healthy atmosphere of corporate sustainability.

There is no country model for CSR and, to a large extent, community investment remains on a philanthropic level. This is especially true for the large Armenian companies, whose oligarchic heads make showy charitable donations in pre-election periods. But this also holds for many other companies, where management has a 'soft spot' for orphanages and children. Many company directors who have been asked about their enterprise's contribution to society have mentioned visiting an orphanage with employees and giving gifts to children, as well as a few random acts of tree planting. There are few examples of structured and strategic CSR initiatives.

▌ Priority issues

The Prime Minister of Armenia listed the main challenges facing Armenia in a speech to Parliament in April 2008. His new government was outlining its programme for the next four years and emphasised tackling the issues of the gap between rich and poor, the 'unhealthy moral and psychological atmosphere', a large shadow economy, corruption, unfair competition and poverty. The priority actions he outlined included maintaining a high rate of economic growth (threatened in 2009 by the global economic crisis), social integration and consolidation, the development of human capital (steps in the fields of education, healthcare, culture and the environment) and the introduction of the principles of corporate governance. Another major issue in the country is the unequal rate of growth in the capital as compared with the rest of the country.

In a survey published by the International Research Exchanges Board (IREX) in March 2009, Armenians saw the top three problems they faced as a country to be unemployment, lack of social security and corruption.

The 2009 Corruption Perceptions Index by Transparency International ranked Armenia 120th out of 180 countries — where first means least corruption (Transparency International 2009) and the OECD Anti-Corruption Network has referred to 'the pervasive tradition of bribe-giving in Armenia' in a past report (OECD 2006).

▌ Trends

A study conducted by the Eurasia Partnership Foundation (2006) is the main source of published information about the level of knowledge of CSR practices in companies operating in Armenia. The study focused on social investment and concluded that the 'comprehension of social investments is poor and the lack of adequate practices among the business community in Armenia does not allow responses to be prioritised in terms of preferred ways and mechanisms to implement them'. Social investments which existed tended to be 'single-term' or 'spontaneous' and would more correctly be characterised as corporate philanthropy, rather than a strategic CSR approach. The study found the attitude in the business community towards public–private partnerships to be 'pessimistic'.

Grant Thornton's (2008) International Business Report also provides some, if limited, insight into the mind-set of the Armenian business community. Their survey found recruitment and retention of staff to be the main driver of corporate responsibility in the country. CSR activities were found to focus mainly on employee safety and well-being, while energy efficiency and waste management measures scored low. Taken in consideration with the study by the Eurasia Partnership Foundation, this suggests that companies have a limited understanding of corporate responsibility, focusing mostly inwards on their staff and not thinking about environmental impact or community involvement.

Since March 2008, four organisations active in Armenia have come together to create an informal CSR working group aimed at promoting the concept of corporate responsibility in the country. The British Council, Eurasia Partnership Foundation, UN Global Compact in Armenia and American Chamber of Commerce organised a conference on the issue in June 2008 and followed that up with a series of one-on-one interviews with leading Armenian companies. Based on feedback received during the conference and interviews, the private sector was divided into four sectors — information technology and communications, banking and finance, manufacturing and industry, and tourism and hospitality — and an informal business luncheon was held for each sector. Invitees discussed the concept of CSR at the luncheons and heard about CSR projects and ideas from each other. In November 2009, a two-day training workshop was also held on CSR and marketing/public relations.

These activities have allowed the CSR working group to generate a wealth of information regarding the understanding and attitude towards CSR held by many companies operating in Armenia, especially in the wake of the global economic crisis which hit the country in early 2009.

There is a clear divide between the international companies — many of whom have well established CSR policies, developed by a central office in Europe or the United States — and the local companies. CSR is well comprehended in the first group, although many of these companies have yet to complete large CSR projects. Coca-Cola, for example, was planning to invest in the water distribution system in 2009, while they had taken these steps in a number of countries earlier.

In contrast, companies owned locally focus mostly on corporate philanthropy, conducted sporadically. Since many large local businesses are owned by oligarchs with political careers, these acts of charity often occur around the election period. Additionally, many local companies organise tree-planting days with their staff members. This is either done in partnership with a nonprofit organisation, which then tends to the saplings, or with no such long-term concerns. CSR remains a blurred concept at best and while the term itself is gaining in popularity, the meaning behind it continues to lack any tangible definition.

CSR is also not yet seen as a separate line of work in Armenia, with only one company boasting a CSR specialist (see K-Telecom in 'Case studies' below). In international companies, most CSR work is done by public relations specialists and in some cases by marketing executives, as part of their regular job description. In local companies, this remains the prerogative of the chief executive officer or company owner (who are often one and the same person), who issues instructions to staff members about philanthropic acts. Companies do not issue CSR reports in most cases (although this is beginning to change with the reporting requirements for members of the UN Global Compact in Armenia) and very few company CSR reports for Armenia are available to the general public.

The economic crisis and increasing unemployment have led to the attitude that any company providing employment opportunities and retaining its staff in the current economic atmosphere is a responsible business, contributing to the development of Armenia.

While this remains the predominant thinking in the business community, there are a number of businesses that are beginning to invest in education and the environment, often partnering with government structures or nonprofit organisations, organising activities that would fall under the definition of CSR, even if they do not go by that name in the given company's strategy.

∎ Legislation and codes

Armenia does not have any legislative measures which reward community investments or philanthropic donations through tax incentives. On the contrary, any and all philanthropic acts are taxed, such that companies donating old equipment to schools find themselves having to make tax payments on the estimated value of that equipment. Furthermore, the government has stated on a number of occasions that there are no plans to provide any tax incentives for such activity any time in the near future. At the same time, a Ministry of Economy representative recently informed the CSR working group that the Ministry was looking to 'set up a separate body to promote CSR' and this structure would presumably take suggestions on board for future action.

Article 15 of the Republic of Armenia's law on the Preservation of Nature states the following:

> Enterprises are obligated to guarantee environmental safety according to existing standards, to secure the uninterrupted and efficient functioning of cleaning equipment, structures and stations, by means of the neutralisation of harmful wastes, by means of investing into environmentally harmless technologies and into water recycling systems. It is forbidden to allow the operation of those objects, which do not guarantee the execution of all environmental requirements. When such objects are given operation permits, the [permitting] committee chairman and committee members are subject to civil and criminal prosecution.

However, there is a general consensus that this law exists only on paper without much practical application. An article in September 2007 in the *Armenian Reporter* concluded on the basis of scientific research, reports and observation that 'Armenian environmental laws are being bypassed, standards are being manipulated, and perhaps even influence is being peddled' — an allegation directed mainly at the mining sector (Sanasaryan and Shirinyan-Orlando 2007). Furthermore, the law is limited to reactive CSR, calling on companies to neutralise the harmful environmental effects of their operations. There are no provisions in Armenian law which would motivate companies to develop strategic CSR policies or increase their involvement in the community.

▮ Organisations

As mentioned, the following four organisations have been closely coordinating efforts to promote CSR since April 2008:

▮ **American Chamber of Commerce in Armenia**. There are 79 companies and organisations among its members; it strives for the creation of a competitive, transparent, free and fair business environment in Armenia. **http://www.amcham.am**

▮ **British Council (Armenia)**. The Council seeks to build strong cultural relations between the United Kingdom and Armenia by facilitating the exchange of ideas. **http://www.britishcouncil.am**

▮ **Eurasia Partnership Foundation**. The Foundation describes its mission as empowering people to effect change for social justice and economic prosperity through hands-on programmes, helping them to improve their communities and their own lives. **http://www.epfound.am**

▮ **UN Global Compact in Armenia**. Launched in Armenia on 17 November 2006, the Global Compact has 31 member institutions. **http://www.globalcompact.am**

▮ Case studies

There are several examples of good practice in Armenia and a few companies have truly integrated CSR into their business approach. However, one company stands out for its reputation in CSR and the widespread perception that it is the leader in this field.

Viva-Cell (K-Telecom)

Viva-Cell is the brand under which K-Telecom provides mobile phone services in Armenia. The company, then Lebanese owned, started providing services on 1 July 2005 and broke into a market that was previously a monopoly, soon becoming the leading mobile services provider. Ownership changed hands and the Russian mobile giant MTS took over, but CSR practices remained largely the same.

K-Telecom is probably the only company in the country to have a manager working on CSR issues full-time and the only one so far to have produced a separate publication on its community activities. Its CEO has become a widely recognised figure, often featuring on the evening news with the latest act of philanthropy by his company. Although he very often uses the term 'corporate social responsibility' in describing this work and rejects the notion that it is charity, it is difficult to see a direct strategic focus in most of K-Telecom's community activities. They are varied and include constructing gas pipelines in villages, donating apartments to earthquake victims, supporting a special school for children with autism, donating equipment to hospitals and much more.

While there has been a lot of debate about whether this is strategically planned or simply meant to garner public support for the company, one can definitely credit the company and its CEO with promoting the idea of community involvement by private businesses in Armenia. **http://www.vivacell.am**

▌ Education

The leading institution in business education in the country is considered to be the American University of Armenia, which is accredited by the Western Association of Schools and Colleges in the United States and is affiliated with the University of California. A prerequisite for graduating from the MBA programme of the university is the completion of a corporate ethics and responsibility course, arguably the only one of its kind in the country. The American University of Armenia was not listed as a participating school for the *Beyond Grey Pinstripes* survey (Aspen Institute 2010).

References

Aspen Institute Center for Business Education (2010) 'Beyond Grey Pinstripes 2009–2010'; http://www.beyondgreypinstripes.org/pdf/2009-2010BGP_Brochure.pdf, accessed 2 June 2010.

Eurasia Partnership Foundation (2006) *Baseline Assessment of the State of Social Investment in Armenia* (Yerevan, Armenia: Eurasia Partnership Foundation).

Grant Thornton (2008) 'Corporate Social Responsibility: A Necessity, Not a Choice' (International Business Report 2008, London: Grant Thornton).

OECD (2006) 'Armenia must crack down on corruption, says OECD'; http://www.oecd.org/document/35/0,3343,en_2649_34857_37846947_1_1_1_37447,00.html, accessed 23 May 2010.

Sanasaryan, H., and A. Shirinian-Orlando (2007) 'Teghut, Drembon, Alaverdi and the Politics of Pollution', *Armenian Reporter*, 1 September 2007.

Transparency International (2009) 'Corruption Perceptions Index'; http://www.transparency.org/policy_research/surveys_indices/cpi/2009, accessed 21 March 2010.

Acknowledgements

I would like to thank the people I consider both partners and friends at the Eurasia Partnership Foundation, UN Global Compact in Armenia and American Chamber of Commerce for providing their frank feedback on the first draft of this document and helping me improve it.

3 Australia

Leeora D. Black
Managing Director, Australian Centre for
Corporate Social Responsibility (ACCSR)

■ Context

At the turn of this century, Australia was widely considered as a lazy backwater when it came to CSR. A decade later, CSR is on the agenda of almost every company director and CEO of at least the larger enterprises in Australia.

In the years following World War II, industrialisation and increasing standards of living did not present acute issues for either business or its regulation. Australia followed the British model of a welfare state, where social needs and infrastructure have been primarily the responsibility of the state. Indeed, government expenditure on welfare and social security rose from 6.9% of Commonwealth budgetary outlays in 1970–71 to 35% in the late 1990s (CCPA 2000). Social issues such as aboriginal reconciliation and poverty remained outside the purview of 'business as usual'. There was not much social unrest and the seemingly inexhaustible supply of natural resources led to little pressure on business or government for change.

The more recent and profound changes in awareness and action on CSR issues have their genesis in events of the 1980s. The then Labour government deregulated the banking industry in 1983. Foreign-owned banks were able to operate in Australia for the first time, and Australian banks became increasingly competitive. The liberalisation was accompanied by an increase in two-way trade between Australia and the rest of the world, and with that trade, increasing exposure to far more complex market and non-market environments, for which CSR is a helpful strategy.

Further, high-profile environmental crises in the 1990s, such as BHP's failed mine tailings dam in Papua New Guinea, business failures in Australia such as HIH and One-Tel in the early 2000s, and crises in corporate accountability, such as at the building products company James Hardie, have led to a greater questioning of the nature of corporate responsibilities within board rooms and executive ranks, in governments and in NGOs.

In 2004, James Hardie's scheme to avoid liabilities for asbestos compensation was exposed, resulting in a New South Wales state government inquiry that led to new long-term funding arrangements for asbestos disease sufferers. The public uproar over James Hardie led to the establishment of two federal government inquiries in Australia into the nature of corporate accountability and responsibility and whether the Corporations Law should be strengthened to directly address the interests of stakeholders. Although both inquiries rejected changes to the Corporations Law, both called for more government encouragement of CSR.

By considering the question of corporate responsibility through these inquiries, company directors and executives were sent a powerful signal that CSR is part of 'business as usual'. It is not an 'add-on', but as the CAMAC report (CAMAC 2006) suggested, 'social responsibility, like effective corporate governance, can be seen as part and parcel of the way a company's affairs are conducted'.

These events have more explanatory power for Australian approaches to CSR than models of CSR developed through scholarship, such as Carroll's (1979) four-part definition, which has been used in Australian studies with mixed results (Black 2001). Although Australian business does clearly prioritise philanthropy and community investment, an authentically Australian approach to CSR balances strategic approaches with social needs. Australian business leaders consider that the major challenge of CSR is to create business behaviours which meet community standards as well as the firm's strategic needs (Birch 2003).

■ Priority issues and trends

The ACCSR (Australian Centre for Corporate Social Responsibility) (2009) research report asked over 500 people with CSR or sustainability accountabilities in their organisations about the priority issues their organisations would face in 2009. The majority (66%) prioritised building internal understanding and support for CSR within their organisations. This high focus is an important finding. It indicates that CSR issues and activities are not yet 'mainstreamed' into many businesses, but that the desire to advance CSR is strong. This may suggest that in future years, as the mainstreaming agenda succeeds, more global CSR leaders will come from Australia.

'Reducing or eliminating the negative environmental impacts of business' ranked a close second priority, with 65% reporting that this will be a 'high' or 'very high' priority in the next 12 months. Similarly, 65% will prioritise understanding the impact of climate change on their organisations. The significant prioritisation of these two environmental issues demonstrates the ways in which environmental concerns have increasingly moved towards the top of CSR agendas. These priorities, particularly understanding climate change, are also likely to be a reflection of the expected implementation of an emissions trading scheme.

■ Legislation and codes

The Australian government has begun to encourage business to take on greater social and environmental responsibilities with the following three substantive initiatives:

The Carbon Pollution Reduction Scheme

Australia is expected to begin a 'cap and trade' Carbon Pollution Reduction Scheme (CPRS) in 2012–13. This is an emissions trading scheme designed to achieve the government's policy commitment to reduce emissions by between 5% and 15% below 2000 levels by 2020. All six greenhouses gases covered by the Kyoto Protocol are included. The Australian Climate Change Regulatory Authority is being established to oversee the CPRS. The CPRS intends to amend the Corporations Act by making emissions units fungible as 'financial products' so that brokers trading emissions units on exchanges will need to be licensed.

The CPRS follows the introduction in 2007 of the National Greenhouse and Energy Reporting Act which provides for the reporting and dissemination of information about the greenhouse gas emissions, greenhouse gas projects, and energy use and production by corporations. The Act will underpin the CPRS, providing the emissions data on which obligations under the CPRS will be based. The Act initially requires only the top 1,000 entities in Australia to publicly report their carbon emissions, but it is expected to lead to a boom in environmental reporting as a swathe of smaller entities see benefits in monitoring and reporting greenhouse gas emissions.

The Responsible Business Practice Project

In 2008, the government commissioned an NGO, St James Ethics Centre, to undertake a three-year project to expand responsible business practice nationally. The Centre established The Responsible Business Practice project to expand the number of Australian companies that are actively engaged in identifying and adopting more responsible business practices, and to improve tools for responsible business practices.

To achieve these goals, St James Ethics Centre has initiated a programme to support CSR development in small and medium-sized enterprises, created a web portal, and entered into agreements with the Global Reporting Initiative and the UN Global Compact to advance their work in Australia. St James Ethics Centre also runs the Corporate Responsibility Index in Australia.

Responsible Investment Academy

In early 2009, the government announced financial support for the Responsible Investment Association Australasia (RIAA) to establish the Responsible Investment Academy, the world's first academic-level centre for responsible investment education, training and innovation. The Academy will provide web-based training for investment professionals on integration of environmental, social and governance issues into investment decisions.

More than 50% of all funds under management in Australia have signed the UN Principles for Responsible Investment. Given that Australia is the world's fourth largest market for managed funds, establishment of the Responsible Investment Academy may signify the emergence of Australia as a leader in shaping the global agenda for the mainstreaming of social, environmental and governance considerations into investment.

▌ Organisations

▎ The **Asia Pacific Centre for Sustainable Enterprise at Griffith University**. The Centre offers research and teaching on sustainability. **http://www.griffith.edu.au/business/sustainable-enterprise**

▎ **Australian Centre for Corporate Social Responsibility**. This consulting and training company is wholly dedicated to building competitive advantage and stakeholder wealth through corporate social responsibility. **http://www.accsr.com.au**

▎ The **Centre for Global Sustainability at RMIT University**. This research institution is focused on creating working models of global sustainability through collaboration with government, corporate, academic and community leaders in the application of global sustainability principles. **http://www.rmit.edu.au/sustainability**

▎ The **Centre for Social Responsibility in Mining at the University of Queensland**. The Centre was established by the University of Queensland in 2001 in response to growing interest in and debate about the role of the mining and minerals industry in contemporary society. **http://www.csrm.uq.edu.au**

▎ The **Centre for Social Impact**. The Centre is a partnership between business schools of the University of New South Wales, the University of Melbourne, Swinburne University of Technology and the University of Western Australia, providing education in social entrepreneurship. **http://www.csi.edu.au**

▎ **La Trobe University Graduate School of Management**. The Graduate School of Management delivers a world-class management education for postgraduate students and business professionals. **http://www.latrobe.edu.au/gsm**

▎ The **Responsible Investment Association of Australia**. This is the peak industry body for professionals working in responsible investment in Australia and New Zealand. **http://www.responsibleinvestment.org**

▎ **St James Ethics Centre**. This not-for-profit organisation promotes and explores individual and organisational ethics and runs The Responsible Business Practice project. **http://www.ethics.org.au**

▌ Case studies

These case studies are extracts reprinted with permission from *The State of CSR in Australia: 2008 Annual Review, Volume 1* (ACCSR 2009).

Delta Electricity

Formed in 1996 as part of the New South Wales government's restructure of the electricity industry, Delta Electricity now generates 12% of the power for the national electricity market.

While most of its output is generated from coal, Delta also identified early on that low-emission electricity is the way of the future. It is currently constructing a 667 MW gas turbine facility, which emits 40% less greenhouse gases than an equivalent coal-fired

power plant, and has two other facilities in development. It has several mini hydro projects and also began the journey to negotiate a joint venture and raise private financial backing for a renewable energy project ten years ago.

In 2008, with the NSW Sugar Milling Co-operative, two 30 MW facilities that convert sugar cane waste (bagasse) to electricity were opened on the north coast of New South Wales. The project is estimated to save 400,000 tonnes of carbon emissions a year, the equivalent of taking 88,000 cars off the road. It also provides the sugar milling co-operative with another source of income.

Delta has also been active in developing sustainable water use. For example, it has put in place a number of measures, including replacing drinking-quality water with seawater for cooling purposes, installing a recycling plant on the central coast to replace a further quantity of fresh water used in the power station processes with recycled water made from treating effluent. Sustainability is a key part of Delta's strategy to gain a distinctive place in a growing market. **http://www.de.com.au**

Lihir Gold Ltd (LGL)

Stakeholder dialogue has been a critical aspect of LGL's community liaison programme on the island of Lihir in Papua New Guinea for over a decade. Stakeholder dialogue shaped the philosophy, structure and programmes that have been implemented in sustainable development plans and benefits packages developed by LGL, together with its Lihirian stakeholders.

The Lihir Sustainable Development Plan (LSDP) outlines how funding from a range of sources is being spent on health, education, training, cultural heritage, utilities, infrastructure and housing. Dialogue has led to decisions about shared equity ventures, such as geothermal power delivery, contract mining, on and offshore accommodation, transport and catering.

The agreement is managed through a joint stakeholder planning and monitoring committee supported by a number of sub-committees and working groups. It is in these forums that LGL's formal daily dialogue with representatives from the landowner association (LMALA) and the three tiers of government takes place. Elsewhere, dialogue within the 35 villages in the Lihir island group is rolled out on a less formal basis through a long-standing weekly communications programme.

The company is also building internal dialogue skills. As the biggest employer in the Lihir island group, 900 kilometres northeast of Port Moresby, LGL recognises that its workforce, including over 750 Lihirians, engage on a daily basis with the Lihir community.

As an outcome of a risk profile exercise with the Centre for Social Responsibility in Mining in 2008, a Social Awareness and Training programme (SAT) was rolled out in 2009 by the community liaison department, in conjunction with the landowner association. Ultimately, SAT is aimed at improving the quality and effectiveness of dialogue through greater understanding and appreciation of the concepts underpinning the sustainable development plan, including the evolving role of both the company's and Lihirian institutions into the future. **http://www.lglgold.com**

Westpac Banking Corporation

Westpac's competitive strategy is to weave corporate responsibility, sustainability and governance into every part of the business. For Westpac, sustainability is about removing risk. One example is its financial literacy programme, Financial First Steps. What began originally as an education tool for staff has now been extended to customers through workshops, one-on-one sessions and a CD-rom, teaching about budgeting for rents and mortgages, and dealing with mobile phone costs and car insurance. With banks now facing big losses through bad debts, Westpac is using this programme as one way to make deep connections with the community in helping to manage money. Along the way, it reduces risk.

Recognised as a global banking leader in the Dow Jones Sustainability Index, Westpac is also using its leadership on environmental issues to recruit talent and work with customers concerned about the impact of the emissions trading scheme on their bottom line. Here, sustainability and corporate responsibility have been turned into a competitive advantage. Indeed, Westpac management believes it is a disadvantage not to have this approach. Thus far, Westpac has continued to deliver sounds results during the global financial crisis. **http://www.westpac.com.au**

▮ Education

Australian universities have been slower than their European and American counterparts to develop university education programmes in CSR.

The first (and, at the time of writing, the only) dedicated CSR course in Australia began at La Trobe University's Graduate School of Management in January 2009. The Graduate Certificate of Corporate Responsibility focuses on issues and dilemmas related to the management of this aspect of an organisation's endeavour. A master's-level programme is expected to begin in 2010. **http://www.latrobe.edu.au/gsm**

The new La Trobe course represents a departure from the traditional sustainability-oriented courses with an environmental focus. These include:

- **Curtin University**. Master of Sustainability Studies **http://sustainability.curtin.edu.au**

- **Monash University**. Master of Corporate Environmental and Sustainability Management **http://arts.monash.edu.au/ges/pgrad/mes/course.php**

- **Griffith University**. Graduate Certificate in Sustainable Enterprise. **http://www.griffith.edu.au/business/griffith-business-school**

- **The University of Melbourne**, **University of New South Wales**, and **Swinburne University of Technology.** Philanthropy and not-for-profit management are the focus of The Centre for Social Impact established in 2008 as a multi-university initiative **http://www.csi.edu.au**

- **Swinburne University of Technology**. Master of Commerce (Social Investment and Philanthropy). New courses in not-for-profit management, corporate social responsibility, philanthropy and social innovation and entrepreneurship are planned **http://www.swinburne.edu.au**

- **La Trobe University** (Graduate School of Management) and **Griffith University** were the first Australian universities to sign on to the United Nations Principles for Responsible Management Education **http://www.latrobe.edu.au**

- **Curtin University of Technology is the only Australian University listed in the** *Beyond Grey Pinstripes* international ranking of MBAs[1]

References

ACCSR (2009) *The State of CSR in Australia: 2008 Annual Review* (Melbourne: Australian Centre for Corporate Social Responsibility).

Birch, D. (2003) 'The Changing Context of Strategic CSR in Australia: Rethinking Business and Civil Society', paper presented at *Managing on the Edge Conference*, Nijmegen, The Netherlands, 2003.

—— (2009) 'CSR in Australia', in W. Visser, D. Matten, M. Pohl and N. Tolhurst (eds.), *The A to Z of Corporate Social Responsibility* (London: John Wiley).

Black, L.D. (2001) 'Towards Understanding Corporate Social Responsibility in Australia', *Proceedings of the International Association of Business and Society 12th Annual Conference*, Sedona, AZ, 15–18 March 2001: 70-75.

CAMAC (2006) *The Social Responsibility of Corporations Report* (Sydney: Australian Government Corporations and Markets Advisory Committee).

Carroll, A.B. (1979) 'A Three-dimensional Conceptual Model of Corporate Performance', *Academy of Management Review* 4: 497-505.

CCPA (2000) *Corporate Community Involvement: Establishing a Business Case* (Melbourne: Centre for Corporate Public Affairs).

1 http://www.beyondgreypinstripes.org/index.cfm

4 Austria

Alice Schmidt
Independent Consultant in CSR and
International Development

∎ Context

The Republic of Austria has 8.3 million inhabitants and covers an area of 84,000 square kilometres in the centre of Europe. It shares borders with eight other countries, namely Czech Republic, Germany, Hungary, Italy, Liechtenstein, Slovakia, Slovenia and Switzerland. Austria's per capita GDP in 2008 was USD52,126.

Social partnership

Austria's social market economy, which postulates not only economic freedom but also social justice and environmental protection, is arguably a fertile ground for CSR. An important part of what is today called CSR, including labour issues and industrial relations, has been addressed through Austria's political tradition of 'economic and social partnership' since the end of World War II. This partnership involves employers and employees being in constant dialogue through their representative organisations about economic and social policy issues, resolving disputes, and engaging in collective bargaining about income and wage levels.

However, beyond the strongly institutionalised and bureaucratic economic and social partnership, there are few joint ventures that bring together business, government and civil society. Related to the strength of the social partnership model is the fact that Austria's business landscape is dominated by small and medium-sized enterprises (SMEs), which represent more than 99% of Austria's businesses and favour collective representation.

History of CSR

While the Ministry for the Environment was established in 1972, it was not until the 1990s, following finalisation of the National Environment Plan, that environmental issues made it onto Austria's agenda more formally and comprehensively. In 2002, the Federal government adopted a sustainability strategy which targets a variety of stakeholders, including the general public.

The concept of CSR was formally introduced in 2002 when business representatives initiated a multi-stakeholder dialogue which led to the development of a CSR Vision (CSR *Leitbild*) encouraging businesses to introduce CSR into their operations and strategies (Konrad *et al.* 2008). The business council respACT was established to provide coordinated communication about CSR to Austrian businesses, and a number of initiatives were created, both by business and by civil society.

Since then, Austria's CSR engine has slowed and political action has been lagging behind business and civil society. It should be stressed that it has been business, especially companies operating internationally, that has been driving Austria's CSR agenda, rather than government.

Today, a number of political actors, including three key ministries, are explicitly responsible for CSR. However, no obvious CSR leader has emerged, leaving gaps in concerted political action; there is no joint government strategy for CSR. Moreover, a common, nationwide understanding of CSR has yet to be developed. This lack of a common definition makes public information and effective communication about CSR — as opposed to specific sub-themes, such as environmental protection — difficult.

The diversity in definitions and approaches to CSR by Austria's key players is also manifested by an array of strategies, guidelines, visions, and lists of criteria and initiatives, ranging from general to very specific CSR instruments. For example, respACT provides specialised CSR guidelines for a number of different industries, including food, fashion, jewellery, construction, etc. Moreover, there is an extensive 'catalogue of criteria' providing companies with indicators to assess their CSR performance put together by the civil society network *Netzwerk Soziale Verantwortung* ('Social Responsibility Network') (NeSoVe). There are also guidelines for the implementation of CSR by the Austrian Standards Institute and initiatives at regional and sub-regional level.

Austria's government sees CSR as an important factor in ensuring competitiveness in a globalised market. Particular emphasis is placed on Austria's geo-economic position between Eastern and Western Europe. This is made explicit in the government's Vision on Foreign Trade (2008).

Debate

While engaging in extensive dialogue, the 'social partners' have not yet developed a common understanding of CSR and a debate on voluntary versus mandatory CSR approaches has persisted for years. Generally speaking, the business camp would like to keep CSR voluntary and sees maintenance and improvement of social standards exclusively as government responsibility. Civil society, on the other hand, fears that CSR may be used to undermine legal obligations; hence, they demand mandatory standards as well as greater transparency and mechanisms for checks and enforcement. These differences in viewpoint and opinion are significant but should not be overemphasised, not least because a recent study shows that only 28% of businesses maintain a strict 'voluntary' position (Ungericht *et al.* 2009).

▌Priority issues

Poverty and inequality

While enjoying high social security and environmental standards, Austria also has its weak points. Poverty and inequality is one area: Austria has traditionally boasted low unemployment of just over 4% and is one of the richest countries in the world. Nevertheless, 12.6% of Austrians were found to be at risk of poverty and 6% to be living in manifest poverty in 2006 (OGPP 2008).

Governance

Governance is another area in which improvements are possible. A report by the Council of Europe (2008) identified problems with independence of the judiciary and police. Furthermore, the report suggests that there are grey areas in respect to parliamentary immunity, which need to be addressed.

Environment

As for environmental matters, the picture is mixed. With more than 13% of the EU's organic farmland and almost 12% of Austria's farms being organic, Austria is the EU's leader in organic farming (Bio Austria 2008). Moreover, Austria has high waste separation and recycling rates, maintains a clear position against genetically modified organisms (GMOs) and has followed a policy against using nuclear power since a referendum in 1978.

However, a number of environmental issues have only been inadequately addressed so far. In 2008 the Court of Audit warned that it was unlikely that Austria would reach its Kyoto Protocol greenhouse gas emissions targets by 2012, adding that as a result, disciplinary action from the EU was likely (Rechnungshof 2008). The 2009 Climate Change Performance Index ranks Austria 50th, just behind China and behind most other European countries (Glocalist Review 2008). Only a part of this disappointing result can be explained by the fact that Austria had a relatively moderate emission level to begin with, and that its status as a transit country for lorry traffic across Europe makes it difficult to control emissions.

Furthermore, despite being one of Europe's key promoters of the Eco-Management and Audit Scheme (EMAS) in the past, Austria today only has 258 EMAS-certified business sites (Umweltbundesamt 2009) and about 500 certified according to ISO 14001 (Schylander and Martinuzzi 2007).

▌Trends

Using media uptake as an indicator it can be said that the concept of CSR has become more prevalent over the last few years. While a search for 'corporate social responsibility' in the Austrian Press Agency's database in 2002 would have revealed only six items mentioning CSR, this figure had increased to 42 in 2004 and to 119 in 2007 (Friesl 2008). The programme of government for the current legislation period (2008–2013) mentions CSR for the second time, pointing out that CSR is important for business success and for improving trust in the economy by the population.

CSR leaders

Austria's CSR leaders display a number of distinctive characteristics. For example, a majority (55%) of CSR leaders — companies participating in the annual TRIGOS competition — sell primarily business to business (B2B). Furthermore, 45% of participants operate primarily in international markets (Friesl 2008). Similarly, a recent study looking at 600 Austrian companies finds that 56% of CSR leaders sell primarily B2B (compared to 24% of companies overall) and identifies a correlation between a company's size and the probability of it being perceived as a CSR leader: 49% of Austria's CSR leaders have more than 250 employees, but this is true for only 1% of businesses overall (Ungericht *et al.* 2009).

As far as content is concerned, charitable giving and sponsoring are leading CSR indicators and account for 26% of projects participating in TRIGOS. Two-thirds of participating companies have concrete CSR strategies. However, CSR activities are generally not yet embedded in corporate strategy but rather driven by individuals with an interest in CSR (Friesl 2008). Most companies only have a vague understanding of CSR, and many focus on just one aspect (e.g. health and safety) rather than taking a comprehensive approach.

Businesses believe CSR to be of little importance to consumers and politicians but think of it as significant within their own business, and to a lesser extent within their industry. Nine per cent of companies even regard CSR as a competitive disadvantage (Ungericht 2009). This confirms earlier findings by the Ministry of Transport, Innovation and Technology. In a study analysing TRIGOS participants it found that many businesses are reluctant to openly account for, or even disclose, voluntary social activities for employees and the local community fearing they will be stopped in order to save operational costs (Jasch *et al.* 2007).

Reporting

CSR reporting is recommended in the government's CSR Vision but is not mandatory and hence not enforced. Currently only an estimated 20–30 Austrian companies produce annual CSR or sustainability reports. Nevertheless, Austria's Ministry for the Environment has been presenting Global Reporting Initiative (GRI)-style sustainability reports since 2004 when it was the first ministry in Europe to do so. Furthermore, a number of publicly listed companies are indeed following the call by investors for reporting on ecological and social performance.

Consumer pressure

Consumer awareness of CSR is low and hence there is little pressure from consumers for companies to act responsibly. Partly as a result of this, businesses do not engage in choice editing. Only 18% of CSR leaders who primarily serve domestic markets think that CSR matters to consumers, and 33% of Austrian companies overall regard this lack of consumer interest as a barrier to acting more responsibly (Ungericht 2009). Consumer protection organisations, however, do demand public development of measurement and monitoring tools in order to be able to guide consumers towards socially responsible businesses, as opposed to those merely using CSR for public relations purposes. Having said this, Austria is one of the fastest growing fairtrade markets and ranks fourth in terms of per capita turnover of fairtrade products (Mandl *et al.* 2007).

Socially responsible investment (SRI)

SRI is still fairly new to Austria. To date, there are no SRI requirements for public pension funds, for example. Therefore, the share of SRI in total investment is only 0.5% (ÖGUT 2007).

(Public) procurement

Austria's approach to public procurement has been fragmented, with different public actors having different areas of focus and hence different standards. However, a CSR policy for public procurement is currently being developed. This may be in response to the fact that 81% of Austria's companies feel that public procurement and bidding should favour socially responsible companies (Ungericht 2009).

Several guidelines on responsible public procurement exist. For instance, the general government guidelines on Green Public Procurement were defined in 1998 and updated in 2004. Furthermore, there is a list of 'green' purchasing criteria called 'Check It!' as well as guidelines on 'green events', which helped event organisers make more responsible purchasing decisions during the Austrian EU Presidency as well as EURO 2008 (Steurer *et al.* 2007). It should be stressed that, due to their voluntary nature, these guidelines primarily act as awareness-raising and information tools. Further, they are clearly focused on environmental as opposed to social issues.

▌ Legislation and codes

Austria is a highly regulated state. There are a number of environmental, labour and social protection laws setting minimum standards for business behaviour. Even the Companies Act dating back to 1966 states that a corporation must be managed in a way that benefits not only shareholders and employees but also the public interest. On the other hand, neither tax law nor regulations concerning trusts and foundations offer incentives to companies to engage in CSR.

In sum, it can be argued that this focus on regulation — as opposed to the establishment of conditions and frameworks — stifles voluntary CSR action. Austrian companies tend to see stringent environmental and labour laws as a competitive disadvantage in international markets and hence fear further CSR regulation by the government.

The Austrian Code of Corporate Governance is reviewed and adapted once a year to reflect changes in legislation and other important developments. It is seen as a valuable instrument in ensuring trust by both shareholders and companies issuing shares.

▌ Organisations

▌ **Austrian Business Ethics Network (Österreichisches Netzwerk für Wirtschaftsethik).** Promotes exchange of information and ideas on moral and ethical questions relating to business and helps its members act in a socially responsible way. **http://www.oenwe.com**

▌ **Austrian Federal Economic Chamber (Wirtschaftskammer Österreich).** By law, this is the representative of the entire Austrian business community; membership is compulsory and comprises all of Austria's almost 400,000 businesses. **http://portal.wko.at/wk/ startseite.wk**

■ **Centre for Corporate Citizenship Austria**. Provides an annual CSR ranking of Austria's top 100 companies, compiles a responsibility index and promotes dialogue and partnerships for CSR by organising 'marketplaces' for stakeholders from different sectors of society. **http://www.ccc-austria.at**

■ **Federation of Austrian Industries (Industriellenvereinigung)**. A voluntary body representing the interests of Austrian industry, currently comprising about 3,500 members. **http://www.iv-net.at/blm50**

■ **Footprint**. An alliance of organisations working on environmental and international development issues. **http://www.footprint.at**

■ **Glocalist**. Offers a daily online newspaper, weekly digital magazine and monthly print magazine on CSR and sustainability. **http://www.glocalist.com**

■ **ICEP (Institut zur Cooperation bei Entwicklungsprojekten)**. Promotes development cooperation by Austrian businesses, for example through its CorporAID initiative which aims to provide Austrian companies with a platform for global CSR and poverty alleviation. **http://www.icep.at**

■ **Initiative Zivilgesellschaft**. A network of civil society organisations working on social and environmental justice issues. **http://www.initiative-zivilgesellschaft.at**

■ **Netzwerk Soziale Verantwortung (Social Responsibility Network) (NeSoVe)**. Established in 2006, this brings together a broad spectrum of civil society representing 25 member organisations working in the area of human rights, development aid, environment, consumer protection and the world of work. **http://www.nesove.at**

■ **RespACT (Austrian Business Council For Sustainable Development)**. RespACT is Austria's leading business platform for CSR and sustainable development. It was founded in 2007 when several older initiatives were merged and today has 134 members. **http://www.respact.at**

■ Case studies

Gugler

Gugler is a print and communication business founded in 1989. Today it has 71 employees and an annual turnover of about EUR70 million (Friesl 2008). All inputs and materials used by Gugler, including not only raw materials but also operating supplies and additives, conform to high environmental standards. Gugler also demands high ecological standards from its suppliers. Its own premises use exclusively green power (two-thirds of the heating is generated through discharged air). A recent programme to save water has resulted in a water usage reduction of 500,000 litres per year and CO_2 emissions were reduced by 25 tonnes. Other efforts, such as an organic canteen, complement the picture of well-rounded sustainability. **http://www.gugler.at**

OMV

With 41,000 employees and a turnover of EUR26 billion, OMV is one of Austria's largest companies and the leading energy business in central Europe. The trigger for OMV's engagement in CSR was strong criticism of its operations in Sudan. This led to the company discontinuing these and the establishment of a CSR taskforce. In 2003, it developed a new code of conduct and CSR strategy. Key elements are: creation of greater CSR awareness among managers and employees; positioning as a responsible business *vis-à-vis* stakeholders; and institutionalisation of stakeholder dialogue. OMV sees CSR as a risk management strategy as well as a response to growing demands by investors and potential partners in joint ventures. However, the company believes it is too early to communicate its CSR activities and positioning more widely to the public. Concrete examples of OMV's CSR activities include: ISO 14001 certification of its refinery near Vienna; offering exclusively sulphur-free fuel to its customers from 2004, five years before the EU deadline; and engaging in international development cooperation and research projects (Friesl 2008). **http://www.omv.com**

Zotter

Zotter produces creative 'hand-scooped' chocolates. It is one of Europe's few 'bean to bar' producers and uses exclusively organic raw materials. With about 100 employees, it is a small enterprise and follows a policy of bypassing supermarkets and big chains in order to promote SMEs itself. Since 2005, Zotter has been supporting three cocoa cooperatives in Nicaragua through knowledge transfer in the areas of environmental and social production and marketing. All inputs purchased in developing countries are certified as fairtrade. Part of its product range supports social initiatives though a joint donation by the company and trade of EUR0.03 per chocolate bar. Furthermore, some Zotter products bear social slogans campaigning for equal opportunities for the disabled (e.g. a chocolate bar calling attention to disability issues with its label written in Braille). **http://www.zotter.at**

▌ Education

There is not yet a clear academic leader in the field of CSR. Several universities and training institutions are in the process of developing CSR diplomas or modules, and CSR research is taking place in a number of Austrian universities, including:

- **Austrian Business Academy for Sustainable Development**. Offers executive education and professional development on CSR. **http://www.asd.at**

- **Bfi University of Applied Sciences**. Offers a one-year part-time course on CSR management. **http://www.fh-vie.ac.at**

- **University of Graz**. Offers lectures on CSR and also hosts a 'business and society' group which conducts CSR research at regional, national and European level. **http://www.uni-graz.at**

- **University of Vienna**. Offers lectures on CSR and is currently working to set up a CSR diploma. **http://www.univie.ac.at**

- **Vienna University of Economics and Business**. Offers lectures on CSR and related issues; houses the Research Institute for Managing Sustainability (**http://www.sustainability.eu**), which analyses sustainability from various angles, including CSR, good governance, innovation research and sustainable consumption. **http://www.wu.edu**

References

Austrian Working Group for Corporate Governance (2007) 'Austrian Code of Corporate Governance'; **http://www.ecgi.org/codes/code.php?code_id=229**.

Bio Austria (2008) 'Anteil des Bio-Landbaus an der Österreichischen Landwirtschaft'; **http://www.bio-austria.at/startseite/statistik**, accessed 21 March 2010.

Bundesministerium für Wirtschaft und Arbeit (2008) 'Das Österreichische Aussenwirtschaftsleitbild', **http://www.bmwfj.gv.at**, accessed 21 March 2010.

Group of States Against Corruption (2008) 'Evaluierungsbericht Österreich' ('Evaluation Report on Austria') (Council of Europe).

Friesl, C. (2008) *Erfolg und Verantwortung: Die strategische Kraft von Corporate Social Responsibility* (Vienna: Facultas).

Glocalist Review (2008) 'Klimaschutzindex 2009', *Glocalist Review* 216 (15 December 2008).

Jasch, C., R. Grasl and R. Köbler (2007) 'TRIGOS CSR Rechnet Sich'; **http://www.ioew.at/ioew/download/TRIGOS-CSR-rechnet%20sich-Endbericht.pdf**, accessed 21 March 2010.

Konrad, A., A. Martinuzzi and Steurer, R. (2008) 'When Business Associations and a Federal Ministry Jointly Consult Civil Society: A CSR Policy Case Study on the Development of the CSR Austria Guiding Vision', *Corporate Social Responsibility and Environmental Management* 15: 270-280.

Mandl, I., and A. Dorr (2007) *CSR and Competitiveness: European SMEs' Good Practice. Consolidated European Report* (Vienna: KMU Forschung Austria).

ÖGUT (2007) 'Systematische Weiterentwicklung des Nachhaltigen Finanzmarkts: Statusbericht und Entwicklungsstrategie'; **http://www.oegut.at/downloads/pdf/nafima_sys_eb.pdf**, accessed 21 March 2010.

OGPP (2008) 'Armuts- und Reichtumsbericht für Österreich'; **http://www.politikberatung.or.at/typo3/fileadmin/02_Studien/5_armut/armutundreichtum2008.pdf**, accessed 21 March 2010.

Rechnungshof (2008) 'Umsetzung der Klimastrategies des Bundes'; **http://www.rechnungshof.gv.at/fileadmin/downloads/2008/berichte/teilberichte/bund/bund_2008_11/bund_2008_11_1.pdf**, accessed 21 March 2010.

Schylander, E., and A. Martinuzzi (2007) 'ISO 14001: Experiences, Effects and Future Challenges; A National Study in Austria', *Business Strategy and the Environment* 16.2: 133-147.

Steurer, R., G. Berger, A. Konrad and A. Martinuzzi (2007) 'Sustainable Public Procurement in EU Member States: Overview of Government Initiatives and Selected Cases' (Final Report to the EU High-Level Group on CSR; Vienna: European Commission; **http://www.sustainability.eu/pdf/csr/Sustainable%20Public%20Procurement%20in%20EU%20Member%20States_Final%20Report.pdf**, accessed 21 March 2010).

Umweltbundesamt (2009) 'EMAS-Statistik'; **http://www.umweltbundesamt.at/umweltschutz/uvpsupemas/emas/emas_statistik**, accessed 21 March 2010.

Ungericht, B., D. Raith and T. Korenja (2009) *CSR in Österreich* (Vienna: Lit Verlag).

5 Azerbaijan

Ahad Kazimov
Corporate Social Investment Program Manager,
Eurasia Partnership Foundation.

■ Context

Historically, charitable activities in Azerbaijan were rooted in Islamic religious beliefs that inspired believers to provide assistance to vulnerable groups. The responsibility of Muslims towards other human beings is given a very strong emphasis in Islam. Moreover, mutual help between members of a Muslim community is strongly emphasised. The Qur'an states that God loves those who are charitable and promises great reward and forgiveness for those who give regularly to others in need.

The very basic rule or obligation regarding charity in Islam is *Zakat,* one of the 'five pillars' of Islam. *Zakat* literally means 'purification' and refers to the almsgiving tax that eligible Muslims distribute annually to poor and needy persons in the Muslim community. Any Muslims who want to give more can do so and they are encouraged to, but 2.5% of one's income is the minimum. A poor Muslim will receive the charity instead of paying it. Another form of charitable action is *sadaqah* (sa-da-kah). This term literally means 'righteousness' and refers to the voluntary giving of alms (charity).

The end of 19th century marked the beginning of the oil boom in Azerbaijan. In that period, a class of national bourgeoisie emerged which developed a reputation as a major philanthropist. Its charitable actions were similar to philanthropic activities in the rest of Russia, presented as almsgiving, patronage of charitable institutions and donations to religious institutions.

The wealthiest Azerbaijanis in Baku belonged to one such charitable organisation — the Muslim Philanthropic Society — which collected money to support vulnerable groups of the population. Other examples include the Caspian–Black Sea Oil Industrial and Trading Society created by the Rothschilds in May 1883, the Council of the Baku Petro-Industrialists, involved in the construction of hospitals and schools, and the Baku Jewish Charitable Society.

One of the prominent philanthropists in Azerbaijan from this period was H.Z. Taghiyev (1823–1924) who established a secular boarding school for Azerbaijani Muslim girls, the first in the Muslim world. This school was considered one of the major solutions to the problem of illiteracy among Azerbaijani girls and acted as an agent of change in the social status of Azerbaijani women at the beginning of the 20th century.

Another famous Azerbaijani philanthropist, Agha Musa Naghiyev (1849–1919), funded several hospitals in Baku, including the First Aid Hospital, built in 1912, that now bears his name. He also built one of Baku's most admired buildings, Ismailiye, in memory of his son who died of tuberculosis at the age of 27. Naghiyev gave this building as a gift to the Muslim Philanthropic Society.

These early philanthropists left a legacy of generosity that reinforces the modern belief in Azerbaijan that it is a business's responsibility to invest in and support social initiatives. Hence, there is an ongoing tradition of Azerbaijan businesses that are active in supporting their communities.

▌ Models

CSR remains mostly at the philanthropic stage of development in Azerbaijan. However, there are several models which local companies use when implementing corporate philanthropic activities. First, there is corporate giving for the sake of society, without any public relations or marketing element. Second, there are social activities undertaken with the intent of improving the company's brand image and reputation. And third, there is strategic social investment that is directly tied to the company's core business, as well as benefiting society.

The latter is typical of the approach promoted by The Eurasia Partnership Foundation since 2006. This defines corporate social investment as a strategic approach to philanthropy that 'addresses important social and economic goals simultaneously, targeting areas of competitive context where the company and society both benefit because the firm brings unique assets and expertise'.

▌ Priority issues

Ethnic conflict

A long lasting ethno-political conflict associated with territorial claims and military aggression on the part of Armenia against Azerbaijan resulted in the Armenian occupation of about 20% of Azerbaijan's territory. This includes the Nagorno–Karabakh region and seven adjacent districts, creating about 1 million refugees and internally displaced persons. Implementing social programmes which will improve conditions and living standards for this group is one the priority issues for the Azerbaijani government, business sector and NGOs.

Unemployment

Another important social issue faced by the country is the high level of unemployment, especially among youth. According to the findings of the first countrywide survey on the economic activeness of the population (conducted in May–June 2003 with financial support from the UNDP and technical support from the ILO), 69% of unemployed people in Azerbaijan are under 35 years old. This problem can be partly ascribed to a mismatch between the education system and labour market, with too many young people graduating with degrees in 'popular' professions and a shortage of professionals in key industries such as engineering and construction. Furthermore, the vocational training system is outdated and ill-equipped and therefore under-utilised, with weak linkages to business.

Corruption

According to Transparency International's 2009 Corruption Perception Index, which measures the degree to which corruption is perceived to exist among public officials and politicians, Azerbaijan ranks 143 out of 180 countries (where first mean least corruption). In response, a governmental commission has been established to act — in cooperation with the President, Parliament and Constitutional Court — as a specialised agency on combating corruption.

Tax regime

The current tax environment neither supports nor acts as a barrier to corporate giving and there are no plans to revise the tax code in favour of charitable contributions. This is partially due to a loophole in a previous tax law, which was repealed in 1999 after businesses were seen to be unduly exploiting it. Azerbaijan's stance is not typical of the region. In the neighbouring country of Georgia, businesses can deduct 8% of their donations to charitable organisations from their taxable profit. Similarly, in Kazakhstan, another former Soviet Union Republic, the law offers corporate tax deductions up to 3% of their income for donations to nonprofit organisations.

An Economic Research Center (2009) survey on CSR in Azerbaijan revealed that 70% of respondents would be willing to engage in CSR activities if they were to receive a tax exemption. In addition to this, 19% of respondents stated they would consider engaging in CSR activities if there was a tax deduction, if not a full exemption.

Trust

Another priority is increasing the level of trust among important stakeholders, especially government, business and civil society. Approximately 22% of companies that participated in a Eurasia Foundation (2005) assessment worked with a third-party organisation to implement projects, yet the business community in general is distrustful and sceptical of the abilities of the local NGO sector to manage projects effectively or manage resources ethically.

Ms Mehriban Aliyeva, First Lady of Azerbaijan and president of the Heydar Aliyev Foundation, stressed in a 2008 interview for the state telegraph agency AzerTac that 'State, civil and business sectors which engage in philanthropic activities can achieve the maximum effect if they work in cooperation with each other. But this cooperation can only take place in the form of equal partnerships.'

■ Trends

According to the Eurasia Foundation (2005) assessment, all of the companies interviewed were engaged in some form of charitable giving. Major areas of philanthropy include donations to orphanages, refugees, internally displaced people, disabled people and education. Another CSR survey among large business companies in Baku, Azerbaijan and conducted by the Economic Research Center (2009) found that 81% claim to be carrying out some form of CSR activity.

Earlier research by the Institute for Social Action and Renewal (Brinkman and Santiago-Adorno 2001) showed that even though Azerbaijani companies are regularly donating to charitable causes, the contribution is done in an unplanned way and lacks a long-term strategy. This ad hoc, philanthropy-driven approach to CSR continuous to this day.

▊ Legislation and codes

There are several key social, environmental and ethical laws in Azerbaijan, including:

- **Law of Azerbaijan Republic on Antimonopoly Activity**, Law No. 526 (1993, amended 1997)
- **Constitution of the Azerbaijan Republic** (1995)
- **Law of Azerbaijan Republic on Copyright and Neighbouring Right** (1996)
- **Law on Industrial and Domestic Waste** (1998)
- **Law of Azerbaijan Republic on Trademarks and Geographical Indications** (1998)
- **Labour Code of the Republic of Azerbaijan** (1999)
- **Law on Environment Protection** (1999)
- **Law on Non-governmental Organisations** (2000)
- **Tax Code** (2000)
- **Law on Combating Corruption** (2004)

▊ Organisations

▊ There are a few business associations and NGOs in Azerbaijan that are promoting CSR (the American Chamber of Commerce, the National Confederation of Entrepreneurs [Employers'] Organisations of AR [ASK] and Eurasia Partnership Foundation).

▊ **American Chamber of Commerce in Azerbaijan (AMCHAM).** Representing over 180 member companies, AMCHAM Azerbaijan advocates the trade and investment interests of its members. In cooperation with the Eurasia Partnership Foundation, they organised several luncheons focused on building public–private partnerships and promotion of corporate social investments and philanthropy in Azerbaijan, which were attended by representatives of local and foreign businesses and international organisations in 2007–2009. **http://www.amchamaz.org**

■ **Azerbaijan Export & Investment Promotion Foundation (AZPROMO).** A joint public private initiative established by the government of Azerbaijan in 2003. AZPROMO is responsible for implementing the Azerbaijan Global Compact Project in cooperation with UNDP and with financial support from StatoilHydro. This project aims to introduce the UN Global Compact to local and international companies operating in Azerbaijan and to help establish the Global Compact network. Currently there are 94 members in Azpromo. **http://www.azpromo.org**

■ **Eurasia Partnership Foundation (EPF).** The legacy institution of Eurasia Foundation (EF), a privately managed nonprofit organisation established in 1992 to deliver seed capital to emerging civil society organisations in the former Soviet countries. EPF has been implementing a Corporate Social Investment Program since 2006. The goal of this is to encourage strategic social investments by local businesses and joint ventures in the long-term social and economic development of Azerbaijan. The programme focuses its activities on three major areas: network development, consulting and capacity development, and information dissemination and publications. More than 40 companies and organisations have been engaged in EPF's Azerbaijani CSI network, regularly participating in the programme's activities. **http://www.epfound.az**

■ **National Confederation of Entrepreneurs (Employers') Organisations of Azerbaijan (ASK).** More than 3,500 entrepreneurial organisations are members of ASK. Cooperation with the International Labour Organisation (ILO) lays the basis for joint implementation of different programmes and projects, including on labour standards, occupational health and safety, gender equality, prohibition of discrimination, female entrepreneurship development, boosting youth employment and eliminating child labour. **http://ask.org.az/en**

■ Case studies

Azersun Holding

Azersun Holding has pursued a policy of CSR since the very start of its activities in 1991. The company primarily supports disadvantaged youth, internally displaced persons (IDPs) and orphanages. To address the problems of vulnerable groups, the company uses the strategy of 'giving a fishing rod to fish, not a fish'. At their packaging plant in Khirdalan near the capital city of Baku all the employees are IDPs. In addition, the company is investing in their staff: in 2008, they provided training for 7,668 employees. Azersun supports the ULDUZ football team consisting of young people with hearing disabilities. The company is also constantly raising awareness about drug addiction, HIV/AIDS and other social problems affecting young people and adolescents, though theatrical performances at the community hall. **http://www.azersun.com/en_holding.asp**

Azercell Telecom LLC

As the leader in the telecommunications sector of Azerbaijan, Azercell Telecom LLC has focused its CSR activities on the most vulnerable population. CSR at Azercell covers different aspects, such as sports, culture, art, education, healthcare, ecology and the economy. From 2007 to 2008, the company spent almost AZN9 million (USD11.25 million) on various social programmes and projects to enhance the social development of Azerbaijan and its population. It was one of the first companies to obtain an International Standard Certificate (ISC) for Investments made into Human Resources among CIS countries. In 1997, Azercell Telecom LLC helped to establish a rehabilitation centre for street children called Umid Yeri (Place of Hope), which has helped nearly 1,000 children to have a normal childhood. The company also sponsored the first Invest in Future conference, dedicated to development of CSR in Azerbaijan and held in May 2008 in Baku. **http://www.azercell.com/en**

Garadagh Cement OJSC

Garadagh Cement is a joint venture with a leading Swiss cement manufacturer (Holcim) and therefore has access to global CSR practices and expertise. Garadagh Cement is the only cement and clinker manufacturing company in Azerbaijan and is committed to supporting and partnering the communities in which their operations are located. The annual CSR budget of Garadagh Cement is USD300,000. Areas of support include a National Oncology Center, the Sahil settlement hospital and a local rehabilitation centre for disabled children (Mushvig). In 2004, the company was awarded the UGUR National Award, recognising their contribution to the economy, business and CSR. **http://www. garadagh.com**

AccessBank Azerbaijan

In 2008, AccessBank formalised its commitment to high ethical standards and responsible banking by joining the UN Global Compact. The company also sponsored the creation of the Yaradan Arts Centre in Baku, which supports the development of young artists. Other areas of support include organisation of work skills training for young people with physical disabilities, culminating in offers of employment to top students and a blood-donation drive to benefit children with blood diseases. AccessBank screens its loans to using environmental and ethical criteria and has adopted detailed procedures for managing anti-money laundering and anti-terrorist financial procedures, which are centred on a strict KYC (Know Your Client) policy. The procedures have been prepared in accordance with FATF (Financial Action Task Force) and other international recommendations. **http://www.accessbank.az**

▌ Education

There are no CSR-related degrees or courses offered by any leading university in Azerbaijan. However, the administration of Khazar University, a leading private university has expressed interest in covering CSR-related topics in other courses on their MBA programme.

In addition, the Eurasia Partnership Foundation, together with the British Council, UNDP and other partners, have offered various CSR training courses since 2008.

References

Brinkman, J., and P. Santiago-Adorno (2001) *Building Civil Society: Strengthening Business–NGO Relations in Azerbaijan* (Baku, Azerbaijan: Isar-Azerbaijan; **http://www.kitab.az/cgi-bin/catlib2/item.cgi?lang=az&item=20031202163109140**, accessed 21 March 2010).

Economic Research Center (2009) 'CSR Survey'; **http://www.erc-az.org/new/view.php?lang=en&menu=0&id=473**, accessed 21 March 2010.

Eurasia Foundation (2005) 'Baseline Assessment of Social Investment Activities in Azerbaijan' (unpublished report; Baku, Azerbaijan: Eurasia Foundation).

6 Bangladesh

Niaz Alam
Board Member, London Pensions Fund Authority

▮ Context

Bangladesh is a densely populated developing country of 145 million people which provides many different perspectives on the role of CSR.

Since gaining independence in 1971, the main drivers of its traditionally agricultural economy have been an export-led ready-made garments industry, which employs over 1.5 million workers. Other export industries include tanneries, tea, generic pharmaceuticals and seafood.

In the last decade, ethical concerns about low wages and child labour in the global garments supply chain have raised the profile of CSR and substantially among Bangladeshi companies. While two-thirds of the population depends on agriculture and around half the population lives below the official poverty line, the impact of growing urbanisation and industrialisation makes labour rights and working conditions a key issue for the economy.

Bangladesh is a low-lying deltaic country subject to regular flooding, which builds up enough soil fertility for three harvests a year. Hence, Bangladesh is particularly vulnerable to climate change and growing attention is given to environmental issues. Some sectors, notably shrimp farming in the mangrove delta and ship salvaging on coastal beaches, have received a high profile in the national and global media for both their environmental impacts and dependence on cheap labour.

Despite political instability and institutionalised corruption, which have held annual GDP growth rate around 4–6% (significantly below other industrialising Asian economies), Bangladesh has been relatively successful in stabilising population growth and making progress against the UNDP Human Development Indicators and the UN Millennium Development Goals.

This is often attributed to the presence of a strongly developed NGO sector in Bangladesh. Best known for two of the world's largest indigenous NGOs — BRAC (formerly Bangladesh Rural Advancement Committee) and the Grameen Bank — NGOs have played a prominent role in advancing rural development and pioneering microcredit across the country. A particularly interesting feature of CSR in Bangladesh is how these and other organisations have been pivotal in developing major social enterprises.

In addition to the large NGO sector that has flourished since independence, ties to the land and the family owned structure of most Bangladeshi enterprises means that there is a deep-rooted paternalistic, philanthropic tradition. The predominantly Muslim demographic of the country (comprising 90%) underpins some of the support by businesses for social welfare and relief aid projects. Although this perception of CSR as charity is increasingly challenged within Bangladesh by a business-case perspective, it does add a further native dimension to the CSR debate and challenges the narrative that CSR is entirely imposed on developing countries like Bangladesh by forces of globalisation.

Nonetheless, the need to compete in the global economy and the key issues of labour rights, working conditions and environmental impacts are the main drivers behind the current development of CSR in Bangladesh. The importance of CSR as a competitive factor is increasingly recognised by the business community, which has welcomed moves announced by the Bangladesh government at the end of 2008 for tax benefits for CSR-based activities.

▋ Priority issues

Corruption and governance

Although political instability after independence (characterised by coups and military rule) formally ended with the resumption of democratic elections in 1991, a tradition of dynastic politics has exacerbated corruption.

The country has regularly featured highly in Transparency International (TI)'s Corruption Perceptions Index (CPI) and even topped polls among business leaders with regard to official and bureaucratic corruption in the last ten years. In 2008, Bangladesh received a CPI score of 2.1 out of 10, giving a ranking of 147 out of 180 countries (with 180 = most corrupt). Concerted calls for tougher action by international aid donors and public support for an official anti-corruption drive are helping to address this issue.

However the overall weakness of the state does mean that enforcement of labour and environmental laws remains poor. Hence, much of the impetus for good practice in CSR is driven by and depends on the private sector (especially multinationals) and NGOs.

Poverty, population and working conditions

Despite some success in stabilising its population growth rate, Bangladesh is one of the world's most densely populated countries, with over 145 million people living in an area approximately the size of England.

As the country becomes increasingly urbanised, with the population of the capital Dhaka increasing from 600,000 to over 14 million in just 38 years since independence, Bangladesh has an urgent need to sustainably develop its economy and raise the living standards of the majority of its citizens who earn less than USD600 a year.

The availability of cheap labour has been a major factor in the export-led growth in the textiles sector. While there has been frequent concern raised about the poor labour practices in some parts of this sector, development organisations have also noted that it provides a way for a predominantly young female workforce of 1.5 million workers to enter the formal economy in a way that was previously not available in a traditionally agricultural, patriarchal society.

Consumer concern about the abuse of workers' rights and prevalence of low pay in the global garments industry supply chain has greatly raised awareness in Bangladesh of issues to do with forced overtime, long hours, lack of respect for freedom of association, sexual harassment and instances of child labour in the textiles sector. The topic has also been intensively studied. See for example the report by the International Federation for Human Rights (2008).

Despite this awareness and the existence of labour standards, competitive pressures and the availability of cheap labour means abuses of workers' rights remain common-place, not only in textiles, but also in sectors such as tanneries and ship salvaging. These concerns are only partly being addressed by media scrutiny and an increasing aware-ness of CSR.

Environmental degradation and climate change

As a traditionally agricultural nation where most people have rural roots, the negative environmental impacts associated with rapid unchecked urbanisation and poor plan-ning in cities is a cause for considerable local public concern. For example, Bangladesh was the first country in the world to ban the sale of plastic bags, which were clogging up the rivers. It also took action in the 1980s to ban the export of frogs' legs.

The environmental impacts of shrimp farming for export and the salvaging of ships containing hazardous wastes on previously pristine beaches in southern Bangladesh have attracted significant media attention, both internationally and locally.

In 2006, there were also widespread public protests against plans by a UK-based min-ing company (AsiaEnergy) for large scale opencast coal mining at Phulbari in north-western Bangladesh, which would have displaced 220,000 people in an important rice-growing region. Although facing a growing need for national energy capacity, the government has (to date) listened to these grassroots protests.

The poor enforcement of environmental and planning laws means that there is often public concern about the unchecked use of chemicals and discharge of effluents by factories, so environmental issues are a growing part of the CSR agenda for business in Bangladesh.

From a macroeconomic viewpoint, the future energy supply of Bangladesh (currently based on a small number of gas fields and oil imports) is a significant concern. As one of the lowest per capita emitters of greenhouse gases and one of the most populated poor countries vulnerable to projected sea level rise, debates about the impact of climate change and development of emissions trading systems are closely followed by Bangla-deshi policy-makers and business.

∎ Trends

Since the early 1990s, pressure on multinational companies for higher workplace and environmental standards in their supply chains has been the main driver of CSR in Bangladesh.

Textile industry bodies such as the Bangladesh Garments Manufacturing Exports Association were forced to develop and implement codes of conduct in response to the threat of consumer boycotts following child labour allegations and formal legislation proposed in the US senate by Tom Harkin in 1992. The Bangladesh garments industry has featured in a number of reform initiatives, primarily through the auspices of the ILO, the World Bank and UNICEF.

Around the same time, a temporary ban was imposed on shrimp exports to the EU on health and hygiene grounds, requiring remedial action and providing a further impetus to the development of CSR in the country.

Much of this activity has been led by international buyers and focused on individual factories supplying garments. Bangladeshi companies themselves have been relatively slow to develop CSR. As recently as 2000, a study of the social and environmental disclosures in corporate annual reports of 87 Bangladeshi companies found that while 62% made disclosures under the categories of human resource development and 87% recognised that 80% of their customers were considered relevant stakeholders, very few or no companies made disclosures under the categories of child labour (0%), equal opportunity (0%) and poverty alleviation (4%).

It has only been with continuing international trade union and campaign group pressure and press attention on labour rights abuses and deaths caused in factory fires in the supply chains of global brands such as Inditex (Zara), Wal-Mart and Tesco that CSR has begun to progress faster among Bangladeshi companies and business organisations. For example, see the reaction to the *Fashion Victims* report by War on Want (*Business Respect* 2008; War On Want 2008).

▌ Legislation and codes

Bangladesh's legal system is based on English Common Law and the state is a signatory to most ILO and UN conventions.

The practices of employers operating in Bangladesh are governed by a regulatory framework which includes the **Factories Act** (1965), **Payment of Wages Act** (1936) and **Workmen's Compensation Act** (1923). Although the framework covers issues such as minimum working hours, a safe and healthy working environment, the right to form trade unions and minimum working age (to ensure no child labour is employed), limited resources means government enforcement of these and other corporate responsibility laws is patchy. In 2006, the Labour Inspectorate of the Ministry of Labour and Welfare, which is responsible for the protection of employees' welfare in 50,000 factories in Bangladesh, only had 20 inspectors and received intense media scrutiny for ineffectiveness and 'bureaucratic tangles and corruption'.

As a result, the vast majority of CSR inspection and enforcement activity is based on self-regulation by industry bodies and individual companies. It has only been due to continued external pressure, supported in some instances by major global brands seeking to enforce their own codes of conduct, that the government has made moves to allow the recognition of trade unions within export processing zones and to raise the minimum wage which until 2007 had not been changed for over 15 years.

The importance of CSR in Bangladesh is increasingly recognised officially. In December 2008, the government approved a tax exemption facility at the rate of 10% on corporate income spent on complying with corporate social responsibility (CSR).

▌ Organisations

▌ **CSR Awards of Bangladesh**. Companies having a record of engaging in not-for-profit activities for social and community welfare are to be considered for these awards. Criteria include tax payment, transparency of accounts, regard for environmental standards and labour laws, product quality assurance, CSR spending and the innovativeness and effectiveness of CSR. **http://www.csraward-bd.com**

▌ **CSR Centre at the Bangladesh Enterprise Institute (BEI)**. Established in June 2005, the CSR Centre is an independent organisation that has been set up to facilitate, promote and advance CSR understanding and learning in Bangladesh. The Centre was launched with private sector start-up funding from eight corporate and non-corporate members. **http://www.csrcentre-bd.org**

▌ Case studies

BRAC (formerly Bangladesh Rural Advancement Committee)

Through its Aarong brand name, BRAC has for many years run a highly successful set of upmarket shops specialising in selling handicrafts made by female-owned cooperatives. BRAC currently employs over 100,000 people in Bangladesh and runs both a major bank and university. **http://www.brac.net**

Grameen Group

The Grameen Group has 7.5 million members in Bangladesh and has successfully collaborated with international companies in developing new socially directed enterprises. These include a joint venture with Danone on low-cost nutritional yoghurt; the establishment of cooperatives to fund solar panels; and the country's largest mobile phone consortium in partnership with Nortel, which within three years of establishment became Bangladesh's largest corporate taxpayer. Founder Mohammad Yunus won the Nobel Peace Prize in 2006 for popularising microcredit globally. **http://www.grameen-info.org**

Other cases

For an overview of the implementation of codes of conduct in the Bangladesh garments sector, see GTZ (2008). The Ethical Trading Initiative and MFA Forum websites also contain examples of good practice and initiatives by individual brands. **http://www.mfa-forum. net   http://www.ethicaltrade.org**

▌ Education

Training courses and seminars on CSR are commonly hosted by public and private universities in Bangladesh as well as by business bodies. There is no formal graduate school of CSR, but business degrees are popular at all levels. **Dhaka University** is the leading national university and contains an Institute of Business Administration. **Brac University** runs wide ranging development programmes which touch on business responsibility issues.

References

Bornstein, D. (1996) *The Price of a Dream: The Story of the Grameen Bank* (New York: Simon & Schuster; Dhaka, Bangladesh: University Press).

Buerk, R. (2006) *Breaking Ships: How Supertankers are Dismantled on the Beaches of Bangladesh* (New York: Chamberlain Bros.).

Business Respect (2008) 'Bangladesh: Primark and other UK retailers accused of suppliers paying "starvation wages" ', *Business Respect* 142 (6 December 2008); http://www.mallenbaker.net/csr/page.php?Story_ID=2330, accessed 2 June 2010.

GTZ (2008) 'Social Codes of Conduct in the RMG Industry'; http://www.gtz-progress.org/2008/files/GTZ_FS_CoC__final%20version(Printable)pdf.pdf, accessed 2 June 2010 *or* search: 'social codes of conduct in the RMG industry'.

International Federation for Human Rights (2008) 'Bangladesh Labour Rights in the Supply Chain and Corporate Social Responsibility'; http://www.fidh.org/IMG/pdf/bg062008en.pdf, accessed 21 March 2010.

Jabed, J.H., and K.M. Rahman (2003) 'Corporate Responsibility in Bangladesh: Where Do We Stand?' (Report 54; Dhaka, Bangladesh: Centre for Policy Dialogue; http://unpan1.un.org/intradoc/groups/public/documents/APCITY/UNPANO18959.pdf, accessed 21 March 2010).

Miyan, M.A. (2006) 'Dynamics of Corporate Social Responsibility: Bangladesh Context'; http://www.researchsea.com/html/article.php/aid/1340/cid/4/research/dynamics_of_corporate_social_responsibility_____bangladesh_context.html, accessed 21 March 2010.

Rahman, A.B. (2008) *Corporate Social Responsibility Reporting in Developing Countries: The Case of Bangladesh* (Farnham, UK: Ashgate).

War On Want (2008) 'Fashion Victims II: How UK Clothing Retailers are Keeping Workers in Poverty'; http://www.waronwant.org/campaigns/supermarkets/fashion-victims/inform/16360-fashion-victims-ii, accessed 2 June 2010).

7 Brazil

Camila Yamahaki
PhD student, Middlesex University, UK

Tarcila Reis Ursini
Director, Ekobé

■ Context

Brazil is the largest economy in South America and the 10th largest in the world, with GDP of over USD1.6 trillion. It is one of the most biologically diverse countries, hosting the largest tropical forest and the largest river basin in the world, as well as an extremely diverse population and culture. The country has one of the highest levels of income inequality: while the poorest 20% of the Brazilian population is responsible for only 2.8% of the GNP, the richest 20% accounts for 61.1%. Moreover, inequality is perceived in relation to distribution of land, assets and social services (SustainAbility 2006).

The social situation in Brazil has its roots in the exploitative nature of the Portuguese colonisation of Brazil, coupled with the exclusion of the black population after the abolition of slavery. The government has proved financially incapable of dealing with the scale of social problems, leaving a gap for the private sector to step in and tackle some of these issues.

Despite a strategic approach to CSR being encouraged in Brazil since the early 1990s, in particular by business associations, CSR activities in the country remain mainly focused on philanthropy and community investment in domestic issues (SustainAbility 2006). The most well-known CSR organisation in Brazil is the Ethos Institute, an NGO founded by a group of companies in 1998 with the aim of promoting CSR in the country. This was responsible for developing the Ethos Indicators in 2002, considered instrumental in disseminating the CSR concept in the business sector (SustainAbility 2006).

Another CSR framework that is influential in the management of many Brazilian companies, especially those that are publicly listed, is the Sustainability Index. This was created in 2005 to select and encourage listed companies with good environmental, social and governance (ESG) performance. It has served as the basis for the creation of Brazilian SRI funds, so encouraging companies to comply with its criteria.

▮ Priority issues

As a strong emerging economy, Brazil is among the biggest players shaping the world's economy today. Since democratic reforms began in the 1980s, the country has been gaining economic and political stability, while developing an increasingly central role in international affairs. However, the nation still faces an extensive range of social and environmental problems, including extreme inequality, land concentration (i.e. highly unequal distribution by ownership), low quality of basic education, corruption in the government, child labour, subtle racial discrimination, deforestation, poor access to health and medication, and pollution in the big cities. Some of these are highlighted below.

Corruption

Corruption is present in all sectors of society, with Brazil ranking 75th in the Transparency International's Corruption Perceptions Index 2009, representing a poor level of public sector ethics. Bribing and buying votes are commonplace. A 2005 survey from Fundação Getúlio Vargas (Lahoz and Onaga 2005) reported that 50% of the companies surveyed had been asked for bribes by government agents. Moreover, more than 8.3 million voters (or 8% of the electorate) were instigated to sell their votes in the 2006 elections. Serious corruption scandals in the current government were revealed, including illegal campaign funding and the bribing of congressmen.

Child labour

Although Brazil has signed most ILO treaties, child labour is still a challenge. The Brazilian Statistics Institute (IBGE 2008) found that 4.5 million children and adolescents from five to 17 years old were working in 2008. Most of these underage workers are employed in the agricultural sector (35.5%), are male (65.8%) and are from the north-eastern region (37.8%). To combat school evasion, the government has implemented the Bolsa Família Programme, covering nearly 46 million people, whereby families are compensated for keeping their children in school.

Racial discrimination

The current situation of Brazil's black population has historical roots, since the slavery abolition process was not accompanied by a governmental policy to include the former slaves. Today, while 73.7% of the 10% poorest population is black, 72.2% of the 10% richest population is white. As far as education is concerned, the white population has an average of 8.3 years of study and the black population has 6.7 years (IBGE 2009). Statistics show that differences in income are explained not only by levels of education, but also by racist attitudes (although these are often subtle and unspoken). On average, whites who have studied for 12 years or more earn 46.7% more than blacks with an equivalent level of education.

Deforestation

Brazil has some of the richest biodiversity in the world, with the largest reserves of water and one-third of the world's remaining tropical forest. Deforestation is a significant concern in terms of the loss of carbon storage capacity that it represents, exacerbated by the expansion of national and international markets for beef, soybeans and cocoa. If emissions from deforestation (i.e. lost carbon storage) were considered, the country would rank as the world's fifth biggest polluter. Ninety-three per cent of the Atlantic Forest, the most biologically diverse forest in the world, has been devastated, while 12% of the Amazon Forest, the biggest tropical forest in the world, has already been lost. Besides climate change, deforestation results in negative impacts on indigenous tribes and the loss of species and genetic material (some of which may have important pharmaceutical properties).

∎ Trends

The CSR culture in Brazil is rapidly disseminating in the private sector. However, the dominant approach is still philanthropic, largely as a consequence of the Catholic tradition of charitable giving, as well as the pressing social needs of the population.

A survey from the Institute for Applied Economic Research (IPEA 2006) indicates that the companies investing in community development rose from 59% in 2000 to 69% in 2004, totalling BRL4.7 billion (approximately USD1.5 billion) or 0.27% of the GNP. The reasons given by companies for community investment include humanitarian motives (57%), requests from different entities (47%) and perceived need to make contributions to the surrounding community (38%). The majority of the businesspeople surveyed believe that it is the government's duty to take care of social issues. Nonetheless, 57% agree that the state alone is not capable of solving all social problems and thus companies have an important role to play (IPEA 2006).

Despite the prevalence of community investment, many companies are taking a more strategic approach. A study from the Dom Cabral Foundation demonstrates that half (53.2%) of the companies that claim to be committed to sustainable development actually incorporate sustainability in their strategy. Particular areas of weakness include transparency and engagement, understanding and commitment at CEO and senior executive levels, balanced management of financial and sustainability concerns, the extension of CSR principles throughout the supply chain and the adoption of suitable ESG indicators linked to corporate goals.

In terms of data related to the institutionalisation of CSR in the country, there are currently seven Brazilian companies listed in the Dow Jones Sustainability World Index (DJSI 2009[1]) and 339 companies that have joined the UN Global Compact. The number of ISO 14000 certifications in Brazil in 2007 was 1,669 (ISO 2008) and for labour standards, Brazil is the nation with the fifth most facilities certified by SA8000 — 96 certified facilities at the time of writing.

Brazilian companies are more likely to publish sustainability reports than Latin American countries such as Mexico and Chile. Sixty-six Brazilian companies adopted the Global Reporting Initiative (GRI) guidelines in 2009 (GRI 2010), although many reports are still regarded as below global best practice.

---

1 http://www.sustainability-index.com

Legislation and codes

In Brazil, as in many other developing countries, legislation is not such an effective driver for CSR. In general, while the quality of legislation is considered good (and even advanced, in the case of environmental laws), the government's capacity for enforcement remains the most serious limitation. Enforcement is further complicated by the judiciary system, which is slow, unreliable and sometimes corrupt (SustainAbility 2006).

Brazilian labour legislation is characterised by its inflexibility and high cost, a legacy of the paternalistic government of Getúlio Vargas in the 1930s. The law offers favourable working conditions for employees with a formal work permit (*carteira de trabalho*), entitling them to retirement benefits, severance payments and paid leave. Nonetheless, rigid labour regulations tend to limit firm size and reduce employment in Brazil, which encourages companies to evade the law.

Brazil has ratified numerous international environmental treaties, but it was only in the 1980s and 1990s that important legal changes increased the level of environmental protection in the country. A national environmental policy was systematised and new judicial and administrative tools were created. In 1988, through the reform of the Federal Constitution, environmental protection was included as one of the fundamental principles to be considered when engaging in social, political and economic activities, a fact that is seen as an innovation in relation to other countries. However, despite the advanced Brazilian environmental legislation, the lack of technical and financial resources by environmental bodies makes the level of enforcement rather weak.

Brazilian legislation also provides tax incentives for individuals or organisations that invest in culture (8,313/1991) or make donations to the Funds for the Rights of Children and Teenagers (8,069/1990). However, the effectiveness of the incentives are questionable, as only 2% of the companies that invest in communities take advantage of the legislation, alleging that the incentive is not substantial enough (IPEA 2006).

In terms of affirmative action, the federal law (8,213/1991) mandates larger companies to employ people with disabilities. Companies with more than 99 workers are obliged to have 2–5% of their workforce comprised of people with disabilities. Although only a minority of companies seems to be complying, the law has stimulated a significant movement for action. A 2007 study showed that 67% of companies had special programmes for hiring people with disabilities, as compared to 32% in 2003 and 41% in 2005 (Instituto Ethos and IBOPE 2007).

Besides government regulation, Brazil has a number of voluntary codes, amongst which the Brazilian Code of Corporate Governance is particularly relevant. Launched in 1999, the Code reflects best practices in corporate governance and has contributed to the promotion of transparency in Brazil, which remains poor by international standards.

Organisations

Brazilian Business Council for Sustainable Development (CEBDS). Established in 1997, CEBDS is the Brazilian representative of the World Business Council for Sustainable Development. CEBDS's mission is to disseminate the concept of sustainable development in the business sector. The organisation has an active role in the development of the national climate change agenda and works in partnership with the federal government. Membership in May 2010 included 50 companies. **http://www.cebds.org.br**

■ **Brazilian Foundation for Sustainable Development (FBDS)**. Founded in 1992, FBDS actively contributes to the debate on sustainable development, using technology and science for formulating projects, scientific discussions and training human resources. **http://www.fbds.org.br**

■ **Brazilian Institute of Corporate Governance (IBGC)**. Launched in 1995, IBGC was one of the main organisations responsible for introducing and spreading the concept of corporate governance in Brazil and is currently the main frame of reference in terms of best practices in corporate governance. In May 2010, 1,348 companies were members. **http://www.ibgc.org.br**

■ **Centre for Sustainability Studies (CES)**. Launched in 2003, CES is an initiative from Getúlio Vargas Foundation's business school. The Centre is becoming a leading institute in research on sustainability in the private sector. **http://www.ces.fgvsp.br**

■ **Ethos Institute**. A membership organisation established in 1998 and committed to encouraging and influencing companies to manage their business in a socially responsible manner. It is considered one of the leading CSR organisations in Latin America and worldwide, with 126 organisations in 2010. The revenues of its associated companies represent approximately 30% of the Brazilian GNP. **http://www.ethos.org.br**

■ **Group of Institutes, Foundations and Enterprises (GIFE)**. An NGO founded in 1995, GIFE focuses on disseminating principles and practices of social investment in the public interest. Membership in 2008 included 112 organisations. **http://www.gife.org.br**

■ Case studies

Banco Real — Santander Group

Banco Real, the former Brazilian branch of ABN AMRO Bank and later acquired by Santander Group, is one of Brazil's leading CSR companies. The bank has received many national and international awards, such as the *Financial Times* Sustainable Banking Award in two categories: the top Sustainable Emerging Markets Bank and the overall Sustainable Bank of the Year. Among its CSR practices, the most recognised include: strong investment in human resources training (e.g. more than 1,800 managers received training in sustainable opportunities); creation of a range of credit lines for sustainable businesses; launching the first socially responsible investment (SRI) fund in Latin America, in 2001; establishment of a Microcredit Programme; development of a department dedicated to supplier relationships that evaluates, monitors, engages and encourages suppliers to be more socially responsible; and internal programmes to stimulate diversity (e.g. programmes for black youths and for people with disabilities, social benefits that are extended to gay, lesbian, bisexual and transvestite (GLBT) employees and policies that encourage the hiring of elder employees).

Natura Cosmetics

Since its foundation 40 years ago, Natura, a leading Brazilian cosmetics company, has been recognised for being a pioneer in sustainability. Its best practices include: analysis of the product life-cycle and control of the impacts of post-consumption waste; non-use of animal testing; a carbon-neutral programme; engagement with stakeholders on environmental, social and governance (ESG) issues; and responsible use of Brazil's biodiversity assets, including contributing to the income of traditional communities in the Amazon Forest through training on how to extract natural resources in a responsible manner.

▌ Education

Teaching in CSR is not widespread, but is a growing area and as more universities offer CSR courses, the number of CSR academics increases and more CSR professionals seek qualification. Some of the institutions currently offering CSR modules include:

- **Fundação Dom Cabral (FDC)**
- **Fundação Getúlio Vargas (FGV)**
- **Serviço Nacional de Aprendizagem Comercial (Senac)**
- **UniEthos**
- **Universidade de Campinas (Unicamp)**
- **Universidade de São Paulo (USP)**

References

GRI (Global Reporting Initiative) (2010) 'GRI Reports List'; http://www.globalreporting.org/GRIReports/GRIReportsList, accessed 18 May 2010.

IBGE (2008) 'Pesquisa Nacional por Amostra de Domicílios' (IBGE; http://www.ibge.gov.br/home/estatistica/populacao/trabalhoerendimento/pnad2008/comentarios2008.pdf, accessed 19 May 2010).

—— (2009) 'Síntese de Indicadores Sociais: Uma Análise das Condições de Vida da População Brasileira 2009'; http://www.ibge.gov.br/home/estatistica/populacao/condicaodevida/indicadoresminimos/sinteseindicsociais2009/indic_sociais2009.pdf, accessed 19 May 2010.

Instituto Ethos and IBOPE (2007) 'Perfil Social, Racial e de Gênero das 500 Maiores Empresas do Brasil e suas Ações Afirmativas. Pesquisa 2007'; http://www.ethos.org.br/_Uniethos/Documents/PesquisaDiversidade2007.pdf, accessed 22 March 2010.

IPEA (2006) 'A Iniciativa Privada e o Espírito Publico: a evolução da ação social das empresas privadas no Brasil' (IPEA; http://www.ipea.gov.br/acaosocial/IMG/pdf/doc-44.pdf, accessed 22 March 2010).

ISO (2008) 'The ISO Survey of Certifications'; http://www.iso.org/iso/survey2008.pdf, accessed 18 May 2010.

Lahoz, A., and M. Onaga (2005) 'O Custo da Corrupção', *Revista Exame* 847; http://portalexame.abril.com.br/revista/exame/edicoes/0847/economia/m0056706.html, accessed 23 July 2009.

SustainAbility (2006) 'Brazil: Country of Diversities and Inequalities' (SustainAbility; http://www.sustainability.com/downloads_public/insight_countrystudies/brazil.pdf, accessed 22 March 2010).

8 Bulgaria

Deyana Marcheva
Lawyer and Researcher in Law, Sofia University
Saint Kliment Ohridski

Nadejda Loumbeva
Independent Consultant and Researcher in
Knowledge Management, CSR and Sustainability

▎ Context

In Bulgaria, there is a widely shared belief in the importance of serving society and the community. This has led to both individuals and business embracing charity and philanthropy. Social responsibility is not, however, generally part of the strategic direction of a business.

Historical perspective

Donating to 'serve the Bulgarian nation' is a longstanding Bulgarian tradition with deep roots in the nation's history. The country was under violent Ottoman rule for approximately five centuries until 1878. During this time, the Ottomans tried to suppress and assimilate the Bulgarian nation, which Bulgarians met with systematic and prolonged resistance, maintaining and cultivating a national self-consciousness. As part of this effort, Bulgarians built and protected schools and churches, where they could teach reading and writing and produce hand-written books about Bulgarian history. As a consequence, there exists a strong and dedicated passion to serving the Bulgarian community and cultivating the spirit of Bulgarian society.

This passion turned into a national cause during the Bulgarian national revival in the 18th and 19th centuries. Out of dedication to their religion, education and culture, Bulgarian communities raised donations to build churches, schools and cultural centres called *chitalishta*. This philanthropic movement grew even stronger after the liberation of Bulgaria from the rule of the Ottomans in 1878. At the end of the 19th and the beginning of the 20th century, generous donations contributed to the construction and establishment of universities, theatres, monasteries and the like (UN Global Compact 2005).[1]

Current view

Despite this history, Bulgaria's 50-year socialist rule during the communist period considerably neglected the culture of philanthropy and giving. Still, because of European Union (EU) integration and the Bulgarian public's change in expectations of the role of businesses in society, CSR began re-emerging in the late 1990s (EU Bulgarian Country Report, 2004). Now CSR practices are gradually being integrated in the business sector, even if the understanding of CSR is still vague and mostly associated with company sponsorship (i.e. philanthropy), compliance with the law and staff welfare (Bristow 2005; Panov 2003).

The widespread view that 'being responsible is abiding by the law' may stem from the legal and institutional uncertainty that characterised the post-communist transition period. Whatever the causes, most businesses in Bulgaria are yet to see CSR as part of a complex and multidimensional business strategy requiring management systems and clear indicators, rather than as a set of one-dimensional approaches that are a mere 'add-on' to the business (BCAF Bulgaria 2005).

■ Priority issues

Corruption

According to Carvajal and Castle (2008), 'Bulgaria is considered the most corrupt country in the 27 member state European Union'. The Centre for the Study of Democracy (2009) says that 'in 2008, the number of corruption transactions has risen to around 175,000 monthly or 2.1 million on an annual basis'. This creates conditions for fraudulent enterprises and companies to emerge, most recently attracted by the flow of EU funds into the country. Sometimes, these seek to forge secret alliances with public officials (in order to protect their business), or infiltrate the government by having their people become public officials. Sometimes people say: 'There is no mafia in Bulgaria as a state; rather, the mafia *is* the state'.

Natural environment

Preserving the natural environment is a key issue for Bulgarian businesses. As there is an increased interest in investing in the transport, energy, tourism, real estate and agricultural sectors, there is also an increasing need to balance environmental preservation with business aspirations and ambitions.

In 2007, the National Statistical Institute provided for the following statistics on business environmental impact. These show a tendency to invest rather than preserve, as shown in Table 8.1:

---

1   Later on, in the 1930s, 6th December began to be celebrated as the Day of the Benefactor, when local communities pay tribute to the most prominent regional benefactors.

Table 8.1 Environmental impact of business in Bulgaria

Environmental expenditure (million BGN)	2006	2007
Expenditure on acquisition of tangible and intangible fixed assets with an ecological destination	609	633
Expenditure on maintenance and exploitation of tangible fixed assets and protection and restoration of the environment	401	532
Total expenditure	1,010	1,165

Standardisation

Adherence to international standards in CSR is a priority for Bulgarian businesses. According to UNDP, in 2007 the number of ISO 9001 certified companies in Bulgaria was 3,121, and of ISO 14001 was 117. Only two companies, TNT Bulgaria (Sofia) and Marvel (city of Sandanski), have been certified to SA8000 which ensures ethical sourcing of goods (UNDP 2007b).

∎ Trends

Generally, CSR tends to be left out of long-term business strategy by Bulgarian businesses. There seems to be no clear concept of CSR and no integral CSR policies. Rather, CSR takes shape in terms of direct provision of funds, in-kind assistance and responding to the social needs of staff. Sometimes, there is also investment in energy efficiency and environmental protection.

In February 2007, the marketing and social research agency Alpha Research presented the findings of a survey on CSR in Bulgarian companies (UNDP 2007b). This revealed that in Bulgaria multinational and large companies are the most active in CSR. The survey identified three distinct approaches to CSR:

- **Caring for employees and their families**. This is the most widespread perception of CSR in Bulgaria and combines two (contradictory?) elements: (i) paternalistic, in which employers see their social roles as benefactors; and (ii) enabling, in which employers see employees as 'social capital' and seek to enhance this through training, qualifications and benefits.

- **Caring for the local community**. This approach typically tries to improve the urban environment and support orphans, children and elderly people in institutions. Such activities are usually ad hoc, adopted on a case-by-case basis and not part of long-term business strategy.

- **Caring for long-term business impact**. This approach tries to implement coherent, long-term CSR strategies. It is seen primarily in large transnational companies with a presence in Bulgaria.

The UNDP study concludes that CSR trends in Bulgaria over the last decade are positive and that — despite their random and casual approach — CSR practices are penetrating the Bulgarian business environment.

▋ Legislation and codes

Although CSR is yet to be formally included in the Bulgarian government's agenda, the legal framework to instil socially responsible practices is gradually being developed, in particular as the Bulgarian law is being harmonised with the EU law.

Labour

In 1997 the **Occupational Health and Safety Act**, including the National System for Occupational Health and Safety, was promulgated. In 2001, employment reforms were introduced in the **Labour Code** in order to institutionalise Social Dialogue (Art. 2 Labour Code) and Tripartite Cooperation (Art. 3 Labour Code), both with the purpose of improving living standards and social security. The **Employment Promotion Law** was also promulgated the same year.

Environment

The **Environmental Protection Act** and the **Water Act** are the main legislative acts in Bulgaria to effectively enable basic environmental policy. They are based on principles such as 'polluter pays', public awareness regarding the state of the environment, shared responsibility, preventive action (control) and integrated management.

Tax

A reform in the **Corporate Income Tax Act** in 2004 introduced corporate donation concessions. Corporations may now treat their donations as expenses. Donations of up to 10% of financial profits are not taxable and may be excluded from taxable income. Article 31, paragraph 1, sub-paragraphs 1–17 of the Corporate Income Tax Act lists the institutions for whose benefit donations may be made. The total expenses for deductible donations may not exceed 65% of the profit. According to Article 177, paragraphs 1–4 of the Corporate Income Tax Act, tax relief is also granted to companies who employ unemployed persons under an employment contract for a minimum of 12 months. In 2005 the **Patronage Act** promoting donations for works of art was also promulgated.

▋ Organisations

▋ **AmCham CSR Committee**. A section in the American Chamber of Commerce in Bulgaria, this is a business organisation uniting over 300 American, Bulgarian and international companies operating in Bulgaria. The CSR Committee is established to encourage and facilitate responsible business practices. **http://www.amcham.bg/ committees/corporate_social_responsibility_committee.aspx**

▌ **Balkan Institute for Labour and Social Policy (BILSP)**. BILSP is an NGO promoting European Union social values in Bulgaria. In particular, it works to implement a regional project for setting up a National Round Table for the Introduction of Social Standards. http://www.bilsp.org/old/eng/index.htm

▌ **Bulgarian Business Leaders Forum (BBLF)**. BBLF promotes socially responsible business practices to benefit both business and society and to achieve social, economic and environmentally sustainable development. http://www.bblf.bg

▌ **Bulgarian Charities Aid Foundation (BCAF)**. BCAF is an expert foundation with a mission to enhance modern philanthropy. It is one of the leaders of promoting CSR in Bulgaria. http://www.bcaf.bg/English/Index.aspx

▌ **Bulgarian Donor Forum (BDF)**. BDF brings together international and local donor organisations and over 30 business and nonprofit organisations with the aim of mobilising sponsorship resources in Bulgaria. http://www.dfbulgaria.org

▌ **Bulgarian Global Compact Network**. This is an informal assembly of companies, NGOs and academia interested and working in CSR. Their aim is to initiate a public dialogue on the issues of CSR. http://www.unglobalcompact.bg/bg/index.php

▌ **Confederation of Employers and Industrialists in Bulgaria (CEIBG)**. CEIBG is the largest association of employers in Bulgaria, with over 230 members. It has adopted a Code of Business Ethics and Corporate Responsibility. http://www.ceibg.bg

▌ **Institute for Social and Trade Union Research (ISTUR)**. ISTUR is a non-governmental research organisation, which is part of the Confederation of Independent Trade Unions in Bulgaria. It was established to promote the European Social Model in Bulgaria. http://www.turi-network.eu/Members/Full-members/Institute-for-Social-and-Trade-Union-Research-ISTUR

▌ **United Nations Development Programme in Bulgaria (UNDP)**. UNDP is the largest UN Agency operating in Bulgaria and the most active promoter of CSR research and practices in Bulgaria. http://www.undp.bg

▌ The **Workshop for Civic Initiatives Foundation (WCIF)**. WCIF is a foundation set up to encourage social development, institutional and business transparency and CSR practices by promoting research, training and education, as well as dialogue among stakeholders. http://www.wcif-bg.org

▌ Case studies

Litex Commerce

For over two decades Litex, as part of its interest in social responsibility and community development, has been investing in the community in the Lovech region. This investment has included:

- Educational projects (Litex Football Academy and Scholarships)

- Art projects (annual Lovech Music Fest)

- Infrastructure facilities projects (improvement of the field, seats, lights and sound system of Lovech city stadium)

- Sponsorship programmes for a number of sports (football, wrestling, volley-ball and horse-racing)

The Litex long-term commitment to support schools, hospitals, social care establishments, cultural centres and local initiatives has turned Litex into the major sponsor and patron of the Lovech region. **http://www.litexjsc.com**

Overgas Inc.

In 2008, Overgas ranked first in the Accountability Rating ™ Bulgaria. This rating makes an assessment of companies' socially responsible practices as well as their economic, social and environmental impact. Overgas was recognised for its CSR integrated policy, covering various practices, such as:

- Educational programmes (Bulgarian School, Overgas Professional Summer Academy, Overgas Basket Academy) and contests (Mathematical and Linguistic Kangaroo contests, the National Literature and Art 'The Soul of a Source' contest)

- Environmental projects such as 'Let us keep Bulgaria green and clean for us and our children', initiated in 2000 and assisting with the reforestation of forests destroyed by wild fires

- Sponsorship of the arts (Askeer Theatre Awards) and sport (Yambol Basketball team)

- Support of local religious communities, such as free connection to the gas grid for the Catholic temple in Yambol

- In addition, Overgas is among the first companies with a presence in Bulgaria to move beyond random sponsorship activities and work to integrate and implement a CSR policy reflecting the philosophy that business prosperity means social responsibility. **http://www.overgas.bg**

Education

CSR is yet to become an area of academic and scholarly interest in Bulgaria. No CSR-related degrees are currently found in the major Bulgarian universities. However, CSR is offered as a separate subject at the New Bulgarian University School of Management in Sofia.

  CSR issues are also referred to in the context of business ethics and management courses taught at:

- **University of Sofia** 'St Kliment Ohridski'. **http://portal.uni-sofia.bg**

- **University for National and World Economy**, Sofia. **http://www.unwe.acad.bg**

- **Economics University**, Varna. **http://www.ue-varna.bg**

- **Economics Academy**, Svishtov. **http://www.uni-svishtov.bg**

In addition, sometimes CSR organisations offer short-term courses on and training in CSR concepts and practices. As a result of this and international conferences (as part of UNDP projects and EU reform initiatives), CSR is now beginning to attract the interest of a growing number of Bulgarian researchers and academics.

References

BCAF Bulgaria (2005) **http://bcaf.bg/Resources/FCK/file/analysis_BG2005.pdf**, accessed 2 June 2010.

Bristow, S. (2005) 'Corporate Governance in Bulgaria: An Outsider's Perspective on Recent Development', paper presented at the *Bulgaria and the European Union: Challenges for Business Education Conference*, Slunchev Bryag, Bulgaria, September 2005; **http://www.bam.bg/nessebar2005/ Bristow.pdf**, accessed 22 March 2010.

Carvajal, D., and S. Castle (2008) 'Bulgarian corruption troubling the European Union', *International Herald Tribune*, 16 October 2008; **http://www.novinite.com/view_news.php?id=97945**, accessed 22 March 2010.

Center for the Study of Democracy (2009) 'Crime without Punishment: Countering Corruption and Organised Crime in Bulgaria', Sofia, Bulgaria; **http://www.csd.bg/artShow.php?id=9583**, accessed 22 March 2010.

EU Bulgarian Country Report (2004) 'European Charter for Small Enterprises: Bulgarian Country Report' (Sofia, Bulgaria: European Union; **http://www.ec.europa.eu/enterprise/enterprise_policy/ charter/2005_charter_docs/report_bulgaria_2004_en.pdf**, accessed 22 March 2010).

Foundation BCAF Bulgaria (2005) 'First regional project launched by UNDP to accelerate implementation of corporate social responsibility in 8 European countries'; **http://www.acceleratingcsr. eu/en/news/view/?id=118**, accessed 2 June 2010.

—— (2007a) 'Corporate Social Responsibility within the Bulgarian Context'; **http://www.bcaf.bg**, accessed 22 March 2010.

—— (2007b) 'The Development of Philanthropy in Bulgaria: 2002–2004'; **http://www.acceleratingcsr. eu**, accessed 22 March 2010.

Panov, L. (2003) 'Philanthropy in Bulgaria: Taxation of Donations'; **http://www.ceetrust.org/article/122**, accessed 2 June 2010.

UN Global Compact (2005) 'Annual Global Compact Report: Bulgaria'; **http://europeandcis.undp.org/ uploads/public/File/Annual_Report_Bulgaria.pdf**, accessed 2 June 2010.

UNDP (United Nations Development Programme) (2007a) 'Baseline Study on CSR Practices in the New EU Member States and Candidate Countries' (European Synthesis Report; UNDP).

—— (2007b) 'Corporate Social Responsibility in Bulgaria: New Challenges 2007' (United Nations Development Programme, Country Office Bulgaria; **http://www.undp.bg/file_dl.php?url=uploads/ images/2457_en.pdf**, accessed 2 June 2010).

9 Canada

Dermot Hikisch
Research Manager, ENDS Carbon

▌ Context

Canada is a recognised world leader in corporate social and environmental responsibility. This leadership is influenced by the country's geography, political history and international relations.

Geographically, Canada contains a wealth of natural resources such as forests, minerals and petroleum. These have been the backbone of Canada's economy, beginning with the fur trade to Europe in the 16th century. Canada has reinvested its wealth from natural resources into education and social services, enabling a large portion of the Canadian population to live healthy lives.

Canada's history as a country with open borders has created a culture that celebrates diversity and gives a relatively high consideration to social prosperity. Although immigration rates have dropped in recent years, Canada was still found to be the friendliest towards newcomers in an HSBC 2008 survey of 48 countries (HSBC 2009).

Progressive government legislation and engaged stakeholder groups have been the driving forces in motivating CSR action in Canada. For instance, in 1971 Greenpeace was founded in Vancouver and the province of British Columbia was the first political jurisdiction in North America to enact extended producer responsibility laws in 1970 by requiring a deposit collection on beverage containers.

The largest campaign of peaceful civil disobedience in Canadian history was in defence of an old-growth forest due to be logged. Through negotiation, the volume of trees removed was significantly reduced and the original multinational logging company has relinquished regional management to a First Nations consortium.

Despite this background, the collapse of the Atlantic cod fishing industry off the coast of Newfoundland in the early 1990s served a loud wake-up call for responsible business. After being stable since the 16th century, the province's number one industry disappeared in just a few short years. As a result of overfishing between competing companies, the northwest Atlantic cod stocks have never returned and still remain at less than 1% of their historical population level.

Although CSR is not yet integrated into all Canadian corporations and full transparency is limited to a few sectors, responsible business practices in Canada are growing.

▌ Priority issues

Tar sands development and greenhouse gas emissions

The rapid development of northern Alberta's tar sands has become a major cause of concern both nationally and internationally. Estimated as the largest hydrocarbon deposit on the planet, the Canadian tar sands hold a huge energy potential. However, the extraction of oil from bitumen is not easy, requiring one barrel of equivalent energy in natural gas to produce five barrels of oil, and two to five barrels of water to steam out a single barrel of oil. In 2007, Alberta's tar sands generated 50% of Canada's GHG emissions growth and tar sands development is increasing.

Canada's tar sands have raised international concern. For example, energy from this source is banned in the state of California. In the Climate Change Performance Index for 2009 Canada ranked second to last on taking action towards climate change.

Canada is currently the world's 7th largest emitter of total GHGs, and in 2007, the acting government dismissed Canada's Kyoto obligations. Whether Canada receives financial penalties post 2012 remains to be seen but Canadian companies may be at risk of losing a competitive advantage should a global climate agreement be reached.

Old growth deforestation and loss of habitat

Canada has the third largest area of forest cover (33.6%) following Russia and Brazil. According to the World Conservation Monitoring Centre, Canada has some 766 known species of amphibians, reptiles, birds and mammals. Of these, 38 species are considered threatened, one of the largest and most recognised being the Woodland Caribou.

Forestry, mining and oil/gas industries have the largest direct impact on wildlife habitat, fuelled by the secondary manufacturing industries to which they provide resources.

Comparatively, Canadian forest practices have improved significantly over the past 40 years, with inclusion of better harvesting and replanting techniques, and the involvement of third party organisations like the Forest Stewardship Council and the Canadian Standards Association's Sustainable Forest Management Standard. After 50 years of continued growth in the total annual area harvested, the trend seems to be levelling off at around 1,100,000 ha/year.

Ninety per cent of all forests harvested still use the clear-cut method, which mimics natural regeneration for boreal forests, but can also lead to a loss of biodiversity. However, with estimates as high as 90% of all logging still occurring in frontier forests, including primary and old-growth forests, the sustainability of the forest industry will be a point of contention for some time.

Canadian fishing industry risks

Canada has the world's longest coastline and has been home to a diverse range of fishing opportunities for industry and tourism on the Atlantic, Pacific and inland.

According to the Marine Trophic Index, a measure of the degree to which countries are fishing down the food chain, Canada recently received a 'D' letter grade for performance on this indicator and finished 12th out of 15 peer developed countries.

From a historical perspective, the sustainability of Canada's fishing industry has been in decline since the 1970s.

Open-net farming of Atlantic salmon on the Pacific coast has become a controversial topic. This farming technique exposes migrating juvenile wild salmon to parasites produced by these farmed fish, further threatening the stability of the population levels of the local wild fish.

Water management

With a population of 32 million, Canada discharges 7% of the world's renewable freshwater supply each year and has about 25% of the world's wetlands.

Nevertheless, water quality is a point of concern in Canada as a result of industrial effluent, water use in oil, gas and mining, municipal sewage and agricultural runoff. Water pollution has led to eutrophication, making water unusable in several parts of central Canada.

National water quality monitoring does not exist; provinces independently outline their own water quality methodology and reporting guidelines and in certain areas, some industries self-monitor their water effluent. This strategy has received significant criticism from groups which claim the environmental risk for a self-monitored system is too high.

Widening demographic gaps

Canada has seen increasing disparity across certain demographics in recent years. According to one World Economic Forum study from 2008, Canada's gender gap is widening and Canadian females now rank 31st in terms of equality in a survey of 130 countries.

A recent OECD report found that after 20 years of closing the income gap between the rich and the poor, the past decade has seen both inequality and poverty rates in Canada rapidly increase to levels now above the OECD international average. The income gap between the middle class and the rich is also growing.

Several factors have contributed to demographic disparity. One unique to Canada, and particularly British Columbia, is unsettled native land claim agreements, which has social ramifications.

∎ Trends

Since 2000, consumers and investors have shown an increased interest in and higher expectations of the private sector to undertake responsible business practices. One indication of this movement was the January 2000 launch of the Jantzi Social Index, a socially screened, common stock index modelled on 60 Canadian companies in the Toronto Stock Exchange. The social screen required these companies to pass a broad set of environmental, social, and governance rating criteria.

According to a 2003 Environics poll, 9 out of 10 Canadian shareholders wanted fund managers to take environmental and social performance into account when valuing companies. The Social Investment Organisation released a 2005 report which estimated that socially responsible investment in Canada had grown to CAD65.5 billion.

With the exception of federal inactivity around climate change, legislation at the national level continues to increase in many CSR issues. For instance, a nationwide proposal for sustainable packaging and extended producer responsibility is in a final consultation phase. If approved, this proposal has the potential to influence businesses across a wide range of sectors.

Company public disclosure is also on the increase, and organisations such as the Global Reporting Initiative have developed training capacity in Canada.

▌ Legislation and codes

The Sustainable Development Act (proposed Bill C474 still moving through parliament) requires the development and implementation of a National Sustainable Development Strategy, the reporting of progress against a standard set of environmental indicators, the appointment of an independent Commissioner of the Environment and Sustainable Development accountable to Parliament and the adoption of specific goals with respect to sustainable development in Canada.

The Clean Air Act, tabled in 2006, Bill C30, amends the Canadian Environmental Protection Act, 1999, the Energy Efficiency Act and the Motor Vehicle Fuel Consumption Standards Act. Bill C30 addresses air pollution as well as GHGs.

The Canada Water Act (1985), C-11 provides for the management of the water resources of Canada, including research and the planning and implementation of programmes relating to the conservation, development and utilisation of water resources.

The Canadian Charter of Rights and Freedoms stipulates that everyone has the following fundamental freedoms: freedom of conscience and religion; freedom of thought, belief, opinion and expression, including freedom of the press and other media of communication; freedom of peaceful assembly; and freedom of association.

Under the Green Energy Act (2009), Ontario became the first area of North America to establish a feed-in tariff for renewable energy projects.

The North American Free Trade Agreement (1994) created a trading bloc between Canada, Mexico and the United States. This agreement has two supplements — the North American Agreement on Environmental Cooperation, and the North American Agreement on Labour Cooperation. As a result, several Canadian environmental laws have been amended to enable consistency between Canada and the United States (although not always in a sustainable direction).

The Canadian Environmental Assessment Act (1995) requires the federal government to conduct an environmental assessment of all projects for which it is the proponent, or for which it provides funding or land or issues a permit or authorisation pursuant to federal legislation.

The Fisheries Act is a federal law that focuses on management and monitoring of fisheries, conservation and protection of fish and fish habitat and pollution prevention.

Canadian companies have also benefited from following the framework set out by the Progressive Aboriginal Relations programme, which establishes performance benchmarks and assesses company performance in this regard over time. This programme, developed by the Canadian Council for Aboriginal Business, enables the use of a hallmark, which can enhance community relations and corporate communications.

▮ Organisations

▮ **Canadian Business for Social Responsibility (CBSR)**. A business-led, national membership organisation of Canadian companies that focus on CSR issues and stakeholder engagement. Activities include the sharing of best practice, capacity building and market research. CBSR currently has 99 corporate members. **http://www.cbsr.ca**

▮ The **Canadian Centre for Ethics and Corporate Policy (CCECP)**. The Centre promotes an ethical culture in Canadian organisations and offers a variety of resources on CSR, including access to speakers, workshops, conferences, CEO roundtables and publications. CCECP currently has 39 member organisations. **http://www.ethicscentre.ca**

▮ The **Conference Board of Canada**. A nonprofit and independent applied research organisation devoted to building leadership capacity and sharing insights on many CSR issues. The Conference Board publishes papers on CSR, holds conferences, issues an annual CSR report and provides links to several executive networks focused on CSR issues. **http://conferenceboard.ca**

▮ **Imagine**. A national programme to promote public and corporate giving, encouraging collaboration and engagement with business to support charity and nonprofit initiatives. Imagine runs the 'Caring Company' programme, where members sign the Corporate Citizenship Commitment and demonstrate leadership in community investment in Canada. This programme currently has 118 corporate members. **http://www.imaginecanada.ca**

▮ **Industry Canada**. Promotes CSR principles and practices to Canadian businesses as a strategy to improve industry competitiveness. The organisation provides a wide range of resources and guidance on social and environmental issues for use by business. **http://www.ic.gc.ca/eic/site/csr-rse.nsf/eng/home**

▮ **National Contact Point (NCP).** An interdepartmental committee chaired by the Department of Foreign Affairs and International Trade. The NCP promotes awareness of the OECD Guidelines for Multinationals and works to ensure their effective implementation. The Guidelines provide recommendations on voluntary principles and standards for responsible business conduct, consistent with domestic and international laws. **http://www.international.gc.ca/trade-agreements-accords-commerciaux/ncp-pcn/index.aspx**

▮ Two organisations provide leading news on CSR issues in Canada: **Corporate Knights**, the Canadian magazine for responsible business, and **CSRwire**, a national distribution service for environmental and CSR news relevant to Canadians. **http://www.corporateknights.ca** and **http://www.csrwire.ca**

▮ There are also a number of nonprofit organisations that interact with business on CSR issues as part of the stakeholder engagement process, including: The Sierra Club of Canada, The David Suzuki Foundation, Pembina Institute, World Wildlife Fund Canada, The Natural Step Canada, The Globe Foundation, The Council of Canadians, Canadian Coalition for Good Governance, and Social Investment Organisation.

■ Case studies

Resort municipality of Whistler

This destination ski resort and host of the 2010 Winter Olympics became engaged in the challenges of rapid growth and overdevelopment nearly a decade ago. Whistler municipality implemented a framework for strategic sustainable development to best plan for economic development while maintaining the region's main attraction, the environment. The resort engaged in a multi-stakeholder feedback process to determine the region's long-term vision. Based on principles of sustainability, *Whistler 2020* was created. This long-term vision for the municipality has resulted in the development of a comprehensive set of measurement indicators, numerous sustainability awards for the region, increased tourism and a new learning centre where other organisations come to learn about how to move in a sustainable direction. **http://www.whistler2020.ca**

Weyerhaeuser

As one of the largest pulp and paper producers in the world, Weyerhaeuser came under scrutiny after purchasing the highly unpopular logging company MacMillan Bloedel in 1999. As a result of this purchase and public concerns around the environmentally sensitive Clayoquot Sound, Weyerhaeuser announced plans to meet standards set by the Forest Stewardship Council and run all operations in the region with a majority share holding (51%) held by the local First Nations group.

■ Education

- **Concordia, John Molson School of Business**. MBA-level courses in CSR issues; *Beyond Grey Pinstripes* global ranking 59.[1] **http://www.concordia.ca/about/jobopportunities/faculty/jmsb**

- **Dalhousie University, Faculty of Management**. MBA-level courses in CSR issues; *Beyond Grey Pinstripes* global ranking 39. **http://management.dal.ca**

- **McGill University, Desautels Faculty Management**. MBA-level courses in CSR issues; *Beyond Grey Pinstripes* global ranking 45. **http://www.mcgill.ca/desautels**

- **Royal Roads University, School of Business**. **http://www.royalroads.ca/programs/faculties-schools-centres/faculty-management/school-of-business**

- **University of Alberta, School of Business.** MBA-level courses in CSR issues; *Beyond Grey Pinstripes* global ranking 53. **http://www.business.ualberta.ca**

- **University of British Columbia, Sauder School of Business.** MBA-level courses in CSR issues; *Beyond Grey Pinstripes* global ranking 23. **http://www.sauder.ubc.ca//AM/Template.cfm?Section=Home**

1 **http://www.beyondgreypinstripes.org/rankings/index.cfm**, accessed 15 June 2009. 149 universities from 24 countries participated in the 2009 Global 100 ranking; 10 of these schools were located in Canada.

- **University of Toronto, St Michael's College**. With the Conference Board of Canada, Certificate in CSR. http://www.utoronto.ca/stmikes/csr

- **University of Victoria, School of Business.** Courses in Corporate Relations and Responsibility. http://www.business.uvic.ca

- **University of Western Ontario, Ivy School of Business.** MBA-level courses in CSR issues; *Beyond Grey Pinstripes* global ranking 21. http://www.ivey.uwo.ca

- **Wilfred Laurier, School of Business and Economics.** MBA-level courses in CSR issues; *Beyond Grey Pinstripes* global ranking 65. http://www.wlu.ca/sbe/cmacro

- **York University, Schulich School of Business.** MBA-level courses in CSR issues; *Beyond Grey Pinstripes* global ranking 3, York also runs the Sustainable Enterprise Academy. http://www.schulich.yorku.ca/ssb-extra/ssb.nsf?open

References

Khare, A. (ed.) (2005) *Emerging Dimensions of Environmental Sustainability: A Canadian Perspective of Innovative Practices* (Edingen-Neckarhausen, Germany: Fachbuch Verlag Winkler; http://www.gerenciamento.ufba.br/Downloads/Emerging%20Dimensions%20of%20Environment%20Sustainability.pdf, accessed 15 June 2009).

HSBC Bank International (2009) 'Expat Explorer Survey 2009'; http://www.offshore.hsbc.com/1/PA_1_4_S5/content/international/2g_pdfs/expat/HSBCInternationalExpatExperienceReport2009.pdf, accessed 15 June 2009.

Natural Resources Canada (2008) 'Corporate Social Responsibility, Lessons Learned'; http://www.businessethicscanada.ca/capacity/tools/file_csr.pdf, accessed 15 June 2009.

10 China

Sam Yoon-Suk Lee
Founder and CEO, InnoCSR

Joshua Wickerham
China Representative, AccountAbility

■ Context

Present-day China is influenced by over 5,000 years of history. In 1949, Chairman Mao Zedong proclaimed the founding of the People's Republic of China and collectivised agriculture, outlawed private enterprise and steered a socialist ship of state. By the early 1980s, China, under Chairman Deng Xiaoping, saw private enterprises re-emerge, transforming China's economy from centrally-planned to market-based.

Since the 1980s, there have been significant economic reforms, a strong state hand and openness to trade, investment and outside culture. China has become a land where, as Chairman Deng Xiaoping said, 'to get rich is glorious', but deep economic divides remain. In 2007, China's Gini coefficient was 0.496, one of the highest in the world. Despite its impressive economic growth, China has mounting social issues and challenging environmental problems.

China joined the WTO in 2001 under Chairman Jiang Zemin. The same year, the Chinese Communist Party (CCP) fully accepted business leaders into its ranks and party congress.

Despite having experienced profound modern socioeconomic changes, China is still greatly influenced by its historic traditions, values and practices. Confucianism, as a mainstay of traditional political and cultural life, still governs the rules and practices of many relationships between people and society. Confucian theories of virtue (*de*) hold that rulers or social elites gain more power by acting in the interest of their followers.

Historically, the philosophical concept of harmony (*he*) has also long been stressed by various philosophical schools, particularly Confucianism and Taoism, and offers some guidance on how businesses and government should engage with stakeholders. Taoism, as China's most influential domestic religious tradition, and Buddhism, China's most mainstream religious import, also contribute to present-day attitudes in establishing various economic, social and environmental responsibilities.

Although during the planned economy period Chinese state-owned enterprises were expected to undertake social responsibilities, these have largely been subsumed by the emergence of a private market and profit-driven goals. Now, as more and more attention is focused on China concerning its economic, social and environmental impact, CSR has gained prominence in public debate and as a policy tool.

▋ Priority issues

China's economic growth of approximately 10% over three decades has often come at the cost of the environment and society. In *Fortune China* magazine's 2009 survey of managerial attitudes towards CSR, designed by the global think-tank AccountAbility, Chinese managers' highest priorities were listed as integrating impact with corporate strategy, improving company governance and strengthening social and environmental impact management.

Environment

According to various estimates, environmental damage costs China between 3% and 10% of its GDP annually. The government has urged businesses to reduce sulphur dioxide gas emissions and energy intensity per unit of GDP and has set targets of 15% renewable electricity use by 2020.

Legal compliance and business ethics

According to the General Industrial and Commercial Administration, there were 6,227 commercial bribery cases in 2008, involving CNY1.654 billion. In the 2009 Corruption Perceptions Index of Transparency International, China ranked 79 out of 180 countries (where rank 1 means the lowest perceived corruption).

Migrant labour and unemployment

China's large 'floating' migrant population of over 100 million people, with high numbers of recent college graduates and shifting models of growth, mean that job creation and high-quality training are among the priorities of both the Chinese government and companies.

Poverty alleviation

Chinese companies look domestically to supplement markets that have dried up during the global economic downturn and have called on businesses to help rural and western regions develop. The World Bank estimates that while 51% of the population was living in poverty in 1981, that number dropped to 8% by 2001 (Dollar 2007). Other World Bank poverty statistics indicate a drop from 64% to 10% from 1981 to 2001 (Ravallion 2009).

Product safety

Repeated product and food safety scandals, such as the melamine scare in dairy and egg products in late 2008 or the Mattel toy safety scandal in 2007, are also a CSR-related government and business concern. According to the Chinese Ministry of Health, 2005 saw 33,000 reported food-related illnesses (Bodeen 2009).

▌Trends

Many contemporary scholars claim that China's first experience with CSR was during the Maoist era of collective agriculture and state-owned enterprises, the period of the so-called 'iron rice bowl'. During Mao's reign, companies were both organised and required to *ban shehui*, or 'administer socially', which meant taking care of everything including workers' food, housing and marriage arrangements. However, this resulted in the social phenomenon called *chi da guo fan*, or 'eating from the same big pot' (getting the same reward or pay as everyone else regardless of individual performance). The 1978 reforms left a vacuum of state and company services that set the stage for debates about CSR from 2001.

Current CSR debates have advanced rapidly since the first Chinese state-owned enterprise (the State Grid Corporation of China) published a CSR report in March 2006. In 2008, more than 120 reports were issued by Chinese companies (Syntao 2008). *WTO Tribune*, a leading research organisation and magazine in the CSR arena, predicted the number of 2009 reports would top 600.

China's CSR has evolved rapidly with its fast-paced economic growth and can roughly be broken down into four categories:

Official scepticism and hesitant engagement (~1994–2004)

During this stage, government attitudes towards CSR ranged from sceptical to hostile. After the economy opened in 1978, the situation for companies in China had improved with Chairman Jiang Zemin's 2001 'Three Represents' theory, which called for the CCP to embrace 'advanced forces of production' (such as corporations) while representing the interests of 'the vast majority of the people'.

Since Chinese government and business attitudes focused on spurring economic growth by developing an industrial, export-oriented economy competing on cost and quality, attitudes towards international CSR best practice, along with statutory and non-statutory standards, were seen as means of discriminating and blocking Chinese enterprises from 'going out, going global', or as a pretext for denying markets for exported Chinese products.

Multinational company-led CSR (2004–2007)

At this point multinational corporations had been publishing CSR reports and integrating social and environmental sustainability into business strategies for several years. The first sustainability report was issued in 1999 by Shell China, and in February 2006 the first national CSR Summit was held in the Great Hall of the People.

Government-led CSR (2008–2010)

On 1 January 2008, SASAC published its 'Notification on issuance of guidelines on fulfilling social responsibility by state-owned enterprises'. This was the first concrete guidance from the Chinese government on how it expected central state-owned enterprises to implement CSR based on the 2006 company law that first mentioned CSR.

In May 2008, the Sichuan earthquake brought CSR to the public's attention. Companies began dealing with the public and other stakeholders in new ways. Not only did companies compete to see which could donate the most money or respond the quickest with supplies to the quake zone, but some companies also 'adopted' villages. Others used their logistical prowess to support the government or nonprofit organisations working in the area. Those companies who failed to react quickly were publicly criticised.

CSR also became more linked to competitiveness. In the 2009 *Fortune China* survey, 81% of respondents felt that 'social and environmental responsibility can improve business performance in the long run', up from 67% in 2007 and 76% in 2008. As more companies operating in China go abroad, they are adopting and promoting global standards and CSR practices acceptable to stakeholders outside of China.

Global hybrid CSR model (2010–)

As Chinese companies continue to use 'going out' strategies, they are starting to pay more attention to the role of international civil society, namely groups that promote voluntary social and environmental standards, campaign for or against companies, or certify products according to values determined by multi-stakeholder governance processes.

▌ Legislation and codes

In addition to the legislation and codes already mentioned, local and provincial CSR standards have been developed and implemented. Currently more than 300 companies in the Shanghai Pudong area are participating in these government initiatives. By developing a responsible competitiveness strategy, the Pudong government has indicated in numerous ways that there will be incentives related to corporate tax for CSR leaders in the area.

Several laws and regulations related to CSR are notable. Since the beginning of 2008, the Labour Contract Law has come into effect to protect the rights of workers, requiring timely wage payment, restrictions on unfair dismissal of workers and other responsibilities. Several other laws including safe production, environmental protection and food safety have also tightened government oversight.

▌ Organisations

▌ **CFCSR (Chinese Federation for Corporate Social Responsibility).** An NGO established in October 2006 and composed of large foreign and Chinese companies, focusing on CSR training, culture and activities. **http://www.cfcsr.org**

▌ **China Entrepreneur's Club.** Comprising China's largest private enterprises, it publishes the *China Entrepreneur* magazine and releases the annual 'China Green Companies' list.

▌ **Golden Bee China CSR Board**. Initiated and organised by China WTO Tribute under the Ministry of Commerce and Golden Bee CSR Development Center. **http://www.csr-china.org**

■ The **Non-Profit Incubator**. Based in Pudong New District, Shanghai, this was set up by founders of the Beijing-based consultancy Corporate Citizenship in Action, with support and funding from the Pudong government. This organisation supports the development of grassroots non-governmental organisations in Pudong. **http://www.npi.org.cn**

■ **NPP (Non-Profit Partners)**. This NGO was established by enterprises and foundations in China in 2006. **http://www.nppcn.com**

■ **Research Center on Transnational Corporations**. This partnership between the Chinese Ministry of Commerce and Chinese Academy of International Trade and Economic Cooperation researches CSR in the context of 'soft competitiveness'. **http://www.tncchina. org.cn**

■ **Society of Entrepreneurs & Ecology**. An NGO dedicated to environmental protection and established by Chinese entrepreneurs in 2004. **http://www.see.org.cn**

■ Case studies

China Mobile

In 2008, China Mobile became the first enterprise of Mainland China to be included in the Dow Jones Sustainability Index, which recognised the telecom's CSR efforts. Joining the international CSR platform has become a significant symbol for Chinese enterprises, greatly improving their image. China Mobile has many CSR initiatives including its Green Action Plan. According to this plan, by applying various energy-saving technologies, and solar and wind power, the power consumption of 2010 should be 60% of that in 2005, saving 8 billion kWh. Its Green Box Plan has recycled more than 3 million wasted cellphones, batteries and parts. **http://www.chinamobile.com**

Guangzhou Baiyunshan Hutchison Whampoa Traditional Chinese Medicine Co. Ltd

Guangzhou Baiyunshan Hutchison Whampoa Traditional Chinese Medicine established a family medicine recycling programme in 2004, exchanging medication that had expired without charge. Now it has 2,100 drug stores across the country implementing the policy. This movement has attracted the attention of the government and influenced the State Food and Drug Administration (SFDA) to consider an industrial standard to regulate the recycling of family medicines. Along with its improved company image and influence, the company's revenue has been increasing by 30% annually.

PepsiCo

PepsiCo introduced a new technology that allows potatoes to be grown in the deserts of Inner Mongolia. PepsiCo's sustainable model has enhanced the lives of more than 10,000 local farmers, helping prevent the desertification of farm land while providing raw materials for its own production at lower cost. Currently, PepsiCo's potato chip brand, Lay's, comprises about 40% of the domestic potato chip market. **http://www. pepsico.com**

Shanghai Pudong Development Bank (SPDB)

SPDB aims at encouraging the development of renewable energies and environment-friendly industries. By the end of 2006, SPDB had granted 14 loans in such fields as urban wastewater treatment, development of clean energy and circulation economy, amounting to CNY2.975 billion. With SPDB as the pioneer, the Banking Association of China announced the guidelines for the CSR of banking institutions in China in January 2009, explicitly urging its financial members to support social, economic and environmental sustainability. http://www.spdb.com.cn

∎ Education

- **China Environment and Sustainable Development Reference and Research Centre (CESDRRC).** Affiliated to the Ministry of Environmental Protection and established in March 1998, it offers classes, references and activities to teach environmental protection

- **China National Textile and Apparel Council (CNTAC)** and the **Responsible Supply Chain Association (RSCA).** CNTAC created and promotes the CSC9000T voluntary CSR management system for the textiles sector and conducted pilot implementation projects on the system

- **CSR Research Center, Law School of Peking University.** Funded by donations, this centre aims to educate policy-makers and the public on CSR

- **Euro–China Centre for Leadership and Responsibility (ECCLAR).** Founded in 2006 and based at the China–Europe Business School (CEIBS), ECCLAR is committed, through research, education and networking, to contribute to the development of responsible leadership in Chinese organisations. http://www.ceibs.edu/ecclar

- **NGO Research Center of Tsinghua University.** Founded in 1999 and headed by Professor Wang Ming, this is China's oldest and most respected NGO research centre. http://www.sppm.tsinghua.edu.cn/english/research/center/26efe4891f406f6b011f5ee4824e0041.html

- **Zhejiang University School of Public Administration.** This school is involved with several local and provincial initiatives to promote CSR in the province of Zhejiang.

References

Bodeen, C. (2009) 'Food troubles in China move to world stage: pet deaths in US underscore purity problems', Associated Press; http://www.cec-ceda.org.cn/english.

CEC (China Enterprise Confederation) and CEDA (China Enterprise Directors Association) (2007) 'Development Report on CSR in China' (CEC and CEDA).

Chinese Enterprise Investigation Team (eds.) (2007) 'CSR in Entrepreneurs' Mind: Report on the Growth and Development of Chinese Entrepreneurs' (Chinese Enterprise Investigation Team).

DLA Piper (2008) 'Corporate Social Responsibility Compliance for Foreign Invested Enterprises'; http://www.dlapiper.com/files/upload/Corporate_Social_Responsibility_compliance_by_foreign_ invested_cos%20_in_PRC.pdf, accessed 22 March 2010.

Dollar, D. (2007) 'Poverty, inequality, and social disparities during China's economic reform' (World Bank Policy Research Working Paper no. WPS 4253; http://econ.worldbank.org/external/default/ main?pagePK=64165259&theSitePK=469382&piPK=64165421&menuPK=64166093&entityID=000 016406_20070613095018, accessed 2 June 2010).

Gefei, Y. (2006) 'China CSR Investigation Report', *China WTO Tribune*.

GERN (Global Education Research Network) (2008) 'Corporate Citizenship around the World; http:// www.bcccc.net/index.cfm?fuseaction=document.showDocumentByID&DocumentID=1237, accessed 22 March 2010.

Kiel, P. (2008) 'Corporate Social Responsibility Training Service Providers in China' (Sino-German Corporate Social Responsibility Project; http://www.chinacsrproject.org/Download.asp?ID=28, accessed 22 March 2010).

Lan, L. (2007) 'The Guideline of CSR Standard Implementation in China'.

Naughton, B. (2007) *The Chinese Economy* (Cambridge, MA: MIT Press).

People's Daily (2007) 'China suffers widening income gap: report', *People's Daily*, 8 January 2007; http://english.peopledaily.com.cn/200701/08/eng20070108_339037.html, accessed 27 September 2009.

Ramo, J.C. (2007) 'Brand China', The Foreign Policy Centre; http://joshuaramo.com/brand-china, accessed 2 June 2010.

Ravallion, M. (2009) 'Fighting Poverty: Findings and Lessons from China's Success', World Bank; http://go.worldbank.org/QX0QI9MP30.

Research Center of Shanghai Security Exchange (eds.) (2007) 'Corporate Governance Report: Stakeholders and Social Responsibility' (Research Center of Shanghai Security Exchange).

Syntao (2008) 'A Journey to Discover Values and an Introduction to China. Sustainability Reporting Resource Center', http://www.syntao.com/E_Page_Show.asp?Page_ID=11026, accessed 2 June 2010.

Youhuan, L. (2008) 'CSR in China: Report from Guangdong on CSR Practice'.

Web resources

China CSR Map (2009) http://www.chinacsrmap.org, accessed 21 March 2009.

SASAC (State-Owned Asset Supervision and Administration Commission) (2009) State-Owned Asset Supervision and Administration Commission, http://www.sasac.gov.cn, accessed 17 March 2009.

11 Colombia

Angela Pinilla Urzola
Postgraduate Researcher, International Centre for Corporate
Social Responsibility, University of Nottingham, UK

■ Context

Colombia is an Andean country, the fourth largest in South America, with a cultural diversity comprising Spanish, indigenous and African traditions. The culture is particularly marked by the Spanish, who conquered the continent centuries ago. This is evident in the organisation of society in a highly stratified social class system, as well as Spanish architecture, sports and cultural traditions, besides the language and Catholic religion.

In Colombia, the concept of social responsibility could have had its origins in Catholic teachings (Gutiérrez *et al.* 2006), where concern for the poor and underprivileged are emphasised. The Catholic Church has influenced a number of areas including education, social welfare, trade union organisation and business. Members of the religious hierarchy have strong ties with members of society who control strategic business positions and have influenced their philanthropic activities. The business sector supports Catholic charities with time and money and provides most of the membership of lay religious associations. In this context, the practice of charity has been a significant driver for CSR (Gutiérrez *et al.* 2006).

Colombian business leaders have collaborated in solving social problems through the establishment of foundations. One of these initiatives, the Family Compensation Foundation, is an organisation created by a group of companies in 1950 to provide social services to families of employees working for affiliated businesses. Today, the fund's reach has expanded to 22% of Colombia's population.

Governmental policies, such as mechanisms allowing social donations to be tax-deductible, have encouraged the creation of foundations, to the extent that there are now 111 foundations in Colombia (Gutiérrez *et al.* 2006). The impact of these governmental policies and traditions can be seen in the conclusions of a study of company perceptions of social responsibility, which was conducted in 2004 by the National Association of Industrialists (ANDI) covering 850 affiliates (Montes 2008):

- Each of the 98 companies that responded to the survey allocated an average of 2.48% of its sales to social investment.

- Half of these companies make an annual social statement.

- A third report on their social investment.

- Three out of four contribute to foundations.

- Their budget for 2004 was COP614.3 million.

Gutiérrez *et al.* (2006) conclude that the total contribution of these businesses in social services for their workers and communities and in donations towards foundations represented 3.34% of their total sales in 2003.

CSR in Colombia can explained by using a convergence of two different models, namely the Virtue Matrix (Martin 2002) and stakeholder theory (Freeman 1984). Taken together, these explain that CSR practices lie within the norms, customs and laws that govern corporate practice in Colombia, while allowing space to innovate with their social programmes and contribute to addressing the country's social injustices (Gutiérrez and Jones 2004). Hence, companies respond to the needs of stakeholders in the country, with the ethical goal of addressing social conflict.

At the national level CSR is also driven by the international agenda, with a strong influence by international actors such as the Inter-American Development Bank, United Nations Development Programme, the head offices of multinational enterprises and international non-governmental organisations (Haslam 2004).

▌ Priority issues

Poverty and inequality

Colombia faces high levels of inequality and poverty, with some of the highest rates in Latin America: 20% of Colombians receive 60% of the national income (World Bank 2009). The most vulnerable to poverty and inequality are women, children, those of African descent, indigenous groups and internally displaced persons. The poverty gap is most evident between rural and urban areas where 62% of the rural population is poor compared to 39% in urban areas. This is also true in the case of extreme poverty; in rural areas 22% live in extreme poverty compared to 9% in the urban sector.[1]

Conflict and human rights

Colombia has suffered decades of violence which has undermined governance systems, to the extent that it determines who controls and influences the country. The conflict started with the 'La Violencia' period in 1948, and intensified when the Revolutionary Armed Forces of Colombia (FARC) and others guerrilla groups were founded in the 1960s and began insurgency campaigns against the Colombian government.

During the last two decades, paramilitary groups have been created as a reaction to the threat represented by guerrilla action. According to Human Rights Watch (2008), paramilitary groups have eliminated numerous opposing voices, including trade unionists, human rights defenders, community leaders, judges and ordinary civilians. In rural

1 http://www.abcolombia.org.uk

areas, they have threatened farmers, indigenous people and people of African origin and then taken their abandoned land, leaving Colombia second only to Sudan as the country with the most internally displaced people in the world.

During the last five years, the government has tried to dismantle the paramilitary groups and reintegrate its members into society. As a result, some paramilitary commanders have confessed to killings and massacres, as well as disclosing some of the names of high-ranking officials in the security forces who worked with them. Subsequently, the Colombian Supreme Court has made unprecedented progress in investigating paramilitary infiltration of the Colombian Congress. However, according to the International Crisis Group (2007), since late 2005 Colombia has also witnessed the emergence of new illegal paramilitary groups.

Cocaine production, conflict and environmental issues

Since the 1980s, Colombia has become the country with the largest illicit coca growing area and cocaine production in the world. The drug business, which is controlled by FARC, paramilitary groups and drug trafficking groups, has been associated with ecosystem degradation, particularly tropical forest deforestation. Research shows that between 1973 and 1996 approximately 82,924 ha of tropical rainforest were converted to other types of land use. Between 1973 and 1985, this was mainly caused by colonisation pressures associated with the intensification of oil industry operations. However, from 1985 to 1996, deforestation was directly related to coca cultivation (Vina *et al.* 2004). In addition, guerrilla sabotage of pipelines has caused severe pollution of the local rivers and land.

Corruption and transparency

The emergence of the drug trade in Colombia gave rise to a high level of corruption which spread throughout the different branches of public power, corrupting values, sacrificing principles and buying political leaders, judges, policemen, soldiers, reporters and academics from municipal to national level (Hoggard 2004). Human Rights Watch (2008) states that paramilitary groups have mafia-style alliances with powerful landowners, businessmen in their areas of operation and state officials, including numerous members of the Colombian Congress. One example of business–paramilitary alliances is the case of Chiquita Brands International, which has admitted to making payments and assisting with the logistical activities of paramilitary groups between 1997 and 2004. Due to this involvement, the government of Colombia is considering a request to extradite Chiquita's board members (*Semana* 2007).

▌ Trends

Gutiérrez *et al.* (2006) highlight the following main CSR stages during the 20th century in Colombia:

- **1900–1960.** The business community supported philanthropic activities created by the Catholic Church. The Social Foundation (Fundación Social) was founded by a Spanish Jesuit Priest, Father José María Campoamor.

- **1960s.** An important group of business foundations emerged and continue to exist today, making a significant contribution to social development.

- **1970s.** Two Colombian companies, Fabricato and Enka de Colombia, started to measure their social performance.

- **1980s.** ANDI developed the first model of social planning, control and reporting for the Colombian industrial sector (Balance Social).

- **1990s.** The private sector created initiatives in areas such as education, health, innovation, productivity, peace, community development, justice and transparency.

- **2000s.** There has been an increase in partnerships between business, non-profit organisations and social investment initiatives.

Despite this evidence showing the interest of the private sector in CSR initiatives — from philanthropy and the creation of foundations to social investment activities and the development of cross-sector partnerships — CSR is still evolving and remains at an incipient stage, especially in the governmental sector, civil society and academia.

▍Legislation and codes

Governmental legislation and policies

Although the Colombian Constitution of 1991 stipulates that the private sector must have a social function, the involvement of the government in the development of policies to promote this is relatively weak. For example, in 2006 and 2007, the Colombian Congress failed to approve proposed legislation to enforce the implementation of CSR programmes and social and environmental reporting practices in the business sector. The initiative did not have the support of the Colombian Business Council (Consejo Nacional Gremial), since it was considered to be in opposition to the voluntary nature of CSR.

Conversely, in the environmental area, the government established **Law 99** (of 1993), requiring large industries or development activities that cause natural resource damage to have a formal environmental (and social) licence. A legal framework for labour rights, the substantive labour code and the procedural code of labour and social security are in the constitution. Health and safety issues are set forth in **Law 100**. The constitution also established new principals of control and transparency, laying out a broader legal basis for controlling corruption.

Corporate codes and international standards

The private sector has developed and promoted several codes of conduct in the environmental and social area, including:

Social Management Guide (Balance Social)

A guide developed by ANDI to plan, organise, control and report social management activities in the business sector. **http://www.andi.com.co**

Green Flowers Guide (Flor Verde)

A guide developed by the Colombian Flowers Association (ASOCOFLORES) to self-regulate environmental and social management activities in the floriculture industry. **http:// asocolflores.org**

CCRE Guide (Indice CCRE)

A guide of indicators developed by the Corporate Social Responsibility Colombian Council to evaluate social performance in the business sector. **http://www.ccre.org.co**

Colombian Technical Guide in Social Responsibility (GTC 180)

A guide developed by the Colombian Institute of Technical Norms (ICONTEC) to plan and report social management activities, including stakeholder participation. **http:// www.icontec.org.co**

Responsible Care® Guide

A programme promoted by the Colombian Plastics Association (ASOCOPLASTICOS) for the chemical sector to implement codes of conduct in areas of community awareness and emergency response, process safety, environmental protection and health and safety. **http://www.acoplasticos.org**

International codes and standards such as the UN Global Compact, Global Reporting Initiative, GEMI and AA1000 standards are followed by some multinational companies and local companies. Colombia had an active participation in the development of the ISO 26000 social responsibility standard.

▌ Organisations

There are several organisations engaged in promoting CSR in Colombia, most notably:

▌ **Colombian Centre for Social Responsibility**. Dedicated to advancing sustainable human development and social responsibility in the business sector through inter-sector promotion and cooperation. **http://www.ccre.org.co**

▌ **Business Ethics Institute**. Dedicated to promoting sustainability reporting and auditing in organisations. **http://www.iletica.org.co**

▌ **Colombian Confederation of Chambers of Commerce (CONFECAMARAS)**. A leader in business ethics and social responsibility in small and medium-sized businesses. **http://www.confecamaras.org.co**

▌ **Investment in Colombia (Compartamos con Colombia)**. Dedicated to incentivising social investments and promoting the social responsibility concept among young entrepreneurships. **http://www.compartamos.org**

▌ **Business Council for Sustainable Development: Colombia Chapter (Cecodes)**. Created in 1993 and dedicated to promoting sustainable development practices and social responsibility initiatives among its 31 members. **http://www.cecodes.org.co**

∎ **ANDI (National Association of Industrialists)**. Founded in 1944 and interested in promoting social initiatives among its 1,100 members. **http://www.andi.com.co**

∎ Case studies

Fundación Social

Fundación Social is a social investment fund dedicated to making investments aimed at removing the structural causes of poverty in Colombia. The fund has invested in ventures ranging from insurance, leasing, construction companies, television stations, savings institutions and banks. A sustainability report is produced covering employee-related matters, wealth generation and distribution, and impacts on society at large. **http://www.fundacion-social.com.co**

La 14

La 14 is a national supermarket chain trading with 30 grower cooperatives in Cali in the western part of the country. Its suppliers are part of Redprodepaz, a peace and development programme. **http://ice.la14.com/ice/index.htm**

Empresas de Narino

Empresas de Narino is a coffee company working with two international government agencies to provide training to 1,080 coffee-growing families. By growing eco-friendly coffee, the participating small farmers are able to secure a premium for their crop.

Indupalma

Indupalma is a crude palm oil company, which was managed as a plantation during its first 30 years. Labour cooperatives emerged as a response to bankruptcy faced at the beginning of the 1990s. Workers formed associations to create cooperatives, micro-enterprises and associations which sold their services to Indupalma. This strategy to engage workers allows them to become owners of the land and cultivation. **http://www.indupalma.com/portal/default.aspx**

∎ Education

The **Universidad de los Andes** is the leading centre in teaching and research in CSR in Colombia, with postgraduate academic programmes in 'social responsibility and development', CSR-related modules in MBA courses and research in CSR. Its business school ranks 95 in the *Beyond Grey Pinstripes* 2007–2008 ranking, and it is a member of the Social Enterprise Knowledge Network (SEKN), founded in 2001 with the goal of advancing the frontiers of knowledge and practice in social enterprise. The business school leads an initiative called 'Mapearse',[2] which is creating an information network map of

2 **http://www.mapearse.net**

social responsibility initiatives in the business sector. **http://administracion.uniandes.edu.co**

Other leading university institutions offering CSR-related modules and postgraduate courses are:

- **Universidad Externado**. http://administracion.uexternado.edu.co

- **Universidad Piloto**. http://www.unipiloto.edu.co/index.php?section=723

- **Universidad Central**. http://www.ucentral.edu.co/rs

- **Universidad Javeriana**. http://www.javeriana.edu.co/fcea/gerse.htm

- **Universidad EAFIT**. http://www.eafit.edu.co/escuelas/administracion/Paginas/grupos-investigacion.aspx

References

Amis, L., A. Hodges and N. Jeffrey (2006) 'Development, Peace and Human Rights in Colombia: A Business Agenda' (London: IBLF; **http://www.iblf.org/resources/general.jsp?id=123802**, accessed 13 March 2010).

Fernandez, D., D. Trujillo and R. Gutiérrez (2003) 'Indupalma and the Associated Labor Cooperatives, 1991–2002' (SEKN Case Studies and Syllabi; **http://www.universitynetwork.org/taxonomy/term/42?page=5**, accessed 13 March 2010).

Freeman, R.E. (1984) *Strategic Management: A Stakeholder Approach* (Boston, MA: Pitman).

Gutiérrez, R., L. Avella and R. Villar (2006) 'Achievements and Challenges of Corporate Social Responsibility in Colombia' (Bogotá, Colombia: Fundación Corona; **http://www.redeamerica.org/Portals/0/Documentos%20gral/RSEmpresarial.pdf**, accessed 13 March 2010).

Gutiérrez, R., and A. Jones (2004) 'Corporate Responsibility in Latin America: An Overview of its Characteristics and Effects on Local Communities', in M.E. Contreras (ed.), *Corporate Social Responsibility in the Promotion of Social Development: Experiences from Asia and Latin America* (Washington, DC: IADB; **http://www.iadb.org/Publications/search.cfm?query=&context=&lang=en&docType=BOOKS&topic=ENVI&country=&searchLang=**, accessed 15 March 2010): 151-254.

Haslam, P. (2004) 'The Corporate Social Responsibility System in Latin America and the Caribbean' (Canadian Foundation for the Americas, Policy Paper; **http://www.focal.ca/pdf/csr_04.pdf**, accessed 13 March 2010).

Hoggard, S. (2004) 'Preventing Corruption in Colombia: The Need for an Enhanced State-Level Approach', *Arizona Journal of International and Comparative Law* 4.2: 578-619.

Human Rights Watch (2008) 'Breaking the Grip', Human Rights Watch; **http://www.hrw.org/en/reports/2008/10/16/breaking-grip?print**, accessed 13 March 2010.

International Alert (2006) 'Local Business, Local Peace: The Peacebuilding Potential of the Domestic Private Sector' (International Alert; **http://www.international-alert.org/peace_and_economy/peace_and_economy_projects.php**, accessed 2 June 2010).

International Crisis Group (2007) 'Colombia's New Armed Groups' (International Crisis Group; **http://www.crisisgroup.org/home/index.cfm?id=1269&l=1**, accessed 13 March 2010).

Martin, R. (2002) 'The Virtue Matrix: Calculating the Return on Corporate Responsibility', *Harvard Business Review* 80.3: 68-75.

Montes, A. (2008) 'La Mano al Bolsillo', *Semana*; **http://www.semana.com/wf_ImprimirArticulo.aspx?IdArt=105914**, accessed 13 March 2010.

Semana (2007) Banana 'Para-Republic', *Semana*; **http://www.semana.com/wf_InfoArticulo.aspx?idArt=101602**, accessed 13 March 2010.

Vina, A., F.R. Echavarria and D.C. Rundquist (2004) 'Satellite Change Detection Analysis of Deforestation Rates and Patterns along the Colombian–Ecuador Border', *Journal of the Human Environment* 33.3: 118-25.

World Bank (2009) 'Colombia: Country Brief'; http://web.worldbank.org/WBSITE/EXTERNAL/COUNTRIES/
LACEXT/COLOMBIAEXTN/O,,contentMDK:22254365~pagePK:1497618~piPK:217854~theSitePK:3249
46,00.html, accessed 13 March 2010.

12 Côte d'Ivoire

Ulf Richter
Profesor e Investigador Principal, Centrum Católica,
Pontificia Universidad Católica del Perú

■ Context

Côte d'Ivoire is a tropical country situated in West Africa, bordering the countries of Liberia, Ghana, Guinea, Burkina Faso and Mali. The official administrative capital is Yamoussoukro while its largest city and economic engine is Abidjan with about 4 million inhabitants. Côte d'Ivoire is an ethnically diverse country with over 70 native languages spoken. The population is around 21 million, with population growth estimated at 2.7% from 2005 to 2009 (IMF 2009).

Traditional export goods of Côte d'Ivoire include agricultural commodities such as cocoa, coffee, cotton, rubber, palm oil, pineapple, banana, tuna and tropical woods. Côte d'Ivoire is the largest cocoa producer in the world and for a long time cocoa was the main source of income (up to 40%). In recent years, newly discovered oil reserves have created an alternative source of income. Further export products include diamonds, iron ore, manganese, cobalt, copper and bauxite.

Côte d'Ivoire has long been a symbol for political stability, ethnic peace and an open economy in West Africa after its independence from France in 1960. A military coup in 1999 ended this period of relative prosperity, creating political instability and civil conflict. A failed coup in 2002 led the country into hostilities and split it into northern and southern territories. During the hostilities an estimated 3,000 people were killed and up to 700,000 persons were displaced (IMF 2008).

In March 2007, Côte d'Ivoire's President Gbagbo and the country's rebel leader, Guillaume Soro, signed the Ouagadougou Accord to establish peace between the government and rebel forces. However, the first post-conflict democratic elections for a new president are still to be held. In April 2004, the UN authorised the UNOCI mission in order to stabilise the war-torn country. As of February 2009, there were over 9,000 uniformed personnel with a budget of USD497.46 million, together with about a further 3,000 French troops, attempting to stabilise the country.

Côte d'Ivoire contributes about 40% to the GDP of the West African Economic and Monetary Union (UEMOA), but is struggling to reclaim its predominant position as the powerhouse and economic engine of francophone West Africa. The private sector is believed to play a crucial role in the re-establishment of a prosperous environment and the creation of economic opportunities and peace.

The CSR approach of most francophone countries in West Africa is different from the UK/US CSR and corporate citizenship models as promoted by Carroll (1979) or Matten and Crane (2005). CSR is widely understood as quality management, often combined with elements of philanthropy. Many corporate executives equate their corporate responsibility with conforming to ISO norms and quality standards including ISO 9001, ISO 14001, OHSAS 18001, SD21000 and AFAQ1000NR.

UK/US CSR standards such as AA1000, SA8000 or the Global Reporting Initiative (GRI)'s Third Generation (G3) guidelines are rarely applied. Grounded in the socio-economic reality, CSR is mainly interpreted as the fight against corruption and poverty, the improvement of labour conditions and philanthropy. In certain cases, CSR approaches are being merged with or adapted to local customs such as the so called 'palaver tree', which is a traditional way to de-escalate conflicts in African communities (Yameogo 2008).

■ Priority issues

Environment

Côte d'Ivoire is facing significant environmental problems. The timber industry has largely destroyed the rain forests, once the largest in West Africa, with disastrous consequences for biodiversity. Chimpanzee populations have been decimated from tens of thousands to an estimated remaining population of 200–300. More recently, water pollution from industrial and agricultural effluents, combined with poor waste management, contamination of water supplies and deteriorating urban conditions, have turned Abidjan, once the 'Paris of West Africa', into a degraded environment.

An example of the environmental hazards faced by the country occurred in August 2006, when the cargo vessel Probo Koala, owned and operated by the Dutch commodities trading company Trafigura, unloaded 500 tons of highly toxic waste in the port of Abidjan and dropped it into 12 randomly chosen sites around Abidjan. At least 17 people died and approximately 90,000 inhabitants suffered from the contamination of the toxic waste.

Conflict

The ongoing conflict continues to affect business activity in Cote d'Ivoire. For instance, in 2007, the Washington-based NGO Global Witness (2007) noted that the lack of transparency in the cocoa sector with respect to the flow of funds and the institutions involved has facilitated the purchase of arms to prolong the conflict.

Conflict diamonds from the north of Côte d'Ivoire, which are banned by the Kimberly Process, continue to appear on the world market, notably in the United Arab Emirates, according to the NGO Partenariat Afrique Canada (2008).

Moreover, about 3,000 children are estimated to be abused as child soldiers (UNICEF 2009).Violence against children and women (in particular sexual abuse), not only by the local population but also by UN peacekeepers and government forces, has also been reported frequently (Amnesty International 2008; UNICEF 2009).

Poverty and labour

The political instability and civil strife have resulted in an economic decline that has reduced living standards and increased poverty. According to the IMF and World Bank, poverty increased from 38.2% in 2002 to 48.9% in 2008. Due to the crisis, the country's ranking in the UN Human Development Index dropped from 154th in 1999 to 163rd in 2009 (out of 182 countries).

The unemployment rate is estimated at 40%, while 32% do not have access to primary school education and 26% do not have access to a hospital (World Bank 2009). A particularly alarming aspect of poverty is the continued existence of child labour in many areas of the economy, in particular in the cocoa sector (Déclaration de Berne 2009).

Public health

Côte d'Ivoire is facing tremendous challenges concerning its state of public health. Life expectancy in 2007 was reported at 47.4 years and mortality for children under five years is estimated at 18%, among the highest in the world, and rising. Only 50% of children are fully immunised (UNICEF 2009).

At the end of 2005, an estimated 750,000 Ivoirians were carrying the HIV/AIDS virus and 7.1% of the population aged 15–49 were HIV-positive. Overall, death caused by HIV/AIDS is estimated at 38,000, leading to about 420,000 orphaned children below 17 years of age (UNAIDS 2009). Moreover, malaria is a common disease often leading to death, in particular affecting the poor.

Corruption

Côte d'Ivoire ranks 154 out of 180 countries in the 2009 Corruption Perceptions Index of Transparency International (2009). Daily small-scale corruption is being accompanied by accusations of large-scale corruption in the public as well as in the private sector (e.g. Bakayoko 2009). Recently, chief executives in the cocoa sector were detained on corruption charges for the misappropriation of over USD224 million allocated for the purchase of a chocolate factory in the United States. A particularly problematic form of corruption is racketeering which, according to a World Bank study, costs between USD230 and USD363.3 million annually (World Bank 2008).

▮ Legislation and codes

The legal infrastructure has been oriented towards the French model. Côte d'Ivoire has embraced the antidumping codes of the UEMOA, and has regulatory frameworks for competition, labour and intellectual property. It is also a member of the Organisation Africaine de la Propriété Intellectuelle (OAPI). The government has established particular regulation for the mining and the petrol sector. Côte d'Ivoire also participates in the Cocoa Initiative that aims to certify cocoa production in order to reduce the worst forms of child labour.

The regulation and protection of the environment in Côte d'Ivoire is under the jurisdiction of the Ministry of Housing, Living Conditions, and the Environment. Côte d'Ivoire is party to the international environmental accords on biodiversity, climate change, desertification, endangered species, hazardous wastes, law of the sea, marine dumping, ozone layer protection, ship pollution, tropical timber 83 and 94 and wetlands. It is not a signatory to the Kyoto Protocol.

■ Trends

The discussion on responsible business practices in Côte d'Ivoire is directly related to the discourse on reviving the economy, alleviating poverty and fighting environmental degradation. Economic activity had slowed down tremendously with the outbreak of the hostilities. Foreign direct investment (FDI) mainly from France traditionally accounted for 40–45% of the total capital of Ivoirian firms. However, many French businessmen and corporations left the country because of the conflict. Much of the empty space has been filled by Lebanese businessmen and, more recently, Chinese, Russian and Indian investors.

The Treaty of Ouagadougou, established in March 2007, instilled a new optimism that has revived the Ivoirian economy. Real GDP in 2008 amounted to USD23.5 billion or USD1,132 per capita. Real per capita GDP had fallen by 15% in 2000–2006 but started growing again by 1.6% in 2007 and 2.3% in 2008. For the first time since 1999, private investments grew substantially, in particular in the telecommunication and construction sectors (IMF 2009). For the time being, the business community is awaiting the official end of the hostilities, as well as the elections for a new president. CSR is only a concern for companies that have a reputation in Europe or the United States to defend.

■ Organisations

■ **Institut des Hautes Etudes Africaines (IHE–Afrique).** The institute organises regular seminars and forums for corporate executives on topics such as sustainable development, environmental regulations, corporate responsibility and business ethics. **http:// www.ihe-afrique.org**

■ **Confédération Générale des Entreprises de Côte d'Ivoire (CGECI).** This private sector association has embraced the fight against the pandemic HIV/AIDS and today about 300 companies are involved. They also organise seminars to improve the quality of the work environment of Ivoirian companies. The initiative is officially supported by the government. **http://www.cgeci.org**

■ **Coalition des Entreprises de Côte d'Ivoire contre le VIH/SIDA (CECI).** With around 30 members, this coalition finances studies and provides information, education, technical support and funds for the fight against HIV/AIDS. **http://www.ceci.ci**

■ **CODINORM.** This is a nonprofit national standards and certification body entrusted with the standards of the International Organization for Standardization (ISO). It was jointly established by the private sector and the state on 24 September 1992, and promotes standards such as the new CSR norm ISO 26000. **http://www.iso.org**

■ **UEMOA**. The organisation recently launched the Programme Qualité de l'Afrique de l'Ouest in order to help companies of the member states to improve their quality management, including the application of CSR standards. The purpose is to render them more competitive in world markets. **http://www.uemoa.int**

■ Case studies

SIFCA

SIFCA is the largest company in the agro-industrial domain in West Africa. In 2007, it had 13,000 employees and a turnover of EUR352 million. The group is West Africa's second largest rubber plantation owner and producer, as well as the second largest producer of sugar in Côte d'Ivoire. SIFCA's group-wide CSR strategy mainly focuses on improving living conditions by building housing and a number of group-wide environmental policies. One of the reasons for their CSR engagement is to attract and satisfy European and US investors enquiring about their CSR policies. **http://www.groupesifca.com**

AZITO O&M

AZITO O&M is a US–French joint venture, active in the energy sector with a focus on electrical power production and plant maintenance. The joint venture set up the Azito power plant, which currently produces a power output of 300 MW, representing 39% of Côte d'Ivoire's energy production. According to the company, it is the best-performing energy producer in terms of reliability and capacity in West Africa. AZITO O&M obtained the triple Quality Safety Environment (QSE) certification in December 2003. The company aims to mobilise stakeholder support through multi-stakeholder dialogue in order to contribute to development and be better rooted in local communities (Yameogo 2008). **http://www.azitoenergie.com**

Nestlé

Nestlé is among the largest companies operating in Côte d'Ivoire. Nestlé sources directly from local farmers, 80% of them smallholders. Despite long-standing criticism following its baby-milk formula sales in Africa in the 1980s, the company is committed, through its directive of 'creating shared value', to sustainable cocoa growing through partnership programmes in order to benefit local cocoa and coffee farmers and increase production. Currently, the company is funding a three-year project with three cooperatives of about 3,000 farmers in Côte d'Ivoire, together with the International Cocoa Organisation (ICCO), the International Cocoa Initiative (ICI) and cocoa exporter ECOM. Before this Nestlé also engaged in projects aimed at increasing access to water and water quality. **http://www.nestle.com**

Olam International

Olam International is a Singapore-based global supply chain manager of agricultural products with extensive operations across Africa. The company is one of the top ten operating in Côte d'Ivoire. It has a very pragmatic approach to sustainable development and the creation of economic opportunities. For instance, the company provides low technology solutions, such as cocoa drying facilities powered by solar energy, free of charge to local farmers. They also help by financing warehouses and provide interest-free loans to farmers to help them buy crops. **http://www.olamonline.com**

■ Education

Higher education on CSR-related topics is very limited. Some higher education institutions have integrated the topics of sustainable development, corporate responsibility and business ethics in their curriculum. However, awareness of these offers appears to be low. The two major institutions are:

- **Centre de Recherche et d'Action pour la Paix (CERAP)**. Offers graduate education on corporate governance, sustainable development and business ethics. The Master en Ethique et Gouvernance is the most comprehensive programme available in Cote d'Ivoire. **http://www.cerap-inades.org**

- **International University of Grand Bassam (IUGB)**. Offers undergraduate courses on business ethics, the environment and sustainable development. **http://www.uigb.org**

References

Amnesty International (2008) *Amnesty International Report 2008* (London: Amnesty International).

Bakayoko, L. (2009) 'Côte d'Ivoire: "Affaire 1 milliard détourné au Crou-A": La Direction générale du Budget mise en cause'; **http://fr.allafrica.com/stories/200901220745.html**, accessed 8 February 2009.

Carroll, A.B. (1979) 'A Three-dimensional Conceptual Model of Corporate Performance', *Academy of Management Review* 4.4: 497-505.

Déclaration de Berne (2009) 'Chocolat Suisse: Le Scandale du Travail des Enfants' (Bern, Switzerland: Déclaration de Berne; **http://www.evb.ch/fr/p25015677.html**, accessed 23 March 2010).

Global Witness (2007) 'Hot Chocolate: How Cocoa Fuelled the Conflict in Cote d'Ivoire' (Washington, DC: Global Witness; **http://www.globalwitness.org/media_library_get.php/.../cotedivoire.pdf**, accessed 23 March 2010).

IMF (2008) 'IMF and World Bank Consider Côte d'Ivoire Eligible for Assistance under the Enhanced Heavily Indebted Poor Countries (HIPC) Initiative' (Washington, DC: IMF).

—— (2009) 'IMF executive board approves US$565.7 million PRGF arrangement for Côte d'Ivoire' (Press Release No. 09/96; Washington, DC: IMF, 27 March 2009).

Matten, D., and A. Crane (2005) 'Corporate Citizenship: Towards an Extended Theoretical Conceptualization', *Academy of Management Review* 30.1: 166-179.

Partenariat Afrique Canada (2008) 'Les diamants et la sécurité humaine: Revue Annuelle 2008', Partenariat Afrique Canada; **http://pacweb.org/Documents/annual-reviews-diamonds/AR_diamonds_2009_fr.pdf**, accessed 23 March 2010.

Transparency International (2009) 'Corruption Perceptions Index 2009' (Berlin: Transparency International; **http://www.transparency.org/policy_research/surveys_indices/cpi/2009**, accessed 24 March 2009).

UNAIDS (2009) 'Ivory Coast' (Geneva: UNAIDS).

UNICEF (2009) 'Côte d'Ivoire' (New York: UNICEF).

World Bank (2008) 'The World Bank and Côte d'Ivoire Wage War on Racketeering' (Washington, DC: World Bank).

—— (2009) 'Ivoirian government commits to reducing poverty rate to 16 percent in 2015' (Washington, DC: World Bank).

Yameogo, U.K.-S. (2008) 'Report of the African Case Study: Company and Stakeholder Involvement in Territory Social Development' (Paris: University of Paris XII Val de Marne).

13 Denmark

Tania Ellis
Speaker, writer and social
business consultant, Inspiratorium®

Jonas Eder-Hansen
Research Director, CBS Center for Corporate Social
Responsibility, Copenhagen Business School

■ Context

Social responsibility in a Danish business context is rooted in Nordic values such as equality, trust, flexibility, balance of power, inclusion, respect for nature and a Protestant work ethic.

For the past 50 years Denmark has — along with Sweden and Norway — developed the Scandinavian model (or the Nordic welfare model) characterised by stable labour relations, reforms in working life and an extensive social welfare system with full employment as an absolute objective.

In the second half of the 19th century, the cooperative movement created a new democratic way of organising business and along with that, different kinds of social enterprises and new business models such as self-owned institutions, which provide various public goods under subcontract.

Since then, companies like Grundfos, Lego, Danfoss and Novo Nordisk have built their organisations around a set of strong corporate values based on ethics and responsibility as an inherent way of doing business.

The Danish tradition for social responsibility, along with its welfare concepts, has contributed to Denmark taking the 6th place in world competitiveness, as well as a global leadership position within responsible competitiveness.[1]

The social responsibility of Danish businesses is based on a multi-stakeholder approach, and is played out in a context of strong cross-sectoral interaction between business, society and the state.

Since the early 1990s, the Danish government has been a key driver of formalised

---

1 In 2007 Denmark was ranked 2nd in AccountAbility's Responsible Competitiveness Index (**http://www.accountability.org**), and 6th in IMD's World Competitiveness Yearbook 2008 (**http://www.imd.ch/wcc**).

approaches to CSR. Relying on the European Union (EU) definition of CSR, a fundamental cornerstone has been to base responsibility initiatives on voluntary commitment, and companies, business associations, trade unions, policy-makers and NGOs
have therefore been involved in the design of legislation, regulation, mandatory requirements, and other CSR-related activities.

As a result, there are today formalised dialogues and social partnerships between private companies, state institutions and local councils, as well as civil organisations, in
order to solve fundamental welfare state dilemmas including employment, education,
climate change and health.

Since 1998, the Danish government has promoted social partnerships on a European
scale through international exchange of experience, publications, conferences etc.[2]

∎ Priority issues

Employment: lack of skilled labour

Knowledge-intensive services and information and communication technologies (ICT)
are amongst the most job- and growth-creating industries in the Danish economy
today. Knowledge production is, however, happening at an increasingly rapid pace. This
places new demands on the general educational level and a risk for increased inequality
between the skilled and unskilled labour force.

Therefore, an inclusive labour market strategy, which since the 1990s has been one of
the predominant CSR issues on the Danish welfare agenda, is still predominant. At the
same time, demographic changes (with fewer young people) are also intensifying the
labour shortage, which has put recruitment of talented employees right at the top of the
Danish corporate agenda.

Lately, surveys among the new generation of professionals with a higher education
show that corporate image, social responsibility and the opportunity to make a meaningful difference are factors that play a role in their choice of workplace.

Globalisation: outsourcing, new markets and competitiveness

The Danish manufacturing industry is, to a large extent, dependent on trade with foreign countries. Since 2001, 40% of Danish companies have already moved or outsourced
activities such as manufacturing and procurement to other parts of the world.

Since the mid 1990s, subsidy programmes have also increased the number of Danish
small and medium-sized companies (SMEs) that have entered new markets and partnerships in Africa, Asia and Latin America. Figures from Statistics Denmark show that
SMEs today account for more than 50% of total Danish trade with developing countries
and growth economies.

These factors have contributed to an increased corporate focus on codes of conduct
and CSR guidelines, with particular emphasis on human rights and responsible sourcing. The Danish government has also developed a strategy for Denmark in the global

2 In 1998, the Danish government opened The Copenhagen Centre for corporate responsibility.
In 2007, all activities were transferred to the Danish Government Centre for CSR (**http://www.
csrgov.dk**).

economy, intended, among other things, to help Danish companies incorporate social, ethical and environmental aspects into their business operations, so they can gain competitive advantages in the global market (Danish Government 2006).

Environment: climate change, renewable energy and COP 15

In common with many other countries, Denmark is faced by issues of securing energy supply, global warming and other environmental challenges, for example the preservation of a high degree of biodiversity, protection of ecosystems and efficient use of resources.

Denmark is already one of the world leaders in the use of wind energy sources, and biomass (including waste) is the single most important source of renewable energy. To strengthen a global position on 'green responsibility', the government launched a vision in 2007 for its future climate and energy policies up to the year 2025, including targets for a doubling of renewable energy's share of overall energy consumption and a doubling of public funding for renewable energy technology.

A Danish Ministry of Climate and Energy[3] was established in addition to the already-existing Ministry of the Environment.[4] Key focus areas of the new ministry include ensuring that the United Nations creates an ambitious, binding climate protocol.

■ Trends

From social welfare politics to economic business affairs

Over the past 15–20 years, the Danish CSR agenda has shifted from the ideal of an inclusive labour market in order to decrease public spending to a business discourse focusing on competitiveness and financial growth.

In the 1990s, the Danish welfare model came under pressure due to the fact that almost 25% of the able-bodied population was supported by social benefits. One of the reasons for this was a tendency towards exclusion of socially marginalised people, handicapped, elderly, ethnic minorities and other groups of people, who found it difficult to participate in the labour market.

As a result, an inclusive labour market strategy was launched by the Danish Minister for Social Affairs in 1994 and companies were encouraged to engage in private–public social partnerships and to employ people unable to live up to normal workforce standards.

In 2001, the inclusive labour market agenda was transferred to the Ministry of Employment and since 2004, the Danish Commerce and Companies Agency (DCCA) (today organised as the Danish Centre for Social Responsibility, CenSa), under the Ministry of Economic and Business Affairs, has been promoting the business case for strategic CSR.

The most significant state-driven initiative on strategic CSR has, so far, been the People and Profit campaign in 2005–2007. It offered free CSR conferences and training materials to more than 12,000 managers and employees in Danish SMEs. The strategic CSR

3 http://www.kemin.dk
4 http://www.mim.dk

agenda was promoted even further in 2008, when the Danish government launched its first national Action Plan for Corporate Social Responsibility.

From implicit to explicit CSR

Implicit CSR has been predominant in Denmark for years, i.e. CSR issues have been addressed by mechanisms implicit in the institutional framework for business and are thus state-defined. Many CSR-related issues have therefore already been included in the legal and institutionalised framework in Denmark and CSR practices of Danish companies have traditionally been a question of companies' individual discretion as a response to needs in the local communities.

As a result, two recent Danish CSR surveys (Dansk Erhverv 2008; TNS Gallup 2005) show that the driver for CSR is a combination of ethical and moral reasons along with business rationales ranging from improvement of corporate image, attraction and retention of employees, customer and partner expectations, as well as a positive impact on financial results.

In order to gain full advantage of strategic CSR as a business case, a more systematic and explicit approach to CSR was called for, and new tools for communicating CSR efforts to stakeholders have emerged.

From CSR to CSI

The number one CSR activity in Denmark is employee-related, followed by environmental activities and activities around local community engagement. Socially-oriented products or services already comprise over half of the turnover for the average SME and thereby constitute a potential for significant economic and competitive benefit.

In 2007, a joint Nordic project was launched to focus on CSR as a key innovation driver.[5] The ambition is to develop a systematic approach to CSR-driven innovation (CSI) to make SMEs break new ground on, for example, low-income markets or strengthening competitiveness by linking innovative solutions to key social or environmental problems.

CSI is often the outcome of social entrepreneurs, who have developed either unique business models or hybrid organisations with both for-profit and not-for-profit characteristics. Therefore, the practitioner field of social entrepreneurship in Denmark is now being supported with the government-funded Center for Social Economy[6]

■ Legislation and codes

In Denmark, CSR practices have been promoted and developed with the use of a combination of laws, regulations, collective agreements, mandatory requirements and voluntary practices.

Current Danish legislation covers many CSR-related areas, such as occupational health and safety, environment, and labour relations. Administrative systems and frameworks, including 'social coordination committees' and 'social chapters' have also been devel-

---

5   http://www.csrinnovation.dk
6   http://www.socialokonomi.dk

oped as a kind of 'soft law' for companies and social partners, which they can interpret and put into practice according to the local context.

Additionally, Danish companies may have to comply with the following legal requirements:

- **The Danish Financial Statements Act (2001).** Requires reporting on intellectual capital resources and environmental aspects in management reports, if it is material to providing a true and fair view of the company's financial position

- **The Green Accounts Act (1995, revised in 2001 and 2002).** Requires certain listed companies to draw up green accounts and include statements from the authorities

- **The 'Social Responsibility for Large Businesses' law (2009).** New legislation for mandatory CSR reporting for 1,100 of the largest Danish companies, both listed and state-owned, in their annual financial reports from 2010 onwards

Guidelines, codes and tools have also been developed around national legislation and international declarations and principles for human rights, labour, the environment and anti-corruption. A full overview of principles, guidelines, accounts and reporting can be found in a report by Oxford Research (2003). Some examples include:

- **The Nørby Code for corporate governance.**
  http://www.corporategovernance.dk

- **The Social Index.** http://www.detsocialeindeks.dk

- **Human Rights Compliance Assessment (HRCA).**
  http://www.humanrightsbusiness.org

- **The CSR Compass.** http://www.csrkompasset.dk

- **The Climate Compass.** http://www.klimakompasset.dk

- **People and Profit: A Practical Guide to CSR** (2008).
  http://www.samfundsansvar.dk

- **A Tool for CSR-driven Innovation** (2009). http://www.csrinnovation.dk

∎ Organisations

∎ **Danish Government Centre for CSR.** Develops and communicates knowledge and tools for businesses and other parties with an interest in CSR. **http://www.csrgov.dk**

∎ **Dansk Erhverv (The Chamber of Commerce).** A private business association with 20,000 member companies. Promotes CSR through surveys, publications, network events, etc. **http://www.danskerhverv.dk**

∎ **Dansk Industri (The Confederation of Danish Industry).** A premier lobbying organisation for Danish business on national and international issues, with 11,000 companies as members. Co-developer of CSR-tools and provider of CSR conferences and consultancy. **http://www.di.dk**

▌ Dansk Initiativ for Etisk Handel (DIEH, The Danish Ethical Trading Initiative). Promotes ethical trade and responsible supply chain management, with 30 members from trade unions, business associations, non-governmental organisations (NGOs) and companies. **http://www.dieh.dk**

▌ Det Nationale Netværk af Virksomhedsledere (National Network of Company Leaders. Includes 15 Danish companies that together employ more than 100,000 people. Focuses on creating an inclusive labour market and acting as an advisory board to the Danish Minister for Employment. **http://www.socialtansvar.net**

▌ Green Network. More than 300 companies and public institutions with a focus on greater sustainability in the fields of environment, social commitment and occupational health and safety. **http://www.greennetwork.dk**

▌ Håndværksrådet (DFSME, The Danish Federation of Small and Medium-Sized Enterprises). The main trade organisation for more than 20,000 companies. Offers a CSR newsletter and consultancy services. **http://www.hvr.dk**

▌ LO (The Danish Confederation of Trade Unions). Comprises 17 trade unions; develops strategies and reports on responsible globalisation policies, global labour market efforts, CSR guidelines, etc. **http://www.lo.dk/Englishversion/Home.aspx**

▌ Rådet for Bæredygtig Erhvervsudvikling (RBE, The Danish Council for Sustainable Business Development). Membership includes 15–20 of Denmark's leading companies. **http://www.rbenet.dk**

▌ Rådet for Samfundsansvar (Social Responsibility Council). Set up in 2009 as part of the Danish Action Plan for Social Responsibility; will be making recommendations to the government, the corporate sector and associations. **http://www.samfundsansvar.dk**

▌ Case studies

Grundfos

Grundfos, a major producer of hydraulic pumps, has a long history of a pragmatic approach to societal problems. An example is the establishment of special workshops for people with reduced capacity to integrate minorities from the local community into the workplace, which provides them with a flexible workforce. **http://www.grundfos.com**

Novo Nordisk

Novo Nordisk is a world leader in diabetes care with 20,000 employees in 78 countries. It is part of the CSR major league with top rankings in the Dow Jones Sustainability World Index and integrated sustainability reporting. It has established the World Diabetes Foundation and partnerships with NGOs and many other CSR initiatives. **http://www.novonordisk.com**

Novozymes

Novozymes is a global bio innovation leader with more than 700 products sold in 130 countries. It generates sustainable solutions as an integral part of its business, including optimising raw materials and energy to enable customers become more sustainable, as well as quantifiable targets for optimising waste recycling, minimising environmental impact, etc. **http://www.novozymes.com**

Specialisterne

Specialisterne is the world's first IT company with an affirmative business model built around the skills of people with autistic spectrum disorder (ASD). It is now expanding its business activities internationally and has become a business case at Harvard Business School. **http://www.specialisterne.dk**

∎ Education

Out of the six leading Danish knowledge institutions shown below, the two leading business schools offer the most CSR-related courses.

Copenhagen Business School (CBS) and **Aarhus School of Business**, University of Aarhus (ASB) are the only institutions offering CSR-related degrees. CBS has a Minor in Sustainable Business and a Minor in Social Entrepreneurship, and ASB has a BSc in Sustainability. CBS is the single Danish entry in the *Beyond Grey Pinstripes* ranking[7] (ranked 63 in 2009 [out of 150]). **http://www.cbs.dk   http://www.asb.dk**

Other universities offering CSR-related courses include:

- **Aalborg University**. http://www.aau.dk
- **Roskilde University**. http://www.ruc.dk
- **Technical University of Denmark**. http://www.dtu.dk
- **University of Southern Denmark**. http://www.sdu.dk

References

Danish Government (2006) 'Progress, Innovation, Cohesion: Strategy for Denmark in the Global Economy: Summary'; **http://www.globalisering.dk/multimedia/Pixi_UK_web_endelig1.pdf**, accessed 2 June 2010.

Dansk Erhverv (2008) 'Erhvervslivets Ansvarlighed: Doing Well by Doing Good', **http://www.danskerhverv.dk/Materialer/Sider/Erhvervslivetsansvarlighed.aspx**, accessed 24 March 2010.

Djursø, H.T., and P. Neergaard (eds.) (2006) *Social ansvarlighed: Fra idealisme til forretningsprincip* (Aarhus, Denmark: Academica).

Ellis, T. (2006) *De nye pionerer: Om Sociale Innovatører, Der Skaber Vækst, Værdi Og En Bedre Verden* (Copenhagen: Jyllands-Postens Forlag).

Haisler, P., and A. Holbech (2008) *CSR-ledelse* (Copenhagen: Børsens Forlag).

---

7 http://www.beyondgreypinstripes.org/rankings/participating_schools.cfm

Hockerts, K., M. Morsing, J. Eder-Hansen, P. Krull, A. Midttun, M. Halme, S. Sweet, P. Davidsson, T.O. Sigurjónsson and P. Nurmi (2008) *CSR-Driven Innovation: Towards the Social Purpose Business* (Copenhagen: Danish Commerce and Companies Agency).

Morsing, M., A. Midttun and K. Palmås (2007) 'Corporate Social Responsibility in Scandinavia: A Turn towards the Business Case?', in S. May, G. Cheney and J. Roper (eds.), *The Debate over Corporate Social Responsibility* (London: Oxford University Press): 98-127.

—— and C. Thyssen (eds.) (2003) *Corporate Values and Responsibility: The Case of Denmark* (Frederiksberg, Denmark: Samfundslitteratur).

——, S. Vallentin and S. Hildebrandt (eds.) (2008) *Forretning eller ansvar? Social ansvarlighed i små og mellemstore virksomheder* (Copenhagen: Børsens Forlag).

Oxford Research (2003) 'Survey and Analysis of Tools in Connection with CSR and Sustainability' (Copenhagen: Danish Confederation of Trade Unions; **http://www.ugebreveta4.dk/upload/LO/Documents/S/Survey_and__1125.pdf**, accessed 24 March 2010).

TNS Gallup (2005) 'Mapping of CSR Activities among Small and Medium-sized Enterprises' (People & Profit Phase 2; **http://www.csrgov.dk/graphics/publikationer/CSR/Survey_Gallup.pdf**, accessed 24 March 2010).

Web resources

Danish Government Portal: **http://www.csrgov.dk** — includes all central surveys, reports and publications initiated by the Danish Government.

14 Finland

Arno Kourula

Project Manager, Aalto University School of Economics

■ Context

Finland is a republic in northern Europe with approximately 5.2 million inhabitants and a land area of 340,000 km^2. Life expectancy at birth is about 79 years and Finland faces the challenges of an ageing population. The literacy rate is 100%, the level of education is high and per capita income is among the highest in Western Europe. Finland has a relatively homogeneous population with Swedish speaking, Russian and Sami minorities. The Lutheran Church of Finland counts 82.5% of Finns among its members.

In the first half of the 20th century, Finland was a farm and forest economy. In paper mill communities, companies ran practically all issues related to workers' lives. Since World War II, Finland has made a transformation to a diversified modern industrial economy and built a Nordic welfare state. In this model, public institutions provided a societal safety net for Finns and levelled inequalities. Corporate responsibility for citizens was transferred to the state and municipalities (Juholin 2004; Mäkinen and Kourula 2008). At the same time, the environmental movement was born, pressuring companies to pay attention to ecological issues.

Since the economic recession of the early 1990s, competitiveness has been emphasised and some state structures privatised. The opening of financial markets, increasing internationalisation and privatisation of the energy and telecommunications sectors made room for the rapid growth of an information and communication technology sector lead by Nokia. In the past few years, Finland has ranked among the most competitive economies in the world (Schwab 2009).

In global comparison, the public sector in Finland is quite large despite the above-mentioned privatisation initiatives. Thus, CSR has been largely implicit in nature (Matten and Moon 2008) — the state is assumed to take care of social issues. This is probably the reason for the lack of a strong philanthropy tradition in Finland. Traditionally, tripartite negotiation between the government, companies and unions has borne the responsibility of employee well-being. Currently, many collective agreements are increasingly open to local negotiation, Finland seems to be moving away from tripartite negotiation and unions have lost some influence. This leaves the primary responsibility of employee well-being to companies.

Finland became a member of the European Union (EU) in 1995 and adopted the Euro currency in 1999. Subsequently, Finnish public policy has been linked to the EU vision of CSR as competitiveness and innovation. The attitude towards honesty is a Finnish cultural characteristic — managers rate honesty as the most important value in business life (Kujala 2004). Indeed, in the past few years Finland has been considered to be one of the least corrupt countries according to Transparency International (2009).

∎ Priority issues

Employment practices

When CSR came into Finnish public discussion in the late 1990s and early 2000s, it was mainly the result of relocations of company operations to low-cost countries and related large-scale dismissals. The social impacts, especially employment in Finland, have been a priority issue in the media.

Ethical consumption

Ethical consumption and responsible purchasing with a focus on labour conditions and child labour in foreign countries are issues related to increasing operations in low-cost countries.

Environment and climate change

Climate change and environmental issues are a central part of Finnish CSR (Heiskanen 2004). Finland has large natural resources of forests as well as large multinational forest companies. The biodiversity of Finnish forests, especially in northern Lapland, is a common subject for CSR discussion.

Cultural adaptation

While Finnish companies have increasingly entered foreign markets such as Latin America, Russia and China, they have had to face new and different institutional, cultural and stakeholder environments. These are central CSR issues for Finnish companies.

Competitiveness

Another CSR topic is its strong link to competitiveness, efficiency and innovation. CSR can be seen as a product and service innovation and as a competitive advantage (Loikkanen *et al.* 2007; Teollisuus ja työnantajat 2001).

∎ Trends

In recent years, CSR has grown in importance in the eyes of Finnish companies. Nonetheless, the growth has been gradual and uneven. There are significant differences in their views of CSR depending on company size, industry and markets in which the company operates. The development of CSR has been gradual in the sense that it expanded from quality and environmental management trends towards a more comprehensive understanding of sustainability. The main drivers of CSR have been legislation, increasing stakeholder pressure, the expression of company values and CSR as a competitive advantage (Loikkanen *et al.* 2007). Companies see CSR as a potential competitive advantage, since consumers are increasingly interested in responsibly produced goods.

The perceptions of Finnish managers towards business ethics and CSR became more favourable in the 1990s and honesty was rated as the primary value in business life in a longitudinal study (Kujala 2004). Panapanaan *et al.* (2003) argue that Finnish companies have been relatively progressive in managing CSR. Additionally, Finnish corporate governance practices have also changed dramatically and US and UK practices have been adopted (Liljeblom and Löflund 2006).

Compared with Europe, Finland scores high on sustainability aspects (Midttun *et al.* 2006). For example, Finnish industry scored the highest in terms of sustainability reporting according to Global Reporting Initiative (GRI) guidelines as well as in KPMG's rating (KPMG 2008). A similar rise in the use of explicit value statements and codes of conduct can be seen. Finnish companies have been some of the most active in Europe in becoming members of CSR organisations and networks such as the WBCSD and UN Global Compact.

With respect to socially responsible investment (SRI), Finland is among the front-runners in the FTSE4Good and Dow Jones Sustainability Index. Finally, in terms of adoption of management standards or ISO 14001, Finland is in an upper-medium position in Europe. These developments indicate that explicit CSR (Matten and Moon 2008) has risen quite rapidly in Finland. In the 2007 State of Responsible Competitiveness evaluation by AccountAbility, Finland is in 3rd place globally (AccountAbility 2007).

▌ Legislation and codes

The Finnish government emphasises the voluntary aspect of CSR in its public policy. Originally, CSR seems initially to have been met with quite a lot of scepticism from government representatives. Compared to other Nordic countries, Finnish public policy has not been to promote the country as a CSR frontrunner. Government representatives tend to hold the view that the primary role of the state is to provide a legal framework within which business operates rather than to force CSR activities — and companies have perceived that the most central CSR component is compliance with Finnish law and regulations (Panapanaan *et al.* 2003).

Key pieces of legislation are the Companies Act, **Employment Contracts Act**, **Employment Accidents Act**, social security legislation and extensive legislation on environmental protection (for a review of human rights legislation for businesses, see Pentikäinen 2009). The Finnish **Accounting Act** includes a CSR focus — company financial accounts need to be accompanied by an annual report containing information about personnel and environmental issues that can affect economic performance. In a global context, Finnish environmental and social legislation is rather advanced and relatively well enforced.

There are no prevalent national codes for CSR. Instead, Finnish companies and public authorities have promoted the implementation of global CSR codes, such as the OECD guidelines, UN Global Compact (ten Finnish member companies), ILO principles,

EMAS, ISO standards, and GRI Guidelines for Sustainability Reporting. European Union initiatives have a significant impact on Finnish CSR.

▌ Organisations

▌ **Association for Environmental Management (YJY).** An association founded in 1996 that has about 500 members, promotes environmental management and aims to improve its members' professional competence. **http://www.yjy.fi**

▌ **Central Chamber of Commerce (ICC Finland).** A business network of about 16,000 companies that is involved in the Finnish CSR discussion and hosts the secretariat of the Council of Ethics in Advertising. **http://www.keskuskauppakamari.fi**

▌ **Committee on Social and Corporate Responsibility.** The council has been organised by the Ministry for Employment and the Economy since 2008, and in a earlier format since 2001. It represents several ministries and a broad set of stakeholders (15 representatives) and gives advice and support for CSR-related public policy decision-making. **http://www.tem.fi**

▌ **Confederation of Finnish Industries (EK** formerly **TT).** This organisation represents Finnish business interests (16,000 member companies) and typically emphasises the voluntary and instrumental nature of CSR and its link to competitiveness. **http://www. ek.fi**

▌ **CSR Research Ring.** A network of about 100 researchers (mostly doctoral students) that was founded in 2003 for academics to get to know each other, keep abreast of CSR research in Finland and organise events. **http://www.tse.fi**

▌ **European Business Ethics Network Finland (EBEN Finland).** An association founded in 2008 that promotes the knowledge and appreciation of business ethics, including national and international discussion on related issues and business ethics research. **http://www.eben-net.fi**

▌ **Finnish Business and Society (FiBS).** An enterprise network founded in 2002 that is funded to a large extent by the Ministry for Employment and the Economy. It has about 100 member organisations (mostly companies), is a national partner of CSR Europe and promotes financially, socially and ecologically sustainable business through workshops, seminars and conferences. **http://www.fibsry.fi**

▌ **Finnish Ethical Forum.** This forum, in operation since 2001, brings together representatives of NGOs, trade unions, church organisations, civil servants and companies to discuss CSR-related issues. **http://www.eettinenfoorumi.org**

▌ **Finnish National Commission on Sustainable Development.** This commission was founded in 1993 and promotes multi-stakeholder participation and high-level political leadership in the implementation of sustainable development. It prepared Finland's national strategy for sustainable development, published in 2006. **http://www.ymparisto. fi/default.asp?node=4270&lan=en**

▮ Case studies

Fortum

Fortum is an energy company focusing on the Nordic countries, Russia and the Baltic Rim area. The company generates, distributes and sells electricity and heat and operates and maintains power plants. It has developed advanced CSR principles and worked in climate change mitigation and renewable energy. Fortum is part of the Dow Jones Sustainability Index and was ranked best in class as the most responsible energy company (Storebrand's evaluation report in 2009). **http://www.fortum.com**

Kesko

Kesko is one of the leading providers of trading sector services in Finland. It has published environmental reports since 1997 and sustainability reports since 2000. Its management philosophy includes a strong stakeholder approach and it has been proactive in developing responsible purchasing (through the SA8000 standard and the Business Social Compliance Initiative) and environmental efficiency (especially carbon disclosure, reduction of CO_2 emissions, energy efficiency and recycling processes). Kesko is a signatory of UNGC and part of the Dow Jones Sustainability Index and FTSE4Good. **http://www.kesko.com**

Neste Oil

Neste Oil is a refining and marketing company focusing on advanced traffic fuels. In terms of CSR, the company has been active, among other issues, in the development of sustainable biofuels and renewable diesel. Neste Oil is a part of the Dow Jones Sustainability Index. **http://www.nesteoil.com**

Nokia

Nokia is a global leading telecommunications company based in Finland. Nokia has published a sustainability report since 2002 and has been a CSR industry leader in environmental issues (ranked 1st in a Greenpeace study of electronics manufacturers). The company has developed responsible purchasing practices with suppliers and through industry collaboration. Nokia has a large number of CSR initiatives with various stakeholders such as communities and NGOs. It is part of the Dow Jones Sustainability Index and FT4Good and a signatory to UN Global Compact. **http://www.nokia.com**

▮ Education

CSR-related courses and/or programmes in Finnish Universities (see Vähäkangas and Peltonen 2007) include:

- **Aalto University**. Formed by Helsinki School of Economics, Helsinki University of Technology and University of Art and Design Helsinki in January 2010, it offers major, minor and various courses. Signatory of UN Principles for Responsible Management Education (PRME). **http://www.aalto.fi (http://www.hse.fi; http://www.hut.fi; http://www.uiah.fi)**

- **Hanken School of Economics**. Various courses. Signatory of PRME. **http://www. hanken.fi**

- **Lappeenranta Technical University**. Various courses. **http://www.lut.fi**

- **Turku School of Economics (TSE)**. Minor and various courses. **http://www.tse. fi**

- **University of Jyväskylä**. Major, minor and various courses. *Beyond Grey Pin- stripes* 2009–2010: 48th out of 149 participating universities globally and 8th in Europe.[1] **http://www.jyu.fi**

- **University of Tampere**. Various courses. **http://www.tay.fi**

In addition, the following universities offer a number of CSR-related courses:

- **Åbo Akademi**. **http://www.abo.fi**

- **University of Helsinki**. **http://www.helsinki.fi/yliopisto**

- **University of Joensuu**. **http://www.joensuu.fi/joyindex.html**

- **University of Kuopio**. **http://www.uku.fi**

- **University of Lapland**. **http://www.ulapland.fi**

- **University of Oulu**. **http://www.oulu.fi/yliopisto**

- **University of Vaasa**. **http://www.uwasa.fi**

References

Aaltonen, T., and L. Junkkari (1999) *Yrityksen Arvot ja Etiikka* (*Company Values and Ethics*) (Hel- sinki: WSOY).

AccountAbility (2007) 'The State of Responsible Competitiveness 2007: Making Sustainable Devel- opment Count in Global Markets' (London: AccountAbility)

Finnish Prime Minister's Office (2006) 'Kohti kestäviä valintoja: Kansallisesti ja globaalisti kestävä Suomi' ('Towards Sustainable Choices: Nationally and Globally Sustainable Finland') (Hel- sinki: Prime Minister's Office).

Heiskanen, E. (ed.) (2004) *Ympäristö Ja Liiketoiminta: Arkiset Käytännöt Ja Kriittiset Kysymykset* (*The Environment and Business: Everyday Practices and Critical Questions*) (Helsinki: Gaud- eamus).

Hockerts, K., M. Morsing, J. Eder-Hansen, P. Krull, A. Midttun, M. Halme, S. Sweet, P. Davidsson, T.O. Sigurjónsson and P. Nurmi (2009) *CSR-Driven Innovation: Towards the Social Purpose Busi- ness* (Copenhagen: Nordic Centre for Corporate Responsibility [NCCR]).

Juholin, E. (2004) 'For Business or the Good of All? A Finnish Approach to Corporate Social Respon- sibility', *Corporate Governance* 4.3: 20-31.

Kauppinen, I. (ed.) (2004) *Moraalitalous* (*The Moral Economy*) (Tampere, Finland: Vastapaino).

Ketola, T. (2005) *Vastuullinen liiketoiminta: Sanoista Teoiksi* (*Responsible Business: From Words to Action*) (Helsinki: Edita).

KPMG (2008) 'International Survey of Corporate Responsibility Reporting 2008' (Amstelveen, Netherlands: KPMG).

---

1   http://www.beyondgreypinstripes.org

Kujala, J. (2004) 'Managers' Moral Perceptions: Change in Finland During the 1990s', *Business Ethics: A European Review* 13.2/3: 143-165.

Lehtipuu, P., and S. Monni (2007) *Synergi: Vastuullisen yritystoiminnan menestysmalli (Synergy: A Model of Success for Responsible Business)* (Helsinki: Talentum).

Liljeblom, E., and A. Löflund (2006) 'Developments in Corporate Governance in Finland', *International Journal of Disclosure and Governance* 3.4: 277-287.

Loikkanen, T., K. Hyytinen and S. Koivusalo (2007) *Yhteiskuntavastuu ja kilpailukyky suomalaisyrityksiss: Nykytila ja kehitysnäkymät (Corporate Social Responsibility and Competitiveness in Finnish Corporations: Current State and Development)* (Espoo, Finland: VTT).

Mäkinen, J., and A. Kourula (2008) 'Yritysvastuun politiikkaa' ('The Politics of Corporate Responsibility'), *Niin & Näin* 59.4: 92-101.

Matten, D., and J. Moon (2008). ' "Implicit" and "Explicit" CSR: A Conceptual Framework for a Comparative Understanding of Corporate Social Responsibility', *Academy of Management Review* 33.2: 404-424.

Midttun, A., K. Gautesen and M. Gjølberg (2006) 'The Political Economy of CSR in Western Europe', *Corporate Governance* 6.4: 369-385.

Panapanaan, V.M., L. Linnanen, M.-M. Karvonen and V.T. Phan (2003) 'Roadmapping Corporate Social Responsibility in Finnish Companies', *Journal of Business Ethics* 44.2/3: 133-148.

Pentikäinen, M. (2009) 'Yritystoiminta ja ihmisoikeudet' ('Business and Human Rights') (Erik Castrén Research Reports 26/2009, Helsinki, Finland: Helsinki University).

Rohweder, L. (2004) *Yritysvastuu: Kestävää kehitystä organisaatiotasolla (Corporate Responsibility: Sustainable Development at the Organizational Level)* (Porvoo, Finland: WSOY).

—— (2008) *Kasvaminen globaaliin vastuuseen: Yhteiskunnan toimijoiden puheenvuoroja (Growing towards Global Responsibility: Addresses from Societal Actors)* (Helsinki: Ministry of Education).

Schwab, K. (ed.) (2009) 'The Global Competitiveness Report 2009–2010' (Davos, Switzerland: World Economic Forum).

Storebrand (2009) 'Best in Class: Environment and Social Performance Index' (Lysaker, Norway: Storebrand; available at **http://www.fortum.com**).

Takala, T. (1991) *Managerial Beliefs Concerning Social Responsibility of the Firm* (Jyväskylä, Finland: University of Jyväskylä).

Teollisuus ja työnantajat (2001) *Yrityksen Yhteiskuntavastuu: Työvälineitä itsearviointiin ja oman toiminnan kehittämiseen (Corporate Social Responsibility: Tools for Self-assessment and Development)* (Helsinki: Confederation of Finnish Industries; **http://www.ek.fi/arkisto/ekarchive/20010124-144202-178.pdf**, accessed 24 March 2010).

Transparency International (2009) 'Corruption Perceptions Index 2009' (Berlin: Transparency International).

Vähäkangas, A., and T. Peltonen (2007) *Etiikan asema liikkeenjohdon opetuksessa ja koulutuksessa Suomessa: Opintorakenteet, oppisisällöt ja motiivit (Ethics in Management Education and Training in Finland: Curriculum, Content and Motives)* (Oulu, Finland: Oulu University).

15 Germany

Nick Tolhurst
Managing Director, Institute for Corporate Culture Affairs

Aron Embaye
Project Manager, Institute for Corporate Culture Affairs

▮ Context

A historical perspective

The Federal Republic of Germany with its 82 million inhabitants is the most populous country among the member states of the European Union (EU) and the third largest economy in the world.

Long before the emergence of CSR as a world-wide phenomenon, the idea that business has duties to society has always occupied a central place in political and philosophical debates in Germany. Germany has also played a crucial role in the development of modern western religion, as it was the birthplace of Martin Luther and the Protestant Reformation — an episode that has had profound effects on the development of modern capitalism. At the other extreme, socialistic thinking owes much to German thinkers including, among others, Karl Marx.

Some of the features that define current CSR thinking in Germany can be traced back to the early stages of industrialisation in Germany. Even before the introduction of a state-centred welfare system by Chancellor Otto von Bismarck at the end of the 19th century, many German businesses were providing social benefits for their employees and local communities.

For example, the Fugger family, the German mercantile and banking dynasty that dominated European business during the 15th and 16th centuries, is widely known for establishing numerous pious and charitable foundations that served the poor and elderly. Similarly, the entrepreneur Robert Bosch was one of the first entrepreneurs in Germany to introduce the eight hour working day in 1906. Similarly, company histories of Faber Castell AG, ThyssenKrupp AG, Volkswagen AG and many others show a deeply rooted culture of social engagement.

More recently, the social market economy, which Germany adopted as its economic model after the Second World War, combines the principle of a free market economy with social justice. The model depends on a shared responsibility of the public and private sectors and allows for participation of labour organisations in business decision-making.

German companies are still distinguished by the high proportion of family owned entities, many of which are not traded on the stock exchange and still exist within the town where the company was originally founded. Such historical embeddedness and nearness to community often creates a strong multi-generational bond between management, owners and workers.

The contemporary CSR model

The traditional German culture of corporatism — with its high level of regulation — still defines the country's economic, industrial and social frameworks. In this regard, various aspects of CSR, such as businesses relations with its employees and the wider community, are well defined. However, change in societal values and expectations, as well as reputation and image-based competition, have compelled many German companies to augment their traditional role with new social and environmental initiatives in their local constituencies.

On the global stage, the increased prominence of CSR both as a norm and a competitive strategy has led big German corporations to adopt a proactive approach to CSR. On a regional level, the EU's view of CSR as a source of competitiveness, entrepreneurial innovation and economic development, together with its various environmental and social laws, are defining the CSR approach of German companies.

▌ Priority issues

In Germany, labour issues, consumer rights, sustainability and environmental concerns are well integrated into the law. Moreover, the social market economy provides ample scope for various business initiatives that can be viewed in the light of CSR. The four CSR priority areas identified by the German Federal Ministry of Labour and Social Affairs are participation, good work, consumer information and environment.

Saving the tradition of participation

The traditional German system of participatory decision-making — known as *mitbestimmungen* — ensured that workers were fairly treated and had a direct say in how their companies were run. This system still exists but is weakening. Among other things, membership in unions is decreasing and more employers are withdrawing from the employers' association — the body that works as a negotiator between labour and management. A recent rise in the number of people employed part-time, as interns, in the shadow economy or outside normal tariff agreements can be seen in relation to the weakening of the traditional system. This issue is already stimulating debates, as can be seen in recent discussions about a minimum wage for Germans.

'Good work' to tackle social problems

The CSR issues that fall under the 'Good Work' category include fair treatment of employees, focus on reconciling family and work life, promoting diversity and giving the young and old an opportunity.

The need to focus on family and work life can be seen in relation to demographic changes in Germany. With a fertility rate of 1.37 children per mother, Germany has one of the lowest birth rates in the world; hence, the German Federal Statistics Office estimates that the population will shrink from 69 to 74 million by 2050. At the same time, with an increased life expectancy, the average age of retirement in Germany has been raised to 67 years. Hence, the work place should accommodate the needs of older employees.

The issue of diversity and opening of opportunity for various groups in society such as women and immigrants is also stimulating a lot of debate, as Germany has one of the highest gender pay gaps in Europe. The average gross hourly earnings of German women are 77% of men's in the public sector and 73% in the private sector. Furthermore, German women are only half as likely as men to hold managerial positions.

Simultaneously, as the traditional power of the unions wanes, the gap between the rich and the poor is growing. With stagnant wages for low-income families and few opportunities for social mobility, there are increasing poverty levels.

As the traditional welfare system is facing increased financial and capacity limitations to satisfy all the needs of the society, there are high expectations for the German private sector to play an important role in dealing with all these important issues.

Consumer information

As in many other parts of the world, ethical consumerism is growing in Germany. For example, according to market research group GfK NOP (GfK Viewpoint 2008), German consumers would pay a 5–10% price premium for many ethical products (similar to consumers in France, UK, US and Spain). Labour standards, human rights, health and safety standards, environmental concerns, animal welfare and corruption are among the most important issues for German ethical consumers. As customers, consumer lobby groups, government agencies and members of civil society organisations continue to demand information on how companies operate, German enterprises will continue to focus on making transparency a major part of their CSR strategy.

Environment

The environmental movement became a social and political force in Germany in the 1970s and the country has a very strong Green Party. In relation to the EU's recent far-reaching legislation on climate change and renewable energy, Germany is expected to take various measures to meet the environmental targets set by the Commission. In this regard, the focus on the environment will remain a major priority for German companies.

Globalisation

Germany has many companies that are considered 'heavyweights' in global markets. Hence, CSR issues such as ethical supply chain management, fair trade and observation of international standards will continue to be among the priorities for Germany companies.

▮ Trends

Awareness of CSR

According to the CSR survey of the top 500 companies in Germany (Riess and Peters 2005), the CSR agenda is a matter of high importance for most companies. For example, 93% of large companies emphasised CSR as one of their primary objectives. The 500 survey participants reported that they feel responsible primarily to their customers (97%), their employees (96%) and to owners, or more specifically shareholders (88%). The majority of the surveyed companies indicated their rejection of the idea of corporations as pure profit maximisers. On future developments in CSR, 67% indicated that companies' commitment to, and engagement with, CSR would continue to gain in importance.

CSR reporting

Another important trend in the German business world is CSR reporting, and 150 companies were surveyed by the Institute for Ecological Economy Research (IÖW) and Future e.V. (2007) (see Table 15.1).

Table 15.1 CSR reporting in Germany

Issue	Companies surveyed
Report on sustainability issues available	38%
Report from international parent company available	16%
Relevant information available in the annual report or on the internet	13%
Site-based or topic-based pamphlet available	4%
Information only on limited topics available in the annual report or on the internet	4%
Very limited information available in the annual report or on the internet	10%
No information available	16%

The survey also indicated that an increasing number of German companies are moving towards online reporting.

CSR standards

Most CSR standards and guidelines, such as the Global Reporting Initiative (GRI) guidelines, UN Global Compact principles, ISO standards and OECD Guidelines, are widely known in Germany. The German Global Compact Network, for example, currently has 103 company participants and around 60% of the Dax 30 companies are members of the Global Compact. According to the 2007 CSR reporting survey cited above, many German companies report being 'in accordance' with the GRI guidelines or have reports based on the guidelines. A close examination of the CSR reports of large German companies also shows their listing in various sustainability indexes such as the Dow Jones Sustainability Index, FTSE4Good Index and Domini 400 Social Index.

■ Legislation and codes

In line with the basic definition of CSR adopted by the EU, CSR is generally understood as a voluntary commitment in Germany. For example, the German Federal Ministry of Labour and Social Affairs defines CSR as being 'about enterprises and other organisations and institutions shouldering voluntary social responsibility beyond and above compliance with their legal obligations'.

However, there are also various laws and codes which promote the adoption of CSR by companies, including:

- **The German tax system**. Donations can be deducted from duties if the recipient is a charitable organisation.

- **Investment criteria for pension funds**. Germany has a law that obliges investment (predominantly pension) funds to disclose the extent to which social, environmental and ethical criteria are accounted for in their investment policy.

- **German Council for Sustainable Development**. Established in April 2001, its task is to promote sustainability as an issue for public discussion and to support the German government in all matters of sustainability.

- **The Round Table on corporate codes of conduct**. The German government established this round table, which aims to improve labour and social standards in developing countries through codes of conduct.

- **Internationally recognised codes of conducts**. The German government also supports many of the codes of conduct developed by various intergovernmental organisations such as OECD, ILO, UN Global Compact and the Equator Principles.

■ Organisations

■ **Bertelsmann Stiftung (Bertelsmann Foundation)**. Projects and publications on CSR, corporate culture and philanthropy. **http://www.bertelsmann-stiftung.org**

■ **Centre for Corporate Citizenship (CCC)**. Conducts interdisciplinary research on strategic corporate citizenship. **http://www.corporatecitizen.de**

■ **Deutsches Netzwerk Wirtschaftsethik (DNWE, German Business Ethics Network)**. CSR publications, events and dialogue. **http://www.dnwe.de**

■ *Forum Nachhaltig Wissenschaften* (*Forum* **Magazine**). The leading CSR publication in Germany, appearing quarterly. **http://www.forum-csr.net**

■ The **Federal Ministry for Economic Cooperation and Development (BMZ)**. Offers CSR guidance, publications, events and dialogue. **http://www.bmz.de**

■ The **German Federal Ministry of Labour and Social Affairs**. Responsible for CSR within the German government. **http://www.bmas.de**

■ **Institute for Corporate Culture Affairs (ICCA)**. A CSR networking, research and consultancy organisation. **http://www.cca-institute.org**

■ **Öko-Institut e.V. (The Öko-Institute)**. Does sustainability-oriented projects and research. **http://www.oeko.de**

■ **Wissenschaftszentrum Berlin für Sozialforschung (WZB, Social Science Research Center Berlin)**. Conducts basic social science research and interdisciplinary research on CSR. **http://www.wzb.eu**

■ Case studies

The BASF Group

BASF is one of the world's leading chemical companies, located in Ludwigshafen, Germany. The company has a sustainability strategy that integrates social and ecological issues into its business processes, which helps the company in opening up new business areas and securing its economic success in the long term. Among other things, BASF's sustainability development strategy comprises: climate protection, energy efficiency, occupational health and safety, education and sustainable investment. In the 2007 Good Company Ranking, BASF was voted Europe's most socially responsible firm. **http://www.basf.com**

Betapharm Arzneimittel GmbH

Betapharm is a medium-sized pharmaceutical company headquartered in Augsburg, Germany. The company was founded in 1993. Despite its youth, the company is considered as one of the CSR pioneers in Germany and carries out its CSR engagements in various directions. The company's foundation — the Betapharm Stiftung — focuses on helping chronically ill children and engages in prevention-oriented measures in kindergartens. The company's Beta Institute focuses on various health-related research activities and various social projects. Recently, the Beta Institute's Papilio Project won the 2008 'Active for Democracy and Tolerance' prize — an award organised by the German Ministries of Internal Affairs and Justice. **http://www.betapharm.de**

Henkel AG & Co. KgaA

Henkel is an international company headquartered in Düsseldorf, Germany. The company operates in three business areas: home care, personal care and adhesives, and sealants and surface treatment for consumer and industrial purposes. Henkel's CSR strategy tackles sustainability challenges in five areas: energy and climate, water and wastewater, materials and waste, health and safety, and social progress. The American Business Magazine *Fortune* gave Henkel the first place as Germany's most admired company in its issue of 16 March 2009. **http://www.henkel.com**

▌ Education

Education on business ethics and corporate governance are well established in German universities. However, teaching of CSR as a stand-alone degree programme is yet to develop. Below is the list of some exemplary universities which offer CSR courses as part of their curriculum and conduct CSR-related research:

- **Humboldt-Universität zu Berlin (Humboldt University of Berlin).** Besides many courses related to CSR, the University has its own biannual CSR conference which is the largest academic conference in its field in Europe. **http://lehre. wiwi.hu-berlin.de/Professuren/bwl/management**

- **Katholische Universität Eichstätt-Ingolstadt (Catholic University of Eichstätt-Ingolstadt).** The University offers an MBA with a focus on corporate responsibility, and combines broad general management studies with CSR-specific management training. **http://www.ku-eichstaett.de**

- **Ludwig-Maximilians-Universität-München (University of Munich).** The University specialises in CSR as social capital and incorporates the influence of ethical behaviour on a company's success and value, as well as the measurement of CSR, analysis of drivers and impacts of CSR and its relation to corporate reputation. **http://www.uni-muenchen.de**

References

GfK Viewpoint (2008) 'Consumers and Ethical Expenditure', GfK; **http://www.gfknop.com/imperia/md/ content/gfk_nop/financial/onthehorrizon/viewpoint_ethicalbranding.pdf**, accessed 2 November 2009.
Institute for Ecological Economy Research (IÖW) and future e.V. (2007) 'Sustainability Reporting in Germany, 2007: Results and Trends in the Ranking 2007'; **http://www.ranking-nachhaltigkeitsberichte. de/pdf/2007/Ranking_2007_Report_English.pdf**, accessed 5 November 2009.
Riess, B., and A. Peters (2005) 'Corporate Social Responsibility. Management Summary. Survey of 500 Top German Companies' (Gütersloh, Germany: Bertelsmann-Stiftung; **http://www. bertelsmann-stiftung.de/cps/rde/xbcr/SID-779316C4-5AAFF60D/bst_engl/excecutive%20summary_ engl._final.pdf**, accessed 24 March 2010).

16 Ghana

Daniel F. Ofori
Head of Department of OHRM at the
University of Ghana Business School

▌ Context

Although CSR took root in Ghana in the mid 1950s, fragments could already be found in 1939, when the National Liberation Council (NLC) government investigated cases of corruption in Ghana. Literature on CSR in Ghana is still evolving as research attempts are being made to understand the nature and form of CSR in Ghana and the entire West African region.

There are no Ghana-specific CSR models. Research suggests that in Ghana CSR concepts are played out in the education, health, community development, sports and philanthropic areas (Ofori 2005, 2006; 2007, 2009; Ofori and Hinson 2007; Ofori and Ofori 2009). Ghana CSR activities broadly follow Carroll's (1979) and more recently, BSR's (2004) model which define CSR from four dimensions: economic, legal, ethical and discretionary. However, it is evident that in Ghana, a lot of philanthropic actions are executed under the discretionary mode (Visser *et al.* 2006).

▌ Priority issues

Environment

The mining industry in particular has significant environmental impacts in Ghana. In one case, Bogoso Gold Mines Ltd were ordered by the Environmental Protection Agency (EPA) to cease operations immediately because the company's operations violated Environmental Impact Assessment (EIA) procedures and regulations (Kwarteng 2005).

Occupational health and safety

This issue applies to the extractive sector, as well as industry in general. In one serious case, Diamond Cement Ghana Ltd began negotiations with communities in its eastern catchment area with a view to resettling them as compensation for the health hazards they are exposed to from cement dust pollution.

Socioeconomic development

In Ghana efforts are being geared towards the provision of free and compulsory education. In 2006 schools in Ghana saw a 16.6% increase in enrolment of school children, totalling more than 616,000 pupils. The northern part of the country experienced the largest increase. This national increase in school enrolment has led to the need for more teachers and classrooms. The poverty level in Ghana is 28% (2005/6) of the population (23.3 million) with a GDP growth rate of 3.7%. In 2009, Ghana ranked 152nd out of 182 countries on the UN Human Development Index.

Governance and corruption

Transparency International ranks Ghana 69th out of 180 countries on their Corruption Perceptions Index (where 1st is the least corrupt) (see South Africa 2 Day 2009).

∎ Trends

The CSR activities of Ghanaian firms have straddled several divides. Ofori (2006) suggests that a cursory glance at recent company actions reveals a somewhat haphazard indulgence in corporate good works by local firms.

Ofori and Hinson (2007) sampled companies in the Ghana Club 100, comparing the adoption of social responsibilities by internationally connected firms in Ghana with those of the indigenous Ghanaian firms. They found that the internationally connected companies are more strategic, moral and ethical in their approach to CSR. Both groups of companies concentrated on a few select areas: education, safety, environmental damage, healthcare, consumer protection and philanthropy.

Ofori (2007) also examined the perception, nature, type and extent of CSR activity among firms on the Ghana Stock Exchange. He noted that listed firms in Ghana are more alive to their societal obligations and responsive to all the concerns of their major stakeholders than their unlisted counterparts.

A recent (2005) African Peer Review Mechanism (APRM) report of the African Union pointed out the need to clarify the concept of CSR in Ghana and make efforts to bring the full import of the concept to all stakeholders, especially government, corporations, communities and civil society organisations.

A report from the Friedrich Ebert Foundation (FES) (2009) also recommended that a CSR policy be developed for Ghana and that the laws that regulate the various sectors of the economy (and aspects of social life) in Ghana be amended to include specific CSR provisions. The report further stated: 'It is recommended that modalities be put in place to ensure some measure of enforcement of business and professional codes of ethics by external stakeholders in order to improve CSR in the country', and 'It recommends that regulatory institutions include in their regulatory efforts, definitive efforts at facilitating the formation and supporting of the activities of CSR advocacy groups.'

The most recent CSR work in Ghana by Ofori (2009) suggests a high degree of awareness by firms of the rationale for and importance of CSR, as well as an appreciation of the place of CSR in business and society. However, this is tempered by the fact that Ghanaian firms' CSR approaches sometimes appear to be haphazardly rather than strategically undertaken. The study also showed that some Ghanaian companies pay heed to global CSR agreements such as the UN Global Compact, while others follow local Ghanaian initiatives, for example the Ghana Business Code. Firms' CSR approaches are based on several generalised CSR concepts, with major rationales for CSR being to improve the image of the business and engaging in socioeconomic development of key stakeholders through initiatives in education and health.

The Deutsche Gesellschaft für Technische Zusammenarbeit (GTZ) GmbH (2009) Sub-Saharan CSR study noted that CSR in Ghana will in the future need to be more closely correlated to firms' core business and concentrated on longer-term projects that include cross-sector partners, the provision of more resources and expansion of intervention areas. The report also proposed the development of industry association codes of practice in CSR that are benchmarked against international best practices, the empowerment of public institutions to enable them to perform better, CSR enforcement and the creation of a CSR Index of Ghanaian firms.

▌ Legislation and codes

There is no comprehensive CSR policy or law in Ghana. Rather there is a variety of social and environmental policies and laws that together provide the CSR framework. In addition, the following voluntary initiatives are significant:

- **The Ghana Business Code.** A 10-point voluntary code aligned to the UN Global Compact addressing human rights, labour standards, the environment, anti-corruption and ethical business practices. The Code's founding members include: the Association of Ghana Industries (AGI), Ghana National Chamber of Commerce and Industries (GNCCI) and Ghana Employers Association (GEA), with support from the Improving Business Practice (IBP) sub-component of the DANIDA-funded Business Sector Programme Support (BSPS). **http://www. ghanabusinesscode.com**

- **The African Peer Review Mechanism (APRM).** Although not strictly a CSR code, this an organ of the African Union that has encouraged the practice of CSR. For instance, the APRM (2005) report stated: 'It is recommended to clarify the concept of CSR in Ghana and make efforts to bring the full import of the concept to all stakeholders especially government, corporations, communities and CSOs.' **http://www.aprm.org.za**

▌ Organisations

▌ Consultancy within Engineering, Environmental Science and Economics (COWI). Operates with a goal of improving business practice in Ghana and developed a code based on the UN Global Compact — The Ghana Business Code — in 2006. **http://www. cowi.com**

▌ Corporate Social Responsibility Movement (CSRM). Formed in 2001, CSRM advocates for organisations to be socially responsible, especially with respect to protecting the environment. **http://www.revitalization.org**

■ **The Ghana Chamber of Mines (GCM)**. The Chamber represents the interests of companies involved in mineral exploitation in Ghana. It was established in 1928 and seeks to ensure that its members are honest, transparent and good corporate citizens. **http://www.ghanachamberofmines.org**

■ **The Ghana Club 100 (GC 100)**. This is a system of ranking the top 100 companies, which was introduced by the Ghana Investment Promotion Centre in 1997. The expectation is that ranking criteria reflect the development goals of the country. One of these criteria (with a 10% weighting) is to have engaged in CSR, including responding to health concerns, education, poverty alleviation, environmental concerns, issues relating to the socially vulnerable and contribution to sports development. The 2009 objectives of the ranking include the development of a uniform basis for assessing CSR of Ghanaian enterprises. **http://www.gipc.org.gh** and **http://www.investinghana.org**

■ **The Ghana National Chamber of Commerce and Industry (GNCCI)**. GNCCI was established in 1961 to promote and protect the commercial and industrial interests of companies in Ghana. One of its core activities is the policy, lobbying and representation of the business community in Ghana. **http://www.ghanachamber.org**

■ **Third World Network-Africa (TWN)**. This is a research and advocacy organisation established in 1994 to promote the protection of the rights of marginalised social groups. It also undertakes capacity building, networking with various civil society groups and lobbying for government policies on development and environmental protection issues. **http://www.twnafrica.org**

■ **Voluntary Workcamps Association of Ghana (VOLU)**. VOLU is an NGO that organises work camps with the aim of helping poor communities and learning more about African and Ghanaian culture. VOLU support the construction of schools, reforestation and the organisation of AIDS campaigns. **http://www.volunteerafrica.org**

■ **WACAM Association of Communities Affected by Mining**. WACAM is an NGO formed in 1983 and is committed to creating networks for protecting the environment, natural resources and the rights of mining communities (especially gold mining). It achieves its mission through advocacy, campaigns and representation of community concerns. **http://www.wacamghana.com**

■ Case studies

ABL SABMiller

ABL SABMiller's sustainable corporate social investment (CSI) focuses on the positive transformation and uplifting of communities by supporting education, health and social development. ABL has established a corporate accountability and risk assurance committee (CARAC) that manages and monitors its social and accountability issues. ABL strives to ensure that its work benefits as many people as possible and is guided by its core values and principles. **http://www.sabmiller.com**

Barclays Bank Ghana (BBGL)

Barclays Ghana was established in 1917. In 2003, the bank signed on to the Equator Principles, which guide project investment in managing social and environmental impacts. In 2008, the bank held a seminar for market traders with a view to fostering inclusive banking. **http://www.barclays.com/africa/ghana**

Ghana Commercial Bank (GCB)

The Ghana Commercial Bank Ltd was established in 1953. To improve its ability to meet the expectations of its customers and shareholders, the bank makes an effort to invest in information technology that improves the efficiency of its operations. To enable its CSR investment, GCB has created a special account from which it makes periodic contributions towards education, health and sports. **http://www.gcb.com.gh**

Multichoice Africa (MCA)

MCA views CSI as a good strategy for maintaining corporate reputation, brought about by positive and proactive stakeholder relations. MCA embraces the triple bottom line approach of economic, environmental and social performance and seeks to leverage its assets and expertise for the development and growth of communities where it operates throughout Africa. **http://www.dstvafrica.com**

UT Financial Services Ltd (UTFSL)

UT was established in 1997 and endorses the concept of CSR as 'the commitment of business to contribute to sustainable economic development — working with employees, their families, the local community and society at large to improve the quality of life, in ways that are both good for business and good for development'. **http://www. utfinancialservices.com**

■ Education

At the time of writing, there were no CSR-related degrees and courses offered by any universities in Ghana. The Improving Business Practice (IBP) project has however partnered the University of Ghana Business School, Legon, to create a course on CSR and the Ghana Business Code for both undergraduate and postgraduate business students in Ghanaian universities. The plan is for this course to be introduced in Ghanaian schools from the 2009/2010 academic year.

References

APRM (African Peer Review Mechanism) (2005) 'Country Review Report of the Republic of Ghana'; **http://aprm.krazyboyz.co.za/index.php?option=com_aprm_documents&Itemid=32&page=documents-category&cid=25&nid=21&id=21**, accessed 2 June 2010.

Atuguba, R., and E. Dowuona-Hammond (2006) 'CSR in Ghana' (report submitted to Friedrich Ebert Foundation [FES]; Accra, Ghana: FES).

Boon, E.K., and F. Ababio (2008) 'Corporate Social Responsibility in Ghana: Lessons from the Mining Sector', International Association for Impact Assessment conference proceedings; http://www.iaia.org/iaia09ghana/documents/cs/CS4-1_Boon&Ababio_CSR_in_Ghana.pdf, accessed 25 March 2010.

BSR (Business for Social Responsibility) (2004) 'Introduction', in P. Kotler and N. Lee, *Corporate Social Responsibility: Doing the Most for Your Company and Your Cause* (New Jersey: John Wiley).

Carroll, A.B. (1979) 'A Three-dimensional Conceptual Model of Corporate Performance', *Academy of Management Review* 4.4: 497-505.

FES (Friedrich Ebert Foundation) (2009) 'CSR in Sub-Saharan Africa 2009' (Accra, Ghana: FES).

Ghana Stock Exchange (1999) 'Listing Requirements' (Accra, Ghana: Ghana Stock Exchange).

GTZ (Deutsche Gesellschaft für Technische Zusammenarbeit) GmbH (2009) 'Corporate Social Responsibility in Sub-Saharan Africa: A Survey on Promoting and Hindering Practice' (Pretoria, South Africa: Deutsche Gesellschaft für Technische Zusammenarbeit [GTZ] GmbH).

Kwarteng, K.E. (2005) 'Close down operations: EPA orders Bogoso Gold', *Graphic Ghana*, 29 September 2005; http://www.minesandcommunities.org/article.php?a=630, accessed 25 March 2010.

LaVerle, B. (ed.) (1995) *Government and Politics: A Country Study. Ghana* (Washington, DC: Federal Research Division, Library of Congress).

New Partnership for Africa's Development (NEPAD) (2005) 'Africa Peer Review Mechanism (APRM) Republic of Ghana, Country Self Assessment', January 2005; http://aprm.krazyboyz.co.za/index.php?option=com_aprm_documents&Itemid=32&page=documents-category&cid=25&id=21, accessed 2 June 2010.

Ofori, D. (2005) 'Book review of *Best Practices in Poverty Reduction* by E. Oyen *et al.* (eds)', *Democracy & Development: Journal of West African Affairs* 5.1: 135-138.

—— (2006) 'Business' Corporate Social Responsibility: Theory, Opinion and Evidence from Ghana', *African Journal of Business and Economic Research* 1.2/3: 11-40.

—— (2007) 'Corporate Social Responsibility, Myth, Reality or Empty Rhetoric: Perspectives from the Ghana Stock Exchange', *African Finance Journal* 9.2: 53-68.

—— and R. Hinson (2007) 'Corporate Social Responsibility (CSR) Perspectives of Leading Firms in Ghana', *Corporate Governance: The International Journal of Business in Society* 15.1: 60-72.

—— and T.A. Ofori (2009) 'Modelling Appropriate Corporate Social Responsibility (CSR) Behaviour in the Gold Mining Sector: Cases from Ghana', paper presented at the *36th AIB Conference*, University of Glasgow, Glasgow, UK, 2–4 April 2009.

—— (2009) 'Corporate Social Responsibility in Ghana: Promoting and Hindering Practice', in *Corporate Social Responsibility in Sub-Saharan Africa: A Survey on Promoting and Hindering Practice* (Pretoria, South Africa: Deutsche Gesellschaft für Technische Zusammenarbeit [GTZ] GmbH).

South Africa 2 Day (2009) 'Ghana among the least corrupt nations', GMRI Afrikalink, 21 November 2009; http://southafrica2day.com/index.php?option=com_content&task=view&id=516&Itemid=1, accessed 2 June 2010.

Visser, W., M. McIntosh and C. Middleton (eds.) (2006) *Corporate Citizenship in Africa: Lessons from the Past; Paths to the Future* (Sheffield, UK: Greenleaf Publishing).

17 Greece

Kiara Konti
Senior, Ernst & Young

▐ Context

The concept of responsibility, since Aristotle first tried to give a systematic account, has ramified and developed throughout the years. Interestingly enough, an etymological perspective sheds some light on both modern Greek CSR appreciation, as well as CSR links to ancient Greece. The English term 'responsible' derives from the Latin *respondēre*, to respond, in the sense of answering questions about one's actions and explaining them in a moral context. In its turn, *respondēre* comes from the Latin *spondēre* (past particle of *spondeo*) which means 'to pledge, to promise', from the Greek word *spondē* (*spondee*), a 'solemn libation'. In this context, the Greek connotation of responsibility goes beyond that of most modern European languages, and relates both to 'responding' as mentioned above, as well as to 'blame', 'burden' and 'charge'. Consequently, one could argue, the appreciation of the concept of CSR in Greece has to some extent been influenced by this dual connotation which can perhaps most effectively be demonstrated by the existence of two different Greek words for the single English term 'responsibility'.

Although global discussions and debates concerning the roots of CSR are expectedly many and long, the existence of CSR links to ancient Greece are well established and reach beyond the etymological links to *spondee*. Eberstadt (1977) argues that practices of CSR date back to ancient Greece and that today's corporate responsibility movement is an attempt to restore a 2,000-year-old tradition of businesses being connected to the community. In this context, perhaps the most characteristic link of modern CSR to ancient Athens is the institution of the *choregia*, the ancient form of sponsorship. (Interestingly enough, the word 'sponsor' also derives from the Latin *spondēre*, as mentioned above). *Choregia* was one of the four liturgies, a system that privately provided public goods, and was perceived as a duty of wealthy Athenians arranged at their own expense. This ancient form of sponsorship may not reflect what CSR is today, but it nevertheless demonstrates a historic link that has in one way or another affected the way that Greeks perceive the interdependence between public and private wealth, the consequent role of the corporation in society, as well as the choices of Greek organisations in order to demonstrate that role.

■ Priority issues

Environmental issues

Environmental issues connected to both illegal and legal landfills are a challenge for Greece. In 2008, there were 2,108 dumps operating illegally, although this was reportedly reduced to around 400 in 2009.

Another environmental issue is Greece's dependency on fossil fuels, especially lignite. Lignite is responsible for high levels of local air pollution, as well as contributing to climate change. The largest lignite centre is located in northern Greece in the Ptolemais–Amyntaion district and comprises 16 units with a total capacity of 4,050 MW. Most of these power units were installed during the 1970s and early 1980s and are using old and highly polluting technologies.

Wildfires, which have been afflicting Greece for decades, also represent one of the top environmental issues for the country. According to the Greek chapter of the WWF, the amount of land burned in the wildfires of August 2007, the worst fire season on record in the past 50 years, was 5% of the whole country.

According to the newspaper *Kathimerini* (2007), more than 750 factories dump their waste into the Asopos River, in central Greece's Viotia region. The drinking water supplied to 10,000 local residents has been shown to contain potentially carcinogenic pollutants, such as chromium, lead and nitrate. Erin Brockovich, the famous activist, requested in late March 2009 that the American ambassador in Greece press the Greek government towards a viable and environmentally friendly solution for the area.

Socioeconomic issues

Immigration has become a central social issue for Greece. According to a survey, conducted in July 2009 by the public opinion research company Public Issue, citizens were more concerned than the previous year about the impacts of immigration on Greek economic and social life. More specifically, 62% believe that immigration hinders the country, while only 19% believe that it benefits Greece.

In terms of the economy, in 2009 Greece fell ten places in the International Institute for Management Development World Competitiveness Yearbook (IMD 2009), ranking in 52nd place overall, and 23rd place among the European Union (EU) member states included in the scorecard.

Another serious issue is corruption. According to Transparency International's Global Corruption Barometer (2009a), 76% of Greek respondents find the government's actions in the fight against corruption ineffective. More specifically, according to the Corruption Perceptions Index (CPI), which indicates the perceived level of public-sector corruption in a country/territory, Greece ranks 71st (as compared to 57th in 2008), where first means the least corrupt country (Transparency International 2009b). According to the report, insufficient efforts against corruption have been made in Greece, while many delays in the bestowal of justice have been noted.

▮ Trends

Despite country-specific challenges and peculiarities that CSR faces in Greece, one of its global problematic commonalities, namely its definitional aspects, also affects its national understanding and implementation. In particular, although the lack of a common definition can be generally supported by the notion that CSR reflects corporate identity and implies a different business case for each organisation, the connotations derived from the term 'social' have had a rather negative effect on the acceptance and sense-making approach to both Greek public opinion and organisations. In other words, the term 'social' seems to lead to confusion about the rationale behind responsible corporate conduct, leading to prejudice and scepticism among the public, and to ineffective implementation by corporations. As far as Greek public opinion is concerned, this can be demonstrated by a combination of evidence. For example, the 'CSR 2008 Survey' (Institute of Communication, Greece) points out that the majority of the Greek public not only doubts the motives behind CSR, but moreover disbelieves the honesty behind social and environmental corporate actions. More specifically, 86.2% believe that corporations project a social profile in order to enhance their brand image and not because they wish to positively contribute to society.

▮ Legislation and codes

According to the 2009 WWF Hellas report 'Unmet Commitments: Environmental Legislation in Greece' (Terzis 2009), Greece is the poorest-performing member state in the EU27 in terms of integration of EU environmental directives into the national legal framework. There is, however, a variety of national social, environmental and ethical legislation, including:

- **Act No. 3488/2006.** Implementation of the principle of equal treatment for men and women as regards access to employment, vocational training and promotion, and working conditions

- **Act No. 3304/2005.** Implementation of the principle of equal treatment regardless of racial or ethnic origin, religious or other beliefs, disability, age or sexual orientation

- **Act No. 3064/2002.** Against trafficking in human beings, offences against sexual freedom, juvenile pornography and the economic exploitation of sexual life in general as well as the assistance for the victims of such crimes

- **Act No. 1650/1986.** On environmental protection

- **Act 2742/1999.** Covers regional planning and sustainable development

▌ Organisations[1]

▌ **Corporate Responsibility Institute**. A not-for-profit organisation founded in 2008, in association with Business in the Community (BITC) UK, to introduce the Corporate Responsibility Index in Greece. The Institute aims to use the CR Index as a management tool to support Greek companies in improving their social and environmental performance. At its inaugural meeting on 14 April 2008 and with the support from the Greek Network for CSR, the Greek Management Association, the Entrepreneurial Club and the Institute of Communication, the Corporate Responsibility Index was introduced to Greek business. **http://www.cri.org.gr**

▌ **EBEN Greece**. A nonprofit association founded in 2005, representing the European Business Ethics Network in Greece. It has 50 members. **http://www.eben.gr**

▌ **EuroCharity**. Founded in 2006, EuroCharity owns, publishes and daily updates Greece's only bilingual (Greek and English) Corporate Social Responsibility directory. It also supports and co-organises conferences, events, awards, competitions and campaigns that focus on raising awareness of numerous issues related to sustainability. It has 343 members. **http://www.eurocharity.org**

▌ **Hellenic Federation of Enterprises (SEV)**. SEV's mission is 'to contribute in a decisive manner towards further modernisation and development of today's Greek enterprise, which amounts to the creation of a competitive national asset, both within European and global economic competition'. In order to further promote CSR, in November 2008 SEV's Business Council for Sustainable Development was launched as a not-for-profit organisation that will comprise the Greek chapter of the World Business Council for Sustainable Development's (WBCSD) regional network. **http://www.sev.org.gr**

▌ **Hellenic Management Association (HMA)**. HMA was founded in 1962. It is a non-profit organisation which aims at the dissemination, development and promotion of the principles, methods and practice of contemporary management, including CSR. Today, HMA has 4,000 members. **http://www.eede.gr**

▌ **Hellenic Management Association (Entrepreneurship Club)**. The Entrepreneurship Club was founded in 1995 by HMA and 24 top businessmen. It is a not-for-profit association that aspires to support entrepreneurs in Greece. It has 72 members. **http://www.leshiepi.gr**

▌ **Hellenic Network for Corporate Social Responsibility**. A business-driven membership-based nonprofit organisation, founded in 2000, whose mission is 'to promote the meaning of Corporate Social Responsibility to both the business community and the social environment, with the overall objective being a balance between profitability and sustainable development'. It has 124 members. **http://www.csrhellas.org**

▌ **Institute of Communication**. A not-for-profit organisation, established in November 2002, with the aim to establish a closer cooperation between the academic and the professional communication sectors. It promotes CSR mainly through campaigns and surveys and has 140 members. **http://www.ioc.gr**

---

1   Information on organisations' memberships was correct as of March/April 2009.

■ Case studies

Titan Group

In 1995, Titan was one of the first companies in Greece to publish a social report. It was ranked 1st in the Accountability Rating™ Greece: 2008. Titan's approach to CSR includes the integration of CSR into its corporate policy and strategy, the establishment of internal structures (a CSR committee and department), various CSR activities focused on the marketplace, workplace, community and environment, and stakeholder engagement. Titan's 2007 CSR and sustainability report was the first Greek report to ever achieve a Global Reporting Initiative (GRI) A+ Application Level, and among the first reports in Greece with independent external assurance. Titan has also taken a leading role in the implementation of the 'CSR and Supply Chain Laboratory' under the EU Business Alliance for CSR.

■ Education

The following list includes leading Greek public universities with CSR-related graduate and postgraduate courses:

- **Democritus University of Thrace**. International Economic Relations and Development department

- **National Technical University of Athens**. Faculty of Mechanical Engineering, Industrial Management and Operational Research departments

- **Panteion University of Social and Political Sciences**. Economic and Regional Development, and Communication, Media and Culture departments

- **University of the Aegean**. Sociology, and Environmental Studies departments

- **University of Crete**. Faculty of Social Sciences and Economics department

- **University of Macedonia**. Business Administration and Accounting and Finance department

- **University of Piraeus**. Business Administration department

References

Adoniou, D. (2009) 'Μεγαλύτερη ανησυχία για μετανάστες' ('Great Concern for Immigrants'), *Kathimerini*, 5 July 2009; http://news.kathimerini.gr/4dcgi/_w_articles_ell_1_05/07/2009_321146, accessed 25 November 2009.

Diakoulaki, D., S. Mirasgentis and M. Tziantzi (2001) 'Environmental Externalities and the Development of Renewable Energy Sources', Laboratory of Industrial and Energy Economics, Department of Chemical Engineering, National Technical University of Athens; http://www.soc.uoc.gr/calendar/2000EAERE/papers/PDF/F4-Diakoulaki.pdf, accessed 31 March 2009.

Eberstadt, N.N. (1977) 'What History Tells us about Corporate Responsibilities', in A.B. Carroll (ed.), *Business and Society Review*, Autumn 1977. *Managing Corporate Social Responsibilities* (Boston MA: Little, Brown).

Hamashige, H. (2007) 'Greek wildfire recovery could take decades', *National Geographic News*, 3 October 2007; **http://news.nationalgeographic.com/news/2007/10/071003-greece-wildfires.html**, accessed 31 March 2009.

Hellenic Network for CSR (2009) 'Ελληνικό Δίκτυο για την Εταιρική Κοινωνική Ευθύνη' ('CSR and SMEs'); **http://www.csrhellas.org/portal/index.php?option=ozo_content&perform=view&id=189&Itemid =143&lang=EN**, accessed 3 April 2009.

IMD (International Institute for Management Development) (2009) *World Competitiveness Yearbook*; **http://www.imd.ch/research/publications/wcy/upload/scoreboard.pdf**, accessed 8 November 2009.

Kathimerini (2007) 'Asopos pollution levels rising', *Kathimerini*, 10 April 2007; **http://www.ekathimerini. com/4dcgi/_w_articles_politics_100010_10/04/2007_82143**, accessed 31 March 2009.

Terzis, V. (2009) 'Unmet Commitments: Environmental legislation in Greece', (Athens: WWF, June 2009; **http://politics.wwf.gr/images/stories/wwf%20nomoreport%202009.pdf**, accessed 8 November 2009).

Transparency International (2009a) 'Global Corruption Barometer'; **http://www.transparency.org/ policy_research/surveys_indices/cpi/2009/cpi_2009_table**, accessed 08 November 2009.

—— (2009b) 'Corruption Perceptions Index'; **http://www.transparency.org/policy_research/surveys_ indices/cpi/2009**, accessed 25 November 2009.

18 Hungary

Attila Kun

Labour Lawyer, Senior Assistant Professor at
Károli Gáspár University, Budapest

▌ Context

CSR is a relatively new phenomenon in Hungary. However, in recent years it has become more and more fashionable. In spite of the gradual spreading of CSR practices, the level of awareness is still low and there are still many structural hindrances.

In Hungary, as with the majority of Central–Eastern European (CEE) post-socialist countries, the socialist legacy has influenced the national vision of CSR. There is still an overwhelming public perception that social responsibility and welfare are not the 'business of business' and that governments should take the lead. The CEE character of CSR lies in the fact that CSR seems to be a contributing tool to solving social problems the state is unable to solve alone. In other words, CSR is a kind of voluntary restriction on 'wild west' capitalism (Hardi 2006: 8).

The social and cultural mentality does not offer adequate public support for the idea of CSR. The power of civil society, NGOs and multi-stakeholder initiatives is still limited. Furthermore, stock market capitalisation is underdeveloped; rather, strategic investors ('blockholders') are dominant. As a result, public and stakeholder influence over corporations is limited. CSR is thus implemented by businesses on a purely voluntary basis. On the other hand, public trust in companies and in managers is very low: according to a survey from 2003, 44% and 54% of the public do not place trust in domestic and multinational corporations respectively (Fekete 2005).

In the socialist era, state-owned enterprises had to follow paternalistic welfare policies and the centrally financed social infrastructure of firms was significant. As a result, on the one hand people have bad memories about ideological corporate culture and about 'voluntary' collective movements. On the other hand, many citizens have nostalgic feelings towards the socialist welfare policies of corporations. Therefore, social expectations towards corporations are confused.

The early years of the transition of the 1990s brought about the overriding focus on core business and the most important goal was to stay afloat in the 'free market': privatised firms divested themselves of their former social obligations, foreign investors mainly had short-term goals and corporations didn't invest much in CSR. Since the mid 1990s, 'wild capitalism' has been mitigated and corporations have started to pay more attention to their social roles. However, the development of CSR in Hungary is not entirely an organic and self-evident process. Rather, it is driven by the following specific — and relatively artificial — factors:

- Formal and exterior motives. On the business level, 'importing' the CSR mechanisms of multinational parent companies and foreign investors; and on the public policy level, the CSR policy of the EU

- Management's ad hoc personal ethics

- The desire for free publicity, positive PR and reputation/image-building

There are two prevailing misunderstandings of CSR in Hungary: first, it is often associated with charity and philanthropy; and second, it is frequently linked to the fulfilment of legal obligations (FIDH 2006: 11). Business leaders and PR managers habitually communicate charity or legal compliance as CSR. Deeper, strategic, governance-oriented understandings of CSR are still largely absent.

∎ Priority issues

The core challenges and priority issues in the Hungarian CSR arena include activating fruitful democratic dialogue among business and social actors; enhancing compliance with already existing CSR-related laws (e.g. labour, environmental protection) and norms; tackling discrimination (e.g. against the Roma people); fighting against the 'grey economy' and boosting the transparency of business life; and motivating coherent and strategic CSR policies instead of ad hoc and superficial ones.

As a World Bank survey shows, Hungarian companies generally understand the term CSR to mean compliance with existing regulations, behaving ethically and assuring environmental protection, but do not think that CSR involves correcting social inequalities or engaging in public relations (World Bank 2005).

According to the CSR Hungary Index 2009 (Perspective Institute 2009), the ranking of the most important CSR activities is:

1. Environmental awareness (37%)

2. Employee-friendly attitude (26%)

3. Sponsorship (16%)

4. Responsible communication (13%)

5. Responsible supply chain issues (13%)

∎ Trends

General

Most CSR activities are connected to donations, philanthropy and communication. Enterprises tend to think more in terms of projects, spectacular events that can be easily communicated, than of responsible operations. In the CEE region, CSR has not yet reached the critical mass that would motivate corporations to change their way of doing their core business (Ligeti and Oravecz 2009). The majority of businesses are yet to appreciate that CSR is not equivalent to merely establishing ad hoc, sporadic environmental and social programmes. Reflecting its peripheral status, CSR staff (where they do exist) are mostly part of the PR or HR department. Hence, comprehensive and systematic management of CSR is the exception.

Codes of conduct and standards

According to a survey, 60% of Hungarian corporations have some kind of CSR code or charter. However, these codes are often from the foreign parent company, while local CSR policies lack specificity (FIDH 2006: 19).

Technical CSR standards (such as SA8000, AA1000) are not commonly used by Hungarian corporations. ISO 14001 is the most widely adopted standard. The Hungarian Global Compact Network was launched in 2006 and in April 2008, there were only 19 national signatories.

Since 2006, Braun & Partners (2008) have compiled an annual Accountability Rating™ of Hungary's highest-turnover companies. In 2008, the top five performers were Magyar Telekom, MOL, TVK, MVM and Hungarian Post.

Reporting and communication

The first CSR report was published in Hungary in 2002. Over the next five years, only 35 reports were issued (Feketéné 2006: 6). The number of reporting firms is still low (15 in 2006), but slowly increasing. Sustainability reports are usually published by half of the 'Top 20' companies but only some of them can be read in Hungarian (Ligeti and Oravecz 2009). Independent assurance is extremely rare. In 2008, only seven Hungarian corporations used the Global Reporting Initiative (GRI) standard.

The online CSR communication of the Top 100 companies was assessed in 2006, finding that 20% do not have a Hungarian website at all and 20% do not mention CSR on their website. Of the remaining websites, there were only four that provided concrete examples and CSR reports (Terra-Idea 2006).

SRI and other key initiatives

Socially responsible investment (SRI) is very underdeveloped in Hungary. Recently, OTP Hungary Fund Management Ltd was considering launching the first SRI fund in the region. However, so far, no clear results have been communicated.

1st June 2006 was named as the First CSR Day in Hungary. Since then, a national CSR event has been organised annually.

The first Hungarian CSR MarketPlace was organised on 14 May 2009 by KÖVET. Nearly 50 companies sent in more than 80 proposals. It is telling that the jury withheld one of the awards because the overall quality of the projects was not convincing or innovative enough.

■ Legislation and codes

In Hungary, systematic and explicit governmental CSR policies are generally absent.

The government's major targeted action in favour of CSR is the Government Resolution No. 1025 from 2006 'for the reinforcement of the social responsibility of employers and for measures to stimulate it'. Although the Resolution clearly announced the public political commitment to CSR (in line with EU CSR policies) and put forward some ambitious proposals (e.g. promoting an extensive public debate on CSR and introducing a state-controlled Social Label), most of the declarations have not been realised so far.

None of the stakeholders seem to be in favour of directly regulating CSR. Also, there is a general opinion that the priority should be more strict compliance with existing norms of 'business and human rights'. Although there are no specifically targeted legal requirements for CSR in Hungary, numerous pieces of recent legislation are indirectly associated with its scope. For example:

- Public aid and public tenders are required to take into account the record of applicant companies on 'sound labour relations' (see relevant articles of **Act XXXVIII of 1992 on Public Finances** and **Act CXXIX of 2003 on Public Procurement**). These CSR-related 'exclusions' have a very limited scope, as they only focus on critical breaches of basic labour laws from a negative perspective and they do not take into account wider CSR criteria (since 2009, the scope of such prohibitions has become even more restricted).

- In line with the relevant EU directive (2003/51/EC), Act C of 2000 on Accounting suggests the possibility (not the obligation) for companies to include non-financial information in their annual business report

- In the national law on Trade, companies with significant market force must comply with fair trading practices and prepare self-regulating codes of ethics dealing with responsible supply chain management (**Act CLXIV** of 2005).

- The state encourages the adoption of self-regulating 'equal opportunity plans' (**Labour Code, Act XXII of 1992**).

- Since 2004, the Budapest Stock Exchange has issued Corporate Governance Recommendations for listed companies. The new Company Act (**Act IV of 2006**) has given legal force to the disclosure obligations regarding corporate governance.

The first **National Sustainable Development Strategy** was adopted in 2007.

The Ministry of Social Affairs and Labour takes the lead in CSR-related public policies. For instance, it takes part in some CSR award schemes such as the Family-Friendly Employer Prize (since 2000) and the Best Workplace survey (carried out since 2001 by Hewitt Inside Consulting). In the former Ministry of Economy and Transport (now Ministry for National Development and Economy) a so-called 'CSR Director' was appointed, but the competence and impact was not significant from a general CSR-related public policy perspective

Nevertheless, in 2007 the Hungarian Economic and Social Council (ESC) adopted 'Recommendations in connection with CSR for the Government, enterprises and civil organisations'. Also, in 2008, in the framework of the UNDP–EU CSR project, strategic recommendations for the government were formulated. More than 100 experts were involved and the document covers five subjects: economic development, environment, consumer protection, equal opportunity/labour and corruption/transparency.

▌ Organisations

▌ **ACC (Association of Conscious Consumers)**. Includes Cégmérce, a database of corporate criticism and ratings. **http://www.tve.hu**

▌ **BCSD (Business Council for Sustainable Development) Hungary**. The national member of the WBCSD. **http://www.bcsdh.hu**

▌ **Braun & Partners**. A leading CSR consultancy. **http://www.braunpartners.hu**

▌ **Budapest Chance**. A nonprofit company offering a Socially Responsible Company qualification and label. **http://www.pestesely.hu**

▌ **Carpathian Foundation**. Runs 'The Way It Works' project, which aims to enhance CSR in the CEE region. **http://www.thewayitworks.org**

▌ **CSR Hungary**. Has organised annual CSR conferences since 2006. It also offers a CSR Award (with the President of the Republic as patron) and constructs a CSR Index. **http://www.csrhungary.eu**

▌ **HBLF (Hungarian Business Leaders Forum)**. A nonprofit association of influential CSR-oriented business executives. **http://www.hblf.org**

▌ **International Chambers of Commerce**. These include AmCham and the British Chamber of Commerce in Hungary, which are important promoters of CSR. **http://www.amcham.hu**, **http://www.bcch.com**

▌ **KÖVET (Association for Sustainable Economies)**. The Hungarian member of CSR Europe and the Global Footprint Network, this is an independent, pragmatic NGO promoting environmentally aware business management and CSR. **http://www.kovet.hu http://www.csreurope.org** and **http://www.footprintnetwork.org/en/index.php/GFN**

▌ **Kurt Lewin Foundation**. An independent civil public interest organisation. Its main focus is on anti-discrimination, democratic civic participation and 'internal' CSR (e.g. workplace-level CSR analysis). **http://www.kla.hu**

▌ **MPRSZ (Hungarian PR Association)**. Hosts many significant CSR projects, e.g. best practice and media competitions. **http://www.mprsz.hu**

▌ **International organisations**. The UNDP is the most important one promoting CSR in the region. The ILO Sub-Regional office is also active (e.g. promoting the law on equal treatment). The National Contact Point (HNCP) of the OECD Guidelines for MNEs is an interdepartmental government body, but its impact is marginal.

NGOs are not identified as significant stakeholders in Hungary, but they are considered as organisations with which to maintain dialogue in order to secure their help in implementing appropriate CSR practices. Thus, as opposed to the traditional roles of NGOs as watchdogs, defending against violations, many engage in consultancy on CSR.

This gives rise to a serious management problem as far as objectivity and independence are concerned (FIDH 2006: 17).

■ Case studies

Bakos

This small firm with 40 employees in the wood industry is the top Hungarian example of a responsible SME, and has won the CSR MarketPlace 2009 prize in the SME category, and CSR Best Practice recognition in 2007.

Coloplast Hungary

Coloplast Hungary won the CSR MarketPlace prize 2009 for a 'truly responsible enterprise'. Environmental and health issues are especially important to Coloplast.

Hungarian Post and Magyar Telekom

The diversity policies of the Hungarian Post and Magyar Telekom are among best practices acknowledged by the ILO SRO (International Labour Organisation Sub-regional Office for Central and Eastern Europe) project: Combating Social Exclusion at the Workplace (Tardos 2007).

IBM

IBM is the founding supporter of the Romaster project (launched in 2007 by HBLF). Romaster is a talent support programme for disadvantaged Roma students.

OTP Bank

OTP Bank's innovative internal CSR training course won first place in the eFestival Hungary 2008 e-learning competition.

Besides these positive examples, some controversial cases are also noteworthy:

Visteon Hungary Ltd

In the framework of the HNCP's grievance mechanism, the liability of Visteon was investigated in a work-related personal injury case (the only Hungarian OECD 'specific instance' case so far). Attempts to agree a trilateral agreement were not successful.

'Győri' Biscuit and Waffle Corporation

Danone bought this traditional firm with the promise not to close it. But some months after takeover, Danone closed the plant. The reaction was a country-wide boycott and the sales of Danone products dropped significantly in Hungary that year (Feketéné 2006).

Education

In general, CSR education in Hungary is still at a very embryonic stage. The list of leading institutions that are engaged in CSR-related teaching and/or research follows:

- **BKF (Budapest College of Communication and Business)**. A CSR management postgraduate training programme was launched in 2008, the first of its kind in Hungary

- **CEU (Central European University)**. Center for Business and Society

- **Corvinus University**. Business Ethics Center

- **KÖVET**. In partnership with several European partners, it is coordinating the innovative EU-funded training project *Train4CSR*

- **University of Szeged**. Institute of Labour Relations and Social Security Studies

References

Braun & Partners (2008) 'Accountability Rating™'; **http://www.arhu.hu**, accessed 2 June 2010.

Fekete, L. (2005) 'Social Welfare Lagging behind Economic Growth', in A. Habisch, J. Jonker, M. Wegner and R. Schmidpeter (eds.), *CSR across Europe* (Heidelberg, Germany: Springer Berlin): 141-49.

Feketéné Csáfor, H. (2006) 'Hungarian Distinctiveness of CSR in Comparison with the EU Practices', Fondazione Eni Enrico Mattei, CSR PAPER 13.2006; **http://core-conferences.net/attach/CSR2006-013.pdf**, accessed 25 March 2010.

FIDH (2006) 'International Fact-finding Mission: An Overview of CSR in Hungary', International Federation of Human Rights Report No. 458/2; **http://www.fidh.org/IMG/pdf/hu-report1309a.pdf**, accessed 25 March 2010.

Hardi, P. (2006) 'Corporate Social Responsibility: Britain in Hungary 2006' (Budapest: British Chamber of Commerce in Hungary; **http://www.bcch.com/content/csr2006.pdf**, accessed 26 March 2010).

Kun, A. (2009) *A multinacionális vállalatok szociális felelőssége* (Budapest: AdLibrum; **http://adlibrum. hu/Kun-Attila**, accessed 2 June 2010).

Ligeti, G., and Á.Oravecz (2009) 'CSR Communication of Corporate Enterprises in Hungary', *Journal of Business Ethics* 84.2: 137-149.

Line, M., and R. Braun (2007) 'Baseline Study on CSR Practices in the New EU Member States and Candidate Countries', UNDP; **http://www.acceleratingcsr.eu/uploads/docs/BASELINE_STUDY_ON.pdf**, accessed 25 March 2010.

Perspective Institute (2009) 'CSR Hungary Index 2009'; **http://www.csrhungary.eu/CSRH2009-eloadasok/CSR-Index.pdf**, accessed 28 Oct. 2009.

Simonyi, Á. (1999) 'Labour and Social Welfare in Competitive Firms', in C. Makó and C. Warhurst (eds.), *The Management and Organization of Firm in the Global Context* (Budapest: Institute of Management Education, Gödöllő University, Budapest University of Economic Sciences, Department of Management and Organisation).

Tardos, K. (2007) 'On the Impact of the "For an Inclusive and Diverse Workplace" Training Program', ILO; **http://www.ilo.org/public/english/region/eurpro/budapest/download/socsec/workplace_diversity. pdf**, accessed 26 March 2010.

Terra-Idea (2006) 'CSR Online 2006', online CSR communication of the Hungarian Top100 companies, Budapest, June 2006; **http://www.terra-idea.com/download/terraidea_csr_online_2006_ summary_en.pdf**, accessed 26 March 2010.

World Bank (2005) 'What Does Business Think about Corporate Social Responsibility? Part II: A Comparison of Attitudes and Practices in Hungary, Poland, and Slovakia' (Washington, DC: World Bank).

19 Iceland

Hanna Thorsteinsdottir

Environmental Specialist, Société Générale, Paris

▌ Context

The Icelandic economy has developed rapidly in past years, with market liberalisation and diversification, from being largely dependent on fisheries to a multi-sector economy, including energy-intensive industries (notably aluminium), tourism and financial services.

Although the concept of CSR has received less attention in Iceland than in other Nordic countries, Icelandic companies operate in accordance with strict environmental and social standards in line with those of European Union (EU) countries.

While the coming years will be economically challenging, Iceland benefits from a strong foundation of renewable natural resources which, when moving forward, will be important for existing as well as innovative sectors. Increased focus on the sustainable aspects of Icelandic industries can help Iceland in reviving the economy and regaining the trust of the international community.

Historical context

Iceland is an island of 103,000 km² with around 320,000 inhabitants (2009 figures). Iceland has a legal system in line with those of Denmark and the other Nordic countries with an emphasis on a strong social system and labour rights.

After centuries of poverty and poor living conditions, the 20th century saw the Icelandic economy and welfare system develop quickly. During the first part of the 20th century cooperatives were a popular form of enterprise which embedded some aspects of CSR in their operations. For instance, they provided financial support for the communities where they operated, including support for education and culture. The philanthropic aspects of the cooperatives (now a rare organisational form in Iceland) have remained prominent in Icelandic companies and form the basis of many CSR initiatives.

In the period 1960–80 living standards in Iceland improved dramatically with advances in fisheries and the emergence of new industries, such as tourism and energy-intensive industries. By 1980 Iceland was in second place on the UN's human development index for the highest living standards in the world. Iceland joined the European Free Trade

Agreement (EFTA) in 1970 and was a founding member of the European Economic Area (EEA) in 1993, which brought about fundamental changes to the Icelandic economy.

The EEA opened up the Icelandic economy to EU/EEA countries and at the same time required Iceland to comply with many EU directives, thereby bringing social and environmental standards largely in line with EU regulations. The last two decades have been characterised by free market capitalism, fostered by the dominance of Iceland's centre-right Independence Party (*Sjálfstæðisflokkur*).

Current state of CSR

While CSR has become an important topic in Western Europe in recent years, little emphasis has been put on the concept of CSR in terms of voluntary corporate practices in Iceland to date. It has generally been considered sufficient that companies provide jobs, pay taxes and abide by rules and regulations, which are strict in terms of environmental and social protection. A noticeable exception to this, however, is the common practice of philanthropy by Icelandic companies. According to a study conducted by the European Commission (2002), around three quarters of Icelandic companies were involved in 'external community causes' (philanthropy). Only Finland and Denmark had a higher percentage.

Possible reasons for the limited corporate focus on voluntary CSR practices, beyond philanthropy, include:

- The small size and generally limited international operations of Icelandic companies (with hardly any operations in the developing world)

- Generally high standards for environmental protection, labour and human rights

- Limited demand for CSR from the stakeholders of Icelandic companies (largely Icelandic), beyond legal requirements

- Dominance of centre-right politics with a key emphasis on economic growth and less on social and environmental issues

- The fact that Iceland is outside of the EU and although it adopts many of the EU's directives through the EEA agreement, it does not have the same exposure to CSR-related guidelines, position papers (such as Green Papers of the European Commission) and relevant debate in the EU

- The absence of serious corporate scandals involving Icelandic companies, until the collapse of the financial sector in 2008

∎ Priority issues

Economy

In October 2008, Iceland was hit by the global financial crisis, which in Iceland started with the fall of the country's three largest banks. For the first time since Iceland joined NATO in 1949, the Icelandic public took to the streets and protested against the government for insufficient oversight of the banks' operations and for failing to prevent their failure.

The roots of the crisis stemmed in part from failures in internal monetary and institutional management, but also from the growing financial troubles internationally. Given the weight of the Icelandic banking system (around nine times larger than the Icelandic economy), the impact of the fall of the banks was enormous, deeply affecting Icelandic society as well as foreign actors who had invested in the fallen banks.

The situation will be likely require a reorganisation of the Icelandic banking system and government measures to prevent a large number of companies and households from facing bankruptcy. After many years of a low unemployment rate, 8.2% were unemployed in January 2009, compared to 1.0% in January 2008. Resolving these economic issues is without a doubt the biggest challenge Iceland will face in the next few years.

Business ethics

Ethics in companies has not been a focus in the national debate until the current economic crisis. A recent study of Iceland's 100 largest companies conducted by students at Reykjavik University found that only 38% had a written code of ethics in 2008, less than in a 1996 study. A majority (71%) stated that ethical standards were relatively or very high. Contrary to these findings, a 2004 survey by Capacent found that more than half of the public considered ethical standards to be low.

The findings imply a certain disconnect between Icelandic companies and their stakeholders when it comes to expectations of ethical standards. The current economic crisis has put the spotlight on ethics in Icelandic companies, notably in the bankrupt banks and associated companies. Relevant investigations have been launched to determine the causes of the failure of the Icelandic banks, which may shed light on ethical aspects of their management. It is likely that ethical standards will play a larger role in Icelandic companies in the future.

Energy resources

Iceland has an abundance of renewable energy resources, primarily in the form of geothermal and hydro power. In 2007 over 80% of the country's total energy usage originated from geothermal and hydro energy. This abundance of energy for Iceland's small population has made the country an attractive location for foreign energy-intensive industries, most notably aluminium production. Iceland currently has three aluminium smelters, all owned by foreign corporations.

Although hydro power is a clean and renewable energy source, it comes at the cost of disrupting the natural state of land and rivers. One of the most controversial power plants in Iceland is the Karahnjukar hydropower project in the eastern part of the country, which entails the harnessing of glacial rivers from Iceland's largest glacier, Vatnajökull. The energy from Karahnjukar is used to power the aluminium smelter of Fjardaal, owned by US company Alcoa. In 2005, Icelandic and international environmental activists protested strongly against the Karahnjukar project. At present, the possibility of new aluminium plants is being debated.

Sustainable fisheries

Although the relative size of fisheries compared to other industries has diminished in recent years, the industry still accounts for around half of Iceland's export income. To protect this valuable natural resource, Icelanders put great emphasis on fishing in a responsible and sustainable way. Key steps towards the protection of Iceland's marine resources were taken in the 1970s when Iceland gradually extended its fishing limit to 200 miles.

The Icelandic Marine Research Institute conducts research on the commercial fishing stocks, marine life and ecosystems and advises on sustainable fisheries, i.e. how much can be caught of a given species while ensuring sustainable maintenance of the stock. In order to communicate the sustainable management of Icelandic fisheries to the relevant stakeholders, a special logo has been designed for Icelandic seafood products with third-party certification in accordance with the UN Food and Agricultural Organization.

▌ Trends

Limited debate on CSR is reflected by little being written on CSR and related topics in Iceland. However there are signs of increased interest in CSR, notably in the last two years, particularly among university students, some of whom have chosen to write their dissertations on CSR-related topics. The establishment of the first Icelandic CSR-focused institute, Ethikos, has in the last year helped increase the debate and awareness, and created a forum for the exchange of best practices and facilitated in bringing relevant expert knowledge to Iceland.

Although integrated CSR reporting, compliant with internationally recognised standards, is not yet practised by Icelandic companies, environmental reporting has become mainstream in companies operating in environmentally sensitive sectors and is required by national legislation on environmental reporting (green accounting) instituted in 2002.

Icelandic subsidiaries of large international companies, such as aluminium companies, put noticeably more emphasis on voluntary CSR than companies solely operating in Iceland. Both the international companies Alcoa and Rio Tinto Alcan have extensive CSR programmes and practices at headquarter levels which extend to their Icelandic operations. Alcoa's subsidiary, Fjardaal, has initiated an ongoing multi-stakeholder sustainability initiative linked with its production (see Case studies). The project is unique in Iceland and has been generally well received by Alcoa Fjardaal's stakeholders. Alcan puts emphasis on CSR in various ways such as responsibility to its employees (training, competitive salaries, free meals, etc.) and strict management of environmental impacts (e.g. it was the first company in Iceland to implement the ISO 14001 standard).

Despite this emphasis on CSR, aluminium companies remain a source of controversy in Iceland due to their environmental impact.

Apart from the environmental side, which is covered by national regulations, there has been little pressure from stakeholders for company practices and initiatives exceeding legal requirements. This is likely to change in light of the recent turmoil in the Icelandic economy, which has focused attention on accountability of companies, the need for transparency, sound ethical standards and good governance. Given the sudden importance ascribed to CSR in Iceland and the critical need for the country to redeem its business sector in the eyes of the world, the stage is now set for a concerted effort to be made to promote CSR. During the preparation of this chapter, Ethikos, together with leading business associations and ministries, were considering the possibility of developing a national CSR strategy.

∎ Legislation and codes

Environmental

- **Law for the scientific conservation of the continental shelf fisheries**. This states that the Ministry of Fisheries will issue regulations regarding areas protected against fishing within the Icelandic continental shelf and that the areas will be subject to Icelandic control aiming for scientifically based protection of fish stocks. Extensions of fishing limits after 1948 (up to the current 200 miles) were based on this law.

- **Law on environmental impact assessments**. Its objective is 'to ensure that an environmental assessment is conducted before a license is issued for any project which can have material impact on the environment because of its location, nature, operations or scope'.

- **Law on greenhouse gas emissions**. The law gives a framework for Iceland's obligations associated with the signing of the Kyoto Protocol of the UN Framework Convention on Climate Change of 1992.

Other key environmental laws concern pollution mitigation and waste management.

Social

- **Social Security Act**. The Act contains legislation on health insurance, unemployment benefits and pension funds for all persons resident in Iceland.

- **Law on maternity and parental leave**. The law covers the right of parents to a total of nine months' paid parental leave.

- **Law on occupational health and safety**. The object of the law is to secure and promote the health and safety of people at work.

- **The European Convention on Human Rights**. Iceland has implemented the European Convention on Human Rights which aim is to protect human rights and fundamental freedoms.

∎ Organisations

∎ **Ethikos**. The first and only CSR-focused institute, founded by several Icelandic companies and the Icelandic Ministry of Foreign Affairs in May 2008. The activities of Ethikos include supplying companies and the government with information regarding CSR, organising conferences and seminars and facilitating the connection between international and national experts on CSR. The goal of Ethikos is to 'increase the knowledge of CSR in Iceland and help companies to become more responsible towards society, the environment and to respect human rights in their daily operations.' http://www.ethikos. is

∎ Case studies

Auður Capital

Auður Capital is a financial services provider founded in 2008 by women with a vision to incorporate feminine values into the world of finance. The values of Auður Capital include integrity, CSR, risk awareness and long term sustainable profits with social benefits. The company's website states that the difference between Auður Capital and other financial services companies is not about what services it provides but how they are provided. http://www.audurcapital.is/english

Marorka

Marorka develops energy management systems for the maritime industry. Marorka's mission is 'to deliver high quality products and services that save energy, increase profitability and reduce harmful emissions'. The company won the Nordic Council's Nature and Environmental Prize 2008. http://www.marorka.is

∎ Education

- **University of Iceland**. Faculty of History and Philosophy: Applied Ethics (course) and Business Ethics (MA degree). www3.hi.is/~mhs/skor/ensskor/hsp. ens.html

- **Reykjavik University**. School of Business: Business Ethics (course); and School of Law: Human Rights in Business (course). http://www.ru.is

References

Danielsson, J., and G. Zoege (2009) 'The Collapse of a Country', 2nd edn, 12 March 2009; http://www. riskresearch.org, accessed 10 February 2009.

European Commission (2002) 'European SMEs and Social and Environmental Responsibility', Observatory of European SMEs 4; http://ec.europa.eu/enterprise/enterprise_policy/analysis/doc/ smes_observatory_2002_report4_en.pdf, accessed 5 January 2009.

Guðmundsson, J. (2002) 'The Fall of the Federation of Icelandic Cooperative', in H. Kjartansson (ed.), *Barn hvers tíma: Samvinnan á Íslandi í meira en 120 ár* (Reykjavík, Iceland: Sögufélag): 97.

Hafsteinsdottir, A., and S. Hall (2008) 'Code of Ethics in Icelandic Business' (unpublished BSc dissertation; School of Business, Reykjavik University, Iceland).

Ildi (2008) 'Sustainability Initiative in East Iceland, Evaluation June 2008'; **http://www.sjalfbaerni.is/assets/sjalfbaerniverkefni_austurl-endurmat.pdf**, accessed 15 February 2009.

Ólafsson, S. (2008) 'The Icelandic Economic Wonder: From Financial Prosperity to Liberalism and Economic Collapse', *Stjórnmál og stjórnsýsla* 2.4; **http://www.stjornmalogstjornsysla.is/images/stories/fg2008h/stefan08.pdf**, accessed 7 January 2009.

Statistics Iceland (2008) 'Statistical Yearbook of Iceland 2008', Statistics Iceland, Reykjavik; **http://www.statice.is/lisalib/getfile.aspx?itemid=8717**, accessed 15 February 2009.

Vinnumálastofnun (2009) 'Status of Labour Market February 2009'; **http://www.vinnumalastofnun.is/files/febrúar09_181539161.pdf**, accessed 20 March 2009.

20 India

Bimal Arora
Independent CSR Scholar

Aparna Mahajan
Independent Consultant in Management, CSR and Development

▌ Context

An ancient civilisation with over 5,000 years of history, India's rich cultural, religious and historical traditions have been influenced by numerous travellers, scholars, invaders and conquerors from across the world. The cultural, religious and historical traditions include the virtues of charity and philanthropy, drawing not just from Hindu mythology and scriptures, but several other religious philosophies and practices — such as Christianity, Zoroastrianism and Islam. Therefore, notions of charity and philanthropy are deeply rooted in Indian society and embedded in traditional ways of life.

India has predominantly been an agrarian economy, but mercantile traditions date back thousands of years. The merchant community enjoyed great respect and frequently supported and patronised temples, constructed night shelters and drinking water facilities and provided relief during natural calamities.

Industrial development in India largely began 150 years ago. India's trading route with Europe was established in 1498AD. The British East India Company entered India in the early 17th century, with primary interests in trading, but later expanded affairs to governance. The British Crown took control of governance of India in 1857 and, after an intense freedom struggle by Indian nationalists, relinquished control in 1947, freeing India from colonial rule. The roots of industrial development were sown during this period.

During colonial times, some early industrial pioneers in India demonstrated leadership through active interest in public life and social reforms. Jamsetji Tata experimented with labour welfare by instituting pension funds, compensating workers in case of accidents, and installing humidifiers and water sprinklers in his textile mill in the 1870s. The philanthropic spirit was further strengthened in the early 20th century with the concept of trusteeship promoted by Gandhi.

Post independence, some business houses — the majority of which were family owned and controlled — engaged in activities such as donations for schools, colleges and hospitals. Several academic institutions, such as the Indian Institute of Science and the Tata Institute of Fundamental Research, stand testimony to the munificence of business families.

▌ CSR models

In academic circles, the most popular CSR model is Archie Carroll's (1979) pyramid, which includes economic, ethical, legal, and philanthropic responsibilities. However, Kumar *et al.* (2001) propose four CSR models that are present in India:

- The **ethical model**, influenced by Gandhi's trusteeship concept, refers to the community welfare acts of companies

- The **statist model** refers to state-led development that emerged with the adoption of a socialist economy by Prime Minister Jawaharlal Nehru

- The **liberal model** was influenced by the thesis of Milton Friedman

- The **stakeholder model** emerged from Freeman's stakeholder theory (Freeman 1984)

Contemporarily, convergence of the four CSR models can be seen in India, especially among large Indian corporations and multinationals operating in India.

▌ Priority issues

India is home to one-sixth of the world's population (1.15 billion in 2008) living on 2.4% of world's land area. Deprivation, inequities and relative poverty across the socio-income classes are major problems in India. There is lack of access to basic needs such as quality education (while 65% of Indian population is literate, 90% lack education and vocational skills), healthcare (over 73% of India's population lives in rural areas and has access to only 25% of healthcare facilities) and social infrastructure (around 60% of rural households lack access to electricity and more than 30% of India's 640,000 villages are still not connected by roads). There is also a severe shortage of employment opportunities, with the formal economy comprising only 12% of the total Indian economy, leading to weakened resilience for millions of people living on the margins of society.

Hence, there are numerous development challenges in India, but here we focus on two crucial issues: demographics and environment/climate change.

Demographic dividend/disaster

The economic policy of liberalisation in India since the early 1990s has unleashed the Indian entrepreneurial spirit and several entrepreneurs, largely operating in the organised manufacturing and services sectors — such as information technology, biotechnology and automobile manufacturing — have put India on the global stage. These industries leveraged the availability of an educated and skilled pool of labour, where over 300 universities and 15,600 colleges provide 2.5 million graduates each year.

However, by 2008, while the share of the agriculture sector reduced to less than 18% of GDP, paradoxically 67.5% (over 600 million) of India's total labour force still derive livelihoods from agriculture. Approximately 90% of India's labour force is agrarian in nature and skills, and unemployable for the growing services and manufacturing sectors.

While most populations in the world are ageing, India is the only country where about 70% of the population is below the age of 35 years. Eminent scholars see this as a 'demographic dividend', but also caution that if adequate attention is not paid to skills development, it may turn into a 'demographic disaster'.

Environmental management and climate change

India's track record on energy efficiency, use of renewable resources, and management of effluent and natural resources, including efficient use of water, has been weak. Civil society pressures, coupled with tighter regulatory monitoring and market-based incentives, are nevertheless creating awareness and environmental management practices are showing signs of improvement.

While India is not currently a major contributor to climate change — as compared to more advanced consumption-driven economies — India's traditional cultural, agricultural and business practices, along with modernising lifestyles, make it a major potential contributor for the future. Besides this, inertia in public governance systems, resistance to change, a large illiterate population and poorly skilled labour force all magnify India's vulnerability to the impacts of climate change.

∎ Trends

Although some large private corporations such as Tatas and Birlas have been conducting community programmes since the 1970s and even earlier, CSR has only gained momentum in India recently and the use of the term CSR had an upsurge around the turn of the century.

In the wake of economic liberalisation in 1991, some NGOs anticipated that the corporate sector would generate unprecedented wealth, and hence started focusing on ways to secure funds for development programmes. Such activities were touted as corporate partnerships by NGOs like Partners in Change and Child Rights and You (CRY). However, some of these NGOs have now shifted focus to promoting CSR, rather than just fundraising. Since 2000, new NGOs have also formed to facilitate the community development initiatives of corporations.

Industry associations initiated CSR promotion among their member companies around the mid 1990s. Some private corporations in India that previously engaged in ad hoc philanthropic activities started systematising corporate giving and focusing on communities surrounding their manufacturing plants. Other initiatives include supporting national causes such as primary education, health and natural disasters.

Since 2000, the level of CSR awareness has increased significantly, supplemented with CSR education being mainstreamed in many business schools. This has been supported by the promotion of various institutional mechanisms for corporate governance, environment, labour, and occupational health and safety issues, including regulatory provisions and penalties. However, these issues still tend to be dealt with and reported upon separately, and in many cases, with a compliance mind-set.

A report by UN Volunteers in 2004 (Mahajan 2004) indicated that while corporate philanthropy is prevalent, many companies were beginning to recognise the value of supporting structured development programmes. In fact, 80% already claimed to have CSR policies and practices and several companies were in the process of mainstreaming CSR as an integral part of their business strategy.

One major biennial study, undertaken by Partners in Change (PiC) since 1996–97, tracks developments and changes in perceptions and practices of CSR among large corporations. The PiC study (2007) — covering 552 leading companies across sectors — suggests that 99% of respondents claimed increased CSR awareness since 2006, as compared to 84% respondents in the 2004 survey.

More interestingly, while 64% in the 2004 survey said philanthropy was the main driver for CSR, in 2007 goodwill and reputation were most cited (by 66%, as compared with 42% in 2004). Other motivating factors included building employee morale, company value realisation, investor relationships, risk management and operational efficiency.

▌Legislation and codes

India has progressive legislation and policies that supports CSR on several fronts. For example, the **Forest Policy** regards sustainability as imperative and seeks ecological balance by preserving and increasing forest cover. This legislation favours the livelihood rights of indigenous, forest-dependent communities over the ambitions of forestry companies.

In terms of codes, the Confederation of Indian Industry has developed a social code for its member companies, while Partners in Change has developed a 'Frame of Reference for Responsible Business in South Asia'. Several international programmes, codes and standards such as the UN Global Compact, ISO, the Global Reporting Initiative (GRI) and Responsible Care are also followed by many corporations.

▌Organisations

▌ **Centre for Science and Environment (CSE).** Founded in 1980, CSE is a public interest research institution and environmental pressure group. **http://www.cseindia.org**

▌ **Confederation of Indian Industry — Social Development Council (CII-SDC).** Over 113 years old, CII is an industry association with membership of over 7,500 organisations and about 380 national and regional industry associations. SDC was formed in 1995 to promote CSR. **http://www.cii.in**

▌ **Federation of Indian Chambers of Commerce and Industry's Socio-Economic Development Foundation (FICCI-SEDF).** FICCI is one of the oldest industry associations with membership of over 1,500 companies and 500 regional chambers. SEDF was established in 1995 to promote CSR. **http://www.ficci-sedf.org**

▌ **Partners in Change.** Partners in Change was established by Action Aid India in 1995 and is among the pioneers engaged in deepening CSR practice in India. **http://www.picindia.org**

∎ **TERI-BCSD**. The Energy and Resources Institute (TERI), established in 1974, has become the national chapter of WBCSD and an independent platform for corporate leaders to promote CSR. **http://www.bcsd.teri.res.in**

∎ Case studies

Lupin Limited

Lupin Limited is India's 7th largest family-owned and managed pharmaceutical company. Lupin has been undertaking substantial community development initiatives in the Bharatpur district of Rajasthan since 1988, through its Lupin Human Welfare and Research Foundation, and has recently started expanding its work to other regions in India. Community initiatives in India are often undertaken in the areas surrounding factories to ensure peaceful operations and to earn a 'social licence to operate'. However, Lupin has no strategic interest in Bharatpur. It illustrates the ethical model of CSR. **http://www.lupinworld.com**

NTPC

NTPC is one of the largest public sector undertakings (PSU) and the largest power company of India. NTPC's CSR initiatives include community development, resettlement and rehabilitation, environmental protection and conservation practices. As part of socialist policies from the 1950s to the 1980s, the Indian government mandated all PSUs to undertake community welfare initiatives and NTPC continues this legacy. Today, all such initiatives, as well as environmental management, have been labelled as CSR. NTPC illustrates the statist model of CSR. **http://www.ntpc.co.in**

RPG Enterprises

RPG Enterprises was established in 1979 and is one of India's largest family-owned and -managed industrial conglomerates with over 20 companies in its fold. The group has a presence in diverse business sectors including power, transmission, tyre, IT, retail, entertainment, 'carbon black' and speciality industries, all of which engage in their own form of CSR. RPG illustrates the liberalist model of CSR. **http://www.rpggroup.com**

Jubilant Organosys Limited

Established in 1978, Jubilant is one of the largest custom drug research, discovery, development and manufacturing companies. Jubilant has developed an impressive CSR programme over the years, which includes corporate governance, environmental performance, contributions to society and profitability for shareholders. It is one of the few Indian companies that publishes a sustainability report, following GRI guidelines. Jubilant illustrates the stakeholder model of CSR. **http://www.jubl.com**

Hindustan Unilever Limited (HUL)

Hindustan Unilever Limited is a subsidiary of global MNC Unilever, and is India's largest fast-moving consumer goods company. Infusing the CSR approaches of its parent company, HUL integrates sustainability aspects into most of its products, processes and practices. HUL has also targeted low-income segments of society in an attempt to tackle poverty through innovation (e.g. projects like Shakti). HUL represents the convergence model of CSR. http://www.hul.co.in

■ Education

CSR education in India is still at a nascent stage and mostly led by and restricted to the interests of individual faculties. Dedicated research and teaching centres in academic institutions are few and far between, and out of over 1,200 business schools in India, only the following three have featured in global rankings such as *Beyond Grey Pinstripes*:[1]

- **Indian Institute of Management, Bangalore**. http://www.iimb.ernet.in

- **Indian Institute of Management, Kolkata**. http://www.iimcal.ac.in

- **Indian Institute of Management, Ahmedabad**. http://www.iimahd.ernet.in

- **SP Jain Institute of Management and Research, Mumbai**. http://www.spjimr. org

In addition, the following institutions also offer CSR-related modules:

- **Management Development Institute, Gurgaon**. http://www.mdi.ac.in

- **Indian School of Business, Hyderabad**. http://www.isb.edu

- **Narsee Monjee Institute of Management Studies, Mumbai**. http://www.nmims. edu

References

Carroll, A.B. (1979) 'A Three-dimensional Conceptual Model of Corporate Social Performance', *Academy of Management Review* 4.4: 497-505.

Freeman, E.R. (1984) *Strategic Management: A Stakeholder Approach* (Boston, MA: Pitman).

Kumar, R., D.F. Murphy and V. Balsari (2001) 'Altered Images: The 2001 State of Corporate Responsibility in India Poll' (New Delhi, India: TERI-India).

Mahajan, A. (2004) 'Enhancing Business–Community Relations, India National Research Report', by UN Volunteers, TERI and New Academy of Business (New Delhi, India; http://www.new-academy. ac.uk/research/businesscommunity/unvpages/index.htm).

Partners in Change (2007) 'Fourth Report on Corporate Responsibility: The Business Perspective (2006–2007)' (New Delhi, India: Partners in Change).

Sood, A., and B. Arora (2006) 'The Political Economy of Corporate Responsibility in India' (Technology, Business and Society Programme Paper Number 18; Geneva: United Nations Research Institute for Social Development [UNRISD]).

1 http://www.beyondgreypinstripes.org

21 Indonesia

Yanuar Nugroho
Senior Advisor, Business Watch Indonesia;
Research Associate, Manchester Business School UK

Jimmy Tanaya
Research Associate, Business Watch Indonesia

Theresia Widiyanti
Researcher, Business Watch Indonesia

Adhitya Hadi Permana
Researcher, Business Watch Indonesia

▌ Context

CSR is an emergent discourse in Indonesia, not only in corporate practice but also in the larger political-economic landscape. The uptake of CSR practices can be observed outside the business realm as well as in government agencies and civil society organisations (CSOs). This mainstreaming is understandable as the corporate practices which CSR addresses have long been scrutinised in the Republic.

While the private sector has positively contributed to Indonesian development, various malpractices have been detrimental to the society and economy, as well as threatening environmental sustainability. Part of the reason for this is that, historically, business practices in Indonesia have long been fuelled by collusion and corruption. This may have been inherited from the colonial era (Kemp 2001), but was also exacerbated during the administration of President Soeharto (1966–1998).

In addition, with a macroeconomic policy favouring the private sector, many firms and companies remained beyond the arm of law enforcement and were unresponsive to pressure exerted by local citizens or NGOs. These conditions have slowly been improving since Soeharto resigned in 1998 and due to rising pressure from NGOs and other CSOs. Most recently, Law No. 40/2007 concerning limited liability companies made CSR mandatory.

Despite this, CSR remains a contested concept in Indonesia, practised mostly by transnational corporations that are pressured by NGOs and consumer groups in the northern hemisphere. This — and the fact that these firms use standards, principles and concepts that are often detached from local contexts — further justifies the perception that CSR is a value-laden Western concept, mostly used by firms in Indonesia for public relations or 'greenwashing'.

At the very least, however, CSR has created a new space for dialogue between government (public bodies), business and society.

▮ Priority issues

Economic crisis and corruption

Indonesia still suffers from the prolonged impact of the Asian economic crisis of 1997 which led to a regime change a year later. Despite having a more democratic administration, unemployment is still rising and poverty is pervasive, with 110 million people living on less than USD2 a day. Indonesia continues to face poor governance, increasing trends of crime (especially in urban areas), widespread corruption in public offices (including business bribery) and religious fundamentalism.

Poverty and basic services

Besides natural disasters like the tsunami in 2004, earthquakes and outbreaks of polio and avian influenza, the country has to deal with the impact of decentralisation on the poor, inadequate allocation of resources from central government and the absence of minimum standards or regulations for basic services. The latest statistics show that 13% of the population above 15 years old is illiterate; infant mortality is 34 per 1,000 live births; 24% of children under the age of five suffer from malnutrition; and only 80% of the population has access to adequate water sources (World Bank 2006).

Environmental degradation

A host of environmental problems remain unchecked, including pollution, over-extraction of natural resources and deforestation. Nearly 50% of Indonesia's natural forests have been lost since 1950 (FWI/GFW 2002), much of it converted into roads, plantations (palm oil, wood processing, etc.) or factories. It is estimated that every minute, 5 ha of forest disappear — which means that a forest area equal to the size of a football field vanishes every 12 seconds. This is all the more tragic when one considers that the lives of 40–50 million Indonesian people are heavily dependent on the forests.

▮ Trends

There are four main CSR trends in Indonesia today:

Community development

Perhaps due to severe poverty, CSR in the form of community development is seen as an effective and convenient way for the private sector to provide assistance to poor people, while at the same time gaining business legitimacy. However, a study by Chapple and Moon (2005) shows that compared to other Asian countries, not only does Indonesia have the lowest levels of CSR penetration, but also the lowest levels of community involvement. This begs the question of the effectiveness of community development as a CSR practice, despite it being overwhelmingly reported by Indonesian companies.

Reporting

CSR reporting is often taken as a proxy of CSR commitment and practice. In January 2008 there were 376 companies listed in the Indonesian Stock Exchange/IDX, of which 168 did not have an official website. Of these listed companies, only 76 publicly reported their CSR programmes, either in their annual financial report, a separate CSR report or on their websites. Assuming companies without official websites do not produce CSR reports, only 27% of listed companies engage in CSR reporting — a rather disturbing finding, given the implied responsibilities of 'going public'. An even more striking fact is that only seven companies produce stand-alone CSR reports.

Multi-stakeholder forums

There are many multi-stakeholder forums in Indonesia, bringing together business, government and social groups (mostly NGOs). Companies joining these forums are expected to be more committed to CSR, not only as community development activities but as a more comprehensive sustainable business practice. In some cases, these initiatives lead to certification and standard schemes, such as the RSPO (Roundtable Sustainable Palm Oil) and ETP (Ethical Tea Partnership), although the latter takes a slightly different approach.

Government initiatives

In certain instances, there has been a revitalisation of government initiatives which were once undermined. For example, PROPER — a government programme run by the Ministry of Environment for public disclosure of environmental compliance — began as a government policy initiative in 1995 and is once again being promoted as a strategy to promote sustainability measurement and voluntary CSR activities.

▌ Legislation and codes

Indonesia is perhaps the only country where CSR has been made mandatory — through the enactment of **Law No. 25/2007 on Investment**, and **Law No. 40/2007 on Limited Liability Companies**, although regulations are yet to be introduced.

Law No. 25/2007 defines CSR as 'the responsibilities attached to every investment so as to maintain a harmonious and balanced relationship that concurs with the environment, local values, local norms, and local cultures'. The responsibilities of investors with regard to CSR are (a) to maintain environmental conservation; (b) to care for the safety, health, comfort and well-being of employees; and (c) to comply with the laws. Infringement of the Law may cause the withdrawal of a business permit. However, the Law still lacks implementation guidelines, principles and standards.

Law No. 40/2007 goes one step further by introducing a requirement to report on CSR. It defines CSR as 'the commitment of the Company to take a role in developing a sustainable economy in order to improve the quality of life and environment function either for the Company itself, or for local communities, or broader society'. CSR however, is only compulsory for firms involved in natural resource extraction and 'other related industries'. Moreover, firms are allowed to treat CSR expenditures as costs in their accounting, subject to the fairness of such expenditures. There will be a sanction, which is as yet undefined, should firms fail to implement CSR.

Prior to these two laws, there were numerous laws and regulations concerning corporate codes of conduct. These are categorised into four areas: environment (**Law 23/1997**); human rights and labour (**Law 39/1999** and **Law 13/2003**); consumer protection (**Law 8/1999**); and anti-corruption (**Law 31/1999** and **Law 15/2002**).

▌Organisations

The main business associations and other organisations that promote CSR in Indonesia include:

▌ **Business Watch Indonesia (BWI).** http://www.fair-biz.org

▌ **Corporate Forum for Community Development (CFCD).** http://www.cfcdcenter.or.id

▌ **CSR Indonesia.** http://www.csrindonesia.com

▌ **Indonesia Business Links/IBL.** http://www.ibl.or.id

▌ **Indonesia Centre for Sustainable Development (ICSD).** http://www.icsd.or.id

▌ **LEAD Indonesia.** http://www.lead.or.id

▌ **KEHATI — Yayasan Keanekaragaman Hayati Indonesia (Indonesian Biodiversity Foundation).** http://www.kehati.or.id

▌Case studies

British Petroleum

When initiating a project in West Papua, BP openly and explicitly stated that, unlike other extractive companies operating in Indonesia, it would not use and work with the Indonesian military force when facing social problems. BP has kept its promise and now intensively liaises and interacts with local indigenous groups using the so-called Community-based Security Approach. This case is a successful example — one of the few among multinational companies operating in Indonesia — where military force and violence are not used as a means of dealing with local concerns. http://www.bp.com/modularhome.do?categoryId=4760&contentId=7009216

Freeport Indonesia

Responding to heavy criticism of its business practices, Freeport Indonesia (PTFI) has initiated various CSR programmes. In 2009, PTFI introduced a recycling bin made from the recycled containers of acetylene plants, provided to local schools in Timika as part of a 3R programme (reduce–reuse–recycle) to educate students and raise awareness of local communities of the importance of waste separation. Another initiative is the *Inisiatif Tunas Lingkungan* (environmental initiative), which began in 2006 and aims to build environmental awareness and concern among junior high-school students. PTFI also started a Tailings Management Programme to investigate the use of tailings as construction materials in the Mimika region and for the drainage systems used by PTFI itself. Among their notable CSR achievements are the use of tailings waste as back-fill materials at Timika Airport and their mangrove colonisation initiative in the Ajkwa Estuary. **http://www.ptfi.com**

Multi Bintang Indonesia (MBI)

In 1978, well before other such initiatives took place in Indonesia, MBI introduced a consultation forum for the trade union and board of directors or commissioners. MBI has also been a pioneer of good corporate conduct in terms of industrial relations, employee consultation and the improvement of work conditions. 1997 saw the 12th collective bargaining round at MBI. The company set up occupational health commit-tees in all of its plants, one of which was awarded a 'Zero-Accident Award' for two con-secutive years. MBI's labour policy complies with the Indonesian Law No. 13/2003 on Labour and meets all requirements relating to working hours, wages, allowances and collective bargaining. MBI also provides additional benefits for employees, such as a cafeteria, regular health checkups, facilities for sport and religious observance and a pension fund. **http://www.multibintang.co.id**

Panasonic Indonesia

'Good Electronics' has been a central motif for the CSR activities of Panasonic Indone-sia, whereby it strives for environmentally friendly production of electronic devices. For example, Panasonic Indonesia has started producing lead-free solder which is far more environmentally friendly than traditional lead solder. Panasonic has also implemented waste disposal management systems, which aim to achieve a zero-waste target by means of increasing material recycling (already 74% in 2002). In addition, there are two well-known community development CSR programmes: *Peduli Pendidikan* (education concern), which provides scholarships for Indonesians to pursue masters' degrees in Japanese universities, and *Peduli Budaya* (cultural concern), which facilitates the pres-ervation of local cultures in Indonesia. **http://panasonic.co.id**

■ Education

The rapid uptake and diffusion of CSR has motivated the following universities and other higher education institutes to initiate CSR-related degrees and courses:

- **University of Trisakti**, Jakarta. Offers an MBA and master's degree in Management Studies focusing on CSR

- **State University of Gajah Mada**, Yogyakarta. Introduced specialisation in CSR Policy in their Master of Public Policy course

- **State University of Sebelas Maret**, Solo. Initiated a doctoral degree in CSR in 2007

- **State University of Indonesia**, Jakarta. Collaborated with PA CSR Ltd and Kofi Annan Business School (KABS) to introduce a Programme Academic Chair in CSR in 2009

- **State Institute of Technology Bandung Business School (SSMB-ITB)**. Established undergraduate and postgraduate courses (MBA, MSc in Management) which have had specialisation in CSR since 2003

References

Bresnan, J. (2005) 'Economic Recovery and Reform', in J. Bresnan (ed.), *Indonesia: The Great Transition* (New York: Rowman & Littlefield): 189-237.

Chapple, W., and J. Moon (2005) 'Corporate Social Responsibility (CSR) in Asia: A Seven-Country Study of CSR Web Site Reporting', *Business & Society* 44.4: 415-441.

FWI/GFW (2002) 'The State of the Forest: Indonesia' (Bogor, Indonesia: Forest Watch Indonesia; Washington, DC: Global Forest Watch).

Kemp, M. (2001) 'Corporate Social Responsibility in Indonesia: Quixotic Dream or Confident Expectation?' (Technology, Business and Society Programme Paper, Geneva: United Nations Research Institute for Social Development).

Khor, M. (2000) 'Globalization and the South: Some Critical Issues' (Discussion Paper No. 147, Geneva: UNCTAD).

—— (2001) *Rethinking Globalisation* (London/New York: Zed Books).

Matten, D. (2006) 'Why Do Companies Engage in Corporate Social Responsibility? Background, Reasons, and Basic Concepts', in J. Henningfeld, M. Pohl and N. Tolhurst (eds.), *The ICCA Handbook of Corporate Social Responsibility* (Chichester, UK: John Wiley): 3-46.

Shiva, V. (1999) 'Ecological Balance in an Era of Globalization', in N. Low (ed.), *Global Ethics and Environment* (London: Routledge): 47-69.

Vogel, D. (2005) *The Market for Virtues: The Potential and Limits of Corporate Social Responsibility* (Washington, DC: Brooking Institution Press).

World Bank (2006) 'World Development Indicators: Data and Statistics' (Washington, DC: World Bank).

22 Iran

Alireza Omidvar
President, CSR Development Centre

■ Context

In Iran, CSR exists in various traditional forms. For example, loans by employers to employees, charity funds for the poor, construction of schools and mosques, or religious payments to the poor or the public like *Zakat*, *Khoms* and *Vaghf*. These activities have been partly driven by the traditional role of business within the Iranian culture backed by Islamic principles. Even prior to the entrance of Islam into Iran, Zoroastrian teachings required its followers to allocate a tenth of their earnings to helping the needy, or society at large.

Many business owners in Iran have traditionally fostered a close relationship with their employees, who have in turn regarded the employer as a father figure. For example, it is not uncommon for an employer to assist employees during sickness, marriage or when purchasing a house. Hence, religion, tradition and patriarchy have played major roles in promoting responsibility by business towards society, especially in the form of charitable actions. Furthermore, corporate philanthropy in Iran is strongly driven by the media attention given to national and international disasters.

A survey of 100 Iranian companies (Omidvar 2005a) reveals that the concept of CSR is mostly translated as: a new concept that is not fully understood; minimum environmental activities; charitable donations; job creation and employee retention; activities that lead to securing certificates such as EFQM and environmental regulatory certificates; and support for seminars and conferences.

Consequently, there are two parallel phenomena in Iran that can be related to CSR: 1) a traditional inclination towards charitable activities and assisting employees; and 2) an increasing understanding and adoption of modern CSR concepts. While the former has emerged as part of the Iranian business culture, the latter appears to be an 'imported' concept which still needs to fully take root in the country. The challenge for Iran is to shift from short-term transactional-based commitments to longer-term values based on building relationships with stakeholders.

However, there are some cultural obstacles to the consolidation of CSR in Iran. For example, within the country's traditional business culture, charitable acts were always meant to remain confidential. Charity has been considered as an act in the relationship between the businessperson and God, not something to boast about in public. This sits uncomfortably against the pressure of modern CSR for transparency, reporting and communication. Another obstacle is the short-termism of Iranian managers, although this could be said to apply to businesspeople all over the world. Finally, many Iranian business leaders consider it the task of the government, rather than private companies, to contribute to sustainable development.

Despite these obstacles, a number of domestic and international processes are increasing awareness about CSR; hence, Iranian companies are gradually warming to the concept. Among the drivers are increased competition in some markets; the reputation of national quality management awards, and willingness of government and quasi-government companies to increase their rankings in these awards; and the increasing international exposure of the Iranian economy.

■ Priority issues

Unemployment

The unemployment rate for the Iranian year 1386 (2007–08) was estimated to be 15.6%, which was significantly higher than the 11.1% of the previous year.[1] Hence, economic growth and job creation are seen as priority issues for CSR. This has implications for supply chain management, where engagement with small and medium-sized companies (SMEs) and social enterprises is critical in creating an economic multiplier effect.

■ Education

Out of a total population of 66 million in Iran, 9 million are illiterate, around 90% of whom are women. The illiteracy rate is particularly high in some provinces. For example, according to the report of the Literacy Movement Organization of Iran, in the province of Sistan it exceeded 32% in 1386 (2007–08). Hence, there is a dual empowerment role for business, in terms of supporting education and gender equality.

Malnutrition

According to the Food and Agricultural Organisation (FAO), Iran has the second highest level of malnutrition in the Middle East and North Africa (MENA) region, with 2.7 million suffering from acute malnutrition. The malnutrition rate among children under 5 is 15%, according to the Mehr News Agency.

Poverty and philanthropy

Poverty was 28% in rural areas and 29% in urban areas in 2004, according to the Ministry of Welfare. The current level of poverty is estimated to be 32%. Raghfar, one of the most famous experts on poverty in Iran, has mentioned that currently the population of the poor in Iran is 20 million (*Social Security Seasonal Journal* 2006).

---

1 Iran Labour News Agency 12/4/1387; **http://ilna.ir**.

Research by Omidvar (2005b) has found that while philanthropy is an important feature of Iranian business organisations, the concept of strategic philanthropy is not widely recognised or practised. Corporate philanthropy in the region is strongly driven by media attention given to certain international disasters, such as the 2004 Bam earthquake relief efforts and the plight of Palestinian children. Of the 37 companies with corporate CSR initiatives identified, 32 of those emphasised their philanthropic contributions. These contributions are generally of a humanitarian nature, and often given to welfare or charity organisation, hospitals and disadvantaged children.

Other issues

Iranian companies list environmental protection initiatives, employee training programmes, social contributions and supporting social projects among their activities in the field of CSR (Omidvar 2005a). In particular, environmental protection and health are major CSR focus areas, probably due to more stringent regulatory obligations imposed by the government on these two issues.

∎ Trends

Iran has a long tradition as a trading economy. In the course of the 20th century and prior to the 1979 Islamic Revolution, the country also developed a substantial industrial base. However, in the post-revolutionary period there was a growing attitude of mistrust towards capital investors as a result of prevailing leftist political and economic policies and the apparent alignment of some socialist theories with Islamic teachings.

These attitudes towards investment created an insecure atmosphere for the business community. The confiscation of assets and prosecution of a number of industrialists caused a further deterioration in the overall commercial climate. Much of this mistrust was directed towards multinational companies operating in Iran, to the extent that the activities of these companies were described as exploitation and attempts at colonisation. Consequently, private sector business was mostly confined to traditional merchant activity for the first post-revolutionary decade.

This began to change in the post-war reconstruction period. The need for private sector investment in the 1990s paved the way for increased activity by domestic and foreign companies, which has led to the emergence of modern management concepts, including CSR. A watershed event in this respect was an international conference on CSR held in February 2004 by the Tehran Chamber of Commerce and the Confederation of Industry, as well as a number of private companies and non-governmental organisations (NGOs).

As Iran's market becomes more competitive and globally integrated, the significance of CSR is set to rise still further. This is supported by the efforts of the Iranian government in areas such as consumer rights, anti-monopolistic behaviour, corruption and corporate jurisdiction legislation, as well as through drafting CSR standards. A growing number of large companies are also pursing international standards, such as those of the European Foundation for Quality Management (EFQM), especially those seeking foreign (especially Western) joint-venture partners.

Iranian NGOs and business associations have also strengthened the process by promoting CSR as an important instrument in achieving sustainable development. Currently, a group of NGOs has joined forces with the UNDP to promote CSR through targeted training for managers under the umbrella of the UN Millennium Development Goals. In addition, new laws and regulations of the Tehran Stock Exchange are putting pressure on listed companies to become more transparent and accountable on issues such as environmental protection and sustainable development.

■ Legislation and codes

The legal context for CSR in Iran is focused in three areas of CSR: the workplace, environment and community. Iran has a relatively developed and stable legal framework that governs social and environmental issues. It mostly conforms to international standards and provides support for mainstream environmental management and compliance to the ILO conventions, with a few notable exceptions.

Workplace

According to the 'decent work' bylaw enacted by government, companies should provide for the present and future well-being of employees, investors, managers, employers and their families, avoiding any material and intellectual damage. Furthermore, all work should be in line with sustainable development and growth of the country, without destroying environmental resources. The concept of 'decent work' is based on four factors: freedom, equality, security and munificence.

A **Code of Corporate Governance** was drafted and ratified by the stock exchange organisation (Exchanges Regulatory Authority), for implementation by the Tehran Stock Exchange in 2010.

Environment

In Iran, environmental protection has been included in the constitution. In the Fourth National Development Plan, which embraced the concept of sustainable development, one chapter was devoted to environment. The Department of Environment administers a variety of enabling, encouraging and punitive policies in relation to the impact of companies on the environment.

Community

There is no legal obligation to allocate a proportion of a company's turnover to charity. Furthermore, for cultural reasons, there are no statistics on corporate donations, nor are companies willing to disclose this information. As a general rule, Iranian managers do not make charitable donations for publicity purposes, but rather as an act that is between them and their God.

In 2008, the *Zakat* law was codified by parliament. According to this law, a central council for *Zakat* will be formed to promote paying and organising issues around the traditional wealth tax. The government is obliged to allocate a budget equal to 110% of all *Zakat* contributions to the Imam Relief Committee. This budget is spent for alleviating poverty through in-kind donations, job creation, empowerment of the poor and improving healthcare infrastructure in rural areas.

Beyond this, industrial companies are obliged to pay a 2% special tax to the government to support infrastructural projects such as education, healthcare and sports. For example, beverage companies must pay 2% special tax to the Ministry of Health for caring for diabetes patients.

▌ Organisations

▌ **CSR Development Center**. CSR-DC is a non-governmental, non-commercial organisation that promotes CSR in Iran. The Center is the first Iranian member of UN Global Compact, a Board Member of Islamic Conference Youth Forum for Dialogue and Cooperation and member of GPN360. **http://www.csriran.com**

▌ **Institute for Productivity and Human Resources Development**. IPHRD was established by the Ministry of Industry and Mines in 2001 to promote productivity through EFQM awards. **http://www.iphrd.com**

▌ **Iran Chamber of Commerce**. The Iran Chamber of Commerce held the first CSR conference in 2004 in cooperation with the private sector, with attendance by Iranian as well as foreign companies operating in Iran. It aimed to increase companies' awareness about the CSR-based business environment and to clarify their role in society and suggest cooperative projects between the public and private sector. Mr Behzadian, former president of the Tehran Chamber of Commerce, stated that a key success factor for promoting CSR is integrating this concept in organisational culture. Also, enterprises should develop their CSR plan according to their own capabilities and characteristics. The Chamber also established an Ethics in Business committee in order to research ways of institutionalising ethics in a business environment. **http://www.iccim.ir/fa**

▌ **Iranian Association for Ethics in Science and Technology**. This association was founded in 2005 by the previous Ministry of Science with the support of distinguished professors and academics. **http://iranethics.irost.org**

▌ **Iran Standards and Industrial Research Institute**. In line with international efforts to formulate CSR standards, the ISIRI introduced SA8000, although it has yet to be implemented. ISIRI has also formed a working group to introduce ISO 26000 to the industrial community of the country. **http://www.isiri.org**

▌ **National Committee on Sustainable Development**. This committee was established by the government's environmental department, with participation by other government agencies, to promote and implement sustainable development in their departments through policies and plans. **http://www.irandoe.org/doeportal/ncsd**

▌ Case studies

Many Iranian companies display concern about social responsibility and make a social contribution, but due to traditional and religious practices, they do not publicise these as CSR. The following cases represent those with a more visible, strategic CSR profile:

Damavand/UNICEF

Provides educational facilities in 12 cities and 96 villages and has an employee volunteer scheme.

Kaveh Bandage, Gauze & Cotton Co (KBGC)

Has allocated 3% of its annual sales to voluntary charitable and cultural programmes. Three specialised committees have the role of policy-making and leading the CSR activities of the company, namely those for research and innovation, education and culture, and health and safety. **http://www.kavehbgc.com**

Melli Bank

Sees CSR as a part of its business strategy and invests in sport and cultural projects as its social responsibility. **http://www.mellibank.com**

Pakshoo

Works with UNICEF in order to improve the health of children in disadvantaged areas. The slogan for this programme is 'be kind with children'. **http://www.gig.co.ir/portal**

Pasargad Bank

Pays the debts of some prisoners each year. **http://bpi.ir**

Tam Iran Khodro

Implements CSR within its EFQM strategy, including cooperation with research institutes and universities, provision of IT and other equipment to the Ministry of Education, and sponsorship of seminars. **http://www.tam.co.ir**

Shell

Involved in the provision of educational grants to medical students, construction of a children's facility in Bam, installing an internet connection in Ahvaz schools and donation of footballs to Ahvaz schools.

Statoil

Invited the Ilam football team to Norway and is involved in the provision of technical and educational courses to oil and gas managers, as well as training of lifeguards for the IRIS.

Companies such as **Behrouz**, **Damavand**, **Tak Makaron** and **Goulrang** cooperate with UNICEF and promote its goals and projects through their marketing campaigns.

▊ Education

CSR education in Iran is still nascent and mostly led by and restricted to the interests of individual faculties. However, the CSR Development Center has reached an initial agreement with the Global Studies Faculty of the **University of Tehran** to launch a CSR Academy Center. Other departments that touch on CSR issues at Tehran University include the Theology Faculty (focusing on professional ethics) and the Medicine Faculty (focusing on medical ethics). In addition, the Economic and Management Faculty of **Sharif University** teaches business ethics.

References

Alvani, M. (1998) *Corporate Social Responsibility* (Tehran: Governmental Management Training Center. 1st edn).

Gharamaleki, A. (2001) *Professional Ethics* (Tehran: Majnun Publication, 2nd edn).

—— (2006) *Ethics Organization* (Tehran: Boshra Publication).

—— (2008) *Professional Ethics in Iran and Islam* (Tehran: Knowledge and Research Institute).

Omidvar A. (2005a) 'Country Report: CSR in Iran', *MENA Development Forum Conference*, Lebanon, April 2005.

—— (2005b) 'Perspective of CSR in Iran', *Iran Strategic Focus* 1.2 (December 2005) (Menas London): 11-14.

—— (2008) 'Public Policy and CSR in Iran', *CSR Research Journal* 1.1 (Center for Strategic Research): 9-89.

Social Security Seasonal Journal (2006) *Social Security Seasonal Journal* 24 (Spring 2006): 3-10

23 Ireland

Tomás Sercovich
Membership Services Manager, Business in the Community Ireland

▌ Context

There are two main elements that need to be considered when analysing the development and current status of CSR in Ireland: the historical context and heritage, and the role of multinational enterprises in developing CSR.

Ireland is a country that until the current economic downturn enjoyed strong economic growth, high employment rates and stability, due mainly to a large influx of foreign direct investment. One of the factors of success behind the 'Celtic Tiger' was the political and economic stability that derived from the series of Partnership Talks, a unique platform for employer and employee bodies to agree with government on a series of issues ranging from employment conditions to taxes, inflation rates and other subsidies. This platform allowed business to grow within a framework that guaranteed a stable environment. The practice of CSR was quite unknown in the way it is today when, in 2000, Business in the Community Ireland was set up as a response to the need to further organise the business contribution to society, which was at the time considered outside the Partnership Talks.

There has always been a strong sense of philanthropy and social justice in Ireland, perhaps due to its political history of division and conflict. There are prominent examples of employers who provided benefits to staff beyond compliance and had a sense of social responsibility, the most notable being the Guinness Brewery in Dublin, where its founder, Sir Arthur Guinness, built housing for staff, provided medical care for employees and their families and had a very generous approach to charitable giving. This tradition of paternalistic and caring employers was alive in many businesses for years.

Another important phenomenon was the role played by business in the 2003 Summer Games of the Special Olympics, one of the biggest sporting events ever organised in Ireland, with thousands of athletes, families, visitors and media participating. The organisation of this event required a huge influx of volunteers throughout the country and a significant amount of sponsorship. Business played a key role in supporting staff to take time off and volunteer, with many businesses faced with the challenge of organising volunteering policies to accommodate this demand. Coupled with this, social and voluntary organisations have played a key role in Irish society, with individual volunteering at the heart of many of these organisations.

Multinational investment brought a new system of company culture and values, including a more developed practice of CSR, mainly in the areas of environmental awareness and health and safety, but also in governance, reporting and communications. Multinational investment heavily influenced the development of indigenous CSR practices in Ireland and is an important factor to help understand the current state of play.

Today, the practice of CSR is widely acknowledged by Irish businesses, whether multinationals or indigenous companies, but the definition of CSR has taken some time to be widely agreed upon and we can still see a divergence in definitions and concepts. For many businesses, as well as for consumers and government, CSR is seen as an issue related mostly to community involvement, charitable giving and volunteering. There are extraordinary examples of best practice in many Irish companies, but still there is a divergence in how businesses understand the concept and the practice of CSR. Another classic dichotomy is on the importance that large businesses and small and medium-sized enterprises (SMEs) give to CSR, with SMEs arguing until recently that this was an issue for the large players only.

Models of CSR

There are no specific CSR models for Ireland. The practice of CSR has followed successful examples derived mainly from the UK and USA, where most of the large multinational companies originate and where most of the Irish export markets are. The UK model has allowed Irish businesses to understand the multi-dimensional nature of CSR, to include not only community and environmental issues but also workplace practices, the marketplace and (more recently) the area of governance and communications.

Stakeholder engagement and consultation have been at the heart of the Irish approach to CSR, as a system to streamline two-way communication between business and society. CSR communications are not as developed in Ireland as in other mature CSR countries, with notable exceptions and a concrete commitment to improve practice in this area. Unlike other countries, the ethical drivers of CSR are not so strong, fewer businesses articulating their CSR commitments in terms of being 'the right thing to do'; rather CSR is important insofar as it impacts the company's bottom line.

▌ Priority issues

Trust in business

Recent reports such as the Edelman Trust Barometer (2009) clearly show that the economic downturn has increased the negative perception of business. In Ireland, trust levels are down to 41% from 47% in 2008 and 50% in 2007. Businesses that would have been seen at the forefront of economic success have been challenged by their failed governance and reporting structures, their questionable decision-making processes and, in some cases, the lack of long-term vision for the company. All of these factors have severely undermined their capacity to recover from the crisis and regain their reputation.

In some cases, CSR has helped companies to articulate their corporate strategies, better manage operational and reputational risk and adapt to customer demands. In other cases, companies that would have been highly regarded for their successful CSR programmes have failed in their business strategy and this has raised questions about whether CSR is indeed a force for positive change or merely a PR stunt. In this sense, while the business case for CSR has been severely challenged by the media and public opinion, it is helping businesses to critically assess the impact and effectiveness of their CSR programmes and initiatives.

Climate change

The discussion on climate change and the role of business is ongoing and gaining relevance. A major issue for multinational corporations is the high cost of energy. Energy sources in Ireland are scarce, and companies rely mainly on imported energy, with the serious threat in terms of security of supply that accompanies such reliance. On the other hand, despite the country's limited capacity to generate electricity from coal, it has yet to tap the potential of exploiting renewable energy sources, mainly wind and tide/wave, which are still at the margins of the energy market.

Current estimations indicate that Ireland will be likely to miss its Kyoto CO_2 emission targets, hence the country needs to determine a realistic and competitive level of CO_2 emissions that should balance the cost of carbon with the requirements of industry and transport. There are significant challenges in terms of the contribution of agriculture to CO_2 emissions, versus its economic and social impact, that need to be resolved.

For business, this means that there is a need to revise processes and business models to adapt to the requirements of a low carbon economy. There are examples of business leadership and real transformation, but the current economic and financial crisis is not helping businesses to look beyond the very short term.

Disadvantaged sectors

Up until the early 1990s, Irish society was fragmented and divided. The economic success of the 'Celtic Tiger' helped tackle this barrier with an increase in employment, better income redistribution, lower taxes and improved social welfare structures. There are still significant challenges today and it is expected that the current economic downturn will reverse much of this social progress. Business has played a key role in social integration through programmes and initiatives to promote employment and education. It is yet to be seen whether the downturn will seriously affect the viability of these programmes.

Economic recovery

Given the major economic challenges expected in Ireland, the Irish business community needs to be prepared for economic recovery. This includes a series of challenges such as investment in cutting edge technologies, especially in the 'green tech' area; an increase in the number of science graduates; a holistic approach to lifelong learning and training; and flexible employment and family-friendly arrangements to ensure that top talent is recruited and retained. The attractiveness of a company as a potential employer is a complex assessment of not only career prospects and financial returns but also the company values and its commitment to society. In order for Ireland to remain competitive, its workforce needs to have the key skills required and offer the infrastructure and legislative backing to promote this type of sustainable economic growth.

▌ Trends

A Business in the Community Ireland (BITCI 2009a) and Ipsos MORI a Survey of Consumer Attitudes in Ireland towards Corporate Responsibility examined how decisions to buy a product or service were made. Eight out of ten people said that an organisation's commitment to social and environmental responsibility is important. Yet almost 80% of consumers could not name one company that treats staff well, offers a good customer service and is mindful of its environmental impact. While 92% of consumers are taking individual actions to limit their own environmental impacts, three out of four people could not name a company doing the same. Furthermore, 81% of consumers said customer service was the most important factor when making a judgement about a company.

According to the Edelman Trust Barometer survey in 2009,

> 83% of survey respondents in Ireland trust business less now than at the same time last year, the highest fall in any of the 20 countries covered. An encouraging sign is the continued faith in the 'knowledge economy', with the technology and biotech sectors ranking as the two most trusted industries in Ireland. However, only 21% of participants believe information they hear from a CEO about their company to be true, and 41% put their faith in conversations with company employees ahead of official channels of information.

Transparency International's recent 'National Integrity System Country Study' (2009) ranks Ireland as the 16th least corrupt country out of 180. However, it found that the country suffers high levels of lawful or 'legal corruption' and has highlighted local government, political parties and the public contracting system as the sectors most vulnerable to fraud, corruption and abuse of power. The study recommended the introduction of laws to protect whistleblowers in the public and private sector, the introduction of a register of lobbyists and the ratification of international conventions against corruption.

▌ Legislation and codes

Government has provided limited guidance on issues related to CSR as an overall business strategy. However, as part of the government guarantee scheme to provide financial stability and under the Credit Institutions (Financial Support) Scheme 2008, the government introduced a requirement for institutions to provide a summary of CSR activities through regular reports to be presented by the Irish Banking Federation.

Some of the main pieces of legislation that relate to CSR aspects include:

- **Equality Act 2004** and **Equal Status Act 2000**. These deal with all issues of equal opportunities and discrimination.

- **Safety, Health and Welfare at Work Act 2005**. Matters relating to health and safety.

- **Competition Act 2000**. Applies to marketplace issues such as price fixing and established the Competition Authority.

- **Waste Management (Amendment) Act 2001**. Relates to the implementation of the plastic bag levy.

- **Sustainable Energy Act 2002**. Established Sustainable Energy Ireland.

Government responsibility for CSR rests on various departments, led by the Department of Enterprise, Trade & Employment. The Department published a sustainable development strategy in 2003–2005, which included the development of activities to encourage and promote the take-up of CSR activities by Irish business.

▋ Organisations

▋ **Business in the Community Ireland**. The largest membership organisation for CSR, with over 58 of the top companies in Ireland as members. The organisation offers bespoke services on all aspects of CSR, as well as several programmes aimed at tacking social exclusion through business impact on education and employability. **http://www. bitc.ie**

▋ **Chambers Ireland Policy Council on CSR**. A working group that advises Chambers Ireland on their positioning on CSR and on the development of their award scheme for CSR; over 12 active members. **http://www.chambers.ie**

▋ **The Irish Business Employers Confederation Sustainable Enterprise Group**. The Group was set up to discuss common approaches and positions related to sustainability and CSR issues in Ireland with over 20 companies participating. **http://www.ibec.ie**

▋ **The National Standards Authority of Ireland ISO 26000 Expert Group**. Set up to provide the Irish input into the development of the ISO 26000 guidance document with over 20 different stakeholders from the business, government, NGO and trade union sectors. **http://www.nsai.ie**

▋ Case studies

The best source of CSR best practice in Ireland are the case studies issued by Business in the Community Ireland, which as of March 2009 included over 180 documented examples (**http://www.bitc.ie/corporate_responsibility/case_studies.html**). Some of the best CSR cases include companies such as:

Irish Life

Has a programme to implement the Plain English standard across all company communications to ensure transparency in customer communications.

Pfizer

Community investment programmes such as their Way to Go campaign on student and parent awareness on child obesity and youth smoking, with a huge impact across the country.

Savills Ireland

Graduate Excellence Programme that has incorporated employee volunteering as an element to develop leadership, negotiation, teambuilding and interpersonal skills with more effectiveness than formal training.

Vodafone

Has a Green Agenda programme; one of the first companies in Ireland to issue a public target for carbon emission reductions in their operations.

▌ Education

Although references to CSR are growing in the curricula of both undergraduate and postgraduate courses, there are no specific degrees or research programmes on CSR. Major business and commerce degrees do mention CSR, business ethics, corporate accountability; almost all universities, business schools and institutes of technology have built CSR into their curricula as stand-alone or elective courses. In 2008 the first executive education course on CSR was launched, delivered by **Nurture Development**, which is accredited by FETAC, the Irish educational accreditation agency.

References

BITCI (Business in the Community Ireland) (2009a) 'Survey of Consumer Attitudes in Ireland towards Corporate Responsibility'; **http://www.bitc.ie/uploads/2009_Survey_Report.pdf**, accessed 27 March 2010.

—— (2009b) 'Green Ireland: The Business of Climate Change'; **http://www.bitc.ie/uploads/Green_ Ireland_The_Business_of_Climate_Change_Full_Report.pdf**, accessed 27 March 2010.

Cunningham, P. (2008) *Ireland's Burning: How Climate Change Will Affect You* (Dublin: Poolbeg Press).

Edelman Trust Barometer (2009) 'Irish Results'; **http://www.slideshare.net/pkelly/edelman-trust-barometer-2009-irish-results**, accessed 27 March 2010.

Heron, R., and O. Long (2005) 'Ireland', in D. Frank (ed.), *CSR World: Jurisdictional Comparisons in the Law and Regulation of Corporate Social Responsibility* (London: The European Lawyer): 85-94.

Sweeney, L. (2008) 'European Sustainability Reporting Association Report for Ireland'; **http://www. sustainabilityreporting.eu/viewreport.php?id=35**, accessed 4 June 2010.

Transparency International Ireland (2009) 'Transparency International Country Study Ireland'; **http://www.transparency.ie/Files/NIS_Full_Report_Ireland_2009.pdf**, accessed 4 June 2010.

24 Israel

Ivri Verbin

CEO, Goodvision Corporate Responsibility Consulting

Dena Freeman

CSR consultant; lecturer in Anthropology, Hebrew University of Jerusalem

∎ Context

Giving charity is a core value in the Jewish religion and has been central to Jewish community survival throughout the ages. The Hebrew word for charity (*tzedakah*) is closely related to the word for justice (*tzedek*) and is seen as a core part of community life. Similarly, volunteering and engaging in community affairs has had a long history in Jewish communities throughout history. Charity and volunteering are thus key values in Israeli society. In a survey conducted in 1998 it was found that 72% of the adult Jewish population in Israel contributes to the community with either money or volunteering (Katz *et al.* 2007).

It was only recently, however, that these values have officially spilled over into the business world. Although many Israeli companies have given small-scale assistance to their local communities for a long time (e.g. restaurants giving surplus food to homeless people in the area), it is a relatively new phenomenon to see corporations engaged in large community programmes. As state spending on welfare has diminished, there has been an explosion of new non-governmental organisations (NGOs) and third sector organisations forming to fill this gap (Ben-Tzuri 2008). Many of these NGOs are partly funded by business donations.

In 1998, Maala (Business for Social Responsibility in Israel) was formed and spearheaded the development of CSR in Israel. One of Maala's aims is to broaden the scope of CSR in Israel, so that companies will expand their activities from simple philanthropy and community programmes and begin thinking seriously about how to integrate social, environmental and ethical concerns into their core business. Whilst still in its early stages, CSR is becoming increasingly recognised and important in Israel's business world.

▌ Priority issues

It would be fair to say that Israeli CSR practitioners are still getting to grips with the 'basics' of CSR and have not yet given much thought to the social, environmental and ethical issues that specifically face companies in the Israeli context (Shamir 2002).

Some local priority issues might include equal opportunities in the workforce for Arab and Bedouin citizens and for new immigrants; labour issues for Palestinian workers and foreign migrant workers in factories and plantations in Israel and in the Occupied Territories; and environmental sustainability. Other priority social issues in Israel include projects aimed at improving coexistence with Palestinians, moves towards peace, poverty in peripheral areas and rising social inequality.

▌ Trends

CSR in Israel started with a focus on philanthropy and community involvement and this approach still dominates. Many companies support a wide and creative range of community programmes, ranging from educational programmes for underprivileged youth in peripheral areas and promoting entrepreneurship among women and new immigrants, to teaching computer skills to Arab youth and providing health information to elderly people on low incomes.

In the past few years some leading companies have begun to expand their CSR activities to include environmental issues and business ethics. Egged, Israel's largest bus company, has been working to reduce the emissions of its bus fleet and also to minimise solid waste, sewage and water consumption. Many other companies have implemented 'green office' policies to reduce the consumption of electricity and to switch to recycling.

To date Israeli corporations are mainly importing CSR principles and practices developed in Europe and America and applying them in Israel. There has been relatively little attention given to considering how CSR might look different in the Israeli context or in addressing Israeli-specific CSR issues.

One important exception to this is in the area of community involvement, where several companies have identified important areas that are very specific to the Israeli context, for example programmes to improve the absorption of new immigrants and those that offer assistance to Arab and Bedouin citizens of Israel, who are often marginalised and discriminated against. A number of companies support such community programmes. For example, IBM Israel gives free computer programming courses to Arab and Jewish students, who then work together in order to develop learning programmes for children in a local hospital.

There has been a separate development of CSR in smaller Israeli companies that supply manufactured or cultivated products to the European and American markets. Many of these companies have implemented ethical codes in their facilities, driven by ethical supplier management programmes from abroad. However, a significant number of plantations and factories remain that do not respect workers' rights or implement local labour laws regarding minimum wages, safe working conditions, holiday and sick pay and other good practices. This situation is worst regarding foreign migrant workers (often from Thailand, China and Africa) and Palestinian workers, both in Israel and in the Occupied Palestinian Territories. These issues are being brought to public awareness by the NGO Kav LaOved (Workers' Hotline).

The first Israeli company to produce a full CSR report was Bank Discount in 2004, although several companies had produced smaller environmental or community reports before that. By 2008 the number of full CSR reports had increased to eight, and seems likely to grow in the future. Of the eight reporting companies in 2008, three are banks, three are telecommunications providers, one is a clothing company and one is a food and beverage company. Several Israeli subsidiaries of global companies also provide CSR data to be included in global CSR reports.

The awareness of CSR among the public is still small, but is slowly increasing. In a public survey by Maala in 2005, 24% said that they had avoided a product or a service in the last three years because of bad performance in CSR issues at least once, while 47% said that knowing that a company performed well in CSR would increase the chances of them buying their products. CSR issues are also getting an increasing coverage in the business press.

Socially Responsible Investment (SRI) is relatively underdeveloped in Israel and it is very unusual for investors to discuss social or environmental issues, or to require particular social or environmental standards in the companies they invest in. However, Israeli investors are beginning to become interested in investing in companies that are developing environmental technologies. 'Clean tech' is growing in Israel as Israeli scientists and entrepreneurs work to develop technological solutions to the environmental problems of today and tomorrow. The Green Fund, for example, was established by the Altshuler Shaham Group in 2005. It is the first mutual fund in Israel that focuses solely on leading edge companies in Israel and around the world which provide innovative technological solutions to global environmental challenges.

▌ Legislation and codes

Israel has over 30 laws that deal with labour and workforce issues, covering such areas as working hours, annual leave, sick pay, minimum wage, severance pay, work safety, workers with disabilities, sexual harassment and so forth. There is also special legislation dealing with the employment of foreign workers and with the use of manpower contractors.

- The **Stock Exchange Regulations (No. 10)** require all publicly listed companies to disclose the value of their philanthropic donations.

- Environmental regulation in Israel is scattered in dozens of laws and different regulations, some of which lack clarity and were legislated many years ago. In recent years there has been renewed interest and considerable development in environmental matters due to the establishment of the Ministry of Environmental Protection, which works to promote environmental legislation and growing public awareness. The **Environment Protection Law** came into effect in 2008. The key principle of this law is that the polluter pays fines or penalties when an organisation causes harm to the environment. The **Clean Air Law** was legislated in 2008, based on the United States' Clean Air Act, and is expected to take effect in 2011.

- There are a number of national voluntary codes regarding CSR. The most general and all-encompassing code is the **Guidance on the Social Responsibility of Organisations** (SI10000) brought out by the Standards Institution of Israel. This code has sections on community, workforce, human rights, environment, product life-cycle, marketplace, consumer behaviour, business ethics, corporate governance, and transparency and reporting. It was published in 2007 but, as yet, very few companies have implemented it.

- There are also a number of environmental codes, also brought out by the Standards Institution of Israel. The **Green Building Code (SI5281)** was published in 2005 and considers the environmental impact of buildings. The **Green Label**, brought out in 1994 by the Ministry of Environment Protection and the Standards Institution of Israel, is a voluntary label granted to products and services with reduced environmental impact relative to comparable products and services. By 2007 some 107 Israeli brands and products had received this.

- The Israeli Stock Exchange Authority brought out a **Corporate Governance Code** (generally known as the **Goshen Code,** after its author) in 2006. All publicly listed companies must adopt the code or explicitly state why they have not.

A number of NGOs have established further voluntary codes dealing with specific issues. The Public Trust Organisation established **The Public Trust Code** in 2006. The code covers advertising, transparency, disclosure, service and product guarantees, honesty in contracts and privacy of information. To date about 300 companies have implemented the code.

▌ Organisations

▌ **The Israel Venture Network**. A venture philanthropy network of high-tech entrepreneurs, business executives, venture capitalists, corporations and philanthropists from Israel and the US. IVN supports community projects which aim to build the capacity of the educational, social leadership and business communities in Israel through the sharing of skills, knowledge and experience that have led to private sector success. **http://www.ivn.org.il**

▌ **Maala (Business for Social Responsibility in Israel)**. The main CSR membership organisation in Israel; founded in 1998, it is modelled on America's Business for Social Responsibility (BSR), with which it is affiliated. Maala compiles an annual CSR index, holds an annual conference and offers training and support to companies developing CSR strategies and programmes. The organisation has over 100 member companies, representing combined annual revenues of USD25 billion and over 170,000 employees. The Maala CSR index ranks some 60 participating companies, representing over 41% of Israel's business, with a turnover of USD50 billion and almost 135,000 employees (Aharoni 2008). Since 2008 Maala has coordinated the UN Global Compact in Israel, which has a small, but growing, number of participating companies. **http://www.maala.org.il**

▌ **Matan**. A leading Israeli NGO specialising in facilitating cross-sector partnerships between businesses and community organisations. Established in 1998, Matan assists companies to develop effective philanthropic and community involvement programmes. Matan has worked with over 100 corporate partners and has facilitated the investment of over USD50 million and 95,000 volunteer hours into community programmes with some 800 organisations. Matan is an affiliate of United Way International and a partner of Business in the Community (UK). **http://www.matanisrael.org.il**

∎ **Tmura (The Israeli Public Service Venture Fund)**. A foundation established in 2002 with the aim of facilitating donations to community activities by high-tech companies. Companies donate equity to Tmura and upon liquidation the proceeds are donated to education and youth-related charities in Israel. Currently, over 100 companies participate in Tmura. **http://www.tmura.org**

∎ **Zionism 2000**. An Israeli NGO focusing on social responsibility. One of their core programmes, Business in the Community, was founded in the early 1990s and encourages companies to develop community programmes and contribute to the local and national community. They have worked with over 120 companies. **http://www.zionut2000.org.il**

∎ The number of CSR consultancies in Israel is growing, and there are now nearly 30. PwC, Deloitte and BDO all have CSR departments and there are several other boutique consultancies specialising in CSR or in particular areas, such as community, ethics or environment.

∎ Case studies

Fishman Group

The Fishman Group is a private investment group, primarily involved in real estate, retail, media and telecommunications. They have a community programme which focuses on disabled and disadvantaged people in Israel. Disabled people comprise 10% of the total population of Israel and unemployment rates within this group reach up to 90%. The Fishman Group and its subsidiary companies seek ways to integrate people with disabilities into their work environment as graphic designers, customer service personnel, internet information managers, warehousing assistants and so on. The company also encourages its staff to learn more about how to work with disabled people and keeps close contacts with special-interest groups. For example, 50 employees recently took a sign language course funded by the Institute for the Deaf. They then started to serve as special representatives to assist deaf and hard-of-hearing employees. **http://www.fishmanholdings.com**

Strauss Group

Strauss is an Israeli company producing various products and brands in the food and drink industry. It is one of the leading Israeli CSR companies and has received the highest ranking in the Maala Index for CSR for the past five years. Strauss takes a broad approach to CSR, aiming to consider the social, ethical and environmental impacts in all of its main business areas, and has CSR programmes operating in all units of the company. Strauss is active in issues such as diversity and inclusion, quality of the environment, healthy nutrition and fairtrade coffee. There is a company code of ethics that is designed to guide the conduct of its staff and workers in different fields, and in relations with stakeholders, in order to promote a just and humane environment. In order to further encourage open discussion on the issue of ethics, ethical trustees were appointed across the company. In 2008 the first corporate responsibility and sustainability report was published and the company joined the Global Compact. **http://www.strauss-group.com**

▌ Education

There are no full BA, MA or MBA degrees in CSR in Israeli academic institutions. However, many business and accounting degrees include semester courses on social responsibility, business ethics and other subjects related to CSR.

References

Aharoni, T. (2008) 'Corporate Social Responsibility in Israel', *The Jerusalem Post*, 27 October 2008.

Ben-Tzuri, R. (2008) 'Social Responsibility and Business Involvement in the Community: Quantitative Indicators' (Jerusalem: Research Directorate, Ministry of Trade and Industry [in Hebrew]).

Katz, H., E. Levinson and B. Gidron (2007) *Philanthropy in Israel 2006: Patterns of Giving and Volunteering of the Israeli Public* (Beersheva: Israeli Center for Third Sector Research, Ben Gurion University of the Negev).

Orit, N., and L Gadot (2003) *Corporate Social Responsibility and the Community: Its Development in Israel and the World and the Contribution of Social Work* (Jerusalem: Ministry of Social Affairs and Social Services [in Hebrew]).

Shamir, R. (2002) *The Commodification of Corporate Social Responsibility: An Israeli Test Case* (Tel Aviv: The Pinhas Sapir Center for Development, Tel Aviv University).

Shipenbauer, L. (2008) *Socially Responsible Investment of Institutional Bodies: Operational Report* (Jerusalem: Ministry of Finance [in Hebrew]).

Zachlinski, N. (2007) *The Encyclopaedia of Corporate Social Responsibility and Social Reporting* (Tel Aviv: BDO [in Hebrew]).

25 Japan

Luke Poliszcuk
CEO, eQualC Sustainability Communications

Motoko Sakashita
Insight Supervisor, McCann Erickson

▮ Context

In Japan, CSR-related ideas existed before the establishment of companies themselves. One example of this is the Tokugawa sustainable forest management practice that started around 1700 in response to deforestation, and continued to evolve over the next 150 years. Another example is the *sanpo yoshi* business philosophy practised by merchants in the Edo period. Literally meaning 'three-way good', *sanpo yoshi* means mutual benefit for both buyer and seller, and the notion that commerce should also benefit society. The founder of Panasonic Corporation, Konosuke Matsushita, is famous for his statement: 'If you do good for society, people, and yourself, you will accomplish your goals.'

Many traditional Japanese religious practices include a CSR perspective. Shinto, Japan's traditional religion, worships the natural environment, with its gods being connected to various aspects of nature, culture and people. Buddhism, another religion that has long been part of Japanese culture, places a strong emphasis on 'harmony', an important factor in CSR.

In post-war Japan, the ideas underlying the concept of CSR became more widespread as a result of environment-related issues. During the rapid post-war economic recovery, environmental pollution became a serious problem. In the 1950s, many people contracted severe illnesses such as Minamata disease caused by the release of methyl mercury in the industrial wastewater from a chemical factory in Minamata city from 1932 to 1968.

▌ Priority issues

Food self-sufficiency

Japan's food self-sufficiency ratio, at around 40%, is one of the lowest in the world. The reasons behind this include limited agricultural land, changing trends in food consumption from domestic to imported foods, and increased consumption of meat, as a low percentage of livestock feed is produced domestically. Additionally, small-lot farming is common in Japan, and higher costs encourage consumers to purchase overseas products.

This lack of self-sufficiency presents several challenges, including the issue of securing a long-term, stable, economically viable food supply. Japan was hit hard by the recent jump in international prices for staples such as rice and corn, as well as increasingly tight supplies due to new demand for raw materials for biofuels, and an increase in food import rates in developing nations.

Product recalls

Recently, a number of companies have been caught up in food mislabelling and other scandals. In 2007, there were three times more food recalls nationwide than in 2006, which had a significant impact on consumer confidence. Consequently, food labelling and food safety have featured prominently in CSR programmes at a number of major corporations.

Climate change

Japan is a signatory to the Kyoto Protocol, and is required to cut CO_2 emissions by 6% by 2012. However, despite the global economic slump and world-leading efficiency at the manufacturing level, emissions have continued to rise, particularly in the utilities sector.

Although Japan looks set to miss its Kyoto targets, the government has not set legal, binding requirements on carbon emissions in any sector. Japan has created a trial carbon trading scheme, with approximately 500 companies participating voluntarily; however, some of Japan's largest emitters have failed to participate.

Some of the current and predicted impacts of climate change in Japan include:

- **Cardio-respiratory-related illnesses and deaths.** These may be increased by a rise in temperature (the annual mean temperature in Japan has increased by about 1°C over the last century).

- **Water restrictions.** These may affect major cities such as Tokyo and Osaka. In addition, Japan is already feeling the impact of water scarcity due to climate change in food-producing nations such as Australia.

- **Flooding.** The conurbations of Tokyo, Osaka and Nagoya account for more than 50% of Japan's industrial production. In these metropolitan regions 860 km² of coastal land is already below the mean high-water level. A 100 cm rise in sea level would enlarge this area to nearly three times its current size and expand the flood-prone area from 6,270 km² to about 8,900 km².

- Other impacts include **changes in agriculture, forests, flora and aquatic eco-systems**, and **energy demand**.

Energy supply

Although Japan is the third largest oil consumer in the world, the second largest net importer of oil, and the largest net importer of LNG, it has virtually no domestic oil or natural gas reserves. Hydroelectric power and renewable energy account for just 3% and 1% respectively of total energy production, despite the abundance of wind, solar, wave and geothermal energy sources. Even with nuclear power, which supplies around 13% of Japan's energy needs, Japan is still only 16% energy self-sufficient.

As the effects of climate change become more noticeable, and oil and gas supplies begin to dwindle, Japan will face serious challenges in securing energy supplies. The manufacturing industry has reached near optimum efficiency levels in many areas and new energy sources are desperately needed. However, the government has yet to launch any policies that will fundamentally alter the current energy mix.

Labour issues

Current working conditions in Japan present many problems. Many employees work long hours, which can result in physical and mental stress, often leading to suicide or even death due to overwork. Combined with the increasing wealth gap, a rise in the number of 'working poor' and anxiety about the future, these work–life issues are making it difficult for people to get married and raise children. One result was that, in 2005, Japan experienced its first decline in population since records began. The decreasing birth rates, combined with a rapidly ageing 'grey nation', have created a shrinking labour force that is creating sustainability problems for companies as well as for society.

One of the core factors in these issues is the decreasing number of permanent staff and the increasing number of non-permanent employees, causing an imbalance in the labour force. From 1997, when the Asian financial crisis occurred, companies started reducing the number of permanent employees to maintain revenue levels, resulting in these employees having to work longer hours and take less paid leave.

In response, at the end of 2007, the government established the 'Work Life Balance Charter', portraying how companies should utilise their human resources and how individuals should change their working styles. Through the Gender Equality Bureau, the government highlighted the importance of not only assisting families in raising their children, but also providing for flexible working styles for both women and men, overhauling fixed gender stereotypes and the participation of men in housework and parenting responsibilities.

▮ Trends

As reported in the KPMG International Survey of Corporate Responsibility Reporting (2008), nearly 80% of the largest 250 companies worldwide issued CSR or sustainability reports, and an additional 4% integrated CSR information into their annual reports. The rate of reporting among the largest 100 companies by revenue in 22 countries is 45% on average, with Japan the leader at 88%. Japan has topped the tables in rates of CSR reporting over the last decade, with an 8% increase in stand-alone reports printed in the last year, and an additional 5% of companies that integrate their CSR and financial reporting.

Reporting in Japan is now the norm for top companies, although for different reasons from most of the rest of the world. Listed Japanese companies adhere to clear environmental performance and reporting regulations, and this is slowly expanding to include economic and social issues. Companies in 16 out of the 22 countries surveyed cited two of the three top drivers: ethical considerations, economic considerations and reputation/brand. France, Norway and Romania cited market position as one of their top two key drivers, while Japan, Mexico and Portugal cited innovation and employee motivation as their top two drivers.

Japan also leads when it comes to CSR strategies and the reporting process, with 86% of companies utilising a CSR strategy and objectives. Second is France, possibly indicating that the involvement of regulatory bodies or stock exchanges in encouraging disclosure of social and environmental data helps to accelerate development of a strategic approach to CSR. In Japan it seems that companies have moved away from a PR and risk management approach to CSR towards one that is integrated deeply in their businesses. Japanese companies also seem to be the most consistent: the vast majority report and do so in the context of a sustainability strategy and quantification of CSR.

Sixty-five per cent of Japanese CSR reports address supply chain risks, another first. However, despite the increasing importance of climate change, Japanese companies are falling behind when it comes to disclosure of their carbon footprints. UK companies lead, with 63% reporting on their own operations (47% in Japan) and 8% on their total value chain (11% in Japan).

Nearly all Japanese companies with business activities that have a direct impact on the environment publish reports. Companies whose business activities have a more indirect effect on the environment issue fewer reports, although the rate is still high. Japan also has the largest number of companies basing their reports on the recommendations of the Global Reporting Initiative (GRI). However, despite the fact that 99% of companies in Japan report on CSR issues in either stand-alone or annual reports, only about 24% utilise a form of formal assurance (independent verification).

At the CSR Symposium 2007, the Nikkei CSR Project conducted a survey on 'the ideal society in 2020'. The results show how people see Japanese companies as the role model for technology and CSR in Asia, especially regarding eco-friendly technology. There are signs that Japan is transforming itself from a 'grey' nation to a 'green' nation, supporting other countries with activities such as clean development mechanism projects and aiming to be a global role model.

∎ Legislation and codes

- **Companies Act**. In 2006, Japan enacted the Companies Act, unifying all corporate law. This abolished the old form of corporations, established two new forms of corporations and changed the roles and responsibilities of auditors and directors.

- **Financial Instruments and Exchange Law**. The Financial Instruments and Exchange Law came into effect in 2007. In total, 89 laws were amended, some of which were consolidated into the new law. This has broadened the scope of instruments covered under the law and is designed to protect investors by enhancing disclosure by listed companies through introduction of statutory quarterly reporting and enhancing internal control over financial reporting.

- **JCGF Principles**. In 2001 the Japan Corporate Governance Forum published its Revised Corporate Governance Principles. The revised code incorporates some new ideas, drops some earlier ones and provides more commentary than the original.

▌ Organisations

▌ **Corporate Governance Japan (CGJ)**. Founded in 2002 by the Japanese government's Research Institute of Economy, Trade and Industry, CGJ is an online forum for the discussion of corporate governance issues in Japan. **http://www.rieti.go.jp/cgj/en/index.htm**

▌ **Japan Corporate Governance Forum (JCGF)**. An organisation that aims to promote and debate corporate governance issues in Japan. JCGF issued the first Japanese corporate governance principles in 1998. **http://www.jcgf.org/en**

▌ **Japan Corporate Governance Research Institute (JCGRI)**. A nonprofit organisation set up by individuals from academia and business, JCGRI aims to promote a deeper understanding of the values of corporate governance in Japan. **http://www.jcgr.org/eng**

▌ **Global Industrial and Social Progress Research Institute (GISPRI)**. GISPRI, established by the Minister of International Trade and Industry, conducts research into issues related to global resources, the environment, industry and society. **http://www.gispri.or.jp/english**

▌ **The Kabunushi (Shareholders') Ombudsman (KO)**. The KO is a nonprofit organisation comprising lawyers, accountants, academics and shareholders. It aims to reform Japanese management practices to incorporate the views of all shareholders in Japanese companies. **http://kabuombu.sakura.ne.jp/archives/english-02.htm**

▌ **Nippon Keidanren (NK)**. The Japan Business Federation, or Nippon Keidanren, is an influential economic organisation that aims to promote and develop a free, fair and transparent Japanese economy. **http://www.keidanren.or.jp**

▌ **Certified Public Accountants and Auditing Oversight Board (CPAAOB)**. CPAAOB was established in 2004 to enhance the function and system of monitoring CPAs and audit firms. **http://www.fsa.go.jp/cpaaob/english**

▌ Case studies

aRigen Pharmaceuticals

This bio-venture company developed ARA-01, a treatment for sleeping sickness (Human African Trypanosomiasis), a major disease in Africa. It was one of the four finalists selected by the Drugs for Neglected Diseases initiative (DNDi). The best reward for these kinds of products, aRigen believes, is recognition from the public rather than monetary returns, so the packaging is to feature the following statement: 'This (not-for-profit) drug is developed by the Japanese for the African People'. http://www.arigen.jp

Sumitomo Chemical

Sumitomo Chemical developed the Olyset® net, a long-lasting insecticidal net that is making a significant contribution to the fight against malaria. In recognition of this, *TIME Magazine* named the Olyset® net one of 'The Most Amazing Inventions of 2004'. To realise its ambition to manufacture Olyset® net locally, Sumitomo Chemical transferred its technology to a Tanzanian company, which now produces 10 million units per year. This transfer has created more than 3,000 jobs in Tanzania, while the profits generated from the sale of Olyset® net help with school construction and other projects. http://www.olyset.net

Toyota

Between 1997 and 2007, Toyota improved the average fuel efficiency of its cars in Japan, the US and Europe by 17.4%. Domestic sales for hybrid cars in 2007 were 85,268 units, 5.5% of Toyota's total domestic sales. From December 2007 to March 2008, total sales of hybrid cars around the world exceeded 1.4 million units, up significantly from 440,000 units in 2007. http://www.toyota.com/hsd

▌ Education

CSR programmes and research in Japan tend to be initiated by companies rather than universities. However, the following are some of the universities active in CSR-related initiatives:

- The **Akio Morita School of Business** and the **Kisho Kurokawa Green Institute**, in conjunction with Anaheim University, California. http://www.anaheim.edu

- **Reitaku University Business Ethics** and **Compliance Research Center**. http://www.reitaku-u.ac.jp/koho/english

- **Hitotsubashi University Graduate School of International Corporate Strategy**. http://www.ics.hit-u.ac.jp

- **University of Tokyo**, Graduate School of Frontier Sciences. http://www.k.u-tokyo.ac.jp/index.html.en

- **Meiji University**, Graduate School of Governance Studies. http://www.meiji.ac.jp/cip/english

References

Asian Corporate Governance Association (2009) 'Annotated Links: Japan'; **http://www.acga-asia.org**, accessed 27 March 2010.

FRCGC (Frontier Research Center for Global Change) of the Japan Agency for Marine-Earth Science and Technology (JAMSTEC) (2007) 'Paper No. 2: Frontier Research Center for Global Change (FRCGC)', in United Nations Framework Convention on Climate Change, 'Ways to Contribute To Climate Modelling, Scenarios and Downscaling'; **http://unfccc.int/resource/docs/2007/sbsta/eng/misc24.pdf**, accessed 4 June 2010.

Gender Equality Bureau (2007) 'Gender Equality in Japan 2007' (Tokyo: Cabinet Office, Government of Japan).

KPMG International (2008) 'KPMG International Survey of Corporate Responsibility Reporting 2008' (Amstelveen, Netherlands: KPMG; **http://us.kpmg.com/RutUS_prod/Documents/8/Corporate_Sustainability_Report_US_Final.pdf**, accessed 27 March 2010).

Ministry of Agriculture, Forestry and Fisheries (2007) 'Annual Report on Food, Agriculture and Rural Areas in Japan FY 2007' (Tokyo: MAFF).

Ministry of Internal Affairs and Communications Statistics Bureau (2009) 'Labor Force Survey' (Tokyo: Ministry of Internal Affairs and Communications Statistics Bureau).

Nishioka, S., H. Harasawa, H. Hashimoto, T. Ookita, K. Masuda and T. Morita (1993) *The Potential Effects of Climate Change in Japan* (Tsukuba, Japan: Center for Global Environmental Research/Environment Agency of Japan).

26 Jordan

Dima Abdeljalil Maaytah
Associate Director, Terra Vertis

▮ Context

The Hashemite Kingdom of Jordan is a constitutional monarchy with a representative government. Jordan has played a key role in promoting peace and stability in the Middle East. In recent years, it has embarked on broad economic and social reforms to improve living standards. Since his accession to the throne, HM King Abdullah II has been determined to transform Jordan into a viable model in the region designed to be a catalyst for building the modern and developed Middle East. As a result, sustainable development, economic growth and social welfare are at the top of the national agenda and are being realised in an environment that safeguards solid political and democratic reforms and social cohesion, in order to provide Jordanians with the necessary tools to contribute to the development of their country.

Jordan's demographic profile is a major factor affecting development opportunities. In 2007, the total population of Jordan exceeded 5.69 million, representing a more than five-fold increase since 1961. The considerable growth is attributed to successive waves of refugees and migrants from Palestine and the region over the past 50 years, combined with the impacts of a high population growth rate, especially until the end of the 1970s (average 4.3% between 1952 and 1979). The current population growth rate of 2.8% has remained constant since 2000, decreasing from 3.6% in 1996.

Despite reasonable economic growth, poverty and unemployment remain serious issues and progress continues to be challenged by regional tensions. Lacking the oil wealth of some of its neighbours and with limited rainfall and arable land, Jordan is classified as a lower–middle income country. The 2009 budget was around USD8.3 billion with a deficit of USD973 million or 4.6% of GDP. The deficit is a result of Jordan's escalating oil bill, growing debt service payment, diminishing foreign aid and an anticipated lower GDP growth.

CSR status

Jordanian society is characterised by its efforts to foster a strong national identity. Religious beliefs, in particular Islamic and Christian faiths, have had a notable influence, as has the tradition of giving back to society and the values that stem from it. Until recently, philanthropy driven by personal beliefs characterised most of the CSR activity practised by Jordanian businesses. Philanthropy, being the most traditional of all CSR initiatives, has historically been a major source of support to communities.

A significant observation of businesses in Jordan is that the concept of duty is ingrained in the personal attitudes and values of the individual or persons directing the businesses, in many cases based on religious belief. CSR is seen predominantly as a social imperative, with ethical and environmental considerations much less evident among organisations. In general, CSR is concerned with 'giving something back to the community' by supporting local individuals, causes and organisations seeking different forms of assistance.

Although CSR in Jordan is an emerging phenomenon and is understood mainly as a philanthropic concept, the fact that business has found 'causes' to engage with is not new; for several years, business in Jordan has proved active on various social causes. Regardless of whether or not these activities can be evaluated as being 'responsible' by international standards and norms, a substantial number of larger national companies have already begun reflecting more strategically on their social, environmental and ethical missions and business strategies.

In the last decade there have been significant political, social and institutional reforms in Jordan. However, given extended family, religious and societal structures, the Jordanian concept of CSR will be likely to remain quite different from the western, corporate, transaction-based approach. Despite these cultural differences, CSR is beginning to take off in Jordan. Many initiatives have been launched whereby the private sector, civil society and government have worked together to produce blueprints for economic and social change. These initiatives have been associated with positive economic impacts, which have provided a sense of empowerment for the non-governmental sectors.

In 2006, the Al Urdun Al Jadid Research Centre (UJRC) published a CSR evaluation report called 'Strengthening Responsible Corporate Citizenship in the Businesses of the MENA Region'. Initiatives in seven Arab nations were discussed, including a review of a regional workshop on CSR held in Jordan and case studies from major business sectors.

In addition, the Greater Amman Municipality held a CSR forum in 2007 under the patronage of HM Queen Rania. The objective of the forum was to encourage new dialogue towards positive, progressive thinking with an impact for healthier communities in mind, body, soul and economies.

In 2009, Excellence, Inc., a not-for-profit organisation, held a conference on CSR. This served as a first opportunity for exploring CSR and summoned private sector businesses and a wide audience of stakeholders including civil society organisations, municipal councils, business associations, trade unions, media, political parties and academia.

The launch of the Global Compact (28 Jordanian companies have so far joined) and the forthcoming ISO 26000 in Jordan is likely to bring multiple benefits: encouraging the private sector to adopt CSR initiatives; creating a positive climate for foreign investments; developing local community; building up civil society; enhancing business ethics and transparency; and protecting the environment and workers' rights, in line with the objectives of the National Agenda.

CSR-related initiatives

The King Abdullah II Centre for Excellence has become the national reference for quality and encouraging excellence in performance and management in all Jordanian institutions, by promoting awareness of the concepts of distinguished performance, innovation and quality in line with international models of excellence. The award criteria include 'societal contributions', which links to CSR activities.

In addition, the Madrasati Initiative, launched by HM Queen Rania in April 2008, brings together public, private and nonprofit partners in an exciting new grassroots initiative to renovate public schools in urgent need of repair. Madrasati seeks partnerships with private sector organisations with the objective of enriching learning environments and enhancing opportunities for children in 500 schools across Jordan.

The Ministry of Labour has started the Golden List Program, which is a code of practice based on implementation of international labour standards. To be added to the list an enterprise must present a certification that all workers are covered by social security; a vocational licence; and a list of the names of foreign workers, their employment permits and their term of validity. In addition, the enterprise must sign an agreement to train and employ Jordanians as part of the National Training and Employment Project.

▋ Priority issues

Unemployment

According to the Department of Statistics, the number of unemployed people in Jordan was estimated at 170,046 in 2006, of which 71% are males and 29% are females. This represents 13% of the labour force and has been relatively stable in the past five years. The National Employment Project mentioned above has stemmed from an agreement signed by the Ministry of Labour with the administration of Sahab Qualified Industrial Zones and some investment companies. The project was funded by USAID.

Education

Despite showing impressive improvement, the education system still has some persistent problems. With a growing youth population (expected to increase by 124,634 between 2008 and 2013), the Jordanian government has to ensure adequate education and skills. However, there is currently a mismatch of skills taught and skills required by employers. Many of the jobs that have been created for Jordanians require low skills, while outdated teaching methodologies, lack of teachers' training and limited use of technology persist. The Jordan Education Initiative was launched to accelerate education reform through a public–private partnership model that drives innovation and capability. The Initiative was developed in partnership between the Government of Jordan and the World Economic Forum and to date incorporates over 17 Jordanian entities as stakeholders in achieving its goals.

■ Trends

According to a survey by Hindeyeh (2007), Jordanian companies are more engaged in social issues than is actually reported. This lack of accurate information may be the reason that Jordan is under-represented in CSR international benchmark studies and indices, which often give the general impression that Jordanian companies are not active in this field.

Hourani and Altaher (2007) find that there is no contradiction between the increasing CSR practices and the rising labour conflicts in Jordan. On the one hand, the large, exposed, export-oriented companies with young management have an understanding of CSR and of the importance of fully realising labour rights and joining global initiatives. On the other hand, small companies, informal sector businesses, unorganised sectors or sectors with weak unions are the entities that witness most, if not all, of the labour conflicts and strikes. This indicates that the private sector is not on the same level of understanding, awareness and applying of labour standards. There are two levels existing in Jordan: a highly matured one among a limited number of companies, and an undeveloped one among the majority of private sector entities.

A study by Mansur (2007) shows that lack of transparency and corruption are barriers that hinder Jordan's development. Yet 73% of respondents said that they had not attempted to implement any anti-corruption mechanisms in their companies. The survey also shows that the introduction of the Anti-Corruption Commission Law in December 2006 and subsequent creation of the Anti-Corruption Commission did not prevent the country's worsening position in the Corruption Perceptions Index, possibly because full implementation of the law is yet to take place.

A report by BSR and FIAS (2008) found that 22% of buyers are starting to phase out Jordan due to the heightened media attention on CSR issues and because of concerns that Jordan is becoming less economically competitive than neighbouring countries. Some investors and manufacturers are also beginning to pull out, citing heightened concerns around the labour shortage, increase in minimum wage and proliferation of CSR audits.

■ Legislation and codes

The following represents a sample of CSR-related legislation:

- **Labour Law No. 8 of 1996**. Includes Regulation No. 7 of 1998 on Forming Committees and Supervisors of Occupational Safety and Health Issued by virtue of Article 85.

- **Standards and Metrology Law No. 22 of 2000**. Includes a set of 94 standards and technical regulations related to environment and occupational safety, e.g. JSNO 1415 on Environmental management: Environment assessment of sites and organisations (EASO).

- **Environmental Law No. 52 of 2006**. Includes Regulation No. 37 of 2005 on conducting Environmental Impact Assessment.

∎ Organisations and education

∎ **Excellence, Inc. (EXI)**. Based on the Centers of Excellence (COE) programme, this was created as a not-for-profit organisation to further COE's efforts in supporting private sector-driven economic growth. EXI realised the potential and need for introducing a new service that tackles CSR. EXI offers consulting services and training programmes that will improve the labour environment and raise CSR awareness among organisations. **http://www.excellenceinc.org**

∎ **Schema**. Their mission is to establish an advisory role on corporate governance and corporate responsibility practices and principles. In 2007, Schema organised their first interactive corporate governance and responsibility forum. **http://www.schematt.com**

∎ **Terra Vertis**. This organisation is a sustainability consulting and training provider. Through a dedicated team of environmental and corporate responsibility experts, Terra Vertis assists clients in developing and implementing key corporate responsibility strategies, underpinned by strong policies and reporting, which helps clients focus on the opportunities and risks in their non-financial performance that are key to protecting and enhancing the value of the business. **http://www.terravertis.com**

∎ Case studies

Aramex

Aramex is a commercial provider of international and domestic express package delivery, freight forwarding, logistics and other transportation services primarily within the Middle East and South Asia. In 2005, Aramex founded Ruwwad, the first privately funded nonprofit organisation in Jordan. Ruwwad runs a series of initiatives such as scholarships and rehabilitation programmes in marginalised communities and aims to expand the successful formula throughout the region, with the goal to positively affect the lives of 1,000,000 people in marginalised and underprivileged sectors of society. In 2006, Aramex published 'Aramex Values and Principles', an internal code of conduct aligned with the Global Compact across ethical, economic, environmental and social dimensions. Aramex also contributed to the establishment of the Mousab Khorma Youth Empowerment Fund, which, since 1999, has awarded more than 100 scholarships a year to marginalised young people. It has also created an emergency and disaster relief fund and is joining forces, through sponsorships, with the Economic Opportunities for Jordanian Youth Program (INJAZ). Aramex published its first sustainability report, the first such report in Jordan and the Middle East, in 2006. **http://www.aramex.com**

Greater Amman Municipality (GAM)

GAM is taking the lead among local authorities through the preparation of its first official Master Plan, the city's blueprint for sustainable development. In 2007, GAM held the first CSR forum and created the Department for Social Services, a stand-alone department for social development that aims to enhance the quality of life in the city, and to help Jordan achieve the objectives outlined by the National Agenda and the UN Millennium Development Goals. GAM is the largest provider of volunteers for major non-governmental organisations (NGOs), and is one of the first institutions in Jordan to have an employee volunteering programme. GAM joined the UN Global Compact Cities Programme in 2008. **http://www.ammancity.gov.jo**

Nuqul Group (NG)

NG is one of the Middle East's leading industrial groups. Its business covers a wide range of products including converted hygienic tissue paper, non-woven fabrics, processed meats, aluminium profiles, ready-mix concrete, synthetic sponge/foam, plastic pipes, stationery and printed packaging materials. NG has been a member of the Global Compact since 2007 and has undertaken many initiatives to promote greater environmental responsibility. The Zero Water Discharge Project treats 1,500 m^3/day of industrial waste water, recycling it back into the manufacturing process. NG has also decreased its overall water consumption in paper mills to 5–6 m^3 /ton of paper while the international standard for the industry is between 10 and 15 m^3/ton of paper. This is a 43% saving in water consumption. NG renews its local community resources through the involvement of its employees in planting tree saplings every year. As of 2008, NG has planted over 1,000,000 trees. **http://www.nuqulgroup.com**

Social Security Investment Unit (SSIU)

The SSIU was established in accordance with the Bylaw for Investing Funds of the Social Security Corporation. The Unit started actual operations in early 2003 after the investment strategies governing its functions were endorsed. The SSIU has recently recognised its duty to spread CSR awareness amongst its corporate partners and suppliers, including the publication of the first Arabic Jordanian Businesses CSR Guidelines. **http://www.ssiu.gov.jo**

Talal Abu-Ghazaleh & Co. International (TAG)

TAG is one of the leading firms of certified public accountants and auditors in the Arab region and has been a Global Compact member since 2003. The TAG Center for Capacity Building opened in 2008 in the Gaza refugee camp near Jerash (north of Jordan). It works on qualifying the young participants of the camp to obtain the TAG Cambridge IT Skills Certificate, and offers a variety of free IT training programmes. The Center is established as an affiliate of a larger institution called the Gaza Camp Community Development Center, operating under the supervision of the UN Relief and Works Agency for Palestine Refugees in the Near East (UNRWA). **http://www.tagi.com**

▌ Education

The organisations listed above are the only ones with CSR training programmes. CSR is not offered at a university level in Jordan yet.

References

Abu-Baker, N.I., and N.M. Abdul-Karim (1997) 'Corporate Social Responsibility and Accountability as a Comprehensive Approach for Developing Reporting and Disclosure Practices in Jordan', *Dirasat: Administrative Sciences* 25.2: 409-428.

Al-Awamleh, N. (1990) 'Indicators of Social Responsibility in the Jordanian Shareholding Companies', *Dirasat: Administrative Sciences* 17.2: 7-38.

Al Urdun Al Jadid Research Centre (2006) 'Strengthening Responsible Corporate Citizenship in the Businesses of the MENA Region'; **http://www.ujrc-jordan.org/pdf/CSR%20Report.pdf**, accessed 4 June 2010.

Basma Bint, T. (2004) *Rethinking and NGO: Development, Donors and Civil Society in Jordan* (London/New York: I.B. Tauris).

Belal, A.R., and M. Momin (2009) 'Corporate Social Reporting (CSR) in Emerging Economies: A Review and Future Direction', in *Research in Accounting in Emerging Economies* series, Vol. 9: 119-143.

BSR and FIAS (2008) 'Competitiveness and CSR in the Jordanian Apparel Industry', Business for Social Responsibility; **http://www.bsr.org/reports/BSR_FIAS_Jordan-Report.pdf**, accessed 4 June 2010.

Hindeyeh, M. (2007) 'Assessment of Corporate Environmental Responsibility in Jordan' (Launching the UN Global Compact Project, UNDP; **http://www.undp-jordan.org/Portals/0/GC%20Environment%20report.doc**, accessed 4 June 2010).

Hourani, H., and M. Altaher (2007) 'Towards Strengthening Corporate Citizenship in Labour Standards and Rights' (Launching the UN Global Compact Project, UNDP; **http://www.ujrc-jordan.org/pdf/Global%20Compact%20Labour%20Study.pdf**, accessed 4 June 2010).

Ibrahim, B.L. (2005) 'Strengthening Philanthropy and Civic Engagement in the Arab World: A Mission for the John D. Gerhart Center', working paper presented at the *Symposium: Promoting Philanthropy and Civic Engagement in the Arab World*, American University in Cairo, Egypt, 30 October–1 November 2005.

Kamla, R. (2007) 'Critically Appreciating Social Accounting and Reporting in the Arab Middle East: A Postcolonial Perspective', *Advances in International Accounting* 20: 105-177.

Mansour, T. (1997) 'Social Responsibility of Public Relations in Jordanian Shareholding Companies', *Dirasat: Administrative Sciences* 24.2: 425-443.

Mansur, Y. (2007) 'Private Sector Anti-corruption Measures in Jordan' (Launching the UN Global Compact Project, UNDP; **http://www.undp-jordan.org/Portals/0/Anti-Corruption%20report.doc**, accessed 4 June 2010).

Naser, K., and N. Baker (1999) 'Empirical Evidence on Corporate Social Responsibility Reporting and Accountability in Developing Countries: The Case of Jordan', *Advances in International Accounting* 12: 193-226.

Social Security Investment Unit (2009) 'CSR Implementation Guidelines' [in Arabic], in D. Maaytah (ed.), at **http://www.ssiu.gov.jo/Portals/0/PDF/csr_book.pdf**, accessed 4 June 2010.

Wiktorowicz, Q. (2002) 'The Political Limits to Nongovernmental Organizations in Jordan', *World Development* 30.1: 77-93.

Zoubi, F. (1990) 'Involvement of Jordanian Executives in Social Responsibility: An Exploratory Study', *Mutah Lil-Buhooth Wa Al-dirasat* 5.9: 52-64.

27 Kenya

Judy N. Muthuri
Lecturer, International Centre for Corporate Social Responsibility,
Nottingham University Business School, UK

Kiarie Mwaura
Senior Lecturer in Law, University of Nairobi

■ Context

CSR has risen to prominence in recent years, and it is an emerging practice among businesses operating in Kenya. The uptake of CSR among companies in Kenya can be explained by specific economic, social, cultural and political factors, which include, among others, the nature of corporations and their role in public administration. As legal entities undertaking commercial activities with a view to profit, private companies have not had a traditional role in the public sector. Instead, it is the state-owned enterprises (parastatals) that have been key providers of public services and goods. Parastatals have been doing so since pre-independence days when the colonial government established them to offer services that were not provided by the private sector, to curb the exploitation of consumers and to redistribute regional income (Mwaura 2007).

Similar economic and social objectives led the post-independence government to establish additional parastatals, with a view to providing low cost services of a monopolistic nature, thereby developing sectors that were not attractive to private investors while Africanising the economy. It is as a result of the latter objective, for instance, that the Kenya Industrial Estate and the Industrial Commercial and Development Corporation were established to foster African socialist goals by assisting local entrepreneurs to increase their participation in the industrial sector.

However, the Kenyan government, like many others in developing countries, has gradually minimised its role in service provision and delivery through the process of privatisation. The belief that resources are likely to be used more efficiently if they are transferred to the private sector, as well as the realisation that the state, as an owner of enterprises, cannot effectively motivate firms to realise competitive business standards, are some of the justifications for privatisation (Estrin 1998).

Although Kenya is one of the largest and most advanced economies in the greater Horn of Africa, it faces numerous social, economic, political and environmental challenges, which include, for example, HIV/AIDS, high levels of poverty, corruption and bad governance. These challenges have contributed to increased stakeholder expectations for the private sector to take on broader social and political responsibilities (Muthuri 2008). Corporations are, therefore, encouraged to engage in social initiatives beyond philanthropy in order to improve the overall well-being of the local communities (SID 2004; UNDP 2003). Positive actions taken by companies have taken a variety of forms and include individual corporate initiatives as well as partnerships with governments and civil society (Bossuyt and Carlsson 2002).

CSR practices can be located within the socio-cultural traditional heritage encapsulated in the concept of 'African Mutual Social Responsibility', which is an institutionalised community development and resource mobilisation strategy popular in Kenya (Gatamah 2005). The concept encourages members of society to work and cooperate with others, through the exchange of resources (time, gifts and money), for the purposes of collective problem-solving and societal prosperity. It involves the norms of reciprocity and building of networks of mutual dependency among members of the society. If corporations are to be considered as citizens, this African philosophy should apply to them as well.

▌ Priority issues

The CSR trends show that corporations are increasingly engaging in social initiatives and many have instituted CSR policies and programmes or even set up corporate foundations (Ngondi-Houghton 2005). The engagement of companies in the administration of social goods, such as education, health and social infrastructure, reflects the particularity of Kenyan socioeconomic conditions which pose significant challenges for companies.

According to a recent survey conducted among 70 companies operating in Kenya (Muthuri and Gilbert 2009), prominent CSR issues are education (61%), environment (48%), HIV/AIDS (41%) and health (35%). Companies are increasingly aware that a healthy business depends on a healthy society and are, therefore, responding to local needs in a strategic manner. Companies have also rallied behind the Kenyan government 'Education for All' agenda to help meet the 'Universal Education' targets as set out in the Millennium Development Goals. The increased attention to environmental issues is an indication of increased global concerns about global warming. In recent years, Kenya has continued to suffer from persistent droughts with the resultant starvation and lack of water bringing untold suffering on her population. The threat of HIV and AIDS is real (UNAIDS 2008) and companies address the problem both in the community and the workplace.

Corporate governance is also becoming an urgent CSR issue owing to a lack of accountability and transparency among institutions in Kenya, as well as the absence of robust enforcement of soft and hard regulations. These factors have, for example, made it difficult to curb corruption in state-owned enterprises, most of which have struggled to remain solvent as a result (Mwaura 2007). Although these issues have attracted corporate attention, the same cannot be said of other equally important matters, such as supply chain standards, policies on fair trade and compliance with legal responsibilities.

■ Trends

CSR in Kenya is embedded within the national context and is motivated by both altruistic and economic rationales (KCDF 2006). Although the predominant wave of CSR in Kenya can be said to be community-based, with corporate philanthropy and cause-related marketing being the most popular modes of CSR (Ngondi-Houghton 2005), ever-rising stakeholder expectations and national needs are key drivers of the CSR agenda. Examples of these drivers include concerns about human rights violations in the agricultural sectors and export processing zones.

The drivers of CSR in Kenya are a combination of normative (i.e. to give something back to society), instrumental (i.e. for public relations and marketing purposes) and strategic (i.e. engagement in CSR as part of the company mission and vision) motives. These variations depend on the companies' country of origin, their size and industry sector (KCDF 2006). Muthuri and Gilbert's (2009) study demonstrates that multinational companies engage in performance-driven CSR intended to maximise profits and enhance competitiveness. Kenyan domestic companies, by contrast, were seen to engage in value-driven CSR (i.e. as a good and right thing to do).

According to Muthuri and Gilbert (2009), companies prioritise shareholders, community, environment and employee stakeholders. No wonder then that companies pay greatest attention to CSR in terms of community (90%) and environmental (74%) issues. It is very clear from various research conducted in Kenya that CSR does not take the form of Carroll's (1991) CSR pyramid, but might more or less resemble Visser's (2006) pyramid for Africa. Hence, economic responsibility as the primary objective of a firm's existence dominates the CSR agenda. Beyond economic performance, the CSR agenda of companies in Kenya is dominated by philanthropic responsibilities, followed by ethical and legal responsibilities respectively.

■ Legislation and codes

The main branch of law regulating companies in Kenya, namely company law, defines the responsibilities of directors through the lens of shareholder value. This is, however, likely to change if the government enacts the draft Companies Bill of 2007, which adopts an enlightened shareholder approach. When enacted, directors will be permitted to act in the way they consider would be most likely to promote the success of the company. In doing so, they will also be required to have regard to specific community interests. This will make the law more accessible and even help directors to take into account more social responsibilities, something that would be unlawful under the present law — especially if the benefits to the company are too remote (Muthuri and Mwaura 2006).

Despite the shortcomings of company law, a number other key pieces of legislation and industry codes have been effective drivers of CSR. These include:

- **Factories Act of 1951**. Safeguards labour rights in the industries.

- **Environmental Management and Coordination Act of 1999**. Established to provide a legal and institutional framework for the management of the environment.

- **Anti-Corruption and Economic Crimes Act of 2003**. Requires directors not to compromise the interests of companies by accepting gifts or donations or to corrupt others with donations, irrespective of their intended benefits to the company.

- A few **industry-specific codes** exist in sectors such as agribusiness.

- These codes are organisation-specific, for example those by the **Fresh Produce Exporters Association of Kenya** and the **Kenya Flower Council** which guides CSR practice in the horticulture and floriculture sectors. These two are membership organisations that seek to foster the responsible and safe production of fruits, vegetables and cut flowers, promote a safe working environment, ensure welfare of all workers and safeguard the environment.

∎ Organisations

∎ **Center for Corporate Governance**. Established in 2002; promotes the implementation of good corporate governance principles and practices in Kenya through training, education, advocacy, monitoring and evaluation. **http://www.ccg.or.ke**

∎ **Horticultural Ethical Business Initiative**. A multi-stakeholder initiative formed in 2003 to guide social auditing and accountability, and the incorporation of gendered needs of employees in the Kenyan horticulture sector. **http://www.hebi.or.ke**

∎ **Kenya Human Rights Commission (KHRC)**. Established in 1992; champions a range of economic, political, social and cultural rights of the people of Kenya. KHRC has contributed to monitoring, documenting and publicising violations of human rights and social injustice by corporations, particularly those in the horticulture industry, the export processing zones and the extractive industries. **http://www.khrc.or.ke**

∎ **The National Environment Management Authority (NEMA)**. A government parastatal tasked with the implementation of all policies relating to the environment. NEMA became operational in 2002. **http://www.nema.go.ke**

∎ **Ufadhili Trust**. Established in 2000 to promote and build local institutional capacity on resource mobilisation, volunteering, philanthropy and CSR in East Africa. **http://www. ufadhilitrust.org**

∎ Case studies

The following four case studies highlight best practices in CSR in the environment, marketplace, community and the workplace.

Bamburi Cement Ltd

Bamburi Cement Ltd was founded in 1951. It is the largest cement manufacturing company in the East Africa region. Due to the nature of its business, the environment and sustainability are priority business concerns. The company has initiated projects to implement, monitor and reduce environmental pollution from its core business pro-cesses. It has become a leading example of land reclamation and biodiversity efforts by companies — its world famous Haller Park, a quarry rehabilitation project, demon-strates the company's commitment to social and environmental responsibility. **http://www.bamburicement.com**

Magadi Soda Company

Magadi Soda Company was founded in 1911 when the primary concern of the colonial government was to administer law and order rather than development. The company, however, inadvertently adopted a social welfare approach to corporate community involvement by, for example, establishing a company town with vital social amenities including housing, water, roads, railway infrastructure, a hospital, schools, entertain-ment facilities and places of worship. The company's participatory and collaborative approaches to CSR demonstrate a commitment to the community (Muthuri 2008). **http://www.magadisoda.co.ke**

Safaricom Limited

Safaricom was started as a department of Kenya Posts & Telecommunications Corpora-tions in 1993 and was incorporated in 1997 under the Companies Act as a private limited liability company. Besides its social initiatives through sponsorship and the Safaricom Foundation, in 2007 the company introduced an innovative product, M-Pesa, which allows Kenyan customers to transfer money by mobile phone texts. An example of a 'bottom of the pyramid' product, M-Pesa allows access to financial services for mil-lions of Kenyans, most of whom are without bank accounts or access to a bank. M-Pesa empowers customers to directly and indirectly engage in social and economic activities. **http://www.safaricom.co.ke**

Unilever Kenya Limited

Unilever Kenya (previously East Africa Industries) was incorporated in Kenya in 1949 following an agreement signed by the Kenya government and the Colonial Development Corporation, now the Commonwealth Development Corporation (CDC). The company employs close to 800 employees and it invests in HIV/AIDS education and prevention, voluntary counselling and testing. In 2002, it launched the 'Neighbours Against AIDS' coalition of eight companies committed to developing a common approach to tackling HIV/AIDS in the workplace. Unilever Kenya has also helped set up the Kenya HIV/AIDS Private Sector Business Council which encourages Kenyan companies to adopt work-place HIV/AIDS programmes by creating and building their capacity to fight the disease and share best practice. **http://www.unilever-esa.com**

▌ Education

CSR education and research is relatively underdeveloped in Kenya and, as a result, most academic institutions do not have dedicated CSR programmes. However, a few business schools in leading universities offer related courses. For example:

- **Strathmore University**. Teaches ethics and corporate governance. In September 2008, it established the Governance Center to promote good governance in the public, private and civic sectors of the East African region. **http://www. strathmore.edu**

- **Kiriri Women's University of Science & Technology**. Has conducted a one-off CSR certificate course. **http://www.kwust.ac.ke**

- **United States International University**. Teaches a business ethics and CSR module. **http://www.usiu.ac.ke**

Findings from an ongoing survey on responsible management education in Kenya reveal that CSR teaching and research is on the whole left to individual faculty members' interests. However, there is evidence that universities are beginning to encourage their staff to reinforce elements of CSR in their teaching (Muthuri and Mwiti unpublished).

References

Bossuyt, J., and C. Carlsson (2002) *Institutional Analysis of Non State Actors in Kenya* (Maastricht, Netherlands: ECDPM [European Centre for Development Policy Management]).

Carroll, A.B. (1991) 'The Pyramid of Corporate Social Responsibility: Toward the Moral Management of Organisational Stakeholders', *Business Horizons* 34: 39-48.

Estrin, S. (1998) 'State Ownership, Corporate Governance, and Privatization', in S. Nestor (ed.), *Corporate Governance, State Owned Enterprises and Privatization* (Paris: OECD): 11.

Gatamah, K. (2005) 'The Corporate Enterprise in Africa: Governance, Citizenship and Social Responsibility'; http://www.corporategovernanceafrica.org, accessed 25 April 2005.

Gilbert, V.E. (2008) 'An Insight into Corporate Social Responsibility in Kenya' (MA dissertation, University of Nottingham, UK).

KCDF (Kenya Community Development Foundation) (2006) 'KCDF Corporate Research Report' (Nairobi : KCDF, August 2006).

Muthuri, J.N. (2007) 'Corporate Citizenship and Sustainable Community Development: Fostering Multi-sector Collaboration in Magadi Division in Kenya', *Journal of Corporate Citizenship* 28 (Winter 2007): 73-84.

—— (2008) 'Corporate Citizenship and the Reconstruction of Governance Roles and Relationships: Corporate Community Involvement of the Magadi Soda Company' (PhD thesis, University of Nottingham, UK).

—— and V.E. Gilbert (2009) 'Corporate Social Responsibility in Kenya: Drivers, Issues and Processes', *International Academy of African of Business and Development (IAABD) Conference*, Kampala, Uganda, 19–23 May 2009.

—— and K. Mwaura (2006) 'The Digital Divide and CSR in Africa: The Need for Corporate Law Reform', in W. Visser, M. McIntosh and C. Middleton (eds.), *Corporate Citizenship in Africa: Lessons from the Past; Paths to the Future* (Sheffield, UK: Greenleaf Publishing): 201-210.

—— and F. Mwiti (unpublished) 'The State of Responsible Management Education in Kenya'.

Mwaura, K. (2007) 'The Failure of Corporate Governance in State Owned Enterprises and the Need for Restructured Governance in Fully and Partially Privatized Enterprises: The Case of Kenya', *Fordham International Law Journal* 31: 34-75.

Ngondi-Houghton, C. (2005) *Philanthropy in East Africa: The Nature, Challenges and Potential* (London: Allavida).

SID (Society for International Development) (2004) 'Pulling Apart: Facts and Figures on Inequality in Kenya' (a report by the Society for International Development Eastern Africa Regional Office; Nairobi, Kenya: SID).

UNAIDS (2008) 'Epidemiological Fact Sheet on HIV and AIDS'; **http://www.who.int/globalatlas/ predefinedReports/EFS2008/full/EFS2008_KE.pdf**, accessed 30 August 2008.

UNDP (United Nations Development Programme) (2003) *Participatory Governance for Human Development. Third Kenya Human Development Report* (Nairobi: UNDP).

Visser, W. (2006) 'Revisiting Carroll's CSR Pyramid: An African Perspective', in E. Pedersen and M. Huniche (eds.), *Corporate Citizenship in Developing Countries* (Copenhagen: The Copenhagen Centre): 29-56.

28 Liberia

Marcus S. Wleh

Corporate Responsibility Manager, ArcelorMittal Liberia[1]

∎ Context

Formally established as a republic in 1847 by freed and resettled slaves, Liberia's history is peppered with political struggles between a small ruling class and the majority of indigenous Liberians. Its 3.49 million people are spread out over 111,370 km² of mostly forested land. A violent overthrow of the former ruling class by a mainly indigenous military in 1980 was followed by more upheavals, which resulted in a 14-year civil war that ended in 2003. The election of a member of the former ruling class in 2005 and the presence of over 14,000 UN peacekeepers has so far kept the peace and maintained stability.

Liberia is endowed with gold, diamonds, iron ore, nickel, cobalt, manganese and, it is believed, oil. It has one of the few remaining rainforests in West Africa. With an estimated 2008 GDP per capita of USD500, Liberia ranks number 176 out of 179 countries on the UN Human Development Index (UNDP 2008). Seventy-six per cent of the population is dependent on subsistence agriculture with official unemployment at around 85% (US CIA, 2009). Average adult life expectancy at birth is estimated at 45 years.

The early years

In the period leading up to the first large investment in Liberia by the Firestone Tire & Rubber Company, a large part of Liberia was in dire need of basic social services such as schools, hospitals and roads. There was an increasing need for opening up the hinterland — the largest part of Liberia was cut off from Monrovia (the country's capital). The official policy espoused by the government during this period was the attraction of foreign capital from many sources for a wide range of investment that would enable the economy to become more diversified, while at the same time yielding development dividends in local communities where foreign businesses operated.

Thus, when Firestone began operation in 1926, it constructed schools, health facilities

---

1 **Disclaimer.** The views expressed in this article are those of the author and do not represent the views and policies of ArcelorMittal or any of its subsidiaries and affiliates.

and roads and provided accommodation for its employees in an area that was essentially a wilderness. Later, this area became a small city, renamed Harbel (after Harvey and Isabel Firestone).

During the iron ore boom beginning in the late 1950s, the three largest iron ore mining companies established and ran various programmes intended to address the socioeconomic needs of communities where they operated. These social programmes were focused on the need for adequate facilities in the concession areas and not for the altruistic aim of contributing to socioeconomic growth and development in poor, rural communities. The companies built schools, hospitals and roads and provided electricity and safe drinking water for their concession areas. In time, the concession areas became small cities in the midst of misery and poverty.

Although the results achieved by these companies are the focus of many discussions on CSR in Liberia, the relative dearth of details makes it difficult to conduct any useful analysis of these programmes. There is also very little physical evidence to indicate that the companies' focus was on improving the lives of the ordinary people in communities where the natural resources were being extracted.

As a major shareholder in the management of the four iron ore companies, the government played a significant role in influencing companies' decisions on CSR. It included a Viable Community Clause in all mining concession agreements to ensure that companies supported agricultural, industrial and commercial enterprises, which promoted self-reliance and sustainability. There were also provisions on employment and training of Liberians, utilisation of local resources and ownership of natural resources.

However, as Barnea and Rubin (2006) found, CSR may create a conflict between different shareholders, when there are opposing views of how high a company's expenditure on social initiatives should be. Despite official provisions, there was a lack of political goodwill by the government to ensure that companies adhered to the Viable Community Clause and other social provisions. As a result, there was often very little perceptible transformational development in many communities where companies operated.

The intermediate period: 1971–1989

In the 1970s and 1980s there was an increase in the role that national and foreign companies played in promoting CSR. Through his concept of humanistic capitalism, President William Tolbert (1971–1980) sought to bring a new approach to relations with business, especially foreign companies. For example, he ordered the renegotiations of old concession agreements in favour of accountability and socioeconomic development. As a result, the Liberia Petroleum Refining Company contributed large sums to provide low-cost housing for Liberians, and the Liberia Electricity Corporation and similar other public corporations established scholarship funds to provide needy students with high school and university education.

However, domestic political instability, capital flight and the global financial crises of the 1980s forced many large mining and agro-based companies to scale down operations or close down. For those that remained, many of the CSR programmes of the 1970s continued into the 1980s, albeit at a reduced pace.

The war years: 1990–2003

The 14-year civil conflict saw a significant reduction in economic activities, with the most vibrant economic sectors being logging and small-scale mining of gold and diamonds. A large proportion of the economy was heavily dependent on foreign aid and foreign remittances.

The activities of logging and mining companies that operated in Liberia during the war years have been documented in many reports and studies. In their operations, some of these companies are alleged to have abused workers' and community rights, encroached on private lands and provided very little benefits to local communities. For example, Global Witness[2] reported that there was widespread environmental degradation and deforestation in communities where logging and mining operations took place. Indeed, it was during this period that Liberia earned a reputation for using 'blood diamonds' to fuel conflicts in the region.

There was very little, if any, investment in social projects to mitigate the effects of companies' activities on local communities. Moreover, due to declining incomes, many public corporations ended their social programmes, thereby placing the responsibility on the UN and non-governmental organisations (NGOs) which operated in Liberia during this period. In 2002, for example, the UN and aid agencies appealed for over USD17.2 million to provide food aid and basic social services for over 0.5 million people in Liberia.

Post-war: 2003 to present

Two main factors have helped propel corporate responsibility issues to the forefront of business in present-day Liberia. The first is the legacy of dependency created by years of relying on aid money for socioeconomic development during the civil conflict. This has created local expectations that companies struggle daily to meet. Another factor is the relative freedom of advocacy on political, economic and social rights, owing partly to the multiplicity of NGOs and human rights organisations. An 'aware society' is constantly confronting companies and government on community rights, justice, peace and socioeconomic development.

There has been a significant growth in investment (or 'returning investment') following the end of the civil war. Companies, especially those in the extractive sectors, now face tougher scrutiny in their operations. The government has led the way in reforming the way business is done in Liberia. It has renegotiated agreements with Firestone and other concessions in order to provide more dividends to the country and to increase investment in social and environmental mitigation projects. New mineral development and logging agreements now place an emphasis on addressing issues related to the environment, workers' rights, community development, and sustainability.

■ Priority issues

Land rights and natural resources

The current growth of investment in forestry, agriculture and mining is taking place against a background of increasing tensions among communities for access to land and its related wealth. For example, in 2007 a Belgian manager of the Liberia Agricultural Company (LAC) was shot and killed in a village in Grand Bassa County, where residents

2   http://www.globalwitness.org/pages/en/liberia.html

were protesting the expansion of the rubber plantation on land they claimed were theirs.

There are significant challenges in relocating and paying just compensation to people who have encroached on the right of way of former railroad tracks and who have occupied properties of former mining, logging and agro-based companies across the country.

Community dividends

Establishing the dividends that accrue to communities whose lives are affected by companies' activities is an important concern for the government and its stakeholders. This issue resonates with current advocacy over ensuring that communities who 'own' the resources benefit the most from their exploitation. In helping to address this, the government has negotiated mining and logging contracts that commit companies to funding social projects in local communities.

In a good example of private sector–civil society–government collaboration, the Liberia EITI (Extractive Industries Transparency Initiative) produced the first report of payments made by extractive companies to the government. The report shows that companies paid nearly USD30 million to the government in the fiscal year July 2007–June 2008.

Conservation versus economic development

Liberia faces a challenge in balancing the need for rapid economic growth with the need to sustain its natural environment and biodiversity. The key revenue earners are located in the extractive sectors, which deplete both renewable and non-renewable resources. Some of the large deposits of minerals lie in virgin, tropical forests. Logging also affects natural habitats and local livelihoods. Dealing with environmental pollution and determining appropriate mitigating and remedial measures are challenges that will have to be addressed.

▌ Trends

The divide between marketing and advertising, and CSR programmes, has grown narrower in Liberia. For example, a company may want to assist a struggling basketball team as part of its CSR. It purchases jerseys and sneakers for the team and emblazons its corporate emblem on them. The public sees the company's actions as philanthropic and the company achieves publicity through an effective marketing strategy.

The pool of studies and academic research on CSR in Liberia is shallow. A few academic theses and dissertations researched the social programmes of former concessionaires. Other research materials cite Liberia as an example of a country where human rights, social development and transparency can be improved in the conduct of business.

One such source is Mohamed Latifi's doctoral thesis (Latifi 2004). He argues that multinational companies in Liberia were not equipped to deal with the complexities of indigenous development, and were more likely to use an intermediary to implement their social programmes. Yet, he found that past governments relied on multinational companies to take responsibility for social development in their concession areas.

Therefore, of the more than USD20 million paid to the government in the form of royalties between 1976 and 1980, no visible development investments were made in rural areas.

Global Witness, Greenpeace, Amnesty International and their affiliates in Liberia are among the organisations that have contributed to propelling corporate responsibility issues to the forefront of advocacy for improved human rights and accountability in Liberia. These organisations were successful in influencing the imposition of UN sanctions on the sale of Liberia's diamonds and timber and in renegotiating investment contracts in post-war Liberia.

There are genuine concerns that the economic downturn of 2009 will force companies to concentrate on survival rather than adhering to international best practices on good corporate citizenship or philanthropy. If CSR is on the lower rung of a company's priority ladder, this may lead to either the postponement or cancellation of social programmes. If, as is feared, the economic crisis leads to the drying up of foreign aid and foreign direct investment, this could fuel unemployment and adversely affect the government's poverty reduction strategy.

▌ Legislation and codes

Liberia has made significant progress in institutionalising best practices in the way businesses operate and the impact their activities can have on local communities. Each major investment sector now has a law or policy that prescribes specific guidelines and regulations geared towards ensuring that international best practices are adhered to and the interests of Liberia are promoted.

The National Forestry Reform Law of 2006 and Liberia's Mineral Policy are good examples. They include specific provisions on programmes to promote community development and to mitigate the impact of a company's operations on the environment. An EITI law now obliges companies to report on all payments to government in the extractive industry sector in Liberia.

▌ Organisations

▌ There are no business associations that promote CSR in Liberia as a core activity. ArcelorMittal Liberia is collaborating with German Technical Cooperation (GTZ) on the establishment of a corporate responsibility forum in Liberia.

▌ Case studies

ArcelorMittal Liberia

ArcelorMittal is one company that is trying to implement international best practices in its CSR programme in Liberia. In the rehabilitation stage of its Liberia Mining Project, the company dealt regularly with competing ownership claims to lands within the concession areas (defined in the Mineral Development Agreement). Other issues were relocation of people, crops and small public infrastructure from the railway right of way and providing alternative income-generating activities for people who had hitherto used the railroad for small businesses. In this process, it used a combination of information dissemination, consultations, impact assessment, conflict resolution and compensation to tackle these issues.

Through its County Social Development Fund, ArcelorMittal is investing USD3 million annually for development projects in the three counties where it operates. The company initiated a groundbreaking environmental and social impact assessment (ESIA) in 2009. The ESIA will help in the formulation of appropriate strategies to mitigate the impact of mining activities on the environment and local communities. **http://www.arcelormittal. com**

Broadway Consolidated

Broadway Consolidated Plc is investing in the grassroots development of sports in Liberia with the aim of promoting the health and well-being of young Liberians. The company has sponsored football and basketball tournaments and has funded training for Liberian athletes abroad. Recently, it distributed football jerseys and boots to local football teams and the Liberia National Olympic Committee. They have launched a Boots for Liberia programme to provide football boots to deprived young children who play football in bare feet. **http://www.bc-plc.co.uk/social-programmes.htm**

Firestone Rubber Company

Prompted by many calls and advocacy, including violent protests, Firestone renegotiated its contract with the government to include specific improvements in employees' welfare, housing and other sustainable development projects. Now, the company is funding scholarships and investing in better healthcare and education for its employees and their dependants. **http://www.firestonenaturalrubber.com**

■ Education

No university in Liberia currently offers courses or degrees in CSR, nor are there training courses or seminars on corporate social responsibility.

References

Barnea, A., and A. Rubin (2006) 'Corporate Social Responsibility as a Conflict between Shareholders', Social Science Research Network Working Paper Series, 10 March 2006; **http://papers.ssrn. com/50/3/papers.cfm?abstract_id=686606**, accessed 4 June 2010.

Global Security (2009) 'Liberia: A Country Study 2000–2009'; **http://www.globalsecurity.org/military/ library/report/1985/liberia_contents.htm**, accessed 4 June 2010.

Latifi, M. (2004) 'Multinational Companies and Host Partnership in Rural Development: A Network Perspective on the Lamco Case' (doctoral dissertation; Uppsala University, Sweden).

LISGIS (Liberia Institute for Statistic and Geo-Information Services), Ministry of Health and Social Welfare, National AIDS Control Program and Macro International Inc. (2008) 'Liberia Demographic and Health Survey' (Monrovia, Liberia: LISGIS; Calverton, MA: Macro International Inc.).

—— and Government of Liberia (2008) '2008 National Population and Housing Census: Preliminary Results', June 2008; http://www.emansion.gov.lr/doc/census_2008provisionalresults.pdf, accessed 4 June 2010.

OCHA (UN Office for the Coordination of Humanitarian Affairs) (2001) 'Consolidated Interagency Appeal for Liberia 2002' (New York: OCHA, November 2001).

UNDP (United Nations Development Programme) (2008) 'Human Development Reports: Statistical Update 2008'; http://hdr.undp.org/en/statistics, accessed March 2009.

US CIA (Central Intelligence Agency) (2009) 'The World Factbook', 5 March 2009; https://http://www.cia.gov/library/publications/the-world-factbook/geos/li.html, accessed June 2009.

Van der Kraaij, F.P.M. (1995) 'Liberia: Past and Present of Africa's Oldest Republic'; http://www.liberiapastandpresent.org, accessed 29 March 2010.

World Bank Group (2008) 'Liberia at a Glance', 12 September 2009; http://devdata.worldbank.org/AAG/lbr_aag.pdf, accessed 29 March 2010.

29 Malaysia

Roger Haw Boon Hong
Professor in Corporate Social Responsibility,
Ansted University; Founder and Chairman of the
Ansted Social Responsibility International Award (ASRIA)

▋ Context

Malaysia is a country of great diversity. The diversity does not only apply to its natural heritage, but also to the multiracial, multi-religious and multicultural population of 26 million. Caring is still part of Malaysian life and although there is no standard CSR model, each organisation has in its own way put CSR into practice.

Strategically located at the crossroads between the East and the West, Malaysia attracted early travellers from different parts of the world. Also, Hindu–Buddhist influences came from India and China. Traders from the Middle East and India sailed to this land, introducing Islam to the local population. The country's independence was proclaimed on 31 August 1957. Kuala Lumpur is the country's capital city. The petroleum industry makes the largest contribution to GDP and the manufacturing sector has transformed Malaysia from an agriculture-based country into an industrial economy.

CSR is not a freshly minted idea to Malaysians; the term might be new to some, but not the concept. CSR principles epitomise the fundamental religious and social values that have held together the very fabric of Malaysian society for millennia.

▋ Priority issues

Community and social welfare

Over 1,000 community and social welfare projects were implemented in 2008, compared to 350 projects in 1998. These range from the setting up of ICT centres in rural Malaysia and improving health through the use of cutting-edge medical technology, to sponsoring children's educational needs and providing convenience facilities, which includes escalator and washrooms/toilets for the disabled community and senior citizens. As a result of these community programmes, the lives of many marginalised and underprivileged people are being improved.

Education

There is a strong emphasis on the provision of scholarships to underprivileged children. Studies have shown that the number of students who obtained scholarships for pursuing various levels of education has increased by 300% within the ten-year period 1995–2005. Companies are also providing vocational training to equip youth and women with marketable skills. In addition, some corporations have set up resource centres in rural and semi-urban areas; others have even established universities. Certain projects make interesting use of IT. For example, employees have been using computers for online distance-learning courses, website design competitions and company internal quizzes, which helps to improve proficiencies in IT and English.

Environment

Environmental projects range from protecting endangered species such as marine turtles, to rehabilitating entire natural habitats, such as mangroves and firefly colonies. Since 2000, almost 55% of companies in Malaysia have prioritised environmental protection plans in their projects, as compared to only 10–15% in 1980. Property developers are building around, and sometimes even creating, 'green lungs', while resorts are adopting eco-friendly initiatives and policies, for example using recycled materials and recycling waste. Companies are also educating the public on important green issues, such as the need to adopt non-wasteful habits.

Workplace practices

According to ASRIA's studies carried out in 2008 (Haw 2008), 47% of companies in Malaysia are practising good workplace ethics to create a vibrant, healthy environment for their employees. Many companies are becoming more flexible with regards to where, when and how employees work. Links between home and office are becoming blurred as companies seek to strike a better work–life balance by creating greater opportunity for social interaction with families of employees. Some companies are even providing scholarships to the children of staff.

Culture and heritage

Whether it is by supporting the work of heritage champions, setting up a fund to promote the local theatre, preserving traditional music or restoring historical landmarks, corporations clearly understand the importance of protecting Malaysia's culture and heritage. In 1980, only 5% of corporations were willing to support cultural and heritage projects or events, compared to 35% today. Through their projects, these companies have also improved the lives of artisans, artists and their families in rural communities, while playing an enormous role in helping to safeguard some of the nation's most precious and irreplaceable assets.

▌ Trends

Awareness

The Ansted Social Responsibility International Award (ASRIA) has helped to raise awareness about the need for business to be legitimate in the eyes of the public, through managing the company's human capital as well as its social, financial, manufactured and natural capital. This is starting to manifest itself through companies in Malaysia that are weaving CSR into their strategy and holding dialogues with stakeholders. These changes are driven in part by more discerning customers and institutional investors, who are beginning to show signs of favouring socially responsible stocks.

Reporting

A recent survey by the ASRIA in Malaysia found that there has been an increase in the number of listed companies reporting on environmental and social responsibilities, compared with the results of a similar study conducted in 2007 (Haw 2007). More specifically, the number of listed companies reporting environmental information has increased from 30 in 1999 to 138 in 2007. Disclosure of social performance has risen similarly, from 28 companies in 2002 to 43 in 2003. Among the companies that embrace such reporting, it is heartening to note that many see a close link between reputation and the importance of CSR. A majority of the companies whose annual reports discuss their CSR activities are multinationals and the large-cap (large or publicly listed) home-grown corporations.

Awards

Prestigious awards such as ASRIA (launched in 2004) (Crowther 2004), MESRA (launched in 2006) (ACCA 2006), the Prime Minister's CSR Awards (launched in 2007) and StarBiz-ICR Malaysia Corporate Responsibility Awards (launched in 2008) aim to recognise companies that have made a difference to the communities in which they operate through their CSR programmes. Launching these awards has helped raise the profile of corporate transparency and responsibility issues in Malaysia. They especially serve to encourage non-reporters to publish information on their social and environmental impacts and, ultimately, help underline the business case for sustainable practices and development. Overall there has been an improvement in the number of entries for CSR recognitions in Malaysia.

Research

In addition to these awards, ASRIA and ACCA regularly conduct research to explore CSR and sustainability issues, including on sustainability accounting in the Malaysian government, social and environmental reporting, ethical investment, social capital and ecological footprint analysis. Growing awareness of the concepts and applications of CSR has prompted strong interest from the media.

SMEs

In 2008, 58% of small companies contributed to society 'in a big way', as compared to 18% in 1998, a 40% increase within a ten-year period. Small companies are 'showing big hearts' by integrating a caring philosophy into their day-to-day operations, from improving the literacy of underprivileged children to campaigning to stop violence against women. Focusing on key issues affecting the community while supporting their businesses, these companies prove that being small is no hindrance to doing great work.

Media

The percentage of media reporting on CSR has increased from 35% to 45% between 1980 and 2003, and from 45% to 87% between 2004 and 2008. Media reporting of the community-based initiatives of corporations is as important as the CSR programmes themselves. Such reporting both serves to increase public awareness of topics of national concern and to motivate other companies to follow in the lead of CSR practitioners. At the same time, media houses are also reporting on issues of justice and fair play, which is contributing towards strengthening the moral fibre of the nation.

▌ Legislation and codes

The Malaysian government is expected to continue to place an emphasis on CSR practices, especially by listed companies. In the 2007 budget, the government announced that all listed companies are required to disclose CSR activities in their annual financial reports, including their employment composition by race and gender, as well as programmes undertaken to develop domestic and *Bumiputera* (ethnic Malay) vendors.

Recognising that the private sector has been successful in implementing CSR projects for the benefit of low-income groups, the government has established a CSR fund, with an initial sum of MYR50 million (USD15 million), to jointly finance selected CSR projects. These include repairing dilapidated houses for the poor and creating more employment opportunities. It is also proposed that tax deductions be granted for CSR investments, even if these investments also benefit the companies.

▌ Organisations

▌ **The Securities Commission Malaysia** and **Bursa Malaysia** provided the starting and reference point for potential CSR practitioners by sharing their CSR Framework, while **Khazanah** drove the CSR agenda for government linked corporations with its guidelines. The guidelines mandate that, whatever good causes companies support, they must ensure that stakeholders' interests are not put at risk.

▌ Other organisations that have supported CSR development are the **Institute of Corporate Responsibility Malaysia**, the **Department of Environment**, the **Ministry of Women, Family & Community Development**, the **Ministry of Culture, Arts & Heritage**, the **Malaysian Institute of Integrity**, **Transparency International Malaysia**, **ACCA** and **ASRIA** in Malaysia.

■ Case studies

DiGi

Ever since 2005, more than 1,000 children have embarked on 'journeys of discovery' with the help of DiGi, through their Amazing Malaysians (AM) programme. AM is DiGi's way of putting substance and meaning into progress and technology. It is a corporate responsibility programme that shares the work of ordinary Malaysians who do extraordinary things to preserve national heritage — whether natural, cultural, artistic, social or architectural. From these amazing heritage practitioners, the children learn about the country's rich legacy. The experience creates lifelong impressions, allowing them to see heritage in a new light — a bridge from past to future. The children have been transformed into 'ambassadors of change' — change for the better, for an enriched nation, proud of its unique identity. **http://www.digi.com.my/aboutdigi/cr/cr_index.do**

Northport (Malaysia) Bhd

CSR in Northport (Malaysia) Bhd is driven all the way from the president down to the management staff. The company is committed to promoting a caring society through its various local community projects, including Adopting Port Klang Project/Port Klang Citizenship Program,[1] Northport Business Safety Initiative, Life Long Education Programme, Employee Sustainability Programme and Community Technology Terminal Initiative. As a result of these positive values, Northport has received an award from ASRIA's CSR-CAP Board. **http://www.northport.com.my**

Telekom Malaysia

Telekom Malaysia (TM) is committed to a CSR programme in the area of education. In line with the Malaysian government's move to promote and encourage higher education, TM has invested over MYR800 million in higher education facilities by establishing the Multimedia University and Multimedia College, as well as by providing financial assistance through the TM foundation. The objective is to contribute towards building a larger human capital pool for the nation in the areas of ICT, multimedia and language proficiency, especially in English. By 2008, the TM foundation had sponsored over 4,000 students in its various scholarship schemes. TM is interested in education because knowledge creates possibilities. **http://www.tm.com.my**

YTL Corporation

The YTL Corporation is doing its part for the environment by incorporating new alternative energy and eco-friendly technologies in every aspect of the business. This helps to tackle the issues of forest fires and climate change. **http://www.ytlcommunity.com/climatechange**

---

1 Port Klang is an international cargo harbour hub located in Klang district of Malaysia. Both these titles are used in referring to the community services in that area supported by Northport (Malaysia).

Other organisations

Other progressive companies on CSR include: **Advanced Micro Devices Export Sdn. Bhd.** (http://www.amd.com), **IJM Corporation Berhad** (http://www.ijm.org), **Ire-Tex Corporation Berhad** (http://www.iretex.com.my), **MERCY Malaysia** (http://www.mercy.org.my), **Nestlé (Malaysia) Berhad** (http://www.nestle.com.my), **Shell Malaysia** (http://www.shell.com.my) and **Tenaga Nasional Berhad** (http://www.tnb.com.my).

▌ Education

CSR education in Malaysia is still very much at the nascent stage. Local institutions in Malaysia do not have any CSR faculty to support and conduct research and development. Therefore, there is no specific diploma or degree programme in CSR, and CSR is not available as a course, but is typically incorporated into business and accounting programmes, often as part of the corporate governance components of MBA courses.

However, a few foreign universities — from the UK (**Nottingham University in Malaysia http://www.nottingham.edu.my**) and Australia (**Monash University–Sunway Campus http://www.monash.edu.my** in Malaysia) — have branch campuses located in Malaysia that are offering graduate degree programmes with majors in CSR.

References

ACCA (ACCA Malaysia) (2006) 'ACCA Malaysia Environmental and Social Reporting Awards (MESRA) 2006', ACCA Malaysia Sdn. Bhd; http://www.accaglobal.com.

Anugerah CSR Perdana Menteri (Malaysia) (2007) '2007 Report', Capital Corporate Communications Sdn. Bhd; http://www.anugerahcsrmalaysia.org.

ASRIA (Ansted Social Responsibility International Award) (2004) 'SRW Social Responsibility World of RecordPedia', Ansted Service Center, ASRIA report 2004, 46-60.

Crowther (2004) 'SRW Social Responsibility World of Recordpedia 2004' (Penang, Malaysia: Ansted Service Center).

Haw (2007) 'ASRIA Survey Report' (Penang, Malaysia: Ansted Service Center).

—— (2008) 'ASRIA Survey Report' (Penang, Malaysia: Ansted Service Center).

MESRA (2006) *Report of the Judges* (Kuala Lumpur, Malaysia: ACCA): 2-23.

Star Bizweek (2004) 'Does corporate Malaysia care?', *Star Bizweek*, cover feature, 13 November 2004: 12-13.

The Edge Malaysia (2008) 'The Northport Edge: Sustaining growth strengthens customer confidence', *The Edge Malaysia*, 7 April 2008: 2-3.

The Sun (2007) 'ACCA Mesra awards 2006, Malaysia', *The Sun*, 7 May 2007: 4-14.

Web resources

Silver Book Guidelines (Malaysia) available from **http://freedownloadbooks.net/synopsis-khazanah-silver-book-pdf.html** (accessed 10 October 2009).

30 Mauritius

Renginee G. Pillay
Lecturer, School of Law, University of Surrey, UK

■ Context

Mauritius is a tiny island of 1,865 km² situated in the Indian Ocean off the south east coast of the African continent. It was uninhabited when the Portuguese discovered it at the beginning of the 16th century. It was first settled by the Dutch in 1598, followed by the French in 1715 and by the British in 1810. The British were in control until 1968, when the country gained independence. Mauritius became a Republic in 1992 and forms part of the British Commonwealth.

Mauritius is one of Africa's richest countries. Its engines of growth have been sugar (under the European Union Sugar Protocol), textiles (under the Agreement on Textiles and Clothing, commonly known as the Multi-Fibre Agreement or MFA, and now under the African Growth and Opportunity Act or AGOA) and tourism.

The very first example of CSR in Mauritius was during the colonial times when, in 1948, the government established the Sugar Industry Labour Welfare Fund (SILWF). The SILWF is a parastatal (quasi-public) body, which is funded by part of a 'cess' (an assessed tax; Government of Mauritius 2005), to which sugar producers contribute. The object of the SILWF is to contribute to the welfare of workers and their children. One of its projects is a scholarship scheme, whereby financial assistance is given to children of sugar workers at secondary and university level and also for vocational training schools. Moreover, the sugar estates built concrete houses for some of their workers and also donated the land on which housing estates have been built by the SILWF.

Forty years later, in 1988, another parastatal body, the Export Processing Zone Labour Welfare Fund (EPZLWF) was established by the government. Like the SILWF, the object of the EPZLWF is to contribute to the welfare of workers and their children. It also operates a number of different projects, including a daycare centre, a scholarship scheme and a household appliances programme.

These two examples are government-led initiatives. Over the last ten years, CSR has also been done by companies on a voluntary basis, mostly in the form of charitable donations. However, recent legislation has now made such donations mandatory.

Since it is a relatively new area of study, no unique CSR model has been proposed in the context of Mauritius.

▮ Priority issues

Cultural issues

Although Mauritius is known as an upper middle-income country, income disparities prevail. In February 1999, week-long riots erupted in Mauritius. These were generally attributed to what has been labelled 'le malaise Créole' (the Creole unease), referring to the appalling conditions in which large numbers of Mauritians of African descent, usually called the Creoles, live. Prior to this, open racial discord had been very rare in Mauritius and the riots were seen as indicative of 'something rotten in the state'.

Investment climate

On the economic front, from the beginning of the new millennium, Mauritius lost the trade concessions it enjoyed in the textiles and sugar industries. As a result, the government embarked on a reform strategy, outlined in the budget for the fiscal year 2006/07, to open up the economy and improve the investment climate. This strategy seems to have paid off as Mauritius topped the ranking in Africa on the ease of doing business, scoring even higher than South Africa and ranked 24th in the world according to the World Bank's 'Doing Business' report of 2009. At the same time, however, social expenditure has been reduced.

Poverty

The first Millennium Development Goal relates to the eradication of extreme poverty and hunger in the world. The target is to halve the proportion of people living on less than USD1 a day by the year 2015. The most recent Mauritian Household Budget Survey in 2006/07, conducted by the Central Statistics Office, showed that the proportion of poor households below the relative poverty line (set at the half median monthly household income per adult equivalent) increased from 7.7% in 2001/02 to 8.0% in 2006/07. Thus, the number of poor households increased from 23,700 in 2001/02 to 26,900 in 2006/07. Although the average monthly household disposable income increased by 33.7% from 2001/02 to 2006/07, it was found that household income did not change significantly after adjusting for inflation.

Income inequality

The survey also indicated a slight deterioration in income distribution: the share of total income going to the 20% of households at the lower end of the income range decreased from 6.4% in 2001/02 to 6.1% in 2006/07. On the other hand, the share of the upper 20% of households increased from 44.0% to 45.7%. Furthermore, the degree of inequality in income can also be measured by the Gini coefficient that ranges from 0 (complete equality) to 1 (complete inequality). This coefficient increased from 0.371 in 2001/02 to 0.389 in 2006/07, confirming the rise in income inequality.

Government response

The government has been trying very hard to come up with policies to address these issues, especially to prevent any potential social unrest. In the 2006/07 budget speech, it launched the 'Empowerment Programme' with the aim of securing viable employment, encouraging entrepreneurship, improving competitiveness, providing transitional support to low-income households for housing, and enhancing education for vulnerable children. The programme has a life span of five years with a project value of MUR5 billion. Moreover, in the 2008/09 budget speech, the government proposed targeted measures to address poverty, such as the setting up of the 'Eradication of Absolute Poverty Programme' and the 'Social Housing Fund'.

∎ Trends

CSR is still very much equated with corporate philanthropy and sponsorship in Mauritius, and CSR activities are usually carried out on an ad hoc basis. However, there is sufficient empirical evidence to suggest that CSR has emerged as a priority for businesses in Mauritius recently, and it is also garnering interest among government, nongovernmental organisations (NGOs) and academia.

It must be noted that the use of the term 'CSR' is very new in Mauritius. The 1999 riots were a wake-up call for some corporations to start thinking of their social responsibilities, specifically in terms of trying to help integrate what are perceived as marginalised and vulnerable groups into Mauritian society. Thus, the 'Fondation Espoir et Développement' (FED) — literally, the 'Foundation for Hope and Development' — was set up by the Beachcomber Group, a hotel consortium, in April 1999. The FED was the first independent entity created by a company to design and implement its CSR commitments, although the term CSR itself was not used at the time.

The 'pioneers' of CSR in Mauritius have been subsidiaries of global multinational enterprises, such as British American Tobacco Mauritius, which in 2003 became the first company to publish a social report in the country. This was the first time that the terms 'CSR' and 'social reporting' were openly referred to. Shortly after, in November 2003, Princes Tuna (Mauritius) Ltd became the second African enterprise to obtain the SA8000 certification. The ever-growing importance of the CSR phenomenon is also evidenced by the number of articles devoted to the subject in the local media: it increased from around ten in 2003 to around 70 by the end of 2008.

Significantly, the government of Mauritius has made CSR a major focus of its social policy objectives in recent years, culminating in new legislation, which came into effect on 1 July 2009, requiring companies to either spend 2% of their profits on CSR activities approved by the government or to transfer these funds to the government to be used in the fight against poverty.

In the last few years, there have been three key studies on CSR in Mauritius. The most comprehensive was a report by Kemp Chatteris Deloitte (2008). This was commissioned in 2006 by the government of Mauritius in partnership with the Mauritius Council of Social Service and the United Nations Development Programme (UNDP) to undertake a review of CSR in Mauritius. The assignment was part of an overall programme set to strengthen the NGO sector in Mauritius. Published in April 2008, it covered 100 companies, divided into 63 large national and international corporations and 37 small and medium enterprises (SMEs) respectively.

One significant finding of the report was that, despite the fact that Mauritian organisations have been involved in one way or the other in CSR undertakings, the country still lags behind Western countries when it comes to the integration of CSR into organisational strategy, structure and operations. This was further highlighted by the fact that CSR activities in Mauritius appeared to be equated with philanthropy and sponsorship: an overwhelming majority (90%) of large companies surveyed carried out philanthropic activities which tend to revolve around three main areas — health and safety, education, and community (including sports) — whilst 83% indulged in sponsorship activities. With respect to SMEs, 87% carried out philanthropic activities while 60% engaged in sponsorship activities. The report also established that the main reason why companies engage in CSR in Mauritius is to enhance their image. In this respect, it is not surprising that philanthropy and sponsorship should rank high as CSR activities.

▮ Legislation and codes

- The **Finance (Miscellaneous Provisions) Act 2009**. As from 1 July 2009, every company was required to set up a CSR Fund equivalent to 2% of its book profits after tax derived in the preceding year to implement approved CSR programmes or finance approved NGOs. Any amount left unspent in the company's CSR Fund at the end of its accounting year will have to be sent to the Mauritius Revenue Authority.

- **Environmental Protection Act 2002**. Companies wishing to undertake works listed under the Act as having an impact on the environment are under an obligation to supply an Environment Impact Assessment. Opponents can contest the project and appeals can be made before the Environment Appeal Tribunal.

- The **Mauritius Employers' Federation Code of Practice for Enterprises in Mauritius**. Published in 1981, it consists of 19 tenets, with the very first relating to the 'Social Obligations of the Enterprise'.

- The **Joint Economic Council Model Code of Conduct for Directors and Employees of Private Sector Companies**. Adopted in 2001, one of its core standards relates to 'Responsibilities to the Community' which comprises care for the environment, participation by companies in community affairs and support to charitable organisations.

- The **Code of Corporate Governance**. Under the Financial Reporting Act 2004, all companies with a turnover exceeding MUR250 million have had to comply with the Code's provisions from the reporting year ending 30 June 2005. Companies have to report regularly to their stakeholders on ethics, the environment, health and safety and social issues.

▮ Organisations

▮ **Joint Economic Council (JEC).** Founded in 1970, the JEC is the coordinating body of the private sector of Mauritius. In 2004, the JEC, the Ministry of Education and Human

Resources, and the UNDP entered into a partnership called the Zones D'Education Prioritaires (Education Priority Zones) Project (ZEP) whereby companies contribute in giving special support and compensatory education in schools in deprived and under-privileged localities. **http://www.jec-mauritius.org**

■ **Mauritius Chamber of Commerce and Industry (MCCI).** The MCCI, established in 1850, is the oldest nonprofit institution representing the private sector in Mauritius. In April 2007, the organisation took on the ZEP Project from the JEC. **http://www.mcci.org**

■ **Mauritius Employers' Federation (MEF).** The MEF was founded in 1962 and is the largest private sector organisation in Mauritius with 913 members. It is the focal point for the UN Global Compact Local Network in Mauritius with the support and collabora-tion of the UNDP. It also offers CSR-related courses from time to time. **http://www.mef-online.org**

■ Case studies

Barclays Mauritius plc

Barclays Mauritius is a subsidiary of the multinational bank. It has a well-structured com-munity programme in Mauritius. Owing to the high prevalence rate of diabetes in the country, it adopted the fight against this disease as its flagship cause in 2006. For World Diabetes Day in November 2007, Barclays Mauritius pledged the sum of GBP174,003 to the cause of diabetes prevention. **http://www.barclays.com/africa/community/mauritius_index.html**

Beachcomber Group

The Beachcomber Group is a pioneer of the hotel industry in Mauritius, having opened its first hotel on the island in 1952. It established the FED in 1999. The organisation provides substantial financial support to NGOs whose main mandate is to help the underprivileged segments of Mauritian society. Moreover, at the beginning of 2009, it implemented a Regional Empowerment Programme in the northern part of the coun-try, which aims to fight illiteracy, train young people and support micro-enterprises in the region. **http://www.fonesdev.org**

British American Investment Co. (Mauritius) Limited (BAI)

Formerly known as British American Insurance Co. (Mauritius) Ltd, BAI is an invest-ments holding company listed on the Stock Exchange of Mauritius since 2003, and is the leading provider of life insurance in Mauritius. In 2008, it launched a large-scale CSR programme to support several community projects on the island. This CSR programme focuses on three key elements: health, education and empowerment of women. **http://www.bai.mu/CSR.asp?CAT=EVOL**

CIEL Group

The CIEL Group is one of the leading industrial and investment groups based in Mauri-tius, with operations in a number of African and Asian countries. The core activities of the Group are sugar, textiles and investment. It set up the 'Fondation Nouveau Regard' (literally 'Foundation New Look') (FNR) in 2004. The FNR, like the FED, provides financial support to 'social' NGOs, and it has set up a portal called ACTogether to support their work (**http://www.actogether.mu**). Since 2007, it has also been working with SAFIRE to help with the plight of street children in Mauritius. **http://www.cielgroup.com/group/social_fondation_nouveau_regard.aspx**

Médine Group

The Médine Group, an indigenous group of companies whose core activities are sugar and investment, set up the 'Fondation Médine Horizons' (FMH) in 2006 as part of what it called its 'Master Plan 2005–2025', the aim being to contribute to the development of the poorest and least developed part of the country (the western region). In December 2008 the FMH, together with the FED, filed a request for funding to the Decentralised Cooperation Programme of the European Union (EU) to promote the work of local craftsmen in the western part of the country. The request was approved and both foundations will be implementing the project in 2010. **http://www.fondation-medine.org**

▌ Education

CSR education in Mauritius is at a very embryonic state. Mauritius has two public universities (the **University of Mauritius**, **http://www.uom.ac.mu** and the **University of Technology**, **http://www.utm.ac.mu**) and a private university (the Charles Telfair Institute, **http://www.telfair.ac.mu**). None features in global rankings such as *Beyond Grey Principles*. However, the two public universities do offer CSR-related modules on their various management programmes.

References

Government of Mauritius (2005) 'A Roadmap for the Mauritius Sugar Cane Industry for the 21st Century'; **http://www.gov.mu/portal/goc/moa/files/roadmap.doc**, accessed 24 May 2010.

Kemp Chatteris Deloitte (2008) 'Review of Corporate Social Responsibility Policies and Actions in Mauritius and Rodrigues: Final Report' (Port-Louis, Mauritius: Kemp Chatteris Deloitte).

MEF (Mauritius Employers' Federation) (2006) 'MEF Survey Report on Corporate Social Responsibility Survey' (Port-Louis, Mauritius: MEF).

—— (2008) *MEF Survey Report on Corporate Social Responsibility Survey* (Port-Louis, Mauritius: MEF).

Ragodoo, N.J.F. (2009) 'CSR as a Tool to Fight against Poverty: The Case of Mauritius', *Social Responsibility Journal* 51: 19-33.

UNDP (United Nations Development Programme) (2010) 'UNDP in Mauritius: Poverty Reduction'; **http://un.intnet.mu/undp/html/mauritius/povertyred.htm**, accessed 24 May 2010.

World Bank Group (2010) 'Doing Business in Mauritius'; **http://www.doingbusiness.org/ExploreEconomies/?economyid=125**, accessed 24 May 2010.

31 Mexico

Leonardo J. Cárdenas
Chair, Graduate Program on CSR,
Universidad Regiomontana

■ Context

Mexico has a very long tradition of social responsibility, which can be tracked back to the indigenous cultures of the region before America was 'discovered'. For example, the Raramori, who still live in the mountains of Northern Mexico in the state of Chihuahua, use the expression *korima*, which means 'to share'. Importantly, *korima* is not philanthropic in the sense of sharing surplus wealth, but is the practice of sharing resources in times of stress.

In the middle of the last century, before social security was part of labour law in Mexico, one of the country's largest and oldest breweries, Cerveceria Cuauhtémoc Moctezuma (CCM), located in Monterrey, voluntarily started providing health services to its employees and their families, including access to medicine, dentists, optometrists and various medical services (X-ray, surgery, etc.). Furthermore, CCM provided its employees and families with sporting, cultural and educational facilities such as libraries and theatres (Cervecería Cuauhtémoc Moctezuma 2007).

During the 1980s and 1990s, several natural disasters hit Mexico and the reaction to these was a demonstration of social responsibility from many organisations. For example, in 1985, a large earthquake hit Mexico City. More than 10,000 people were killed and more than 30,000 injured (BBC 1985). In response, hundreds of construction companies provided equipment and labour to help remove debris and rescue trapped people. Similarly, privately owned hospitals opened their doors to anyone in need.

In 1988, the urban area of Monterrey was hit by hurricane Gilbert, flooding most of the city, killing hundreds and leaving thousands homeless (El Norte 1988). In the aftermath, a non-governmental organisation (NGO) called Asociación Gilberto was formed with support from several private organisations to provide housing to those affected. Asociación Gilberto continues working today to help victims of diverse disasters.

In 1990, a flood hit the state of Chihuahua. Hundreds of families lost all their material possessions. The response from industry owners was to ask the state congress to charge companies with a special tax for one year to help repair damaged areas and provide new shelter for those families. This scheme was so successful that industry leaders asked for the tax to become permanent and managed by an independent trust fund. This gave birth to FECHAC (Federation of the Chihuahuan Industry), an NGO supported by more than 38,000 industries which make voluntary annual contributions (FECHAC 2009).

These examples are indicative of the embedded attitudes to CSR in Mexico.

∎ Priority issues

Environment

Mexico is a relatively large country with close to 2 million km^2 of surface (Instituto Nacional de Geografía y Estadística 2009), a diverse climate and biomes ranging from deserts to tropical forests. Water availability ranges from less than 200 l per person per year in some northern states, such as Baja California Sur, Baja California and Coahuila, to more than 10,000 l per person per year in southern states such as Veracruz, Chiapas and Oaxaca (Instituto Nacional de Geografía y Estadística 2009).

As a result, Mexico is one of the ten richest countries in terms of species diversity in the world (UNEP, 1997). This situation challenges Mexico to balance ecological integrity with economic growth and the needs of its large population — estimated to be over 103 million people (Instituto Nacional de Geografía y Estadística 2005).

According to Achim Steiner, Executive Director of UNEP:

> Mexico is at the cross-roads of the Green Economy politically, physically and practically. Firstly it still has many challenges, from high air pollution in cities and dependence on fossil fuels to land degradation and the need to fight poverty. But Mexico is also emerging as one among a group of developing economies who are bringing much needed leadership to the need for a new, comprehensive and decisive climate treaty. (UNEP 2008)

Among the goals set by the Mexican government are:

- **To increase the land surface covered by forest**. During the decade between 1993 and 2002, Mexico lost 2.5% of its forests.

- **To reduce the carbon dioxide emissions both per capita and globally**. Between 2000 and 2002, there was a reduction in Mexico from 4.11 to 3.90 tons/person, although this still represents a 6.6% increase from the level in 1990 (as compared with a 20% increase in global emissions since 1990).

- **To have at least 87.7% of the population with access to drinking water and 79% with access to sanitary systems**. This goal has almost been achieved, with 87.1% having access to drinking water and 84.4% having access to sanitary systems in 2005.

Social issues

Social issues in Mexico have mainly to do with providing healthcare, education and the eradication of discrimination (especially gender discrimination). Among the goals set by the government are:

- To achieve 100% literacy among 15 and 24 year-olds. As of 2008, the rate was 97.9%.

- To achieve 100% completion of primary education (which is mandatory). In 2008, the rate was 90.5%.

- To improve job opportunities for women in the non-agricultural sectors. In 2008, 39.3% of women worked in these sectors.

Economic issues

The economic challenges in Mexico have to do with the population at the base of the economic pyramid, especially those who lack access to basic nutrition. The government has set the goal to reduce the malnourished population to less than 1.25%. In 2006, the level was 1.51%.

▌ Trends

The origins of CSR in Mexico, as in many other parts of the world, can be traced back to various philanthropic activities. Only more recently has this broadened to include a more business-oriented approach. Two of the most active business associations in Mexico are the Mexican Union of Social Business (USEM), founded in 1957 and probably the oldest voluntary business association in Mexico with social goals, and the Alliance for Corporate Social Responsibility in Mexico (ALIARSE), founded in 2001. These associations, as well as many others, have encouraged companies to become conscious of their role as corporate citizens.

CEMEFI (The Mexican Center for Philanthropy), an NGO founded 20 years ago, has more recently started a CSR programme with the goal of coaching industry in the business case for CSR: doing what is right for society, not only because it is morally right, but also economically beneficial. In 2000, it also launched the Socially Responsible Industry Awards (CEMEFI 2009a), given to organisations that demonstrate their CSR performance (using a self-evaluation scheme). In 2009, 392 organisations in Mexico and Latin America received this award. The criteria for the CEMEFI award has significantly influenced the trend of CSR in Mexico, so that it is now considered to go beyond pure philanthropy.

CSR is typically adopted in five stages by most organisations in Mexico, which can be described as follows:

1. **Philanthropic activities**. Charity and donations towards worthwhile social and environmental causes.

2. **Responsible marketing**. Matching marketing campaigns with donations to recognised social organisations or causes.

3. **Responsible governance**. Setting up organisational governance policies and procedures to improve the quality of life within the organisation.

4. **Business ethics**. Implementation of ethical codes that apply not only to employees, but also to the way the organisation engages in its business.

5. **Management system integration**. Integrating CSR throughout the organisation and considering the environmental, social and economic performance.

Most organisations undertaking CSR in Mexico are between stages 2 and 4, with some still at stage 1 and relatively few that have moved to stage 5.

▌ Legislation and codes

Legislation in Mexico in areas related to social responsibility, such as labour and the environment, is vast and tends to be applied quite efficiently. The main reason is that, since Mexico joined NAFTA in 1994, US and Canadian companies can be taken to court in their countries for failure to adhere to Mexican social and environmental legislation. In the area of social involvement, legislation covers issues such as infrastructure for the physically challenged and inclusion of minorities in political bodies such as the congress and the senate.

Voluntary CSR standards (besides the two mentioned before) include:

- **Best corporate practices code**. A code of practices to achieve a good corporate governance (Consejo Coordinador Empresarial 2006).

- **Family responsible industry model**. Giving recognition to industries that adopt good labour practices in the areas of gender equity, prevention of work violence and sexual harassment, as well as actions and policies that favour their employees attending to their family responsibilities (Secretaria del Trabajo y Previsión Social 2002).

- **Inclusive industry award**. An award that recognises actions to include vulnerable groups (handicapped, elders, HIV/AIDS and others) (Secretaria de Trabajo y Previsión Social 2007).

▌ Organisations

▌ **ALIARSE (Alliance for Corporate Social Responsibility)**. A group of organisations which aims to support and create industries committed to CSR. **http://www.aliarse.org.mx**

▌ **Caux Round Table Mexico**. The national chapter of the international network of principled business leaders working to promote moral capitalism. **http://www.cauxroundtable.org**

▌ **CEMEFI (Mexican Centre for Philanthropy)**. A centre that gives the Social Responsible Industry award annually. This is the most recognised CSR award in Mexico. CEMEFI also delivers an annual award for best practices in social responsibility. It also makes an annual award for the best practices in social responsibility (CEMEFI 2009b). **http://www.cemefi.org.mx**

▌ **FECHAC**. The independent and autonomous organisation in the state of Chihuahua dedicated to the allocation of business grants as soft credits to finance social projects. **http://www.fechac.org.mx**

■ **USEM.** A voluntary organisation (more than 50 years old) of businessmen and leaders who help industries improve in a socially responsible way. **http://www.usem.org.mx**

■ Case studies

CEMEX

The third largest cement producer in the world has established the programme My House Today (*Patrimonio Hoy*), where CEMEX offers credit on purely verbal agreements to groups of low-income families and provides them with technical assistance, so they can build cement and block houses (the most-used construction materials in Mexico). **http://www.cemex.com**

Cerveceria Cuauhtémoc Moctezuma

This brewery, more than 100 years old, was the first alcoholic beverage company in Mexico to develop a country-wide designated driver programme. This is a complete programme, including training waiters and monitoring of bars throughout Mexico; and it has literally saved hundreds of lives, especially of young people. **http://www.ccm.com. mx**

Cinepolis

This is one of the largest movie theatre chains in Mexico. Linking to its core business, it promotes a campaign and organises medical services to perform several hundred of eye operations a year that allow children to gain or regain their sight. **http://www.cinepolis. com.mx**

Met-Mex Peñoles

As with all large mining companies, this one uses large amounts of water in its industrial process. In 1972, it built and has since operated an urban wastewater treatment plant that allows it to use 100% of treated urban waste water in its process. **http://www.penoles. com.mx**

Sabritas

This subsidiary of PepsiCo in Mexico is a large producer of chips, peanuts and other foods. In 2007 it started a very vigorous programme to integrate mute people into its workforce, including the training of fellow workers in sign language to train and communicate with the mute workers. **http://www.sabritas.com.mx**

■ Education

- **Universidad Regiomontana in Monterrey**. This University has one of the world's few graduate programmes devoted to CSR. It is called a master in Corporate Social Responsibility, with subjects such as environment, economics, social integration and CSR business management. Students from Mexico and Europe have already graduated from this programme. It is available both in campus and online. http://www.ur.mx

- **Universidad de Anahuac in Mexico City**. This University has a master's programme in social responsibility, mainly directed to the management of NGOs dedicated to philanthropic activities, such as fundraising for hospitals and making food available to communities that have been affected by natural disasters. http://www.anahuac.mx

References

BBC (1985) 'Mexico suffers devastating earthquake', BBC News; http://news.bbc.co.uk/onthisday/hi/dates/stories/september/19/newsid_4252000/4252078.stm, accessed 31 March 2009.

CEMEFI (2009a) 'Empresas Distintivo ESR 2009'; http://www.cemefi.org/esr/index.php?option=com_content&task=category&sectionid=4&id=26, accessed 31 March 2009.

—— (2009b) 'Concluye Seminario Mejores Prácticas'; http://www.cemefi.org/spanish/content/category/35/18/25, accessed 1 December 2009.

Cervecería Cuauhtémoc Moctezuma (2007) *Historia de Cervecería Cuauhtémoc Moctezuma* (Monterrey, Mexico: Cervecería Cuauhtémoc Moctezuma).

Consejo Coordinador Empresarial (2006) *Código de Mejores Prácticas Corporativas* (Mexico City: Consejo Coordinador Empresarial).

El Norte (2008) '¡Es el peor desastre!', *El Norte*, Redacción, 18 September 1988.

FECHAC (2009) '¿Qué es FECHAC?'; http://www.fechac.org/web/fechac.php, accessed 1 December 2009.

Instituto Nacional de Geografía y Estadística (2009) 'Aspectos Generales del Territorio Nacional', http://www.inegi.org.mx/inegi/default.aspx?s=geo&c=909, accessed 1 December 2009.

Nacional de Geógrafia y Estadística (2005) 'Cuadro: Población Total por Entidad Federativa Según Sexo, 2000 y 2005'; http://www.inegi.org.mx/est/contenidos/espanol/proyectos/conteos/conteo2005/bd/consulta2005/pt.asp?s=est&c=10401, accessed 1 December 2009.

Secretaria del Trabajo y Previsión Social (2002) 'Empresa Incluyente: Manual de Orientación para Empresarios' (Mexico City: STPS).

STPS (Secretaria de Trabajo y Previsión Social) (2007) 'Modelo de Reconocimiento "Empresa Familiarmente Responsable" Manual de Aplicación' (Mexico City: STPS).

UNEP (United Nations Environment Programme) (1997) *Global Environmental Outlook-1* (UNEP; http://www.unep.org/geo/geo1).

—— (2008) 'Mexico to Host World Environment Day Under the Theme "Your Planet Needs You" '; http://www.unep.org/documents.multilingual/default.asp?DocumentID=545&ArticleID=5928&l=en, accessed 1 December 2009.

32 The Netherlands

Jennifer Iansen-Rogers[1]
Senior Manager, KPMG Global Sustainability Services

■ Context

The Netherlands has strong social traditions, rooted in its history, Christian beliefs and culture which support the principles of social responsibility. Its geography provides the background to its concern for environmental issues.

Small but densely populated, the Netherlands has a strong history of international trading and economic success. Its strong Christian (Catholic and Calvanistic) beliefs support labour rights, social security and equality at home and its provision of international aid. A long history of international trade has produced a relatively high number of well-known multinationals such as Shell, Unilever, Philips and Heineken, and the country is also a leading financial centre.

In its recent history, Dutch socioeconomic development was based on the Rhineland model — a stakeholder-based approach for economic development which promotes the principles of solidarity and cooperation between the owners of companies, government, employees and customers. It provides a balance between free market-forces and social and environmental responsibility for longer-term societal stability.

Based on a market economy, the model promotes intervention by the state in industry and the labour market to ensure just working conditions for employees and to prevent social inequality, for example through the funding of a comprehensive social security system.

This model has developed further into the 'Polder Model', which describes the current consensus-based decision-making model in Dutch politics and economics. Its use is thought to date from the Wassenaar Accord (1982), an agreement between government, employers and companies to revitalise the economy by increasing employment through wage restraint and shorter working hours. This tripartite relationship also supports the tradition of volunteering.

The Netherlands is a country built on a major river delta and requires a complex system of dykes and pumping stations to keep the water at bay. Over the centuries it has

1 **Author's note:** all information correct at time of writing. The author accepts no responsibility for action based on information in this chapter.

battled with major flooding in the lower reaches of its rivers and the low-lying coastal areas. For the last 60 years the Zuiderzee project (enclosing the IJsselmeer) and the Delta Project in Zeeland (after the flood disaster of 1953) have protected the country, but both the population and the economy are particularly vulnerable to a rise in sea level caused by global warming. As a result climate change is too serious and too urgent an issue to be ignored.

Models of CSR

The Netherlands has a long record of corporate philanthropy (e.g. through foundations) and was at the forefront of developments around environmental auditing and management systems in the 1980s and 1990s. Since the late 1990s many companies have adopted the Triple Bottom Line (Triple P or People, Planet, Profit) model (Elkington 1994) for CSR and some have their own company-specific approaches such as Shell's 'Trust me, Tell me, Show me, Involve me' model.

While many aspects (such as labour and human rights, and emission regulation) have been incorporated in legislation, unique partnerships have developed to promote the practice of CSR which reflect the Dutch consensus model. These include the Social and Economic Council of the Netherlands (SER) which brings together employers' representatives, union representatives and independent experts to help shape Dutch policy and legislation on social and economic affairs. Its role is to interpret signals from society and to offer advice based on the objective of social prosperity in its widest sense, encompassing not only material progress (increased affluence and production), but also social progress (improved welfare and social cohesion) and a high-quality environment in which to live (environmental and spatial factors). This does not mean that everyone agrees with the views expressed by the SER — its 2008 advisory report on globalisation and development initiated a heated debate in the Netherlands between politicians, NGOs, religious organisations and business.

∎ Priority issues

Many social and environmental priorities are already embedded in comprehensive legislation and regulation, including the implementation of European Union (EU) Directives. Current environmental challenges for the Netherlands are climate change (including energy and water management) and land management, while in the social sphere the main concerns revolve around the changing demography (age and immigration) alongside equal opportunities and diversity.

Climate change

Climate change already affects the Netherlands: milder winters, warmer summers, more extreme rainfall and, last but not least, the rise in sea level. Failing cooling systems in power stations, increased storm damage as well as the risk of flooding threaten the population, agriculture and the economy. In line with the EU, the Dutch government's policy is to address climate change in two ways: mitigation (energy and emission reduction) and adaptation (water management).

To meet its commitment to reduce greenhouse gas emissions by 30% by 2020 (base year 1990), the government introduced a range of policy instruments for both industry and citizens in its work programme 'Clean and Efficient'. This includes measures to reduce energy use (e.g. higher taxes on fuel and emission-related variable taxation for cars) and to stimulate renewable energy (wind energy and biofuels) to achieve 20% of total energy use (2% in 2007). It also extends emission trading to sectors that fall outside the European programme (ETS sectors).

Water management policies have also been updated as part of the policy programme to adapt to climate change. The 'weakest links' in coastal water defences are being strengthened and areas reserved to allow flooding along major rivers. However, if climate change continues, innovative solutions will be needed to protect the country from the longer-term effects.

Land management

Due to its size, a growing population and changes in demography, land use is currently the focus of debate and discussion. Industry, commerce, transport, housing, recreation and nature all complete for limited land resources. While some worry about increasing traffic congestion (despite excellent public transport) and may welcome the many motorway widening schemes that are in progress, the 'green heart' of Holland is shrinking. Areas of the country are liable to flooding which may increase if rainfall patterns and sea levels change. The government has set up a new programme 'Holland beautiful' with a budget of EUR13 million (2009–2011) to subsidise projects in the area of land renovation and efficient land use.

Demography, equal opportunities and diversity

An ageing population and a rise in immigration over recent years have implications for social infrastructure and community relations. Ethnic minorities account for about 10% of the Dutch population and the country attracts large numbers of workers from the new EU states, putting education, health and social security systems under pressure. Recent government policies to address these issues focus on 'integration' and ensuring equal opportunities in education and work. On the other hand, it has resulted in a move to the right in the political landscape and a tendency towards a 'blame' culture which threatens national values of equality, social justice and tolerance.

∎ Trends

The Netherlands was a pioneer in environmental policy planning, auditing and management systems and many issues (waste, water pollution, soil contamination) are now under control. It has a good reputation in recycling (household, cars and electronic waste) and renewable energy.

KPMG's latest survey of CR reporting (KPMG 2008) shows that of the top 100 Dutch companies the number with a separate CR report has doubled since 2005 to 60%, while 50% had CR issues (partially) integrated in their annual reports. Reporting still varies across sectors from 100% (communications, utilities and automotive) down to a surprisingly low 25% for retail.

The 2008 Transparency Benchmark analysed 146 reports (of 170 listed and non-listed companies). The overall score increased slightly from 2007, with the financial sector holding the top three positions. As in KPMG's survey, the retail sector again scored badly with nine of 170 retail companies without a report. Four companies achieved maximum points for supply chain. Increasing attention for this issue is also supported by the 2007 VBDO (Dutch Association of Investors for Sustainable Development) Benchmark on supply chain management where the leaders — Philips, Unilever and Shell — helped to raise the average score compared to the previous survey.

The 2007 and 2008 reports of MVO Nederland provide some indications of trends in CSR. Overall, understanding of the concept of CSR is high amongst Dutch SMEs (5–99 FTEs) at 68% although embedding of CSR in business processes was much lower at 34%. Alongside energy and CO_2 emissions, supply chain management and sustainable purchasing emerge as key issues, the latter influenced by the 2010 targets for sustainable purchasing in the public sector which together spend more than EUR40 billion.

Companies are also acutely aware of the interest of the financial community, especially institutional investors, in socially responsible investment (SRI). With a long history of ethical investment, the Netherlands boasts two 'sustainable' banks, Triodos and ASN Bank, while all major Dutch banks offer ethical investment products. In 2007 around EUR3.8 billion was invested in sustainable funds, an increase of 17% from 2006 (compared to a decrease of 4.8% in regular investment funds). This is expected to increase following the banking crisis which led to the nationalisation of a major Dutch bank.

Taking recycling a step further, the Dutch government is also promoting the 'Cradle to Cradle' (CTC) principle.[2] Companies and regions have responded with a range of initiatives, from an electric waste truck (Van Gansewinkel) that uses energy from the waste it collects, to the local authority of Venlo which aims to be the first Cradle to Cradle region and is using C2C principles in its plans for the 2012 Floriade (World Horticultural Expo).

▌ Legislation and codes

The Netherlands has a strong legislative framework for many aspects of CSR including environment, health and safety, labour, human rights and corporate governance. It has implemented most EU directives and regulations in this field. Voluntary codes and standards such as UNGC, OECD/ILO, PRI, the Equator Principles and certification (ISO 14001) are also strongly embedded in corporate society.

Existing environmental legislation covers environmental planning (by the authorities), permits, surface water pollution, air quality and emission standards and trading. Managed and enforced by the regional/local authorities, these are currently under review and some will be consolidated, for example in a new law for environmental and building permits and a new Water law.

On 19 December 2008 a **Declaration of International Corporate Social Responsibility** was signed by employers and employee organisations under the auspices of the SER. This declaration — incorporating international codes such as ICC guidance on supply chain responsibility (2007) and ICC guidelines for responsible purchasing: integration of social and environmental aspects in the supply chain (2008) — is designed to stimu-

2   http://www.cradletocradle.nl/home/321_wat-is-cradle-to-cradle.htm, accessed 4 June 2010.

late and provide further structure and content to CSR in Dutch companies. The consultation draft of the national Annual Report Guidelines 400, published in September 2009, has been extended to cover supply chain management. The Netherlands is one of the few countries to have a specific (accountants) standard for assurance on sustainability reporting (COS 3410 of the Royal NIVRA).

The updated **Dutch Corporate Governance Code** (also called the Code Tabaksblatt, 2004) was presented in December 2008 and includes changes to supervisory board responsibilities including due regard for relevant CSR issues as well as diversity in the composition of the board.

▌ Organisations

▌ **CSR Netherlands (MVO Nederland)**. Set up by the Ministry of Economic Affairs in 2004, this has more than 800 partner organisations. It is a knowledge and network organisation that stimulates CSR in business. **http://www.mvonederland.nl**

▌ **Global Reporting Initiative (GRI)**. This international CSR organisation is based in the Netherlands. It pioneered the development of the world's most widely used sustainability reporting framework. **http://www.globalreporting.org**

▌ **Greenpeace International** (**http://www.greenpeace.org**) and **FoE International** (**http://www.foei.org**) are also located in Amsterdam

▌ The Dutch government, in particular the **Ministry of Economic Affairs (EZ)** (**http://www.ez.nl**) and the **Ministry of Housing, Spatial Planning and the Environment (VROM)** (**http://www.vrom.nl**) both continue to play key roles in CSR in the Netherlands

▌ **SenterNovem**. An agency of the Dutch Ministry of Economic Affairs, this promotes sustainable development and innovation, both within the Netherlands and abroad, in particular by helping to translate government policy into practice in the areas of energy and climate change, environment and spatial planning. **http://www.senternovem.nl**

▌ The **Social and Economic Council of the Netherlands (SER)**. Established in 1950, this an independent advisory body of employers' representatives, trade unionists and independent experts which aims to create social consensus and advises the Dutch government on major (inter)national socioeconomic issues. **http://www.ser.nl**

▌ **VBDO (The Association of Investors for Sustainable Development, Vereniging van Beleggers voor Duurzame Ontwikkeling)**. With more than 1,000 individual and institutional members, this represents the interests of investors in sustainable companies. **http://www.vbdo.nl**

▌ **VNO-NCW (The Confederation of Netherlands Industry and Employers)**. This is the largest employers' organisation in the Netherlands with a membership of over 130 (sector) associations representing more than 115,000 enterprises. It also houses the secretariat of The Netherlands Network of the Global Compact (GC NL). **http://www.vno-ncw.nl**

■ Case studies

Rabobank

A leader in stakeholder engagement and sustainability in mainstream banking, this Dutch cooperative bank has achieved wide recognition for its approach to CSR, including transparency. It was one of the first banks to report these issues and has been ranked 1st in the Transparency Benchmark for three years. It is a leader in the Netherlands in stakeholder engagement including partnerships with NGOs. **http://www.rabobank.com/content/about_us/corporate_social_responsibility**

Royal Philips Electronics

Philips, a company with a long history of social responsibility, was also a pioneer in EMS (environmental management systems). In recent years the focus has been on supply chain management, product design and responsibility as well as diversity. Their 4th EcoVision programme contains challenging targets including 25% improvement in energy efficiency of operations, EUR1 billion for green innovations and 30% of total revenues from green products by 2012. They are well on the way to achieving 15% women executives in 2012 (compared to 5% in 2005). It was global sector leader in the DJSI (Dow Jones Sustainability Indexes) 2007/8. **http://www.philips.com**

Unilever

Unilever is a Dutch company that has achieved a leading reputation in best practice in CSR in recent years, with a focus on agriculture, water and fish. In the 2008/9 DJSI it achieved top place in its sector for the eighth year. **http://www.unilever.com**

Other Dutch companies that have also achieved global recognition in CSR are **Akzo** and **DSM** (chemicals) and **TNT** (transport).

■ Education

Many of the universities and polytechnics (Hogescholen) in the Netherlands offer either bachelor's courses or modules in CSR (MVO), sustainable development or specific aspects of CSR such as environmental and natural sciences, international development studies, environmental and social science, and human rights. Specialist masters' courses in this field include:

- **Erasmus University School of Assurance and Accounting (ESAA) (Rotterdam).** CSR management and accounting. **http://www.esaa.nl**

- **Groningen University.** Planning and sustainable development related to development. **http://www.rug.nl/cds/education/researchmaster/index**

- **Maastricht University.** Human rights and democratisation. **http://www.maastrichtuniversity.nl**

- **Rotterdam School of Management (RSM, Erasmus University)**. International MBA (*Beyond Grey Pinstripes* Global 100 Ranking 2009: 7th overall and 3rd for student exposure to environmental and social issues [Aspen Institute 2010]). http://www.rsm.nl/home

- **Utrecht University**. Sustainable development. http://www.uu.nl/EN/informationfor/internationalstudents/sd/Pages/study.aspx

References

Albert, M. (1991) *Capitalism against Capitalism* (London: Whurr Publishers).

Aspen Institute (2010) 'Aspen's Global 100: Beyond Grey Pinstripes 2009–2010'; http://www.beyondgreypinstripes.org/pdf/2009-2010BGP_Brochure.pdf, accessed 5 June 2010.

Elkington, J. (1994) 'Towards the Sustainable Corporation: Win–Win–Win Business Strategies for Sustainable Development', *California Management Review* 36.2: 90-100.

KPMG (2008) 'International Survey of Corporate Responsibility Reporting' (KPMG; http://www.kpmg.com/Global/en/IssuesAndInsights/ArticlesPublications/Documents/International-corporate-responsibility-survey-2008.pdf, accessed 4 June 2010).

Van Weperen, E.J. (2007) 'VBDO Benchmark Maatschappelijk Verantwoord Ketenbeheer' (Projectnummer P673; VBDO; http://mvoplatform.nl/publications-nl/Publication_2334-nl/at_download/fullfile, accessed 4 June 2010).

33 Nigeria

Kenneth Amaeshi
Doughty Centre for Corporate Responsibility,
Cranfield School of Management, UK

Chris Ogbechie
Lagos Business School, Pan African University, Nigeria

▮ Context

Nigeria has a population of about 140 million and is rich in natural and human resources. Despite its rich natural resources, Nigeria has a per capita income of less than USD1,000 per annum and a life expectancy of 45 years (World Bank 2006). The country suffers from poor infrastructure (bad roads, poor power supply etc.) and the education system is under-funded, with a literacy rate around 40%. The doctor:patient ratio is almost 1:1,000. The public sector is very weak and corruption threatens to crumble the country. The three major sectors of the economy are oil and gas, financial services and telecommunications. These sectors co-exist with thriving traditional agricultural and trading economies. This context of poverty, poor infrastructure and weak institutions provides a fertile ground for some multinational corporations (MNCs) in Nigeria to engage in CSR in order to make up for failures of governance by the government and at the same time protect their business interests in the country (Amaeshi *et al.* 2006).

The meaning of CSR in Nigeria largely reflects the local reality. In an environment where basic human needs and infrastructure are a luxury, CSR is mainly seen from a philanthropic perspective. To many Nigerian executives, CSR is the corporate act of giving back to the immediate and wider community in which they operate (Amaeshi *et al.* 2006). This philanthropic understanding is dominant in the framing of CSR by both the Nigerian business and public policy communities.

■ Priority issues

Poverty

Poverty is one of the most critical challenges facing Nigeria. According to the UNDP's *2006 Human Development Report* (UNDP 2006), Nigeria has a high percentage of people living on less than a dollar a day (70.8%). The Human Development Index ranks Nigeria 158 out of 177 countries. About 64% of households in Nigeria consider themselves to be poor while 32% say the economic situation has worsened since 2007. Over the years, successive Nigerian governments have initiated various poverty alleviation programmes. Despite these efforts, most Nigerians still live in abject poverty and the public health facilities are inadequate to take care of the increasing population, which is continually threatened by diseases, hunger and death.

Corruption

Tied to the challenges of poverty is the issue of corruption. Corruption is endemic in Nigerian society and polity. During decades of military rule, corruption thrived and became the dominant 'way of life'. Since Nigeria has traditionally lacked the institutional capacity to address corruption, the venom has become assimilated. Political corruption has been inadvertently encouraged as there are limited pieces of evidence of successful prosecution of corrupt political office holders. In addition, while recent Nigerian government regulatory measures to address corruption have attracted considerable admiration, they have also attracted significant scepticism and criticism with regards to their sincerity. Specifically, government campaigns aimed at addressing corruption have been perceived to be witch-hunt exercises to settle personal grudges. The pervasiveness of corruption in Nigeria is corroborated by independent corruption indexes. For example, Transparency International (2008) ranks Nigeria 121st out of 180 countries in its Corruption Perceptions Index, where 180th represents the highest perceived corruption.

Environment

Nigeria has a high deforestation rate of primary forests according to the Food and Agriculture Organization of the United Nations (FAO). Between 2000 and 2005 the country lost 56% of its primary forests. Logging, subsistence agriculture and the collection of fuel wood are cited as leading causes of forest clearing in Nigeria (Butler 2005). In addition, gas flaring by the extractive industries is still a major environmental concern, especially in the Niger Delta region.

■ Trends

The popularity of the contemporary usage of the term CSR can be linked to the renewed surge of economic activities after the 1999 return of political democracy in Nigeria. This is particularly the case in the financial services sector following the 2005 consolidation exercise in the banking industry. Some non-governmental organisations (NGOs), both local and international, have also contributed to the growth of CSR awareness in Nigeria.

Since 2000, for example, the Growing Business Foundation (GBF) has collaborated with some MNCs and local corporations to promote economic development and sustainable entrepreneurial growth, especially among disadvantaged communities and groups.

This growing awareness of CSR is confirmed by Amaeshi *et al.* (2006). Notwithstanding the progress, about 85% of the respondents surveyed stated that growing CSR awareness was not matched by significant action. The survey confirmed that the few CSR activities were focused mainly on education (46%). Poverty alleviation received the least attention (8%). Some of the drivers of CSR activity in Nigeria identified by the survey include: local needs and public pressure (46%), globalisation (38%), competition (38%), public relation (38%), regulation (31%) and firm's success (31%).

There is also an emerging interest in setting up corporate foundations, especially in the telecoms and financial services sectors. The main targets of these corporate foundations are usually in one or more of these areas: (1) education, (2) health (3) poverty alleviation, and (4) the environment. This confirms the view that the dominant mode of CSR is philanthropy (in the form of corporate social investments), which does not show any signs of waning in the very near future.

▮ Legislation and codes

Nigeria is one of the few countries in the world to legislate on CSR. A bill, which proposes that businesses spend about 3.5% of their gross profits on CSR, is currently making its way through the Nigerian National Assembly. This bill has attracted very strong negative criticism from private sector companies, NGOs, the general public and some international commentators. The main issue is whether CSR in Nigeria should be approached only on a voluntary basis or should be complemented with a compulsory regulatory framework. Despite the negative publicity, it has, on a positive note, further raised the awareness of CSR in the Nigerian public discourse.

There are some international codes and standards (such as the UN Global Compact, ISO, Global Reporting Initiative [GRI] and Responsible Care) that are being adopted by some firms in Nigeria, although the diffusion of such practices is still extremely low. Only a negligible number of firms (mainly MNCs) in Nigeria produce CSR reports.

▮ Organisations

▮ **Development Partnership International** was established in 2004 to help in building the capacity of young activists and their organisations for effective innovation, and proactive social change and development actions, as well as to empower them for sustainable livelihoods. **http://www.developmentpartnership.org**

▮ **Growing Businesses Foundation (GBF)** commenced operations in October 1999 as a non-governmental, nonprofit organisation, against the backdrop of increasing socio-economic imbalance in Nigeria. It tackles issues of national concern, such as mass poverty, corruption, unemployment, rising crime rates, rural urban migration, entrepreneurs' lack of access to credit, environmental degradation, dilapidated infrastructure, poor public amenities and educational standards in the formal and informal sectors.

GBF helps corporations in promoting CSR especially in the area of entrepreneur development and capacity building. **http://www.gbfng.org**

■ **National Agency for the Control of AIDS** was established in 2000 to coordinate the various activities on HIV/AIDS in Nigeria. **http://www.naca.gov.ng**

■ **New Nigeria Foundation** was incorporated in Nigeria in November 2000 as a not-for-profit, non-governmental organisation. It represents a new institutional paradigm that provides a platform for mobilising non-traditional resources through promotion of public–private partnerships to spur sustainable development efforts. **http://www.nnfng.org**

■ **Nigerian Conservation Foundation (NCF)** was established in 1980 and formally registered as a charitable trust (no. 1917) in 1982. NCF has maintained a lead role in the promotion of nature conservation and environmental protection and has remained an institutional symbol of environmental protection in Nigeria over its 27 years of existence. **http://www.ncfnigeria.org**

■ **Niger Delta Development Commission** was established by the Nigerian government in 2000 with the mission of facilitating the rapid, even and sustainable development of the Niger Delta into a region that is economically prosperous, socially stable, ecologically regenerative and politically peaceful. **http://www.nddc.gov.ng**

■ **Positive Action for Treatment Access** is a non-governmental organisation working to ensure that every individual has access to treatment education and every person can access qualitative, affordable, ethical and humane treatment. **http://pata-nigeria.com**

■ Case studies

Diamond Bank Plc

Diamond Bank Plc began as a private limited liability company in 1991 and became publicly listed in 2005. In 1999, the bank had a major policy rethink in the area of CSR to strengthen the positive impacts of its operations on the most needy in society. The bank's policy on CSR is driven by the imperative to directly and positively touch the lives of its stakeholders, with special emphasis on the indigent section of the society. The bank does not act through third party charity organisations and care givers but gets involved directly. The major areas of CSR activities are healthcare, education and economic empowerment. **http://www.diamondbank.com**

MTN Nigeria

MTN Nigeria is a part of MTN Group, Africa's leading cellular telecommunications company, and was established in 2001. The company provided the first GSM network and started full commercial operations in Lagos, Abuja and Port Harcourt in August 2001. MTN has been undertaking substantial community development initiatives in Nigeria since 2005 through the MTN Foundation in the area of education, health and economic empowerment. MTN's involvement in CSR activities is based on its philosophy that good business ethics and social well-being will bring about the development of a vibrant private sector, sustainable quality of life for the people and the growth of society in general. **http://www.mtnonline.com**

Nestlé Nigeria

Nestlé SA Switzerland is the parent company of Nestlé Nigeria which began its operations in 1961 and has grown into a leading food manufacturing and marketing company. For Nestlé, CSR is creating shared values for shareholders, consumers, employees, business partners, local communities and the national economies in which they operate. Its focal areas are eradicating poverty and hunger, supporting primary education, empowering women, reducing child mortality, improving maternal health, combating HIV/AIDS and ensuring environmental sustainability. **http://www.nestle.com**

Nigerian Brewery

Nigerian Brewery Plc is the foremost and largest brewing company in Nigeria. Established in 1946, it produced its first bottle of Star Lager Beer in June 1949 at its Lagos brewery. CSR underpins the company's concern for the sustainable economic development of Nigerian communities. Over the years, Nigerian Brewery has fostered meaningful collaborations with businesses and individuals to translate their strong commitments into action. The company's CSR activities are mainly in the areas of education, healthcare, sports development, protection of the environment and the development of the young Nigerian entertainment industry. The company is also engaged in promoting responsible consumption of alcohol. **http://www.nbplc.com**

Shell Nigeria

In 1938 Shell Nigeria started operations in Nigeria as Shell D'Arcy, with the first successful drilling in Oloibiri in 1956. As a leader in the oil and gas industry, Shell feels that the way it handles environmental issues and employee relations can have a negative or positive impact on shareholder value. In 1995 the company faced various social and environmental challenges linked to the execution of human rights activist Ken Sara Wiwo. Since then, and despite, or more likely because of these, Shell has had a strong focus on employee relations, engaging in sponsorship of community events and tackling environmental issues. Ongoing criticism notwithstanding, the company's CSR activities are based on the aspiration of finding sustainable ways for development and social change within and beyond their areas of operation. **http://www.shell.com/nigeria**

United Bank for Africa (UBA)

UBA was established in 1961 and in 2005 it merged with Standard Trust Bank and later with Continental Trust Bank to become one of the leading banks in Nigeria, with operations in about nine African countries. At UBA, enabling social progress is part of the business strategy. This is why the UBA Foundation was set up to drive the bank's CSR activities. The major areas of focus include education, environment, youth development and economic empowerment of local communities. The bank's programmes in these areas have proved to be very effective in meeting its CSR goals and addressing the overall concerns of its stakeholders. **http://www.ubagroup.com**

■ Education

Academic institutions and researchers focusing specifically on corporate social responsibility in Africa are still very few and immature (Visser *et al.* 2006). In a review of the CSR literature on Africa between 1995 and 2005, it was found that only 16% of the articles on CSR focused on Nigeria (Visser 2006). This review partially reflects the high media profile generated around CSR issues and the oil sector, especially focused on Shell and their impacts on the Ogoni people (Ite 2004).

CSR education in Nigeria is still in its infancy and is led by the **Lagos Business School (LBS), Pan-African University**, Nigeria. Since 2005, the LBS has run annual CSR executive education programmes targeting middle and senior management personnel in oil and gas sectors, telecoms, financial services, manufacturing, the public sector and the NGOs. Tied to the interest in CSR, the LBS also runs an annual lecture series on corporate governance in Nigeria. **http://www.lbs.edu.ng**

References

Amaeshi, K., A.B.C. Adi, C. Ogbechie and O.O. Amao (2006) 'Corporate Social Responsibility in Nigeria: Western Mimicry or Indigenous Influences?', *Journal of Corporate Citizenship* 24 (Winter 2006): 83-99.

Butler, R.A. (2005) 'World Deforestation Rates and Forest Cover Statistics, 2000–2005' (Nigeria: FAO; **http://news.mongabay.com/2005/1115-forest.html**, accessed 20 October 2009).

Carroll, A.B. (1991) 'The Pyramid of Corporate Social Responsibility: Toward the Moral Management of Organisational Stakeholders', *Business Horizons* 34.4: 39-48.

—— (2004) 'Managing Ethically with Global Stakeholders: A Present and Future Challenge', *Academy of Management Executive* 18.2: 114-1.

Chandranayagam, D. (2009) 'Nigeria: Legislating CSR', *The CSR Digest*, 2 March 2009; **http://www.csrdigest.com/2009/03/Nigeria-legislating-csr**, accessed 12 May 2009.

Federal Military Government (1992) 'Federal Environmental Protection Agency (Amendment) Decree No. 59 of 1992' (Abuja, Nigeria: Federal Environmental Protection Agency, 2 August 1992).

ILO (International Labour Organization) (1995) 'National Human Rights Commission Decree 1995 (No. 22 of 1995), 1995. Official Gazette (Decrees 1995), 1995-10-06, Vol. 82, No. 28, pp. A853-A590'; **http://bravo.ilo.org/dyn/natlex/natlex_browse.details?p_lang=es&p_classification=01.05&p_country=NGA**, accessed 30 March 2010.

Ite, U.E. (2004) 'Multinationals and Corporate Social Responsibility in Developing Countries: A Case Study of Nigeria', *Corporate Social Responsibility and Environmental Management* 11.1: 1-11.

Limbs, E.C., and T.L. Fort (2000) 'Nigerian Business Ethics and their Interface with Virtue Theory', *Journal of Business Ethics* 26: 169-179.

UNDP (United Nations Development Programme) (2006) 'Statistical Update 2006/2007: Country Fact Sheets: Nigeria'; **http://hdrstats.undp.org/en/2006/countries/country_fact_sheets/cty_fs_NGA.html**, accessed 12 May 2009.

Visser, W. (2006) 'Research on Corporate Citizenship in Africa: A Ten-Year Review (1995–2005)', in W. Visser, A. Macintosh and C. Middleton (eds.), *Corporate Citizenship in Africa: Lessons From the Past; Paths to the Future* (Sheffield, UK: Greenleaf Publishing): 18-28.

——, A. Macintosh and C. Middleton (eds.) (2006) *Corporate Citizenship in Africa: Lessons From the Past; Paths to the Future* (Sheffield, UK: Greenleaf Publishing).

World Bank (2006) *World Development Report* (Washington, DC: World Bank Group; **http://publications.worldbank.org/ecommerce/catalog/product?item_id=4849133**).

34 Norway

Inge Aarhus
Director, Environment Lillehammer/
Green Business Network Norway

∎ Context

The Norwegian approach to CSR has to be seen in the context of the Nordic welfare model where some key elements are egalitarian values, equal distribution of income, low poverty, income maintenance and good healthcare and education services.

A survey conducted in 2008 among 300 Norwegian companies with activities abroad showed a relatively vague understanding of the term CSR, which was mainly understood in terms of labour conditions for workers (in Norway), as well as support of the local community and civil society. Nevertheless, 54% of the companies stated that they have written guidelines on how CSR should be practised.

A governmental perspective

In 2007, the Norwegian Ministry of Foreign affairs hosted an international conference on CSR and partnerships for sustainable development. Most notably this conference led to the Norwegian government's White Paper on CSR: 'CSR in a Global Economy'. The process was open, and Norwegian stakeholders were invited to contribute during the process.

This White Paper sets corporate responsibility firmly in the context of global sustainability challenges and the competitiveness of Norwegian business in the global economy. The importance of ethical frameworks and transparency are key elements throughout the document. Furthermore, the Norwegian government's position is that CSR involves companies integrating social and environmental concerns into their day-to-day operations, as well as in their dealings with stakeholders. CSR means what companies do on a voluntary basis beyond complying with existing legislation and rules in the country in which they are operating.

The Norwegian government views the following areas as central when it comes to CSR in international operations: respecting human rights, upholding core labour standards and ensuring decent working conditions, taking environmental concerns into account, combating corruption and maximising transparency.

The White Paper describes roles and responsibilities of the state and public spheres as well as the role of the corporate sector. Furthermore, Norwegian enterprises also recommended to position themselves within the global development agenda, especially the UN Millennium Development Goals. In this context, the paper provides guidance on how companies can make responsible use of their supply chains.

The government emphasises the significance of CSR for value creation and for bringing about changes that benefit people, the environment and society at large, suggesting that:

- State-owned enterprises must lead the way in demonstrating social responsibility. The government will seek to promote this by actively exercising ownership rights.

- The ethical guidelines for the Norwegian government pension fund are currently being revised. The government will devise requirements for its own suppliers.

- CSR will be integrated as a cross-cutting theme in the administration of all Norwegian development assistance funds.

The Norwegian government pension fund has ethical guidelines, based on two premises:

- The fund is an instrument for ensuring that a reasonable portion of the country's petroleum wealth benefits future generations.

- The fund should not make investments which constitute an unacceptable risk that the fund may contribute to unethical acts or omissions, such as serious violations of human rights, gross corruption or severe environmental damages.

A business perspective

Today, enterprises have a clear self-interest in conducting business in a socially responsible manner. Norwegian enterprises have almost unfailingly supported their local communities and demonstrated concern for their employees. Major Norwegian enterprises and business federations have shown a growing attention to CSR for several years. The Federation of Norwegian Commercial and Service Enterprises and The Confederation of Norwegian Enterprises have developed several CSR tools as guidance for companies and businesses, for instance a training manual on anti-corruption, a checklist for human rights, ethical guidelines and guidelines for whistle-blowing.

▌ Priority issues

Climate challenge

The Norwegian government's 2007 White Paper on climate policy contains various proposals for concrete measures to reduce greenhouse gas emissions. In fact, all Norwegian political parties except one agreed on an improved national policy on climate change issues, with the goal of Norway as a carbon-neutral country by 2030.

To reduce greenhouse gas emissions, Norwegian businesses and industries strongly advocate an international market-driven pollution permit trading scheme. The Norwegian Forum for Environment and Development (ForUM) — a network of more than 50 non-governmental organisations that focus on environment and development — proposes the following actions: to reduce Norwegian CO_2 emissions by 60–80% by 2020; increased energy efficiency; increased use of renewable energy, including solar, wind and bio-energy; and green taxes.

Human rights

The Norwegian government expects enterprises to respect fundamental human rights, including the rights of children, women and indigenous peoples, in line with international standards and conventions. Business attitudes in Norway towards human rights issues are accordingly becoming more important, with implications for reputation as well as profit. Already in 1998 the Norwegian Confederation for Enterprises developed a checklist, intended to be a tool for companies interested in devising their own strategies for dealing with human rights in line with internationally recognised standards.

Supply chain

The Norwegian government is taking a lead on supply chain issues in terms of its Action Plan for Environmental and Social Responsibility in Public Procurement, and the private sector is similarly implementing standards for supply chain integrity.

In support of this goal, Ethical Trade Initiative Norway seeks collaboration to ensure that international trade does not contravene human rights, labour rights, economic development and the environment. This is undertaken by strengthening the support for ethical trade issues and supporting members in developing ethical trade practices.

Operations in fragile states

Operating and investing in regions marked by war, civil war and other serious forms of political instability involve considerable risks. As an example of a business response to this issue, ForUM's working group for peace, environment and development works for the conversion of resources from military purposes to those that promote sustainable development.

▌ Trends

The government's White Paper on CSR expresses support for the OECD Multinational Enterprise Guidelines Mechanism, the UN Global Compact and the Global Reporting Initiative (GRI). It can therefore be expected that these international standards will set the trend for CSR in Norwegian companies.

CSR in the supply chain looks set to gain in importance, as indicated in two studies financed by the Norwegian Research Council and carried out in the period 2006–2009: C(S)R in Global Value Chains by CSR Norway. and CSR in the Clothing Industry by IRIS.

■ Legislation and codes

- **The Pollution Control Act**. To protect the outdoor environment against pollution, to reduce existing pollution, to reduce the quantity of waste and to promote better waste management.

- **The Product Control Act**. To prevent products from causing damage to health or the environment in the form of disturbances of ecosystems, pollution, waste, noise, etc.

- **The Greenhouse Gas Emission Trading Act**. To limit emissions of greenhouse gases in a cost-effective manner by means of a system involving trade in greenhouse gas emission allowances.

- **The Working Environment Act**. To secure a working environment that provides a basis for a healthy and meaningful working situation, one that affords full safety from harmful physical and mental influences and that has a standard of welfare at all times consistent with the level of technological and social development of society.

- **The Norwegian General Civil Penal Code**. Among others this Code contains provisions on corruption and trading in influence. Gross corruption has a sentencing framework of up to ten years.

- **The National Insurance Act.** The National Insurance Act is one of the most important statutes that provides for the central national insurance and welfare schemes in Norway. Within the National Insurance Act there are provisions for benefits related to unemployment, sickness, and the course of life and family situations; retirement pension; and rules for processing cases.

- **The Labour Market Act**. To facilitate an inclusive working life through a well-functioning labour market with high levels of occupational employment and low unemployment. The Act also imposes duties on employers related to job vacancies that the employer seeks to fill, and has rules governing mass redundancies and layoffs.

- **The Social Welfare Act**. This Act governs the responsibilities of each local authority in respect of a number of social welfare services provided to the municipality's inhabitants, such as practical help for those with assistance needs, places in health institutions and so on.

■ Organisations

■ Confederation of Norwegian Enterprises (NHO). Has a membership of more than 18,500 companies ranging from small family-owned businesses to multinational companies. NHO's mission is to work in the best interests of member companies in a way that also benefits society, as the creation of value and welfare are closely linked. **http://www.nho.no**

■ **Federation of Norwegian Commercial and Service Enterprises (HSH)**. Has about 12,000 businesses as members. HSH offers services to employers on a wide range of employment, commercial and social issues. **http://www.hsh-org.no**

■ **Green Business Network Norway (GBNN)**. A network of enterprises, business federations, governments, universities and non-governmental organisations; has hosted four national conferences on CSR (in 2002, 2003, 2005 and 2008). GBNN is also a member of CSR Europe's National Partner Organisations network. **http://www.gbnn.org**

■ **KOMpakt**. The Norwegian government regards economic engagement in developing countries as both necessary and positive, and established this consultative body in 1998. The aim is both to discuss and to raise awareness regarding human rights and other CSR issues, particularly with reference to developing countries. KOMpakt has the following stakeholders: business federations, unions, research institutions, human rights organisations and the government.

■ **Norwegian Confederation of Trade Unions (LO)**. The largest and most influential workers' organisation in Norway, LO has a strong position in society and has set its stamp on society's development for more than 100 years. Internationally, LO focuses particularly on workers rights. **http://www.lo.no**

■ Case studies

Kommunal Landspensjonskasse (KLP)

KLP is one of Norway's largest life insurance companies. Its operational guidelines incorporate various CSR issues, including responsible investment criteria; KLP ownership guidelines; ethical guidelines for employees; and environmental guidelines. **http://www.klp.no**

Telenor Group

Telenor provides telecommunication services in 13 countries across Europe and Asia, and its role in society is to help people communicate. Telenor's approach to CSR is based on two principles: to extend the benefits of communications to as many people as possible, and to conduct business responsibly. It aims to maximise the enabling effect of mobile telecommunications; promote safer products and services; minimise the company's carbon footprint; and make responsible business practices an integral part of its operations. **http://www.telenor.com**

Vinmonopolet

A key element in Norwegian alcohol policy has been to remove the private profit motive from sales of wine, spirits and strong beer. Hence, Vinmonopolet (wine monopoly) is a government-owned alcoholic beverage retailer and the only company allowed to sell beverages containing a volume percentage higher than 4.7% alcohol in Norway. **http://www.vinmonopolet.no**

■ Education

Masters' and bachelors' programmes and CSR training are offered at several Norwegian universities and college universities, notably:

- **Bodø University College**. http://www.hibo.no

- **Norwegian School of Economics and Business Administration (NHH)**. http://www.nhh.no

- **Norwegian School of Management (BI)**. http://www.bi.no

- **Norwegian University of Science and Technology (NTNU)**. http://www.iot.ntnu.no/csr

- **University of Life Sciences (UMB)**. http://www.umb.no

A survey conducted in 2008 among 11 Norwegian business schools found that business ethics is not high on the curriculum agenda. The leading university was Bodø University College which performs well, both at bachelor and master levels. Both the University of Life Sciences and the Norwegian School of Economics and Business Administration are also doing well at both levels. The Norwegian School of Management includes ethics at master level, but ethics are not mandatory at bachelor level. The University of Agder also performs well in giving mandatory courses on business ethics at bachelor level.

References

Aronsen, E., and J.B. Olsen (2008) 'Arbeidsnotat 06/2008: Lite etikk i norske økonomistudier: En undersøkelse av etikkundervisningen ved norske høyskoler og universiteter', http://www.framtiden.no/200812012438/arbeidsnotater/etikk-og-naringsliv/lite-etikk-pa-timeplanen.html, accessed 4 June 2010.

Johansson, H., and B. Hvinden (forthcoming) 'New Models of Participation in Nordic Welfare States: Can they also include groups at the margins of society?'; http://www.nova.no/asset/3681/1/3681_1.pdf, accessed 14 May 2010.

Langhelle, O., B. Blindheim, A. Blomgren, R. Fitjar and T. Laudal (2009) 'Conceptions of Corporate Social Responsibility. Case: The Clothing Business' (Rapport IRIS — 2009/247; Stavanger, Norway: International Research Institute of Stavanger).

35 Pakistan

Khadeeja Ashaah Balkhi
Sustainability Consultant;
Editorial Director, *tbl — triple bottom-line*

▌ Context

Most cultures within Pakistan are founded upon hospitality and sharing material blessings, including money. Family unit cohesion, together with cultural and religious traditions, manifest in high levels of philanthropy.

As a country founded in the name of religion, Islamic practices permeate behaviour and legislation in Pakistan. Islam encourages ethical business, reinforces transparent written contracts, decent working conditions and fair exchanges both for natural resources and human effort. As guardians of this earth, Muslims have, in the *Sharia* (Islamic law), holistic codes of social behaviour. This includes guidelines on business ethics and managing public resources, including the environment.

For example, *zakaah* is akin to a wealth tax Muslims pay on most assets they have had for a lunar year. Additionally, a strong religious belief is that philanthropy pays back multifold, in this world and the hereafter. In the holy month of Ramadan, for instance, Pakistanis donate PKR70 billion. About half of this amount is collected into the *Bait ul Maal*, or welfare treasury, via the government's Zakaat and Ushr Committee: on the first day of Ramadan banks deduct the 2.5% obligatory religious, charitable tax from savings accounts not opting for exemption.

The *Waqf* Islamic model, akin to an endowment or trust, is an inalienable religious endowment for charitable or educational purposes, often in the form of property. For instance, in 1906 the Said brothers founded the Hamdard Dawa Khana (House of Medicine herbal pharmacy) and the family leadership of the next generation declared it a *Waqf* in 1953 as it prospered. Other examples include Hamdard University and the Forqan orphanage. To many, these are the quiet pioneers of CSR in Pakistan — businesses that not only add economic value, but are also dedicated to social work. According to independent researcher Shadab Fariduddin, the centuries-old *Waqf* model 'institutionalises the sustainability of social institutions'.[1]

---

1 Presentation at a Roundtable organised by *tbl*.

There are numerous CSR models that have emerged in Pakistan, including the **Cross Company CSR (C3)**, proposed by Zohare Ali Shariff of *tbl — triple bottom-line*. This model seeks to tangibly leverage commonality in the value chains of diverse companies towards a larger cause, thereby connecting companies with each other, not just with nonprofit organisations.

The **Cross Subsidy Food Aid Model**, proposed by Salman Abedin of Frontline Consultants, is based on the premise that feast and famine go hand in hand. This model recommends building in small amounts into affluent consumer dining outlets' charges to cross-subsidise a nutritionally balanced boxed meal.

The **Low Income Housing Model**, proposed by Jawad Aslam of Ansaar Management Company enables lower-income segments to own homes in healthy communities. It provides vibrant housing developments in an environmentally, socially and financially sustainable manner by engaging a wide range of stakeholders including foreign investors, financial institutions and non-governmental organisations (NGOs).

The **CSR Progression Model**, proposed by M. Siddique Sheikh of the Standing Committee on CSR, FPCCI, suggests a progression from compliance to excellence, including from corporate legal responsibility (CLR) to corporate intellectual responsibility (CIR) and corporate spiritual responsibility (CSR).

■ Priority issues

Poor governance

There is a general lack of accountability and transparency permeating all levels in Pakistani society. Non-implementation of existing policies and laws, for instance, results in environmental degradation despite good environmental legislation. Educational and healthcare systems are ailing, with women's literacy less than 35% and a quarter of the population undernourished.

Terrorism

Pakistanis confront terrorism in their daily lives — not only from within their own borders but also the effects of terrorism in neighbouring countries. According to the Ministry of Finance's conservative estimate (Ministry of Finance 2009b), the war on terror within Pakistan has cost Pakistan USD35 billion since 2001–02. This estimate was calculated before the latest of several crises over internally displaced persons peaked in the summer of 2009.

Labour issues

Labour laws are frequently flouted. Unfair, usually undocumented, economic activity contributes to deepening income disparities. The Pakistan Institute of Labour, Education and Research identifies nine sectors where 'forced' labour is common in Pakistan: agriculture, brick kilns, construction, carpet weaving, mining, glass bangles, tanneries, domestic work and beggary. Despite Pakistan being an agrarian economy, the feudal system means that the scale and state of bonded labour is worst in the agricultural sector.

Poverty

Pakistan has a population growth rate of 2.2%, with over 60% living below the USD2/day poverty line, according to UNDP's Human Development Indices (UNDP 2008: 35). In addition to the obvious manifestations, Pakistan's infrastructure cannot cope. For example, the Karachi Water and Sewerage Board (KWSB) claims that the sewage treatment system can only handle 40% of the sewage generated. According to their own statistics, 90% is released untreated into water bodies (UNEP claims only 6% is treated). Karachi alone discharges 150 million gallons of untreated effluents into the sea every day.

Environmental degradation

Environmental issues in Pakistan include water pollution from raw sewage, industrial waste and agricultural runoff; limited natural fresh water resources; poor access to potable water; deforestation; soil erosion; and water logging, salinity and desertification.

For example, between 1990 and 2005, Pakistan lost 25% of its forest cover, or 625,000 ha of forests, including centuries-old juniper forests. Less than 2.5% of the country is under forest cover.

The impacts of industrial and vehicular pollution are also evident. For instance, in a 2006 study, the Pakistan Environment Protection Agency found that the average suspended particulate matter in Pakistan cities is 6.4% higher than WHO guidelines.

▌ Trends

Fariduddin (2007) highlighted three current CSR-related trends:

- **Competition to cooperation**. Instead of stand-alone departments undertaking end-to-end projects, a partnership model with NGOs and development agencies is on the rise.

- **Command to demand orientation**. Instead of corporations determining what is best for the community or society and then supplying that service, there is marked awareness of the need to be responsive to the people whom CSR is supposed to serve. CSR is now more demand-driven.

- **Outsourced versus in-sourced fund management**. While the phenomenon of setting up an in-house foundation or a welfare trust is not new, the recent trend of setting up corporate foundations or trusts seems to have a genuineness of purpose. As a result serious efforts are made to address pressing social issues.

Fariduddin argues that these trends manifest themselves via the following four strategies:

- **Politically motivated CSR strategy**. A company's CSR strategy is aligned with a current political slogan which seldom captures a real grassroots need.

- **Globally aligned CSR strategy**. This is typically practised by multinational corporations operating in Pakistan, driven either by headquarter requirements or because centralised CSR makes good economic sense given the lowering of implementation costs and maximising global branding.

- **Externally imposed CSR**. This is legally or trade-imposed CSR, such as many supply-chain labour standards.

- **Philanthropic and responsive CSR**. This is based on a broad 'do good' principle. A charitable budget is reserved and funding takes place when requested or on an ad hoc basis.

According to the Pakistan Centre for Philanthropy (PCP) corporate giving survey, Pakistan is ranked as the 6th most philanthropic country in the world. While larger companies tend to give the most in terms of monetary amounts, local companies are the most philanthropic, giving a larger percentage of their profits. In PCP's most recent survey, the profit before tax donation percentage ranged from as high as 48.6% to 4.8% among the top 25 public limited (mostly local) companies.

Corporate philanthropic trends have been rising, from PKR228 million in 2000 to PKR1.87 billion in 2007. Even this underestimates the true value, since many people give for spiritual upliftment, so their donations remain undocumented.

A CSR-related survey of the leadership of 16 Pakistani companies[2] found that:

- The motivation for CSR is influenced by cultural values and religious beliefs.

- External pressures drive the adoption of CSR practices in some industries (e.g. export-based textiles).

- There is evidence of substantial financial CSR activity in Pakistan, both in the corporate sector and by individual businesspeople.

- CSR appears to be limited to concepts of corporate (and personal) philanthropy.

- Often little attention is paid to responsibility towards stakeholders such as customers.

- Some industries are attempting to set standards of ethical, socially responsible behaviour.

- Inconsistencies abound, with considerable gaps between best and common practice.

▌ Legislation and codes

- The **1973 Constitution of the Islamic Republic of Pakistan**. Prescribes essential human rights-based principles. The state is, for example, responsible for ensuring full participation of women in all spheres of national life (Article 34); just and humane conditions of work (Article 37); and well-being and basic

---

2 Conducted by Jas Ahmad, researcher, in 2006.

necessities of life, such as food, clothing, housing, education and medical relief for all persons, while reducing income disparity (Article 38).

- The **1997 Pakistan Environmental Protection Act**. Provides the framework for the implementation of the 1992 National Conservation Strategy including sustainable development funds, protection and conservation of species, conservation of renewable resources, establishment of environmental tribunals, appointment of environmental magistrates and environmental impact assessments. It includes jurisdiction of the National Environment and Quality Standards (NEQS), parameters for municipal and liquid industrial effluents, industrial gaseous emissions, motor vehicle exhaust and noise.

- The **1996 PSQCA Act**. Governs the Pakistan Standards and Quality Control Authority, which has full authority in relation to use of any Authority Marks. It also enforces and assists with the implementation of quality and environmental management systems ISO 9001:2000 and ISO 14000.

- **Securities and Exchange Commission of Pakistan (SECP)**. Covers governance and transparency-related policies for public companies, including the 2002 Code of Corporate Governance.

- The **2007 Trade Organizations Ordinance**. Led to the following inclusions in the Memorandum and Articles of Association of the FPCCI: 'To . . . adopt measures of such nature which aim at social growth of industrial workers' and:

    > To set up different departments of the FPCCI to deal with various aspects of its business, including a Social Welfare Department to work exclusively for the promotion of Social Welfare in Pakistan and to meet all expenses on account of or arising from the work of these departments

- **Other corporate governance-related laws** include: The Companies Profits (Workers' Participation) Act, 1968; The Securities and Exchange Ordinance, 1969; The Monopolies and Restrictive Trade Practices (Control and Prevention) Ordinance, 1970; The Workers' Welfare Fund Ordinance, 1971; The Companies (Appointment of Legal Advisors) Act, 1974; The Companies Ordinance, 1984; The Securities and Exchange Commission of Pakistan Act, 1997; and The Listed Companies (Substantial Acquisition of Voting Shares and Takeovers) Ordinance, 2002.

❚ Organisations

❚ **CSR Standing Committee, FPCCI**. Works to create practical awareness and facilitate implementation throughout its member network of 33 chambers and 76 trade and professional associations. **http://www.fpcci.com.pk/about-csr.asp**

❚ The **Overseas Investors Chamber of Commerce and Industry (OICCI)**. Tracks CSR-related work with their 175 multinational members. **http://www.oicci.org**

▌ **Pakistan Centre for Philanthropy**. Involved in corporate philanthropy research, awards and NGO certification. **http://www.pcp.org.pk**

▌ The **Pakistan Institute of Corporate Governance (PICG)**. A nonprofit public–private partnership that creates awareness, undertakes research and publishes resource materials while providing a forum for discussion on corporate governance. **http://www.picg. org.pk**

▌ The **Responsible Business Initiative (RBI)**. Involved with disclosure and capacity-building interventions that promote sustainable development and reinforce ethical behaviour. **http://www.rbipk.org**

▌ *triple bottom-line (tbl)*. A platform, centred around a bi-monthly CSR publication, that aims to facilitate the germination of sustainable organisational growth, sharing specific triple bottom-line knowledge and tools such as training journalists for reporting on CSR. It had print and online readership over 18,000 in mid-2009. **http://www.tbl. com.pk**

▌ **United Nations Global Compact (UNGC)**. The Employers Federation of Pakistan (EFP) hosts the UNGC and has over 60 members. It aims to provide practical guidance and help develop the social outlook of business organisations as a new competitive edge.

▌ Case studies

The Dairy Project

Pakistan is the fifth largest producer of milk in the world. This project includes Engro Foods, Nestlé and UNDP. As of late 2008, 1,066 rural women have been trained by the project as lady livestock workers (LLWs), with their income enhanced by PKR2,000–4,500/month each. In total, 594 villages have benefited via livestock skills development, improved livelihoods and food security at the household and community level. The milk production-related companies have, in turn, an improved quality and much steadier supply of milk, thereby reducing idle plant capacity. **http://unbeta.globalhand.org/ en/documents/300**

The Engro Group

Led by Engro Chemicals the group includes Engro Polymer, Engro Energy, Engro Foods and many others. Engro Chemical was the first Pakistani company to publish a sustainability report, winning several awards. Its telemedicine project in rural Sindh is one of the group's many integrated initiatives, mainly around its industrial operations. **http:// www.engro.com**

National Foods Limited

National Foods is among the few companies that began its CSR realisation without any external pressures. Commencing with a thoroughly researched CSR strategy that is still stewarded at board level, the company is working in three main areas: value chain empowerment, in terms of capacity and livelihood development mainly for small farmers or share-croppers in rural Sindh who grow its raw materials; workforce empowerment; and fortified food products to tackle malnutrition in Pakistan. **http://www.nfoods.com**

The Pakistan Competitiveness and Compliance Initiative

Most textile companies adhere to numerous voluntary CSR-related compliances — a requirement from supply-chain ethics-conscious global buyers. Initiated in 2001 by Pakistan's textile industry — which generates over half the nation's foreign exchange earnings — the PCCI seeks to bring all social, environmental and security compliances into one scorecard. An ambitious project, it has achieved negotiation and global-buyer agreement milestones, but has yet to fully develop the scorecard.

▌ Education

While some institutions are developing CSR degrees and programmes, none are currently offered. Most institutions however (including those not listed), offer a course on an area directly related to CSR. Several professors now routinely discuss CSR in courses ranging from social marketing to social entrepreneurship. Ethics-based courses tend to be part of required curricula. Offerings include:

- **Forman Christian College University, Lahore**. Course on ethics and CSR. **http://fccollege.edu.pk**

- **Institute of Business Administration (IBA)**. Courses in ethics and CSR and in business and society. **http://www.iba.edu.pk**

- **Institute of Business and Management**. Courses on CSR and corporate governance. **http://www.iobm.edu.pk**

- **Lahore University of Management Sciences (LUMS)**. Social Enterprise Development Center. **http://sedc.org.pk/portal/index.php**   **http://www.lums.edu.pk**

- **University of Central Punjab (UCP)**. Course on business ethics and CSR; organised national conference on CSR. **http://www.ucp.edu.pk**

- **University of the Punjab**. Electives on CSR. **http://www.pu.edu.pk**

- **Shaheed Zulfikar Ali Bhutto Institute of Science and Technology (SZABIST)**. General and dedicated courses on CSR. **http://www.szabist.edu.pk**

References

Fariduddin, S. (2007) 'Corporate Social Responsibility: Trends and Types in Pakistan', *NGORC Journal* 8.1: 4-7.

Ministry of Finance (2009a) 'Overview of the Pakistan Economy 2008–2009', Government of Pakistan; **http://www.finance.gov.pk/finance_blog/?p=238**, accessed 20 September 2009.

—— (2009b) 'Poverty Reduction Strategy Papers — II' (Pakistan Ministry of Finance).

Population Reference Bureau (2008) 'World Population Data Sheet' (Islamabad: Pakistan Government).

UNDP (United Nations Development {Programme) (2008) 'Human Development Indices'; **http://hdr.undp.org/en/media/HDI_2008_EN_Tables.pdf**, accessed 9 April 2009.

Waheed, A. (2005) *Evaluation of the State of Corporate Social Responsibility in Pakistan and a Strategy for Implementation* (Karachi, Pakistan: Securities and Exchange Commission of Pakistan and United Nations Development Programme; **http://www.secp.gov.pk/Reports/CSR_Study_FinalReport_November.pdf**, accessed 10 April 2009).

36 Perú

Cristian Loza Adaui
Auxiliary Professor and Adjunct Researcher,
San Pablo Catholic University, Perú

▌ Context

The current Peruvian context is the heir of two great cultural traditions: on the one hand, the legacy of several Andean cultures that enabled the configuration of the Inca civilisation and empire (1430–1534 BC); on the other, the cultural heritage and tradition of Western civilisation received through the Spaniards in the mid 16th century.

Both cultural traditions have had religious, social, ecological and economic influences on CSR and its particular development in Perú. For example, the concept of 'Andean reciprocity' can be thought of as an historical precedent for CSR (Franco 2007: 4). In a culture that did not utilise money as a medium of exchange, reciprocity defined the interaction between individuals, not only in social and economic contexts, but also in religious and ecological terms as well. This characteristic of Andean culture continues to have influence through endemic perspectives on social relations and the way some people in the Peruvian Andes relate to the environment and to responsibility.

During colonial times, and with the installation of the Spanish Viceroyalty in Perú until the 19th century, the Catholic Church, as part of its evangelisation process, engaged in and promoted philanthropic activities, even in secular settings. Hence, the role of the Catholic Church has been essential in shaping a charitable social ethos, not only in Perú but also throughout Latin America (Franco 2002; Puppim de Oliveira 2006). The tradition of Catholic 'Social Thought' and its influence over Peruvian history has also shaped contemporary management practices, especially in the approach to philanthropy and CSR.

Since Perú became a republic in 1821, society and business culture have been influenced by other factors too. For example, extensive population migration from rural to urban areas since the mid 1950s reconfigured the appearance of cities and many social customs. Then, between 1968 and 1980, two military governments hampered state–business relations with expropriations and nationalisation policies, shrinking the business sector (and thus its social action) and generating an economic crisis that led to fragmentation and profound social upheaval, fuelling terrorism and the worsening of the economic crisis during the 1980s.

Only at the end of the 1990s did an economic recovery and relative stability allow the country's business elites to engage more proactively in activities with a social purpose (Durand 2008). During the 21st century, this has increasingly adopted the face of CSR, the development and dissemination of which has accelerated in recent years.

More specifically, the contribution of businesses to the Peruvian society in recent decades has been twofold: first, through the creation of corporate foundations focused on funding solutions to the social problems afflicting the country (Portocarrero *et al*. 2000); and, second, through the creation of business organisations such as Perú 2021. This organisation recommends the prioritisation of seven key stakeholder groups: shareholders, employees and their families, customers, suppliers, government, community and the environment (Canessa and García 2005). Perú 2021 also proposes a set of CSR indicators and offers a practical guide for stakeholder engagement, thereby helping to spread the stakeholder model throughout the country (Canessa and Cuba 2006; Rizo Patrón *et al*. 2007).

Today, CSR in Perú is experiencing diffusion and growth within the private and public sectors, promoted by such factors as the ratification of various international trade treaties, the creation of the Ministry of Environment, the emergence of CSR-specialised media (e.g. Revista Stakeholders and Semanario Empresa Responsable), the supply of CSR educational programmes and the development of national initiatives that seek to bring more players into the CSR movement.

▌ Priority issues

The priority issues regarding CSR in Perú are the building of confidence and social reconciliation; the overcoming of corruption, poverty and inequality; the improvement of the education level; and environmental management.

Building confidence and social reconciliation

The Truth and Reconciliation Commission (Comisión de la Verdad y la Reconciliación 2003) estimates approximately 69,280 victims and around USD9.2 billion as social and economic costs of the terrorism between 1988 and 2000. As a result of the havoc caused by terrorism and human rights violations (35,229 acts of human rights violations are documented), there is still widespread distrust and extensive social fragmentation in Perú.

Corruption

According to Transparency International's (2009) Corruption Perceptions Index, Perú was ranked in 75th place of 180 countries (where 1st shows the least corruption). The sectors perceived as more corrupt were the political parties and the judiciary sector (Transparency International 2007a: 16; 2007b: 22).

Poverty and inequality

In recent years Perú's positive macroeconomic performance has unfortunately not yet been reflected in important improvements at the microeconomic level. A high proportion of the population are still living in poverty (36.2%) and extreme poverty (12.6%) (INEI 2008). There is economic and geographical inequality — in Perú the Gini coefficient is 49.6, with the richest 10% of the population earning 38% of the income and the poorest 10% of the population only 1.5% of the income (UNDP 2009). More than 6.5 million Peruvians live in rural areas, where 65% of the people are in poverty. In terms of human development, Perú was ranked 78th of 182 countries in the UN Human Development Index for 2009 (UNDP 2009).

Education

More than 2.5 million Peruvians are illiterate, with just six out of ten children finishing primary school and one in every four children working. In rural areas, just the half of the population has access to primary school. Despite awareness of the importance of education for development, and modest state efforts, Perú ranks in last place on reading, literacy and mathematics in Latin America (LLECE 2008). Only about 5% of Perú's students perform at the OECD average (World Bank 2007: xiii).

Environmental management

The deterioration of the environment and natural resources is an issue of major concern (Grupo de Trabajo Multisectorial Preparación del Ministerio del Medio Ambiente 2008), especially:

- **High levels of water pollution**. For example, there are more than 800 environmental mining liabilities from past mining activities.

- **Poor disposal of solid waste**. There is only one official landfill for hazardous solid wastes and the improper collection of solid waste has produced losses of at least USD45 million.

- **High urban air pollution**. This is mainly caused by the obsolete vehicular fleet and poor fuel quality. It is estimated that in Perú approximately 4,000 people die each year from diseases caused by poor air quality

- **Loss of agricultural land through erosion, salinisation and deteriorating soil fertility**. For example, 8 million ha are severely eroded and 31 million ha moderately eroded.

- **Destruction of forests through illegal logging, and the loss of native crops and their diverse genetic wealth.** At least 10 million ha of forest have been destroyed. In the Peruvian Amazon, which represents 13% of the Amazon rainforest in South America; 221 species of fauna are in danger of extinction; and ethnic groups and their cultures have been gradually disappearing.

In response to these and also to other problems, the Ministry of Environment was created in 2008 with the intent of addressing and managing these environmental issues.

▌ Trends

The 1990s marked the beginning of the CSR debate in Perú and led to a series of studies — focused on transnational corporations — which showed an underdeveloped interest in CSR among the Peruvian business community. Nevertheless, an appetite for developing CSR activities was present, despite unsupportive legal and tax frameworks and a lack of state intervention in these matters (Portocarrero *et al.* 2000).

According to Benavides and de Gastelumendi (2001: 51), the business sectors most actively engaged in CSR in Perú are mining, banking, telecommunications and electricity, motivated primarily by corporate image and employee relations. While environmental issues, supplier relations and the responsible use of publicity showed improvements, the most significant developments were in relationships with internal stakeholders. This study also identified poor diffusion of CSR, a gap between the motivation and practice of CSR, non-strategic implementation of CSR and lack of vision by managers and decision makers.

The mining sector in Perú deserves a special mention, not only because of its importance to the Peruvian economy, but because despite its engagement with CSR, social conflicts related to mining activity remain a serious problem (Portocarrero *et al.* 2007; de Echave *et al.* 2005; Caravedo 1998). Many of these conflicts are linked to environmental issues and problems with local communities. In recent years concern has been generated about environmental protection and improvement of communication strategies with communities in the mining areas. Another study (Garavito *et al.* 2004) showed that some CSR claims by transnational companies were not necessarily implemented. This created a negative perception of CSR in the public sphere and scepticism about this topic.

A recent study (Del Castillo and Yamada 2008) has placed renewed emphasis on the relationship between CSR and the Peruvian labour market. In particular, CSR is being seen as an additional incentive to take on labour standards that allow the companies to benefit from the recent trade promotion agreements (TPAs) signed between Perú and other countries.

According to Portocarrero *et al.* (2006), CSR in micro, small and medium enterprises (MSMEs) is a thinly applied but widespread practice, albeit sporadic and at the owners' discretion. The most common CSR practices in MSMEs are directed inwards, seeking improved working environments and responding to economic, as well as ethical and religious motivations. External CSR in MSMEs tends to reflect the owners' social networks, often taking the form of 'sponsoring' (*apadrinajes*), while the tackling of environmental issues is chiefly motivated by cost reduction and efficiency, rather than a real concern for the environment.

Despite the limitations of CSR in MSMEs, there is increasing recognition of the potential for collaboration with large enterprises, through activities aimed at promoting production chains and bottom of the pyramid markets (BOPM). A recent study (SNV 2008: 14) states that in Perú:

> many firms incorporate BOPM in their production process as part of CSR policies, having identified these populations as important allies who can be integrated into their production chain. Others focus on BOPM consumers because the country's economic growth has helped to transform BOPM into an interesting business niche, and a way to access new consumers in the face of increased competition within higher segments of the economic spectrum.

Whether the renewed interest of companies in the BOPM only answers to economic motives or really to the desire to contribute to sustainable development of the country remain to be investigated.

The launch of two major initiatives in 2008 marked an important year for the development of CSR: first, the Lima Stock Exchange (Bolsa de Valores de Lima 2008) launched the Corporate Governance Index; second, the '*Responsabilidad Social: Todos*' project brought together over 250 people, including state representatives, business, academia and civil society, with the aim of thinking about social responsibility as a tool for sustainable development (Caravedo 2008: 18). The initial results of this initiative have been published by the UNDP (Caravedo 2008).

■ Legislation and codes

The role of Peruvian law in the promotion of CSR has been discussed by de Belaunde *et al.* (2001) and partially reviewed by Schwalb and García (2003: 90). In addition to the labour and tax laws, the recent creation of the Ministry of Environment has resulted in considerable restructuring of Peruvian environmental laws. The following represents some of the major CSR-related legislation.

Labour rights

- **Texto Único Ordenado de la Ley de Productiviad y Competitividad Laboral D.S.003-97-TR** (March 1997).

- **Texto Único Ordenado de la Ley de Compensación por Tiempo de Servicios D.S. 001-97-TR** (March 1997).

Workers with disabilities

- **Ley General de la Persona con Discapacidad, Ley 27050** (December 1998).

- **Reglamento D.S. 3-2000-PROMUDEH** (April 1999).

Pension funds

- **Ley de Modernización de la Seguridad Social en Salud Ley 26790** (May 1997).

- **Ley del Sistema Privado de Pensiones D. Ley 25897** (December 1992).

Non-discrimination

- **Ley contra actos de discriminación, Ley 26772** (April 1997).

- **Ley 26626** concerning workers with HIV (June 1996).

Employee profit sharing

- **Decreto legislativo 677** (October 1991) and **Decreto Legislativo 892** (November 1996).

Environment

- **Ley General del Ambiente, Ley 28611** (October 2008).

Since November 2009, a very complete Compendium of Environmental Laws in Perú has been available on the website of the Ministry of Environment.[1]

▮ Organisations

▮ **Centro de Investigación de la Universidad del Pacífico (CIUP)**. Since 1996 CIUP has carried out research on nonprofits, philanthropy and social responsibility, the results of which have been published through the Library of Social Responsibility. **http://www. up.edu.pe/ciup**

▮ **Ministerio del Ambiente (MINAM)**. Created in May 2008 with the mission to preserve environmental quality and to ensure present and future generations have the right to enjoy a balanced environment suitable for the development of life. **http://www.minam. gob.pe**

▮ **Perú 2021**. A business organisation founded in 1994, aimed at achieving a shared long-term national vision and the dissemination and promotion of social responsibility as business management methodology. It has 47 corporate members. **http://www. peru2021.org**

▮ **Seguimiento Análisis y Evaluación para el Desarrollo (SASE)**. A nonprofit association devoted to work in social responsibility, founded in 1990, and a pioneer in CSR in Perú and Latin America. **http://www.sase.com.pe**

▮ Case studies

Several successful CSR experiences implemented in Perú have been documented and published, for example the series: 'Casos de Responsabilidad Social' presents a total of 15 successful CSR projects between the years 2003 and 2005 (Schwalb *et al*. 2004; Schwalb and García 2004; Schwalb *et al*. 2006). Other case studies are documented by Molteni and Rossato (2007: 137-155); some experiences on corporate philanthropy and volunteering are documented by Portocarrero and Sandborn (2003); and, more recently, successful experiences regarding corporate governance can be found in Franco *et al*. 2009.

In addition, Perú 2021 conducts an annual contest of CSR best practices. Beginning in 2005, they sought to locate the projects submitted in seven categories, corresponding to the seven prioritised stakeholder groups of its CSR model. The last publication of Perú 2021 (2008) includes 26 CSR best practices projects in different economic sectors.

---

1 The Compendium of Environmental Laws in Perú can be accessed at **http://www.minam.gob.pe/ index.php?option=com_content&view=article&id=426&Itemid=81**, accessed 27 May 2010.

∎ Education

CSR education in Perú has recently gained momentum. The first master's programme in CSR was launched in 2009 (offered by **CENTRUM Católica**), which is complementary to existing specialised CSR programmes. There are no Peruvian business schools in global rankings such as *Beyond Grey Pinstripes* (Aspen Institute 2003, 2005, 2008, 2010), but two business schools adhere to the Principles for Responsible Management Education: **CENTRUM Católica Business School of the Pontificia Universidad Católica del Perú (PUCP)** and **Universidad ESAN**.

Furthermore, **Universidad del Pacífico** is also seeking to integrate CSR into the entire curriculum (Caravedo 2007). Other universities that have shown an academic interest in CSR include: Universidad Católica San Pablo (Arequipa), Universidad Católica de Santa María (Arequipa), Universidad de Piura (Piura), Universidad Privada Antenor Orrego (Trujillo).

There is also a model of university social responsibility (USR) developed by a scholar of the PUCP. This model is presented as a form of ethical management of the university's impacts, categorising them in terms of organisational effects (labour and environmental), educational effects (academic teaching), cognitive effects (research and epistemology) and social effects (extent, social projection) (Vallaeys 2008). In this regard there has been not only academic discussion, but also specific initiatives whose results are being analysed.

References

Aspen Institute (2003) 'Beyond Grey Pinstripes 2003' (New York: Aspen Institute; http://www.aspencbe.org/documents/bgps_2003_brochure.pdf, accessed 25 May 2010).

—— (2005) 'Beyond Grey Pinstripes 2005' (New York: Aspen Institute; http://www.aspencbe.org/documents/bgp_ranking_2005.pdf, accessed 25 May 2010).

—— (2008) 'Beyond Grey Pinstripes 2007–2008' (New York: Aspen Institute; http://beyondgreypinstripes.org/rankings/bgp_2007_2008.pdf, accessed 25 May 2010).

—— (2010) 'Beyond Grey Pinstripes 2009–2010' (New York: Aspen Institute; http://www.beyondgreypinstripes.org/pdf/2009-2010BGP_Brochure.pdf, accessed 25 May 2010).

Benavides, M., and G. de Gastelumendi (2001) *Responsabilidad Social Empresarial: Un Compromiso Necesario* (Lima: Centro de Investigación de la Universidad del Pacífico [CIUP], SASE and Perú 2021).

Bolsa de Valores de Lima (2008) 'Índice de Buen Gobierno Corporativo'; http://www.bvl.com.pe/indicegob.html, accessed 20 February 2009.

Canessa, G., and C. Cuba (2006) *Indicadores de RSE* (Lima: Perú 2021).

—— and E. García (2005) *El ABC de la Responsabilidad Social Empresarial en El Perú y el Mundo* (Lima: Perú 2021).

Caravedo, B. (1998) *El Impacto Social de las Empresa Mineras en el Perú* (Lima: IDEM).

—— (2007) *La Sociedad Oculta: El Espacio de la Transformación* (Lima: SASE).

—— (coord.) (2008) *Responsabilidad Social: Todos, hacia un encuentro de todos los peruanos* (Lima: PNUD).

Comisión de la Verdad y la Reconciliación (2003) 'Informe Final'; http://www.cverdad.org.pe/ifinal/index.php, accessed 20 February 2009.

De Belaunde, J., D. Muñoz and B. Parodi (2001) *Cómo Promover la Responsabilidad Social Empresarial en el Perú: Marco Legal e Institucional* (Lima: CIUP and Perú 2021).

De Echave, J., A. Diez, L. Huber, B. Revesz, X. Ricard and M. Tanaka (2005) *Minería y Conflicto Social* (Lima: IEP, CIPCA, CBC and CIES).

Del Castillo, E., and G. Yamada, (2008) *Responsabilidad Social y Buen Clima Laboral: Una Fórmula Ganadora* (Lima: CIUP).

Durand, F. (2008) 'Empresa y responsabilidad social empresarial: el caso peruano', in C. Sanborn and F. Portocarrero (eds.), *Filantropía y cambio social en América Latina* (Lima: CIUP and David Rockefeller Center for Latin American Studies Harvard University; trans. by A. de la Cadena and E. Neyra of *Philanthropy and Social Change in Latin America* [2005]): 233-264.

Franco, P. (2007) *Diagnóstico de la Responsabilidad Social en el Perú* (Lima: CIUP; http://www.up.edu. pe/_data/ciup/documentos/20080107112404_DD-07-15.pdf, accessed 20 February 2009).

——, G. Pipoli and C. Varela (eds.), (2009) *El Gobierno Corporativo en el Perú: reflexiones académicas sobre su aplicación* (Lima: CIUP).

Garavito, C., M. Carrillo and A. Hernandez (2004) *Panorama de la Responsabilidad Social Empresarial: Sector Comercio, Minero y Telecomunicaciones* (Lima: PLADES and FNV).

Grupo de Trabajo Multisectorial Preparación del Ministerio del Medio Ambiente (2008) 'Diagnóstico Ambiental del Perú' (Lima: Grupo de Trabajo Multisectorial Preparación del Ministerio del Medio Ambiente; http://www.scribd.com/doc/4641761/DIAGNOSTICO-AMBIENTAL-DEL-PERU, accessed 25 February 2009).

INEI (Instituto Nacional de Estadística e Informática) (2008) 'Informe Técnico: Situación Sobre la Pobreza en el 2008'; http://censos.inei.gob.pe/DocumentosPublicos/Pobreza/2008/Informe_Tecnico. pdf, accessed 30 August 2009.

LLECE (Laboratorio Latinoamericano de Evaluación de la Calidad de la Educación) (2008) 'Los Aprendizajes de los Estudiantes de América Latina y el Caribe' (Santiago, Chile: Oficina Regional de Educación para América Latina y el Caribe de la UNESCO; http://www.anep.edu.uy/ documentos/serce/primer_reporte.pdf, accessed 30 August 2009).

Molteni, M., and E. Rossato (2007) *Responsabilidad social y resultados de empresa. Hacia una síntesis sociocompetitiva* (Lima: Universidad Católica Sedes Sapientiae).

OECD (Organisation for Economic Cooperation and Development) and UNESCO Institute of Statistics (2003) *Literacy Skills for the World of Tomorrow: Further Results from PISA 2000* (Paris: OECD).

Perú 2021 (2008) *IV Premio Perú 2021 a la Responsabilidad Social y Desarrollo Sostenible: Recopilación de Casos y Documento de Discusión* (Lima: Perú 2021).

Portocarrero, F. (2002) 'La filantropía peruana en perspectiva histórica: Una terra incógnita, un blanco móvil', *ReVista*, Spring 2002; http://www.drclas.harvard.edu/revista/articles/view/554, accessed 20 February 2009.

——, and C. Sanborn (eds.) (2003) *De la caridad a la solidaridad: filantropía y voluntariado en el Perú* (Lima: CIUP).

——, C. Sanborn, S. Llusera and V. Quea (2000) *Empresas, Fundaciones y Medios: la responsabilidad social en el Perú* (Lima: CIUP).

——, B. Tarazona and L. Camacho (2006) *Situación de la Responsabilidad Social Empresarial en la Micro, Pequeña y Mediana Empresa en el Perú* (Lima: CIUP).

——, C. Sanborn and L.A. Camacho (eds.) (2007) *Moviendo montañas: empresas, comunidades y ONG en las industrias extractivas* (Lima: CIUP).

Puppim de Oliveira, J.A. (2006) 'Corporate Citizenship in Latin America: New Challenges for Business', *Journal of Corporate Citizenship* 21 (Spring 2006): 17-20.

Rizo Patrón, C., D. Diaz, and M.K. Filomeno (2007) *Relación y Compromiso con los Grupos de Interés: Guia Práctica para las Empresas Peruanas* (Lima: Apoyo and Perú 2021).

Schwalb, M.M., and E. García (2003) *Evolución del Compromiso Social de las Empresas: Historia y Enfoques* (Lima: CIUP).

—— and E. García (eds.) (2004) *Buenas Prácticas Peruanas de Responsabilidad Social Empresarial Colección 2004* (Lima: CIUP).

——, E. García and V. Soldevilla (eds) (2006) *Buenas Prácticas Peruanas de Responsabilidad Social Empresarial. Colección 2005* (Lima: CIUP).

——, C. Ortega and E. García (eds.) (2004) *Casos de Responsabilidad Social* (Lima: CIUP).

SNV Netherlands Development Organization (2008) 'A Firm-Level Approach to Majority Market Business: Private Sector Mapping Project'; http://www.inclusivebusiness.org/2008/06/ private-sector.html, accessed 25 May 2010.

Transparency International (2007a) 'Informe Global de la Corrupción 2007: Corrupción en los Sistemas Judiciales' (Buenos Aires, Argentina: Editores del Puerto; **http://www.proetica.org.pe/ Descargas/GCR2007.pdf**, accessed 30 August 2009).

—— (2007b) 'Report on the Transparency International Global Corruption Barometer', **http://www. proetica.org.pe/Descargas/GCB_2007_report_en_02-12-2007[1].pdf**, accessed 30 August 2009.

—— (2009) 'Corruption Perceptions Index 2009'; **http://www.transparency.org/policy_research/ surveys_indices/cpi/2009/cpi_2009_table**, accessed 25 May 2010.

UNDP (United Nations Development Programme) (2009) *Human Development Report 2009* (New York: UNDP; **http://hdr.undp.org/en/media/HDR_2009_EN_Complete.pdf**, accessed 30 August 2009).

Vallaeys, F. (2008) 'La Responsabilidad Social Universitaria: ¿Cómo Entenderla para Quererla y Practicarla?', *Brújula* 16: 25-35.

World Bank (2007) 'Toward High-Quality Education in Peru: Standards, Accountability, and Capacity Building. A World Bank Country Study' (Washington, DC: World Bank; **http://siteresources. worldbank.org/INTINDIA/4371432-1194542322423/21542208/TowardhighqualityeducationinPeru. pdf**, accessed 30 August 2009).

37 The Philippines

Francisco L. Roman

Deputy Executive Director, Ramon V. del Rosario Sr.
Center for Corporate Social Responsibility of the
Asian Institute of Management

Maria Elena B. Herrera

Faculty Fellow, Ramon V. del Rosario Sr.
Center for Corporate Social Responsibility of the
Asian Institute of Management

▌ Context

In the Philippines, the concept and practice of CSR is rooted in cooperative and community associations involving business and society. The spirit of *bayanihan* is a Filipino tradition characterised by mutual assistance of one's neighbours. The legitimacy of CSR depends on at least two factors:

- The Philippine Constitution defines the state's role in promoting equality and the common good, and

- The Corporation Code enforces the responsibility of boards and directors to practice good governance.

CSR in the Philippines evolved through five stages (Velasco 2009; Roman and Alarilla 2005), described briefly below:

- **The decade of donation (1960s)**. Characterised by social inequity, and unrest eventually resulting in protest demonstrations. Companies donated to charitable institutions in cash and in kind but efforts were sporadic, fragmented and uncoordinated.

- **The decade of organisation (1970s)**. A number of business associations/organisations were established to address the common concerns of the poor based on the realisation that a weak network reduced both the impact and efficiency of philanthropy. This decade represented the first step in establishing CSR as 'true' CSR.

- **The decade of involvement (1980s)**. Another period of unrest. Many companies responded and offered assistance through community relations (COMREL) to promote stable and peaceful business operations by increasing the range and funding of company-to-community activities and services, and by incorporating stakeholders in the design and implementation of the CSR programmes.

- **The decade of institutionalisation (1990s)**. This period highlighted the emergence of corporate citizenship, the understanding that corporations must contribute to the well-being of society beyond COMREL. Many companies began to consider CSR concerns in strategy formulation.

- **The decade of engagement (early 21st century)**. Social organisations became involved, utilising management frameworks to better serve the poor. In turn, CSR involved the integration of values, goals, resources and skills between business and other sectors, broadening its scope beyond the concerns of families and immediate communities.

▮ Priority issues

Education

Education is a key priority for both the public and private sectors. For 2008, the country's Department of Education received 11.8% of the national budget, the highest among all the departments. However, one in ten Filipinos (6.8 million of the population) never attended school; one in six Filipinos (9.6 million of the population) is not functionally literate; one in three young Filipinos (11.6 million of the population) is not in school; and one in every three entrants to Grade 1 drops out.

Poverty

Fighting poverty is another key priority. According to the 2008 survey by the Social Weather Station, 52% or about 9.4 million Filipino families consider themselves as *Mahirap* (poor); 24% put themselves on the borderline; 42% of Filipino families (an estimated 7.7 million) consider themselves as food-poor; and 30% put themselves on the food-borderline.

Environment

The third key priority is the environment. Air pollution affects the major cities, with solid waste disposal continuing to be a challenge. Illegal logging in the south induces landslides, lakes in Central Luzon are polluted and mining operations result in numerous oil and chemical spills. Exposure to water pollution, poor sanitation conditions and hygiene practices account for one-sixth of reported disease cases, with treatment costs and lost income amounting to PHP6.7 billion (USD134 million) annually. Air pollution is a primary cause of respiratory diseases, which annually costs the country PHP7.6 billion (USD153 million).

▌ Trends

Education, poverty reduction and environmental programmes are priorities for most corporations and are expected to remain the focus for future CSR programmes. In a 2008 survey of CSR practitioners conducted by the AIM RVR Center on the State of Corporate Citizenship in the Philippines, 42% reported a focus on primary education and 42% also mentioned global climate change; about 36% reported active engagement in the pursuit of improving conditions in poor communities.

The survey findings also concluded that CSR initiatives are CEO-driven and that most companies operating within the community are under pressure to act more responsibly. The overall lack of funds, employee support and direction are the major hindrances for companies conducting CSR programmes.

Within the last decade, CSR in the Philippines has moved rapidly from a broad discourse on issues to strategies for implementing and sustaining CSR initiatives. As the five-decade framework suggests, CSR began with a search for an identity or role and progressed to pursuing sustainability partly through networks. Perhaps the next decade will see a closer alignment of business core values to national and societal values.

▌ Legislation and codes

According to Dr Romulo Emmanuel Miral, Executive Director of the Congressional Planning and Budget Department of the Philippine House of Representatives Congress, legislation offers societal economic value when the social marginal cost is higher than private marginal costs, for example in the case of a mining company causing pollution. In other instances, the social marginal benefits may be higher than the private marginal benefits (e.g. schools, hospitals, water utilities, etc.) and society's welfare would be enhanced if the firm increases its operation beyond its most profitable level. However, a firm must be profitable in order to fulfil its social obligations. Hence, legislation should enable a corporation to offset the costs of, and derive benefits from, its social activities. The following represents the key CSR-related legislation:

- **Philippine Constitution of 1987**. All Philippine laws and codes emanate from the Constitution. Article II, Section 9 states that 'the State will promote a just and dynamic social order . . . and free the people from poverty through policies that provide adequate social services, promote full employment, a rising standard of living, and an improved quality of life'.

- **Environment**. The Philippine Mining Act promotes 'sustainable mining' by ensuring compliance among mining companies and providing community programmes within the impacted areas through a percentage allocation of their income to environment and social-related issues. The Clean Air Act and Clean Water Act provide a legal framework for the use and discharge of industrial waste, while the Wildlife Resources Conservation and Protection Act and the Animal Welfare Act ensure protection of wildlife within forested areas where companies operate.

- **Governance**. The Code of Corporate Governance requires public companies to maintain transparency and accountability.

- **Labour**. The Labor Code and the Magna Carta for Disabled Persons provide a framework of equal opportunity and employee protection and benefits, while the Act of Prohibition on Discrimination against Women addresses gender equality in the workplace.

- **Education**. The Adopt-a-School Act allows companies to integrate education into their CSR programmes. The Children's Television Act of 1997 promotes the airing of children-oriented educational programmes.

- **Health**. The Comprehensive Tobacco Regulation Act regulates the tobacco industry, the Cheaper Medicines Act ensures that pharmaceutical companies promote the production of generic medicines, and the Philippine Milk Code promotes the practice of breast-feeding over substitutes.

- **Small business**. The Magna Carta for Small Enterprise offers financial support and the creation of a council that oversees the development and the promotion of small and medium enterprises (SMEs). The private sector's role is to participate in government programmes for SMEs.

▌ Organisations

▌ **Asian Institute of Management: Ramon V. del Rosario Sr. Center for Corporate Social Responsibility**. A research and programme centre focusing on corporate citizenship relative to the competitiveness of firms and its impact on society. The Center runs surveys and advocacy forums. Its flagship project is the annual Asian Forum on Corporate Social Responsibility and Asian CSR Awards, which are held each year in different Asian countries. **http://www.rvr.aim.edu**

▌ **Jollibee Foundation**. The Foundation has 37 programme partners and its mission is to improve access to education for youth, promote livelihood programmes for small farmers and small-scale entrepreneurs, ensure leadership development for local organisations and become active in disaster relief. **http://www.jollibeefoundation.org**

▌ **League of Corporate Foundations**. The League includes 50 corporate foundations and business organisations, two non-governmental organisation (NGO) networks and six associates. It evolved in 1991 to engage in external advocacy work, including a benchmarking project and the celebration of the country's first ever CSR Week, mandated by a presidential proclamation. **http://www.lcf.org.ph**

▌ **Makati Business Club**. The Club comprises over 800 senior executives, representing almost 450 corporations. Its programmes include Children's Hour, the Corporate Network for Disaster Response, and Promoting English Proficiency. Furthermore, 1% of all cardholders' charges made via the MBC–Bankard Visa go to a charitable pool of funds. **http://www.mbc.com.ph**

▌ **Management Association of the Philippines (MAP)**. The Association has 835 members from business, government and academia. MAP's advocacy includes external and internal campaigns on corporate governance, CSR, and environment and sustainability; and also projects such as the MAP Recognition Program for Responsible Businesses, teachers' training, and a Climate Change Contest. **http://www.map.com.ph**

▋ Philippine Business for Education. This organisation has 40 corporate members striving for consensus on education reform. Its initiatives include the 1,000 Teachers Program Scholarship Award to attract the best into the teaching profession and the 57–75 Campaign to reverse the education crisis and raise the national achievement test scores from 57% to 75%. **http://www.pbed.ph**

▋ Philippine Business for Social Progress. This organisation, formed around 1970, focuses through its 238 members on poverty alleviation, information technology and leadership in CSR through partnerships between government, NGOs, civil society and donor institutions. In 1991, it established the Center for Corporate Citizenship, which focuses on social investment, environmental stewardship, workplace concerns and corporate–community partnerships. **http://www.pbsp.org.ph**

▋ Pilipinas Shell Foundation, Inc. The Foundation is the social arm of the Shell Oil Company in the Philippines. It runs programmes covering two million beneficiaries for the development of leadership; technical and vocational skills; health, sanitation and safety; livelihood and entrepreneurship; educational improvement; and environmental stewardship. **http://www.shell.com.ph**

▋ Synergeia. This organisation with 61 individual fellows and 57 institutional partners is a coalition whose goals include raising proficiency in English at graduation from elementary school to 85% through four initiatives for governance in education. It has ten initiatives for special communities and 32 initiatives under the reading and mathematics proficiency programme. **http://www.synergeia.org.ph**

▋ Case studies

Ayala Foundation

Ayala Foundation tries to bridge the digital divide through its Gearing up Internet Literacy, and Access for Students programmes. It has 24 partners and 383 donors. By 2010, all public high schools could be linked to the internet. **http://www.ayalafoundation.org** and **http://www.gilas.org**

Gawad-Kalinga

Gawad-Kalinga aims for the creation of a 'slum-free, squatter-free nation through providing land for the landless, homes for the homeless, food for the hungry'. It currently has over 100 partners and 900 communities in the Philippines and other developing countries. **http://www.gk1world.com**

Intel Philippines

Intel Philippines focuses on volunteerism. Its efforts include programmes for the environment, education and training. Volunteerism increases camaraderie and unity among community members, helping them address the immediate needs of their community. **http://www.intel.com**

Lamoiyan Corporation

Lamoiyan Corporation is a medium-sized company driven by faith-based CSR that is focused on providing equal employment opportunities for the hearing impaired. **http:// www.lamoiyan.com**

Lopez Group Foundation

The Lopez Group Foundation, Inc. coordinates the work of nine foundations and the CSR activities of other Lopez Group companies to create synergies and share experiences on its CSR programmes. For them, 'a business whose primary goal is not to earn the biggest profit but to serve the larger interests of the public will remain not only profitable but also survive much longer than any self-serving competitor'. **http://www. lopezgroup.org**

Rapu-Rapu Polymetallic Project

The Rapu-Rapu Polymetallic Project represents misaligned CSR practice, spending over PHP23.5 million (more than USD450,000) on CSR projects in education, health, and livelihood but failing in its primary social responsibility area, namely the protection of the environment. The project experienced two mine tailings spills which contaminated the nearby creeks used by the community. **http://www.rapu-rapumining.com**

Philippine Investment Management Consultants Inc. (PHINMA)

PHINMA integrates CSR into its business strategy. According to the organisation's President and CEO, Mr Ramon R. del Rosario, Jr: 'Services to the poor, in order to be sustainable, must be profitable. High quality education, profitability and affordability are not separate objectives. They are one and the same. This is PHINMA's direction in CSR — citizenship that goes beyond programmes and foundations'. **http://www.phinma.com.ph**

▌ Education

CSR, as part of the education curriculum in most leading universities, is usually embedded in existing courses such as ethics and responsible business leadership.

Ranked 97th in the 2009–2010 *Beyond Grey Pinstripes* report, the **Asian Institute of Management (AIM)** was the only academic institution listed among Philippine universities. AIM offers a one-week course called Reinventing CSR and a course via video conferencing in partnership with the Tokyo Development Learning Center and World Bank Institute. CSR is also taught in all its degree programmes.

Three universities — **Ateneo de Manila University**, **De La Salle University** and the state-run **University of the Philippines** — have no diploma courses on CSR but offer MBA subjects related to CSR such as business ethics, corporate leadership, law and business environment, business and professional discourse, career and family life, labour law, and collective bargaining as core and elective subjects.

There are universities outside Metro Manila (the Manila metropolitan area) that regularly teach CSR-related topics. For example, **Siliman University** in Negros Oriental runs an undergraduate course in business ethics and social responsibility. The **University of San Carlos** in Cebu runs three programmes:

- The BSBA in Development Management aims to lead and promote development-geared organisations and projects.

- The BSBA in Environmental Management is designed to work towards protecting and preserving the environment while engaging in the business world.

- The USC Master in Business Administration contains CSR subjects that include business ethics and CSR.

References

Asian Institute of Management and De La Salle Professional Schools Ramon V. del Rosario, Sr. Graduate School of Business (2007) 'Doing Good in Business Matters: CSR in the Philippines: Frameworks and The Practice' (Makati City, Philippines: Asian Institute of Management and De La Salle Professional Schools Ramon V. del Rosario, Sr. Graduate School of Business).

Aspen Institute Center for Business Education (2010) 'Beyond Grey Pinstripes 2009–2010'; http://www.beyondgreypinstripes.org/pdf/2009-2010BGP_Brochure.pdf, accessed 7 June 2010.

Dumangas, J.I. (2008) 'The State of Corporate Citizenship in the Philippines' (AIM-RVR Working Paper; Makati City, Philippines_.

Guerrero, L., J.B. Baylon, G. Sandoval and I. Labucay (2006) 'Judging Companies' Performance: Corporate Social Responsibility in the Philippines' (SWS Occasional Paper; Quezon City, Philippines).

Magno, F.A. (2006) 'Promoting Corporate Environmental and Social Responsibility in Developing Countries' (DLSU-SDRC Research Paper No. 2006-05; Manila, Philippines).

Maximiano, J.M.B. (2007) 'A Strategic Integral Approach (SIA) to Institutionalizing CSR', *Corporate Social Responsibility and Environmental Management* 14.4: 231-242.

National Statistical Coordination Board (2008) *2008 Philippine Statistical Yearbook* (Makati City, Philippines: NSCB).

Roman, F.L., and M.C.I. Alarilla (2005) 'A Note on Networks in CSR' (AIM-RVR-CSR Working Paper; Makati City, Philippines).

—— and R.V.L. Uy 'The Evolution of CSR: Stages, Issues and Trends: A Comparison between the United States and the Philippines', *Journal of Asian Management* 1.1: 43-58.

Velasco, G.T. (2009) 'Corporate Philanthropy in Asia: The Philippine Case', Center on Philanthropy and Civil Society Working Paper'; http://www.philanthropy.org/publications/online_publications/asia.pdf, accessed March 2009.

Web resources

Philippine Congress: http://www.congress.gov.ph

Acknowledgements

The authors wish to thank Dr Romulo Emmanuel Miral for his insights on a framework for CSR-related laws in the Philippines.

38 Poland

Liliana Anam
Founder and Manager, CSRinfo

■ Context

Poland is a democracy situated in the centre of Europe, between the Baltic Sea and the Carpathian Mountains. With a size of 312,679 km² it is one of the largest countries in the European Union (EU). The population is 38.1 million and the society is homogenous, without any significant ethnic or religious minorities. Roman Catholicism remains the central religion, influencing public debate.

To understand Poland one should look at its contemporary history. The country went under the influence of the Soviet Union after the Second World War and was separated from the rest of the Europe by the 'iron curtain'. In 1989, the opposition and communist authorities reached a number of agreements through the 'roundtable negotiations'. They legalised the Solidarity Trade Union and announced free elections in 1989. As a result of these elections, the first non-communist government was formed in the region, giving an impulse to major changes throughout communist Europe.

Since 1989 Poland has been going through a fast transformation from communist regime to democracy and from a central planned economy to a market economy. Therefore, the crucial players from the perspective of CSR development (i.e. the private sector as well as civil society) are relatively young when compared to developed Western European countries.

During the first years of its transformation, Poland was inspired by an American style of capitalism focused on individual entrepreneurs. This business attitude combined with the legacy of the communist regime, which regularly misused the word 'social', did not contribute to the dissemination of the CSR concept among business (Filek 2006). It has gradually changed since Poland joined the EU in 2004. At that time the European Commission's Green Paper on CSR had already been published and the EU had started actively promoting the concept.

A recent analysis (Brzozowski *et al.* 2007) outlines five stages of CSR development in Poland: silence (1997–1999), opposition (2000–2002), growing interest (2003–2004), projects involving various areas of companies' operations (2004–2005) and linking CSR with other strategies such as communication and marketing (2006–2007). To this division I would add a sixth phase (2008 to the present), where one can observe the attempts of companies to integrate CSR with business strategy.

▮ Priority issues

A recent report analysing Poland 20 years after recovering independence (Boni 2009 *et al.*) distinguishes the top five priorities in the upcoming decade as follows:

Growth and competitiveness

Although the divergence from a centrally planned economy secured growth at an average level of GDP at 4.3% between 1992 and 2007, it was slower than other emerging economies such as Hong Kong or Spain. Furthermore, in the Global Competitiveness Report 2008–2009, Poland was ranked 53 out of 134. The low position in comparison to mature economies is caused mainly by three factors: out-of-date technology, the state of physical capital and unexploited potential of human capital.

Demography

While Poland is a relatively young society in the context of the EU, one can observe two trends: a declining population growth rate and a gradually ageing society. The prognosis for 2030 is that people over the age of 60 will number about 10 million (out of a population of 38 million), while the number of professionally active persons will not change. That creates a significant pressure on social security issues.

Labour resources

The average employment rate in the EU 15 in 2008 was 67%, while in Poland it was 59%, the lowest rate in Europe. Furthermore, the proportion of permanent unemployment in the unemployment rate is the highest among European countries. To face these challenges Poland has to reform its labour market. The changes are necessary to increase personal activity and to utilise the labour potential.

Infrastructure

Poland experiences deficiencies in both the transportation network (density and quality) and the availability of broadband internet. According to European Road Statistics (2009), Poland has one of the lowest proportion of motorways in the EU compared to the total road network. Monitoring by the Information Society Index, which includes 53 countries, ranked Poland at 33rd place in provision of information and telecommunication infrastructure in Poland. It is a low position in comparison with other Central European countries. This situation creates a considerable barrier to workforce mobility and communication.

Energy and climate

Energy and climate issues in Poland are driven by two factors: EU policy and a reliance on coal by the Polish economy. According to Eurostat (2009), Poland relies on coal and lignite for 92% of its electricity production. However, in 1988–2005 Poland achieved the substantial greenhouse gas reduction of 32% (Ministry of the Environment 2007) because of environmental investments.

Climate issues are related to the tensions caused by lack of coherence between environmental protection objectives and economic development. For example, the distribution of protected areas, such as Poland's forests that make up 29% of its territory, raise difficulties in the development of the necessary road infrastructure.

In addition, the issue of protecting water resources is becoming a significant problem. According to the World Resources Institute, internal renewable water resources per capita (in cubic metres) in Poland stands at a figure of 1,391, while the statistic for Europe as a whole is 9,089. Furthermore, Poland uses its groundwater resources at a level of between 3.5–4.8 km^3 per year, which constitutes 26–35% of total annual resources.

∎ Trends

CSR is a relatively new concept in Poland, where the market economy has only been operational for 20 years. Analysis of companies through the CSR lens suggest division into three categories: multinationals, large Polish companies and SMEs. Brzozowski *et al.* (2007) find that the pioneers of CSR tend to be international companies with mature global strategies. The uptake of CSR among Polish companies, including those that are state-owned and without access to previously-defined CSR policies and tools, is rather modest. A qualitative study among SMEs (ARFP *et al.* 2005) shows that half of the entrepreneurs surveyed did not undertake any CSR programmes. However, in more recent research (GfK and PSDB 2008), almost half of SMEs exploited environmental attributes in marketing. This indicates that SME managers are not fully aware of their CSR performance, even when introducing environmental, health and safety management systems (Grupa BOSS 2006).

The first study among managers from the national top 500 companies (Rok *et al.* 2003) showed that most of them understand CSR as compliance with ethical norms and adequate treatment of employees. Further research (World Bank 2005a) confirmed that in Poland, businesses mainly associate CSR with ethical conduct (almost 80%), and transparency in operations (50%). Addressing stakeholder concerns and building partnerships were mentioned by less than 50% of surveyed companies.

Nevertheless, companies perceive a real value in CSR implementation. The main returns mentioned were business sustainability (19%), competitive advantage (17%), compliance with regulations (17%) and employee loyalty (16%). Among the perceived external benefits were reputation (51%) followed by the country's sustainable development (11%) and environmental preservation (10%).

Since 2002, Forum Odpowiedzialnego Biznesu has published an annual report, *Responsible Business in Poland*, presenting best practices in CSR. These reports suggest that companies prioritise social engagement first, followed by practices related to market and workplace issues. However, in the last year, environmental practices took second position.

Brzozowski *et al.* (2007) found that the most developed CSR performance is in the field of building strategy and stakeholder engagement, while management, public disclosure and assurance require major improvements. World Bank research showed that less than 40% of companies in Poland issued environmental or social reports. At the beginning of 2009, there were fewer than ten sustainability reports adhering to the Global Reporting Initiative (GRI) guidelines. However, recent translation of GRI Sustainability Guidelines into Polish, as well as the development of professional services to support companies in this area, might contribute to broader disclosure.

Poor CSR practices are explained by the barriers and risks associated with adopting CSR practices. The barriers distinguished in the World Bank's research are grouped in three categories: (1) financial, such as no visible link to financial success, a short-term perspective and direct costs; (2) governmental, such as lack of government involvement and changeable polices; and (3) human, such as cultural differences or management resistance.

Since the 1990s, the CSR concept has been through different stages of development. However, it seems that currently CSR is gaining momentum in Poland. The changes include:

- **Benchmarks**. The Warsaw Stock Exchange launched the first responsibility index in Poland, the Respect Index, in Autumn 2009. The index includes 16 companies: KGHM, PKN Orlen, TP S.A., PGNiG, ING BSK, Bank Handlowy, Lotos, Swiecie, Elektrobudowa, Ciech, Bank BPH, Apator, Azoty Tarnow, Barlinek, Zywiec and Ropczyce.

- **Established leaders**. Companies with CSR strategies are recognised by the CSR ranking prepared by the Centre of Business Ethics at Akademia Leona Kozminskiego and FOB. In 2010 the top companies were Danone Polska, Kompania Piwowarska and Procter & Gamble.

- **Rise in awareness**. CSR has become a fashionable topic taken up by the media. Press monitoring by Instytut Monitorowania Mediow (a company monitoring the media) presents a rapid growth in the number of articles devoted to CSR in leading newspapers from fewer than 100 in 2005 to more than 1,500 in 2009. This contributes to a nationwide understanding and dissemination of the concept (World Bank 2005b).

- **Stakeholder engagement**. The programmes financed by the European Social Fund now attract more CSR-related interest. Consequently, trade unions, consumer organisations and academia are building projects dedicated to CSR at the regional level. In almost half of all provinces there were or are ongoing projects, which contribute to the competitiveness and adaptability of companies or developing SME potential while utilising the CSR concept.

- **Government engagement**. Government institutions are responding more actively to stakeholders' expectations through a national stakeholder dialogue (UNDP 2008). In May 2009 the Polish Prime Minister appointed the Intragovernmental CSR Working Group, which will coordinate governmental efforts and will continue the stakeholder dialogue.

▌ Legislation and codes

An analysis of the legal environment distinguishes three levels of regulation regarding CSR:

The Constitution of the Republic of Poland

This establishes the main principles of governance and underlines the importance of human rights, social dialogue and sustainable development.

Policies and regulations

These are developed by the Polish regulator as well as imposed by the EU. The key legislation includes:

- **Ustawa o swobodzie działalności gospodarczej (2004)**. Economic Freedom Act.

- **Ustawa o ochronie konkurencji i konsumentów (2007)**. Competition and consumer protection.

- **Ustawa o zwalczaniu nieuczciwej konkurencji (1993)**. Unfair competition.

- **Prawo ochrony środowiska (2001)**. Environmental law.

- **Kodeks Pracy (1974)**. The Labour Code.

Voluntary international and Polish standards

Companies in Poland adhere to voluntary standards such as the Global Compact, SA8000, GRI G3 and ISO. The OECD Guidelines for Multinationals are moderately recognised. There are number of codes developed by Polish business associations and industries, for example The Best Practices of WSE Listed Companies, the Ethical Code of Employees developed by PKKP and the 'Lewiatan' or principles of good banking practice adopted by the Polish Bank Association.

▌ Organisations

▌ **Business Centre Club**. A multilevel organisation supporting enterprises in Poland. More than 1,200 companies are BCC affiliates. http://www.bcc.org.pl

▌ **Centrum CSR.PL**. A foundation that popularises CSR as an integral strategy. It cooperates with the OECD Watch Network. http://www.centrumcsr.pl

▌ **CSRinfo**. A company providing information and services to the CSR community in Poland. It is a GRI Organisational Stakeholder. http://www.csrinfo.org

▌ **Forum Odpowiedzialnego Biznesu (FOB)**. An association and business member organisation with 45 companies as members. FOB belongs to the CSR Europe network and also acts as representative of WBCSD in Poland. http://www.fob.org.pl

▌ **Konfederacja Pracodawców Polskich (Confederation of Polish Employers)**. An organisation of employers in Poland, with over 7,000 companies as members. http://www.kpp.org.pl

▌ **Krajowa Izba Gospodarcza (Polish Chamber of Commerce, PCC)**. A self-governing economic institution grouping more than 140 business organisations. http://www.kig.pl

▮ **PKPP Lewiatan (Polish Confederation of Private Employers Lewiatan)**. A nation-wide representation of employers and trade unions. It comprises about 3,000 companies. http://www.pkpplewiatan.pl

▮ **UN Global Compact**. Promotes the principles of CSR. It has 74 members. http://www.globalcompact.org

▮ Case studies

British American Tobacco

Stakeholder dialogue

BAT was the first company in Poland to conduct a stakeholder dialogue according to AA1000. Since 2003, there have been two phases of the dialogue, which contributed to the development of local partnerships and empowerment of local communities around the factory. The process also brought the company valuable feedback and resulted in reputational gains. The experience of BAT inspired other companies, which are now planning to start similar dialogue programmes. http://www.odpowiedzialnosc.pl

Citi Handlowy

Community investment

City Handlowy combines employee volunteering with community investment programmes led by their corporate foundation. Their strategic approach is supported by tools and management systems, resulting in wide recognition of their volunteering performance and a significant impact of their community investment programme. One of their respected programmes in financial education is 'Moje finanse'. http://www.citibank.pl

Lotos Group

Sustainability reporting

In 2007 Lotos Group, one of the largest of the 25 top Central and Eastern Europe companies, developed a five-year comprehensive Strategy of Corporate Social Responsibility. This included sustainability reporting according to the GRI Guidelines, and the implemented reporting system and report itself were distinguished in a Polish competition as the best sustainability report. http://www.lotos.pl

▮ Education

In Poland, corporate social responsibility is almost absent in the curricula. Research among students (LOB and Oikos 2006) shows that 70% are unfamiliar with the concept. However, in some universities there are subjects such as business ethics or social engagement, usually as elective modules. In 2009, two schools launched postgraduate studies in this field: **Akademia Leona Koźmińskiego** in Warsaw and **Wyzsza Szkola Europejska im. Jozefa Tischnera** in Cracow.

References

ARFP, FOB and PKPP Lewiatan (2005) 'Survey: Perception of Responsible Business and Social Participation among Polish Entrepreneurs', Exploration Survey; http://www.konkurencyjnafirma.pl/dokumenty/fob_raport_short.ppt, accessed 7 June 2010.

Boni, M., *et al.* (2009) 'Poland 2030: Development Challenges', The Chancellery of the Prime Minister, Board of Strategic Advisors to the Prime Minister of Poland; http://www.zdp.kprm.gov.pl, accessed 7 June 2010.

Brzozowski, A., I. Kuraszko, M. Panek-Owsianska, B. Rok and L. Wieciech (2007) 'Corporate Social Responsibility in Poland' (Baseline Study; United Nations Development Programme; http://www.acceleratingcsr.eu/uploads/docs/Corporate%20Social%20Responsibility%20in%20Poland%20Baseline%20Study.pdf, accessed 7 June 2010).

European Union Road Federation (2009) 'European Road Statistics 2009'; http://www.erf.be/media/stats/ERF-2009%20European%20Union%20Road%20Statistics%20BOOKLET_V07_update.pdf, accessed 7 June 2010.

Eurostat (2009) 'Panorama of Energy: Energy Statistics to Support EU Policies and Solutions'; http://epp.eurostat.ec.europa.eu/cache/ITY_OFFPUB/KS-GH-09-001/EN/KS-GH-09-001-EN.PDF, accessed 7 June 2010.

Filek, J. (2006) 'Spoleczna odpowiedzialnosc biznesu: Tylko moda czy nowy model prowadzenia dzialalnosci gospodarczej' (Warsaw: UOKIK [Office of Competition and Consumer Protection]; http://www.uokik.gov.pl).

GfK and PSDB (2008) 'The Potential of Small and Medium Enterprises in Developing New Innovative Products: Environmental Solutions, Sample of 1005 Companies' (Warsaw: GfK and PSDB).

Grupa BOSS (2006) *Rozmowy o dobrym biznesie* (Warsaw: Grupa BOSS).

Jackiewicz, J. (2007) 'EU SDS Member States' Input' (Ministry of the Environment).

Karbowski, A., A. Bielinska, M. Dyglowicz, M. Selwa, M. Chlebek and L. Makuch (2006) CSR oczami studentów' (LOB and oikos; http://www.lob.org.pl/cms_a/upload/file/Raport_CSR_oczami_studentow.pdf, accessed 7 June 2010).

Rok, B., S. Stolorz and D. Stann (2003) *Menedzerowie 500 i odpowiedzialny biznes* (Warsaw: ARFP, FOB and World Bank; http://www.csrinfo.org/images/stories/publikacjedo2008/2003_managerowie500.pdf, accessed 7 June 2010).

UNDP (United Nations Development Programme) (2008) 'Multi-stakeholders' Agreement on National Corporate Social Responsibility Development Agenda in Poland'.

World Bank (2005a) 'What do businesses think about corporate social responsibility? Part II: A Comparison of Attitudes and Practices in Hungary, Poland and Slovakia. Polish Sample: 154 Companies'; http://www.csrinfo.org/images/stories/publikacjedo2008/worldbanksummary.pdf, accessed 7 June 2010.

—— (2005b) 'Public Expectations for Corporate Social Responsibility in Poland' (Washington, DC: World Bank).

39 Portugal

Maria Lemos

Founder CEO, Sustainable Side of the Street

■ Context

Corporate Social Responsibility (CSR) is known in Portugal as Responsabilidade Social Empresarial (RSE).

Portugal, on Europe's west coast, has an area of 93,033 km². In 2008 the resident population was 10.6 million. As of 2010 the economic active population is 5.6 million, of which 2.6 million are women (46% of the total). The average monthly earning (2006) was EUR933, and the dominant religion is Catholicism (94%).

Three importance influences on Portuguese society have been the Roman Catholic Church, the country's tradition of mutuality and self-help, and its history of authoritarian political control. The recent development of key elements of a modern welfare state and a growing reliance of state agencies on private nonprofit groups should also be taken into account. Historically, these influences have created tension between the state and nonprofit institutions, limiting their interdependence and confining each to a relatively narrow field of activity until recently.

The Portuguese nation state has existed since 1143 and organised charities existed even before this, inspired mostly by the Roman Catholic Church. The influence of the Roman Catholic Church tended to be paternalistic in providing assistance. However, there was also a counter-trend towards mutualism, solidarity and self-help. In the 12th and 13th centuries, crafts corporations (*corporações de mestres*) appeared in Portugal and various brotherhoods (*confrarias*), including the seamen's brotherhoods (*confrarias dos mareantes*). Similarly, and unrelated, there were also common granaries (*celeiros comuns*).

By the late 15th century, a new type of Church-related institution appeared — the Holy Houses of Mercy, or *Misericórdias*. These reflected the growing influence of Franciscan and Dominican ideas that link 'works of mercy' to the achievement of salvation, targeting those increasingly enriched by the Portuguese maritime exploits of the era. *Misericórdias* were a response to the rise of poverty: many women and children were left behind as a consequence of these maritime exploits. These *Misericórdias* established a strong base of nonprofit social institutions throughout the country that persists to this day.

In the first quarter of the 19th century these traditions took different institutional formats, such as workers' associations, mutualist associations (*Associações de Socorro Mútuo*), humanitarian institutions of voluntary firemen (*Associações de bombeiros voluntaries*) and agricultural mutuals (*Mútuas agrícolas*). The lack of resources, legal frameworks and state support led to the failure of many of these initiatives.

By contrast, the mutualist organisations that emerged among the middle class (state officers, liberal professionals and merchants) were more successful. Examples include Montepios and Caixas económicas, the Lisbon Commercial Association (*Associação Comercial de Lisboa*) and the Porto Commercial Association (*Associação Comercial do Porto*), the latter two both created in 1834.

The coup d'état of 28 May 1926 that put Oliveira Salazar in power was concerned with creating an '*Estado Novo*' or New Order reflecting 'solid, prudent and conciliated nationalism'. The New Order created opportunities for the creation of cooperatives. However, freedom of association was seen as contrary to the national interest and therefore forbidden. Consequently, the New Order resulted in a decline of nonprofit organisation in general and the mutualism movement in particular.

The revolution of 25 April 1974 put an end to authoritarianism in Portugal. With the adoption of the Constitution of the Republic in 1976 and the re-establishment of freedom of speech and association, several movements and institutions appeared.

The new post-Salazar regime has not been wholly supportive of civil society. In addition, Portugal's accession to the European Union (EU) in 1986 had equally ambiguous implications for Portuguese civil society: the access to funding required association among those concerned and, on the other hand, the income inflows from EU structural funds reinforced state responsibility for matters that were covered by the mutualism movement and civil society associations.

▌ Priority issues

Education

With a low education level Portugal is the worst rated country among the EU-25. According 2004 data, only 21% of people aged between 25 and 64 had completed secondary school and 45% still abandoned school before completing the compulsory nine years of education.

Similarly, lifelong training has not been strong. According to the 2001 official report on professional training published by the Portuguese Ministry of Social Security and Labor (MSST), only 17% of companies (excluding micro companies) organised training courses.

Social issues

Low productivity, low adherence to implemented security policies at work and a high rate of car accidents are some examples of the poor performance of Portugal among the EU-15 in most of the ratios related to social development.

The balance between working and private life is also a problem. Surveys in 1994/5, 2000 and 2005/6 show a noticeable relative increase in expenditure on housing, health, culture and recreation, as compared to food, beverages and transport. The inefficiency of public transportation, especially in major cities such as Lisbon and Porto, adds to the problem. Transportation is mainly by road and there is a strong negative impact on the environment and on the quality of life of Portuguese people.

The risk of poverty shows differences based on gender (not very significant), age (quite high for the elderly), household composition (detrimental to self-employed) and labour intensity of non-dependent household members. In 2007 the unemployment rate in Portugal was higher than both the EU(15) and the EU(25) average by 1% and 0.9% respectively (*Statistical Yearbook of Portugal* 2007).

The Delta Cafés company is a good example of finding socially responsible solutions to the problem of unemployment, resulting from delocalisation of factories in labour-intensive industries. Rui Nabeiro, the founder and owner, is known to have refused several proposals to sell the company because he would not like to see it removed from Campo Maior, a small town where 70% of the inhabitants depend on Delta Cafés for a living.

Environmental issues

Environmental problems have never been considered a serious problem in Portugal because pollution levels were low compared to other European countries. This is partially explained by the fact that, in 2006, 79% of enterprises were concentrated on the tertiary (services) sector, generating 63% of national employment and turnover. However, due to EU pressure and financial support, there are now more restrictive laws governing issues such as air and water pollution, construction and natural heritage.

Despite general improvement, government expenditure on environmental protection decreased by 2.0% in 2006 to EUR903 million, which accounts for only 0.6% of GDP. Waste management continues to absorb the main share of expenditure (46%), while protection of biodiversity and landscape, and waste water management are second and third in terms of relative importance (Statistical Yearbook of Portugal 2007).

Climate change is also a concern, with CO_2 emissions of 66,670 tons in 2006. Although greenhouse gas emissions diminished in 2007, they remain above the 11% national target of the Kyoto Protocol (as compared with 1990 levels). One of the contributors is transportation. In 2007, there was an 8.1% increase in the volume of freight transported by road in mainland Portugal, and a 6.6% increase in the volume of freight transported by railway.

Portugal made water scarcity and drought a priority theme for its EU presidency in 2007, a problem that had — until the advent of climate change — been of major concern only in southern countries. Rising consumption and the current drought have had a marked impact on flow in Portuguese rivers, according to the Portuguese Water Institute. Water prices for domestic consumers have risen 9% on average since 2002.

As a result, demand management measures such as price incentives, public awareness campaigns and more efficient water management are being given priority. The Portuguese government approved an eco-tax on agricultural, industrial and commercial water use. This came into force in July 2008 and it is specifically designed to apply the principles of 'user and polluter pays'. On the supply side, newer desalination and wastewater reuse technologies should be preferred to more traditional dam building and water transfer solutions.

∎ Trends

In March 2010 Sair da Casca (**http://www.sairdacasca.com**) published a study on the role of companies in society — 'O Papel das Empresas na Sociedade' — whereby it showed that more than EUR65 million were invested in the community, support was given to institutions in various fields such as culture, health, education, and that there had been a significant increase in the number of voluntary programmes by companies.

In August 2007 the Portuguese government approved its National Strategy for Sustainable Development (ENDS 2015) and the Implementation Plan for the National Strategy for Sustainable Development (PIENDS). Both documents are aligned with the strategy of the European Council of 9 June 2006.

The social economy is now receiving greater recognition at the EU member state level because it represents an important source of entrepreneurship and jobs. In Portugal, the civil society sector had 2002 expenditures equal to 4.2% of GDP, engaging nearly 250,000 full-time equivalent workers. In fact, nonprofit organisations employ more people in Portugal than sizeable industries such as transportation.

In 2002 the Portuguese Enterprise Association (AEP), the Aveiro University and the Porto Catholic University published exploratory research on ethical management and CSR in Portugal. One trend is the significant increase in CSR reporting among the 100 largest companies, although few have their report externally assured.

There are now CSR toolkits available for Portugal, such as the Business Council for Sustainable Development Portugal's *Procurement Sustentável — Guia Prático de Implementação* published in 2008.

Journalists tend to be less familiar with the CSR concept than companies, according to 2003 research conducted by Sair da Casca in association with Multiviária. The media complain they do not have enough CSR information, and also that they are wary of companies misrepresenting the data, and showing only the positive side of their operations.

In 2003, Portuguese companies collectively held 243 ISO 14001 certifications, 14 EMAS registrations, 54 OSHAS 18001 certifications and one SA8000 certification, with more than 25 published CSR reports (Pinto 2004). In 2004, there were also 43 different eco-labelled products from 18 different companies, eight of which were national Portuguese companies.

∎ Legislation and codes

Portugal is a member of the UN and signed the Universal Declaration of Human Rights of 1948. Portugal is also a member of the ILO, having ratified 77 ILO conventions since 1919. Portugal has also signed and ratified more than half of the Council of Europe Conventions (99 out of 195).

Portugal signed the Kyoto Protocol on greenhouse gases, which came into effect in 1997. The Treaty of Lisbon entered into force on 1 December 2009 after ratification by all 27 Member States.

At the national level, important legislation includes the Commercial Societies Code and the Real Estate Code. Equally important is the Labour Code that came into force on 1 December 2003. Article 2 refers to the total or partial transposition into Portuguese legislation of a list of European directives. Training, health and safety at work, labour accidents and others related areas are not yet regulated, however.

Several companies follow international standards such as the UN Global Compact, ISO standards, SA-8000 and the Global Reporting Initiative (GRI) guidelines.

▌ Organisations

▌ **ACEGE**. This Christian association was created in August 1960. **http://www.acege.org**

▌ **APEE**. A nonprofit organisation with over 30 members. **http://www.apee.pt**

▌ **BCSD Portugal**. A nonprofit organisation of 114 members established in October 2001. **http://www.bcsdportugal.org**

▌ **Equalskills**. Created in 2004 by ECDL Portugal, the aim of Equalskills is to show the use and role of technology in the everyday lives of all people, regardless of status, education, age, ability or understanding. **http://www.equalskills.com**

▌ **GRACE**. A nonprofit organisation with over 30 associates created in February 2000. **http://www.grace.pt**

▌ **IPCG**. A nonprofit organisation created in May 2004 by 130 businesspeople, managing directors, jurists and academics. **http://www.cgov.pt**

▌ **MÃO-NA-MÃO**. This is a business movement created in September 2001. **http://www. ptinovacao.pt/noticias/2005/abr5%20maonamao.htm**

▌ **MECENATONET**. This is a project for managing, advertising and fundraising. **http:// mecenato.net**

▌ **OIKOS**. This nonprofit organisation created in February 1988 is known internationally as ONGD. **http://www.oikos.pt**

▌ Education

The universities listed below offer CSR–related degrees and/or courses although none features in global rankings such as *Beyond Grey Pinstripes*:[1]

- **Universidade do Algarve**. **http://www.ualg.pt**
- **Universidade Autónoma de Lisboa**. Escola de Gestão e Negócios. **http://www. egnegocios.ual.pt**
- **Universidade Católica das Beiras**. **http://icm.crb.ucp.pt**
- **Universidade Católica de Lisboa**. **http://www.fcee.lisboa.ucp.pt**
- **Universidade Católica do Porto**. **http://porto.ucp.pt/crp**

---

1 **http://beyondgreypinstripes.org/rankings/participating_schools.cfm**

- **Universidade de Coimbra**. Faculdade de Economia. **http://www.uc.pt/feuc**

- **Universidade de Évora**. **http://www.uevora.pt**

- **Universidade Lusíada de Lisboa**. **http://www.lis.ulusiada.pt**

- **Instituto Superior de Ciências do Trabalho e da Empresa (ISCTE)**. **http://iscte.pt**

- **Instituto Superior de Gestão (ISG)**. **http://www.isg.pt**

- **Universidade Técnica de Lisboa, Instituto Superior de Gestão e Economia (ISEG)**. IDEFE. **https://aquila.iseg.utl.pt/aquila/instituicao/ISEG**

References

Franco, R.C., S.W. Sokolowsky, E.M.H. Hairel and L.M. Salamon (2005) *The Portuguese Nonprofit Sector in Comparative Perspective* (Porto, Portugal: Uniarte Gráfica).

KPMG (2006) 'Estudo da KPMG sobre a Publicação de Relatórios de Sustentabilidade em Portugal'; **http://www.bcsdportugal.org/files/983.pdf**, accessed 8 June 2010.

—— (2008) 'KPMG International Survey of Corporate Responsibility Reporting 2008'; **http://www.kpmg.nl/docs/Corporate_Site/Publicaties/Corp_responsibility_Survey_2008.pdf**, accessed 8 June 2010.

Pinto, G.R. (2004) *Corporate Social Responsibility: State of the Art in Portugal 2004* (Lisbon: CECOA).

'Presidência do Conselho de Ministros Resolução do Conselho de Ministros nº109/2007: ENDS2015 PIENDS' (Plano de Implementação da Estratégia Nacional de Desenvolvimento Sustentável) (Lisbon: Diário da República).

Rego, A., M.P. Cunha, N.G. Costa, H. Gonçalves and C. Cabral-Cardoso (2006) *Gestão Ética e Socialmente Responsável* (Lisbon: Editora RH).

Statistical Yearbook of Portugal (2007) *Statistical Yearbook of Portugal* (Lisbon: Instituto Nacional de Estatística, IP).

40 Romania

Rodica Milena Zaharia
Professor, Academy of Economic Studies, Bucharest, Romania

Alin Stancu
Assistant Professor, Academy of Economic
Studies, Bucharest, Romania

Liviu Chelcea
Senior Lecturer at the University of Bucharest, Romania

▮ Context

Romania is the only country in the Balkans whose language is of Latin origin. It gained its unity and independence during the late 19th and early 20th centuries. After the Second World War, Romania went through a difficult period, struggling to avoid Communism and to preserve democracy. However, in less than five years, the Communist regime installed itself for a half a century, making Romania part of the Communist world.

Between 1948 and 1989, Romania experienced forced industrialisation and followed an import substitution strategy. The motivation was both ideological and economic. Socialist countries developed their economies according to Communist world needs, not according to their national potential and characteristics, in order to protect themselves from capitalist ideology and to reduce economic dependency on the capitalist world. Farmers were moved from villages to new communist cities and from land work to new industrial specialisation.

Industry was considered to be the heart and engine of the entire economic system and industrial spatial distribution followed natural endowments and equal repartition around the country. Heavy industry was particularly valued, while agriculture was neglected. This quantitative phase was not followed by a qualitative stage. Much of Romanian industry remained at the level of 1970s technology.

The 1980s brought a period of severe scarcity at all levels. Imports shrank dramatically, while there was pressure to achieve export targets without any respect for efficiency. In 1989, after a bloody revolution, the communist regime was replaced and a new era started. Romania faced a tough period of transformation into a democratic society ruled by the principles of a market economy.

An important role in the development of socially responsible behaviour has been played by philanthropy. Early on, the Orthodox Church developed orphanages for abandoned or lost children; houses for young, unmarried girls; and asylums for widows. Since the 14th century, various monasteries hosted proto-hospitals, such as asylums for the sick poor, orphans and the elderly sick. Towards the end of the 1700s, the local administration in Bucharest created the institution of the 'head doctor of the town', whose main mission was to oversee the free care of the sick and poor (Mănoiu and Epureanu 1996: 6-17; Buzducea 2009).

Another aspect of philanthropy was that the state, non-governmental associations, and industrialists and businesses offered care. In 1881, the capital city of Bucharest developed a public care system based on donations of various buildings by the rich families. It focused mainly on fighting the growth in the numbers of beggars, but it also contained night asylums, popular eateries, subsistence help for the poor, education, and support for young girls to marry (Mănoiu and Epureanu 1996: 6-17).

The large-scale factories and industrialists of the 20th century were involved in philanthropic activities and had various forms of commitment to their employees, such as food and board. The Anghelescu chocolate factory in Bucharest offered 200 beds for their employees. Malaxa Steel Works, a giant steel and railway equipment company, constructed family houses for its engineers in the 1930s.

Some of these trends were discontinued during the communist regime, while others were transformed and continued. Philanthropic issues remained at an individual level owing to the fact that social problems were identified and resolved only by the state. Also, many factories, all of which became state-owned after 1948, had extensive social functions. They received state allocations for housing, eateries, medical centres and sport facilities.

▮ Priority issues

Economic issues

After the fall of the communist regime in 1989, Romania took the first steps towards a market economy. Important changes took place in Romanian society that generated increasing unemployment, privatisation of Romanian companies, bankruptcies, increased inflation and reduced purchasing power for the population. However, the political desire for European Union (EU) integration put pressure on Romanian companies to align with EU legislation (*acquis communautaire*). This encouraged the harmonisation of Romanian legislation with Europe in various fields and fostered increasing debates about the social responsibility of companies.

Environmental issues

Romania is one of the poorest performers in Europe with respect to protecting the environment. Water pollution is the major problem. Only 65% of the population has access to water facilities and only 21% of the used water is properly treated. The lack of investment in waste-water treatment plants and in water supply systems is one of the major impediments for security of water supply. Another problem is industrial and urban waste. Only 30% of industrial landfills are licensed and many are poorly located and not monitored for impacts.

Air quality is also a concern. Although Romania is considered a country that meets Kyoto Protocol requirements (achieving an 8% greenhouse gases reduction against 1990 levels), this performance is not due to the improvements in technology, but to shrinking economic activity. The main sources of pollution are thermal power plants, vehicles, electric power plants, and the glassware, lime and cement industries. Another cause of low air quality is dust caused by the lack of green areas around the cities. Deforestation has also contributed to soil degradation, desertification and climate change in some areas.

Social and ethical issues

The most important ethical issue is that employees are not considered as a key stakeholder (Diaconu 2009). Often, they are not informed about work-related risks, they are poorly educated about their rights and they are not involved in the decision-making process.

Consumer protection is another important aspect of companies' ethical behaviour. In Romania, consumer rights are not fully respected, although there are laws in this area. Romanian consumers are not properly informed and conscious about companies' responsibilities. They are not encouraged to set up and run self-help consumer associations.

The lack of adequate social welfare is a major issue in Romania, largely due to the scarcity of governmental resources for sustaining a proper social protection policy.

■ Trends

The 2008 KPMG report on corporate responsibility reporting indicates a much greater percentage of multinational companies with CSR reports than national Romanian companies. Among the largest 100 Romanian companies, 24% report their CSR activities. The sectors that issued the most reports were electronics and utilities. Market position and economic considerations are the main drivers of CSR, which shows a lower level of maturity in the local companies.

The Top 10 Corporate Philanthropists selected by the Donors Forum in Romania reveals an increase in the budgets allocated to social responsibility, from EUR3 million in 2006 to EUR7.7 million in 2008. The top ten companies in 2008 were Vodafone Romania, Petrom SA, Banca Transilvania, UnicreditTiriac Bank, GlaxoSmithKline, Alexandrion Group Romania, Agricola SA, Mol Romania, IBM Romania and SC Pasmatex.

Stakeholders are becoming increasingly sensitive to companies' involvement in CSR activities. Companies also recognise that CSR translates into good awareness, brand consolidation, sound risk management and better relations with stakeholders (Sgârcitu 2008). EU integration will also drive improved CSR standards in Romania. In addition, media involvement in CSR campaigns is expected to generate increasing recognition of responsible behaviour.

In the context of a prolonged financial and economic crisis, it is expected that CSR activities will focus more on social and employee problems. NGOs and multinationals are expected to remain the drivers of CSR, as the contraction of economic activity will affect SMEs more acutely.

▌ Legislation and codes

Several laws on environmental protection and ecology have been enacted in Romania. In 1990, the National Program for Environmental Protection was established and in 1995 the framework Law for Environmental Protection was introduced. Laws have also been passed on bribery and corruption (Law no. 31/1990 and Law no. 503/2002, known as the Anticorruption Law), competition (Competition Law no. 21/1996) and working conditions (Law no. 319/2006). Both European legislation and international requirements (such as those of the OECD) were taken into account in drafting these laws.

There are two specific laws pertaining to social responsibility: the Sponsorship Law, which allows a company to direct 0.3% of its turnover and up 20% of its tax on profits towards a social cause, and the '2% Law' (in terms of the Fiscal Code), which allows every citizen to redirect 2% of personal income tax to a nonprofit organisation. As a result of the 2% Law, the amount donated by citizens was USD4.5 million in 2005 and USD17.7 million in 2006. The number of donors increased from 145,000 to 586,000 over the same period.

In 2007, the Ministry of Labor, Family and Equal Opportunities established a Direction for Corporate Social Responsibility. Its mission is to identify and develop policies related to social responsibility, to disseminate and implement such activities, and to assess the social effects of the operating programmes.

Besides these developments, the most important CSR-related laws are:

- **Law against Unfair Competition** no. 11/1991

- **Competition Law** no. 21/1996

- **The Romanian Company Law** no. 31/1990

- **Sponsorship Law** no. 32/1994, amended and supplemented

- **Anticorruption Law** no. 503/2002

- **Fiscal Code Law** no. 571/2003, amended and supplemented

- **Labour Code** no. 53/2003, amended and supplemented

- **Labour Safety and Security Law** no. 319/2006

- **Environment Protection Law** no. 137/1995

- **Human Rights Law** no. 30/1994

▌ Organisations

▌ **The Association for Community Relationships (ARC).** A nonprofit organisation that aims to contribute to the mobilisation of local financial resources for the benefit of local communities. The association is a member of Business in the Community, AmCham, LBG and CSR360 Global Partner Network. Its main activities are to develop the capacity of NGOs to attract resources from the community, the promotion of the 2% Law and the realisation of a favourable environment for philanthropic actions. **http://www.arcromania. ro**

■ The **Association to Save the Danube and the Delta (SDD)**. A national environmental organisation founded in 2004 in order to protect the Danube Delta Biosphere Reserve. The Danube Delta is the second largest delta in Europe and the best preserved delta in the world. The main activities of the organisation are the reduction of the effects of human impacts on the Danube Delta biosphere. **http://www.salvatidelta.ro**

■ The **Chamber of Commerce and Industry of Romania (CCIR)**. Founded in 1990, this is the biggest association of Romanian businesses, comprising 42 local chambers of commerce and industry, bilateral chambers of commerce and professional associations. CCIR has been a partner in the project 'Mainstreaming CSR among SMEs: CSR and Competitiveness. European SMEs' Good Practice' coordinated by KMU Forschung Austria, an institute researching SMEs. **http://www.ccir.ro**

■ The **Romanian Donors Forum (RDF)**. This was set up in 1999 as a network of grant making organisations that aim to create a sustainable civil society. Among the RDF members are the Allavida Foundation, The Resource Center for Roma Communities, The Resource Center for Ethnocultural Diversity, Carpathian Foundation, Open Society Foundation, The Foundation for Partnership, The Princess Margarita of Romania Foundation, Sensiblu Foundation and the Trust for Civil Society in Central and Eastern Europe. **http://www.forumuldonatorilor.ro**

■ Case studies

OVM Petrom

The largest company in Romania, OMV Petrom, is considered to be one of the most responsible enterprises. Through the platform Respect for the Future, Petrom has developed and supported several pro-environmental and social programmes, such as Parks of the Future, Parenting Education and Resources for the Future. Petrom is among the few companies that have a special area for CSR on their website. **http://www.petrom.com**

Realitatea TV and partners

This partnership between Media trust Realitatea TV (a private television company), *Academia Catavencu* (a private magazine), Romsilva and the NGO *Mai mult Verde* (More Green) has significant CSR activities. The campaign aims to plant over 40 million trees in five years. The campaign was launched in October 2008, on a budget of EUR500,000. The timing was strategic, right before elections, in order to involve more political figures and thus to increase the number of sponsors and participants. **http://www.maimultverde. ro**

Vodafone and SMURD

The partnership between Vodafone and SMURD (Mobile Service for Emergency, Reanimation and Descarceration), under the campaign 'A Partnership for Life', is another example of CSR oriented to social problems. In 2005 and 2006, Vodafone funded SMURD with EUR380,000 for buying modern ambulances equipped with vital apparatus and communications systems. Vodafone is a presence in many campaigns that are addressing social issues. http://www.vodafone.ro

∎ Education

Romania is in an early phase regarding academic programmes dedicated to social responsibility. Some institutions include particular courses on CSR, including:

- **The Academy of Economic Studies**, **Bucharest**. The Social Responsibility of Companies. http://www.ase.ro

- **West University from Timişoara**. Ethics and social responsibility in business. http://www.uvt.ro

Other institutions include CSR-related subjects in the syllabus, such as business ethics, environmental law, environmental economy, environmental economy and protection, sustainable development management, change management and social-political marketing.

References

Brady, A. (2007) 'Însemnări din România: responsabilitatea socială corporatistă în Europa Central-Estică', *Revista* 22 (12 January 2007); http://www.revista22.ro/insemnari-din-romania-responsabilitate-sociala-corporatista-in-europa--3370.html, accessed 25 May 2009.

Buzducea, D. (2009) *Sisteme moderne de asistenţă socială. Tendinţă globală şi practici locale* (Iaşi, Romania: Polirom).

Dehelean, D. (2008) 'Raport de cercetare: Bilantul Responsabilitatii Sociale pe 2008'; http://www.responsabilitatesociala.ro/editoriale/raport-de-cercetare-bilantul-responsabilitatii-sociale-pe-2008.html, accessed 23 May 2009.

Diaconu, B. (2009) 'Angajatul'; http://www.creditareresponsabila.ro/2009/02/18/angajat, accessed 23 May 2009.

Mănoiu, F., and V. Epureanu (1996) *Asistenţa socială în România* (Bucharest: Editura All).

Oprea, L. (2005) *Responsabilitea socială corporatistă: de la teorie la practică* (Bucharest: Tritonic).

Sgârcitu, L. (2008) 'Responsabilitatea Socială: Un pilon important al strategiei de afaceri' (Bucharest: Selenis; http://www.csr-romania.ro, accessed 12 April 2009).

Stoian, C., and R.M. Zaharia (2009) 'Corporate Social Responsibility in Romania: Trends, Drivers, Challenges and Opportunities', *International Journal of Economics and Business Research* 1.4: 422-37.

Acknowledgements

This work was supported by CNCSIS/UEFISCUS project PNII-IDEI code 1888/2008.

41 Russia

Alexey Kostin

Executive Director, CSR Russian Centre, Moscow

▪ Context

CSR has in recent decades been the subject of quite a substantial, albeit controversial, evolution in Russia. There have been many voluntary CSR initiatives from the most conscientious and strategic private big businesses. However, CSR in Russia does not yet involve small and medium-size enterprises, which have so far preferred to confine themselves to some charity work at a local scale, viewing it as the main form of their social engagement.

A group of leading Russian companies with some basic experience in this field has come to realise that CSR is not merely a function of public relations, but an essential part of sustainable development and corporate governance. Hence, CSR in these companies has become part of their strategic thinking, in order to improve their business image, competitiveness and market capitalisation. For these leading Russian companies, CSR and sustainable development are two sides of the same coin.

Beyond these leading companies, however, CSR has been very slow in penetrating large and medium-sized state companies and companies that are predominantly state controlled, as well as unitary federal and municipal enterprises. This is largely due to a general lack of transparency in Russian business. According to annual research carried out by Standard & Poor's since 2005, the level of transparency in Russian government-owned business is much lower than in private business, although the latter is also not on a par with world standards.

▪ Priority issues

Economic and social issues

The negative consequences of the world financial and economic crisis are quite substantial for social and environmental development in Russia. According to the World Bank, in 2009 Russia's real GDP was predicted to contract by about 8%, unemployment to rise to 13% and poverty to increase by 17% (World Bank 2009). Russia's middle class measured by household consumption was also expected to shrink by about 10%.

The outlook going forward is brighter. The World Bank revised its estimates of Russia's GDP growth in 2010 from 0% to 2.5%, and the OECD from –0.7% to 3.5%. Both revisions are based on expectations that prices for raw materials will not go down, and the government's economic incentives will be effective. OECD economists also think that inflation in Russia will fall to 8% in 2009 and to 6.5% in 2010, although the World Bank estimated inflation at 11–13% in 2009.

Environmental issues

The Russian economy remains among the most energy intensive in the world. Forecasts of emissions and discharges of major pollutants show that urban air pollution will remain a serious problem, while water pollution and drinking water quality will become more serious in the long run. The rate of land degradation and ecosystem fragmentation threatens the security and wealth of future generations. In addition, climate change will pose new threats to the population and economy, in particular in the Russian Arctic and the southern regions.

Though coverage of the land area by forests remains high (50%) and access to safe drinking water is relatively good (96%), indicators such as GDP per unit of energy use (USD1.6, as compared to USD3.3 in Canada and USD4.4 in Sweden), as well as CO_2 emissions, show that even the significantly downsized post-Soviet economy is not yet environmentally sustainable. Steps are being taken by the Russian government, but not enough to offset Russia's ecologically costly economic growth, combined with limitations in its environmental legislation and deficiency of investment in environmental protection.

▌ Trends

Russia's leading companies, by embracing CSR and sustainable development, are gaining a more socially responsible image domestically and bringing themselves closer to the level of international leaders.

There is still vigorous debate about the essence, scope and goals of CSR. Most Russian business leaders tend to view CSR as incorporating two interconnected components: social and environmental responsibility required by law, and additional voluntary public responsibility which is beyond the requirements of the law.

For about 30 leading Russian companies, CSR is becoming a component of corporate governance rather than merely a part of public relations. This is what is new about CSR in Russia: companies are increasingly complying with international best practice and 'soft' global standards, such as the Global Reporting Initiative (GRI) Guidelines and AA1000 SES.

Socially responsible business conduct, which is reflected in a system of economic, environmental and social performance indicators, and which is realised through a regular dialogue with the community, is gradually becoming a part of the strategic planning and corporate governance practices of these companies. Therefore, decisions regarding CSR are increasingly made by company owners, boards of directors and senior management.

Some advanced companies have established special working groups and committees to address CSR and non-financial risks. Some are including non-executive directors responsible for CSR matters on the board, as well as introducing systems for non-financial risk management. Unfortunately, the financial crisis has substantially slowed down this positive trend in the country's CSR development.

Russian companies have begun to issue CSR reports, but still lag behind much of the rest of the world. According to the register of the Russian Union of Industrialists and Entrepreneurs (RUIE), by October 2009 74 companies had published 193 non-financial reports since 2001. Of these, 112 were social reports, 48 sustainability reports, and 33 environmental reports. Approximately one third used methods and indicators from voluntary international standards, such as GRI and AA1000S.

Among the leading CSR reporters are Norilsk Nickel, Lukoil, RAO UES of Russia, Tatneft, Gazprom, Rosneft, Euras Holding, Group EuroKhim, Group Ilim and Sakhalin Energy Investment Company Ltd. Russian Railways, RUSAL and some others have based their non-financial report on the ten Global Compact principles.

The role of regional and local government in fostering CSR in Russia is crucial. Russian regional and municipal authorities are starting to realise the need to establish stable relationships with business. Until recently, the authorities used to turn to business in an ad hoc way to assist with social, environmental, or infrastructural challenges. However, governors, regional legislatures and city mayors increasingly prefer to draw up joint medium-term public–private partnership plans and programmes. to tackle social and (less often) environmental issues.

At the federal government level, there is no empowered body or department dealing with the social responsibility of Russian business. Since December 1997, the government-approved state strategy of sustainable development has never been properly implemented or reviewed. The impression is that the state bureaucracy, absorbed in the recent ineffective administrative reforms and controversial anti-crisis activities, not to mention grappling with social problems, has no motivation for identifying and formulating strategic goals related to CSR and sustainability.

∎ Legislation and codes

Although various social, labour and environmental laws exist in Russia, there is no legislation or officially approved public framework specifically for CSR. Hence, CSR remains in the sphere of companies' voluntary initiatives and activities.

In 2004, RUIE introduced a Social Charter of Russian Business that has been signed by 220 companies and organisations. This code is quite similar to the UN Global Compact's principles and stimulates the participants to follow various CSR principles and practices. The UN Global Compact's Network in Russia, officially formed in April 2008, unites 35 companies and non-governmental organisations (NGOs).

In 2009, UNDP Russia and the UN Global Compact Russia Network launched a multi-year project for 'engaging Russian business in Global Compact driven sustainable development'. This aims at the joint development and implementation of sustainable socioeconomic development projects by UNDP and Russian and foreign multinational companies that are participants in UN Global Compact Russia. The main current priority of this project is to minimise the economic, social and environmental fallouts of the financial and economic crisis.

∎ Organisations

∎ **Agency of Social Information**. A leading association in the social sphere. **http://www. asi.org.ru**

∎ **Business & Society Consortium**. Uniting and promoting CSR and corporate philanthropy best practices and publishing a magazine of the same name. **http://www.b-soc.ru**

∎ **CSR–Russian Centre**. A think-tank in CSR methodology, policy formulation and CSR practical in-company applications. **alexey.kostin@mail.ru**

∎ **National Council on Corporate Governance**. A key association, publishing annual reports on corporate governance development, including CSR aspects. **http://www.nccg. ru**

∎ **Russian Managers Association**. Makes regular nationwide reports on social investments in Russia. **http://www.amr.ru**

∎ **Russian Union of Industrialists and Entrepreneurs (RUIE)**. Responsible for introducing the Social Charter of Russian Business, accumulating best CSR practices and registering non-financial reporting. **http://www.rspp.ru**

∎ **UNDP Russia**. Coordinating the UN Global Compact–Russia network. **http://www.undp. ru**

∎ Case studies

Several studies of CSR best practice were made during last five years by the RUIE, UNDP and Russian Managers Association. The main aspects which Russian best practices in CSR cover are personnel development, charity projects, community stakeholders' engagement, corporate governance and non-financial reporting.

Among the leading Russian companies in CSR are:

- **Group EuroKhim**. http://www.eurochem.ru
- **Gazprom**. http://www.gazprom.com
- **Group Ilim**. http://www.ilimgroup.com
- **Lukoil**. http://www.lukoil.com
- **Sakhalin Energy Investment Company Ltd**. http://www.sakhalinenergy.ru
- **Tatneft**. http://www.tatneft.ru

More details of CSR and sustainable development of the leading Russian companies can be found in the register of non-financial reports of RUIE. **http://rspp.ru**

∎ Education

CSR education does not yet exist in Russia, though some special training is organised in-company with participation of Western experts from organisations such as GRI and AccountAbility. Some of the companies have also founded their own corporate universities for the permanent development of personnel. A few state-owned universities are introducing the first CSR courses for students, including:

- **The Higher School of Economics**. http://www.hse.ru

- **Moscow Lomonosov State University**, Faculty of Economics. http://www.econ.msu.ru/cd/121

- **Saint-Petersburg State University**. http://www.econ.pu.ru

References

Russian Business and the UN Global Compact (2007) *Social Responsibility in Practice* (Moscow: United Nations Development Programme).

Russian Managers Association (2008) 'The Report on Social Investments in Russia 2008: Integrating CSR Principles into Corporate Strategy' (Moscow: Russian Managers Association; http://amr.ru/en/research).

UNDP (United Nations Development Programme) and RUSAL (2008) 'From Russia with Love: A National Chapter on the Global CSR Agenda' (Moscow: UNDP and the Economist Intelligence Unit).

World Bank (2009) 'Russian Economic Report No. 19: From Crisis to Recovery' (Washington, DC: World Bank; http://web.worldbank.org/WBSITE/EXTERNAL/COUNTRIES/ECAEXT/RUSSIANFEDERATIONEXTN/0,,contentMDK:22222555~pagePK:141137~piPK:141127~theSitePK:305600,00.html, accessed 8 June 2010).

42 Saudi Arabia

Tareq Emtairah
Research Fellow, International Institute for Industrial
Environmental Economics, Lund University

▌ Context

> Giving to society is not new to Saudi businesses. We have a great history of generosity and goodwill from both business people and companies. We need, however, to move a step further with our corporate social work to make it more effective. Facing the development challenges requires us to institutionalise an integrated approach to development linked with human development, social progress and the preservation of our environmental and cultural assets
>
> *Asya Al Alshaikh, MD, Tamkeen International,*
> *Jeddah Economic Forum, February 2007*

Between the old notion of corporate charity and the emergent expectations of greater business accountability to stakeholders, CSR is still a confusing term to many Saudi companies. While many companies in the country like to perceive themselves as engaged in CSR, a growing number of voices are sceptical about the traditional models of corporate engagement with the public good. A 2006 survey of the top 100 Saudi companies revealed mixed views among business leaders regarding the concept of CSR, particularly in terms of the expected role of business in the society (Emtairah *et al.* 2009). In this context, culture and faith — more than stakeholder considerations — still dominate the shaping of the CSR construct in Saudi Arabia, where the duty to give back to society through the Islamic pillar of *Zakah* is strongly prevalent (Nelson and Murphy 2009).

At the same time and since the transformation of Saudi Arabia into a modern state following the discovery of oil in the 1930s, another story line about the role of business in society has taken root in some parts of the country. The narrative of Aramco (the state oil company) provides another familiar anchor for an alternative construct of CSR. From the 1950s to the early 1970s, Aramco played a pivotal role in building the public infrastructure in the eastern province of the country. The company did this through extensive engagement in local community building activities, ranging from basic services in education and healthcare to human resource development and local suppliers' development programmes.

Between these two story lines, the potential for Saudi corporate engagement in sustainable development has yet to mature. The relatively high GDP per capita, as well as the opportunities provided by the oil economy, has given Saudi-based companies distinctive opportunities to become regional powerhouses. In terms of size, the Saudi capital market is considered the largest in the Arab world and ranks among the top ten emerging markets. In contrast, the CSR practices of Saudi companies hardly measure up against peers of similar size in the global arena.

Part of the explanation lies in the relative absence of stakeholder pressures on Saudi corporations relative to peers in developed economies. Most of the typical drivers of CSR found in developed economies are not functioning well in the Saudi context. There is a near absence of civic organisations such as consumer protection agencies, professional and labour unions or advocacy organisations that could articulate social or environmental expectations *vis-à-vis* products, services or general corporate conduct.

The role of the media is not fully enabled in driving CSR either. Most journalists feel constrained by customary law in their ability to expose corporations engaged in irresponsible conduct (Emtairah *et al.* 2009). Furthermore, the tax system can not be leveraged to generate private subsidies from social investments, since most corporations do not pay taxes beyond the 2% stipulated for *Zakat*.[1]

Finally, because of industry specialisation in the country, Saudi companies face hardly any of the supply chain pressures so typical in countries such as China or India. Most Saudi exports are related to hydrocarbons, mainly sold to governments and large business consumers. These buyers are reluctant to place constraining demands on strategic commodities. Therefore the adversarial tensions between business and society, which to a large extent were influential in shaping the construct of CSR in liberal democracies, play a lesser role in the Saudi context.

▌ Priority issues

Human capital development

According to the 8th five-year plan, a number of key priorities were identified for achieving the goals of Saudi Arabia Vision 2025 (MEP 2009). Among these are the need to address unemployment among young people, sustainability of natural resources and balanced regional development. Saudi Arabia is facing a formidable challenge with the influx of young people onto the job market, as the current education system is unable to prepare them adequately for employment. A CSR survey conducted by Tamkeen in 2007 found that close to 90% of business respondents were concerned about the adequacy of the national education system to provide the skills demanded by Saudi corporations (Emtairah *et al.* 2009).

Resource pressures

Saudi Arabia is in a similar position to other Gulf countries of the region with regard to dwindling water resources, rapid urbanisation and increasing pollution. According to

---

1 Under *Sharia* (Islamic) law, individuals and companies are obliged to pay *Zakat* to a government-appointed council as a form of donation for the needy. Companies cannot claim their own CSR donations to be *Zakat*-deductible.

the latest UNDP Arab human development report (UNDP-RBAS 2009), Saudi Arabia is among the countries facing significant water stress and is experiencing one of the fastest growth rates in CO_2 emissions. At the same time both the issues of water scarcity and CO_2 emissions have been given little attention from either corporate or public policy actors.

Responsible business climate

As the country is striving to improve the overall business climate and enhance Saudi's competitive position globally, a number of priorities have been highlighted in the recent report from the general investment authority (SAGIA) with regard to the role of business (MacGillivary and Emtairah 2009). Among these is the need to improve corporate communications with stakeholders, improve transparency of business transactions with public bodies, enforce regulations, combat corruption and encourage responsible advertising.

Health

The country is also experiencing many of the health concerns related to rapid urbanisation, rapid expansion in car transport and changing lifestyles. For instance, Saudi Arabia is experiencing the highest growth rates globally in child obesity, diabetes and cancer. The food and healthcare industries are increasingly under the spotlight on issues of responsible product information and advertising.

∎ Trends

Questions of how Saudi companies are viewing CSR and how they are responding to societal challenges have been the subject of two recent assessments in the country: the Tamkeen study of 2007 and the SARCI index assessment report of 2008. With regard to how CSR is perceived in the country today, a growing number of executives are calling for a broader construction of corporate responsibilities combining adherence to international standards and norms with Islamic values and traditions. For instance, the Islamic tradition of *Zakat* may provide cultural or religious support to private sector CSR initiatives. One of the five pillars of Islam, *Zakat* is an obligation to give a percentage of one's income to charity. Many executives believe that this deep-seated tradition of giving can offer a strong starting point to further integrate CSR practices into business.

On the other hand, competitive market pressures seem to increasingly drive corporate interest in social initiatives relating to human resource development. Both surveys indicate that the business community is well tuned to the competitive implications of skills gaps and the integration of women into the job market. Thus it is no surprise to see the majority of CSR investments among Saudi companies going into human development initiatives.

The direction of CSR towards environmental protection has lagged behind other efforts. In spite of growing evidence of the relevance of environmental concerns to Saudi Arabian long-term competitiveness, environmental issues are seldom included in the CSR or risk management plans of most companies. For instance, discussions of climate change and industry responsibilities are hardly debated in the public media.

▌ Legislations and codes

Saudi Arabia seems to lag behind other countries of the region in terms of the role governments can play in creating appropriate incentives and drivers for CSR. Aside from the *Responsible Competitiveness Initiative* by SAGIA and the occasional royal patronage of certain CSR events, the government seems totally absent from the CSR scene. On the other hand there is noticeable progress within a number of CSR-related policy areas, such as environment, labour and corporate governance.

In 2001, the Presidency of Meteorology and Environment (PME) introduced the first comprehensive legal framework in Saudi Arabia for the management of environmental impacts from industrial facilities and projects (General Environmental Law and Rules for Implementation 28 Rajab 1422 H, 15 October 2001). Industry was given a grace period of five years for implementation and since 2006 companies have started to become more environmentally concerned. However, this concern remains within the boundaries of legal compliance, with limited proactive corporate environmental initiatives.

Labour policy is of particular concern for Saudi Arabia due to its high dependency on migrant workers and the need to encourage local employment in general and woman in particular. To address some of these concerns, the Ministry of Labour introduced major amendments to the law in 2005 (National Labor Law M/51 — 23/8/1426 H, 2009). In this context, companies are increasingly linking their CSR agendas to the ministry's goals regarding the employment of women and Saudi nationals.

In the area of corporate governance, Saudi Arabia is the second country after Oman in the Gulf Corporation Council to adopt corporate governance regulations for its public companies. The Capital Market Authority (CMA) of Saudi Arabia issued the first code of corporate governance in 2006 as a voluntary code. In 2009, most of the clauses in the code were made into legal requirements for listed companies, including disclosures in the directors' annual report as to whether companies have complied, and if not, to explain why (CMA, 2009).

▌ Organisations

▐ **King Khalid Foundation**. This is a foundation focusing on the development of the not-for-profit sector in Saudi Arabia. In its efforts to engage the business community, the foundation launched the King Khalid Award for Responsible Competitiveness in 2008. **http://www.kkf.org.sa**

▐ **Saudi Arabian General Investment Authority (SAGIA)**. This is the government agency in charge of promoting inward investments into Saudi Arabia and improving the national business climate for ease of doing business. SAGIA became interested in CSR as a way to drive improvements in business ethics, employment of women and environmental protection. In 2008, SAGIA launched an index under the name of SARCI to benchmark Saudi companies along seven thematic areas such as responsible labour practices, resource efficiency and responsible communications. **http://www.sagia.gov.sa**

▐ **Tamkeen Sustainability Advisors**. Starting in 2006 as a private consulting firm, today Tamkeen is credited with catalysing a renewed debate on the role of business in the national development agenda, through a number of high profile initiatives. These initiatives include the publication of the first survey on CSR in Saudi Arabia (2007), the launch of the first public–private partnerships on water conservation under the name Wafeer (2008), and the launch of the first Saudi Index on Responsible Competitiveness with Accountability. http://www.tamkeenconsult.com

∎ **Local chambers of commerce and industry** have also created specialised units dedicated to promoting CSR and community investments. However, most of their CSR activities tend to focus on engaging their members in various charitable causes.

∎ Case studies

ALJ Group

Founded in 1945 by the late Abdul Latif Jameel, the ALJ Group is recognised today as the sole distributor of Toyota vehicles in Saudi Arabia and provider of consumer financing. After the launch of ALJ community service programmes in 2003, the group's brand shot into prominence as the leading example of CSR among private family businesses in Saudi Arabia. While the CSR model of ALJ fits more within a philanthropic orientation, the systematic efforts taken by the group's community services unit to address the challenge of reducing unemployment among young Saudis was seen as highly unusual, coming from a private concern, and hence attracted considerable praise from the government and the public. Under the community services programmes, in 2004 ALJ created Bab Rizq Jameel (BRJ), a specialised unit providing training programmes ending with employment or micro loans for young Saudi men and women. Since its inception, the unit claims to have created close to 14,000 job opportunities. http://www.alj.com

The National Commercial Bank (NCB)

The NCB is considered the largest bank in Saudi Arabia. Founded in 1953 as a general partnership, the bank was restructured in 1999 with the government acquiring a majority holding. NCB is another celebrated example in Saudi Arabia for the extent and coverage of its community service programmes. However, it also represents the first generation of companies in Saudi Arabia to adopt a more comprehensive approach to the integration of CSR across the various functions of the organisation. Though still limited in comparison with international best practices, NCB is the first bank in Saudi Arabia to publish a sustainability report, institute a formal stakeholder consultation process and assign responsibilities for sustainability at senior management level. http://www.alahli.com.sa

∎ Education

In terms of CSR-related activities in the educational sector, **King Saud University** created the first chair in CSR and business ethics in 2008 with funding from a local bank.

References

CMA (2009) 'Corporate Governance Regulations'; **http://www.cma.org.sa**, accessed 28 October 2009.

Emtairah, T., A.Alshaikh and A. Al-Badr (2009) 'Contexts and Corporate Social Responsibility: The Case of Saudi Arabia', *International Journal of Sustainable Society* 1.2: 134-148.

MacGillivary, A., and T. Emtairah (2009) 'The Saudi Responsible Competitiveness Index 2008'; **http://www.tamkeenconsult.com**, accessed 20 October 2009.

MEP (2009) 'The Long Term Strategy for the Saudi Economy'; **http://www.mep.gov.sa**, accessed 30 October 2009.'

MoL (2009) 'Rules and Regulations'; **http://www.mol.gov.sa**, accessed 28 October 2009.

Nelson, J., and S. Murphy (2009) 'Corporate Social Responsibility in Saudi Arabia and Globally: Key Challenges, Opportunities and Best Practices: A Report of the First Leadership Dialogue' (CSRI Report No. 33; Cambridge, MA: Harvard Kennedy School).

UNDP-RBAS (2009) *Arab Human Development Report 2009: Challenges to Human Security in the Arab Countries* (New York: United Nations Publications).

43 Senegal

Oumhany Sy
Corporate Responsibility Officer, ArcelorMittal Mining, Senegal

▌ Context

Senegal has a long cultural tradition of solidarity and sharing, which is even reflected in its name. 'Senegal', although said to be derived from the Portuguese explorers of the 15th century, was taken up in the indigenous Wolof language as 'Sunugal', which means 'our boat'. Even today, this boat metaphor is frequently invoked by politicians and opinion formers as a call to unity and working together, to keep the country 'afloat'.

The country is also known as 'Senegal, Pays de la Téranga', meaning the country of hospitality. Hence, solidarity and philanthropy are part of the country's values. These found early expression in forms of tradition-based organisation, rooted in communitarianism and religion, which continue to this day. For example, it is common to see a car stopping in the streets to distribute a meal to homeless children, beggars or mosques. These gestures are mainly based on the religions practised in the country (Islam, Catholicism and Animism), of which Moslems represent the majority (90%).

Islam rests on five fundamental pillars, the third of which is *Zakat*, the giving of alms or charity to the poor. Hence, every 'good Moslem' has an obligation to be a philanthropist. Many Senegalese imagine that *Zakat* procures a kind of divine protection. Therefore, when there is a perilous incident like a fire on the commercial site of a prosperous businessman, it is common to hear people saying that he simply lost the portion that he didn't return to the people: it is a heavenly punishment!

The practice of *Zakat* intensifies during religious festivals such as Ramadan, when companies offer support to mosques, whose mission is to redistribute supplies to those most in need.

Models of CSR

In the 19th century in the city of Touba, a Senegalese worshipper, Cheikh Ahmadou Bamba, created a religious fraternity called *Mouride*, which incorporated a model of a mutually dependent economy that has become widely adopted in the country. Much like Protestantism in Europe, it is a religious philosophy that proposes productivity or labour as a path to salvation. This cooperative model is still used in the agricultural sector, notably peanut farming, as a community system for the collection and redistribution of benefits (*Hadiya* and *Zakat*).

Today, the Mourides come together in socio-professional and religious associations named *Dahiras*, under the guidance of the General Khalife. A successful Mouride tradesman will recruit youngsters from his fraternity and train them so that they can open another business. In effect, they act as entrepreneurial incubators in the economy. Their socioeconomic support system includes 'popular savings accounts', which can be redistributed within the group, as well as an interdependent system of international funds transfers, based on mutual confidence.

The migrant Mourides' (*Modou-modou*) contribution to GDP was estimated to be 10% in 2007 or XOF543 billion. The construction of the city of Touba, which is the fraternity's stronghold, has come to symbolise their culturally embedded CSR practices. Most of the city's infrastructure was built as a result of successive Khalifes, with grants from their relatives and profits made in the Mouride economy. For instance, in 2008, in a bid to support the government's efforts to upgrade the city's drainage, road, water and lighting infrastructure, the Khalife succeeded in raising XOF19 billion of capital through the solidarity-based contribution of the Mourides.

▌ Priority issues

Rural poverty

Senegal's rural population includes 10 million people living in poverty, of whom 70% are farmers. These rural areas face many socioeconomic problems, including declining real incomes, resulting in a decrease in the use of agricultural inputs, soil depletion and environmental deterioration; poor access to credit; unavailability of sufficient good quality seeds; obsolete agricultural equipment; urbanisation, resulting in an ageing rural population; low quality production facilities; insufficient infrastructure for storage and processing; and lack of competitiveness between industries (Ndiaye 2006).

These problems remain, despite numerous national and multilateral policies and economic programmes to boost the rural economy. Today, therefore, there is increasingly a call for genuine participation of the private sector in securing sustainable socioeconomic development.

Education

Access to education is still limited in Senegal, according to the Poverty Reduction Strategy Paper (DSRP II) (2006), the reference document of the Senegal government for economic and social policy. There have been advances in the schooling rate in recent years, rising from 69% in 2000 to 82% in 2005. However, the number of pupils per teacher averages 51 in Senegal, as compared with 44 in Sub-Saharan Africa. Poor schooling is partially the result of a high incidence of child labour. Research by the Senegalese government and UN Children's Emergency Fund at the end of the Decade of Childhood ('MICS 2') showed that 38% of children aged 5–15 (Government of Senegal and UNICEF 2000). As a result, only 39% of children older than 15 can read and write.

Water

Inadequate access to clean water in many parts of Senegal accelerates exposure to water-related diseases. For instance, diarrhoea affects 26% of children under the age of five. Water for human consumption is generally stored in canaries (traditional terracotta containers), mostly in rural areas where 90% of the population use these canaries, as compared with 48% in urban areas (Government of Senegal and UNICEF 2000).

Water provision in Senegal's cities does not reach the World Health Organization (WHO) minimum of 35 l water per capita per day. In Dakar, it is less than 30 l in many poor districts (IMF 2002). Poor access to potable water not only causes health problems, but also impacts economic development. Indeed, women in rural areas can spend hours fetching water, which is time that could otherwise be used in agricultural or commercial activity.

Health

As with other social services, the health sector is under-resourced and services are unevenly distributed between the regions. Only 39% households have access to maternity care. As a result, infant mortality is still 58%, and 510 out of 100,000 women die during childbirth (450 and 950 women per 100,000 in urban and rural areas respectively). Malaria is the primary cause of morbidity, with around 25% of declared cases among pregnant women and children.

Transparency

The national press and human rights associations frequently denounce political corruption, non-transparent management of public business and various power abuses. In 2008, Transparency International classified Senegal in the critical zone, ranked 85th out of 180 countries on the Corruption Perceptions Index. Nevertheless, some public efforts have been made, such as a commission for fighting against corruption, a national programme for good governance, the establishment of regulatory agencies in various sectors (public, audiovisual markets, telecommunication, etc.) and a Public Procurement Code.

Environment

Many of Senegal's natural resources are overexploited due to population growth, a weak economy and poverty in rural areas. There is the problem of desertification as a result of massive deforestation, with severe implications for household access to energy resources in the form of wood to burn as charcoal. The Food and Agriculture Organization of the United Nations (FAO) reports in the 'State of the World's Forests' that Senegal loses 45,000 ha or 0.5% of its forests per year (FAO 2007).

▋ Trends

In Senegal, the concept of CSR is still in the initial stages of development. Hence, while there is very little in the way of literature or surveys, CSR is beginning to be discussed. For example, due to the actions of a local non-governmental organisation (NGO) called

La Lumière in Kédougou, international NGOs such as Oxfam America have stimulated a debate on the responsibility of newly-established mining companies in Senegal.

Many of the themes of CSR — such as the struggle against poverty, the establishment of democratic practices, good governance and the preservation of natural resources — are not new in Senegal. However, these have mainly been the focus of NGOs and public institutions. It is only more recently that companies — especially subsidiaries of multinationals and foreign-based companies — are taking an active interest in helping to solve the country's 'social emergencies'.

CSR activities in Senegal take various forms: supporting artists and their work, drilling water wells and installing solar panels in villages, organising campaigns for blood donations, investment in the fight against AIDS by signing a national charter of corporate commitment, and the provision of equipment to rural women to lighten their domestic chores.

Beyond these practices, several studies have looked more broadly at the challenge of sustainable development in Senegal. For example, Diop *et al.* (2004) looked at the impact of structural adjustment programmes, while Diallo (2009) investigated the connection between mining exploitation and sustainable development, using the gold mining activities of Mineral Deposits Limited (MDL) in Sabodala as an example. Fall and Ndiaye (2008) also conducted a survey to allow mining company ArcelorMittal to better adapt its CSR strategy to the socioeconomic realities of the region.

▌ Legislation and codes

- The **Code of Environment**. Reviewed and updated in 2001 by Law no. 2001/01, this legislation covers nuisances, pollution, waste management, preservation of natural resources and biodiversity. It includes the provision (in Article L 48) that 'all development projects or activities susceptible to affecting the environment, as well as the policies, plans, programmes, regional and sectoral studies, shall be subject to an environmental assessment'.

- **International Treaties**. Senegal has ratified the Rio Convention on Biodiversity, the Montreal Protocol on Substances that Deplete the Ozone Layer and the Kyoto Protocol of the UN Framework Convention on Climate Change.

- The **Mining Code**. This national legislation (established by Law no. 2003/36) defines the conditions for the exploration and execution of mining operations, including provisions to preserve the environment whereby applicants for mining licences must create a plan of environmental management (Article 83).

- The **Mining Corporate Social Programme**. In November 2007 the Senegalese government, in consultation with the population and socioeconomic actors of the mining region, established a Mining Corporate Social Fund, to which the mines all contribute. Investments are planned in education, health, drinking water, energy and various economic and cultural activities and are executed by companies. The fund amount is about XOF3 billion over five years.

- The **Public Procurement Code**. This is a national regulatory code defining the procedures of procurement in public institutions. It was established in order to build good governance and transparency in the management of public finances.

- **Company's Charter Against AIDS**. The charter is the Senegalese application of the recommendations from the ILO regarding the UN system-wide workplace programme on HIV. It is promoted by the AIDS Fighting Council for prevention campaigns, protection of sick workers and the fight against discrimination of those with AIDS in the workplace.

▌Organisations

▌**AIDS Fighting National Council (CNLS)**. Created in 2001, the CNLS is responsible for the execution of the AIDS Fighting National Programme. Corporate leaders are encouraged to address HIV/AIDS by signing an AIDS charter, implementing workplace projects and co-financing awareness and testing activities inside their companies. **http://www.cnls-senegal.org**

▌**Oceanium**. The oceanium is a diving centre that uses ecological movies to promote awareness about protection of the environment. In 2008, their 'Plante Ton Arbre' ('plant your tree') initiative engaged 32,500 people from 11,000 villages in planting 6 million mangroves on 1,200 ha, thereby fighting deforestation and desertification. **http://www.oceanium.org**

▌**RSE Senegal**. This is a network of socially committed enterprises, established by the consultancy CFPMI for the purpose of sharing CSR good practices and with the goal of 'ensuring that more enterprises carry out their activities with due consideration for social cohesion and sustainable development'. **http://www.rsesenegal.com**

▌Case studies

ArcelorMittal

ArcelorMittal established itself in Senegal during the integrated Mining, Rail and Port construction project. The company has become known for the fight against poverty through its community investment programme, including drilling water wells, constructing a local community-based health centre and financing the struggle against malaria. ArcelorMittal has also demonstrated best practice through its community-based communications approach, including holding dialogues with the local population and their leaders in the definition and execution of its CSR programme. **http://www.arcelormittal.com**

Eiffage Senegal

Eiffage Senegal is most well known for its sponsorship of the arts. For many years, the company has supported Senegalese artists through the organisation of exhibitions, promotion of talent and publishing of artwork. Eiffage is also involved in the protection of Senegal's cultural heritage through the renovation of historic buildings. **http://www.eiffage.sn**

Senegalese Sugar Company (CSS)

CSS has distinguished itself in the area of waste management. In 2007, the company created an ethanol distillery using the treacle extracted from sugar cane. The factory generates sales of XOF10 billion for a yearly production of 10–12 million litres of ethanol. In addition to this business venture, CSS contributes extensively to the protection of the environment and the promotion of biofuels. **http://www.css.sn**

Sonatel

Sonatel was Senegal's first telecommunications company. Its main CSR achievements came through the social actions carried out by its foundation. In particular, the company has enabled the modernisation of health services with the introduction of digital medical imaging at Ziguinchor Hospital, as well as supporting the fight against malaria and promoting education through a programme for scholarships. **http://www.orange.sn**

∎ Education

Although CSR has not been addressed as a specific educational topic, the universities have been key leaders in addressing issues relating to the environment, renewable energy and sustainable development. These include:

- **Centre for Studies and Research on Renewable Energies**. http://cerer.ucad.sn

- **Faculty of Sciences and Technics (UCAD)**. Offers a master's degree in Environment. http://www.crefast.ucad.sn/mpe

- **The Institute of Environmental Sciences, Dakar University (UCAD)**. http://www.ucad.sn

- **Institute of Management of Development, Supdeco Group**. http://www.supdeco.sn

- **University of Saint-Louis (UGB)**. Offers a master's degree in Project Management. http://www.ugb.sn

References

Commenne, V. (2006) *Responsabilité Sociale et Environnementale: L'engagement des Acteurs Economiques* (Clamecy, France: Charles Léopold Mayer).

Copans, J. (1980) *Les Marabouts de l'arachide: La Confrerie Mouride et les Paysans du Sénégal* (Paris: Le Sycomore).

Diallo, M.L. (2009) 'Mine d'Or et Développement Durable', *Revue Echo Géo* 8 (March–May 2009); http://echogeo.revues.org/index11103.html, accessed 8 April 2010.

Diop, M.C., A. Adjamagbo, P. Antoine, D. Gaye, A. Diagne, F.B. Dial, A. Diaw, E.H. Ly, M. Samb, F. Sow, E.S.N. Touré and A.A. Wane (2004) *Gouverner le Sénégal: Entre Ajustement Structurel et Developpement Durable* (Paris: Karthala).

Fall, P.N., and A. Ndiaye (2008) 'Analyse des Dynamiques Economiques et Sociales des Zones d'Intervention d'ArcelorMittal Sénégal' (ArcelorMittal Global Survey Report).

FAO (Food and Agriculture Organisation of the United Nations) (2007) 'State of the World's Forests 2007' (Rome: FAO; **http://www.fao.org/docrep/009/a0773e/a0773e00.HTM**, accessed 8 June 2010).

Government of Senegal (2002) 'Document de Stratégie de Réduction de la Pauvreté (DSRP)'; **http://www.dsrp-senegal.org**.

—— (2006) 'Document de Stratégie de Réduction de la Pauvreté II 2006–2010' (DSRP II); **http://www.dsrp-senegal.org/resume.htm**, accessed 8 June 2010.

——and UNICEF (2000) 'Rapport de l'Enquête sur les Objectifs de la fin de Décennie sur l'Enfance (MICS II)'; **http://www.childinfo.org/files/senegaltables.pdf**, accessed 8 June 2010.

IMF (International Monetary Fund) (2002) 'Republic of Senegal: Poverty Reduction Strategy Paper', May 2002; **http://www.imf.org/External/NP/prsp/2002/sen/01/index.htm**, accessed 8 June 2010.

Ndiaye, A. (2006) 'Agriculture, Genre et Budget' (Internal Report for the Gender Laboratory of the Fundamental African Institute of Dakar).

Ministry of Mines and Regional Agency for Development of Senegal (2008) 'Programme Social Minier' (Tambacounda Senegal); **http://www.industrie.gouv.sn/services%20usagers_dmg.htm**, accessed 8 June 2010.

Salem, G. (1981) 'De la Brousse Senegalaise au Boul'mich: Le Système Commercial Mouride en France', *Cahiers d'Etudes Africaines* 81–83: 267-286.

Samb, A. (1974) *L'Islam et l'Histoire du Senegal* (Hilal).

St-Martin, Y.J. (1989) *Le Sénégal Sous le Second Empire* (Paris: Karthala).

44 Sierra Leone

Nicole Porto
Independent CSR Consultant

▌ Context

Early inhabitants, expeditions and migrations have all contributed to shaping Sierra Leone's rich cultural, religious and historical traditions, with archaeological evidence suggesting that people have occupied Sierra Leone for at least 2,500 years.

Religion plays a prominent role in Sierra Leonean society, with followers of Islam comprising 60% of the population, Christianity 30% and African indigenous religions 10%. Muslims and Christians coexist peacefully, and religious respect and tolerance is the norm. Principles of charity and philanthropy are deeply ingrained in Sierra Leonean society and traditional ways of life.

Kinship networks are also prominent in society and extremely important in everyday matters, in that one is obligated to assist one's family throughout life. This practice was intensified by the war and the resultant pervasive poverty. Diaspora remittances are high, amounting to USD168 million according to recent International Fund for Agricultural Development estimates, and have been particularly crucial in poverty alleviation.

Historically, Sierra Leone was an important centre of the transatlantic slave trade until the close of the 18th century, when it began to be outlawed and Sierra Leone became a resettlement site for freed slaves. The first resettlements were carried out by the St George's Bay Company, comprised of British philanthropists concerned about the welfare of the unemployed black poor on the streets of London. The subsequently established Sierra Leone Company also facilitated the return of several groups of formerly enslaved Africans, who founded Freetown in 1792.

Post independence, some companies engaged in quasi-philanthropic activities in response to stakeholder requests — for example, in the areas of the arts and education — but these activities were haphazard and often politically and tribally based. The advent of the civil war in 1991 caused many businesses to cease operations and over the next decade much of the formal economy and socioeconomic infrastructure were destroyed. Since the end of hostilities in 2002, many companies have engaged in CSR-related activities in ad hoc and informal ways, but CSR is far from being institutionalised.

Models of CSR

The principal arena for discussing CSR in Sierra Leone is in academic circles. However, the capacity of the few CSR professors to undertake research to maintain abreast on international CSR issues is severely limited, with funding as a primary constraint.

While academics agree that Archie Carroll's pyramid model, which includes economic, legal, ethical and philanthropic components, is helpful, all maintain that Sierra Leone's private sector is far from adopting such a comprehensive model.

Frequent examinations of corporate activity in Sierra Leone have yielded two CSR models that academics believe characterise the current climate. The first, which some academics call the Marketing Model, relates to the motivations behind companies' CSR activities. Hence, CSR is economically driven with a focus on profit maximisation and maintaining a strong competitive position. The telecommunications companies, which are spearheading the modern CSR movement in Sierra Leone, are somewhat typical of this approach.

The second example, the Stakeholder Model, refers to companies responding to the needs of their stakeholders, primarily customers and communities. While this model has been present in Sierra Leonean history periodically to small degrees, it has become more prominent in the years after the civil war. Hence, CSR activities are philanthropically driven, with a focus on stakeholder requests for aid and support.

∎ Priority issues

The economic history of Sierra Leone shows a country with abundant mineral and marine resources, and vast agricultural and tourism potential. Unfortunately, since independence the nation and its leaders have been unable to utilise these resources to transform the country and make lasting improvements in the welfare of the people. Successive governments have been characterised by corruption, mismanagement and inefficiency, only perpetuating the poor governance practices of their predecessors. This cycle has caused extensive societal damage.

Poverty

Sierra Leone ranks 180th out of 182 on the UNDP Human Development Index 2007. Over 70% of the population live below the national poverty line, i.e less than SLL2,111 per day, and an estimated 26% live in extreme poverty — meaning that they do not earn enough to buy an adult recommended minimum nutritional requirement of 2,700 calories a day. The majority of Sierra Leoneans, especially in rural areas, lack access to basic social services and social infrastructure.

Food security

Subsistence agriculture comprises the mainstay of the rural Sierra Leonean economy. It represents the largest single sector, producing about 45% of GDP and employing over two-thirds of the population. However, according to the country's Poverty Reduction Strategy Paper, farmers, especially subsistence food crop farmers, are among the poorest in the country. The agrarian crisis, perpetuated in part by poorly developed rural infrastructure, continues to be a major cause of poverty and has hindered private sector investment in agriculture. Currently only 11% of the total arable land has been cultivated and private sector investment to address related social issues remains absent.

The development of agricultural infrastructure could attract increased private sector investment and generate high export earnings, while simultaneously playing a considerable role in alleviating poverty by providing food security. Consultations held by the World Bank and ENCISS in 2008 stressed the particular importance of Bonthe District with its potential independently to produce enough rice to feed the country, while also providing a huge surplus for export to other countries.

Unemployed urban youth

With 42% of the population residing in urban areas, and urbanisation increasing annually, the large number of unemployed urban youth in Freetown and other cities is considered a source of instability and disorder. According to the 2004 Population and Housing census, youth between the ages of 15 and 35 make up 39% of the population, and the proportion under 15 is even larger. Furthermore, between 60% and 70% of all Sierra Leonean youth are unemployed and many already reside in cities and engage in informal market activities. They lack the education and skills needed to secure employment that could provide economic and social stability.

The government has set employment creation and building the skills and capabilities of youth as a primary task. A reinvigorated private sector will be instrumental in achieving this through the creation of sustainable jobs, as will be preparing young people for entering jobs in growth sectors in the economy.

Environmental degradation

Sierra Leone suffers from severe environmental degradation arising mainly from demographic, economic and social pressures. Increasing demands on the physical environment have led to rapid deforestation, land degradation, biodiversity loss and uncontrolled exploitation of natural resources.

Slash-and-burn cultivation for agriculture, logging, clearing for cattle grazing, fuel wood collection and mining have resulted in a dramatic drop in forest cover since the 1980s. UNDP estimates for 1995–2000 indicate that 87% of total forest area has been cleared. Unsustainable large scale and artisanal mining activity have also had adverse impacts on the environment, including deforestation, land degradation and water and air pollution.

The government has expressed a commitment to strengthening environmental management for sustainability. However, its inability to monitor existing environmental policies and develop effective conservation programmes has allowed for severe, continual abuse.

∎ Trends

CSR is not new in Sierra Leone, but it has yet to be mainstreamed among the wider population. As a result of sensitisation by non-governmental organisations (NGOs) and the large-scale CSR marketing campaigns of the telecommunications and banking institutions, a large portion of the public, albeit mainly in Freetown and mining-affected communities, supports the notion that companies are responsible for developing the communities in which they operate and contributing to poverty reduction.

The need for responsible private sector investment as an engine for poverty reduction and development is clear. However, political instability since independence has been a major impediment to the country's progress and has deterred foreign investment. Furthermore, the condition of the country's infrastructure remains poor. Since the end of the war in 2002, massive infusions of outside assistance have helped Sierra Leone begin to recover. However, the economy is still in a desperate state and most companies remain focused on economic performance above all other considerations.

Historically, business philanthropy has been practised in Sierra Leonean society, albeit minimal and haphazard. In the 1970s and 1980s, with theatre and the arts burgeoning, struggling artists approached companies for support, with limited success. The German, US and Chinese embassies were more responsive and banks soon followed suit.

With the advent of the war in 1991, major companies ceased operations and business owners fled the country, in effect bringing such philanthropic acts to a standstill. In 2000, with the establishment of the first telecommunications company, Celtel, the focus was on making money. It was not until the arrival of fierce competition with the establishment of three other major telecommunications companies that CSR really became visible in Sierra Leonean society. The pervasive poverty resulting from the war created an influx of requests for aid, and companies, feeling a heightened need to compete with one another, began responding to these requests.

Despite public acknowledgement that society has benefited from such acts, there is a concurrent perception that CSR has mainly been a marketing ploy. This demonstrates the need for CSR mainstreaming and sensitisation to show how CSR can more effectively promote poverty reduction and development. Furthermore, CSR activities are neither reported on nor monitored, which limits discourse on the effectiveness and impact of CSR programmes.

A study by the Foreign Investment Advisory Service (FIAS, 2006) on CSR in Sierra Leone highlighted the growing interest in Sierra Leone from investors, philanthropic and nonprofit groups to promote tourism in a way that addresses poverty, environmental degradation and the sustainable development of local communities. However, it also concluded that Sierra Leone needs to develop a profitable tourism economy before it can fully benefit from the guidelines on pro-poor tourism (tourism that results in net benefits for poor people) or CSR in this sector.

With regard to the mining sector, FIAS observed an emerging 'clash of expectations' about the benefits that will accrue to the government, local communities and businesses respectively, following the reactivation and expansion of large scale industrial mining. This clash of expectations, FIAS argues, provides the rationale for CSR and explains why it is one factor that will encourage and sustain foreign investment in the mining sector.

∎ Legislation and codes

While Sierra Leone has passed some progressive policies on environment and labour, these are poorly implemented and lack proper monitoring and oversight mechanisms.

- The **Mines and Minerals Act of 1994** requires mining lease applicants to submit particulars of the effects of the proposed mining activities on the environment and the health of the local community together with a programme for their mitigation and compensation measures.

- The **2003 Core Mineral Policy** aims to ensure that the development of the minerals sector is achieved in ways that will protect the environment and are socially responsible and economically viable.

- The **Environmental Protection Agency (EPA) Act of 2008** established the EPA and requires environmental impact assessments for projects in various sectors, which must include the environmental, social, economic and cultural effects of projects and measures to avoid, mitigate or remedy them.

- The **Forestry Act of 1988** requires the preparation of a forest management plan, with provisions on forest protection and reforestation measures.

- The **Regulation of Wages and Industrial Relations Act of 1971** established Trade Group Negotiating Councils for most sectors, which are responsible for negotiating wages and other conditions of service for workers and settling disputes between employers and employees.

- The **Investment Policies and Incentives for Private Sector Promotion in Agriculture in Sierra Leone** (January 2009) is a proposed set of policies that contain a section on CSR, mandating an investor to clearly describe support to be given to host communities or to use 5% of annual net profit to accomplish that responsibility. It further states that such demands require serious vigilance and monitoring by both the government and the host community.

▮ Organisations

While there are several business associations in the country, those most active lack the knowledge and capacity to promote CSR. Furthermore, the government's current focus on remedying administrative barriers to investment, for example, has not created an environment encouraging to the active consideration of CSR issues by these organisations.

The one possible exception is the **Sierra Leone Chamber of Commerce, Industry and Agriculture (COCSL)**, established in 1961 to provide an advocacy role on behalf of the private sector. It has a membership of about 180 companies and while its major functions do not currently include CSR promotion, it has featured speakers discussing CSR-related topics at its annual luncheon for members. **http://www.chamberofcommerce.sl**

Case studies

Africell

Established in Sierra Leone in 2004, Africell is the biggest telecommunications company in terms of subscriber base. Although it supports projects across various sectors, it has been primarily active in supporting the arts and sports. Its projects are all undertaken in response to stakeholder requests. Examples include sponsoring the Amputee Football Club and the National Beach Volleyball and Football leagues. Its 'Sing with Africell' programme supports artistic expression. Other projects include rehabilitating infrastructure at Fourah Bay College, donating provisions to religious institutions and large cash giveaways to subscribers. Its most recent endeavour is financing the rehabilitation of a football stadium and construction of shops in what will be called Africell City in the village of Mokanji. **http://www.africell.sl**

Standard Chartered Bank Sierra Leone Ltd

Operating in Sierra Leone since 1894, Standard Chartered Bank has stated its commitment to building a sustainable business and to upholding high standards of corporate governance, social responsibility and environmental protection. Its corporate policy is to devote 0.75% of the previous year's profits to CSR activities. The bank's Community Partnership Programme is very active in addressing issues in the health, education and environment sectors. Projects undertaken include 'Living with HIV/AIDS' education, the construction of the Wellington Orphanage, the Bo Government Hospital Outpatient Wing and skills training centres at schools for the blind and the handicapped. **http://www.standardchartered.com/sl**

Transnational Sierra Leone Ltd

Established in 1986, Transnational SL Ltd has actively supported a range of education, health and infrastructure-related projects in Sierra Leone. Along with its work to support Pikin Bizness, an NGO founded in 2001 by CEO Adonis Abboud to help children with serious heart problems receive life-saving treatment abroad, other initiatives are undertaken in response to stakeholder requests for assistance. The philanthropic work of the company began with the donation of a satellite system to Fourah Bay College in 1990, followed by similar donations to all other major universities. It has also equipped numerous secondary schools with direct learning systems, providing educational programmes via satellite. In total, 40–42 educational and social institutions have benefited from such donations and more are planned. **http://www.dstvafrica.com**

Education

CSR education in Sierra Leone is still at a nascent stage. With only one business school in the country, courses on CSR-related issues are in short supply. Below are the leading institutions that offer CSR-related modules:

- **Institute of Public Administration and Business Management (IPAM)**. University of Sierra Leone, Freetown. **http://www.tusol.org**

- **Fourah Bay College (FBC)**. University of Sierra Leone, Freetown. **http://www. tusol.org**

Reference

FIAS (Foreign Investment Advisory Service) (2006) 'Competitiveness and Corporate Social Responsibility in Sierra Leone: Industry Solutions for Tourism and Mining' (9989623; Washington, DC: FIAS).

45 Singapore

Thomas Thomas
Executive Director, Singapore Compact
for Corporate Social Responsibility

▊ Context

The history of modern Singapore began when the British East India Company established a trading post on the island of Singapore. The place prospered and grew from a sleepy fishing village to a cosmopolitan city with migrants from Asia and beyond. Consequently, British commercial interests took precedence. Under these circumstances, individual philanthropy, as well as community self-help initiatives organised along ethnic, clan and religious lines, have been cornerstones of Singapore's social network ever since. In essence, philanthropy and community self-help initiatives responded to a lack of social welfare provisions under the colonial government (Mohamed *et al.* 2008: 17).

Immediately after World War II, the British colonial authorities allowed the formation of trade unions and set up the Social Welfare Department. The agency mainly dealt with providing emergency relief for war victims, as well as housing for the homeless. It addressed the then acute problems of poverty, juvenile delinquency and prostitution (Mohamed *et al.* 2008: 17). Unions that came into being were involved in both the political struggle for independence and efforts to improve the lives of workers.

Singapore achieved full independence in 1965, with acute problems of unemployment, housing shortage and low living standards. The early years of nation-building were characterised by competition between political parties over the right to define the philosophical and ideological foundations of the newborn nation. The social sector, that had until then been largely based on the delivery of social services, came to be infused with a sense of social advocacy (Mohamed *et al.* 2008: 18).

The foundations and origins of the national compact for social responsibility that dominate social relations in Singapore to this day, can be found in the early years of industrialisation, since the 1960s. From the outset, the Singapore government has been conscious of the need to achieve sustainable growth and development. It has consistently put into place legislation and policies that has sought to create a conducive environment for businesses, to attract foreign investment and ultimately to create quality jobs to raise people's living standards and quality of life.

In order to achieve this, the government established tripartism as a consultative decision-making framework in which government, labour and business collectively address the challenges of industrialisation. Coupled with the overarching aim of attracting foreign investment, tripartism in Singapore has resulted in a dramatic reduction in the number and frequency of labour disputes. The spirit of industrial peace with justice ensured that industrial disputes were settled amicably, without the need for labour to resort to industrial action.

Beyond industrial relations, the National Trades Union Congress (NTUC), formed in 1961, moved towards establishing various cooperatives, with the aim of promoting the welfare of its members and their families (Chandran 2005: 230-232). NTUC today has 12 social enterprises and 4 related organisations that are owned by more than 500,000 workers, with the core mission of creating better life in the community. These social enterprises have social objectives that combine with commercial approaches. NTUC also has initiatives that aim to increase the employability of workers, through training and skills-upgrading programmes.

In May 2004, with support from national and tripartite leaders in Singapore, a CSR forum was organised to launch the National Tripartite Initiative (NTI) on CSR. The NTI was represented at the International Organization for Standardization (ISO) conference on CSR in Stockholm in June 2004. Subsequently, the initiative chaired the national ISO Mirror Committee as Singapore's official country contact point, with the aim of providing consultative input to the ISO26000 Working Group.

In January 2005, the Singapore Compact for CSR was launched by Mr Heng Chee How, the then Minister of State for Trade and Industry and Mayor for the Central Singapore Community Development Council. The Singapore Compact was created as a national society with a mission to provide impetus to the CSR movement in Singapore, and had as its founding members the NTUC and the Singapore National Employers Federation (SNEF). In the same year, the United Nations Global Compact (UNGC) country focal point was officially launched in Singapore, bringing together signatories from ten companies and the NTUC, SNEF and the Singapore National Co-operative Federation. By 2009, the number of signatories to the UNGC had increased to 72.

▌Priority issues

Job creation

Economic growth has consistently been one of the foremost priorities of the Singaporean government. During an interview with UCLA professor Tom Plate, Prime Minister Lee Hsien Loong stated that 'the whole business environment has to be favourable so that people come here and say this is where I want to live, this is where I want my business to be and I can do the business of business, which is to make money and the place can prosper' (Plate 2007).

In the context of Singapore, economic growth is essential not only as a validation of the government's political legitimacy, but more crucially as a guarantee of job creation and employment. One of the reasons why employment is important in Singapore is that it entitles a Singaporean to access the Central Provident Fund (CPF). Employment contributions to CPF, a compulsory savings scheme that serves as an old-age pension fund, are calculated as a percentage of an employee's monthly income, and paid by both employees and employers.

Skills shortages

Today, re-employment is also important for Singaporeans in order to have enough savings for retirement due to higher life expectancy; many seek to work beyond retirement age. This is also to overcome labour and skill shortage issues. Economic growth was supported by foreign workers and the treatment and status of these workers are being monitored by NGOs, government and unions.

Employment practices

Tripartite leaders have also emphasised the importance of fair employment practices. On 10 February 2009, Halimah Yacob, deputy secretary-general of NTUC, stated at the inaugural tripartite conference on fair employment practices that 'it is absolutely important that if companies are going to downsize or they have to retrench, they have to communicate with employees that sense of fairness. It is not only important for those that are being retrenched but those that are left behind' (Frois 2009).

Emphasis on flexibility and diverse skills in education is also one of the priorities in the era of uncertain change. Along with education, Singapore is building up its research and development to 3% of GDP, with a focus on three major thrusts: biomedicine, interactive and digital media and water technology (Plate 2007). With a growing aged population and incoming international companies, the biomedical sciences sector is expected to create up to 1,000 jobs in 2009, almost double the number created in 2008 (Kelly 2009).

Water

Singapore imports 40% of its water from Malaysia under two international agreements, one expiring in 2011 and the other in 2061. In just four decades, Singapore has overcome water shortages despite its lack of natural water resources, flooding and pollution in its rivers in the 1960s and 1970s. Its water supply now comes from four water 'taps' — imported water, reclaimed water, rainwater capture and desalination. By integrating the system and maximising the efficiency of each of the four taps, Singapore has ensured a stable, sustainable water supply capable of catering to the country's continued growth.

Due to sound watershed management, effective water treatment processes and continued investments in research and development, Singaporeans have been enjoying good quality water for the last four decades. The tap water is well within the World Health Organization drinking water guidelines, and is suitable for drinking without any further filtration.

▌ Trends

Many companies in Singapore devote significant time and resources to 'giving back to the community'. Asian businesses in Singapore have traditionally displayed care for their employees, and have often given back to the community by means such as building schools, running hospitals and helping the needy. Community spirit is one of Singapore's shared core values, and provides the context in which philanthropy and volunteerism are encouraged and recognised.

Broadly speaking, companies in Singapore are likely to view contributing to society as an activity that takes place outside of their core business activities, rather than a use of their specific strengths to more effectively respond to needs of the community, as well as to broader economic, social and environmental challenges.

This does not mean that Singaporean companies are socially irresponsible. In fact, the Singaporean context — the sum of national legislation, policies and social norms that companies there abide to — has obliged companies to be, *de facto*, good corporate citizens. Companies in Singapore are expected to meet the codes of practice and legislation concerning issues such as corporate governance, safety standards, pollution control and environmental health requirements.

Nevertheless, a national survey commissioned by the Ministry of Trade and Industry (2008) revealed a very low level of awareness of CSR among companies operating in Singapore (Yang 2008). Out of the 507 companies surveyed, 40% were aware of the term 'CSR'. This suggests that there is a gap between local companies' understanding of business responsibility and international definitions of CSR.

Awareness of CSR was higher in larger and foreign-owned companies and lower among local SMEs, the latter making up 70% of the survey's respondents. According to the survey's findings, CSR is generally understood as paying back to society, by means of corporate philanthropy and volunteerism. The survey showed that companies that abstained from CSR initiatives did so due to the lack of allocated budgets, time and know-how, as well as the perception that CSR is neither relevant to their business nor financially worthwhile. Respondents also identified public incentives, as well as awareness-building seminars, as initiatives that would encourage them to pursue CSR initiatives.

In terms of CSR, Singaporean companies do more than they think. However, some issues remain relatively neglected and require further scrutiny, including migrant workers, companies operating overseas, more disclosure and reporting, and practices of companies that are not listed.

▌ Legislation and codes

Over the past 44 years, the Singaporean government has succeeded in putting in place a comprehensive set of regulations that have established high standards of responsible business practices. This is despite the fact that there has been little formal emphasis on CSR. Regulations have focused on three main areas, namely labour rights, corporate governance and environmental protection, all of which aim to protect the interest of different stakeholders in Singapore.

- The **Code of Corporate Governance** encourages Singapore-listed companies to enhance shareholder value through good corporate governance. In order for shareholders to have a sound basis on which to make investment decisions and to assess the adequacy of a company's corporate governance practices, companies must provide appropriate disclosure of their corporate governance framework and practices. Such disclosure also allows other market participants to play a more active role in promoting good corporate governance.

- The **Inter-Ministerial Committee on Sustainable Development** was set up in February 2008 to formulate a clear national framework and strategy for sustainable development in Singapore. Co-chaired by Mr Mah Bow Tan, Minister for National Development, and Dr Yaacob Ibrahim, Minister for the Environment and Water Resources, the Committee also included the Ministers for Finance and Transport and the Senior Minister for State for Trade and Industry.

- The **Environmental Protection and Management regulations** set high standards on various issues including food hygiene, emission control, boundary noise limits for factory premises, ozone-depleting substances, energy conservation, public cleansing, toxic industrial waste and quality of piped drinking water.

- **Employment and industrial relations** practices are covered by legislation and tripartite guidelines formulated by government, business and labour. These guidelines are widely implemented.

- The **Work Injury Compensation Act** provides a simple system of liability and compensation beneficial to both employees and employers. Employees, regardless of their level of earnings, are entitled to receive compensation quickly without having to prove fault, while the liabilities of employers are capped.

▌ Organisations

▌ **Consumers Association of Singapore (CASE).** CASE is a nonprofit, non-governmental organisation that is committed towards protecting consumers' interests through information and education, and promoting an environment of fair and ethical trade practices. http://www.case.org.sg

▌ **National Trades Union Congress (NTUC).** NTUC is the sole national trade union centre in Singapore. It helps working people to earn a better living and live a better life. http://www.ntuc.org.sg

▌ **National Volunteer and Philanthropy Centre (NVPC).** NVPC is the national body that promotes and develops volunteerism and philanthropy across all sectors and networking agencies to foster the giving spirit in Singapore. http://www.nvpc.org.sg

▌ **Singapore Business Federation**. SBF is the apex business chamber that champions the interests of the Singapore business community in trade, investment and industrial relations. SBF has a Sustainable Development Group to promote sustainable practices among member companies. http://www.sbf.org.sg

▌ The **Singapore Compact for CSR.** The Compact is a national society committed to bringing the CSR movement forward. Its mission is to provide a multi-stakeholder platform for collaboration, in developing coordinated and effective strategies to promote CSR policies and practices in Singapore. http://www.csrsingapore.org

▌ **Singapore Environment Council (SEC).** SEC's main objects include promoting greater public awareness of and concern for the living and natural environment and encouraging the public to be more environmentally conscious and display a greater sense of environmental responsibility. **http://www.sec.org.sg**

▮ **Singapore National Employers Federation**. SNEF aims to help employers achieve excellence in employment practices and strengthen their role in the tripartite partnership. **http://www.sgemployers.com**

▮ Case studies[1]

City Development Limited (CDL)

City Development Limited (CDL) was the first private developer in Singapore to be awarded the ISO 14001 (Environmental Management System) certification by the local governing body, the Building Construction Authority (BCA), for its commitment to raising environmental standards in its projects and incorporating eco-friendly features. It is the only Singaporean developer listed on the London FTSE4Good Index since 2002. CDL is also the first Singaporean company to publish a sustainability report under the Global Reporting Initiative (GRI) G3 framework in 2008. **http://www.cdl.com.sg**

FairPrice (NTUC)

Established in 1973, NTUC FairPrice Co-operative Ltd is the leading supermarket retailer in Singapore. Many of its projects are aimed at adding value to the well-being of the community in which it operates. In recognition of its achievements in work–life strategies, FairPrice won the Work–Life Achiever Award in 2006 conferred by the Tripartite Committee on Work–Life Strategy. **http://www.fairprice.com.sg**

▮ Education

There are an increasing number of higher educational institutions introducing CSR-related modules:

- The **National University of Singapore** has an MBA course with a module on managerial decision-making and ethical values. **http://bschool.nus. edu.sg/TheNUSMBA/ProspectiveStudents/TheNUSMBA/ProgrammeInformation/ ProgrammeSchedule/tabid/2261/default.aspx**

- **Ngee Ann Polytechnic** has two-year diploma in Social Entrepreneurship, indicating growing interest in ethical business among students and educational institutions. **http://www.np.edu.sg/hms/courses/bzse/Pages/default.aspx**

- The **Singapore Management University**'s core modules include business, government and society; and ethics and social responsibility. **http://knowledge.smu. edu.sg/category.cfm?cid=11**

---

1 See also Wong 2009.

References

Chandran, R. (2005) *Singapore: Employment Law in Singapore* (Singapore: Pearson/Prentice Hall).

Frois, C. (2009) 'Employers urged to adopt fair employment practices', *Channel NewsAsia*, 10 February 2009.

Kelly, R. (2009) 'Biomedical sciences' job creation expected to almost double in 2009', *Channel NewsAsia*, 12 March 2009.

Ministry of Trades and Industry (2008) 'National CSR Survey' (Singapore Compact for CSR, October 2008).

Mohamed, S.M., *et al.* (2008) *Social Space Singapore* (Lien Centre for Social Innovation, Singapore Management University; **http://www.lcsi.smu.edu.sg/socialspace2008.asp**, accessed 8 June 2010).

Plate, T. (2007) 'Transcript: Interview with Lee Hsien Loong', *Asia Media* (Los Angeles, CA: UCLA), 22 February 2007.

Singapore National Employers Federation (2009) 'Why is Re-employment Important?', **http://www.re-employment.sg/web/contents/contents.aspx?contid=165**, accessed 28 March 2009.

Wong, E. (2009) *CSR for Sustainability and Success* (Singapore Compact; Singapore: Marshall Cavendish).

Yang, H. (2008) '40% of Singapore firms aware of social responsibility: Poll', *Straits Times*, 7 October 2008.

46 South Africa

Mervyn E. King
Chairman, King Report on Corporate Governance in South Africa;
Chairman, Global Reporting Initiative

Derick de Jongh
Director, Centre for Responsible Leadership,
University of Pretoria, South Africa

René Carapinha
Research Associate, Centre for Responsible Leadership,
University of Pretoria, South Africa

■ Context

In the broadest sense, CSR refers to the role of business in society. It entails how business is governed, and how it contributes to a just and sustainable society. In South Africa (SA), CSR is also called corporate citizenship, corporate social investment and corporate social and environmental responsibility. Corporate governance is largely seen as an element of corporate citizenship.

The development of CSR in SA was greatly influenced by the county's history of apartheid. While this period saw business implicated in the exploitation of black labour, as well as low occupational health, safety and environmental standards, it also gave rise to early manifestations of voluntary business initiatives that pushed for government policy changes (Carapinha and de Jongh 2008).

CSR in post-apartheid SA has been strongly influenced by the socio-political mandate of nation building (Alperson 1995). A call for business to contribute to development is repeated in various White Papers and public policy documents, all of which are aligned with the country's Constitution. In this sense, the South African government has gone much further than many other governments to legislate social issues in management (Hamann 2008).

CSR is also informed by a culture of business self-regulation and market drivers. First, CSR is being shaped by the growing realisation that the major shareholders of JSE-listed companies are pension funds and financial institutions, representing ordinary citizens.

Second, the concept and rationale of CSR are strongly informed by the King Code for Corporate Governance. Now in its third edition, the King Report was the first report on corporate governance that embraced the concepts of stakeholder engagement, ethics and environmental management, and actively encouraged an inclusive approach to these issues (Rossouw *et al.* 2002: 300).

Third, through the King Report confidence is placed in the entrenchment of African values into corporate governance, of which *Ubuntu* (African humanism) is the most evident. The notion of *Ubuntu* resonates with the reciprocal nature of CSR in SA, making it a dominant cultural driver of CSR.

Most CSR strategies in South Africa are modelled as a partnership between sectors of society, with each sector or partner contributing strengths and resources (Pretorius 2002). For business, this entails contributing financial and often human resources through philanthropic donations and employee volunteering. Through business coalitions, business also contributes leadership in problem-solving, as seen in collaborative initiatives such as Business Against Crime.

CSR in SA is generally seen and treated as a business investment in the community or environment, on which a return on investment is expected. This expectation is characteristic of Corporate Social Investment (CSI), which closely resembles strategic philanthropy. What remains a challenge for most SA businesses is to measure this return in quantifiable terms (Hamann 2008).

Although the CSI approach to CSR is most dominant in SA, its value is increasingly being questioned (Bezuidenhout *et al.* 2007; Carapinha and de Jongh 2008). Fundamentally, it is perceived as lacking the integrity and participation that leads to empowerment (Carapinha and de Jongh 2008). Furthermore, differentiation between what is important to the corporation and the real needs of the community is often very vague. And, even though CSI initiatives have no doubt been making important development contributions, they are generally not integrated or aligned to core business (Carapinha and de Jongh 2008).

As a result, the role of business in society is going through a transition. Some argue that this shift represents the integration of a systemic approach to responsibility that closely resembles sustainable business models (Carapinha and de Jongh 2008). Others characterise the shift as moving from social investment to sustainable development and collaborative governance (Hamann 2008).

▮ Priority issues

HIV and AIDS

SA is currently at the epicentre of the AIDS pandemic and the disease is affecting all aspects of South African society. Prevalence rates have increased from 0.7% among 15–49 year-olds in 1990 to 18% at the end of 2007 (AVERT 2009). The Actuarial Society of SA estimate that 5.4 million people were living with HIV in 2006, or around 11% of the total population (Dorrington *et al.* 2006). It predicts that the number will exceed 6 million by 2015, by which time around 5.4 million South Africans will have died of AIDS. The response of corporate SA to HIV/AIDS has been slow, partial and erratic (Dickinson 2004).

Skills development and job creation

SA's unemployment rate is around 24% and unemployment remains the country's greatest economic challenge. Job creation and skills development are consequently a major national development objective to address poverty and develop the economy. Although the South African government's Expanded Public Works Programme (EPWP) more or less achieved its main objective of creating 1 million jobs for the poor by 2009, significant and sustained poverty alleviation is unlikely without business creating long-term employment and training opportunities (Hemsen 2007).

Energy

Energy issues are high on the political agenda ever since the January 2008 energy crisis and subsequent blackouts, during which more than 20% of SA's electricity-generating capacity was out of commission (Dagut and Bernstein 2008). Plans to address the power supply crisis are summarised in a policy document issued by the Department of Minerals and Energy (RSA, 2008). Strategies aimed at promoting energy efficiency and deterring energy inefficiency include reducing demand by increasing the price of electricity and conserving power by allocating quotas (EIA 2009). Hence, energy conservation is one of the most important sustainability issues facing companies (Trialogue 2008). It is increasingly becoming an integral part of many business strategies due to energy conservation pressures and incentives.

∎ Trends

There is a long history of the use of codes of conduct in SA. The most influential and enduring is probably the Sullivan Principles (Mangaliso 1997), which promoted employee rights in multinational companies during apartheid. Other examples include mandatory CSR reporting for companies listed on the JSE Securities Exchange and the King Code (IOD 2009), which endorses the Global Reporting Initiative (GRI) and AA1000 Standard, and strongly encourages companies to comply with industry standards. The latest version of the King Code (King III) strongly argues in favour of external assurance of sustainability reports becoming a mandatory requirement.

It is expected that, as a result of these self-regulatory measures, a rise in CSR will result, at least in the medium term (Beszuidenhout *et al.* 2007). A rise in CSR reporting is already evident, as research suggests that South African companies report more frequently and in more depth on CSR relative to the Fortune Global 100 companies (Dawkins and Ngunjiri 2008). In particular, reporting of community investment, diversity, and employee relations were significantly more than the global norm. This illustrates not only the positive impact of self-regulation but also the impact of legislation.

In general, it is mostly large companies, especially those with international interests, which adopt global standards such as the UN Global Compact (UNGC). To date, there are 29 active Global Compact business participants in SA. Although participation is increasing, the comparatively lower prominence of the UNGC in SA is attributed to the perception that it offers very little additional and differentiating value in comparison to the many other existing CSR reporting practices, codes of conduct and regulatory frameworks in the country (Reith *et al.* 2007).

The most prevalent certification scheme in SA is the ISO 14001 standard (Bezuiden-hout 2007; Visser 2005). As many as 530 certifications were issued by 2007, which is a slight drop from 540 in 2005 (ISO 2008).

▌ Legislation and codes

National legislation significantly informs the nature of CSR as the government has legislated several social issues in management and in the workplace since the democratic dispensation in 1994 (Visser 2005). Nonetheless, implementation and enforcement are challenging, even to the extent that compliance in some instances is treated as 'an issue of business voluntarism' (Hamann 2008).

Premised on a progressive constitution, there have been numerous legislative developments that are pertinent in shaping the country's CSR landscape. The following are some of the more prominent legislative influences on CSR:

- **Companies Act No. 61 of 1973** and **Closed Corporations Act No. 69 of 1984**

- **Occupational Health and Safety Act No 85 of 1993** and **Mine Health and Safety Act No. 29 of 1996**

- **Compensation for Occupational Injuries and Diseases Act No 130 of 1993** and the **Occupational Diseases in Mines and Works Act No 78 of 1973**

- **Labour Relations Act No. 66 of 1995** and **Basic Conditions of Employment Act No. 75 of 1997**

- **Constitution No. 108 of 1996** (contains the Bill of Rights)

- **National Water Act No. 36 of 1998**

- **Employment Equity Act No. 55 of 1998**

- **Competition Act No. 89 of 1998** (amended in 2000)

- **Skills Development Act No 97 of 1998**

- **National Environmental Management Act No. 107 of 1998**

- **Promotion of Access to Information Act No. 2 of 2000**

- **Promotion of Equality and Prevention of Unfair Discrimination Act No. 4 of 2000**

- **Mineral and Petroleum Resources Development Act No. 28 of 2002**

- **National Black Economic Empowerment Act No. 53 of 2003**

The SA government is also party to numerous international treaties and conventions that have a bearing on CSR issues. These include (but are not limited to) the core conventions of the International Labour Organisation (ILO); the conventions and protocols relating to biodiversity; climate change; ozone-depleting substances; the handling and transportation of hazardous waste and the phasing-out of persistent organic pollutants; and various conventions and treaties relating to the protection of humans rights.

▌ Organisations

▌ **African Institute of Corporate Citizenship (AICC).** AICC is a non-governmental organisation (NGO) committed to promoting responsible growth and competitiveness in Africa by changing the way companies do business there. The Institute focuses on the development of relevant corporate responsibility standards for South African companies operating in Africa. **http://www.aiccafrica.org**

▌ **Business Against Crime SA (BACSA).** Since 1996, BACSA has been assisting the government to enhance the efficiency of the Criminal Justice System (CJS). **http://www.bac. co.za**

▌ **Institute for Corporate Citizenship (ICC).** The ICC at UNISA provides training and education, conducts research and creates a platform for information sharing and professional advice. The Centre also assists organisations in transforming and integrating corporate citizenship into their management practices. **http://www.unisa.ac.za/ccc**

▌ **Centre for Responsible Leadership (CRL).** The CRL at the University of Pretoria is a multi-disciplinary, inter-faculty unit that aims to develop a new generation of responsible leaders committed to social and environmental justice. **http://www.up.ac.za**

▌ **National Business Initiative (NBI).** NBI is a voluntary membership-based group of leading national and multinational companies, working together towards sustainable growth and development in SA through partnerships, practical programmes and policy engagement. **http://www.nbi.org.za**

▌ **South African Business Coalition on HIV and AIDS (SABCOHA).** SABCOHA aims to coordinate a private sector response to the HIV/AIDS epidemic. It is a member-driven organisation that produces research and practice models, and it lobbies for policy change. SABCOHA reported having 178 members in March 2009. **http://www.sabcoha.org**

▌ Case studies

Pick 'n Pay

One approach to CSR is where practices are perceived as informal, unsystematic or even 'whimsical', as they are directed by the paternalistic 'whim of a company chief executive or chair' (Friedman *et al.* 2005). Such CSR is based on the values of senior leadership, as is typical of Pick 'n Pay, a chain of family-owned retail and franchise stores operating throughout SA and abroad. Pick 'n Pay's CSR is based on 'a vague notion of what will attract favourable publicity rather than an analysis of society' (Friedman *et al.* 2005). Pick 'n Pay supports diverse programmes, although they all tend to address major developmental challenges, such as HIV/AIDS, education, joblessness and economic growth. However, the company does not focus on any particular areas of need or social concern. Instead, the philosophy is to benefit as many people and projects as possible with the aim of receiving positive publicity. A closer look at this type of CSR illustrates that social investment and marketing is closely intertwined (Friedman *et al.* 2005). **http://www.picknpay.co.za**

AngloGold Ashanti

A second typical approach to CSR is based on systematic decision-making guided by institutional policies. Operationally, CSR is approached as a professional area that requires good management. Relationships with societal stakeholders — often aimed at communities wherein the business operates — are purposeful with clear parameters. Planning, budgeting and screening of applications are typical of the professional and systematic approach (Carapinha and de Jongh 2008). The mining company AngloGold Ashanti epitomises this type of CSR (Friedman *et al.* 2005) which, although not new, is significantly influenced by mandatory guidelines such as the Mining Charter and other codes aimed at standardisation and accountability. **http://www.anglogold.com**

BHP Billiton (SA)

The third practice type is a promising approach aimed at integrating CSR into all business strategies and processes. BHP Billiton (SA) is emerging as a leader and innovator in institutionalising CSR. The 2007 Accountability Rating™ (CSRNetwork *et al.* 2007) awarded BHP Billiton the first prize in overall performance for the second time. The 522 page Sustainability Report released by BHP Billiton provided a robust description of the company's dual strategy that integrates its core business with broader sustainability dimensions. The company has also developed a Sustainable Development Road Map, which is a strategy map embedded at the strategic, operational and commodity level to ensure compliance, risk management, responsibility and innovation. BHP Billiton clearly recognises the importance of social, environmental and broader economic (SEE) issues to the growth of the company. Material issues are identified and the processes, by which these issues are addressed, are described. A clear linkage between various stakeholder groups and their corresponding material issues are also noted. **http://www.bhpbilliton.com/bb/home.jsp**

■ Education

A review of the 17 accredited MBA programmes in SA revealed that CSR is minimally integrated into core course curricula (Hamann *et al.* 2006). However, CSR is more prominent in elective course offerings. It is concerning that at least 30% of schools included no explicit reference to CSR themes whatsoever in their curricula.

Three South African MBA programmes are listed in the 2007–2008 *Beyond Grey Pinstripes* survey by the Aspen Institute (2008):

- **Graduate School of Business at Stellenbosch University** (ranked 70th among Global 100 in 2007–2008 and 39th in 2010) (ranked 10th of Top Ten International Schools). **http://www.usb.sun.ac.za**

- **Rhodes University Investec Business School** (ranked 80th among Global 100). **http://www.ru.ac.za/businessschool**

- **University of Cape Town Graduate School of Business** (ranked 96th). **http://www.gsb.uct.ac.za**

Over and above the CSR course offerings in MBA education, various institutes and executive training programmes offer CSR education and training. In comparison, these course offerings seem to address the need for pragmatic knowledge and skills aimed at addressing and managing CSR (Hamann *et al.* 2006).

References

Alperson, M. (1995) *Foundations for a New Democracy: Corporate Social Investment in South Africa* (Johannesburg: Ravan).

Aspen Institute (2008) 'Beyond Grey Pinstripes 2007–2008: Preparing MBAs for Social and Environmental Stewardship'; http://www.beyondgreypinstripes.org/rankings/bgp_2007_2008.pdf, accessed 10 April 2009.

AVERT (2009) 'HIV and AIDS in South Africa'; http://www.avert.org/aidssouthafrica.htm, accessed 16 March 2009.

Bezuidenhout, A., D. Fig, R. Hamann and R. Omar (2007) 'A Political Economy of Corporate Social and Environmental Responsibility in South Africa', in D. Fig (ed.), *Staking Their Claim: Corporate Social and Environmental Responsibility in South Africa* (Pietermaritzburg, South Africa: University of KwaZulu-Natal Press): 13-94.

Carapinha, R., and D. de Jongh (2008) 'The Meaning and Nature of Corporate Citizenship in South Africa: A Review of Historical and Contemporary Drivers', in *Trends in Corporate Citizenship: A Study of Global vs. Local Perspectives* (Commissioned by the Global Education and Research Network; Boston, MA: Boston College for Corporate Citizenship): 58-79.

CSRNetwork, Accountability and Unisa Centre for Corporate Citizenship (2007) 'Accountability Rating™ 2007: An Analysis of the Financial Mail Top 51 Companies of South Africa', October 2007; http://www.unisa.ac.za/contents/colleges/col_econ_man_science/ccc/docs/Accountability%20Rating%202007%20Report.pdf, accessed 27 May 2010.

Dagut, S., and A. Bernstein (2008) 'South Africa's Electricity Crisis: How did we get here? And how do we put things right?'; http://www.cde.org.za/article.php?a_id=312, accessed 1 April 2009.

Dawkins, C.D., and F.W. Ngunjiri (2008) 'Corporate Social Responsibility Reporting in South Africa: A Description and Comparative Analysis', *Journal of Business Communication* 45.3: 286-307.

Dickinson, D. (2004) 'Corporate South Africa's Response to HIV/AIDS: Why So Slow?', *Journal of Southern African Studies* 30.3: 627-50.

Dorrington, R.E., L.F. Johnson, D. Bradshaw and T. Daniel (2006) *The Demographic Impact of HIV/AIDS in South Africa: National Provincial Indicators for 2006* (Cape Town, South Africa: Center for Actuarial Research, South African Medical Research Council and Actuarial Society of South Africa).

EIA (Energy Information Administration) (2009) 'South Africa Energy Data, Statistics and Analysis: Electricity'; http://www.eia.doe.gov/cabs/South_Africa/Electricity.html, accessed 10 April 2009.

Friedman, S., J. Hudson and S. Machey (2005) 'Like Chalk, Like Cheese: Professionalism and Whim in Corporate Giving at AngloGold Ashanti and Pick & Pay. The State of Social Giving in South Africa' (Report Series Research Report 2; Durban: Centre for Civil Society, University of Kwa-Zulu Natal; http://www.ukzn.ac.za/ccs/files/Corporate%20Giving%20Steven%20Friedman.pdf.pdf, accessed 8 June 2010): 1-36.

Hamann, R. (2008) 'CSR in South Africa: On the Role of History, the Government, and Local Context', in S.O. Idowu and W.L. Filho (eds.), *Global Practices of Corporate Social Responsibility* (Berlin: Springer): 435-459.

——, L. Van Duin, C. Appels, E. Taylor and E. Akor (2006) 'Corporate Citizenship in South African Business Education', *South African Journal of Business Management* 37.2: 45-53.

Hemson, D. (2007) 'Mid-term Review of the Expanded Public Works Programme: Perceptions of the EPWP by Government Officials'; http://www.hsrc.ac.za/research/output/outputDocuments/5470_Hemson_MidtermreviewofEPWPResearchreport.pdf, accessed 1 April 2009.

IOD (Institute of Directors) (2009) 'King Report on Corporate Governance for South Africa 2009' (Johannesburg: Institute of Directors).

ISO (International Standards Organization) (2008) 'The ISO Survey 2007' (Geneva: ISO Central Secretariat; **http://www.iso.org/iso/survey2007.pdf**, accessed 10 April 2009).

Mangaliso, M.P. (1997) 'South Africa: Corporate Social Responsibility and the Sullivan Principles', *Journal of Black Studies* 28.2: 219-38.

Pretorius, R. (2002) 'Social Development Partnerships between the Corporate Sector, the Government and Nonprofit Organisations' (MA thesis, University of Stellenbosch, South Africa).

Rieth, L., M. Zimmer, R. Hamann and J. Hanks (2007) 'The UN Global Compact in Sub-Saharan Africa', *Journal of Corporate Citizenship* 28 (Winter 2007): 1-15.

Rossouw, G.J., A. Van der Watt and D.P. Malan (2002) 'Corporate Governance in South Africa', *Journal of Business Ethics* 37: 289-302.

RSA (Republic of South Africa) (2008) 'National Response to South Africa's Electricity Shortage'; **http://www.info.gov.za/otherdocs/2008/nationalresponse_sa_electricity1.pdf**, accessed 1 April 2009.

Trialogue (2008) 'The CSI Handbook' (ed. H. de Wet; Johannesburg: Trialogue Publications).

Visser, W. (2005) 'Corporate Citizenship in South Africa: A Review of Progress since Democracy', *Journal of Corporate Citizenship* 18 (Summer 2005): 29-28.

Whiteside, A., and C. Sunter (2000) *AIDS: The Challenge for South Africa* (Cape Town, South Africa: Human & Rousseau Tafelberg).

47 South Korea

Angela Joo-Hyun Kang

Founder and CEO, G-CEF (Global
Competitiveness Empowerment Forum)

Sam Yoon-Suk Lee

Founder and CEO, InnoCSR

∎ Context

South Korea, officially called the Republic of Korea (ROK), is situated in the southern half of the Korean peninsula with a population of 48 million. South Korea was a recipient country of the World Bank in the 1960s but successful modernisation, the so-called 'Miracle of Han River', made it a G-20 member country as the 13th world economic power with a GDP of USD20,820 per capita in 2008.

South Korea has a long and volatile history. Its founding father, Dangun, established Go-Joseon in 2,333 BC. The Shilla dynasty united the Korean peninsula in the year 668, ending the Three-Kingdom period. After the Koryo Dynasty (918–1392), Chosun Dynasty (1392–1910) and the Japanese colonisation (1910–1945), the Korean peninsula was divided into South and North Korea as an outcome of the Korean War (1950–1953). During the administration of President Rhee Syng-Man (1948–1960), reconstruction from the 'ashes' was a national focus.

From 1962, the government led economic development with a series of five-year economic development plans. President Park Chung-Hee (1961–1979), President Chun Doo-Hwan (1979–1988), President Rho Tae-Woo (1988–1993) and the first civilian President (after 32 years of military rule) Kim Young-Sam (1993–1998) all strived for industrialisation. South Korea successfully hosted the 1988 Seoul Olympics. It also overcame the 1997 Asian financial crisis. President Kim Dae-Jung (1998–2003) and President Roh Moo-Hyun (2003–2008) tried to reform the centralised economic system and corporate governance. Facing the 2008 global financial crisis, President Lee Myung-Bak's administration (2008–present) lays the emphasis on an economy based on pragmatism.

The business community has been a powerful force in social change and national development. For example, during the Chosun Dynasty, it is known (Park 2008) that élite merchants with management and trade leadership influenced social innovation of the four-class social structure: scholars, farmers, artisans and merchants, in descending order. Large conglomerates, known as *Chaebols*, governed by families, accumulated economic influence by rebuilding the economy and encouraging the growth of sophisticated industrial structuring such as the semiconductor, IT and auto industries. Research on socially responsible investment (Choi and Shin 2007) shows that from 1986 to 2006, of the 50 largest corporations in South Korea, 20 belonged to four *Chaebols* (Samsung, LG, Hyundai and SK Groups) and had approximately 40–57% of sales relative to GDP and 56–69% of assets relative to GDP.

Civil society organisations (CSOs) have played an important role in achieving democratisation including the national election of the President in 1987. CSOs have advocated economic, social and environmental justice and transparent relationships between businesses and the government, to overcome the adverse effects of compressed economic growth.

CSR models that are found currently in South Korea are rooted in historical, religious and cultural traditions. The founding philosophy of South Korea is *Hong-Ik-In-Gan* (弘益人間), which means 'benefiting all humankind widely'. It has become the central virtue of South Korean *noblesse oblige*. South Korea's spiritual heritages of Buddhism, Confucianism, Christianity and Chondogyo are also a good foundation for respecting stakeholder interests.

The key virtue of Confucianism, *In* (仁), meaning 'goodness and empathy for human beings', is regarded as a fundamental value that enables solidarity between self and others, and peace of *Gong-Dong-Che* (共同體), or 'community'. This incorporates *Gong-Dong-Che* customs such as considering 'we' rather than 'I'. *Hyang-Yak* is a cooperative precept based on Confucianist principles which recommend moral and social support. *Doo-Rae* is a voluntary grassroots farming practice to help with harvesting labour, and *Poom-Ahat-Yi* is similar to *Doo-Rae*, though on a smaller scale (Lee *et al*. 2005).

Another virtue of Confucianism, *Zhong-Yong* (中庸), or 'mean', pursues the ideal of moderation, avoiding excesses and deficiencies. It is reflected by wise resource consumption, economic and social value creation and balance between shareholders and stakeholders. It is believed that it can be obtained by realisation of the 'ethical self' as a principal of action (Lee *et al*. 2005).

Christian missionaries have also influenced the philanthropic practices of individuals, corporations and faith-based social service organisations.

Models of CSR

There are five CSR models in South Korea at present, and these are shown in Table 47.1. They are not stage-based developmental models. Key concepts are merely drawn to show the most distinctive characteristic of model categorisation and can be associated with other models as well. Multiple models can exist within a corporation.

▌ Priority issues

Environment

Low-carbon green growth is one of the major policies of the current President Lee's administration to address climate change, reduce greenhouse gas emission and foster green technology. The Climate Change Committee, the National Energy Committee and

Table 47.1 CSR models in South Korea

No.	Model	Key concepts	Focus	Leadership
1	Individual philanthropy	*Hong-Ik-In-Gan*	*Noblesse oblige* and socioeconomic enterprise	Founder, owner and/or CEO
2	Corporate community involvement	*In and Gong-Dong-Che*	Corporate philanthropy, domestic and overseas corporate volunteerism	Employee volunteer corps, often joint engagement with their families, business partners, customers and social service organisations
3	Ethical management	Self-purification as ethical self	Anti-corruption, transparency, accountability, environment and quality management, etc.	Internal departments such as business ethics, compliance, audit, general affairs and HR
4	Cross-sector alliance	*Gong-Dong-Che*	Social enterprise focusing job creation for independence of the disadvantaged	Government-led partnerships with corporations, social service organisations and academic institutions
5	Sustainability management	*Zhong-Yong*	Environment, social and governance (ESG)	Socially responsible investors and corporations, themselves with holistic organisational structures

the Korean National Commission on Sustainable Development were merged into the Presidential Committee on Green Growth, which leads national green strategy and has the goal of making South Korea the seventh green power country in the world by 2020.

Labour

Social issues include an unstable labour market and unemployment. The middle class has declined from 65% to 60% between 1997 and 2005. The Federation of Korean Trade Unions states that 54% of the working population are irregular workers, about twice the proportion of the OECD country average. In 2008 their wages were only 50% that of the regular workforce. The unemployment rate continues to increase and was around 4% as of February 2009. Hence, job creation has become a key issue on the national agenda. In 2009, the National Tax Service announced that corporations engaged in job creation and sharing will be exempt from tax audits.

Corporate governance

Illegal inheritance, excessive exercise of corporate ownership, limited independence of corporate board directors, accounting fraud and stock price manipulation are issues that result in what is known as the 'Korea Discount', referring to undervalued stock prices of South Korean corporations. In 2006, the Federation of Korean Industries (FKI) surveyed 1,000 members of the public and 201 businesspeople on their perception of business. Positive recognition was 14% whereas negative recognition amounted to 48%. In a similar survey conducted in 2005, 68% of business participants felt that anti-business sentiments were serious and 74% wanted to overcome this with ethical and transparent management. In 2006, South Korea ranked 21st of 30 countries in Transparency

International (TI)'s Bribe Payers Index (where 1st is best). In 2005, TI Korea acted as a catalyst to produce the Social Pact on Anti-Corruption and Transparency (K-PACT), the first national alliance of public, private, civil society and political sectors.

▮ Trends

We can see trends across all five CSR models.

Individual philanthropy (Model 1)

In 2008, the Center on Philanthropy at the Beautiful Foundation and School of Social Welfare at Yonsei University announced the Yuhan-Kimberly Giving Index regarding the Korean public's recognition, attitude and status of giving and volunteering in 2007.

Corporate community involvement (Model 2)

The FKI 2005 survey showed that the contribution to national and social development ranked as the top priority of South Korean corporations (26%), followed by customer satisfaction (23%) and profit maximisation (20%). FKI noted a six-fold increase in corporate philanthropy budgets from 1996 to 2006. In 2005, the Korea Nonprofit Academic Association and FKI launched the Korea Social Contribution Index assessing companies' social vision, strategy, implementation, infrastructure, stakeholders, communication, evaluation and employee volunteering.

Ethical management (Model 3)

FKI launched FKI-BEX (FKI-Business Ethics Index) to assess ethical management policies and practice with sector-specific consideration. FKI's 2008 survey of 200 member corporations showed that 95% had adopted a code of conduct and 91% held business ethics training. Over 60% responded that ethical management increased revenue, competitiveness and brand awareness.

Cross-sector alliance (Model 4)

Corporate community involvement also utilises cross-sector alliances, but Model 4 focuses especially on hybrid corporate community involvement programming to support social enterprises for job creation for the vulnerable, collaborating with the government and non-governmental organisations (NGOs). As of 2009, 251 social enterprises have been certified by the Ministry of Labor. The business school community (Social Enterprise Conference 2009 [KDI and Columbia Business School 2009]) advocates that state-led social enterprise momentum should go beyond social services by maximising market mechanisms for higher scalability and impact on society.

Sustainability management (Model 5)

The number of sustainability reports from South Korea increased almost fourfold from 11 to 42 between 2005 and 2008. Electronics, computers, utilities, and oil and gas sectors are the most active in reporting.

As of September 2009, Lotte Shopping, POSCO, Samsung Electronics, Samsung Electro-Mechanics, Samsung SDI and SK Telecom became members of the Dow Jones Sustainability Indexes.

The Business Institute for Sustainable Development launched by the Korea Chamber of Commerce & Industry announced the Korea Climate Change Index to gauge corporate responses to climate change and external corporate environmental changes. The 2008 Carbon Disclosure Project surveyed the top 50 Korean corporations on climate change risk management, and found that 88% of respondents had already taken detailed action or were preparing to do so.

In 2008, the National Human Rights Commission of Korea, Center for CSR and KO-CSR undertook a survey and analysis of human right policies and management practices of major Korean corporations including questions on key ILO standards to 100 corporations listed in the World Index of the Financial Times Stock Exchange.

The Korea Corporate Governance Service conducts annual corporate governance ratings. In 2008, Korea Telecom, KT&G, POSCO, SK Telecom and Woori Financial Group were praised for upholding the rights of small shareholders and the independence of the board of directors.

The Economic Research Institute for Sustainable Society issued the 2008 Sustainability Review of Korea's Top 100 Companies with Samsung Electronics ranking as number one.

▮ Legislation and codes

There is a wide range of legal requirements related to corporate responsibilities (Rho 2009), including the **Constitution**, the **Civil Act**, the **Commercial Act**, the **Consumer Protection Act**, the **Labor Standards Act**, the **Framework on Environmental Policy**, the **Anti-Corruption Act** and the **Monopoly Regulation and Fair Trade Act**.

More specifically, the **Social Enterprise Promotion Act** (July 2007) proposed by the Ministry of Labor provides certification of social enterprises and financial and tax benefit support, thereby supporting the cross sector alliance model of CSR.

The addition of the ninth clause defining sustainability management to the **Industrial Development Act** (August 2007), proposed by the Ministry of Knowledge Economy (the former Ministry of Commerce, Industry and Energy) relates to the sustainability management model of CSR.

The **Low Carbon Green Growth Act** proposed by the Presidential Committee on Green Growth became active on 14 April 2010.

▮ Organisations

The following CSR-related organisations exist in South Korea:

- **Business Institute for Sustainable Development of Korea Chamber of Commerce and Industry**. http://www.bisd.or.kr

- **Center for Sustainability Management**. http://csm.ips.or.kr

- **Community Relations Center**. http://www.crckorea.kr
- **Global Compact Korea Network**. http://www.unglobalcompact.kr
- **Hankyoreh Economic Research Institute**. http://www.heri.kr
- **Korea Standards Association**. http://www.ksa.or.kr
- **Korea Sustainability Investing Forum**. http://www.kosif.org
- **Korean Business Council for Sustainable Development**. http://www.kbcsd.or.kr
- **Social Cooperation Department of the Federation of Korean Industries**. http://www.fki.or.kr
- **Sustainability Services Center of Korea Productivity Center**. http://www.kpc.or.kr

∎ Case studies

Hyundai-Kia Motors Group

Hyundai-Kia Motors Group designed 'Easy Move' cars for the physically challenged through collaboration between its research and development, technical engineering and corporate community involvement departments. SCEM (Supply Chain Environment Management), SCEP (Supply Chain Equal Partnership) and SCCM (Supply Chain Carbon Management) are all green partnership programmes under sustainability management. The company's CSR committee is headed by its Group Chairman, Chung Mong-Koo, to orchestrate horizontal and vertical organisational structure in both headquarter and overseas networks.

Kyobo Life Insurance

Kyobo Dasomi Care Service is a hybrid programme of corporate community involvement and social enterprise collaborating with the Work Together Foundation and the Ministry of Labor. It enables women with low incomes to be trained as patient caregivers, providing nursing services for disadvantaged and senior patients.

Samsung Group

Samsung Group's Community Service Corps was established in 1997 and was followed by a flourishing of employee volunteerism in other *Chaebols*. Reflecting *Gong-Dong-Che* (共同體) or community value and cooperative customs in agricultural society, Samsung Group's employee volunteering programme, One Company One Rural Village was praised by the Chinese *Renmin Daily* in 2006.

SK Group

The philosophy of SK Group is embedded in the SK Management System (SKMS). Chey Tae-Won, its current Chairman, is a UN Global Compact Board member and a strong advocate of CSR. SK Telecom's Mobile Safety Net programme utilises its mobile technology for: searches for missing children; emergency rescue; donation-giving; and e-counselling. Employees' families, business partners and customers participate in the Group's nationwide 'Sunny' volunteer programme. SK Telecom's ethical management provides an online hotline to report any grievance by internal and external stakeholders and provides direct access to the Chair of the Audit Committee, an independent board member.

Yuhan Corporation

Dr New Il-Han, an independence movement activist, educator and entrepreneur, founded Yuhan Corporation in 1926 based on his philosophy that only healthy people can restore their nation's sovereignty and overcome Japanese colonisation. Yuhan Corporation was the first pharmaceutical company to be publicly traded and to adopt an employee stock ownership programme in 1962. Dr New founded Yuhan University and Yuhan Technical High School. He passed away in 1971 leaving all his wealth to the public foundation Korean Society and Education Aid Trust Fund. Its joint venture with Kimberly-Clark, Yuhan-Kimberly Ltd, is recognised in Korea, Asia and North America for its leading corporate citizenship efforts as well as harmonious labour relations.

▋ Education

- **Kookmin University** provides a Business Ethics course in collaboration with its Sustainability Management Center.

- **Korea Advanced Institute of Science and Technology (KAIST)** School of Business offers a Business and Society course for various MBA programmes cooperating with its CSR Research Center.

- **Yonsei University** School of Business and College of Engineering run social entrepreneurship courses collaborating with Yonsei Social Enterprise Center (YSEC). Interdisciplinary curriculums integrating engineering and business skills will also be introduced.

References

Choi, J.-S., and J.-K. Shin (2007) '2007 Report: SRI in Korea' (Seoul: KOSIF [Korea Sustainability Investing Forum]).

KDI and Columbia Business School (2009) 'International Conference on Social Enterprise 2009' (Seoul: Yonsei University/KAIST, 11–12 March 2009).

Lee, D.-C. *et al.* (2005) *Eastern Philosophy in the 21st Century: Future of East Asia Opening with 60 Keywords* (Seoul: Eulyumunwha-Sa).

Park, E.-S. (2008) *History of Market: Changing History of Market and Merchant* (Seoul: Yeoksabi-pyeong-Sa).

Rho, H.-K. (2009) 'Seminar Presentation about Korean Government Policy towards CSR', in H.-K. Rho, *CSR with Three Perspectives: Materiality, SRI and Government* (Seoul: Konrad Adenauer Stiftung and KOSIF, 19 February 2009).

48 Spain

José Manuel Almela Burgos
Independent consultant on CSR

Germán Granda Revilla
Managing Director, Forética

Ricardo Trujillo Fernández
CSR Analyst, Forética

∎ Context

Spain has an area of 504,645 km² and a population of 46 million, being the 9th world power according to nominal GDP.[1] Although it has traditionally been an agricultural country, and is currently still one of the largest producer of agricultural goods in Europe, the industrial growth created in the mid 1950s quickly displaced agriculture as the leading economic activity of the country.

Spanish business has always internalised diverse responsible actions that might be considered good CSR practices, albeit unconsciously and in an ad hoc way. Its historically determined mix of cultures and the role of Catholicism in education have instilled values such as charity or helping one's neighbour. These might be considered the precursors of CSR.

Another important factor is the immigration flows that Spain has experienced, especially in recent years. This diversity of coexisting cultures has developed a spirit of cooperation and integration of minorities into society, making Spain open to the emergence of sustainability.

Models of CSR

Spain's history has been shaped by the Anglo-Saxon world, and this is also true for CSR, especially among large transnational companies. During the last decade, an increasing number of companies have started to voluntarily implement various social initiatives to control or compensate for the social or environmental externalities resulting from their

---

1 IMF World Economic Outlook Database, April 2009.

activities. There are, however, different points of view on CSR among the main societal actors.

As a country committed to sustainable development, the Spanish government is working on a policy for CSR that is shaped by negotiations between civil society, business and workers. These efforts are placed within the Social Negotiating Table, which is informed by a multi-stakeholder advisory board, the CSR State Council.

Different professional or civil society organisations are spreading the concept of CSR, including Forética, AECA, the Observatories of CSR of the Trade Unions CCOO or UGT, and the CSR Commission of the General Council of Economists Association. They have taken the role of researcher and educator. Employers, in their turn, are beginning to understand that CSR is about a long-term investment that will yield returns in terms of competitiveness.

■ Priority issues

Sustainable growth

Since 2006, various working committees have contributed to the creation in 2008 of the 'State Council of CSR'. In January 2010, the State Fund for Employment and Local Sustainability was launched. It was established in terms of RD 13/2009 of 26 October and was worth EUR8 billion, to be funded through municipal authorities and focusing on the environment, economic innovation and social initiatives.

Small and medium-sized enterprises (SMEs)

One of the main problems facing Spanish industry is fragmentation. According to the National Statistics Institute,[2] 99% of Spanish companies have fewer than 50 workers. In addition, from a total of 3.3 million companies registered in January 2007, 51% were micro enterprises, where the owner was also the sole employee. As a result, the State Council of CSR has marked the development of specific tools to promote CSR in SMEs as one of its main areas of interest.

Unemployment

National unemployment stands at 3.7 million, which reflects an upward trend.[3] According to IMF forecasts, unemployment in late 2009 will be 18.2%, rising to 20.2% by the end of 2010. This makes job creation one of the major political and economic issues of the next few years.

Renewable energy

Spain is betting heavily on clean energy, targeting 20% of energy from renewable sources by 2020 and thus becoming a technological leader in this emerging market. Already, more than 100 Spanish companies are specialising in sustainable energy technologies and preparing to penetrate international markets.

2 Instituto Nacional de Estadística, INEbase, 2007 figures.
3 *Ibid.*, September 2009.

Environment and climate change

The main environmental problems affecting Spain, aggravated by climate change, are the loss of water resources; coastal regression; loss of biological diversity and natural ecosystems; and increases in soil erosion processes, all causing serious impacts on various economic sectors. In 2007, the Ministry of Environment defined the Spanish Strategy for Climate Change and Clean Energy with a first horizon in 2012. Included are a series of policies and measures to mitigate climate change and achieve energy consumption compatible with sustainable development.

■ Trends

An analysis of CSR in Spain shows an encouraging, albeit complex, picture, with progress still needed to align with the CSR directives and guidelines of the European Union (EU).

Perhaps the greatest challenge is achieving CSR penetration within Spanish SMEs. According to Report Forética (2008a), more than 90% of companies have fewer than ten workers and only 48% of them know what the CSR is about. Nevertheless, 70% of the companies polled agreed that CSR is going to become more important in the future.

In terms of CSR integration into strategy, CSR management systems are increasingly influential in Spain. Around 60 companies are certified to SGE 21, which is an auditable and verifiable standard covering nine CSR management areas.

With regard to communication, Spain is a leader in sustainability reporting. According to the Global Reporting Initiative (GRI) in 2008, more than 12% of CSR reports worldwide come from Spain, with 75% of them reported as A+.[4]

Despite this progress, a survey by CECU (2008) found that 75% of Spanish people cite the lack of information as a key constraint in achieving more responsible consumption. Furthermore (and perhaps reflecting the global economic recession), according to Report Forética (2008a), only 55% of consumers were prepared to pay a premium for socially responsible products or services in 2008, as compared with 61% in 2006.

■ Legislation and codes

Some of the most significant CSR-related legislation includes:

- **LISMI Law 13/1982.** This law provides for the social integration of handicapped people. Among other measures, it establishes the obligation of hiring a minimum quota of 2% of handicapped people in companies with more than 50 workers.

- **LO 3/2007.** This regulates for equality between women and men in society in general, and the workplace in particular.

---

4   Based on a response on each core G3 and Sector Supplement indicator with due regard to the Materiality Principle by either: (a) reporting on the indicator or (b) explaining the reason for its omission; in addition, the report should be externally assured.

- **Regulation PRE/116/2008**. This enacted the Green Public Bid Plan of the General Administration of the government and its public bodies, whereby environmental criteria are applied in the procurement of civil services.

- **Royal Decree 221/2008**. This set up the State Council of Social Responsibility of Companies. It is an advisory body for the government consisting of representatives from different areas of civil service, business, trade unions and CSR-related organisations.

- Another significant CSR-related initiative in Spain is the **Código Conthe** (Code of Good Government). It establishes a series of good practices for the management of Spanish entities listed on the stock market.

- Another voluntary standard is **SGE 21: 2008, System of Ethics and Socially Responsible Management** (Forética 2008b), the first certifiable company standard for CSR.

Organisations

Asepam. A Spanish association of the UN Global Compact set up in 2004, with the objective of supporting, promoting and spreading the incorporation of the ten principles of the Global Compact into the strategic vision of companies and into their daily operations. **http://www.pactomundial.org**

Club de Excelencia en Sostenibildidad. A business association consisting of large companies with the goal of sustainable growth from the economic, social and environmental perspective. **http://www.clubsostenibilidad.org**

Empresa y Sociedad. An organisation that, since 1995, has been promoting social inclusion among companies and savings banks. It has 125 members. **http://www.empresaysociedad.org**

Forética. A nonprofit organisation set up in 1999 involving more than 220 companies, CSR professionals and other organisations (universities, NGOs, etc.) with the aim of promoting social responsibility by providing knowledge and useful tools to successfully develop a competitive and sustainable business model based on CSR. **http://www.foretica.es**

Foro de Reputación Corporativa. A forum for convening meetings, analysis and spreading of trends, and the provision of tools and management models about corporate reputation, founded in September 2002. It has 11 members. **http://www.reputacioncorporativa.org**

■ Case studies

Caja Navarra (CAN)

Caja Navarra is a Spanish savings bank that has introduced a new CSR-based business model founded on transparency and customer participation. For example, they allow customers to contribute to social causes through a 'civic account'. CAN also provides information on the loans it has made to support social organisations and what the activities of these organisations are. Social organisations can also present their projects to be funded by clients, in a programme called 'You Choose, You Decide'. They can also meet people from the organisations they support (encounter points) and work with them as volunteers (VolCan programme).

Ferrovial

Ferrovial is one of the world's leading infrastructure companies, with operations in 48 countries across a range of sectors including construction, airports, toll roads, car park management and maintenance, and municipal services. They are committed to foster CSR within their more than 80,000 suppliers through a supplier agreement model that incorporates CSR and transparency. They also apply a buyer's Code of Ethics.

Sanitas

Sanitas is a leading Spanish insurance company, offering medical and healthcare cover. As a healthcare specialist, the company is strongly engaged in issues of disability. For example, they offer customised healthcare insurance for disabled people and a fully accessible network of hospitals and clinics. They are also committed to employing and integrating disabled people in their organisation, as well as supporting scientific research in this field and the Spanish National Paralympics Team.

■ Education

Some of the universities that offer specific training on CSR are the **University of Alcalá de Henares (http://www.uah.es)** in collaboration with **CIFF (http://www.ciff.net)** or the **University of Barcelona (http://www.uab.cat)**. Business schools of renowned prestige such as **IESE (http://www.iese.edu)**, **ESADE (http://www.esade.es)** and **IE (http://www.ie.edu)** also offer modules on CSR.

References

Asepam (2009) 'Guía de la Gestión Responsable de la Cadena de Suministro. Una alternativa de gestión' ('Guide to the Responsible Management of the Supply Chain. A Management Alternative') (Asepam; **http://www.unglobalcompact.org/docs/issues_doc/labour/tools_guidance_materials/Guxa_Cadena_de_suministr_versixn_Web.pdf**, accessed 8 June 2010).

CECU (2008) 'La Opinión y Valoración de los Consumidores sobre la Responsabilidad Social de la Empresa en España' ('Opinion and Evaluation by Consumers of Social Responsibility in Spain') (Madrid: CECU, 3rd edn; **http://www.cecu.es/GuiaRSE3.pdf**, accessed 8 June 2010).

Dirección General de la Pyme (2008) 'Retrato de las Pymes 2008' ('Portrait of Small and Medium-sized Enterprises 2008') (Madrid: Ministerio de Industria y Comercio).

European Commission (2006) 'Implementing the Partnership for Growth and Jobs: Making Europe a Pole of Excellence on CSR' (COM[2006]136 final; Brussels: European Commission, 22 March 2006).

Forética (2005–2009) 'Colección Cuadernos Forética' ('Forética Notebooks Collection') (series of small-format books analysing specific aspects of CSR; Madrid: Forética; http://www.foretica.es/es/index.asp?MP=31&MS=73&MN=3, accessed 2 April 2010).

—— (2008a) *Informe Forética 2008. La evolución de la Responsabilidad Social de las Empresas en España* (*Forética Report 2008. The Evolution of Social Responsibility of Companies in Spain*) (Madrid: Forética; http://www.foretica.es/es/index.asp?MP=34&MS=89&MN=2&TR=A&IDR=1&iddocumento=480, accessed 8 June 2010).

—— (2008b) *SGE 21:2008 Sistema de Gestión Ética y Socialmente Responsable* (*SGE 21:2008 System of Ethical and Socially Responsible Management*) (Madrid: Forética; http://www.sge21.foretica.es/es/index.asp?TR=C&IDR=214, accessed 8 June 2010).

—— (2008c) *El modelo de empresa del siglo XXI: Hacia una estrategia competitiva y sostenible* (*The Management Model of the 21st Century: Towards a Competitive and Sustainable Strategy*) (Madrid: Forética; http://www.foretica.es/recursos/doc/Biblioteca/19507_263263200894817.pdf, accessed 8 June 2010).

Observatorio de la RSC (2008) 'La RSC en las memorias del IBEX 35' ('CSR in the Reports of IBEX 35') (Madrid: Observatorio de la RSC; http://www.observatoriorsc.org/images/stories/audio/Proyectos/Informe_Memorias_RSC_2008.pdf, accessed 8 June 2010).

Acknowledgements

The authors would like to acknowledge the work of Yasmina Almela Burgos in translating this chapter from Spanish.

49 Sri Lanka

Lalith Gunaratne
Director and Co-Founder, Sage Training Ltd/
LGA Consultants Ltd

Ravi Fernando
Chief Executive Officer, Sri Lanka Institute
of Nanotechnology (Pvt) Ltd

▌ Context

Sri Lanka, an island of 19 million people, has a written history of 2,500 years. Buddhist culture defines a way of life with compassion and generosity as basic tenets. Hindu, Christian and Moorish influences add to the diversity and underscore the principle of charity.

Over the last 30 years, two ethnic communities have polarised — Sinhala in the south and Tamil in the north. The conflict has ended, yet much will be required to reconcile, rebuild and regenerate the nation. This is an ideal time for corporate responsibility to help bring about a sustainable peace through investment in the war zone to create socioeconomic stability.

Sri Lanka was ruled by monarchs as a whole or in parts until the Portuguese landed in 1505 to govern the coastal regions. Colonial rule prevailed under the Dutch (between 1698 and 1795) and British, until the country became independent in 1948.

Sri Lanka has not had corporate philanthropists as such, but there have been wealthy individuals who donated funds to develop schools, hospitals and support religious institutions, thereby promoting social progress among the people.

After independence, a state-led model of corporate responsibility evolved as Sri Lanka adopted a mixed economy with a socialist focus. With large public sector and state-owned companies, boundaries between the state and society were defined. Labour laws were introduced, thereby creating a framework for corporate responsibility in relation to community and worker relationships.

Liberalisation

A neo-liberal model of CSR evolved after 1977 following economic liberalisation and institutional privatisation. CSR was passed onto owners of businesses, who regarded it as a 'new' responsibility.

During this period, companies focused on obeying the law, generating wealth and paying taxes. The government's responsibility was still the welfare of the people. Hence, to give charitably was a choice an individual or a business made on their own. This further broadened the divide between Sri Lankan business and social responsibility.

Political leaders, such as the late President Premadasa, did involve businesses in the development process from the 1980s. However, donations were seen as a way to procure favoured status with the government, including lucrative contracts, rather than authentic acts of social responsibility.

Philanthropy, or *dhana*, is an integral part of Sri Lankan culture, but most businesses have not taken on board the more secular, humanitarian and social development reasons for engaging in CSR.

Global influences and local action

With globalisation in the 1980s interlinking the world and citizens' campaigns against irresponsible business practice, consumer rights movements in the West generated a stakeholder model of CSR, especially in Sri Lankan export industries such as garments and tea. Businesses had to meet their social obligations, closely monitored by external agencies. This brought pressure on shareholders of businesses to not merely look at profits, but also at their impact on society and the environment, both internally and externally.

In the early 1990s, influenced by the new global interest in CSR, many other businesses embraced it, but more as a fad or fashion than an embedded philosophy. This led to CSR getting a bad name as the public became cynical about its use in image building.

Nevertheless, the stakeholder model has started taking root in the 21st century. With so many Sri Lankan companies now doing business internationally, there has been a migration from 'simple' CSR to embedding social responsibility and sustainability as an integral part of the business. A survey by TERI Europe, LGA Consultants and New Academy of Business undertaken for the report 'Sri Lanka: Altered Images' (2003) showed that this is particularly true in larger export businesses. Others display more limited activities such as sponsoring sports and responding to disasters such as the 2004 tsunami.

The new emerging paradigm is strategic sustainability, where enlightened Sri Lankan companies are now embedding triple bottom line initiatives that include social aspects as one of the three pillars of responsibility (along with environmental and economic).

Roles and responsibilities for the corporate sector

Being a developing country, the Sri Lankan government cannot take on the development burden alone. With coordination, there is an opportunity for business to participate in meeting long-term development goals.

A survey by International Alert (2005) showed that the public expects businesses to play a major role in bringing peace to Sri Lanka. The public also expects companies to address social issues for the betterment of society through employment opportunities, by helping the poor, providing relief to customers and through social welfare. When asked about the likelihood of businesses addressing social issues, over 50% of the public said 'somewhat likely'.

Correspondingly, when the business community was asked, over 95% overwhelmingly agreed that they have a role in the betterment of society. When asked whether their businesses should play a role in achieving peace, over 80% said 'yes'. This is not entirely consistent with their historical 'silence' during the most crucial period of Sri Lanka's conflict.

▮ Priority issues

Internally Displaced People (IDP) in the north

Sri Lanka currently has 250,000 IDPs and there is an opportunity for businesses to engage in support programmes, such as the provision of food and other amenities in the short term and helping communities to resettle and re-establish themselves in the longer term. The focus can include assistance with basic infrastructure such as water and sanitation, rebuilding schools, and support in bringing the different ethnic communities back together.

Water

According to UNEP/UN forecasts presented at the CEO Water Mandate, Sri Lanka will be one of the few nations in Asia in 2025 with 'abundant water resources'. However, 'physical and economic water shortages' may prevail in the future. There is therefore an opportunity for corporate Sri Lanka to play a role in securing this resource.

Social dislocation

Over 100,000 Sri Lankan domestic helpers work outside the country in West Asia, and many families are becoming fragmented and socially disoriented due to the absence of mothers. In the short term, there is a need to educate people on the emotional and social impact on their families when they leave them, while in the longer term corporate Sri Lanka could invest in rural areas where most of the migrating women live.

Education

Sri Lanka invests 2.2% of GDP to ensure universal access to education for its citizens. However, investment in Science and Technology is only 0.14% and is reflected in the lack of innovation and patents as an outcome of research and development. There is an opportunity for corporate Sri Lanka to play a vital role in changing this paradigm by steering the education sector towards science and technology and investing more in emerging areas such as nanotechnology.

This left-brained development process needs to work in tandem with 'high touch' and 'high concept' right-brain development, so the new generation is balanced emotionally and spirituality too.

Trends

In 2004, the Ceylon Chamber of Commerce launched its 'Best Corporate Citizen' award. This has become an annual event, with Hayleys winning it three years consecutively. However, the narrow definition of CSR resulted in rewarding only 'outreach programmes' and not embedding the WBCSD definition covering 'employee, community and society' or the UN Global Compact concept of 'spheres of influence'.

In 2008, a Voluntary Agenda for Responsible Business was developed in partnership with the Employees' Federation, Federation of Chambers of Commerce and Industry, ILO, UNDP, International Alert, the Global Compact Network of Sri Lanka, the Corporate Volunteerism Network and with the support of the Sri Lankan government. The Agenda covers the following:

- **Core business activities**. How business is run while keeping to values, ethics and principals internally and externally.

- **Social investment**. How business participates in development programmes to alleviate poverty.

- **Policy dialogue**. How business influences government policy towards sustainable development, poverty alleviation, justice and peace.

- **Co-ordination and action**. How business integrates first and then collaborates with civil society and government to implement the sector-specific responses to Sri Lanka's developmental challenges.

With education and awareness creation, more businesses are looking at the community and environment around them. The **Voluntary Agenda for Responsible Business** — developed by the Ceylon Chamber of Commerce and partners from government, civil society and the donor community — advocates that business should mount a coordinated effort with government and civil society to adopt and implement CSR.

Legislation and codes

Key CSR-related legislation includes the **Penal Code**, **Nuisance Ordinance**, Offences Against Public Property Act, Criminal Procedures Code, **Police Ordinance**, **Bribery Act** and **Public Bodies Ordinance: Corruption**.

Sri Lanka is a signatory to 27 ILO conventions (including those relating to child labour) and adheres strictly to them. The ILO's Decent Work initiative was developed together with the Employer's Federation, trade unions and government (Ministry of Labour Relations and Manpower). Decent Work includes four strategic objectives: fundamental principles and rights at work and international labour standards; employment and income opportunities; social protection and social security; and social dialogue.

Today, labour is protected through many statutes, with the law tending to favour employees in labour disputes, reflecting the socialist leanings of Sri Lankan policy. Many unions that protect workers' rights have strong political associations.

Sri Lanka is also a signatory to other international agreements, such as the Kyoto and Montreal Protocols.

▌ Organisations

▌ The **Board of Investments**. The Board encourages foreign investment and promotes environmental norms and guidelines, as well as regulations for employment of labour. It publishes labour and employment standards covering the industrial relations and labour laws of Sri Lanka.

▌ The **Central Environmental Authority**. The CEA was established in 1980 and regulates business to protect the environment, including land, soil, water, atmosphere, climate, sound, odours, tastes and biological aspects of animals and plants. Manufacturing businesses are obliged to obtain approval through Environmental Impact Examinations and Assessments, on the wastes and pollutants produced, based on the National Environmental Act.

▌ The **Consumer Affairs Authority**. The CAA operates the Fair Trade Commission, Department of Internal Trade and Department of Weights and Measures. It has established consumer societies around the country.

▌ The **Employers' Federation of Ceylon**. The Federation has spearheaded the promotion of legislation and voluntary adherence to codes of practice in good corporate behaviour. It was formed in 1929 by a few enlightened employers after a series of strikes by the labour movement. It has a Responsible Business Initiatives Unit and created schemes such as the Disability Network to encourage the employment of disabled people. It also has codes of practice on gender and HIV/AIDS. **http://www.employers.lk**

▌ *Lanka Market Digest* (*LMD*). In 2008, LMD ratings of top businesses for CSR highlighted the different stages of involvement. They ranged from a focus on corporate sustainability embedding CSR in mainstream business strategy (social and environmental sustainability) while still reflecting the philanthropy paradigm. Among the top ten were: Dialog Telekom MAS, Hayleys, Aitken Spence, Commercial Bank, Brandix, Hemas and John Keells. **http://www.LMD.lk**

▌ The **UN Global Compact (UNGC)**. The Sri Lanka network has 32 members committed to the ten UNGC principles. One member, the Sri Lankan company Hayleys, has played a key role in the Global Platform on the CEO Water mandate.

▌ Case studies

Cargills: Food City

Cargills operates a chain of supermarkets in Sri Lanka and works closely with rural farmers who supply fruit, vegetables, spices and rice. They pay 20% above market prices for produce and guarantee a minimum price to cushion downward price movements. Cargills provides farmers with technical input on the latest agricultural developments and supports methods such as drip irrigation. They have a network of collection centres and work in collaboration with local non-governmental organisations (NGOs) to ensure localised cleaning, processing and packaging, thereby adding value to the local economy. Cargills also guarantees loans for farmers through banks and micro finance. **http://www.cargillsceylon.com**

Hayleys Group

Hayleys has diversified into agriculture, engineering, hospitality, exports and transport. The company was Corporate Citizen of the Year in Sri Lanka 2004–2006 and has been a champion of value-added exports in plantations and agriculture. In 2007 they were globally recognised for their 'Ethical Tea' initiative and commitment to the CEO Water mandate. INSEAD School of Business has written case studies on Hayleys' initiatives. **http://www.hayleys.com**

Hemas Group

Hemas operates in FMCG (fast-moving consumer goods), healthcare, transportation, leisure and strategic investments. The Piyawara programme, launched in 2002, is its primary CSR project. Developed in partnership with the Ministry of Child Development and Women's Empowerment, this focuses on early childhood care and development. They operate 32 child-friendly preschools using a holistic approach to education. This includes teacher training, parental awareness programmes and the provision of children's parks for recreational activities. **http://www.hemasgroup.com**

Jinasena Group

Jinasena Group (pump manufacturers) and its subsidiary Loadstar (a hard rubber tyre manufacturer) have various good CSR practices, such as their internal employee welfare programmes and community development initiatives in the areas where their factories are situated, although they tend not to publicise these activities. **http://www.jinasena.com**

MAS Holdings

MAS is a high-end apparel manufacturer. Its strategic CSR initiative is the Women Go Beyond (WGB) project launched in 2003. The three dimensions of the project cover personal motivation and care of employees; the community surrounding MAS (women and children); and society as a whole. The programme promotes career advancement, computer skills, English language and leadership. WGB trains women in work–life balance, emotional intelligence, communications and managing stress. MAS has gained international recognition and is used as a case study at the INSEAD School of Business. This raised the profile of Sri Lanka as an ethical manufacturer and led to the Garments without Guilt initiative of the Sri Lanka Apparel Manufacturers Association. **http://www.masholdings.com**

References

De Silva, S., and F. Amerasinghe (2004) 'Corporate Social Responsibility: Issues, Problems and Challenges' (Colombo, Sri Lanka; Employers' Federation of Ceylon, August 2004).

The Environmental Foundation Ltd (2006) *Your Environmental Rights and Responsibilities: A Handbook for Sri Lanka* (Colombo, Sri Lanka: Environmental Foundation Ltd).

Gunaratne, L. (ed.) (2008) 'Voluntary Agenda for Responsible Business' (Colombo, Sri Lanka: Ceylon Chamber of Commerce, International Alert, UNDP, ILO, Employees' Federation of Ceylon, Global Compact Network–Sri Lanka, Corporate Volunteerism Network and FCCISL).

—— and R. Vanderwall (2005) *The CSR Handbook* (Colombo, Sri Lanka: Ceylon Chamber of Commerce).

International Alert (2005) 'Peace through Profit: Sri Lankan Perspectives on Corporate Social Responsibility' (Colombo, Sri Lanka: International Alert, January 2005).

Kumar, R., D. Murphy, R. Mortier, C. Rathnasiri and L. Gunaratne (2003) 'Sri Lanka: Altered Images. The 2003 State of Corporate Responsibility' (New Delhi, India: TERI Europe, LGA Consultants and New Academy of Business).

Liyanage, U. (2006) 'Strategy and Society: From CSR to SRB', *Sri Lanka Journal of Management* 10–11 (June 2006): 53-88.

50 Switzerland

Heiko Spitzeck

Lecturer, Doughty Centre for Corporate Responsibility,
Cranfield School of Management, UK

■ Context

Switzerland is known for high-quality products, chocolate, cheese fondue, skiing and for its political neutrality. However, the country also has a rich tradition of responsible and sustainable business rooted in its Protestant ethic.

The Swiss Confederation consists of 26 states (so called Cantons) and unites nearly 8 million people. The city of Berne is the capital of this federal republic which dates back to 1 August 1291 when the first three Cantons joined into a confederation. Today Switzerland is one of the richest countries in the world measured by GDP per capita and cities such as Zurich and Geneva are highly ranked in terms of quality of life. The country has four official languages, French, German, Italian and Romansh.

The oldest religious traditions of the Cantons are Catholic and visibly represented by cathedrals all across the country. The Abbey of St Gallen, for example, holds one of the richest medieval libraries in the world, with over 400 handwritten books that are more than 1,000 years old. This demonstrates the Swiss tradition of science and study, which are still central elements today. However, the reformation brought forward by Calvin and Zwingli in the 16th century split the country into Catholics and Protestants. The famous sociologist Max Weber wrote *The Protestant Ethic and the Spirit of Capitalism* in 1905 and traced economic success to Protestant belief. Protestant thought, which was dominant in financial centres such as Zurich and Geneva, lends support to a capitalist culture and therefore might explain why Switzerland has become an international economic powerhouse.

Another root of its success might be related to its international politics. After Napoleon's invasion in the 18th century, the Congress of Vienna re-established Switzerland's autonomy in 1815 which marks the last time Switzerland fought in an international war. Ever since, the Swiss stance is to apply diplomacy during times of war. This also helped to build a strong sense of unity. Internal politics contain an unusually strong element of direct democracy. In a few Cantons, citizens vote publicly by coming together at a central place for public debate and raising their hands to vote (e.g. in Appenzell Inerrhoden).

Switzerland's economy is built on finance, engineering, chemicals, pharmaceuticals, luxury goods (such as watches) and international organisations. Swiss banks contribute more than 10% to the country's GDP and contain world-famous brands such as UBS, Credit Suisse, Swiss Re and Zurich Financial Services. Famous Swiss corporations include ABB, Adecco, Glencore, Hoffman-La Roche, Holcim, Nestlé, Novartis, Swatch and Xstrata.

Apart from these global players, the Swiss economy is dependent on many innovative SMEs. The country is also host to some of the most important international organisations, such as the IOC (International Olympic Committee), FIFA (Fédération Internationale de Football Association), the Red Cross, UEFA (Union of European Football Associations), UNCTAD (United Nations Conference on Trade and Development), WEF (World Economic Forum), WHO (World Health Organization) and the WTO (World Trade Organization). The presence of these international organisations underlines the fact that Switzerland is a deliberative country of open debate and discussion.

■ Priority issues

There are many issues on the Swiss CSR agenda such as mobility, energy, construction and waste. However, based on the country's strengths in financial services, issues in the public limelight are tax competition and money laundering. Apart from that, the country's approach to climate change might be an interesting case to learn from in order to overcome the traditional regulatory response to social and environmental issues.

Tax competition

Switzerland is an attractive place for doing business and ranked 21st in the ease-of-doing-business index of the World Bank in 2009.[1] With a tax level of 2.7% (tax on corporate income as a percentage of GDP), it offers one of the lowest corporate tax rates within the OECD. As the tax system is based on federal and cantonal taxes, different Cantons compete within Switzerland to attract industry by offering low taxes. A report by PwC in 2006 showed that Canton Obwalden provided the lowest corporate tax of 13.1% (including federal tax) (PwC 2006).

While this tax competition supports industry growth, it also has international consequences and Switzerland has been accused of 'harmful tax competition' by the OECD. Tax competition is considered harmful because the exchange of information between tax authorities is hampered. Swiss banking secrecy has been accused of facilitating tax evasion for foreign nationals who transfer their funds to Swiss accounts. UBS reported in 2002 that 56% of their customers were foreign nationals depositing CHF3.324 billion (Thielemann and Ulrich 2003: 84). Tax evasion refers to individuals employing illegal means so as not to pay their fair share of taxes. In 2008, the European Union (EU) threatened tax havens by blacklisting uncooperative countries, and in March 2009 Switzerland agreed to facilitate the exchange of transparent information allowing foreign authorities to track tax evasion more efficiently.

---

1   http://www.doingbusiness.org/economyrankings, accessed 13 March 2009.

Money laundering

Bank secrecy in Switzerland is based on the Swiss Banking Act of 1934 by which banks are enabled to protect personal information about account holders, for example by the use of numbered bank accounts. This practice has been criticised for facilitating organised crime such as money laundering and tax evasion.

Money laundering refers to the transfer of funds to conceal the fact that they have been obtained by illegal means such as drug trafficking. Led by Transparency International, a group of international banks agreed on the Wolfsberg Principles to fight money laundering. The Wolfsberg Principles have been recognised internationally as a responsible answer to money laundering by Swiss banks.

Climate change

As part of the Kyoto Protocol, Switzerland has agreed to lower CO_2 emissions by 2012. The so called *Klimarappen* (Cent for the climate) was introduced by the oil industry in 2008 as a voluntary charge on petrol to avoid a mandatory CO_2 tax. However, the Swiss CO_2 law mandates the introduction of the tax if the effect of the *Klimarappen* does not show the desired results. Further initiatives to reduce CO_2 emissions in transport are alternative fuels such as bio-ethanol and increasing the usage of public transport or car sharing. Car sharing, combined with rail travel, is increasingly popular in Switzerland and more than 85,000 citizens use 2,300 cars offered at 1,100 service stations by Mobility. The Swiss energy mix relies on water and nuclear power, which is low on CO_2 but raises other serious issues. By international comparison, Switzerland makes use of a high percentage of renewable energy sources.

▮ Organisations

▮ **Netzwerk für sozial verantwortliche Wirtschaft**. The Network for Responsible Business is a platform that connects individuals and organisations interested in socially responsible business. **http://www.nsw-rse.ch**

▮ **Novartis Foundation.** The Novartis Foundation for Sustainable Development promotes development with a human face. **http://www.novartisfoundation.org**

▮ **Öbu**. A think-tank for sustainability and management topics with more than 330 corporate members. **http://www.oebu.ch**

▮ **oikos International**. oikos is the international student organisation for sustainable economics and management and a leading reference point for the promotion of agents for sustainability change. **http://www.oikos-international.org**

▮ **St Gallen Symposium**. The St Gallen Symposium aims at generating stimuli for the sustained success of companies and societies in a globalised world. **http://www.stgallen-symposium.org**

▮ The **Sustainability Forum Zürich**. The Sustainability Forum Zürich provides a dialogue platform for sustainability leaders, primarily in the financial industry. **http://www.sustainability-zurich.org**

■ **Schwab Foundation**. The Schwab Foundation promotes social entrepreneurship as a key element to advance societies and address social problems. **http://www.schwabfound. org**

■ **World Business Council for Sustainable Development (WBCSD)**. WBCSD is a CEO-led, global association of some 200 companies dealing exclusively with business and sustainable development. **http://www.wbcsd.org**

■ **World Economic Forum**. The World Economic Forum is an independent international organisation committed to improving the state of the world by engaging leaders in partnerships to shape global, regional and industry agendas. **http://www.weforum.org**

■ **WWF International**. The mission of the World Wide Fund for Nature is to stop the degradation of the planet's natural environment and to build a future in which humans live in harmony with nature. **http://www.panda.org**

■ Case studies

There are hundreds of companies worthy to be mentioned in this section. In the financial industry one might think of **Alternative Bank Switzerland (http://www.abs.ch)**, **Bank Sarasin (http://www.sarasin.com)** or **Zürcher Kantonalbank (http://www.zkb.ch)**. Other companies with a reputation in sustainable management are **Baer** (Swiss cheese, **http:// www.baer.ch**), **Coop** (retail, **http://www.coop.ch**), **Ernst Schweizer** (construction, **http://www. schweizer-metallbau.ch**) or **responsAbility** (social investments, **http://www.responsability. ch**). In order to cover different industries and organisations of different sizes the following five are described in more detail.

Freitag

Inspired by the trucks passing by their student apartment in the centre of Zürich, Markus and Daniel Freitag — both design students — had the idea of crafting bags from used truck tarp (tarpaulin). They went to a shipping company, and obtained some used truck tarp ready to be thrown away, at no cost. From this they created their first prototype bag, which now has become a symbol of Swiss quality and fashion. The bag is made of 95% recycled material, truck tarp being the main component; the brothers took seat belts for straps and used a spare bicycle inner tube to keep the edges from fraying. The Freitag brothers won the Swiss design award in 1997. Their bags can be found on display in the Museum of Modern Art in New York, Tate Modern in London and the Museum of Design in Zürich. The company produces over 150,000 products every year with an estimated average price of CHF100, leading to annual sales of CHF15 million. **http://www.freitag.ch**

Holcim

Holcim is a leading provider of cement and aggregates (crushed stone, sand and gravel). The company employs more than 48,000 people in over 70 countries. Its vision is to provide a foundation to society's future and its efforts in sustainable development have been recognised by the Dow Jones Sustainability Index, where the company was ranked the leader in its industry from 2005 to 2008. One of many examples of how the company provides value to stakeholders is given by the 'Mi casa' project of Holcim-Apasco in Mexico. To make the construction of homes more affordable to customers of lower income, the company provides standard components at low cost and trains their customers on how to build a quality house. Through this initiative, it is estimated that Holcim-Apasco has supported the construction or improvement of approximately 400,000 homes all over Mexico. **http://www.holcim.com**

Migros

Gottlieb Duttweiler opened his retail business with five trucks selling basic products in the streets of Zürich on 25 August 1925. From the very beginning the company placed great emphasis on values and sustainability. Migros is today one of Switzerland's largest enterprises (with more than CHF25 billion in sales in 2008), the largest supermarket chain and the largest employer (with more than 80,000 employees). In 1941 Migros converted from being a public listed company into a cooperative by giving out membership vouchers to customers and employees. Migros has a proven track record in sustainable management. It has introduced product labels such as Marine Stewardship Council (MSC) and Forest Stewardship Council (FSC) and was rated 'fairest retailer worldwide' in 2007 by the independent company oekom research AG. Ethical guidelines rule their employment practices and the company has a long history of philanthropic engagement. **http://www.migros.ch**

Precious Woods

Precious Woods is a leading company in sustainably managed tropical rainforests. Apart from growing, trading and selling FSC-labelled wood, the company uses waste wood to produce energy. This local energy production saves CO_2 emissions, which are traded under the Kyoto regime and provide a further income stream to the company. The Swiss company employs 2,300 people worldwide with subsidiaries in Brazil, Costa Rica, Nicaragua, Gabon and the Netherlands. In 2008, Precious Woods reported sales of USD116.7 million. The company was selected to offset all emissions caused by the WEF meeting in 2009. **http://www.preciouswoods.com**

Sustainable Asset Management (SAM)

Sustainable Asset Management was founded in 1995 with an exclusive focus on sustainability investments. Today, the company is considered a global leader in terms of sustainability investing. In cooperation with Dow Jones, SAM compiles the Dow Jones Sustainability Index and has launched similar indexes worldwide. This in turn spurred sustainability innovation in different industries around the globe, as companies are trying to demonstrate their sustainability performance by becoming listed in the index. **http://www.sam-group.com**

∎ Education

Its religious origins have given Switzerland a strong tradition in science, research and education. One of the most famous academics who researched in Switzerland is Albert

Einstein, a pop icon of science. Next to him 113 Nobel Prize winners had a relation to the country and nine Nobel Peace Prizes have been awarded to institutions based in Switzerland.

Among its most prestigious universities is the **Eidgenössische Technische Hochschule (ETH)** in Zürich. The ETH hosts a dedicated centre on the management of Sustainability and Technology (**http://www.sustec.ethz.ch**), investigating how different industries and firms are affected by climate change and carbon constraints and what their response strategies are. The university created an umbrella for sustainability-related research at the end of 2008 (**http://www.sustainability.ethz.ch**). Another high profile research organisation is the European Organization for Nuclear Research (**http://www.cern.ch**), which hosts the world's largest particle physics laboratory.

Research on corporate sustainability and responsibility is spread throughout Switzerland. In the west of the country, researchers at the **HEC** in Lausanne (**http://www.hec.unil.ch**) investigate corporate social responsibility, leadership, corporate branding and the theory of democracy. Close by is the **IMD**, which hosts the Alcan Professor for Environmental Management (**http://www.imd.ch**). A team at the **University of Zürich** researches ethical questions in business and organisational theory (**http://www.iou.uzh.ch**). In eastern Switzerland, the **University of St Gallen** hosts two institutes, one with a focus on economic and business ethics (**http://www.iwe.unisg.ch**) and another on business and the environment (**http://www.iwoe.unisg.ch**).

Genuine Swiss CSR research reflects some of the cultural particularities of the country. Its deliberative roots of direct democracy might have led to the fact that researchers such as Palazzo, Scherer and Ulrich take a Kantian deontological approach. They refer to the insights of the German sociologist Jürgen Habermas, especially his theory of communicative action which serves as a common sociopolitical point of departure. Ulrich has gained a reputation in the German-speaking region as being the founding father of the 'St Gallen Business Ethics School of thought' (see Ulrich 2008).

References

Basu, K., and G. Palazzo (2008) 'Corporate Social Responsibility: A Process Model of Sensemaking', *Academy of Management Review* 33.1: 122-36.

Dyllick, T., and K. Hockerts (2002) 'Beyond the Business Case for Corporate Sustainability', *Business Strategy and the Environment* 11.2: 130-41.

PwC (PricewaterhouseCoopers) (2006) 'Switzerland: Lower corporate tax rates take hold', International Tax Review; **http://www.internationaltaxreview.com/default.asp?Page=10&PUBID=35&ISS=21268&SID=609227**, accessed 12 March 200).

Scherer, A.G., and G. Palazzo (2007) 'Toward a Political Conception of Corporate Responsibility: Business and Society Seen from a Habermasian Perspective', *Academy of Management Review* 32.4: 1,096-120.

Spitzeck, H., M. Pirson, W. Amann, S. Khan and E. von Kimakowitz, (eds.) (2009) *Humanism in Business: Perspectives on Responsible Business in Society* (Cambridge, UK: Cambridge University Press).

Steger, U. (2004) *The Business of Sustainability: Building Industry Cases for Corporate Sustainability* (Basingstoke, UK: Houndmills; New York: Palgrave Macmillan).

Ulrich, P. (2008) *Integrative Economic Ethics: Foundations of a Civilized Market Economy* (Cambridge, UK: Cambridge University Press).

Thielemann, U., and P. Ulrich (2003) *Brennpunkt Bankenethik* (*Focus Banking Ethics*) (Bern: Haupt).

51 Tanzania

Sarah Lauwo

PhD student, Essex Business School;
Lecturer, University of Dar es Salaam

▮ Context

Tanzania, an East African country with abundant natural and human resources, shares a similar policy climate of economic and political transformation with other developing countries as they move towards greater integration into the global economy (Kulindwa 2002). An economic downturn in the 1970s and 1980s, brought about by oil price rises, unfavourable climatic conditions and growing external debt, resulted in Tanzania pursuing economic liberalisation, privatisation and deregulation reforms typical of IMF-led Structural Adjustment Programmes of the time.

Although Tanzania's economy became more linked into the global capitalist system as a result of these reforms, the IMF-imposed policy conditions resulted in drastic cuts in social expenditure, removal of food subsidies, retrenchments, currency devaluation and the introduction of user fees for education and healthcare (Kilimwiko 1994). Meanwhile, Tanzania remained a periphery economy offering cheap raw materials with minimal environmental, labour and tax regulations (Chachage 1995).

The political, social and economic reforms in Tanzania during the 1990s led to the proliferation of multinational corporations (MNCs) in the lucrative extractive sectors of the economy. These MNCs are often criticised for creating environmental degradation, social unrest and economic decline, and yet, with the government unable to adequately provide public services, it is these same MNCs that provide healthcare, education and infrastructure for the community. Hence, CSR in Tanzania is essentially philanthropic in nature.

Companies in Tanzania are increasingly facing demands to improve their accountability and transparency and reduce their social and environmental impacts. Pressure groups such as non-governmental organisations (NGOs), trade unions and the media are calling for MNCs to be more proactive in addressing the indirect effect of their activities on the quality of life of local communities (Doh and Guay 2006). However, the absence of strong state support and empowered stakeholders (including pressure groups interested in CSR and corporate governance) leaves CSR comparatively weak in Tanzania (Melyoki 2005).

▌Priority issues

Combating poverty

Tanzania is among the poorest countries in the world, ranked at 151st of 184 in 2007, with a Human Development Index (HDI) of 0.53, life expectancy of 55 years, and 96.6% of its population living on less than USD2 a day (UNDP 2009). Tanzania's gross national product (GNP) of USD400 per capita has remained very low and is far less than Sub-Saharan Africa and low-income countries' average of USD952 and USD578 respectively (World Bank 2007). Healthcare services in Tanzania are still very poor and inaccessible, leading to an under-5 mortality rate of 116 per 1,000 in 2007 (UNDP 2007) and an increase in the maternal mortality rate from 529 (per 100,000 live births) in 1999 to 578 in 2008 (URT 2008). While 45% of the population in Tanzania has no access to improved and clean water, only 31% of the urban population are using improved sanitation facilitation (UNDP 2009).

Tanzania faces a mature, generalised HIV pandemic, and the impact of the HIV/AIDS pandemic is felt in all social and economic sectors of society, leading to significantly increased health costs, rising infant and childhood mortality, poverty and a growing number of orphans, estimated at 2.6 million (UNDP 2007). Indeed, the privatisation of the health sector and the introduction of 'user fees' in the 1990s has severely reduced access to health services for the majority of poor people living in the rural regions of Tanzania.

▌Education

Tanzania faces considerable challenges in providing an enabling environment for learning. The government lacks the resources to improve educational facilities, so the education service has been deteriorating over recent years, with an index of 0.673, combined gross enrolment ratio of 57.3% and an adult literacy rate of 72.3% in 2007 (UNDP 2009). In most of the poorer regions, the quality of education is significantly low, with only one desk for every 38 pupils, one textbook for every four children, and a gross enrolment of 431 pupils who share two classrooms only (*Guardian* 2010). The pupil-to-teacher ratios are high, with 56 students to one teacher in 2005 (UNICEF 2006).

Environmental issues

Environmental issues are a matter of public concern in Tanzania, particularly relating to pollution of water bodies and other environmental degradations (Chachage 2005). The National Environmental Policy (1997) identified six major problems that require urgent attention: loss of wildlife habitats and biodiversity; deforestation; land degradation; deterioration of aquatic systems; lack of accessible good-quality water; and environmental pollution. The government of Tanzania urges investors to adopt environmentally sustainable natural resource management practices in order to ensure that long-term sustainable economic growth is achieved.

▮ Trends

CSR has recently become an important issue in Tanzania, with increasing numbers of companies embracing it as part of their corporate strategy. To understand CSR trends, it is important to appreciate the historical development of Tanzania towards a market economy in the 1990s.

The modern history of Tanzania began after independence in 1961, with an economy structurally tied to the advanced capitalist economies of Europe (Edie 1987). However, Tanzania struggled to break free from the sociopolitical domination by the former colonial powers (on which the country remained economically dependent) and the economic exploitation by large corporations that controlled trade and finance (Talbot 2000). As a newly independent state, the government of Tanzania was competing for capital inflow from foreign investments; hence, little or no emphasis was given to corporate governance and CSR issues. The government also suffered from inefficiencies and corruption.

In 1967, when former President Julius Nyerere called for the policies of self-reliance and protectionism, encapsulated in the Arusha Declaration, an era of socialism began, which led to a serious sociopolitical and economic crisis. The state-owned enterprises were characterised by corruption, embezzlement, nepotism, managerial incompetence and political interference, with government subsidisation of failing corporations (Melyoki 2005). In the Arusha Declaration itself, little emphasis was given to CSR issues such as employee protection, environmental protection and human rights.

The Structural Adjustment Programs (SAPs) of the 1980s and liberalisation of the 1990s caused the rolling-back of government from active involvement in economic activities, and MNCs became the key players in the production process and economic development of Tanzania. Now, in light of the increased importance of CSR around the world, corporations in Tanzania also find themselves confronted with systematic pressure for organising and incorporating structures responsible for improving CSR and overall corporate governance. This has been mainly through philanthropic initiatives such as corporate investment in education, healthcare, community support and sponsorship.

▮ Legislation and codes

With the support of the World Bank and the IMF, the government of Tanzania has been reforming its laws and regulations to address corporate governance, accountability and CSR issues. However, the institutional frameworks in Tanzania continue to be influenced by its previous colonial experience.

- The **Companies Act of 2002**. This replaced the Companies Act of 1932 (CAP 212), which was enacted in 1929 during British colonial rule, but has incorporated little to curb the social and environmental impacts of MNCs or protect employee rights (Chachage 2005).

- The **Environmental Management Act No. 20 of 2004**. This replaced the National Environment Management Council (NEMC) Act of 1983 and includes provision for sustainable management of the environment, impact and risk assessment, prevention and control of pollution, waste management, environmental quality standards, compliance and participation. For example, section 81 of the Act states: 'An Environmental Impact Assessment (EIA) shall be undertaken for all proposed activities that are likely to have significant adverse impacts on the environment prior to commencement or financing of a project or undertaking in Tanzania' (p. 57).

- The **National Environmental Policy (NEP, 1997)**. This also recognises the importance of EIAs and calls for accountability and control in managing the environment, with the following overall objectives: to ensure sustainable and equitable use of resources without degrading the environment or risking health or safety; to prevent and control degradation of land, water, vegetation, and air which constitute the essential life support systems; to conserve and enhance natural and man-made heritage, including the biological diversity of the unique ecosystems of Tanzania; to improve the condition and productivity of degraded areas including rural and urban settlements in order that all Tanzanians may live in safe, productive and aesthetically pleasing surroundings; to raise public awareness; to promote individual and community participation; and to promote international cooperation (p. 13).

- The **Employment and Labour Relations Act (2004)**. This Act was formulated to address issues such as child labour, forced labour, discrimination in the workplace, employees' rights and freedom of association.

- The **Occupation Health and Safety Act (2003)**. This was enacted to require companies to protect employees against hazards to health and safety arising out of or in connection with activities at work.

- The **Capital Market and Securities Act (1994)**. Amended in 1997, this Act was formulated to enable the creation and development of capital markets that are efficient, transparent, orderly, fair and equitable.

The effectiveness of these policies in addressing CSR in Tanzania, especially their adequacy and compliance, remains questionable and continues to attract criticism within and outside Tanzania (Kulindwa *et al.* 2003; Chachage 2005; Lissu 1999).

▌Organisations

While CSR is still in its infancy in Tanzania, there are a few organisations that have been actively engaged in advocating and promoting CSR practices (Lissu 1999). These include churches, community groups and human rights organisations, which have been challenging the government to change its institutions and address issues such as human rights and environmental protection.

▌ **Christian Aid** has been working closely with the **Lawyers' Environmental Action Team** (LEAT) and the **Norwegian Church**, through its Kenyan office, to promote CSR in Tanzania. **http://www.christian.org.uk**

▌ **Joint Environment and Development Management Action (JEMA)** is a voluntary, nonprofit, action-oriented education programme founded in 1996 at the University of

Dar es Salaam. It comprises a multi-disciplinary team of students, academic staff and graduates who voluntarily contribute and share their knowledge, expertise and time in addressing environmental issues through collaborative actions. **http://www.Jemaudsm. blogspot.com**

▌ **Lawyers' Environmental Action Team (LEAT)** is the most active NGO, established in 1995 with the mission of encouraging sound natural resource management and environmental protection in Tanzania. **http://www.leat.or.tz**

▌ **Norwegian Church Aid in Tanzania** was formed in 2005 to support other civil society organisations in poverty reduction and addressing the problem of environmental degradation. **http://www.norway.go.tz**

▌ The **Christian Council Church** and *National Council of Muslims in Tanzania* have also been working closely with LEAT, especially in promoting CSR in the mining sector. **http://www.cct-tz.org**

▌ Case studies

The mining sector represents one of the industries active in implementing CSR. Mining companies have reported their commitment in supporting the local communities, healthcare and education. Best practice companies include Barrick Gold Corporation in Tanzania (**http://www.barrick.com**), Anglo Gold Ashanti (**http://www.anglogoldashanti. com**) and Resolute Mining Limited (**http://www.resolute-ltd.com.au**), to mention but a few. Beyond the mining sector, other good-practice cases include:

Tanzania Breweries Company Limited

The company has been very active in sponsorship. For example, in the sustainable development report (2008), the company claimed to have a commitment in the fight against malaria and in measuring, monitoring and evaluating CSI investments. The company also claims to manage carefully and exclude any risk of bribery or corruption in its Tanzanian operations. **http://www.sabmiller.com**

Tanzania Celtel Company

A mobile phone company which in 2006, for example, set aside USD100,000 for its CSR initiative under the 'Build of Our Nation' (BON) project. **http://www.tz.zain.com**

Vodacom

A leading cellular network in Tanzania; the company claims to have the responsibility of giving back to society in a way that will not only make a difference and mean something but in a way that can also be sustained. **http://www.vodacom.co.tz**

■ Education

CSR education is still at an early stage in Tanzania. With fewer than 30 higher learning institutions in total and only one business school, there are very few CSR research and teaching opportunities in Tanzania. An exception is the Centre for Environmental Studies (CES) at the University of Dar es Salaam. Other institutions which can offer CSR-related subjects include:

- **College of Business Education**

- **Dar es Salaam School of Accountancy**

- **Faculty of Business and Management of the Open University of Tanzania**

- **Faculty of Public Administration and Management of Mzumbe University**

- **Institute of Finance and Management**

- **University of Dar es Salaam Business School**

References

Chachage S.L. (1995) 'The Meek Shall Inherit the Earth but not the Mineral Rights: The Mining Industry and Accumulation in Tanzania', in P. Gibbon (ed.), *Liberalized Development in Tanzania: Studies in Processes and Local Institutions* (Uppsala, Sweden: Scandinavian Institute of African Studies): 37-108.

Chachage S.L. (2005) Can Africa's Poor Inherit the Earth and all its Mineral Rights?', conference paper presented in *Council for the Development of Social Science Research in Africa*, 11th General Assembly, Maputo, Mozambique, 6–10 December 2005; **http://www.codesria.org**.

Curtis, M., and T. Lissu (2008) 'A Golden Opportunity? How Tanzania is Failing to Benefit from Gold Mining'; **http://www.policyforum-tz.org/node/6823**, accessed 10 June 2010.

Doh, J.P., and Guay, T.R. (2006) 'Corporate Social Responsibility, Public Policy, and NGO Activism in Europe and the United States: An Institutional-Stakeholder Perspective', *Journal of Management Studies* 43.1: 47-73.

Edie, C.E. (1987) 'Socialism, the State and Rural Development in Tanzania and Jamaica', *Journal of African Studies* 14.3: 141-51.

Egel, N. (2005) 'CSR in Electrification of Rural Africa: The Case of ABB in Tanzania', *Journal of Corporate Citizenship* 18: 75-85.

Guardian (2010) 'Just one teacher in a school of 200 pupils', *The Guardian*, 15 February 2010; **http://www.ippmedia.com**.

Kaiser, P.J. (1996) 'Structural Adjustments and the Fragile Nation: The Demise of Social Unity in Tanzania', *Journal of Modern African Studies* 34.2: 227-37.

Kilimwiko, L. (1994) 'IMF Brings Disaster to Tanzania', *Green Left Online* (*GLW*) 151 (July 1994); **http://www.greenleft.org.au/back/1994/151**, accessed 6 April 2010.

Kulindwa, K. (2002) 'Economic Reforms and the Prospect for Sustainable Development in Tanzania', *Development Southern Africa* 19.3: 390-403.

——, O. Mashindano, F. Shechambo and H. Sosuwele (2003) *Mining for Sustainable Development in Tanzania* (Dar es Salaam, Tanzania: Dar es Salaam University Press).

Lissu, T. (1999) 'Plunder Unlimited: The Social, Economic and Environmental Implications of Foreign Investments in Africa with Reference from Tanzania', paper presented at *CSAE Conference*, St Anne's College, Oxford, UK, 15–16 April 1999.

Melyoki, L.L. (2005) 'Determinants of Effective Corporate Governance in Tanzania' (PhD dissertation, University of Twente, Netherlands).

Msambichaka, L.A., N.E. Mwamba and O.J. Mashindano (2006) *Globalisation and Challenges for Development in Tanzania* (Dar es Salaam, Tanzania: Dar es Salaam University Press).

Reed, D. (1996) *Structural Adjustment, Sustainable Development and the Environment* (London: Earthscan).

Rodney, W. (1972) *How Europe Underdeveloped Africa* (London: Bogle-L'Ouverture Publications).

Shivji, I. (2004) 'Reflection on NGOs in Tanzania: What we are, what we are not, and what we ought to be', *Development in Practice* 14.5: 689-95.

Talbot, A. (2000) 'Book Review of *Justifying the Role of Imperialism in Africa: Aid to Africa: So Much to Do, So Little Done,* by Carol Lancaster', 4 August 2000; http://www.wsws.org/articles/2000/aug2000/afri-a04.shtml, accessed 10 June 2010.

UNDP (United Nations Development Programme) (2007) 'Human Development Report 2007/2008. Fighting Climate Change: Human Solidarity in a Divided World (New York: United Nations Development Programme; http://hdr.undp.org/en/media/HDR_20072008_EN_Complete.pdf, accessed 10 June 2010).

—— (2009) 'Human Development Report 2009 Overcoming Barriers: Human Mobility and Development' (New York: United Nations Development Programme; http://hdr.undp.org/en/media/HDR_2009_EN_Complete.pdf, accessed 10 June 2010).

UNICEF (2006a) *The State of the World's Children 2007: Women and Children, The Double Dividend of Gender Equality* (New York: UNICEF).

United Nations Tanzania (2006b) 'United Nations Development Assistance Framework (UNDAF, 2007–10)'; http://www.unicef.org/about/execboard/files/Tanzania_results_matrix_FINAL_July_2006.pdf, accessed 10 June 2010.

URT (United Republic of Tanzania) (2008) 'Millennium Development Goals Report: Mid-way Evaluation 2000–2008'; http://www.tz.undp.org/docs/MDGprogressreport.pdf, accessed 10 June 2010).

Wangwe, S.M. (2000) *Overcoming Constraints on Tanzanian Growth: Policy Challenges Facing the Third Phase Government* (Dar es Salaam, Tanzania: Mkuki na Nyota Publishers).

World Bank (2006) 'World Development'; http://iresearch.worldbank.org, accessed 6 April 2010.

—— (2007) 'World Development Indicators' (Washington, DC: World Bank; http://search.worldbank.org/data?qterm=Tanzania&language=EN&format=html&_topic_exact=Economic+Policy+%26+Debt, accessed 10 June 2010).

52 Thailand

Alex P. Mavro Jr
Founder and Lead Consultant, Social Impact
Ventures Asia, Bangkok, Thailand

▋ Context

Until 1932 Thailand was an absolute monarchy. Since that time, it has been a constitutional monarchy. While it is also a self-described democracy, the Kingdom has endured long periods of military rule under unelected leaders. Rather like China, the system has not always been 'one person, one vote', but it has generally been responsive to popular demands — through the intercession of His Majesty the King, when necessary.

Critical for this treatise is the royal — which is to say paternalistic — heritage. Commercial enterprise before 1932 was nominally under sufferance of the monarch, whose officers controlled everyday life. The tradition of strong centralised control carried over to modern times, with the result that government–business bonds have remained strong. All of the early Thai-owned initiatives were either government- or royally-inspired, and many of those companies continue in business today.

The owners of these companies (up to and including the recent dollar billionaire Prime Minister, Taksin Shinawatra) are generally Thai-Chinese. Thais themselves have a tradition of living within their means and off the land: 'In the water are fish; in the fields, rice' is a common saying. The inference is that if only one is patient enough, all will be provided. The Chinese (in Bangkok and the far south) and the Vietnamese (along the Mekong, in the northeast), form the body of the entrepreneurial class, in a sense estranged from both government and monarchy.

As a result the Thai world-view encompasses business as well as everything else, and is predominately paternalistic, with the wealthier looking after the less well-off when necessary. Those entrusted with power are expected to wield it with discretion and with concern for the greater good, even if that may mean pain for a few individuals. It is a classic patron–client social model.

Interestingly, many in Thailand (and in Asia in general) claim that CSR's historic roots are to be found in the indigenous culture, but it was not called CSR. If you were to oversimplify and consider CSR as consisting of twin tree trunks, intertwined, you might say that one trunk was the 'do no harm' path and the other trunk, the 'correct previous harm' or 'add value' path. In those terms, there is no question that a Buddhist tradition firmly fits into the 'do no harm' context. Among other things, Buddhism teaches moderation in action on the one hand and respect for all life, right down to the lowly mosquito, on the other. Hence, to a degree, Thai claims of cultural affinity to the imperatives of CSR may be accurate.

As for the second path, namely that of 'correcting previous harm', Thai businesses were originally focused on philanthropy, viewing constituents as clients in need of patronage, as government officials used to do. What has been lacking until very recently is a sense of responsibility for the environment, whether in the narrow (green) sense or in the broader sense of 'the people'. Stakeholders were shareholders, and only shareholders merited consideration.

As a result, 80% of the country's original old-growth forests have been destroyed. Fishermen in the Gulf of Thailand have almost exhausted fish stocks, despite repeated warnings, and now poach in neighbouring waters. North of Bangkok, factories pour untreated waste directly into a river that serves millions of people and animals. One of the original government-owned industrial parks, Map Ta Phut, on the Gulf of Thailand, has created a festering, poisonous environment that has driven villages and schools away from the area.

Government efforts to halt these activities have been desultory, at best. Nevertheless, His Majesty the King of Thailand (HM), still hugely influential in public and private affairs, has postulated a lifestyle designed around what he calls the Sufficiency Economy (not to be confused with a 'self-*sufficient* economy') Philosophy (SEP).

The SEP has its roots in the Gross National Happiness paradigm originated by the King of Bhutan (the two royal families are known to be close). But it is also a natural outgrowth of sustainable development thinking, which in turn can be compared to CSR. The end result of both sustainable development and CSR at the corporate level would be a sustainable business. At the national level, that would be a sufficiency economy. (The Thai academic view is that SEP is a more holistic approach to doing business sustainably as compared with CSR.)

Moreover, to live a life of sufficiency is to live and act with respect for those around us, husbanding available resources out of concern for future generations. It is both an individual and a societal imperative. While CSR mandates similar conduct, it is by definition focused on companies and organisations. Both CSR and SEP attempt to describe sustainable systems, capable of existing in perpetuity, similar to the natural world.

The main points of SEP are:

- Sufficiency entails three components: moderation, reasonableness and the requirement for a self-immunity system which is able to cope with shocks from internal and external changes.

- Two underlying conditions are necessary to achieve sufficiency: knowledge and morality.

- In terms of the first condition, knowledge, the Sufficiency Economy requires breadth and thoroughness in planning, and care in applying knowledge and in implementation of those plans.

- The Sufficiency Economy enforces moral and ethical criteria: people are to possess honesty and integrity, while conducting their lives with perseverance, harmlessness and generosity.

- In sum, the Sufficiency Economy is a holistic concept of moderation and contentment. It sets out to shield the people and the country from adverse shocks, and acknowledges interdependency among people at all levels as an approach, against the backdrop of globalisation. It emphasises the use of knowledge wisely with due consideration. Its values include integrity, diligence, harmlessness and sharing. Finally, it seeks to achieve balance and sustainability.

Introduced with little fanfare over three decades, the SEP today inspires political leaders and businessmen alike, though in truth more as a result of HM's personal charisma than from any innate appeal the propositions may hold. CSR, on the other hand, is far less recognised and even then, not well understood. The corollary is that to increase the level of awareness for CSR, one strategy would be to emphasise the linkage to the SEP.

▋ Priority issues

Governance

Without a doubt the topmost issue on the Thai CSR agenda, in terms of urgency from the company viewpoint, has to be governance. The first critical theme to be addressed is the basic concept of rule of law. Whoever believes 'the law is an ass' would feel at home in Thailand, where that attitude prevails. Acknowledging this reality is fundamental to understanding Thai attitudes and practices. For example, if it is commonplace to flout the law, what good is it to announce the best environmental protection legislation in the world?

The lack of rule of law means that businesses with proper connections can safely ignore oversight constraints. Labour treatment, even with harsh laws (or perhaps, because of them) results in recurring examples of labour abuse — some truly egregious. The other theme within governance that remains critical is that of transparency in general, and corruption in particular. These are sensitive issues, but the current government under the Democrat party is openly addressing and making sincere efforts to rectify them.

▋ Environment

The priority issue in terms of importance is the state of the environment at the micro level, with global warming slowly beginning to appear over the horizon at the macro level. Originally, the focus was on illegal logging and the consequent deforestation of the once teak-rich north. Countrywide, photographic surveys show that in 1960, 56% of the Kingdom was forested; by 1990, that figure was halved. Despite the government declaring half the remaining trees to be permanent reserved forest, the trend continues.

Attention is now turning to a second environmental threat, that of overfishing in the Gulf of Thailand and the simultaneous destruction of reef and mangrove sanctuaries necessary to support the fish stocks. As the fish have declined, more desperate attempts have been made to increase yields, including the use of dynamite or poison in the reef waters normally rich in fish. From a net-fishing yield of 300 k/hour in 1961, today's average is under 30 k/hour. The Gulf is in danger of becoming a desert.

Finally, there is inappropriate land use. This covers everything from the non-existent zoning code in the capital city of Bangkok, and elsewhere, to the transmutation of farmland (and temple land) into golf courses, housing developments and industrial estates — often technically illegal, but usually successful. At a time when agriculture is increasingly important to the Kingdom, there is less land to till.

Other issues

Some might wonder why health is not on the list of troubling subjects. Surprisingly, Thailand is coping rather well with health challenges. Even outlying rural areas of the Kingdom receive good outpatient medical treatment, and most towns have excellent in-patient care. AIDS and tuberculosis remain potent threats, but awareness and treatment options are growing.

∎ Trends

Thailand is at the entry level when it comes to CSR. There is very little in the way of hard data to rely upon. The only broad-based community survey of CSR awareness is based on 2005 data. The results showed an overwhelming tendency to identify community service and philanthropy as vehicles to express CSR. It would be interesting to update the survey and measure the change in expectations since then.

There remains considerable reluctance to expand CSR thinking beyond philanthropy and community service, to innovation and sustainable practices. A related hurdle is the hesitancy to commit strategies that ultimately benefit the company to CSR. In the popular mind CSR must be painful, a sacrifice which must not benefit the company.

Aside from the 2005 consumer study already mentioned, the Kenan Institute has also extrapolated corporate awareness of CSR issues. Again, there is only one study (reported in 2007) so there is no trend, but the top concern for corporates proved to be governance. The environment had a relatively low priority. It is clear that the environment is now of greater importance.

∎ Legislation and codes

There is neither required reporting nor mandated CSR. There are moves afoot, however, to require listed companies to provide CSR, sustainable development or SEP reports annually — and with only peer pressure, nearly half already do so. The Global Reporting Initiative (GRI) standard format is popular but by no means universal.

There are Thai corollary standards for all the major ISO standards and guidelines, overseen by the Thailand Industrial Standards Institute.

Rather annoyingly for the sake of standardised communication, there is a sub-dialogue in Thailand that uses non-standard terminology. CSR 'in process' versus CSR 'after process' and CSR 'as process', which are supposed to represent respectively [in] product/service innovation, [after] palliative measures to atone for harm done, and [as] charity.

Finally, each stakeholder group brings to the table not only differing outlooks, but also a different understanding of what constitutes CSR. The government, now peppered with CSR institutes and committees, has many different views but often thinks of labour and employee issues as being central; corporates continue to view philanthropy as the touchstone; NGOs consider their roles to be that of policemen. This is slowly changing, but CSR practitioners who visit Thailand cannot help feeling they are experiencing a 'blast from the past'.

▌ Organisations

Five years ago there were few CSR-focused organisations. Now, there are dozens, of which a sampling is listed below.

▌ **Kenan Institute of Asia**. An NGO resource and consultancy. **http://www.kiasia.org**

▌ **Moral Center**. A government-sponsored network of organisations promoting business ethics and sustainability. **http://www.moralcenter.or.th**

▌ **Net Impact Professional Chapter**. The Thailand chapter of a US-based MBA organisation founded by Business for Social Responsibility. **http://www.netimpact.org**

▌ **NGO Biz**. A civil society network of organisations promoting business ethics and sustainability. **http://www.ngobiz.org**

▌ **Social Venture Network**. The Thai branch of the US-based organisation. **http://www.svn.org**

▌ **Stock Exchange of Thailand (SET) CSR Institute**. Establishes CSR guidelines for SET membership. **http://www.csri.or.th**

▌ **Sufficiency Economy Working Group (SEWG)**. Formed in 2001, this is a joint NESDBi and Crown Property Bureau effort to interpret and elaborate on the SEP. **http://www.sufficiencyeconomy.org**

▌ **Thailand Business Council for Sustainable Development**. A government Sufficiency Economy think-tank. **http://www.tei.or.th/tbcsd**

▌ **Thaipat Institute**. An NGO resource and consultancy. **http://www.thaipat.org**

▌ **Thailand Environmental Institute**. A nonprofit NGO think-tank. **http://www.tei.or.th**

▌ Case studies

Bangchak Petroleum

Highly regarded for its engagement with the local community and its philanthropy, Bangchak is a Thai multinational in the extraction business. It has issued sustainability reports in English annually since 2006 (but these use the confusing 'in/as/after' terminology already mentioned). Much of the attention Bangchak receives is probably as much to do with the size of their community projects budget as on the strategic value of their activities. **http://www.bangchak.co.th**

Siam Cement Group (Paper Division)

This Thai multinational organises its efforts around the triple-bottom-line model. While initially focused on community work in the environs of its plants, the company strategy continues to develop breadth, as indicated in its second and most recent sustainability report, which merits a GRI 'B' rating. **http://www.scg.co.th/en**

Wonderworld Products

Wonderworld Products is a well-respected SME with 500 employees, whose inspiring Managing Director, Suthichai Eamcharoenying, is the current president of the Social Venture Network. First alerted to the CSR challenge by his customers (Mattel, for example), he quickly responded by changing the raw material for his wooden toys to rubber tree wood, which had traditionally been incinerated. At the same time, he looked internally and began a series of enlightened programmes for staff that resulted in a 50% reduction in his staff turnover. Suthichai is the closest Thailand has to a Ray Anderson.[1] **http://www.wonderworldtoy.com**

▌ Education

At the time of writing there were no Thai universities offering an undergraduate CSR major and only a few offering graduate programmes in CSR — most notably **Chulalong-korn University**.

Other institutions offering topical lectures on CSR, usually in the context of business ethics, include the Sasin Institute, Dhurakit Bundit, Mahidol, Assumption and Thammasart Universities.

---

1 Ray Anderson has become an icon in the CSR world for turning his carpet tile manufacturing business, Interface, into a model of sustainable practice.

53 Turkey

Dixie O'Donnell
Security and Development Specialist

▌ Context

Turkey represents an interesting case of CSR agendas in the developing world. The dual contexts of a maturing democracy, increasing civil involvement and both formal and informal international pressure to safeguard the environment, human rights and workers' rights have brought about substantial progress on some fronts, but Turkey still has a long way to go.

Communal values and extended family ties remain strong and children are highly valued in Turkish society (Ararat and Göcenoğlu 2008). Commercials for consumer products often emphasise sharing. Some traditional informal networks are breaking down as the economy modernises, however, and nationalism is also very strong among the general population. This is an excellent time to launch CSR campaigns, because citizens are becoming more vocal, and business leaders are calling for an improved regulatory environment to facilitate development and trade. These can appeal to strong communal values and national pride (though they should be careful to stress cooperation with all citizens of Turkey, rather than emphasising the Turkish race), and providing a better future for Turkey's children.

The CSR agenda in Turkey, even within foreign multinational corporations (MNCs), is strongly influenced by the Ottoman Turkish tradition of *vakifs*, or endowments. Though the word is derived from Arabic and formerly connoted religious endowments, Turkish *vakifs* need not be religious in any way. They are basically philanthropic entities. In the Ottoman era, successful merchants or nobles would often establish a *vakif*, which would act as a fund that could be used to maintain a mosque, pay for education, public works such as plumbing or water fountains, healthcare facilities, or sponsor the fine arts. Today, powerful business families such as the Sabancis and Kocs, which now run successful multinational corporations, have decades-old *vakifs*. *Vakifs* generally make one-time donations in cash or kind or continually sponsor activities or facilities in health, education, sport and the fine arts.

Foreign MNCs that enter the Turkish market often set up their own *vakifs*. Vodafone and HSBC are two examples. Rather than installing comprehensive CSR programmes with advice and expertise from head offices, these two corporations followed the Turkish model, setting up *vakifs* as vehicles for public sponsorship and donation.

Because Turks expect major corporations to engage in philanthropic activities, these MNCs find it is in their interest to engage in such activities (Ararat and Göcenoğlu 2008). As Turkish democracy has deepened over the past eight years, Turks are slowly becoming more aware of the power of voting, as well as civil society, and therefore the sizeable middle class, as well as the population in general, respond to firms that seem to have respect for their host market.

Now there are NGOs, community organisations, multilaterals, academics and business professionals promoting CSR in Turkey, and more firms are interested in adopting CSR practices. Most still adopt a *vakif* or philanthropic model, rather than incorporating comprehensive strategies for reducing pollution or introducing better health and safety regulations for labourers. However, a shift has begun over the past three years, and firms are beginning to move away from sponsorship and the *vakif* model towards creating sustained CSR agendas[1]. According to *Euromonitor International*, Turkish consumers, particularly women, are responding to products labelled as environmentally friendly and they prefer to purchase such products if they can afford to.

Some Turkish businesses have engaged in substantial development work without any formal CSR agenda. In central Anatolia, private businesses built roads, clinics, even a police station, when the government could not afford or was unwilling to do so. In the Kayseri province, private donors spent 66% more on education than the government between 2002 and 2005. This region is home to many firms that became multinationals, and local businessmen began competing to donate the most to causes and projects deemed necessary in local towns (ESI 2005). All of this occurred without any sort of formal CSR agenda, within a context of valuing entrepreneurship, hard work, and giving back to the community.

∎ Priority issues

A 2001 survey by Environics International found that rather than promoting social development or protecting the environment, job provision is seen as the prime social responsibility of business in low-income countries (Ararat and Göcenoğlu 2008). Unemployment in Turkey reached 13.6% in March 2009 according to *Forbe.com*. However, as access to education, the internet and other media have improved substantially in recent years, health and environmental concerns are becoming more prevalent.

Environment

The environment is becoming a major priority in CSR initiatives in Turkey, unlike labour and human rights. Greenpeace, TEMA and other NGOs have been working to raise awareness of environmental issues, particularly over the last decade. Turks have become much more aware of these issues due to public campaigns and internet access.

As an example of a corporate response, in 2007 Garanti Bank introduced a credit card that donates money to fight climate change. According to a 2008 *Eurobarometer* study, 60% of Turks see climate change as the most serious threat facing the world, compared

---

1 Ozturk, personal communication, 23 February 2009.

to 62% of Europeans (although economic concerns are likely to have overtaken environmental ones in recent months).

Education

Education is highly valued in Turkey as it is seen as the surest way to be lifted out of poverty. Therefore many *vakifs* make much of providing scholarships and donating computers and funds to schools. This resonates well with the general public.

Educational provision is improving in Turkey, which has a large national public education system. However, this is still characterised by rote learning, and the number of students helped by scholarships remains quite small (Bıçakçı 2008). Businesses rarely work with schools to improve curricula or help schools to develop skills that are sorely needed in the private sector but which most graduates lack. Many leave school at a middle or secondary level to take manufacturing jobs, to work as labourers, or in the informal sector, which still makes up an estimated 30–50% of Turkey's GDP, mostly represented by small and medium-sized enterprises. Educating one's children, especially sons, remains a high priority for most Turkish families. Nevertheless little is being done to introduce critical thinking or project-based learning into public schools.

Healthcare

Healthcare is another traditional priority for philanthropy in Turkey. As the internet and other media have spread and matured, and NGOs and corporations have begun to support public health campaigns regarding specific health problems such as STDs, AIDS, smoking and obesity, the Turkish public is becoming much more aware of health issues. Unilever and other food producers label products as 'heart healthy' and free of preservatives. *Vakifs* donate funds to hospitals and clinics, which are often understaffed and stretched for funds. However in eastern Turkey healthcare facilities are severely lacking. In Hacilar, a small town outside Kayseri in central Anatolia, private donations from local businesses were used to build the local clinic, as the town was lacking one (ESI 2005).

Governance

Turkey has changed rapidly politically, socially and economically in the last decade, let alone over the past 40 years. The power balance has shifted from domination by the secular elites and the military to a democratic government dominated by the mildly Islamicist and pro-market Justice and Development party. The military is no longer able to muster public support for coups.

∎ Trends

There are as yet no comprehensive longitudinal studies on CSR practices in Turkey, which is a rather new field in this country. The prevalence of SMEs and the informal economy can also hinder the development of CSR and make accurate measurements hard to come by, and many businesses operate without any formal code of ethics. Western and Eastern Turkey also represent very different environments, with the latter largely rural and underdeveloped and the former quite wealthy by comparison and highly urbanised.

However the economy is maturing and understanding of CSR is moving towards more comprehensive models to be incorporated into overall corporate strategies. Public awareness on health, education and environmental issues is improving. As citizens become more aware of their rights and comfortable in using their voices in a more liberal, if still highly politicised, public space, they are becoming more demanding of both business and government.

The UNDP (2008) produced a baseline study on the state of CSR in Turkey, as well as many relevant materials on entrepreneurship, SMEs and development. Signatories to the Global Compact must submit annual reports on their progress to remain part of that group, so these could be useful tools to track progress. Türkiye Üçüncü Sector Vakfi (TUSEV) conducts surveys and establishes focus groups on issues related to the civil society in Turkey, though not CSR specifically.

■ Legislation and codes

There is very little specific CSR legislation in Turkey. Labour codes, though improving, remain weak. However, as the European Union (EU) consumes the majority of Turkish exports, Turkish firms that wish to sell there must meet particular EU supply-chain regulations. Turkey has also been a member of the European customs union since 1996. This is a powerful incentive to improve working conditions and environmental practices in Turkish firms. Turkey is also a signatory to ILO conventions, including conventions on Freedom of Association and Protection of the Right to Organize; Rights to Organise and to Bargain Collectively; Abolition of Forced Labour; Minimum Wage; Occupational Health and Safety; Termination of Employment; and Elimination of the Worst Forms of Child Labour.

Donations to educational causes are 100% tax deductible, which reflects the high value Turks put on education. *Vakifs* were formerly required to invest in public banks, but now are free to invest in private banks. Corporations such as Sabanci, Koc or HSBC may donate up to 5% of their annual profits to their respective *vakifs*. Civil society organisations are exempt from corporate taxes, but must pay others. There are very few tax benefits available for foundations or for those who donate to them.[2]

Since the AKP became the strongest party in parliament in 2002 and began aggressively pursuing EU membership, many legal reforms have been introduced that relate to civil society organisations. The current constitution was written by the military after a coup in 1982 and carries severe restrictions on the freedom of association. However in March 2005 the **Associations Act** was amended to allow civil servants to join associations. The authority for monitoring NGOs was also moved from the Department of Security to the Ministry of the Interior.

However the pace of reform faltered in 2007 and the implementation of many laws relevant to CSR as well as civil society are not being monitored.

2 Meydanoglu, personal communication, 21 January 2009.

■ Organisations

■ **The British Council** is very active in promoting CSR education, raising awareness and sponsoring networking events for professionals interested in CSR working in countries around the region. **http://www.britishcouncil.org/Turkey**

■ The **Corporate Social Responsibility Association** is a Turkish CSO based in Istanbul and Ankara. It works with private businesses and the Global Compact to raise awareness and to advise on CSR programmes as well as raise awareness. **http://www.csrturkey.org**

■ **TUSEV** promotes linkages between domestic and international NGOs, provides data on NGOs and other nonprofits in Turkey for domestic and foreign firms. Its main goal is to build the capacity of CSOs in Turkey and help them to develop international relationships. It encourages CSR by putting foreign and domestic firms in contact with appropriate CSOs. **http://www.tusev.org.tr**

■ The **UN Development Programme** does a great deal of work with the private sector in Turkey. It works with small- and medium-sized enterprises to develop capacity and bring their business practices in line with international norms and best practice. It often supports youth initiatives and encourages entrepreneurship. It also runs the local Global Compact programme. The signatories include domestic and foreign businesses, as well as the influential Turkish Industrialists' and Businessman's Association (TUSIAD). **http://www.undp.org.tr**

■ Case studies

British Petroleum

British Petroleum has been a leader in promoting sustainable business practices in Turkey. Its impact assessments in the Baku–Tbilisi–Ceyhan project area in Turkey were adopted by Turkish state-owned hydrocarbon pipeline operator BOTAS to assess the impact of subsequent projects on local populations. Within the BTC project area, BP also conducted needs assessments. It then identified projects both needed and wanted by the local population and began training local project leaders on researching and obtaining funding from Turkish sources and abroad, with particular focus on income-generating projects. BP has also increased knowledge and expertise on biodiversity conservation projects by sponsoring local environmental organisations and groups of students in projects that study biodiversity in the project area. **http://www.bp.com**

Yesim Tekstil

Yesim Tekstil is a Turkish company that has taken the CSR agenda to heart by adopting comprehensive, company-wide best practices. Responsibility and direction come from the top and are present in every department. The firm's goal is to become 'the social responsibility leader in world apparel industry'. Its code of conduct addresses compliance with laws and regulations (which a weak regulatory environment and the large informal sector can render irrelevant for most domestic firms not willing to follow them), forced labour, harassment and abuse, wages and benefits, hours of work, discrimination, health and safety, freedom of association (Turkish employees may be fired for joining a trade union in most firms), environment, customs compliance, security and management. It has a social compliance department reporting directly to the general manager. **http://www.yesim.com.tr**

■ Education

Turkey has as yet no CSR courses, let alone masters' degrees, in CSR. There are some encouraging developments however. **Sabanci University**, a private institution established by the VAKSA, the *vakif* associated with Sabanci Holding, has a strong reputation and requires its business administration students to take courses in business ethics. This covers issues that are most important to Turkey's continued economic development, such as corporate governance. Melsa Ararat, an expert on corporate governance who has written articles on CSR practices and public demand, teaches there. Its undergraduate programme in management offers courses such as Civic Involvement Projects and Law and Ethics, and Business and Society. Ethics in Business is a core course in the MBA programme.

Koc University (established by the Koc family, which owns Koc Holding and is associated with the Koc Vaf) offers an MBA special topic course in corporate social responsibility.

Otherwise, professionals and students seeking to learn more about CSR must look at the organisations listed above to attend courses, workshops or networking events to learn about CSR.

References

Ararat, M., and C. Göcenoğlu (2008) *Drivers for Sustainable Corporate Responsibility: Case of Turkey* (Ankara, Turkey: CSR Turkey).

Bıçakçı, İ.C. (2008) 'The Capitalistic Function of Education-Directed Social Responsibility Projects in Turkey within the Context of Relationships between the Private Sector and NGOs', *Journal for Critical Education Policy Studies* 6.1 (May 2008).

Bikmen, F. (2003) 'Corporate Philanthropy in Turkey: Building on Tradition, Adapting to Change', *SEAL: Social Economy and Law Project Journal* 2 (Autumn 2003).

BP Turkey (2006) 'Sustainability Report 2006'; **http://www.bp.com/sectiongenericarticle.do?categoryId= 9032863&contentId=7060187**, accessed 8 June 2010.

British Council (2007) *The Network Effect* (Istanbul: The British Council; **http://cgft.sabanciuniv.edu/ eng/AnaSayfa/documents/BCNetwork.pdf**

ESI (European Stability Initiative) (2005) *Islamic Calvinists: Change and Conservatism in Central Anatolia* (Istanbul: European Stability Initiative).

Euromonitor International (2009) 'Consumer Lifestyles: Turkey 2008' (London: Euromonitor International).

UNDP (United Nations Development Programme) (2008) 'Turkey Corporate Social Responsibility Baseline Report' (Ankara, Turkey: UNDP).

54 Uganda

Cedric Marvin Nkiko

Senior Stakeholder Engagement Officer,
Derbyshire County Council UK and
Doctoral Researcher, Portsmouth Business School, UK

David Katamba

Chairman, Uganda Chapter for Corporate Social
Responsibility Initiatives (UCCSRI) and
Assistant Lecturer, Makerere University Business School (MUBS)

■ Context

Uganda is often regarded as the birthplace of humanity and the 'crib' of civilisation. It is also endowed with tremendous natural beauty, wildlife, diversity and friendly people, leading Sir Winston Churchill to describe it in 1908 as a 'beautiful garden where the staple food of the people grows almost without labour. Does it not sound like a paradise on earth? It is the Pearl of Africa'.

Uganda's business activities can be traced back to the 17th century, when the Arabs introduced Islam and various forms of long distance trade, including the slave trade. In 1890, Uganda was colonised by Britain and remained under British rule until it gained its independence in 1962. Despite these 'outside' influences, Uganda is largely characterised by the norms and beliefs of African traditional society.

Theorists such as Okot P'bitek preached and campaigned for societal ethical values as early as 1950, with an emphasis on helping the needy, and wealthy families taking care of orphans (Imbo 2002). In many different communities, especially in central Uganda, it was also common practice to form small welfare groups called *muno mukabi'* which provided assistance after the loss of loved ones or a bad harvest.

Other early influences on CSR include religious practices such as Catholic tithing (typically, giving one-tenth of personal annual income to support church welfare activities) and Islamic *Zakat*— a form of wealth tax for the relief of the poor and disadvantaged (Nkiko 2009). Christian missionaries also brought a tradition of voluntary community activity, such as building churches, schools and hospitals.

Models of CSR

While there is no single nationally applied and accepted CSR model in Uganda, a few models developed elsewhere are being adopted. For example, a recent UCCSRI study proposed that Freeman's stakeholder dialogue — centred around workplace, community, marketplace and environment — is the dominant approach to CSR in Uganda (Katamba and Gish-Boie 2008). Within these stakeholder categories, there are some distinctive Ugandan features. For example, under the workplace dimension, businesses focus on HIV/AIDS, and prohibition of child labour is a key focus.

The other CSR model that has gained some traction is Carroll's (1979, 1991) CSR pyramid, made up of economic, legal, ethical and discretionary (or philanthropic) responsibilities. Scholars such as Wanyama *et al.* (2006) have challenged the relevancy and applicability of Western corporate governance models to developing countries such as Uganda. Similarly Visser (2008) challenges the accuracy and relevance of Carroll's CSR pyramid in developing countries, suggesting a different order of CSR priorities from the classic American ordering. For example, in African countries, the CSR pyramid would more typically prioritise economic and discretionary (or philanthropic) responsibilities ahead of legal and ethical issues. This more accurately reflects the Ugandan experience of CSR, where the government has played little or no part in creating a policy platform for CSR (Nkiko 2009).

∎ Priority issues

Poverty

Uganda ranks among the 20 poorest countries, with over 50% of the population living below the poverty line (FSD 2006). For decades, the country has been perpetually paralysed with problems of starvation, HIV/AIDS and widespread diseases, despite 50 years of continuous international aid-giving. Hence, businesses' engagement with CSR is now believed to play a critical role in alleviating poverty (DFID 2003; Wambura 2007).

Corruption

With a Corruption Perception Index score of 2.5, Uganda ranks as the 130th most corrupt nation in a world of 180 countries (Transparency International 2009), which in turn is hampering its achievement of the Millennium Development Goals and sustainable development. A recent UCCSRI study (Katamba and Gish-Boie 2008) revealed that corruption is especially prevalent in procurement, taxation, customs, regulatory functions, licensing and inspection of operational business areas in Uganda. According to the African Peer Review Mechanism report (Olupot 2008), corruption in procurement has adversely impacted on services aimed at improving the quality of life, especially health and education. The report presented to the Ugandan President further revealed that corruption, especially in the private sector, exacerbates poverty in Uganda.

Estimates of the scale of Uganda's corruption are diverse and extremely high. For example, the Global Integrity's 2006 report (Biryetega 2006) revealed that the Uganda Debt Network and Transparency International estimated Uganda's annual loss to corruption to be USD108 million and USD950 million respectively. The same report showed that the Public Procurement and Disposal of Public Assets Authority (PPDA) estimates over USD184 million being lost annually to corruption in procurement. Unsurprisingly the World Bank believes the country would save USD18 billion (UGX30 trillion) annually by eliminating losses from corruption in public procurement alone (Olupot 2008). Similarly, the 2005 Auditor General's Report estimated that 20% of the value of public procurement (which accounts for 70% of public expenditure) was lost through corruption, prompted by weak public procurement laws. In addition to the Directorate of Ethics and Integrity's existing national efforts in fighting corruption, CSR can be part of the solution by adopting transparency practices such as sustainability reporting and 'publish what you pay' (disclosing financial flows to and from government).

Environmental issues

Common environmental concerns include deteriorating soil fertility; uncontrolled expansion of agricultural land; soil erosion; encroachment of forest reserves; deforestation (particularly outside protected areas) and the overgrazing of rangelands; decreasing quality and availability of water; water pollution due to industrial and domestic waste; unregulated encroachment and degradation of wetlands; decreasing fish stocks; water hyacinth infestation in Lake Victoria; and widespread poaching.

According to the World Bank (2004), 80% of Uganda's urban population and 47% of the rural population had access to clean drinking water. The annual increase in deforestation in 2005 was 2% compared to 0.8% for all of Sub-Saharan Africa. In addition, many wetlands have been drained for agricultural use. In 2002, permanent pasture comprised 26% and irrigated cropland covered 10.7% of the land area, as compared with 35% and 1% respectively for Sub-Saharan Africa. The invasive water hyacinth on Lake Victoria covers around 5,998 ha, or approximately 5% of the lake. Human pressure, along with traditional cultural, agricultural and business practices, have increased environmental degradation in Uganda and contributed to climate change globally.

Human rights

Human rights are provided for in Uganda's 1995 Constitution. Despite this, the country has a poor track record of human rights violations. The most serious problems, which are the focus of improvement efforts, include extra-judicial killings by security forces, disappearances, abductions, restrictions on the right to a fair trial, harsh prison conditions, torture, restrictions on press freedom and freedom of speech, violence and abuse of children.

In the business arena, the main issues are fair wages, labour rights, child labour, equal opportunities, non-discriminatory treatment, health and safety, consumer rights and obligations with regard to environmental protection. A recent United Nations report highlighted the negative impact of businesses' failure to uphold human rights in Uganda (Hamann *et al.* 2009). In particular, malpractices such as underpayment of employees, child labour, discrimination, poor health and safety and bullying at work were reported.

Trends

As previously mentioned, socially responsible practices in Uganda can be traced back to the 1950s when the communal values of African traditional society prevailed. Following the historical influences of Arab traders, Christian missionaries engaged more with communities on developmental issues such as building hospitals, schools and roads during the 1970s. Large local businesses used the same tradition of community engagement by engaging in charitable money-giving (philanthropy) to social causes. Among the early pioneers were Madhivani, Uganda Breweries Ltd (now East African Breweries Ltd) and Kakira Sugar Works.

From the 1970s, there was a fundamental shift from this philanthropy-based CSR to stakeholder engagement-oriented CSR. This period was characterised by globalisation and international trade, which fostered the introduction of CSR policies by multinational corporations (MNCs) such as Coca-Cola, Shell, Barclays Bank and MTN. Most of these MNCs have adopted voluntary CSR standards, such as those of the International Organization for Standardization (ISO), despite the lack of CSR-driven legislation in Uganda.

Since 1990, CSR has been embraced by all MNCs and a few SMEs. Unsurprisingly, there is a large difference in CSR practices between large and small businesses (Asongu 2007). For example, Tallow Oil plc (a large company) built a school in Kaiso-Tonya, whereas Bee Natural Uganda Ltd (an SME in Arua) makes an annual provision of two primary school scholarships for girls.

The 2000s have witnessed new trends in CSR in Uganda, such as environmental responsibility, mandatory requirements within the supply chain and voluntary CSR reporting. Environmental protection and climate change are now included in the CSR strategies of nearly all businesses. Furthermore, businesses within the supply chain of an MNC are now required to show some evidence of their CSR policies and practices, including those concerned with labour, the environment, and worker health and safety. A few companies, such UTL, MTN and Thermocool Ltd are also informally communicating their CSR efforts to the public via their websites.

Legislation and codes

There is legislation relating to CSR in Uganda, even though adherence and enforcement is weak. These includes the Employment Act 2006, Fisheries Policy 2000, Forest Policy 2001, Labour Disputes Act 2006, Labour Union Act 2006, Land Act Cap 22726, Mining Act 2003, National Energy Policy 2000, National Environment Act Cap 153 (19 May 1995), Occupational Health and Safety Act 2006, Tree Planting Act 2003, Uganda Wildlife Act 1996, Cap 200 of 2000, Wetlands Policy 1994 and Wildlife Policy 1999.

Organisations

Business Council for Sustainable Development Uganda. Voluntary group working with businesses towards sustainable growth and development. **http://www.bcsdu.org**

▌ **Directorate of Ethics and Integrity**. Responsible for the formulation, coordination and implementation of national anti-corruption policy. **http://www.dei.go.ug**

▌ **Donor agencies**. These include DED (German Development Service), USAID and NORAD.

▌ **Federation of Uganda Employers (FUE)**. An umbrella organisation that advocates for workers rights and occupational issues. **http://www.employers.co.ug**

▌ **Institute of Corporate Governance Uganda**. Builds the capacity of companies to implement corporate governance principles. **http://www.icgu.or.ug**

▌ **National Environmental Management Authority (NEMA)**. Supervises, assesses, coordinates and monitors all aspects of the environment. **http://www.nemaug.org**

▌ **Uganda Chapter for Corporate Social Responsibility Initiatives (UCCSRI)**. A voluntary initiative promoting CSR. **http://www.uccsri.com**

▌ **Uganda Manufacturers Association**. Promotes, protects and coordinates the interests of industrialists. **http://www.uma.or.ug**

▌ **Uganda National Bureau of Standards (UNBS)**. Enhances the application of standards in trade, industry and consumer protection. **http://www.unbs.go.ug**

▌ Case studies

Mobile Telecommunication Network: Uganda Ltd (MTN)

MTN is one of the leading providers of communication services, offering cellular network access and business solutions in Uganda, including payphone, fixed lines, fax and data, internet and mobile services. Through the MTN Foundation, the company builds capacity among Ugandan communities. The MTN Foundation has interventions in six programme areas which include education (science and technology); health and HIV/AIDS; music, arts and culture; environment; community development; and habitat for humanity. **http://www.mtn.co.ug**

Tullow Oil Plc (Uganda) Ltd

Tullow Oil plc is one of the largest independent oil and gas exploration companies, with operations in 22 countries. In Uganda, the company operates in Kaiso-Tonya near Lake Albert, where it practises CSR within the community. CSR activities include health and hygiene initiatives (tackling water, malaria, infant mortality and lifejacket availability), provision of access to villages (new roads and airstrips), a beekeeping initiative (supporting a substantial honey market) and education (building schools and providing teacher training). **http://www.tullowoil.com**

Uganda Telecom Ltd (UTL)

UTL is the leading provider of telecommunications services (both fixed and mobile networks) in Uganda. Its CSR initiatives include empowering the youth through educational programme sponsorships and leadership forums, running a child help line, and providing solar powered mobile recharge centres in areas of the country where the electricity grid has not yet reached. The company is well known for its philanthropic sports sponsorships and providing ICT for development. **http://www.utl.co.ug**

▪ Education

There are no CSR courses in the current Ugandan higher education curriculum. However, the following universities are engaged in CSR knowledge transfer through seminars, conferences and training:

- **Makerere University Business School.** **http://www.mubs.ac.ug**
- **Kampala International University (KIU).** **http://www.kiu.ac.ug**
- **Uganda Christian University, Mukono (UCU).** **http://www.ucu.ac.ug**
- **Uganda Management Institute (UMI).** **http://www.umi.ac.ug**

References

Asongu, J.J. (2007) 'The History of Corporate Social Responsibility', *Journal of Business and Public Policy* 1.2 (Spring 2007): 1-18.

Biryetega, S.R. (2006) 'Global Integrity 2006 Country Report Uganda', Global Integrity; **http://www.globalintegrity.org/reports/2006/pdfs/uganda.pdf**, accessed 15 October 2009.

Carroll, A.B. (1979) 'A Three-dimensional Conceptual Model of Corporate Social Performance', *Academy of Management Review* 4.4: 497-505.

—— (1991) 'Corporate Social Responsibility: Evolution of a Definitional Construct', *Business and Society* 38.3: 268-95.

DFID (Department for International Development) (2003) 'DFID and Corporate Social Responsibility: An Issues Paper' (DFID; **http://www.dfid.gov.uk/Documents/publications/corporate-social-resp.pdf**, accessed 15 October 2009).

FSD (Foundation for Sustainable Development) (2006) 'Uganda: A Development Overview'; **http://www.fsdinternational.org/country/uganda/devissues**, accessed 15 October 2009.

Hamann, R., S.Woolman and C. Sprague (eds.) (2009) *Sustainable Development in Africa: Human Rights, Partnerships, Alternative Business Models* (Pretoria, South Africa: Unisa Press).

Imbo, S.O. (2002) *Oral Traditions as Philosophy: Okot P'bitek's Legacy for African Philosophy* (Boston, MA: Rowman & Littlefield).

Katamba, D., and S. Gish-Boie (2008) 'CSR in Uganda: Perceptions, Approaches and Needs of Companies' (UCCSRI report; **http://www.livingearth.org.uk/africa_programmes/uganda/CSR_study.pdf**, accessed 21 April 2009).

Nkiko, C.M. (2009) 'Corporate Social Responsibility: Small Medium Enterprise Contribution towards Sustainable Development in Developing Economies: The Case of BCSDU' (unpublished DBA thesis; University of Portsmouth, UK).

Olupot, M. (2008) 'Corruption costs sh500b a year', Newvision, 21 January 2008; **http://www.newvision.co.ug/D/8/12/607777/Uganda:%20Corruption%20Costs%20Sh500b%20a%20Year**, accessed 14 October 2009.

Transparency International (2009) 'Global Corruption Report 2009: Corruption and the Private Sector' (Transparency International; **http://www.transparency.org**, accessed 15 October 2009).

Visser, W. (2008) 'Corporate Social Responsibility (CSR) in Developing Countries', in A. Crane, A. McWilliams, D. Matten, J. Moon and D. Siegel (eds.), *The Oxford Handbook of Corporate Social Responsibility* (New York: Oxford University Press).

Wambura, E. (2007) 'Corporate Social Responsibility: Key to Poverty Alleviation', *The African Executive*, 21–28 November 2007; **http://www.africanexecutive.com/modules/magazine/articles. php?article=2699**, accessed 14 October 2009.

Wanyama, S., B.M. Burton and C.V. Helliar (2006) 'Corporate Governance and Accountability in Uganda: A Stakeholder Perspective', in W. Visser, M. McIntosh and C. Middleton (eds.), *Corporate Citizenship in Africa: Lessons from the Past; Paths to the Future* (Sheffield, UK: Greenleaf Publishing): 54-66.

World Bank (2004) 'Environment at a Glance 2004: Uganda' (Environment Department; **http:// siteresources.worldbank.org/INTEEI/Data/20859150/Uganda.pdf**, accessed 14 October 2009).

55 United Arab Emirates

Aparna Mahajan

Independent Consultant in Management, CSR and Development

■ Context

As a young and vibrant country, the United Arab Emirates (UAE) is characterised by rich cultural, historical and religious traditions which have had a strong influence on its business environment. Islam, the country's official religion, has widely impacted and shaped the CSR culture. Charity or *Zakat* (giving alms to the poor) is held in high esteem in the Holy Qur'an. During the early centuries of Islam, the *Zakat* revenues were kept in a central treasury and disbursed for public, educational and civic projects, for care of the orphaned and needy (Ayoub 2006).

The traditional culture of the Middle East suggests that social sensitivity was deeply rooted, especially among traders who treated their workers as family members. Inspired by religious teachings concerning responsible conduct on earth, practices such as living in harmony with nature and giving portions of the harvest to the poor and needy in order to merit the *Baraka* (blessings) were commonplace. Philanthropic donations were often made for building mosques and schools, paying for healthcare and for the well-being of unprivileged people. Businesspeople also provided advisory services to local government (Chakaki 2009).

The modern UAE has emerged as an international strategic business hub with many global companies and burgeoning sectors of manufacturing, trade, finance, real estate and tourism. Although philanthropic initiatives stemming from *Zakat* values remain the most common, the international context means that UAE increasingly draws on a number of global CSR models, especially ethical CSR (as a voluntary initiative), statist CSR (based on state ownership/legal requirements) and liberal CSR (which is shareholder-driven). In addition, stakeholder-driven and convergence (integrated within the business) approaches seem to be slowly emerging.

Attempts to devise CSR models based on the national socioeconomic environment juxtaposed with international guidelines and a regional focus are being initiated by, for instance, the Dubai Centre for Corporate Values.

∎ Priority issues

UAE is one of fastest-growing economies of the world, driven not only by a rise in value of the oil and gas sector (18.2% increase in 2007), but also by impressive performance of the non-oil sector. Dubai in particular has witnessed extensive growth as a world-class financial and commercial centre, resulting in challenges such as environmental degradation and high demand for skilled labour.

Environmental challenges

Rapid urbanisation, population growth and industrial expansion have increased pressure on the environment, in particular on water resources. UAE residents are among the highest per capita water users in world, consuming an average of 550 litres per day. Electricity consumption is also high at around 11,000 kW hours per person per year and demand for water and electricity is still rising as a construction boom sweeps the region, fuelled by oil income (UAE 2009).

The coastline and marine environment is under stress due to urban development, ballast water discharge and landfill seepage. There are also high levels of domestic waste. For example, per capita household waste is an average annual 730 k in Abu Dhabi and 725 k in Dubai.

Energy and climate change

Reducing energy use in order to cut greenhouse gas emissions to combat climate change is a critical issue. There has been a rapid increase in the consumption of energy and fossil fuels in the UAE. Efforts have begun to adopt zero emission flaring technologies, and a transition to natural gas in power and desalination plants to curb emissions of greenhouse gases (Environment Agency 2009).

One landmark initiative in UAE is the project to create a zero carbon, zero waste city — Masdar. Established by Abu Dhabi, Masdar is a global cooperative platform for finding solutions to energy security, climate change and sustainability. It is a comprehensive investment in future energy solutions and clean technology — from design to research laboratory to mass deployment with projects targeting solar, wind and hydrogen power, carbon reduction and management, sustainable development, education, manufacturing, and research and development (UAE Embassy in Washington 2009)[1].

National human resource development

UAE's population growth rate is estimated at 5.6% and the population is projected to reach 5.06 million by the end of 2009 (Tanmia 2005). One striking feature of the country is its diversified demographic profile, with UAE nationals accounting for 20% and non-nationals 80%. This exceptionally large and culturally diverse expatriate workforce, with high levels of temporary migration (exceeding 80% of the workforce) and high turnover among professionals, has led to poor labour practices (Ben Brik 2008). Hence, addressing industrial relations is imperative.

Upgrading the quality of education and the creation of job opportunities for nationals, with reduced dependence on a foreign workforce, is particularly important for long-

1   See also **http://www.masdaruae.com**

term sustainable human development in UAE. The UAE Ministry of Economy estimates that the unemployment rate will increase to about 4% in 2009. However, this masks the fact that the rate of unemployment among UAE nationals is around 16% — nearly 20% among women and 9% among men. One response by the UAE government is the 'Emiratisation' initiative, to promote employment of its nationals. Emiratisation targets are set for each industry and specify that individual businesses hire a certain percentage of nationals.

▋ Trends

UAE is a melting pot, with a workforce comprising over 120 nationalities from various cultural, religious and ethnic backgrounds. The integration of traditional culture and Islamic influences within international businesses operating locally presents unique opportunities for CSR action.

CSR in UAE draws on deep-rooted Arab–Islamic traditions that promote endowments and community initiatives. For example, in the holy month of Ramadan, business makes large donations. In the private sector, chambers of commerce have led in creating CSR awareness and these efforts have gained momentum in recent years. Various awards have been created, including the Arabia CSR Awards, Mohammed Bin Rashid Al Maktoum Business CSR Awards and Abu Dhabi CSR Awards. Emirates Environmental Group, a top NGO, has formed a CSR Network and is the focal point of UN Global Compact in the UAE.

The sheikhs (rulers) and leadership of the Emirates have also given support and provided a vision for CSR activities in UAE. For example, Sheikh Zayed, ruler of Abu Dhabi and first president of UAE, was a firm proponent of environmental conservation and believed that the resources of the country should be used for the benefit of the people. The government is generally supportive of social responsibility and some of its initiatives include setting up a Social Responsibility Fund and Community Development Authority.

While the government-owned businesses are responsive to CSR initiatives (DCCI 2006), increased focus is being placed on the private sector to contribute to public health, education and environmental conservation. Masolia (a national CSR programme by the Abu Dhabi Chamber of Commerce) and Zayed's Philanthropic Initiative are encouraging steps in this direction.

Some research studies have been conducted in the country to assess the trends in CSR. Research on CSR in UAE by the Dubai Chamber of Commerce and Industry (DCCI 2006) found that 72% of entrepreneurs and CEOs were highly aware of CSR. Another survey on CSR in Dubai by this Chamber (Ben Brik 2008) found that most companies agree that regulatory compliance, business growth and workplace health and safety are top roles that companies play in society. Environmental and social reporting is practised by very few organisations.

Rettab and Ben Brik (2008) find that 59% companies are aware of CSR, 34% have CSR guidelines, 8% comply with international CSR standards and 3% publicly report on CSR. This survey showed that tourism and manufacturing sectors are more likely to be aware of CSR than construction, trade, transport and real estate sectors.

▋ Legislation and codes

UAE's national legislation is generally in compliance with international labour standards. New regulations by the Ministry of Environment and Water include air quality guidelines, noise, health and safety practices, and regulation of impacts on the environment in areas adjacent to quarry sites. The country's quarrying industry, producing rock and gravel for use in construction projects in coastal areas, is subject to tight controls.

To combat climate change, UAE is actively seeking to upgrade its environmental protection codes at the federal level to be in line with the global agenda to reduce greenhouse gas emissions. A new Green Building Code has been introduced by Dubai Municipality that requires compliance by all proposed building plans in Dubai. The Emirates Green Building Council has launched a building sustainability assessment system for UAE, based on the US Green Building Council's Leadership in Energy and Environmental Design (LEED) rating system, with modifications to account for local environmental conditions. A few companies are using other guidelines such as the Global Reporting Initiative (GRI), UN Global Compact and ISO14001.

▋ Organisations

▋ **CSR Middle East**. A nonprofit platform promoting CSR in the region. **http://www. csrmiddleeast.org**

▋ **Dubai Centre for Corporate Values (DCCV)**. Formed by Dubai Technology and Media Free Zone Authority, Dubai International Financial Centre and Dubai Airport Free Zone Authority, DCCV aims to promote CSR awareness. **http://www.cse-net.org/Contents. aspx?CatId=82**

▋ **Dubai Centre for Responsible Business (CRB)**. As part of the Dubai Chamber of Commerce and Industry, CRB supports Dubai chamber members in responsible business practices. **http://www.dubaichamber.ae**

▋ **Emirates Environmental Group (EEG)**. A voluntary NGO which, through its CSR network of 50 companies, aims to position UAE as CSR leader in the region. **http://www. eeg-uae.org/csr**

▋ **Emirates Foundation**. Established by General Sheikh Mohammed Bin Zayed Al Nahyan, Abu Dhabi Crown Prince and Deputy Supreme Commander of the UAE Armed Forces, the foundation is a philanthropic organisation that encourages public–private partnerships and community-based initiatives. **http://www.emiratesfoundation.ae**

▋ **International Humanitarian City (IHC)**. An independent free zone authority created by the Dubai government as a global humanitarian and aid hub, which also promotes CSR. **http://www.ihc.ae**

▋ **Mohammed Bin Rashid Al Maktoum Foundation (MBRF)**. A personal initiative by HH Sheikh Mohammed bin Rashid Al Maktoum, Prime Minister of UAE and Ruler of Dubai, which aims to develop a generation of future leaders. **http://www.mbrfoundation. ae**

■ Case studies

ABB UAE

The ABB Group of companies is a leader in power and automation technologies and operates in around 100 countries, employing about 130,000 people. ABB follows a triple-bottom-line approach to sustainability, with priorities in energy efficiency, climate change (emissions cutting), lowering environmental impact, health and safety, stakeholder engagement, product innovation and supply chain sustainability. The UAE arm of ABB won the first-ever Arabia CSR Award in 2008 for its active CSR initiatives over 14 years in the Middle East. ABB UAE is one of the founding members of the Green Building Council, WWF, CSR Network, Emirates Environmental Group and the GCC Global Compact. ABB supports UAE's green building initiative in Dubai to cut water and energy use, and supplies automation control technology for homes to reduce power consumption and emissions. The company encourages the professional development of women, provides a Middle East pension plan scheme, and engages staff in environmental programmes such as the 'Clean up the U.A.E.' campaign. **http://www.abb.com**

Dubai Holding

Dubai Holding, a privately held company, was created in 2004 to consolidate and lead Dubai's large-scale infrastructure and investment projects. Dubai Holding's strategy is in tune with the government's Dubai Strategic Plan for 2015. In early 2008, there were around 250 companies owned by Dubai Holding, having presence in four continents over 20 countries. Through its seven member companies — Jumeirah Group, TECOM Investments, Dubai Group, Dubai Properties Group, Tatweer, Sama Dubai and Dubai International Capital — it operates in 13 industries. CSR by Dubai Holding focuses on Emiratisation, and social and community-oriented projects in the areas of healthcare, education and charity, including support to sporting organisations and environmental sustainability. **http://www.dubaiholding.com/en**

Emaar Properties

Emaar Properties Public Joint Stock Company, based in Dubai, is one of the world's largest real estate companies listed on the Dubai Financial Market. With six business segments and more than 60 active companies, Emaar has a collective presence in over 36 markets around the world. The company's CSR initiatives focus on Emiratisation, environmental protection and community development. 'Green Emaar' is a facet of the company's vision for 2010. To promote green buildings, it has partnered with Dubai Municipality on a water use efficiency initiative. Other initiatives include financial donations for community development and facilitating volunteering programmes. **http://www.emaar.com**

Kanoo Group

The Kanoo Group, a family-owned business which has been in existence for more than a century in the Middle East and with headquarters in Dubai, is an established name in shipping, travel, machinery, courier, property, IT, oil and gas, power, chemicals and logistics. The Kanoo Group supports various social endeavours, including investing in education and the environment, besides being committed to recycling used paper, being an active member of the Emirates Environmental Group and actively supporting Emiratisation drives. One key initiative of the Group is its water recycling plant for efficient water use. **http://www.kanoogroup.com**

Shell UAE

Shell in UAE has four businesses — Shell Markets (Middle East) Ltd, Shell Exploration & Production, Shell Gas & Power, and Shell Global Solutions. A multi-stakeholder approach focusing sustainable development and community schemes guides the Group's CSR efforts. Shell sponsored the First International CSR Summit in Dubai in 2004. Environment initiatives include Enviro-spellathon (environmental education to children in over 400 schools in UAE), The Coral Reef Project off Abu Dhabi, 'Better Environment' awards and sponsoring environmental research projects. Community initiatives include Intilaaqah Abu Dhabi (training young UAE nationals in starting their own business), Shell Simulation Centre (a virtual look by college students into the operation of a crude distillation unit and natural gas liquids recovery plant), supporting various charitable organisations and the Emirates Businesswomen Award. **http://www.shell.com/ home/content/are**

▋ Education

CSR Education in UAE encompasses training workshops and courses by some organisations and academia, with a few schools including CSR in MBA programme modules. Leaders among these are:

- **Dubai Center for Responsible Business, Dubai**. http://www.dubaichamber.ae

- **Dubai Women's College, Dubai**. http://www.dwc.hct.ac.ae

- **Emirates Environmental Group, Dubai**. http://www.eeg-uae.org/csr

- **IIR Middle East, Dubai**. http://www.iirme.com

- The **INSEAD Centre for Executive Education and Research, Abu Dhabi**. http:// www.insead.edu/centreinabudhabi

- **University of Wollongong, Dubai**. http://www.uowdubai.ac.ae

References

Ayoub, M.M. (2006) *Islam: Faith and History* (Oxford, UK: Oneworld Publication England).

Ben Brik, A. (2008) *UAE Corporate Citizenship Summary, Corporate Citizenship around the World: How Local Flavor Seasons the Global Practice* (Boston, MA: Global Education Research Network and Boston College Center for Corporate Citizenship).

Chakaki, R. (2009) 'Regional Culture, Heritage and Corporate Social Responsibility (CSR): Dubai and the Middle East'; http://www.dubailime.com/dubai-guide/csr/csr-corporate-social-responsibility-in-dubai.html, accessed 26 August 2009.

DCCI (Dubai Chamber of Commerce and Industry) (2006) 'Corporate Responsibility Awareness in the United Arab Emirates' (Dubai: DCCI).

Environment Agency (2009) 'State of the Environment Abu Dhabi: Climate Change' (Abu Dhabi: Environment Agency; **http://www.soe.ae/Abu_Themespage.aspx?m=43**, accessed 26 August 2009).

Rettab, B., and A. Ben Brik (2008) 'Winds of Change: The State of Corporate Social Responsibility in Dubai, 2008' (Dubai: Dubai Chamber Centre for Responsible Business).

Tanmia (National Human Resource Development and Employment Authority) (2005) 'Human Resources Report' (Abu Dhabi: Tanmia).

UAE (2009) *United Arab Emirates Yearbook 2009* (London: Trident Press and the National Media Council, Abu Dhabi).

UAE Embassy in Washington (2009) 'Energy and Climate Change'; **http://www.uae-embassy.org/uae/ energy/climate-change**, accessed 26 August, 2009.

56 United Kingdom

David Grayson CBE
Director of the Doughty Centre for Corporate Responsibility,
Cranfield School of Management

▌ Context

In Britain, debates about how business should be conducted date back at least to the 18th-century controversies around the activities of the British East India Company, which held a monopoly on trade with India and, for an extended period, effectively administered much of India. The idea that companies should be judged not only on the size of their profits but also on the way that they treat their workers and the impact they have on the environment and the community became more prominent in Britain in the second half of the 19th century, after rapid industrialisation.

A number of the prominent industrialists of the time, such as Cadbury, Rowntree, Boot (Boots) and Lever (Unilever), practised what would now be defined as Corporate Responsibility (CR). Some of these businessmen were strongly influenced by their Quaker religious convictions. They believed that looking after their workers and customers made sound business sense (Bradley 2007).

A century later, a combination of the Great Depression, World War II, nationalisation, corporate consolidations and the emergence of industrial conglomerates, had left business as a much-diminished force in British society. Indeed business was reduced to funding campaigns to promote the worth of free enterprise and careers in business to university students whose preferred destinations were the law, public service or the professions. The link between top management and their corporate presence in different parts of the country had also been greatly diminished.

What turned the tide and made the UK one of the earliest and most enthusiastic modern promoters first of corporate community involvement and subsequently of CR and sustainability?

The severe economic downturn, and industrial restructuring of the 1980s encouraged by the Conservative government led by Margaret Thatcher (1979–90), and the consequent mass unemployment, inspired big business to act. Many of the business leaders who were Thatcher's most prominent business supporters were among those who understood that the *quid pro quo* for less government intervention and market liberalisation was that they themselves had to be prepared to take action. Businesses created a number of organisations to facilitate action and share learning during the 1980s.

These included Business in the Community (BITC), the local enterprise agencies (public–private partnerships to help new and small businesses), the network of environment-focused Groundwork Trusts, and education–business partnerships. Government encouraged this business activism through a series of 'Challenge grants' — matched funding for favoured activities such as education business links, enterprise promotion and small business development, and urban regeneration. At the end of the 1980s, it devolved responsibility for skills training and urban regeneration away from government agencies and local authorities and towards business-led, quasi-autonomous agencies such as the Training and Enterprise Councils (Fogarty and Christie 1990).

The evolution from corporate community involvement to Corporate Social Responsibility (CSR) and then to responsible business practice and sustainability began piecemeal from the early 1990s. Examples include BITC campaigns on business and the environment, and equal opportunities in the workplace, and with a few vanguard companies such as The Co-operative Bank and the late Anita Roddick's Body Shop, which recognised its value to their brands.

Companies such as Unilever started to work on environmental challenges in the 1990s leading, for example, to the establishment of the Marine Stewardship Council. Shell's reputational crisis in 1995 over the disposal of its Brent Spar North Sea oil exploration platform, its operations in Nigeria, and the company's consequent soul-searching about society's expectations of business, led it and many other companies to make public commitments to corporate responsibility. Over the years, there were also several reports initiated by business and governments about how to encourage more corporate responsibility (Bush *et al.* 2008).

A few years earlier, the social philosopher and management guru Charles Handy had asked 'What is a company for?' in a seminal lecture at the Royal Society of Arts (RSA) in London in 1990. This led the RSA in 1993 to initiate a business-led 'Tomorrow's Company' inquiry into 'the role of business in a changing world'. The findings, published in 1995, introduced the concept of an inclusive approach to business success and led to the establishment of the Centre for Tomorrow's Company (1995).

By the millennium, the centrality of business in most economies and societies, the erosion of public trust and the dynamics of a networked society had created what the then chairman of Business in the Community, Sir David Varney, called a 'Perfect Storm' for business. The corporate scandals in the early 2000s, such as Enron and Equitable Life, created the eye of this perfect storm, namely reputational risk which Varney described as 'the risk of failing to manage your company's reputation consistent with the goals and values of your enterprise'.

▮ Priority issues

Priority issues for the UK include climate change and wider environmental concerns such as reducing use of non-renewable natural resources, biodiversity, pollution and waste reduction. The Carbon Reduction Commitment (CRC) is a mandatory cap-and-trade scheme which aims to drive down energy consumption and improve energy efficiency in businesses.

Workplace practices are also prioritised, including 'great place to work' initiatives, equal opportunities and encouraging diversity, as well as responsible downsizing and outsourcing. A number of organisations focus on workplace issues. These include the Employers' Forum on Disability and the Employers' Forum on Age.

Responsible marketing is another area of concern, which includes protection of vulnerable customers, advertising practices, misuse of a company's products and services, and development of sustainable products and services, as well as responsible supply chain practices and engaging the supply chain in improved environmental, social and governance performance.

Key community issues include business–education links, both to improve UK competitiveness and to reduce social exclusion and inequalities (Cleverdon and Grayson 2008) and local economic regeneration. There is also increasing attention to bribery, corruption and the protection of human rights — wherever UK businesses are doing business.

▋ Trends

Many might consider the UK to have an 'enabling environment' for CR, with government encouragement, broad political consensus, network of business-friendly organisations to support, etc., and widespread adoption of at least some aspects of CR. Nevertheless the then CEO of BT observed: 'Until now, Corporate and Social Responsibility (CSR) has been seen in many companies as something which has to be done, a box which needs to be ticked, in all too many cases, without much enthusiasm'.[1]

The emphasis now, therefore, is on embedding CR and sustainability, making an explicit link to corporate purpose and strategy, setting tone from the top, trying to involve all employees and integrating responsibility into each business function. The vanguard companies are beginning to emphasise not just risk reduction but also business opportunities and competitive advantage from their embedding. There is also emphasis on ensuring adherence to codes of business principles or sustainability policies wherever the company is doing business around the world.

Various NGOs such as Greenpeace, Oxfam and Save the Children have engaged in high profile campaigns against a number of alleged corporate abuses (although some of these NGOs are also now working on partnerships with certain companies on shared goals). A number of these initiatives which began in the UK — such as the Marine Stewardship Council and the Ethical Trading Initiative — have gone international.

In 2000, a number of NGOs — including Amnesty International, Action Aid, Friends of the Earth, Traidcraft, War on Want and WWF (UK) — formed the Corporate Responsibility (CORE) Coalition to seek 'changes in UK company law to minimise companies' negative impacts on people and the environment and to maximise companies' contribution to sustainable societies'.[2]

Partly prodded by NGOs and other external stakeholders, UK-headquartered companies have been among the earliest CR reporters, with almost all the FTSE100 largest publicly quoted companies now regularly producing a CR or sustainability report.

Ipsos MORI has tracked consumer, employee and general public attitudes to corporate responsibility since the early 1990s. Asked whether companies will continue to

---

1 Ben Verwaayen, CEO of BT, 23 June 2006.
2 **http://corporate-responsibility.org**, accessed 9 June 2010.

invest in corporate responsibility despite a tougher economic climate, 85% of Ipsos MORI's Reputation Council (senior communications professionals within companies) agree they will do so, and 70% of corporate responsibility experts (CR commentators and advisory organisations) and 64% of NGOs (UK-based non-governmental organisations, e.g. campaigners and charities) also agree.

The UK was also one of the first countries in the world to customise the CR messages, language, agenda and examples for small firms. The UK Small Business Consortium began in 2001 with the encouragement of the government. The Consortium brought together BITC and the NGO Accountability with most of the leading national organisations representing smaller firms, including the British Chambers of Commerce and the Federation of Small Businesses. The Consortium has developed a website and advisor training, shared expertise among participating organisations and produced the *Better Business Journey* guide for small businesses.

▌ Legislation and codes

The general approach of successive Conservative and Labour administrations has been to create an enabling environment. This is reflected in limited legislation mandating CR, as opposed to adherence to general environmental, labour, health and safety and other related legislation.

Among the notable laws in the past two decades have been regulations amending pensions legislation, requiring pension fund trustees to disclose 'the extent (if at all) to which social, environmental or ethical considerations are taken into account in the selection, retention and realisation of investments'. Stephen Timms MP — the then Pensions Minister — later wrote 'it was light touch legislation, designed to promote cultural change' (Gribben and Gitsham 2006: 1). The same approach is foreshadowed in a report commissioned by the then leader of the main opposition party (Ethical Corporation Institute 2008).

The **2006 Companies Act** extended the duties of company directors. In promoting the success of their company, the directors are required to have regard 'amongst other matters' to: '. . . the interests of the company's employees; the need to foster the company's business relationships with suppliers, customers and others; the impact of the company's operations on the community and the environment; the desirability of maintaining a reputation for high standards of business conduct; and the need to act fairly as between members of the company'.

The **Climate Change Act 2008** imposes legally binding reductions on CO_2 emissions such that the net UK carbon account for all six Kyoto greenhouse gases for the year 2050 should be at least 80% lower than the 1990 baseline. The Act aims to enable the UK to become a low-carbon economy and gives ministers powers to introduce the measures necessary to achieve a range of greenhouse gas reduction targets.

The UK was also the first country to appoint a minister for Corporate Responsibility, although the rapid turnover of appointees over the last decade has reduced the impact of most of the occupants of the post.

▌ Organisations

▌ **Business in the Community (BITC)** was founded in 1982. This is a business-led charity in the UK with over 800 member companies. Its purpose is to inspire, challenge, engage and support business in continually improving its positive impact on society. Together, member companies employ over 12.4 million people across 200 countries. In the UK, members employ over one in five of the private sector workforce. Among its activities is an annual, voluntary benchmarking of companies' progress in embedding CR: the Corporate Responsibility Index, run since 2002. **http://www.bitc.org.uk**

▌ The **Centre for Tomorrow's Company** describes itself as a 'think and do tank', with the vision of 'a future for business which makes equal sense to staff, shareholders and society'. It grew out of the 1995 Tomorrow's Company report from the Royal Society of Arts (RSA). **http://www.tomorrowscompany.com**

▌ The **Corporate Responsibility Group** provides CR professionals working in major UK organisations with mutual support and development. It was established in 1987. **http://www.crguk.org**

▌ **Forum for the Future** is a charity committed to sustainable development. It focuses on the root causes and connections between big issues such as climate change, social inequality and environmental degradation. It was founded in 1996 by the environmental campaigners Jonathan Porritt, Sara Parkin and Paul Ekins. **http://www.forumforthefuture.org.uk**

Several specialist print and online CR publications are based in the UK, such as:

- **Business Respect**. http://www.businessrespect.net
- **CSR International Research and News Digests**. http://www.csrinternational.org
- **Corporate Citizenship Briefing**. http://www.ccbriefing.co.uk
- The **ENDS Report**. http://www.endsreport.com
- **Ethical Corporation**. http://www.ethicalcorp.com
- **Ethical Performance**. http://www.ethicalperformance.com

▌ Case studies

BITC runs annual awards for excellence, in collaboration with the *Financial Times*, various government departments and other partners. These awards include Company of the Year and Small Business of the Year. Short profiles of award winning companies are posted on the BITC website. These examples are the most recent companies of the year 2006–2009.

United Utilities

United Utilities is the UK's largest listed water company, owning, operating and maintaining utility assets including water, wastewater, electricity and gas. They have a comprehensive approach to corporate responsibility, with senior managers all playing a part in tackling issues of sustainability. **http://www.unitedutilities.com/EnvironmentCommunity. htm**

Co-operative Financial Services (CFS)

CFS incorporates The Co-operative Bank and Insurance Society. The Bank explicitly embraced ethical business practices in the early 1990s, screening out customers whose activities were deemed unethical. Customers are involved in choosing the bank's social campaigns, funded by cash generated when customers use their bank charge cards. Most recently, CFS has consulted customers on investor engagement strategies. **http:// www.cfs.co.uk**

British Telecommunications (BT)

BT privatised in the early 1980s and (now operating in 170 countries) has embedded sustainability as part of its business purpose, and appointed managing directors to champion each of the key pillars of its sustainability strategy. **http://www.btplc.com**

Marks & Spencer (M&S)

M&S is an iconic British retailer founded in 1884. It has had a long tradition of corporate philanthropy and fair trading. Following a failed, hostile takeover bid in 2004, the company launched a ground-breaking, 100 point sustainability strategy Plan A ('because there is no Plan B'). **http://corporate.marksandspencer.com/howwedobusiness**

∎ Education

- **Ashridge Centre for Business in Society** was established in the early 1990s. **http://www.ashridge.org.uk/ACBAS**

- **Cardiff University's Centre for Business Relationships, Accountability, Sustainability and Society (BRASS)** was funded by the government's Economic and Social Research Council (ESRC). **http://www.brass.cf.ac.uk**

- The **Corporate Citizenship Unit at Warwick** was established in 1996, supported by BP, but has now been dismantled

- The **Doughty Centre for CR at Cranfield** was created in 2007 with a donation from an MBA alumnus, Nigel Doughty. **http://www.doughtycentre.info**

- **Nottingham University's International Centre for CSR (ICCSR)** was created through an endowment from British American Tobacco (BAT) in 2002. **http:// www.nottingham.ac.uk/business/ICCSR**

- The **University of Cambridge Programme for Sustainability Leadership** (formerly Cambridge Programme for Industry) is the oldest CR-related learning institution in the UK, already over 20 years old. **http://www.cpsl.cam.ac.uk**

Various other UK universities also have CSR or sustainability postgraduate programmes, including for example Lancaster, Leeds, London, Middlesex and Strathclyde. Several of the UK schools were also among the founders of the **European Academy for Business in Society** (EABIS) **http://www.eabis.org**

References

Bradley, I. (2007) *Enlightened Entrepreneurs: Business Ethics in Victorian Britain* (London: Lion Hudson).

Bush, G., D. Grayson, A. Jordan and J. Nelson (2008) *Engaging Business in the Community: Not a Quick Fix* (London: The Smith Institute).

Centre for Tomorrow's Company (1995) *Tomorrow's Company: The Role of Business in a Changing World* (London: Centre for Tomorrow's Company).

Cleverdon, J., and D. Grayson (2008) *A Responsibility for Education: Learning from the Examples of Business Engagement with Education* (London: The Smith Institute).

Ethical Corporation Institute (2008) 'A Light but Effective Touch: The Conservative Party Working Group on Responsible Business' (London: Ethical Corporation Institute).

Fogarty, M., and I. Christie (1990) *Companies and Community: Promoting Business Involvement in the Community* (London: PSI Publishing).

Grayson, D. (2007) *Business-Led Corporate Responsibility Coalitions. Learning from the Example of Business in the Community: An Insider's Perspective* (CSR Initiative, Kennedy School of Government, Harvard).

Gribben, C., and M. Gitsham (2006) 'Will UK pension funds become more responsible? A Survey of Trustees' (Just Pensions/Ashridge Centre for Business and Society; **http://www.ashridge. com/website/IC.nsf/wFARATT/Just%20Pensions%20-%20Will%20UK%20Pension%20Funds%20 Become%20More%20Responsible/$file/Just_Pensions_2006_Report-Will_UK_Pension_Funds_ Become_More_Responsible.pdf**, accessed 9 June 2010).

Small Business Consortium (2006) 'Better Business Journey'; **http://www.smallbusinessjourney.com**, accessed 7 April 2010.

57 United States of America

Audra Jones

Americas Director, International Business Leaders Forum (IBLF)

■ Context

In the US, Corporate Social Responsibility (CSR) evolved in the first part of the 20th century, led by a few visionary business leaders such as Rockefeller, Carnegie, Ford, Hewlett and Packard. It could be argued, however, that the growth of US CSR as a business imperative is due to regulation. Beginning in the late 1960s and early 1970s, the US government established regulatory agencies that shaped much of the CSR benchmarks guiding business operations. For example, the Occupational Safety and Health Administration (OSHA), Equal Employment Opportunity Commission (EEOC), Consumer Product Safety Commission (CPSC) and Environmental Protection Agency (EPA) created standards and legislation for responsible corporate business practices which have become thresholds for good behaviour by a corporation. Today, government continues to regulate corporate behaviour. Recent examples of industry-specific and sector-wide regulation include the Community Reinvestment Act in the banking sector, the Clean Air Act and, post-Enron's collapse, the Public Company Accounting Reform and Investor Protection Act.

US corporate philanthropy also accelerated due to regulation. The formalised efforts of philanthropy in the early part of the 20th century by the Rockefellers and Carnegies fostered the first regulatory response to CSR in the form of the tax-break to corporations making charitable contributions to nonprofit organisations. Without that incentive, many corporations would not have engaged in philanthropy. This remains true in parts of the developing world where no such tax incentive exists.

In the last 20 years, there has been a shift in CSR from regulatory compliance towards harnessing the potential for CSR to contribute to reputation, public policy and core business practices. This evolution has been encouraged by pressures on business from new stakeholders, such as institutional investors creating socially responsible investment funds (SRIs), which consider investments in corporations based on environmental, social and corporate governance criteria in addition to standard financial analysis. The Dow Jones Sustainability Indexes were launched in 1999 as the first global indexes tracking the financial performance of the leading sustainability-driven companies worldwide. Business sees the CSR opportunity, and in the 1990s many corporations began participating in voluntary principles such as the Global Reporting Initiative (GRI). More recently consumers have expectations of business, a trend highlighted later in this chapter.

As US business integrates CSR into core business, there is increased pressure on defining the value of corporate investment in CSR. A 2009 McKinsey survey asked CFOs (chief financial officers), investment professionals, institutional investors and corporate social responsibility professionals from around the world to identify whether and how environmental, social, and governance programmes create value and how much value they create. The results indicate agreement that programmes focused on environment, social, and governance issues do create shareholder value; however the current economic crisis has increased the need of governance programmes and lessened that of environmental and social investments. A high level of respondents expected environmental, social, and governance programmes to create more value in the next five years.

▮ Priority issues

Energy and climate change
Climate change was one of the top two issues among the 274 business leaders surveyed in the GlobeScan State of Sustainable Business Poll (BSR 2009). Climate change topped the list of 'very significant' priorities in the next twelve months as selected by 41% of respondents. Respondents further indicated that energy efficiency is the priority within their climate strategy. Business concerns in addressing climate strategies are related investment costs (given the recession) and the limited policy frameworks to reinforce the associated low-carbon market economics.

Job creation
In September 2009, US unemployment reached 9.8% and the number of long-term unemployed rose to 5.4 million, a more than four-fold growth in this group since the start of the recession. Given the potential for a continued rise in global unemployment and likely social unrest, the IBLF and partners looked at how corporations, in partnership with other stakeholders, can make people more employable and create more jobs. 'The Business of Jobs', a recently published working paper, examines 20 global case studies where companies are contributing to skills and enterprise development, and outlines their approach, rationale and benefits derived. Examples focus on collaborative projects where companies have partnered with other companies, governments, NGOs, or academic institutes to pool financial and people resources, tap diverse expertise, reduce risk, increase likelihood of success and enable scale and replication.

Human rights

For any US business operating globally, human rights has become a material concern, ranking the second highest concern in the BSR (2009) Poll. The IBLF produced the report 'Human Rights Translated: A Business Reference Guide' in collaboration with Monash University. A reference for companies attempting to navigate the business case for human rights, the publication gives managers a fuller understanding of stakeholder expectations. It builds on the fact that over 5,000 companies across 130 countries are signatories to the UN Global Compact and have committed themselves to the Global Compact's ten principles including six that address human rights and labour standards.

Consumer health

According to the report by DeVol *et al.* for the Milken Institute (2007), 'The Economic Burden of Chronic Disease', the cost of chronic disease is at least USD1 trillion annually on the US economy. The Milken Institute further determined, 'with modest improvement in preventing and treating disease, by 2023 the US could avoid 40 million cases of chronic disease and reduce the economic impact of chronic disease by 27% or USD1.1 trillion annually. On obesity alone this same modest improvement could lead to USD60 billion less in treatment costs and USD254 billion in increased productivity'.

▌ Trends

There are several major trends affecting CSR in the United States:

Global recession

The first trend affecting US CSR is the global economic recession. Many feared initially that the impact of the recession could be dramatic. However, Boston College Center for Corporate Citizenship (Googins *et al.* 2009) surveyed US CEOs in early 2009 and determined that, despite upheaval in the economy, a majority of US companies are not significantly changing their corporate citizenship practices. In fact, 15% of companies are increasing research and development for new sustainable products; 11% are increasing corporate citizenship marketing and communications; and 10% are increasing local and/or domestic sourcing or manufacturing. Of those that reduced CSR spending, 38% reduced philanthropy/giving, 27% increased layoffs, and 19% reduced research and development for sustainable products.

Declining public trust in business

The global recession not only affected business earnings but seriously damaged public trust in business, some sectors more than others. The BSR (2009) Poll concluded that the two industries that have acted most responsibly in terms of their sustainability efforts in the past few years were consumer products/retail (56%) and information and communications technology (32%), up from 50% and 18% respectively in 2007. At the bottom of the list of responsible industries were financial services (1%) and media and entertainment (2%).

The Googins *et al.* survey for BCCCC (2009) survey found that among 70% of respondents, 'reputation' was a driver for corporate citizenship, tied for first place with 'it fits our company traditions and values'. The same BCCCC survey also revealed that companies should take two key actions to rebuild public trust in business that dropped as a result of the economic crisis: demonstrate positive social and environmental impacts, and innovate for sustainability.

Business partnering with government

Corporations are increasingly looking to take the principles of CSR into their mainstream business, developing products and services that address societal issues such public health, water, food security and energy. This trend was positively reinforced as a result of the recession. The Googins *et al.* BCCCC (2009) survey identified that the top two themes facing CEOs were (1) that CSR is critical to business; and (2) that business needs to work closely with government on addressing major public issues. It also found that 'most U.S. senior executives believe business should be more involved than it is today in addressing major public issues including healthcare, product safety, education, and climate change. Surveyed in June, just as the national debate on healthcare began to intensify, some 65% said business should increase its involvement in this issue'.

Consumer expectations

US consumers increasingly expect business to do more than make money. In their third Annual Global Consumer Study, Edelman (2009) undertook to identify trends in consumer expectations of brands by interviewing 6,000 consumers from ten countries. Over the past three years, the Good Purpose™ Study has identified an evolving trend — when choosing between two brands of similar quality and price, consumers rank 'social purpose' highest (43%) over 'design & innovation' (34%) and 'brand loyalty' (24%). Over half of consumers believed the interests of society and the interests of businesses should have equal weight in business decisions, and 66% of people believe it is no longer enough for corporations to simply give money away to a good cause; they need to integrate good causes into their daily business.

▌ Legislation and codes

The US government regulates on key social, consumer and environmental issues.

Environmental laws

Some of the most important regulations are found in this area. The US Environmental Protection Agency (EPA) issues approximately 130 substantive regulations that apply nationwide. Those that are considered major (with the potential to impose cumulative costs of USD100 million a year) include:

- **Clean Water Act** (33 U.S.C. §1251 *et seq.* (1972), which regulates both discharge of pollutants into the waters of the US and quality standards for surface waters.

- **Energy Policy Act** (42 USC §13201 *et seq.* (2005), which addresses energy production in the US.

- **The Clean Air Act** (42 U.S.C. §7401 *et seq.* (1970), which regulates air emissions from stationary and mobile sources.

National employment law

Federal law establishes minimum wages and workplace safety standards for most workers in the private and public sectors, but allows the states to provide more stringent standards. The US Congress has not ratified the ILO Convention on the Freedom of Association and Protection of the Right to Organize Convention (1948) or the Right to Organize and Collective Bargaining Convention (1949). The **National Labor Relations Act (1935)** (the 'Wagner Act') was the first legislation giving private sector workers the right to choose union representation and resulted in the establishment of the National Labor Relations Board (NLRB).

Occupational and safety law

The Health Act 29 U.S.C. §651 *et seq.* (1970) was designed to ensure worker and workplace safety, free from recognised hazards to safety and health.

▌ Organisations

▌ **AccountAbility**. A global, not-for-profit network of leading business, public and civil institutions. **http://www.accountability21.net**

▌ The **Aspen Institute**. An international, nonprofit organisation dedicated to fostering enlightened leadership and open-minded dialogue. **http://www.aspeninstitute.org**

▌ **Boston College Center for Corporate Citizenship (BCCCC)**. A membership-based research organisation associated with the Carroll School of Management. It is focused on research, executive education and partnerships with its 350 corporate members. **http://www.bcccc.net**

▌ **Business for Social Responsibility (BSR)**. Works with its global network of more than 250 member companies to develop sustainable business strategies through consulting, research and cross-sector collaboration. **http://www.bsr.org**

▌ **Business Roundtable**. An association of chief executive officers of leading US companies focused on direct research, position papers, policy and lobbying Congress. **http://www.businessroundtable.org**

▌ The **Conference Board**. Leading business membership and research organisation. Best known for the Consumer Confidence Index and the Leading Economic Indicators. **http://www.conference-board.org**

▌ **International Business Leaders Forum (IBLF)**. A global, not-for-profit, membership organisation that provides strategic advice to over 100 companies to enable them to understand and respond to development challenges, particularly in transition and emerging economies. **http://www.iblf.org**

∎ **Net Impact**. An international nonprofit network organisation of MBAs, graduate students and professionals. **http://www.netimpact.org**

∎ **US Chamber of Commerce: Business Civic Leadership Center**. A 501(c)3 affiliate of the US Chamber of Commerce that promotes better business and society relations. **http://www.uschamber.com/bclc**

∎ **US Network of UN Global Compact**. A strategic policy initiative for businesses that are committed to aligning their operations and strategies with ten universally accepted principles in the areas of human rights, labour, environment and anti-corruption. **http:// www.unglobalcompact.org**

∎ Case studies

Coca-Cola Enterprise (CCE)

CCE has a goal to reduce its carbon footprint by 15% by 2020. To meet that goal, CCE is more than doubling its current fleet of 142 hybrid electric delivery trucks by adding an incremental 185 hybrids, making the CCE fleet the largest hybrid fleet in North America. CCE facilities are concentrating on becoming more sustainable with the activation of their subsidiary, Coca-Cola Recycling, which is focused on developing recycling solutions for its business and communities, and the installation of water-saving technology and energy-efficient lighting in its facilities. CCE was ranked the number one food and beverage company in sustainability among Fortune 500 Companies by *Newsweek Magazine*. **http://www.cokecce.com**

IBM

In November 2008 IBM's CEO, Sam Palmisano, made a speech at the Council on Foreign Relations outlining a new corporate initiative called Smarter Planet. This is IBM's strategy for using technology to improve the world by specifically addressing issues such as energy, food, healthcare, water, education, public safety and more. To help deliver the Smarter Planet, IBM invests over USD2.5 billion a year in support of the IBM Business Partner Ecosystem, including co-marketing to help partners grow. The Partner Ecosystem will help develop the four key areas within IBM's Smarter Planet initiative: dynamic infrastructure, green and beyond, new intelligence and smart work. **http://www.ibm.com/ us/en**

The Walt Disney Company

Serving millions of meals a year in Disney Parks and Resorts, licensing food products bearing Disney brands and characters and producing and broadcasting popular children's entertainment, Disney developed a strategy to have an impact on encouraging healthy eating. In 2006, the company announced new food guidelines aimed at giving parents and children healthier eating options including limits on calories, fat, saturated fat and sugar. Beyond offering healthier food portions, Disney is integrating health messages into its children's' programmes such as *Hannah Montana* to encourage good nutrition and active lifestyles. **http://disney.go.com**

▐ Education

US graduate schools are increasingly focused on educating socially responsible business leaders. The Aspen Institute undertakes *Beyond Grey Pinstripes*,[1] a biennial survey and ranking of business schools to spotlight MBA programmes integrating issues of social and environmental stewardship into curricula and research. The top-ranked schools are:

- **Harvard University**. John F. Kennedy School of Government: Mossavar-Rahmani Center for Business and Government, Corporate Social Responsibility Initiative. **http://www.hks.harvard.edu/m-rcbg**

- **Stanford Graduate School of Business**, California: Center for Social Innovation. **http://www.gsb.stanford.edu**

- **University of California, Berkeley**. HAAS School of Business: Center for Responsible Business. **http://www.haas.berkeley.edu**

- **University of Michigan**. The Frederick A. and Barbara M. Erb Institute for Global Sustainable Enterprise. **http://www.bus.umich.edu**

- The **University of Notre Dame Mendoza College of Business**. Center for Ethics Research. **http://www.business.nd.edu**

- **Yale School of Management**. Center for Business and the Environment, The Millstein Center for Corporate Governance and Performance. **http://www.mba.yale.edu**

References

Beardsley, S.C., L. Enriquez and R. Nuttall (2008) 'Managing regulation in a new era', *McKinsey Quarterly;* **http://www.mckinseyquarterly.com**, accessed 21 October 2009.

Bonini, S., D. Court and A. Marchi (2009) 'Rebuilding Corporate Reputations', *McKinsey Quarterly,* June 2009; **http://www.mckinseyquarterly.com/Rebuilding_corporate_reputations_2367**.

BSR (2009) 'GlobeScan State of Sustainable Business Poll October 2009'; **http://www.bsr.org/research/reports.cfm**, accessed 17 October 2009.

Castan Centre for Human Rights Law at Monash University, IBLF (International Business Leaders Forum), Office of the United Nations High Commissioner for Human Rights and UN Global Compact Office (2008) 'Human Rights Translated: A Business Reference Guide'; **http://www.iblf.org/~/media/Files/Resources/Guides/HumanRightsTranslated.ashx**, accessed 9 June 2010.

DeVol, R., A. Bedroussian, A. Charuworn, A. Chatterjee, I.K. Kim, S. Kim and K. Klowden (2007) 'An Unhealthy America: The Economic Burden of Chronic Disease Charting a New Course to Save Lives and Increase Productivity and Economic Growth' (The Milken Institute; **http://www.milkeninstitute.org/research/research.taf?cat=health**).

Edelman (2009) 'Goodpurpose™ Consumer Study'; **http://www.edelman.com/news/ShowOne.asp**, accessed October 2009.

Googins, B., V. Veleva, C. Pinney, P. Mirvis, R. Carapinha and R. Raffaelli (2009) *State of Corporate Citizenship 2009: Weathering the storm* (Boston, MA: Boston College Center for Corporate Citizenship; **http://www.bcccc.net/index.cfm?pageId=2053**, accessed 7 April 2010).

---

1 **http://www.beyondgreypinstripes.org/index.cfm**; 2009–2010 report available at **http://www.beyondgreypinstripes.org/pdf/2009-2010BGP_Brochure.pdf**.

McKinsey (2009) 'Valuing Corporate Social Responsibility: McKinsey Global Survey Results', *McKinsey Quarterly*, February 2009; **http://www.mckinseyquarterly.com**, accessed 17 October 2009.

US Department of Labor (2009) 'Commissioner's Statement on the Employment Situation New Release' (Bureau of Labor Statistics2 October 2009; **http://www.bls.gov/news.release/archives/jec_10022009.htm**, accessed 17 October 2009).

58 Venezuela

Perla Puterman Szomstein
Founder and moderator of the Ibero-American
Virtual Forum on Social Responsibility

∎ Context

As in most of the Latin American countries, social responsibility actions in Venezuela began in the 19th century as an initiative of the private sector. Many such initiatives were based on charitable work and private donations of an ethical or family-related nature from individual philanthropists.

Even though the literature on CSR in Venezuela is scarce, it is known that CSR was first introduced in the first decade of the 20th century. According to Méndez (2003) the first initiatives were carried out mainly by foreign oil companies and certain entrepreneurs, focusing on the well-being of workers and their families and their integration within the community. From the 1940s on, entrepreneurs also began to develop activities of a social nature which were not directly linked to productive activity. Hence, they started to address social well-being and the need for companies to help in the solution of problems, not as charity but as an investment of the company.

Models of CSR

Recently in Venezuela, two CSR models have been applied. The first is based on the model of social responsibility and corporate ethics applied in two dimensions — ethics, oriented to human rights, and strategy, projected towards entrepreneurial responsibility and positioning as a consequence of the social commitment of companies (Guédez 2008), which has been in place for the last five years.

The second model is based on the sustainable human development approach introduced by the United Nations Development Programme (UNDP) which includes productivity, equity, sustainability and empowerment dimensions (Machado *et al.* 2002).

Vargas (2009) states that the last three years have marked the need to regard CSR as a way of doing business within the global community: 'No one in the corporate world can run a business without giving proper consideration to economic, social and environmental issues, making use of resources in a responsible manner and offering value to their stakeholders.'

Similarly, for Pizzolante (2009):

the model to be adopted by organizations should be based on the transcend-ence of CSR programs and projects to develop an awareness of the fact that what makes a business responsible is the result of its actions through the day-to-day management process. That is to say that a business could be responsi-ble or not, complying, at the same time, with its mission but before complying with the projects or processes for third parties.

■ Priority issues

Like in many Latin American countries, Venezuela faces a range of problems of a social, political and economic nature, which take a higher priority than environmental issues. The five more fundamental issues are: violence, health, unemployment, transparency and corruption.

Violence

The first issue of serious concern is the national rate of violence. According to Rob-erto Briceño León, Director of the Venezuelan Violence Observatory, an increase in violence has been registered in the last ten years, both in quantity and in the grade of the violent occurrences, going from 4,700 murders in 1994 to 14,600 in 2008. This was unprecedented in Latin America in terms of magnitude and speed of increase. The rate of murders rose from 19 per 100,000 inhabitants in 1998 to 50 for every 100,000 in 2008 (Mondolfi 2009).

Health

A study by PROVEA (2008) indicates that most of the public health services have col-lapsed, due to problems in infrastructure, insanitary conditions and lack of medical staff. The study states that 'the weakening of the health conditions and policies has significantly affected the life and well-being of Venezuelans during the past years. The worsening trends in some aspects reveal situations of concern.' The same study indi-cates that infant mortality rate has remained the same while maternal mortality rate has increased.

Unemployment

According to the National Institute of Statistics (INE), the current rate of unemploy-ment, registered in January 2010 was 6.6% (*El Universal* 2010). However, according to Luis Pedro España, Director of the Institute of Social and Economic Sciences of the Andrés Bello Catholic University, the unemployment appears to be the second or third concern of the country in all opinion polls related to employment (España 2010). Evi-dences of this situation are an increase in poverty levels, lowering of the purchase power of the population, and an increase in the incidence of violence.

Transparency and corruption

Another of the characteristic features of the country is the lack of information by offi-cial entities regarding subjects of national interest, including the presentation of official financial statements related to public expenditure by local, municipal, state and national governments. According to figures from Transparency International (2009), Venezuela occupies 162nd place, of a total of 180 countries, in the world ranking of corruption levels. In a 2009 World Bank study, Venezuela was ranked 9.2% as a percentile in terms of governance and control of corruption, as compared, for example, with Chile, which was ranked at 87% (Kaufmann *et al.* 2009).

∎ Trends

The most important longitudinal studies have been carried out on CSR by the VenAm-Cham Social Alliance (Machado *et al.* 2002; Vargas 2006; Berti *et al.* 2008).

The most recent study researched the social investment patterns of 86 member companies of VenAmCham. The study underlined the importance of investments in health, education and nutrition, since they are linked to the reduction of poverty, social exclusion and inequity. The report also emphasised the need to go beyond the mere transfer of resources, and to strengthen training and capacity building. Investment was encouraged in the quality of life of workers, their families and communities, as well as in science, technology and innovation.

∎ Legislation and codes

A series of CSR-related laws has been enacted in Venezuela, establishing the values and governing principles of CSR, as well as determining the obligations to be fulfilled. These include:

- **Law for Persons with Disabilities** (Official Gazette No. 38.598, dated 5 January 2007). Establishes the means and mechanisms 'to guarantee the wholesome development of persons with disabilities in a complete and autonomous manner in accordance with their capabilities in order to achieve their integration to family and community life'. It requires organisations to hire persons with disabilities, making up not less than 5% of their workforce.

- **Organic Law of Science, Technology and Innovation** (Official Gazette No. 38.242, dated 3 August, 2005). Establishes guiding principles in the areas of science, technology and innovation and their applications, and is oriented to the social appropriation of knowledge (Puterman 2008).

- **Organic Law of Prevention and Working Conditions and Environment (LOPCYMAT)** (Official Gazette No. 38.236, dated 26 July 2005). Aims to guarantee the protection of workers (their physical, mental and social well-being) and to prevent any event that could harm their health, while providing a dignifying job, adequate to their aptitudes and capabilities.

- **Organic Law of the Environment** (Official Gazette No. 5.833 Ext., dated 22 December 2006). Establishes the guiding principles and dispositions for managing the environment, including that environmental management within the framework of sustainable development is a right, making it a fundamental issue for the state and for society, in order to contribute to the safety and well-being of the population and the sustainability of the planet.

- **Law of Community Service of Higher Education Students** (Official Gazette No. 38.272, dated 14 September 2005). Establishes mandatory community service by higher education students having completed over 50% of the academic requirements of their careers. Such service corresponds to 120 academic hours over a period of not less than three months.

- **Law of Social Services** (Official Gazette No. 38.270, dated 12 September 2005). Aims to define and regulate the Social Service Severance Benefit Regime for the Elderly and Other Categories of Persons, its governance, organisation, operation, financing, determination of severance benefits, requirements for obtaining them and management, in conformance with the provisions of the Constitution of the Bolivarian Republic of Venezuela.

▌ Organisations

▌ **Alianza Social de VenAmCham**. Dedicated to promote and encourage corporate social responsibility activities within private businesses. http://www.venamcham.org/index.php?option=com_content&view=article&id=74&Itemid=2&lang=es

▌ The **Center for the Dissemination of Economic Knowledge for Freedom (CEDICE)**. An organisation for the dissemination of Economic Knowledge for Freedom. http://www.cedice.org.ve

▌ The **Center for the Popular Action Service Social Group (CESAP)**. A private organisation of public interest; comprises 31 organisations at the national level which carry out social programmes and projects in small villages, towns, communities and cities. http://www.cesap.org.ve

▌ **Dividendo Voluntario para la Comunidad**. The first joint effort of private businesses to channel social actions. http://www.dividendo.org

▌ The **Federation of Trade and Production Associations of Venezuela (FEDECAMARAS)**. A top business organisation working on CSR through its Social Responsibility Commission, through 2005–2007. http://www.fedecamaras.org.ve

▌ The **National Association of Civil Society Organizations (SINERGIA)**. A democratic space for the articulation, cooperation and creation of opportunities for the participation and strengthening of civil society organisations. http://www.sinergia.org.ve

▌ **Venezuela Competitiva**. A not-for-profit organisation constituted to promote permanent initiatives aimed at strengthening the competitive capabilities of the Venezuelan people and organisations. http://www.venezuelacompetitiva.com

▌ **Venezuela Sin Límites (VSL)**. A private organisation established to contribute to the strengthening of Social Development Organisations (SDOs) dedicated to improving the life conditions of persons in situations of risk, vulnerability and social exclusion. http://www.venezuelasinlimites.org

■ The **Venezuelan Executive Association (AVE)**. An institution that promotes good managerial practices, whose vision can be summed up as 'being a center of knowledge and managerial practice updating'. **http://www.ave.org.ve**

■ Case studies

BanGente

The Bank of Entrepreneurs, better known as BanGente, is the first private commercial bank exclusively dedicated to microfinance. It was established in 1995 as an initiative of the Bank of the Caribbean and non-governmental organisations (NGOs) such as The Eugenio Mendoza Foundation, the Social Group CESAP and The Popular Housing Foundation (Fundación para la Vivienda Popular). BanGente became the first Venezuelan private bank totally committed to providing financial services to those who have no regular access to a formal banking service, especially with respect to credit. **http://www. bangente.com.ve**

CEMEX de Venezuela

Before its recent nationalisation, CEMEX de Venezuela had a reputation as a pioneering company in the deployment of community support programmes. In 2005, it launched its 'Solidarity Cement' programme, through which the population could purchase the product at a very low price and, additionally, received assistance in building social-interest houses in conjunction with The National Housing Institute (INAVI). Another programme which had a great social impact was Patrimony Today, which assisted in building houses in low-income sectors, offering communities a no-interest credit system, a plan for improving individually owned houses and the provision of low-priced construction material. **http://www.cemex.com**

Empresas Polar

Since its beginning in 1941, Empresas Polar has assumed a genuine commitment towards society through the generation of well-being for its workers, their families and their communities. The projects undertaken by Empresas Polar are focused on three priority areas: community development, health through donations and hospitals, and education. The company has promoted social projects providing support to supply chains, contributing to the integral development of communities and also encouraging the development of micro businesses in the country. **http://www.fundacionempresaspolar. org**

Proagro-Protinal

By means of its PROMEVIV programme, a financing plan for housing remodelling, Proagro-Protinal provides a benefit to its workers who (in conjunction with The Popular Housing Foundation and the Mercantil, Venezuela and Banesco Banks) can obtain credits to aid the improvement and remodelling of their houses. This is a two-stage programme — the first consists of an assessment to check the condition of the house, resulting in recommendations for improvement, and the second consists of the supervision of the corresponding improvement work on the house. **http://www.agp.com/ProtinalProagro**

Santa Teresa

The Santa Teresa Rum group of companies demonstrates its commitment to the sustainable well-being and social inclusion of the people of the Revenga Municipality of Aragua State through various worker and community initiatives. The state government participated in the building of 100 houses, and Santa Teresa also helped to create the NGO Consetuors, in alliance with local and state governments and the private sector, to further develop tourism in the area. **http://www.fundacionsantateresa.org**

▌ Education

During the last few years, several university courses on CSR have been developed, including:

- **Andrés Bello Catholic University (UCAB)**. Diploma in Managerial Development and Corporate Social Responsibility. **http://www.ucab.edu.ve**

- **Carabobo University, School of Economic and Social Studies (FACES)**. An academic course on values. **http://www.faces.uc.edu.ve/webfaces**

- **Continuing Education Center, Executive Development and Organizational Consultancy (CENDECO-UNIMET)**. A CSR course. **http://www.cendeco.unimet.edu.ve/faces/home/index.jsp**

- **Institute for Higher Studies (IESA)**. A course on Design and Evaluation of Social Projects. **http://www.iesa.edu.ve**

- **Metropolitan University (UNIMET)**. Postgraduate specialisation in CSR. **http://www.unimet.edu.ve**

- **Simón Bolívar University (USB)**. A CSR Diploma. **http://www.usb.ve**

References

Berti, Z., Y. Sánchez and L. Godoy (2008) *Perfil Social de la Empresa en Venezuela: El ciclo de la práctica de la Responsabilidad Social* (Caracas: Venezuela: Alianza Social de VenAmCham).

El Universal (2009) 'Tasa de desempleo en Venezuela se ubica en el 6,6 por ciento al cierre 2009', *El Universal* (online), 8 January 2010; **http://www.eluniversal.com/2010/01/08/eco_ava_tasa-de-desempleo-en_08A3265571.shtml**, accessed 27 May 2010.

España, L. (2010) 'Problemas 3 — soluciones 0', *El Mundo*, 'Economía y Negocios' (online); **http://www.elmundo.com.ve/Default.aspx?id_portal=1&id_page=15&Id_Noticia=18069**, accessed 27 May 2010.

Guédez, V. (2008) *Ser Confiable, Responsabilidad Social y Reputación Empresarial* (Caracas, Venezuela: Editorial Planeta Venezolana).

Kaufmann, D., A. Kraa and M. Mastruzzi (2009) 'Governance Matters. VIII. Aggregate and Individual Governance Indicators: 1996–2008' (World Bank; **http://www-wds.worldbank.org**, accessed 3 August 2009).